L. FRANCIS HERRESHOFF

YACHT DESIGNER

L. FRANCIS HERRESHOFF YACHT DESIGNER

BY ROGER C. TAYLOR

VOLUME 1 • 1890-1930

Mystic Seaport®
The Museum of America and the Sea®
Mystic, Connecticut

Mystic Seaport
75 Greenmanville Ave.
Mystic, CT 06355
www.mysticseaport.org

First edition 2015

Project managed by Mary Anne Stets

Edited by Andrew W. German
Mystic, Connecticut

Copy edited by Connie Stein

Designed by Trish Sinsigalli LaPointe
tslapointedesign.com

Printed by GHP, West Haven, CT
www.ghpmedia.com

ISBN 978-0-939511-43-3

Taylor, Roger C.
L. Francis Herreshoff : yacht designer / by Roger C. Taylor -- Mystic, Connecticut : Mystic Seaport, c2015.
p. : ill. ; cm.
Includes bibliographic references and index.

1. Herreshoff, L. Francis (Lewis Francis), 1890-1972. 2. Naval architects--United States--Biography.
3. Yacht designers--United States--Biography.

VM 140 H4 T3.9 2015

This book is dedicated to anyone and everyone who has built or will build a yacht to a design by L. Francis Herreshoff. You enable sailors to reap the ultimate benefit of his genius.

It is also dedicated to Kathleen Elizabeth Carney, my wife, who has made many a sacrifice, large and small, in its support.

The publication of this book was made possible by the generosity of the following individuals and organizations:

Jack Deupree

Llewellyn Howland III

Peter Kellogg

William I. Koch

Kyle Endowment for Intellectual Property
Development at Mystic Seaport

Norfolk Charitable Trust

Walter C. Paine

CONTENTS

Preface XI
Acknowledgments XIII
Introduction 1
Prologue 5

1. Seeds of Genius 7
2. A Marine Nursery 23
3. Detour 41
4. A True Apprenticeship 67
5. The R-Boat *Yankee* 113
6. The Chosen Son 143
7. To Marblehead 167
8. From Frustration to Fun 211
9. From the *Walrus* to the 30-Square-Metres 281
10. The *Istalena* 335
11. The *Whirlwind* 359

Chronology 399
Endnotes 409
Bibliography 433
Index 439
Chronological Index of Designs 447

MILTON
MASSACHUSETTS

Apr. 28, 1948.

Dear Mother,

Things are certainly going well here at present. The news from Harvard is great.

Wednesday was a great day. The First Class had no school as the rest of boys were taking some kind of Aptitude Tests. Thank God we're through with those. Dave and I drove up to Marblehead in the Pierce's car and visited Francis Herreshoff. He lives along side of Graves Shipyard on a rise of ground that is used for a park. His house is a miniature stone castle.

– 1 –

You go through a stone archway, up a flight of stone steps to a small wooden, varnished front door like this. You ring the bell and pretty soon out comes L. Francis looking very young and active, with frank, blue eyes behind a nice pair of black steel bifocles. He leads you into his dining room talking a blue streak all the while, and you can just glimpse a long, narrow kitchen with gleaming copper pots hanging on the wall before you turn up a narrow, twisting flight of steps. Upstairs is found a large living room filled with straight back chairs, old books, dusty statuettes, ticking clocks, and a large stone fireplace. You sit and talk awhile and then climb a neat wooden ladder into his designing room. His ladder is too heavy to be pulled up after him, however. Here in the designing room is a large drawing table, another

– 2 –

big fireplace. also a couple of small lathes, oodles of wonderful lithographs and paintings of yachting scenes, and some hundreds of plans that he has drawn during his life. After spending a good deal of time here looking at plans, you go up a sort of companion ladder and out onto the roof. There is a wall around it with a notched top which I have forgotten the name for. Here you get a fine view of the boatyard and harbor, and a good sniff of the outdoors before going down to the living room for some more talk. L. Francis is a very fine talker for he can not only tell you a great deal about what you want to know, but he can also listen when the time comes. I find this last quality quite necessary for a good

– 3 –

conversationalist.

In the afternoon we played baseball against a good Huntington team who had us down several times in the game. Finally we got five runs in the eighth inning and won 9-6 at the end. So it seemed a worthwhile day all the way around.

The Cabots are driving up this weekend so I will get a ride home Saturday night arriving at about 9:00 P.M. I should suppose. It will be great to get home and see you all again.

Lots of love from

Roy.

(You'd better save this so I can turn it in for a descriptive theme in English.)

– 4 –

When the author was a schoolboy at Milton Academy, he wrote to his Mother describing a visit to L. Francis Herreshoff at The Castle in Marblehead.

Apr. 28, 1948
Dear Mother,

Things are certainly going well here at present. The news from Harvard is great.

Wednesday was a great day. The First Class had no school as the rest of the boys were taking some kind of Aptitude Tests. Thank God we're through with those. Dave and I drove up to Marblehead in the Pierce's car and visited Francis Herreshoff. He lives along side of Graves Shipyard on a rise of ground that is used for a park. His house is a miniature stone castle.

You go through a stone archway, up a flight of stone steps to a small wooden, unfinished front door like this (sketch of door). You ring the bell and pretty soon out comes L. Francis looking very young and active, with frank, blue eyes behind a nice pair of black steel bifocles. He leads you into his dining room talking a blue streak all the while, and you can just glimpse a long, narrow kitchen with gleaming copper pots hanging on the wall before you turn up a narrow, twisting flight of steps. Upstairs is found a huge living room filled with straight back chairs, old books, dusty statuettes, ticking clocks, and a huge stone fireplace. You sit around and talk awhile and then climb a neat wooden ladder into his designing room. His ladder is too heavy to be pulled up after him, however. Here in the designing room is a huge drawing table, another big fireplace. Also a couple of small lathes, oodles of wonderful lithographs and paintings of yachting scenes, and some hundreds of plans that he has drawn during his life. After spending a good deal of time here looking at plans, you go up a sort of companion ladder and out onto the roof. There is a wall around it with a notched top which I have forgotten the name for (sketch of notched top). Here you get a fine view of the boatyard and harbor, and a good sniff of the outdoors before going down to the living room for some more talk. L. Francis is a very fine talker for he cannot only tell you a great deal about what you want to know, but he can also listen when the time comes. I find this last quality quite necessary for a good conversationalist.

In this afternoon we played baseball against a good Huntington team who had us down several times in the game. Finally we got five runs in the eighth inning and won 9-6 at the end. So it seemed a worthwhile day all the way around.

The Cabots are driving up this weekend so I will get a ride home Saturday night arriving at about 9:00 P.M. I should suppose. It will be great to get home and see you all again.

Lots of love from Rog

(You better save this so I can turn it in for a descriptive theme in English)

PREFACE

L. Francis Herreshoff attracted me, along with many others, as a powerful magnet draws bits of iron. Some of us were crazy over boats and were mesmerized by his designs and his writings, presented in *The Rudder* magazine, and later in books. We made the pilgrimage to The Castle in Marblehead, where the great man lived, and found, if we were attentive and not proud of our own accomplishments on the water, a man of wisdom and good humor, who talked to us as if we were capable of understanding all manner of things, nautical and otherwise.

I never spent enough time in Mr. Herreshoff's presence (I remember one visit he terminated when it became obvious that at age sixteen I knew everything there was to know about boats) to become well acquainted, but I kept returning, in spirit if not in person, to the Herreshoff well, and by age forty I had learned enough to realize that it would be a service to preserve Francis Herreshoff's artistry, wisdom, and wit in further books than were already available. So, at International Marine Publishing Company, we brought out *Sensible Cruising Designs*, presenting many of his plans, and *An L. Francis Herreshoff Reader*, a book of his writings. The preface to the former was the last thing he wrote. Twenty-five years later, Llewellyn Howland III, an experienced seller of maritime books, suggested that Mystic Seaport, holder of the L. Francis Herreshoff Collection of his plans, letters, and memorabilia, publish a biography of the designer and that I write it. Neither the Museum nor I could resist Louie Howland's persuasions.

I have approached the task with mixed feelings. My long love affair with boats and writing has given me a measure of confidence, but the responsibility for presenting the life and work of such an important figure in art and yachting has given me an equal measure of trepidation. Moreover, I have worked under the constant knowledge that Mr. Herreshoff placed a high value on his privacy and that, had he been buried in a grave, he would have moved mightily in it had he known that his life was being probed and publicized, and by one who had never designed a yacht. I have had to keep reminding myself that human genius deserves, even demands, explication.

My work has been done also in the shadow of the sureness that the best way to get to know Mr. Herreshoff is to study his plans of yachts and read his writing. I have worried that it's all there and that a biography is superfluous. But I have been encouraged to persuade myself that an interpretive presentation of Mr. Herreshoff's life and work will be of value to his friends and devotees and may add to the circle of artists and boat people attracted by his magnetism. I believe, at least, that it is a service to bring his drawings together in a collection that can be viewed readily and to quote some of his writings as they bear particularly on his life and work.

Despite my mixed feelings about writing Mr. Herreshoff's life, I have enjoyed the long labor. Many a time of discouragement and perplexity has been relieved by the pleasure of turning to one of his drawings and admiring again a profile, a shape of bow, or a perfectly proportioned ketch rig. My task has often been sweetened by a vicarious voyage in one of his yachts. My conversations with dozens of Mr. Herreshoff's friends and acquaintances have been rewarding, and the required research of sailing boats built to his designs has been bliss.

As you will see in the acknowledgements, bibliography, and endnotes, I have had much help with this book. There is no lack of interest in and opinions on Mr. Herreshoff. I hope I have made clear when I was reporting the opinions of others and when I was writing my own ideas. I am most grateful for all the help I have received. My greatest hope is that this account of his life and work does justice to L. Francis Herreshoff.

—Roger C. Taylor

P. S. Advisory to LFH afficionados: while the Notes contain mostly references, you can also find therein random scraps of information too esoteric for the text.

ACKNOWLEDGMENTS

My first thanks must go to Llewellyn Howland III, who threw my name in the hat as author, when he proposed that Mystic Seaport publish a biography of L. Francis Herreshoff, as a way to share the highlights of its collection of his plans, letters, and photographs. Ever since, Louie has been a source of encouragement and of insights, especially about Herreshoff's friend and mentor, W. Starling Burgess.

But it was my wife, Kathleen Carney, who persuaded me to accept the challenge of writing Francis Herreshoff's story. Having done so, she has been unstinting with her moral support and her editorial acumen. Every word that you read in this book has been read aloud to her and subjected to her judgment. She can listen to one of my long, convoluted sentences and turn it right side out, like a sock coming out of the laundry.

Joseph Gribbins, who died far too young, welcomed the concept of the book with enthusiasm as the man in charge of publishing at Mystic Seaport. Andrew German and Mary Anne Stets continued the Museum's publishing support, and Andy later took on the task, as a freelance editor, of "tweaking," as he says, my copy. I can tell you that he has done a good job with it.

Thanks be to all those dedicated Mystic Seaport staffers over the years who have acquired, preserved, organized, and presented the L. Francis Herreshoff Collection and who gave me access to it. They are: Maribeth Bielinski; Maynard Bray; J. Revell Carr; Maria Christenson; Kelly Drake; Kathleen Foulke; Dana Hewson; Mindy Matheson; Brandon Morgan; Carol Mowrey; Dennis Murphy; Paul O'Pecko; Leah Prescott; Andy Price; Peggy Tate Smith; Connie Stein; Doug Stein; Mary Anne Stets; Ellen Stone; Barry Thomas; Marifrances Trivelli; Louisa Watrous; Pat Wilbur; Suki Williams; and Georgia York. And thanks be to Muriel Vaughn and her daughter, Elizabeth R. Vaughn, for their generosity in making the collection available.

The late Carlton Pinheiro, for many years curator at the Herreshoff Marine Museum, Bristol, Rhode Island, an expert on the Herreshoff family, pulled from his museum's archives invaluable photographs and racked his memory to share with me his detailed knowledge. It was he who made me aware of the remarkable half model that Francis Herreshoff carved at age sixteen. Kurt Hasselbalch, at the Hart Nautical Collections at the MIT Museum, made available plans from Burgess, Swasey, and Paine. Joann Kowalski, at the University of Rhode Island, unearthed details on Francis's career as a student at the school.

I would like to pay homage to Philip C. Bolger's outstanding essay on L. Francis Herreshoff that Joe Gribbins published in the *Nautical Quarterly*, a piece of writing with which I have had a dual relationship. While it has been a source of inspiration, it is so good that it has made me wonder if a biography was really necessary.

Arthur Brendze, who, as a young man was a confidant of L. Francis in the last four years of his life, and later became a boatbuilder and then a psychologist, has been a tremendous help to me in understanding Francis's personality and, particularly, his relationship with his father. Cynthia Bourgeault, editor extraordinaire and small-boat sailor, helped me shape a good course early in the voyage.

A lot of people have advised me as to when they thought I should get this book written. Doc Buttermore is the one who said, "Take your time."

I particularly appreciate the cooperation in my research of Francis's nephews, Halsey Herreshoff and Nathanael Greene Herreshoff III, and of his late niece, Natalie Herreshoff. They provided insights about their uncle that could have come from no other sources. Nat was particularly helpful on the history of the Herreshoff family.

It has been an honor and a privilege to meet and converse with so many friends of L. Francis Herreshoff, as well as so many who have admired him, or not, as the case may be, from a distance. As the reader may note from the dates of interviews in the endnotes, this book has taken me a long time to research and write. The most unfortunate side effect is that a number of helpful and generous interviewees have not lived to witness their invaluable contributions to the story of a man, who, in many cases, they loved.

Everyone I asked shared their reminiscences and opinions of Skipper Herreshoff, as most of them called him, and were open to my questions. I thank: Lloyd Bergeson; Stan Bishoprick Jr.; Philip C. Bolger; Anne Lawrence Bondy; Dan Brayton; Maynard Bray; Arthur Brendze; Andrew W. Britt; John N. Brown; Paul G. Brown; Dale Calloway; Peter Coe; Steve Corkery; Edmund A. Cutts; Charles Darcy; Charles Doersam; Dieter Empacher; Suzy Fernberger; Adrienne Franklin; Christopher Franklin; John Gardner; Paul Glynn; Mrs. Charles D. Gowing; Stan Grayson; Anne Greer; Jay Greer; Lucile Bonner Hanscom; William Harding; Anne Burgess Hopps; Llewellyn Howland III; Harmon Hunt; John Kendall; Bruce King; O. Lie-Nielsen; Bradley Noyes; Christopher Parker; Carlton Pinheiro; Edith Welch Potter; C. Seaver Robinson; Bobby Russell; Allen D. Slater; Hope Welch Slater; Margrete L. Stinnes; Olin J. Stephens II; William Strawbridge III; Barry Thomas; Tasha Tudor; Muriel Vaughn; Katherine Jones Vosburgh; William Wallace; Nat Wilson; and Marjorie Young Wolff.

I couldn't possibly list all the people who have helped me with this book. Of hundreds of favors, here are just two examples: David P. Jackson, born and raised in Marblehead, shared his memories of the harbor and suggested Marbleheaders to interview; Darryl Reach, an expert on cars, answered questions on Francis's early involvement with the automobile. I am grateful to all who have shared their knowledge with me.

I thank my children, Roger, Dean, Rebecca, and Stephen, for their love, support, and advice. They are all students of human nature, and they are all good writers. I thank my sister, Phoebe Franklin, for her near-Mystic-Seaport hospitality and for her wisdom about books and writing, shared over the last seventy-five years.

The most fun of all was that Len Hornick took Kathleen and me cruising in his replica of the schooner *Joann*; and Matt Gineo took me sailing in the 30 Square Metre *Oriole*. I also have had the pleasure of sailing in nine other Francis Herreshoff designs that will be covered in Volume 2.

INTRODUCTION

L. Francis Herreshoff lived from 1890 to 1972. He was a New England Yankee yacht designer known for his beautiful, fast boats.

L. Francis is sometimes confused with his world-famous father, Nathanael G. Herreshoff, designer and builder at the Herreshoff Manufacturing Company, Bristol, Rhode Island, of fast steam yachts and torpedo boats, America's Cup defenders, and many one-design classes of racing yachts, large and small.

Whereas N. G. Herreshoff was a highly disciplined worker of primarily scientific mind, but also natural artistic ability, who made, himself, perhaps 600 half-hull models and produced designs that resulted in upwards of 12,000 drawings, his son, L. Francis, sought artistic and functional perfection in far fewer designs. His sense of proportion gave him the ability to produce construction plans that were equally scientific to those of his father. He completed only about 125 designs to the point where they could be built, and only about 70 of his designs resulted in finished vessels, though multiple boats were built to some 25 designs. The drawings he and his handful of draftsmen made number scarcely more than 10 percent of the drawings of his father's Herreshoff Manufacturing Company. But of L. Francis's 125 designs, 55, in my judgment, either approached aesthetic perfection, or performed nearly perfectly, or both. And these varied from dinghies to the largest of racing yachts, and from small, simple cruisers to big, elaborate pleasure craft, both sail and power. I can give no other American designer than L. Francis's father credit for so many outstanding designs. And despite Nathanael G. Herreshoff's unparalleled achievements in the design and construction of yachts, L. Francis Herreshoff brought yacht design even closer to perfection than had his more famous father.

L. Francis is the designer of the great, 72-foot ketch *Ticonderoga*, a yacht built as a daysailer and short-range cruiser in 1936. She is thought by many to be the most beautiful yacht in the world, and she has set records for the fastest time over sixteen different ocean racing courses, more than any other yacht. He designed a dozen hauntingly beautiful, double-ended racing yachts, including the successful M-boat *Istalena* (1929) and the unsuccessful J-boat *Whirlwind* (1930). He designed the best racing boat ever in the R Class, the *Yankee* (1926). He designed the H-28 (1942) for *The Rudder* magazine, a simple and pure little cruising ketch that has been built by hundreds around the world. He designed the Meadow Lark (1948), a cruising sailboat drawing 15 inches of water that was another popular *Rudder* craft. And he designed the Rozinante (1956), a slim, 28-foot, double-ended ketch whose sweet form is timeless.

Like his father, but again on a smaller scale, L. Francis is responsible for important innovations in the construction and rigging of yachts. He was the first to apply longitudinal construction to wooden yachts (1925). He was first with mast tangs and hollow, rectangular spars (1923).

L. Francis was born and raised in Bristol, Rhode Island. In his youth, he got invaluable experience for his chosen art through much sailing of diverse types of boats and yachts and through exposure to many parts of the Herreshoff Manufacturing Company. He showed an obvious ability for the designing of yachts, yet his father didn't want him in the business and decreed that he was to run a farm that belonged to Francis's mother. Francis dutifully ran the farm for seven years, until he was liberated by naval service during World War I. He never went back.

Instead, Francis became a black sheep in the Herreshoff family by going off to work for one the country's other leading yacht designers, W. Starling Burgess. He stayed with Burgess for five-and-a half years and learned a lot from this mentor. When Burgess closed his design business in Boston—the year was 1926—and moved to New York to open another, L. Francis started to design yachts on his own in Marblehead, Massachusetts. He lived in this yachting center for the rest of his life. He produced his last design in 1963 but retained a lively interest in the field until his death. L. Francis died believing that his work was misunderstood and even ridiculed, but in fact, through his designs and writings, he had great influence on the surprising revival of wooden boatbuilding and sensible yacht design in the years after his death.

L. Francis wrote 234 articles for *The Rudder*, most under the encouragement of its talented editor, Boris Lauer-Leonardi. The articles were gathered into seven published books, including what is the best book on yacht design, *The Common Sense of Yacht Design*, and an admiring and detailed biography of his father, *Capt. Nat Herreshoff: The Wizard of Bristol*. By writing for *The Rudder*, L. Francis opened his mailbox to the world. His writings exuded knowledge and experience, and any sailor with a question seemed to feel free to address him. L. Francis became per force a prodigious letter-writer, answering every correspondent promptly, courteously, and expertly.

L. Francis was a sensitive man, who, in the style of the time, sought to bury his emotions. His emotions were particularly strong around his father, whom he admired and respected greatly, but who also frustrated and angered him by failing to acknowledge his son's gifts. L. Francis was proud, shy, and judgmental; he developed lifelong friendships with some of his clients and was not on speaking terms with others.

L. Francis's much loved and revered mother died when he was fifteen. He was a bachelor all his life. He once loved a girl far younger than he, and she loved him too, but, under the guidance of her father, she broke off the romance. It was Francis's first and last. Thereafter, he nurtured the façade of a proper Edwardian gentleman, and unfounded rumors of his desire for male intimacy were heard amongst occasional speculation as to the true status of this or that lady friend.

The pain of his personal losses drove L. Francis inward. He cultivated boundaries behind which he could compensate, by creating art. He designed and drew beautiful, functional yachts, not only as a conscious vocation, but also as a subconscious spiritual practice.

He made many elegant objects out of wood and metal. His craftsmanship was of the highest order. The masterpieces he made and gave to his friends would fill a warehouse.

L. Francis was a consummate sailor and an experienced kayak paddler, who was, however, just as happy making imaginary voyages as real ones. Much as he loved the water, he loved his fireside just as much. And he loved his lathe and drawing board even more.

He lived in a small, exquisite, stone castle in Marblehead for the last twenty-eight years of his life. Never was a dwelling better suited to its occupant. The upstairs ballroom became his workshop and drafting room; the roof turrets were his lookouts over Marblehead Harbor. Every nook and cranny of the great hall was filled with some part of the superb collection he amassed over the years of all manner of antiques and art and books. There was the "Tower," a separate garage for his latest sports car. And there was a small, lower room in The Castle, a sort of "keep," where Francis lived and entertained his closest friends. Lucky were those whom he invited in.

Certain myths have grown up around L. Francis: the bad blood with his father, his irascibility, his unfailing genius. The myths are based on reality, but none is strictly true.

L. Francis Herreshoff was the consummate artist, in his values, his personality, his lifestyle, and, above all, in his creation of beautiful yacht designs. The chapters that follow, with their illustrations, presented in two volumes, will tell the story of the life and work of this remarkable artist.

PROLOGUE

The Escape from Bristol

The lanky man sat on the hard, wooden seat of the speeding trolley, shoulders squared, feet flat on the rocking floor, long, delicate hands resting on his knees. His combed and brushed hair was fine and straight, the color of wet, New England beach sand, trimmed short above large ears. A full moustache, several shades darker than his hair and tinged with red at the edges, all but covered his mouth. The hint of a dimple softened his prominent chin. It was only his dancing blue eyes that betrayed his excitement. The car was flying along at ninety miles-an-hour, roaring, screeching, and swaying on the rails from Fall River, Massachusetts, to New Bedford. On this day late in 1920, L. Francis Herreshoff, a month past his thirtieth birthday, was not just indulging his love of speed; he was putting miles between himself and his family home in Bristol, Rhode Island. It was the most important journey of his life: he was on his way to Provincetown, at the outermost tip of Cape Cod, and his first job as a yacht designer. He was leaving behind in Bristol a father who would not acknowledge his son's ability, Nathanael G. Herreshoff, a father who was the most famous yacht designer in the world.

Francis could have taken the boat train directly from Fall River to the Cape, but more likely, he chose trains that went the long way around, via Wareham, so that he could enjoy this fast, interurban trolley. And rather than take the train all the way to Provincetown, he arranged to be met in Truro, where he climbed into the passenger seat of a big, 200-horsepower Mercedes Benz, the very car that held the Daytona Beach speed record at 151 miles per hour. The great car's owner and driver was Francis's new employer, W. Starling Burgess. As they drove, Starling, who loved telling a good story, regaled Francis with the tale of a mishap on the way to Truro. He had been trying the Mercedes' speed, when the left front tire flew off and wedged itself between the twin trunks of a tree. He used an axe to pry it out and was pleased that he managed to free the tire without damaging it. Francis must have been more impressed by Starling's ability to control a speeding car that had thrown a tire. Working with this man was going to be quite an adventure.[1]

The noisy, chain-drive Mercedes rolled into Provincetown and turned onto Commercial Street, which runs along the harbor; Starling brought it to a stop at No. 555, on the water side of the street. Francis would have noticed the smell of the place. Provincetown Harbor, formed by the hook at the end of Cape Cod, was sandy-shored and close to the ocean, with more than twice the tidal range of Bristol Harbor, well up Narragansett Bay. The waterfront smell here was sharper and saltier than at home.

Francis was not only to work for Burgess, but also was to live with him in the modest dwelling that Starling had built on Provincetown Harbor with the help of his young son, Frederic. Francis would have been delighted to discover that his new home had a fireplace, an inglenook with built-in benches, for he loved the light and warmth of a hearth. He would come to appreciate the conviviality of gathering around the fire with friends, for Starling often played host. Sometimes there would be good conversation, inevitably turning to boats, and sometimes Starling would hold the group spellbound with his expressive reading of poetry, while a flask of gin circulated.

Francis came to a Provincetown that was no longer simply the bustling maritime town he had seen as a boy of eleven, cruising with his family in his father's steam yacht, the *Roamer.* The upheaval of social mores in the aftermath of World War I affected everything, from modes of personal behavior and dress to mobility. In the Roaring Twenties, Provincetown became a magnet for artists and writers, a critical mass of creative and adventurous souls who sought to explore the limits of the exciting, new times. Francis, raised in a conservative family in a conservative town, was thrust into a Bohemian atmosphere that must have amazed and fascinated him. In the summer, there would be supper parties on a long wharf, where diners could chat with Eugene O'Neill before seeing the debut of his latest play, performed by waiter-actors. There was plenty of booze, despite Prohibition. People wore whatever they wanted. Midnight bathers swam from a boathouse launching ramp, and often the clothes were left behind. Starling Burgess, no mean social experimenter himself, encouraged Francis to join the party. Francis Herreshoff had landed very far away from his Bristol home.[2]

CHAPTER 1

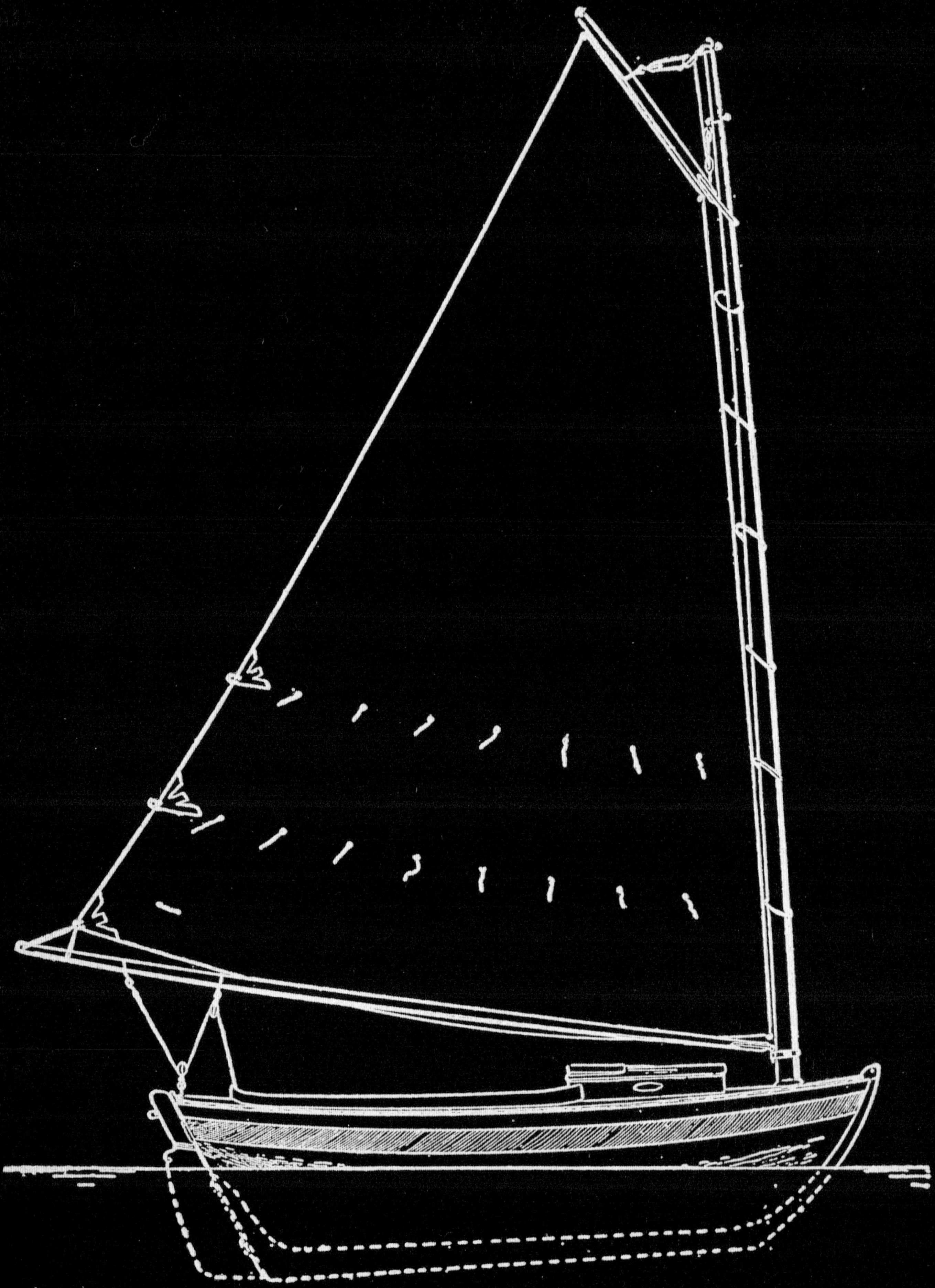

SEEDS OF GENIUS

"There is no doubt that Captain Nat inherited some of his strong characteristics from this remarkable woman, his grandmother"

—L. FRANCIS HERRESHOFF, 1949

Francis Herreshoff's great-grandmother, Sarah Brown Herreshoff, was born in 1773 in Providence, Rhode Island, where, as a daughter of John and Sarah Smith Brown, she grew up with every advantage. John Brown, great-great-grandson of one of the founders of Providence, carried on his father's business as merchant and shipowner. One of the wealthiest men in the American colonies, he was described as "a man of magnificent projects and extraordinary enterprise." He was also a patriot who profited from providing the Continental Army with cannon from his factory in Cranston and gunpowder carried on his ships, and he was not above profiting as well from smuggling, privateering, and slaving. The slave trade, a relatively small part of the mercantile enterprises of John and his brother Moses, was just more business to John, but not to Moses. While John was upset merely about the financial loss when the majority of slaves died on the first such voyage the brothers tried in 1764, Moses was horrified by the inherent cruelty of the business, death at sea or not. John continued in the trade, but Moses became an abolitionist.[1]

In 1787, when Sarah was fourteen, her father built a square, three-story, brick mansion at 52 Power Street that was—and still is—one of the finest buildings in Providence. Sarah, bright and curious, pursued the traditional interests of young ladies of her class and time: music—she was a skilled singer and harpsichordist—and religion—she studied the Bible and "was exact and methodical in her daily devotions." But that was not enough for Sarah, and she had been born into a family with both the means and the will to indulge her thirst for knowledge. The Browns believed in education; in 1767, John and Moses promoted free education in Providence. In 1770, John Brown laid the cornerstone for the first building of the College in the English Colony of Rhode Island and Providence Plantations—later renamed Brown University—which was transplanted from Warren to Providence at the urging of and with the financial support of the Browns, and erected on part of the Brown holdings that were sold to the colony.[2]

The Brown home was graced with a fine library and a steady stream of worldly visitors, and Sarah was a diligent student of both. She excelled at mathematics and acquired considerable knowledge of astronomy, rare accomplishments for a young woman of the eighteenth century. Avid curiosity about all manner of scientific subjects, the mental discipline to satisfy that curiosity, and the drive to succeed were traits bequeathed by Sarah Brown to her Herreshoff descendants.[3]

On July 2, 1801, Sarah Brown, at age twenty-eight, married Charles Frederick Herreshoff in the drawing room of the Power Street mansion, after a courtship of eight years and over the objections of her father. Karl Friederich Herreschoff, Sarah's senior by a decade, was born in Minden in the Kingdom of Westphalia in 1769. His father was probably a Corporal Eschoff, a Prussian Guard, despite the belief by at least two descendants that Karl Friederich was a bastard son of no less a personage than Frederick the Great. His mother, Agnes Muller, died when her son was five years old, from injuries suffered in a carriage accident. Corporal Eschoff went into depression, abandoned his child to the care of a friend, and disappeared into Italy. The friend seems to have been a professor, and a man who had more access to King Frederick II than had a corporal of his Prussian Guard. Through this connection, the King took a great interest in the boy, apparently was responsible for naming him, saw to his education at the Philanthropium school at Dessau, and brought him to Court as a cultured gentleman who, like himself, was an accomplished flutist. King Frederick's death prompted Karl Friederich Herreschoff to start a new life in America, and he emigrated to New York and Anglicized the spelling of his name in 1787.[4]

In New York, Charles Frederick tried, without success, to start an importing business. Then he met John Brown's New York agent, who seems to have hired him as an assistant. Charles Frederick began traveling to Providence on business, met Sarah, and soon found reasons to make the trip as often as he could. He was well over six feet tall, handsome, poised, and gentlemanly. From his mother he had inherited grace and an artistic bent. He and Sarah shared a love of music; she would accompany his singing on the harpsichord, and he would play the flute while she sang. Music bridged the gap between their backgrounds. But Charles Frederick, for all his European education and courtly charm, had no money, and it was partly this lack that made John Brown less than enthusiastic about having him for a son-in-law. Perhaps more important, John saw that Charles had neither the temperament nor the ability to earn money, qualities that the Browns admired above all.[5]

Nevertheless, John Brown gave the newlyweds a country estate in Bristol, a few miles down Narragansett Bay from Providence, a property that he had received in return for his help in financing the War for Independence. The Byfield manor house was built in 1680 on Poppasquash Neck, with an easterly view across Bristol Harbor to the town. Sarah and Charles Frederick named it Point Pleasant Farm. Charles enjoyed making the farm more beautiful and comfortable, but he did not make it more productive. He and Sarah raised six children at the farm, but their home was not entirely happy. Charles Frederick, the former European courtier, earned nothing, while dissipating much of the money Sarah inherited when her father died in 1803. Though not a prudent man, Charles was honorable, and he determined to change his ways about income and expense, perhaps with helpful pressure from Sarah's Uncle Moses.[6]

Sarah's sister Abby had married John Francis, and her husband had become a partner of John Brown. When one of Brown's ships arrived in New York with a cargo worth $210,000, John Francis had the responsibility of redeeming the value. Unaccountably, he traded it for 210,000 acres of Adirondack wilderness. This property became known as the Brown Trust.

Charles Frederick was offered the chance to try to develop the Brown Trust into a money-making enterprise. In 1811, he moved west to the woods of Township 7 in the Adirondack

Mountains, leaving his family behind in Bristol. His initial plan was to develop productive farms, which would increase the value of adjacent lands that could then be sold off to more settlers. But the man who could not develop one productive farm was no more successful on a larger scale. Next, Charles tried raising sheep on the land. He built a 300-foot shed and had a large herd driven out from Providence. Cost exceeded income. By 1817, he was trying iron mining. He built a forge and mined and smelted iron ore. But the product was low-grade and cost a dollar a pound at the site, too high to be profitable.

At first, Charles would return home to Bristol for visits with Sarah and the children, but as financial success eluded him and discouragement set in, the visits became less frequent, then stopped. His gracefully written letters home, showing a character of pride and independence, depicting a man bearing hardships and misfortune with quiet dignity, gradually betray his losing hope. Sensing this himself, he decided not to write again until he had good news. It never came.

With Charles's three unsuccessful attempts at making money on the Brown Trust, family backers refused further money for investment. Financial disaster had caught up with Charles Frederick Herreshoff. On Sunday, December 19, 1819, Charles dressed in his best as usual. A man rushed into his house to report that a new mine was flooding and caving in. Charles immediately went to the scene to survey the damage, fortunately only to property. Then he returned to his house and shot himself. The site of his efforts to redeem himself is now the village of Old Forge, New York.[7]

SARAH AND CHARLES Frederick's fifth child, born in 1809, was named for his father, although he would not have remembered him. The only Herreshoff of his generation to marry, young Charles wed Julia Ann Lewis in 1833. His wife, like his mother, was a daughter in a prominent New England mercantile family. Her father was Joseph Warren Lewis, the sea captain and merchant in Boston who gave his name to Lewis Wharf. Julia was a well-educated young woman, exposed throughout her childhood to the literary and artistic circles of Boston. She traveled abroad with her father. Like Sarah Brown, Julia was an accomplished musician, and she brought her harpsichord along when she came to Bristol with her family for summer holidays. Most likely, it was music that brought Julia and Charles together. As with his parents, their duets turned romantic.[8]

Between 1834 and 1854, nine children were born to Charles and Julia, who proved to be

LEFT: **Sarah Brown Herreshoff, Francis's great-grandmother, at age thirty-seven. Sarah Brown brought strong traits of curiosity, intelligence, and determination into the Herreshoff family.** (Herreshoff Marine Museum, Bristol, Rhode Island) RIGHT: **Sarah's courtly, ne'er-do-well husband, Charles Frederick Herreshoff the elder (original spelling, Karl Friederich Herreschoff), in his late forties.** (Herreshoff Marine Museum, Bristol, Rhode Island)

remarkable parents. They fostered their children's inherited talents and gave them the inspiration, the encouragement, and the tools—in every sense of the word—to do extraordinary things. Their brood grew up to be determined and accomplished individuals, a formidable older generation for Francis to admire and be measured against.[9]

There was genius among Charles and Julia's children. Perhaps the most brilliant was John Brown Francis, the eighth child, known as "Francis." He became a chemical engineer and, in about 1880, developed the standard electrolytic process for refining copper, improved the method of manufacturing sulfuric acid, and invented the Herreshoff electric furnace for casting steel. His innovations resulted in such an increase in the output of both copper and sulfuric acid that, by 1900, US producers of these two critical materials accounted for half the world supply. J. B. Francis Herreshoff made a significant impact on his country's industrial strength.[10]

Four of the Herreshoff children were afflicted with blindness at a young age. The cause remains unknown. Julia taught them Braille and school subjects, and both parents invested their blind children with the same expectations and opportunities as the sighted ones. The children rose to the challenge. Lewis studied music abroad and became a linguist and author, as well as an excellent oarsman. He always had the news read to him, and had an opinion on all of it. Sally was a gifted musician, and she kept up a wide correspondence with other blind people. Julian Lewis, the youngest, became a linguist, schoolmaster, and musician. He learned German, French, Spanish, Russian, and Chinese and was the teaching principal of the Westminster School of Languages and Music in Providence. And John started the boatbuilding enterprise that became the Herreshoff Manufacturing Company and managed it to greatness.[11]

IT WAS BOATS that made the Herreshoff name famous, and it was Charles Herreshoff who taught his sons about boats. His Uncle James Brown had experimented with outside ballast on a sailing boat as early as 1800 (the experiment failed; he used too much). Charles—Francis's grandfather—was the first Herreshoff to design and build boats, the first Herreshoff to design and build boats with the purpose of sailing faster than other boats, the first Herreshoff to develop innovative, superior boat gear.[12]

Charles built his first sizeable craft in 1834, when he was in his mid-twenties, a 23-foot catboat along the lines of a Newport Point boat, a local type that had been developed for carrying and fishing around Narragansett Bay. He named her *Julia* and sailed her on the Bay for twenty years. By his mid-forties, Charles had experimented with a number of sailing models and, in 1854, built his second *Julia*. Charles eventually made the *Julia II* the fastest boat on Narragansett Bay. It took him ten years and an unusual device. He fitted his boat with a box containing 550 pounds of ballast, a box that could be rolled across the boat to shift the weight to the windward side. In effect, Charles's rolling ballast box gave him the equivalent of four extra crewmen hiking out to windward when needed.[13]

TOP LEFT: **Charles Frederick Herreshoff the younger, and his wife, Julia Ann Lewis Herreshoff, in about 1880.** (© Mystic Seaport, 1990.37.1154) BOTTOM LEFT: **Julia Herreshoff, seated center, and her nine children. Francis's father, Nathanael, stands at far left. Next to him (left to right) are Charles, J. B. Francis, and Lewis. Seated next to Julia (left to right) are John, Caroline, James, and Sally. Seated in front is Julian. Francis was about three years old when this photograph of his formidable family was made.** (© Mystic Seaport, 1990.37.191)

By about 1870, the *Julia II* probably had an improved anchor, for Charles designed his own version of the old-fashioned, symbol-of-hope anchor, making subtle changes to the shape of its flukes, arms, shank, and stock to increase its holding power without increasing weight. This is the "Herreshoff Anchor," usually credited to his son Nathanael, but developed by Charles and later improved by Nathanael.[14]

Charles Herreshoff passed on not only his penchant for innovation, but also his love of the water and boats, to his sons James, John B., and Nathanael Greene. James, the eldest and the most intellectually creative of the Herreshoffs, was a prolific inventor. Among his diverse inventions were ankle braces for skates, a thread-tension regulator for sewing machines, and a sounding machine for measuring the depth of water. While still in his twenties, he developed the formula for baking powder and made enough money from this one achievement to allow him to dabble, for the rest of his life, in whatever interested him, which, to a great extent, was boats. He designed a vee-bottomed boat, the *Tadpole*, in 1854, the first on Narragansett Bay and a forerunner of a type that would become common. He was an early experimenter with fin keels on model sailboats, and he built windmill-driven model boats that, given enough wind, would go faster than those that were sail-powered. He liked to row and contributed to the development of both the sliding seat and the forward-facing rowing apparatus. In 1873, James invented the coil steam boiler, an important improvement on the boilers of the time because of its light weight and fast start-up. James's patented boilers would give his brother John's boatbuilding enterprise an edge over its competitors.[15]

Born in 1841, John lost his sight in one eye when he was seven, the first of the children to be afflicted with eye disease. At age ten, demonstrating the mercantile instincts of his Brown and Lewis forbears, he was raising and selling vegetables. Three years later, he built a ropewalk and manufactured cotton rope up to 1/2-inch in diameter and 300 feet long. Then, when he was fourteen, tragedy struck. He was blinded in his good eye while he and his brother Charles were roughhousing with a stick. At the time, he was building his first boat, a 12-foot, vee-bottomed sailing craft of his own design, inspired by James's *Tadpole*. Francis later wrote, "When he … lost his sight, J. B. was very despondent for a few months but his energy to do things soon returned." He took up the boatbuilding project again and finished the *Meteor* two years later, with the help of

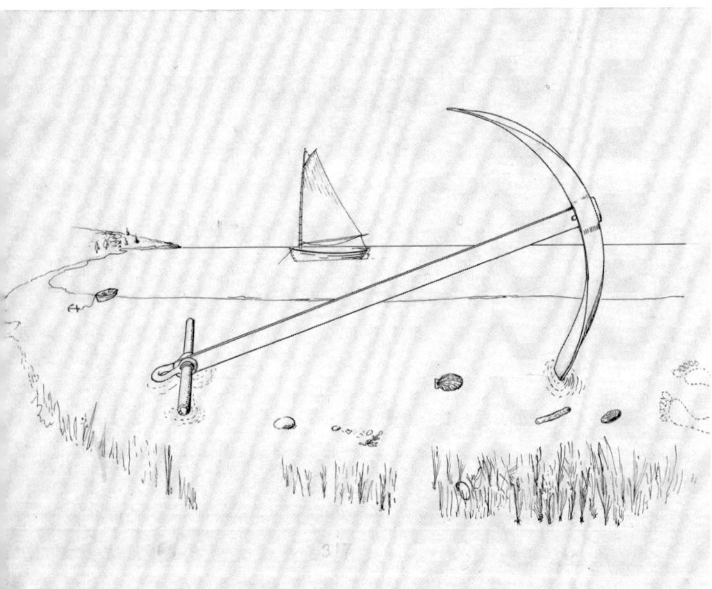

LEFT: **Francis's drawing of his grandfather's anchor, as improved by his father, with the *Julia* in the background. The sketch was used as an illustration in Francis's *Common Sense of Yacht Design*.** (© Mystic Seaport, Daniel S. Gregory Ships Plans Library, SP38.303.1) RIGHT: **Francis made this drawing of his grandfather's first catboat, the *Julia*, to illustrate his 1953 biography of his father, *Capt. Nat Herreshoff*.** (L. Francis Herreshoff, *Capt. Nat Herreshoff*, New York: Sheridan House, 1953, 39)

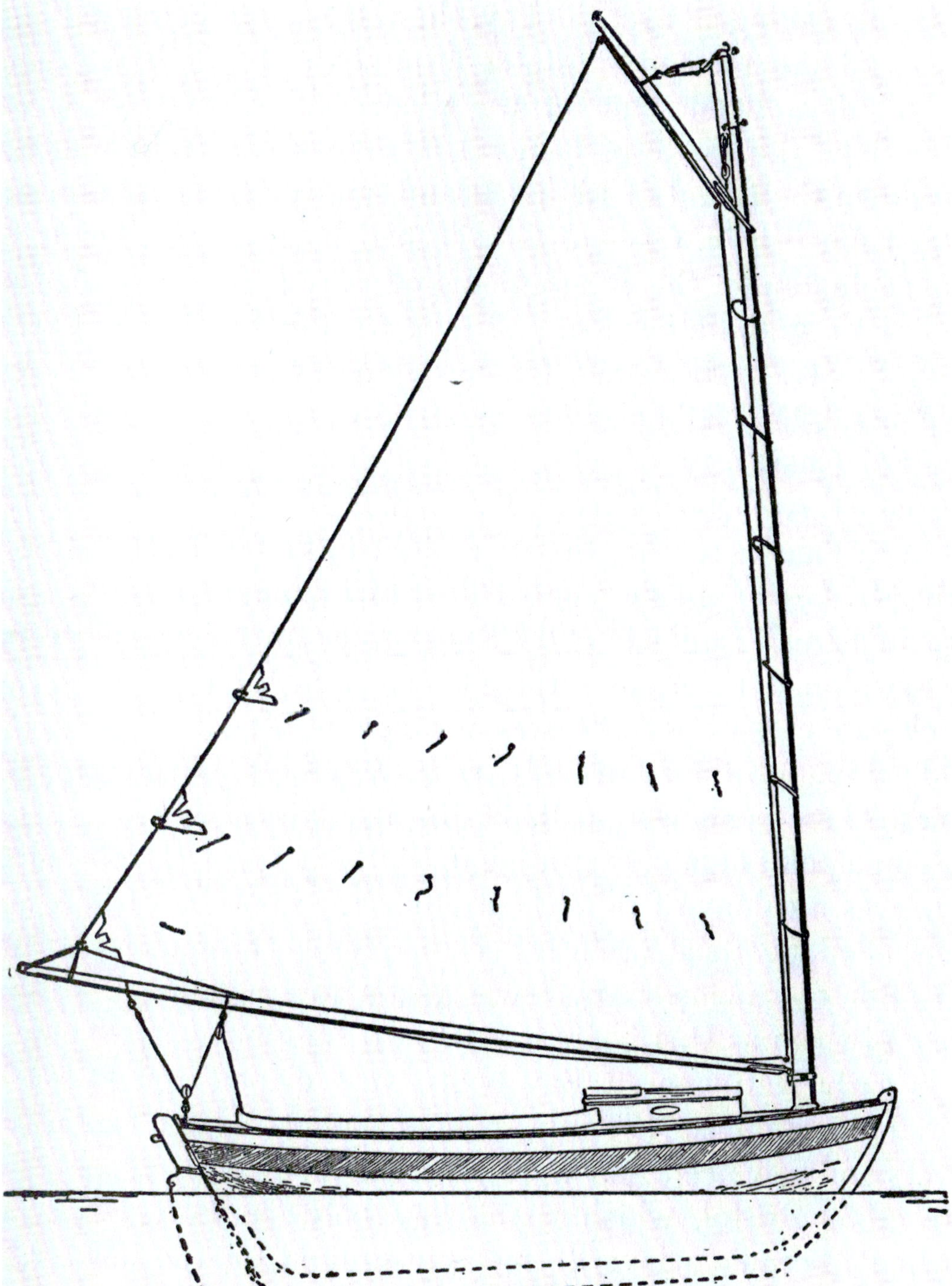

his father. Young John was determined to continue designing, building, and racing boats. To do so, he needed "eyes." He assigned the role of visual guide to his next youngest sighted brother, eight-year-old Nathanael Greene Herreshoff.[16]

So it was that Francis's father, Nathanael, born in 1848, had responsibility and a rigorous work ethic thrust upon him while still a child. Francis wrote: "J. B. was a dynamo of energy and had an indomitable ambition which forced little Nat to do things ... which are generally far beyond the capacity of children of his age." Whether in the boatshop or on the water, Nathanael was John's alter ego, guiding his hands at the lathe, steering his boats in races, and doing it all to John's exacting standards. And John had to put absolute trust in his little brother. It wasn't all smooth sailing. "John had [a] violent temper when things did not go right," Nathanael wrote many years later, but the boys developed the working relationship that would later drive the Herreshoff Manufacturing Company.[17]

In 1856, the family moved from Point Pleasant Farm to a Federal-style house, built in 1800, across the harbor at 142 Hope Street in the south end of Bristol. The house had a good view of the water and gave the big family more space. An adjoining section became fifteen-year-old John's shop, where he set up his four lathes. Just across Hope Street on the waterfront was a vacant building that had been a tannery. By 1859, Charles had secured the use of it for a boatshop, and John began his boatbuilding business. The Tannery was the original site of the Herreshoff Manufacturing Company.[18]

In the winter of 1859-60, John and his father modeled a 20-foot centerboard sloop, which they launched on June 28, 1860, as the *Sprite*. They had definite ideas about how to modify traditional hull shape to gain greater stability and speed, and they made models together that put those ideas into a form that John could "read." The sense of touch is perhaps more useful than the sense of sight when creating and judging a boat's hull shape in three dimensions on a small scale, and John's fingers told him whether or not a given model had achieved what he had in mind. John and his father took away bulk from the hull shape and made their boats gradually narrower and deeper. The finer lines made for a faster boat, and the greater depth lowered the center of gravity of increased inside ballast to provide ample stability, enabling their boats to carry more speed-giving sail area. The *Sprite* was a fast, successful boat; she won her first race against three bigger local boats, needing only a little of her time allowance against one of them. Twelve-year-old Nathanael was her helmsman.[19]

Nathanael never revealed how he felt about spending his childhood glued to the side of his

RIGHT: **John B. Herreshoff in 1865. He has been blind, and has been building boats, for nine years, with help from his father and brothers, particularly Nathanael.** (Herreshoff Marine Museum, Bristol, Rhode Island) OPPOSITE PAGE: **Nathanael G. Herreshoff's high school graduation photo, June 1, 1865. As well as being a high school graduate, he is a competent boatbuilder and designer, an innovator in the design of steam engines, and a skilled helmsman of racing sailboats.** (Herreshoff Marine Museum, Bristol, Rhode Island)

driven, blind brother. What is certain is that he learned a great deal and became accomplished far beyond his years. He later wrote: "I thus got a rather early training in machine work and in boatbuilding and sailing. Even when ten or eleven I became quite apt at tempering small tools, and when eleven had the job of taking the sections from a model [the *Sprite*] and scaling them up to full size, what we call today laying down the lines." But the young Nathanael had to pay a psychological price for his precociousness. John's demands were like running high-voltage current through small wires: something had to give. One effect was to drive Nathanael toward self-centeredness.[20]

By age sixteen, Nathanael was a competent draftsman and an adept woodworker and metalworker. And at that young age, like John, he was putting his own ideas for the improvement of hull shape into the models he carved. He was just sixteen when he modeled a 25-foot sloop that he hoped would be fast. One of the three boats built from the model was the *Violet*, launched two years later, in 1866. Nathanael tried her out in a race against an older boat designed and sailed by his father, and he and the *Violet* were beaten. "Nat was so disappointed," Francis wrote later, "that as soon as he got home he took an ax and chopped up the model from which *Violet* had been built so that no other boats would be built from it." This is the only model of the hundreds Nathanael made that is not still in existence. Despite this early loss, the *Violet* raced successfully in Boston waters for fifty years.[21]

After high school, Nathanael enrolled in a three-year mechanical engineering course at the Massachusetts Institute of Technology in 1866. MIT, which began instruction in 1865, did not offer a marine engineering curriculum until twenty years later. Not long after arriving at the school, Nathanael described to one of his professors a small rotary steam engine that he had designed during his prolific sixteenth year. The professor was intrigued and relayed the story to the school's president, William B. Rogers, who asked Nathanael to demonstrate the engine before the prestigious Society of Arts.[22]

Also during his first year at MIT, Nathanael formulated a breakthrough time-allowance table of racing sailboat handicaps for the newly founded Boston Yacht Club. His table enabled a race committee to read directly without computation the minutes and seconds per mile sailed that any yacht rating from 20 to 80 feet would be required to give any smaller yacht. Nathanael's computations were arranged like a table of distances between points. The handicapper entered the table horizontally at the side with the rated length of one yacht and vertically at the top with the rated length of a second yacht; where the horizontal and vertical columns met, he read the time per mile that the bigger boat gave the smaller. Nathanael's method of equating rated length with speed stood up for years through many rating rule changes with only minor modifications. L. Francis Herreshoff's father N. G. was a prodigy.[23]

After Nathanael finished his studies at MIT in 1869—he didn't receive a diploma, which was reserved for four-year students—he went to work as a draftsman at the Corliss Steam Engine Company in Providence, a leading builder of large steam engines. An enormous Corliss engine that Nathanael helped design would power 8,000 machines in Machinery Hall at the Centennial Exhibition of 1876 in Philadelphia, and Nathanael, age twenty-eight, was in charge of setting up the

engine and getting it running—but not on Sunday, for George Corliss would not allow it.[24]

While working for Corliss, Nathanael found time to design boats and steam engines for John's boatbuilding business in Bristol. In 1870, he modeled a 36-1/2-foot sloop as a study. John was impressed with the model and decided to build a boat to it. The model was beamy and deep, with much-hollowed-out garboards. There was a large amount of inside ballast, kept low, and the breadth of the topsides was increased for extra stability, so the boat could stand up to a big sail plan. The *Shadow* would be a landmark design. Although she was unaccountably not successful in the hands of her first owner, a Dr. Sisson, who had the reputation of being a fine helmsman, she soon came under different management and was invincible, winning nearly 150 racing prizes.[25]

Before the Centennial Exhibition in 1876, Nathanael took a leave from Corliss to spend

LEFT: **Nathanael in his late twenties, when he was working for the Corliss Steam Engine Company. He had greenish-brown eyes, brown hair, and a reddish beard.** (Herreshoff Marine Museum, Bristol, Rhode Island) ABOVE: **The *Shadow* close-hauled in a light breeze with a big spread of sail.** (Herreshoff Marine Museum, Bristol, Rhode Island)

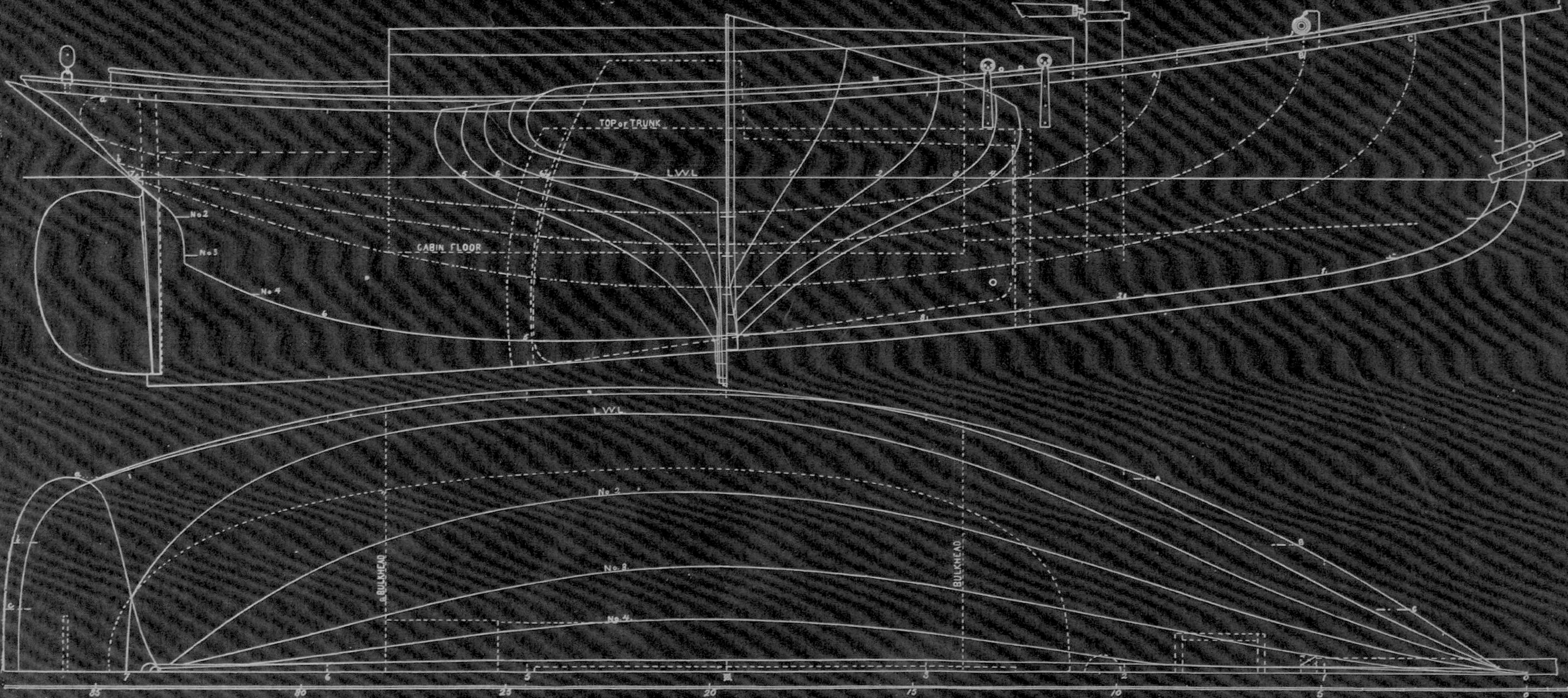
TOP of TRUNK
LWL
CABIN FLOOR
No 2
No 3
No 4
LWL
No 2
No 3
No 4
BULKHEAD
BULKHEAD

more time on his experiments with catamaran design. He designed, and John built, the *Amaryllis*, with twin hulls 25 feet long that could pitch independently of each other. A lateen sail set inside the legs of a bipod mast was not successful, so Nathanael designed a generous gaff sloop rig for the catamaran. If the windward hull lifted clear of the water in a gust, the craft would bear off dangerously, so he put more of her sail area into an extra-large jib that could be eased to ensure luffing and avert a capsize. On June 23, 1876, the *Amaryllis* easily beat the fleet at the head of Long Island Sound in an Open Centennial Regatta. Encouraged by this success, Nathanael took off more time from Corliss in order to make a try at the catamaran business. On April 10, 1877, he obtained a patent on his catamaran design because of the innovations in its details, and by May 10 he had brought out a circular, "A New Era in Yachting: The Patent Catamaran or Double Hulled Boat," announcing that he would build his patented catamaran in 20-, 25-, and 32-foot lengths, and giving their speeds, respectively, as 14, 16, and 20 miles per hour "with a good beam wind." "Sailing in them is the perfection of enjoyment," he wrote. Nathanael, not yet thirty years old, went on to say, "I also hold myself in readiness for consultation in all matters in Naval Engineering, and for furnishing models, drawings, specifications, etc. for Yachts and other sailing vessels." He built half a dozen more catamarans in John's shop, improving on his ideas, but the type would not become popular for a century, and Nathanael's attempt to create a business for himself came to nothing. He went back to Corliss.[26]

While Nathanael was at MIT and Corliss, John was earning a reputation for building fast steamers, vessels designed by Nathanael with engines fed steam by coil boilers invented by James. The coil steam boiler, with very long, light, tapered tubes for rapidly converting feed water to steam, reduced the weight of the plant significantly and resulted in higher speeds in steam-driven craft of all types. The new, light boilers also made small steam launches more practical—John built and sold many of them. James's coil steam boiler, as improved by Nathanael, was a key reason why John could build the steamers that attracted customers.[27]

John took on Dexter S. Stone as a partner in 1864, but the arrangement lasted only until 1867. For the next twelve years, he managed the business on his own with help from his father and his brothers Nathanael and James. Another brother, Charles Frederick, also helped John with his boatbuilding at this time, but Charles's genius lay in enjoying himself. He was a gentleman farmer at Point Pleasant Farm, and he loved to sail, fish, and hunt. Unusual for a Herreshoff, he was a good-natured extrovert. The ladies would tease him with, "Mr. Charles, most of your brothers are famous for something, now what are you famous for?" And Charles would answer, "About all I can claim fame for is being a rather good judge of whisky and tobacco."[28]

In 1878, John persuaded thirty-year-old Nathanael to leave Corliss and join him full-time as partner. They incorporated a new company under the name Herreshoff Manufacturing Company, with the two brothers as sole owners. John was president of the company, but Nathanael had veto power over major decisions.[29]

John gained a partner who could design superlative steam plants and steam vessels, as well as sailing craft, and supervise their construction. He need not worry about the quality of the yard's vessels. Nathanael gained a partner who could

LEFT: **The lines of the *Shadow* were published in *Forest and Stream*, July 28, 1887.** (© Mystic Seaport, Daniel S. Gregory Ships Plans Library, SP38.272.1)

attract customers, purchase materials, and deal with the financial side of the business. He would be free to develop his design and construction ideas to the fullest. The partners divided responsibilities and did not intrude on each other. Each had confidence in the abilities of the other. This was a partnership that would last.

THESE WERE the Herreshoffs: bright, driven, talented, successful. John Brown Francis was one of the country's leading chemical engineers. James was a prolific inventor. John, though blind, was the successful manager of a premier yacht-building firm. Nathanael would become the greatest yacht designer and builder of his era—many would say the greatest ever.

In 1883, Nathanael would marry and sire a new generation of Herreshoffs. Like him and his siblings, some would become yacht designers, engineers, innovators. They would inherit genius. They would have much to live up to.

The Herreshoff family in about 1884. Charles and Julia are seated at top center. John is on his father's right. Sally and Nathanael are on their mother's left. Nathanael's wife Clara is in front of Nathanael; Julian is in front of Sally. Caroline is at the center, below her parents. Standing at the far left are Charles and James, holding James's daughter, Jeannette. Standing at right is J. B. Francis. Lewis is absent. This picture was made about six years before Francis was born. (Herreshoff Marine Museum, Bristol, Rhode Island)

CHAPTER 2

February 20 1898

Dear grandma. mr alpheus was here

today. It has been a very rainy day.

james is married

aunt Flofato is in Brooklyn

Lewis's grandfater is dead

from Francis.

A MARINE NURSERY

"I have made naval architecture a study since childhood under the most favorable conditions in preparation for making the same my life's work."

—L. FRANCIS HERRESHOFF, 1918

"A son born at 4-35 A. M." With this brief entry in his diary, Nathanael G. Herreshoff recorded the arrival of his fifth child, Lewis Francis, on November 11, 1890. Nathanael's diary contained much about the Herreshoff Manufacturing Company and the yachts it produced, and enough weather data to be published as a meteorological record, but little about his family. The baby's mother wrote more in the notebook she kept about her children: "Lewis Francis Herreshoff was born Nov 11 at 4.40. A. M., weighed 9-1/2 lbs. A very nice baby with a very pretty face."[1]

Nathanael Greene Herreshoff had married Clara Ann DeWolf on December 26, 1883. He was thirty-five, she, thirty. Like Sarah Brown and Julia Ann Lewis, Clara was descended from successful shipowners and captains, but by the time she married Nathanael, she and her widowed mother were living on the family farm, struggling to keep it going, with the help of their friends, the Herreshoffs.

Lewis Francis was born at "Love Rocks," a handsome residence that his father had designed. It had porches, gables, and a tower and was built so close to the eastern shore of Bristol Harbor that it needed a seawall to protect its narrow lawn from erosion. The DeWolf Farm, only a mile from Love Rocks, across Bristol Neck facing Mount Hope Bay, became the family's summer home.

In Clara's notebook entry for May 22, 1892, she refers to Lewis Francis simply as Francis, choosing his androgynous name, and the name Lewis is never again used for him. He is still "very pretty, lovely yellow hair and blue eyes." Francis was an early talker, before eleven months, and a late walker at nearly two years old. Both parents recorded his fourth birthday. "Francis 4 years old," Nathanael wrote in his diary. Clara was more effusive: "I have dear little Francis at home with me [his four older siblings were in school]. He is four years old today Nov. 11, 1894. He is quite a tall boy still in dresses with long light hair." The next year, Francis was displaced as the baby of the family when his brother Clarence arrived.

Francis's mother still doted on him, as she did on all her children. Her loving, caring nature was a vital antidote to Nathanael's taciturn, driven

LEFT: **Nathanael and Clara, September 22, 1884, nine months after their marriage.** (Photo by Heald & Giles, Providence, Rhode Island, Herreshoff Marine Museum, Bristol, Rhode Island) RIGHT: **Francis's portrait, taken at the Rose Studio in Providence, November 4, 1893, a week before his third birthday.** (Herreshoff Marine Museum, Bristol, Rhode Island)

personality. Francis adored her. While his father was often stern and unapproachable, forceful and determined, and absorbed in his work, Clara was Francis's source of warmth and affection. Francis never experienced the devotion of his mild, tolerant grandfather, for Charles had died two years before he was born.[2]

Nathanael had "made a verbal agreement with John that if I joined him, our entire efforts would be given to business." Nathanael certainly lived up to his side of the bargain. He began work at 6:30 in the morning, and he worked until 10:00 at night. Francis and the family saw him at meals, and on board his boats on Sundays when the weather served, and on summer cruises. Breakfast was at eight o'clock, lunch at one, and supper at half past six. These were half-hour meals during which the father might ask his children for reports on their activities. He took his responsibility as a parent seriously and wanted his children to be achievers, as he was. But they were a handful for him, often more interested in having fun than in studying.[3]

Agnes Muller, the eldest, born in 1884, was serious enough, but she and her father matched strong wills that led to tension between them. Next to his mother, Agnes was Francis's favorite in the family. He was less fond of his three older brothers: Algernon Sidney DeWolf, born in 1886, named for Clara's father, and known as Sidney; Nathanael Jr., born in 1888; and Alexander Griswold, born in 1889, and known as Griswold. Francis was the different child, and his brothers let him know it. Francis later wrote, "When quite young (four or five years old) I was somewhat of a nuisance at home, for I had a nervous disposition." Francis was not athletic, as his brothers were. He confided to an acquaintance many years later, "When I was a little shaver, my brothers raised hell with me." And he told a friend that his big brothers often turned mean to him in physical play. The normal competition between brothers was certainly played out in the Herreshoff family, and Francis, with his sensitive nature, survived by surrendering his childhood spontaneity. He turned inward and escaped into his own dream world, a world that, increasingly, was involved with boats.[4]

Francis, more than the other children, could aggravate his father. On a beautiful, sunny, spring morning, Nathanael would be up early working in his model room on the third floor of Love Rocks. In the next room, Francis would be lying in his bed, daydreaming. Such behavior baffled and irritated Nathanael.[5]

Unsuited to offering the kind of support and encouragement he had received from his own father, Nathanael nevertheless helped his sons in concrete ways in keeping with his own nature. He had designed the house at Love Rocks for himself

and Clara as newlyweds in 1883. In 1894, with a family of seven, Nathanael replaced his handsome porches, gables, and tower with a tall, square, austere structure that provided more living space. On Christmas Day of that year, he recorded in his diary: "Children's playroom finished and decorated. A happy day for them"—and for Nathanael, as well, who had provided his sons with all the "toys" that he himself would have liked. Many years later, Francis described the playroom to an interviewer as "crammed with steam engines, boilers, hulls, for the boys 'to fiddle with.'" Nathanael also made them model yachts and saw that they had their own workshop with plenty of tools. When Francis was quite young, he took a full-hull model of his father's into the playroom workshop, dismounted it from its stand, made a rig for it, and sailed it. Doubtless, Francis didn't realize the significance of the model. It was a fifty-year-old model of the most famous yacht in the world, the schooner *America* herself, the vessel that had crossed the Atlantic in 1851, beaten the best British yachts in a race round the Isle of Wight, and given her name to the America's Cup. And the model had been made by George Steers himself, the *America's* designer. Nathanael gave Francis a tanning.[6]

ABOVE: **A formal portrait of Francis and his siblings when he was about ten. From left to right are Agnes, Clarence, Sidney, Nathanael Jr., Francis, and Griswold.** (Photo by Anderstrom Photography Studio, Bristol, Rhode Island, Herreshoff Marine Museum, Bristol, Rhode Island)

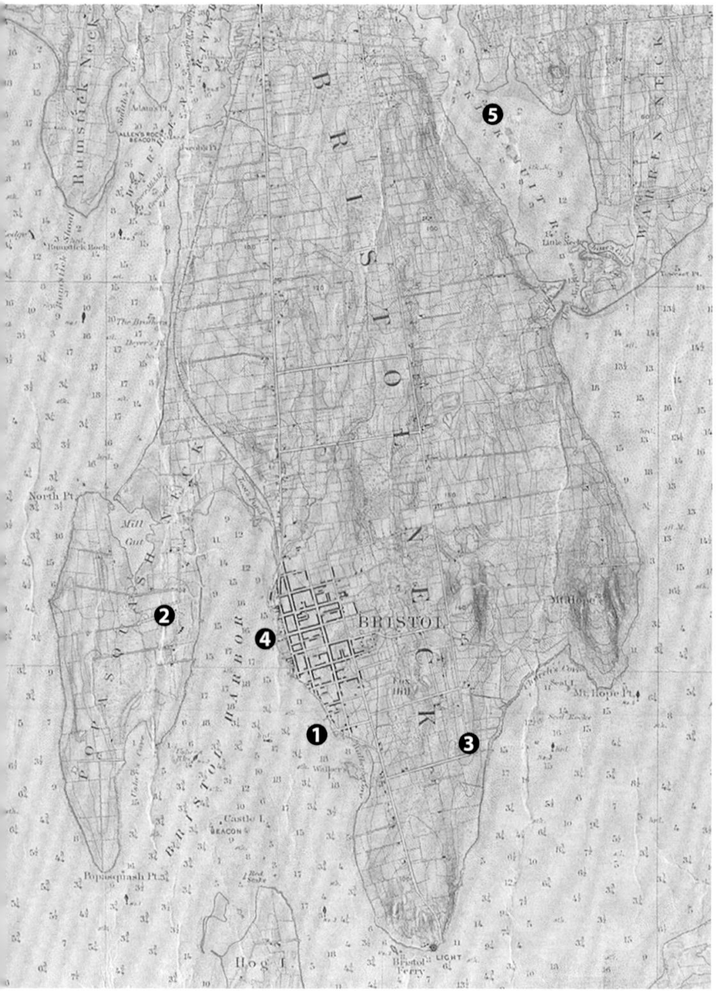

The DeWolf Farm was a happy place for Francis in the summer. It was an operating dairy farm, run by tenant farmer Charlie Luther; buff-colored pencils with white "milk bottles" in place of erasers advertised "Herreshoff Farm—Quality Milk." There were all the barnyard smells, including that of fresh, setting milk. A barefoot Francis dipped his fingers to get a taste. But on a Herreshoff farm, even agriculture was invaded by boats. There were three ponds on the farm, and one of them, a hundred feet by fifty, with firm banks, was perfect for sailing little boats. Nathanael and his eldest son, Sidney, provided "pretty good log boats" for the younger boys to play with. The farm also had more than a quarter mile of shoreline on the east side of Bristol Neck, fronting Mount Hope Bay. There was a good beach for swimming, and the family convened there for holiday picnics. Francis was amphibious as a youngster, and he also did plenty of swimming in Bristol Harbor, off the dock at Love Rocks.[7]

Francis's earliest memory of working on a boat in his father's yacht yard was of the day in the spring of 1895 (he was four years old) when Nathanael summoned him from play in the house at Love Rocks to do a crucial job, one that could only be performed by someone very small. Nathanael had Francis brought to the South Construction Shop, where the first riveted steel mast lay under construction for the *Defender*, that year's America's Cup boat. Nathanael handed little Francis a bucking hammer for the rivets with instructions on how to use it. With the end of a line that had been run inside the length of the mast, Nathanael tied a bowline around his son's small chest. Next to Francis, on the line, was a big bag of rivets. Then Francis squeezed his fragile form inside the tube of the great spar. As he was pulled slowly along in the dark, cramped cylinder, Francis was to insert a rivet into each pair of matching holes in the seam that ran the 100-foot length of the mast. Then he had to hold the weight of the hammer against the rivet as hard as he could while the man outside pounded the other end of the rivet

ABOVE: **Bristol, Rhode Island. (1) Love Rocks; (2) Point Pleasant Farm; (3) The Farm; (4) Herreshoff Manufacturing Company and the Herreshoff Homestead at 140 Hope Street; (5) Kickamuit River.** (Detail from US Coast & Geodetic Survey, Narragansett Bay, Chart 353, 1889, G. W. Blunt White Library, Mystic Seaport) RIGHT: **A barefoot Francis at The Farm, at about age seven. With him are Griswold and his younger brother Clarence. Their cousin, Katherine K. Herreshoff, Uncle John's daughter, took the photo.** (Herreshoff Marine Museum, Bristol, Rhode Island)

over to form a head. (We can only assume that the mast was positioned so that little Francis at least had gravity on his side.) Each rivet had to draw up tight. For want of a tight rivet, the America's Cup could be lost. The deafening noise, he would recount as an adult, was "terrifying."[8]

It seems incredible that the Herreshoff Manufacturing Company had to depend on the strength and nerve of a four-year-old to help rivet the mast of a Cup defender. And that the four-year-old Francis, could do it. Had the great Nathanael G. Herreshoff planned, from the beginning, that the construction of the first riveted mast would require the services of a tiny person? Apparently not. The way Francis told the story, the problem of backing rivets inside a mast had taken his father by surprise, "so he came up to the house to fetch me, much to my mother's objections."[9]

Francis told his story repeatedly. Being chosen to save the day on the construction of a Cup defender's mast was a heady experience for young Francis, even though acting the hero had been scary and exhausting. He was rarely the "chosen one" in the Herreshoff family. His accomplishment that day would be a source of pride for him all his life. Still, it is difficult not to take Francis's story of bucking the hundreds of rivets inside the *Defender*'s mast without a dash of skepticism. Could a slight child of four really have the strength and stamina to do that? We will find Francis as an adult being disingenuous at times in order to paint the picture he wants seen, but we will not find him making up a story from nothing. There is no doubt that Nathanael sent his small son inside that mast, but there is no way to know if or how much Francis may have embellished his tale of that day.[10]

Another of Francis's early memories of the yard was far more pleasant: the smell of wood shavings piling up on the floor of the shop, where he "worked" among the builders of small craft for rowing and sailing, whom he later described as "some of the most kindly men I have ever seen." The workers in the Row Boat Shop, particularly the foreman, Malcolm "Mac" MacNaught, kept a friendly eye on five-year-old Francis; after all, he was one of "Mr. Nat's" sons. Moreover, Mr. Nat let it be known that he had selected the Row Boat Shop as the best place for Francis precisely because

---

ABOVE: **The Herreshoff children at the launching of the America's Cup boat *Defender*, June 29, 1895. Francis, still in curls, is four-and-a-half. Standing, left to right, are Nathanael Jr., Agnes, and Sidney. Griswold is seated in the foreground.** (Herreshoff Marine Museum, Bristol, Rhode Island) RIGHT: **The machine shop at the Herreshoff Manufacturing Company at about the time Francis started taking it all in as a youngster.** (Herreshoff Marine Museum, Bristol, Rhode Island)

he thought its crew to be the most genteel family men in the whole yacht yard. He hoped they would keep his little boy out of trouble.[11]

The Row Boat Shop was at the harbor end of a narrow building sandwiched between the huge North and South Construction Shops. Francis spent a good part of his days there, watching the builders at tasks like planing the long bevels on the edges of planks so they would fit perfectly when laid up against their neighbors on a lapstrake dinghy. Mac MacNaught gave Francis jobs like sweeping the floor and holding the backing iron against the blows of his hammer as he set the small copper rivets used in fine lapstrake construction. At the latter job, Francis was probably almost an expert after his time inside the *Defender*'s mast. Francis worked in the Row Boat Shop after school, on Saturdays, and in the summer at least until he was ten, gradually doing more and more of the work of a boatbuilder. He helped build a number of the 14-foot Columbia lifeboat tenders that his father designed along the lines of the boat that the big Cup defender was required to carry for safety. Beginning at age five, Francis was absorbing the details of boatbuilding as only a young mind can. Many years later, Francis would write to Mac: "I surely remember the days in the row boat shop when you were so very nice to me and taught me a

great deal of what I know about wood working and light construction."[12]

Francis earned 7 1/2 cents an hour for his work in the Row Boat Shop, and one day Nathanael told him that he was going to Providence on business and would take some of Francis's savings and buy him good hand tools. Francis kept some of these tools all his life, tools his father had shown him, by example, how to sharpen and use.[13]

As a youngster, Francis had the run of all the Herreshoff shops. As long as he stayed out of the way and didn't bother any of the 300 workmen with questions, he could watch what they were doing to his heart's content. And watch he did. His uncle and father had built a big, new machine shop for their expanding company, a three-story addition to the old Burnside Rifle Company building that John had leased over thirty years earlier. John filled the new space with every available modern machine for working metal, all driven by leather belts from overhead shafting powered by a Herreshoff steam engine. A boy could climb to either of the second floor galleries that ran most of the length of the space to watch men working at lathes, milling machines, and drill presses. Amid the cacophony of whirring shafts, slapping belts, and squealing cutters, the sweet smell of oiled metal filled the air. A boy who was fascinated with how things are made, as Francis was, could absorb much about how a careful mechanic went about making parts for steam engines and pumps, and about how the parts were assembled to form a finished machine. Late in life, Francis could remember and explain to his automobile mechanic just how a steam engine was balanced, by mounting it on springs, attaching a pencil recorder, running the machine through its speed range, and making adjustments until the pencil remained nearly stationary. Francis knew the ways many things were done at the Herreshoff Manufacturing Company, knowledge he began to acquire as a young child.[14]

The South and North Construction Shops had been put up on the waterfront a few years before Francis was born. These buildings, too, had galleries from which he could look down to see upside-down wooden hulls being planked, or perhaps even to witness the exciting operation of turning them over with two overhead traveling cranes. Most of the big metal vessels were built in the South shop, and when he was eight, Francis doubtless saw the elegant, bronze-and-steel, 131-foot hull of the *Columbia* being framed and plated, right side up, since she was too big to turn over.[15]

He might also have seen the *Columbia* being created in miniature, for sometimes, before he went to bed, Francis was allowed into Nathanael's model room, and, as long as he was quiet, he could watch his father's hands gouge and plane away wood until the new hull shape he had in mind emerged. When Francis couldn't resist asking his father what sort of boat he was making, Nathanael would always answer, "If you watch carefully you will see." Francis did watch carefully, and many years later, he could describe in detail the process by which his father made his half-models.[16]

The *Columbia* was launched on the evening of June 10, 1899, and Francis later wrote about the great event: "As she appeared outside the construction shop calcium lights were played on her so that her polished bronze bottom glistened like gold while her white topsides reflected the strong light so brightly that the assembled thousands broke into a cheer that could be heard for miles. As she took the water an immense silk yacht ensign was raised on a staff aft." The *Columbia* was Nathanael's third America's Cup defender, was chosen over his three-year-old *Defender* to meet the challenge of Sir Thomas Lipton's first *Shamrock*, and defeated the English yacht in three straight races. On the evening after the final victory, the whole Herreshoff family came to the front door of the DeWolf Farm, Nathanael raising little Clarence to his shoulders, to receive the vociferous congratulations of the proud citizens of Bristol. Francis remembered later that the crowd emptied a whole barrel of cider.[17]

"As a boy, living right next door to the Herreshoff plant was a constant holiday," Francis said many years later. "Every day a boat was being launched, rigged and run on her builder's trials. . . . Whenever I could get away from my work [in the Row Boat Shop] or school lessons, I sailed with my father on these trial runs when he checked each boat personally."[18]

Busy as Nathanael was, designing a large number of diverse types of yachts, supervising their construction, and conducting trials of them, he saw to it that his children had their own boats. Francis recalled: "My first command was a nine-foot sailing skiff . . . a dear little ship . . . designed by the same man who designed the Cup defender *Columbia*. . . . I remember very well the first day I sailed in her alone. It was under the lee of a very small island where the water was shallow, and as I sailed back and forth over the eel grass, her speed seemed to me to be terrific, and I have never had such a thrill since."[19]

Francis also rowed a variety of family boats all round Bristol Harbor, over to its protecting Hog Island, and even, on a calm day, around Bristol Point and up to the beach at the DeWolf Farm, or beyond, to enter Church Cove and circumnavigate Seal Island. The boat he liked to row best was narrow, so she went easily, and quite long, so she was stable.[20]

Francis's first memory of sailing was on a family outing when he was five in his father's 16-foot, open cat yawl, the *Coquina*. Nathanael had designed her and had her built for his own use three years before Francis was born, and he sailed her as often as his busy work schedule would allow. She was usually his choice for a Sunday day-sail in Narragansett Bay with members of the family. She was kept hoisted out on davits in the boathouse at Love Rocks; her masts and rig could be set up quickly after she was lowered into the water and moved outside to the dock. His diary contains a good many entries saying simply, "Off in *Coquina* with boys." Nathanael loved to sail and always handled his boats with great care and skill. He was

ABOVE: **The *Roamer* moored at Love Rocks in a photo by Francis's sister Agnes M. Herreshoff.** (Herreshoff Marine Museum, Bristol, Rhode Island)

as good a racing helmsman as there was. Even a celebrated professional skipper like Charley Barr, who knew more about handling a large yacht in a race than anyone, would turn over the wheel of a Cup defender to Captain Nat in a crucial racing situation, for he believed the designer could get a little more speed out of her than he could. Starting as a young child in the *Coquina,* and later in others of his father's boats, Francis could observe how a master sailor handles a boat.[21]

Francis was taken out on a steam yacht at an even earlier age: "The first time I boarded ship was in a baby carriage." He was only twenty months old when his father wrote in his diary: "Started on cruise in *Tranquilo* to Eastward with all the family." It was, for Francis, the first of many cruises and day trips in steam yachts, all designed by his father and built at the Herreshoff Manufacturing Company. The summer before he turned seven, there was a sixteen-day cruise to Bar Harbor, Maine, and back in the *Neckan*, a 109-footer, chartered from her owner, H. C. Baxter. Clara recorded: "We had a delightful cruise. The children all enjoyed it very much." What Francis liked to do most on these trips, aside from eating huge quantities of the good food turned out by the yacht's cook, was to go down into the engine room, with its steamy, hot-oil smells, and watch, fascinated, "the moving parts of the engine as the pant of the air pump kept time with each stroke."[22]

In 1901, when Francis was eleven, Nathanael designed a 94-foot steam yacht to take his family cruising. For the *Roamer*, he devised an exceptionally compact steam plant, so that the yacht could accommodate a dozen people, besides a crew of five, including the all-important cook. For the next decade, this vessel lived up to her name: "she visited most every harbor from Bar Harbor to Sandy Hook." In 1902, the *Roamer* left Bristol on August 6 (having been to New York in July) and, by her return on August 29, had called at Vineyard Haven; Provincetown; Marblehead; Bath, Maine; Bar Harbor; Gloucester; Boston; Plymouth, Nantucket, and Westport, Massachusetts. On many of the trips, Nathanael mixed business with pleasure by observing sailing races in which his yachts were competing. In the late summer of 1903, he took the *Roamer* to Sandy Hook, and the family watched his huge *Reliance*'s successful defense of the America's Cup against the *Shamrock III*. Francis must have thrilled to the sight of a spectator fleet that included many of the prominent yachts of the day, and to the racing between his father's beautiful and spectacular creation—the

Reliance spread more than 16,000 square feet of sail—and the British contender. This was match racing, boat against boat, and whichever boat crossed the finish line first won. Match racing appealed to Francis more than handicapping; when he used to race models at the farm with his chums, "the first yacht that crossed the pond was at once hailed as the winner." He later wrote, "it seemed stupid to me to watch an Astor Cup Race all day, and at the end of the long-drawn-out affair not always know who was the winner until next day, on account of corrected time."[23]

As he grew up, Francis had the use of family boats. The long wharf with its boathouse at Love Rocks harbored a dozen smallcraft propelled by paddle, oar, sail, or power. Francis and his brothers were even allowed to take out their father's delicate *Riviera*, the 17-foot, vee-bottomed sloop that Nathanael and his brother Lewis had built at Nice, France, in 1874 for cruising the coast she was named after and some of the rivers of Europe. She was very lightly built and had to be handled carefully, even under the much-reduced sail plan Nathanael gave her for sailing on Narragansett Bay.[24]

Probably the best times Francis had with his brothers was when some of them would go off cruising together in one of the family's day-sailers. Reluctant to tow a tender astern of a modest-sized sailboat, they would instead take a milk can. Then, when they were at anchor and wanted to go ashore to explore, they would pack clothes and a towel in the can, put on its tight cover, and tow it ashore, swimming. Many of Francis's childhood memories would be painful, but many were also magic. At times, Francis was an outcast from the life of

LEFT: **In this photo by his sister Agnes, Francis has decorated himself with kelp on the beach at Block Island, where the *Roamer* has called on August 7, 1904.** (Herreshoff Marine Museum, Bristol, Rhode Island) ABOVE: **Francis, top, and his brothers climb the tower on the hill at Cuttyhunk Island on a *Roamer* cruise, July 15, 1906. Below Francis are Nat Jr., left; Clarence, center; Sidney, top right; and Griswold, lower right. Francis is proving himself to his brothers and to his sister Agnes, who took the photograph.** (Herreshoff Marine Museum, Bristol, Rhode Island)

his family, but at other times, he was very much a part of it.[25]

At the age of sixteen, Francis graduated to the command of the *Kildee*, a 25-foot, gaff-rigged, knockabout. Nathanael had designed her in 1895 for the use of Clara's sister, Florence, who won many local races in the boat before turning her over to Nathanael, who then passed her on to Francis. On the Bristol racecourses, the *Kildee* continued her winning ways with Francis at the tiller. In one race, he beat his father, who was trying out a new, slightly larger sloop, the *Delight*. Nathanael didn't destroy her model, but he soon sold the *Delight*. In the *Kildee*, Francis made his first cruises as skipper. He later recalled that when he was about to start out on a trip, his father would walk down the wharf and caution him, "Now, Francis, don't forget the water." Francis early learned from his father what was essential to have on a boat and what could be left ashore. Nathanael gave Francis the responsibility "to take the small boats on their trials, to check the fittings, and see that everything was adjusted and in proper working order before the boat was turned over to the owner." Francis had learned sailboat rigging under the stern tutelage of one his father's yard's great characters, chief rigger Frank Chase, so he was well trained for this enjoyable task.[26]

As a son of Nat Herreshoff, Francis was often asked to crew on Herreshoff racing boats. He acquitted himself well enough on foredeck or mainsheet to be asked back. When he was fifteen, he joined the crew of one of the new 30-footers of the New York Yacht Club. Francis had the opportunity to see how the best new racing yachts sailed and also could note how they were handled by owners of varying skill. And he observed the performance of all the parts of a yacht that he had watched being made.[27]

The Herreshoff Manufacturing Company was at its highest plateau of success during Francis's childhood and youth. Neither the financial panics nor the labor unrest of the times bothered it. Huge Herreshoff racing yachts kept the America's Cup safely at the New York Yacht Club, winning eighteen out of twenty races. Rich and famous members of the Club, along with many other customers, ordered hundreds of yachts, large and small, sail and steam, from the yard of the "Wizard of Bristol," as Nathanael was becoming known. "I didn't know it then," Francis was later quoted, "but my father's yard was probably the finest place in the world to learn the various techniques of boat and yacht building at the time. It was the top yard in the United States and had an international reputation." Francis grew up at the center of the US yachting universe, and he learned a great deal.[28]

FRANCIS'S formal education in the Bristol schools, however, was not such smooth sailing. Francis had difficulty learning to read and spell, and he had to repeat first and fourth grades; thus, it took him twelve years to get through the then-standard, ten-year public school program. His particular nemesis was Miss Cora Hill, who taught English to generations of Bristolians. One of her students recalled: "I don't recollect that I ever saw her smile." Francis would later describe himself as "one who made a complete failure of English at school." And he would write years later to Mac MacNaught of the Row Boat Shop, "Tell Cora Hill that I was a better student under you than under her." The Row Boat Shop provided Francis with the vital adult approval that he failed to get at school, or, except from his mother, at home.[29]

Francis blamed his troubles in English class on lack of attention. He later wrote that in the schoolroom "my thoughts were almost altogether either in working in the boat shop or sailing." At the time, neither Francis nor his parents, nor Miss Cora Hill, could have recognized that he had a problem more serious than daydreaming about boats: specific learning disabilities in reading and spelling, or two forms of dyslexia. Although the term had been coined three years before Francis was born, he went through school years before research on how reading is learned was advanced or widespread. Cora Hill could not give him a diagnosis of his disability or training in how to cope with it. Even more important, no one could counsel him that dyslexia often indicates above-average intelligence and ability in the visual arts. When Francis was in school, slowness in reading or trouble with spelling was equated with low intelligence or laziness. He had to suffer the self-doubt, the stigma, the pain of not being able to keep up with his school chums. And when Nathanael saw the school's early reports on Francis, he might well have made up his mind that his fourth son would certainly not be the one to carry on his achievements in yacht design. Neither Francis's father nor his schoolteachers recognized his intuitive, artistic talent. Francis struggled on through the Bristol schools; his brothers nearest him in age, Griswold and Clarence, went off to a private college preparatory school, Milton Academy.[30]

Because of his disability, Francis was not seen for who he really was at home or in school. Though he must have known, on some level, that the things being said about him were not true, still, they were painful and damaging, and, with constant repetition must have left Francis with the impression that something was wrong with him. And underlying his "nervous disposition," Francis may have been wrestling with homosexual tendencies. If so, there is no evidence that he ever acted upon them. In any case, whatever his sexual impulses

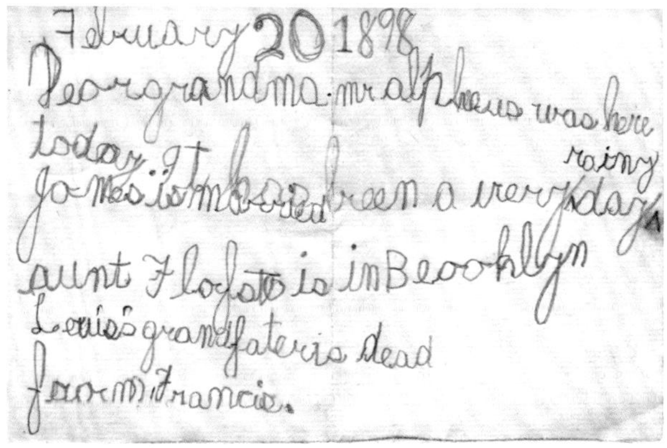

may have been, they would always be submerged. His survival required that early in life he put up boundaries, boundaries that left him isolated and that turned him inward. He would use these defenses all his life, letting in only those whom his intuition told him he could trust.[31]

ABOVE: **While Francis was repeating first grade, he wrote this letter to his grandmother Clara and illustrated the back of it with a drawing of the USS *Boston*. "Mr. Alpheus" is Alpheus Packard, his father's construction superintendent at the Herreshoff Manufacturing Company. "Aunt Floylste" is his mother's sister Florence, or Flossie. The *Boston* is one of the US Navy's first steel warships and will soon fight under Admiral Dewey at Manila Bay. Although Francis's spelling and overwriting show sub-par writing skills for a seven-year-old (yet with a burst of near-genius at the difficult name Alpheus), his drawing of the *Boston*, in which he has emphasized her rig, is brilliant for such an age, and his open numerals for the letter's date already presage his professional drafting style.** (Herreshoff Marine Museum, Bristol, Rhode Island)

DIFFICULT as school was for young Francis, he had to deal with a greater trauma. When he was thirteen, his mother was diagnosed with cancer, and despite the best possible medical attention, she suffered much pain during the next two years. She died at Love Rocks in the early morning hours of November 28, 1905. She was fifty-two. For Francis, at age fifteen, the brightest light in his life went out. Clara's mother, Clara Dimon DeWolf, already living at Love Rocks with the family, took over the household. While Francis loved his grandmother, she could never be the mediator and buffer that his mother had been, the person who smoothed Nathanael's occasionally harsh, sometimes negligent ways with his children. On Clara's gravestone is inscribed, "Her children rise up and call her blessed."[32]

Francis missed his mother terribly. Her illness and death, when he was a vulnerable adolescent, added an element of sadness to his life that perhaps never passed away. His father, grieving and at a loss without the faithful wife who had relieved him almost entirely of any household responsibility so he could concentrate on his work, "withdrew from most human interests and became partly estranged and almost severe with his immediate family." One morning, Francis was late for the usual breakfast of hot johnnycakes. His father said, "Francis, if you can't be down to breakfast at eight o'clock, you'd better get out." Francis replied, "Very well. I will." He went to live, for a time, in the former chauffeur's quarters at the family home of a Bristol friend, Carl B. Rockwell. In an autobiographical poem Francis wrote much later, he referred lovingly to his mother and grandmother, but there is no mention of his father.[33]

Nathanael buried himself in his model room. He had long been self-centered, perhaps initially a reaction to his being forced at a young age to center his attention on the wants and needs of his blind brother. His grief made him more narcissistic than ever. Francis, struggling to succeed around the yacht yard and at school, craved his father's attention. He couldn't get it. Nathanael used his

work to protect himself from facing grief and loss. Coping with trouble, Nathanael did everything he could to avoid looking inward. Francis, coping with trouble, looked inward instinctively. Their different ways of dealing with loss separated them, and, on some unconscious level, the difference made the impenetrable father fear the introspective son. For Francis, the separation and fear meant that he couldn't get the love and recognition he wanted from his father; he would search for it his whole life.[34]

FRANCIS CONTINUED to absorb all he could about yacht design and construction as practiced at the Herreshoff Manufacturing Company. By careful observation, he was acquiring, above all, a sense of proportion in yacht design and construction. And Francis's observational skills were far above normal, a benefit of his dyslexia, which amplifies and sharpens visual memory. He was able to absorb, internalize, and understand all that he saw. He learned not only about the interrelationships of hull and rig dimensions and their performance, but also he learned to recognize just the right size for each part of a boat to be strong enough, but no stronger than necessary. He could have learned from no finer examples than the many yachts produced by his father.

Francis had loved to whittle for as long as he could remember and began to make his own models. In emulating his father's model carving, he found an ideal way to use the gifted talents in visual arts that are so often present with dyslexia.

In June of 1907, the year before he graduated from high school and before his seventeenth birthday, Francis carved a half-hull model that proved he was every bit the prodigy that his father had been at the same age. Francis transformed the idea for a hull shape that was in his mind into the three-dimensional shape of a half model that is similar to designs for racing boats that would not appear until thirty years later. The shape he carved was perhaps more inspiration than conscious choice. Francis, the daydreamer, had an unusual relationship with his unconscious mind. He was not afraid to allow his thinking to be informed by it, even

OPPOSITE PAGE, LEFT: **Francis's personal photograph of his mother, the saintly Clara Ann DeWolf Herreshoff.** (© Mystic Seaport, 1990.37.172) OPPOSITE PAGE, RIGHT: **Francis at The Farm with a bow and arrow, a month before his fifteenth birthday and two months before the end of his mother's two years of suffering with cancer.** (Herreshoff Marine Museum, Bristol, Rhode Island) ABOVE: **Francis on a sail-powered bicycle boat at Love Rocks with an unidentified anchorman, October 28, 1906. The "hull" looks like a modification of an iceboat.** (Herreshoff Marine Museum, Bristol, Rhode Island)

if it took him in unconventional directions. All his life, he would exhibit a strong preference for learning by doing over cognition. This was a sign of his genius. With this model, Francis was not copying his father. Even in the face of Nathanael G. Herreshoff's strong will and enormous skill, his sixteen-year-old son found his own identity and voice and a way to express them.[35]

This remarkable model provided tangible proof of Francis's ability to design yachts. Nathanael was well aware of the model, for the notations on its back—"WL [waterline] 22' 5"; 465 [square feet] sail; Rateing 17.5"—are in his handwriting. He must have recognized the obvious ability that the model demonstrated in his son, but he ignored it and, subconsciously perhaps, even feared it. As we will see, Nathanael had already forced two nephews, both talented yacht designers, out of his drafting room after brief employment. Now, far from encouraging Francis to follow in his footsteps, Nathanael decreed that when Francis finished high school, he was to attend the Rhode Island College of Agriculture and Mechanic Arts and take courses in the Agriculture curriculum to prepare him to take over the management of "Herreshoff Farm—Quality Milk."[36]

The half model of a lovely, long, slim racing boat that Francis carved when he was sixteen. She was to have a waterline length of 22 feet, 5 inches, but this was a study model from which no boat was built. The keel of the model is broken off. This advanced hull should have proved to Nathanael that his son Francis had the genius to be a superlative yacht designer, but it didn't. (Herreshoff Marine Museum, Bristol, Rhode Island)

CHAPTER 3

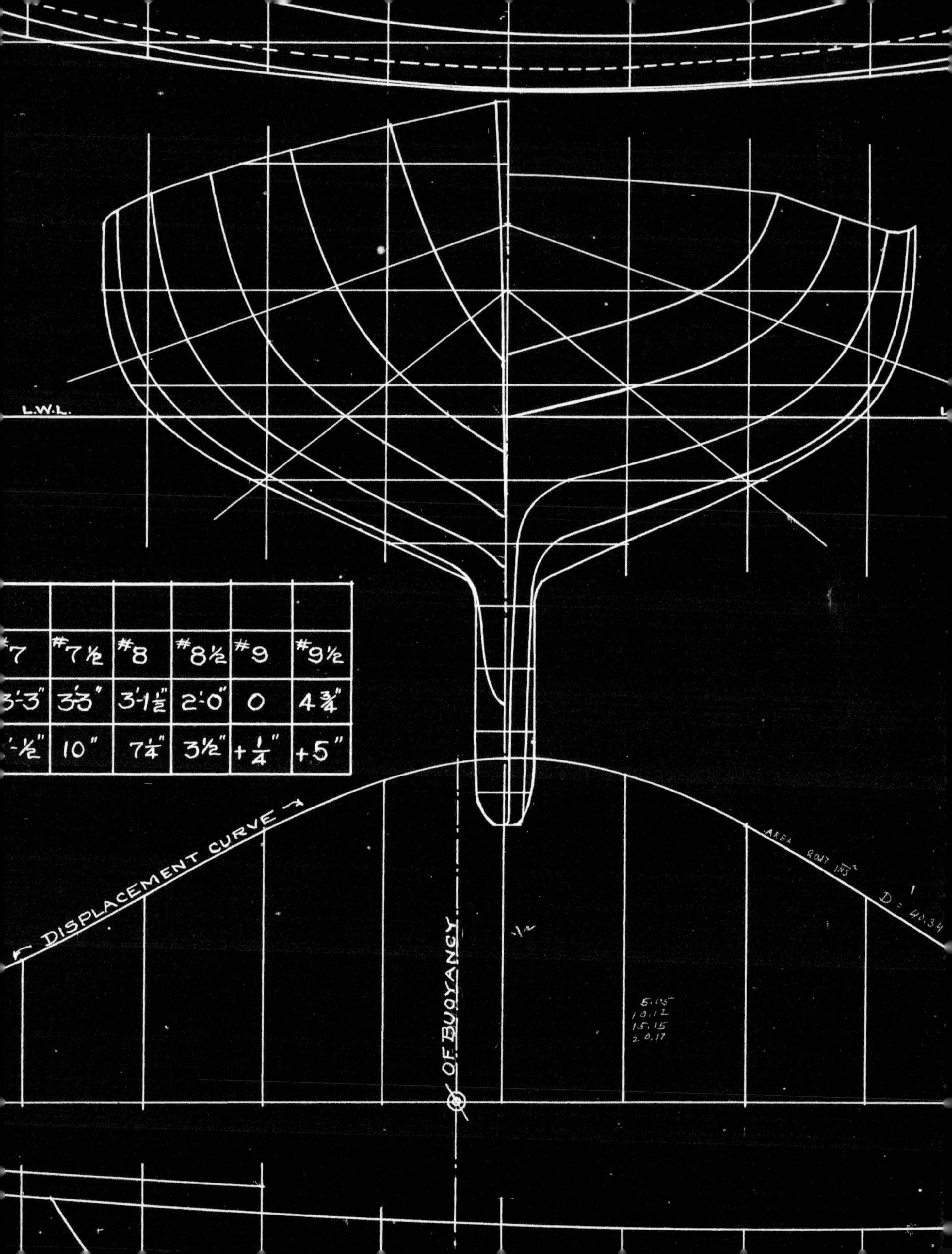

#7	#7½	#8	#8½	#9	#9½
3'-3"	3'3"	3'-1½"	2'-0"	0	4¾"
-½"	10"	7¼"	3½"	+¼"	+5"

DETOUR

"In those days fathers made decisions like that and no one ever questioned them."

—L. FRANCIS HERRESHOFF, 1967

When L. Francis Herreshoff met his twenty-eight classmates at Rhode Island State College at Kingston in September of 1908, he introduced himself as "Fuz" Herreshoff. He and his siblings had concocted three-letter nicknames for each other. Sidney, Nathanael Jr., and Griswold were the obvious "Sid," "Nat," and "Gid." Francis was "Fuz," Clarence was "Ber," and Agnes was "Ugh," or sometimes, more kindly from her brothers, "Zit," pronounced Zeet, short for the Spanish for Little Agnes, Inazita.[1]

As he went off to learn to be a farmer, Francis could reflect, undoubtedly with occasional feelings of bitterness, on the fates, very different from his, of the brothers and sister he was leaving behind. Sid, as the oldest boy, was the chosen one, selected by Nathanael to follow in his footsteps on a straight and narrow path at the Herreshoff Manufacturing Company. Sid had studied naval architecture at MIT for four years, had done well, had left the school without a degree, and, at about the time Francis was sent to agricultural school, had started work in his father's company's drafting room. Nat was in his second year of the naval architecture curriculum at MIT after graduation from Bristol High School. Gid had graduated from Milton Academy and had also entered MIT. Ber was getting ready to follow Gid to Milton. Even Zit, the oldest, though disqualified by her sex from taking an active role in the family business, was able to follow her chosen hobby of photography and make pictures of many of the yachts her father designed and built.[2]

Francis would say many years later that his three older brothers had been educated to run the yacht business, but that "I was educated as a farmer, sent to agricultural school. The plan was for me, the fourth son, to take over the estate [The Farm]. In those days fathers made decisions like that and no one ever questioned them." Indeed, Nathanael's decision to educate Francis as a farmer wasn't questioned by Francis, or anyone else, but it hurt Francis deeply. He had taken every advantage of growing up at the Herreshoff Manufacturing Company to prepare himself to be the yacht designer he wanted to be and that his father wanted him to be. He had told his father that he wanted to be a yacht designer. He had demonstrated, with

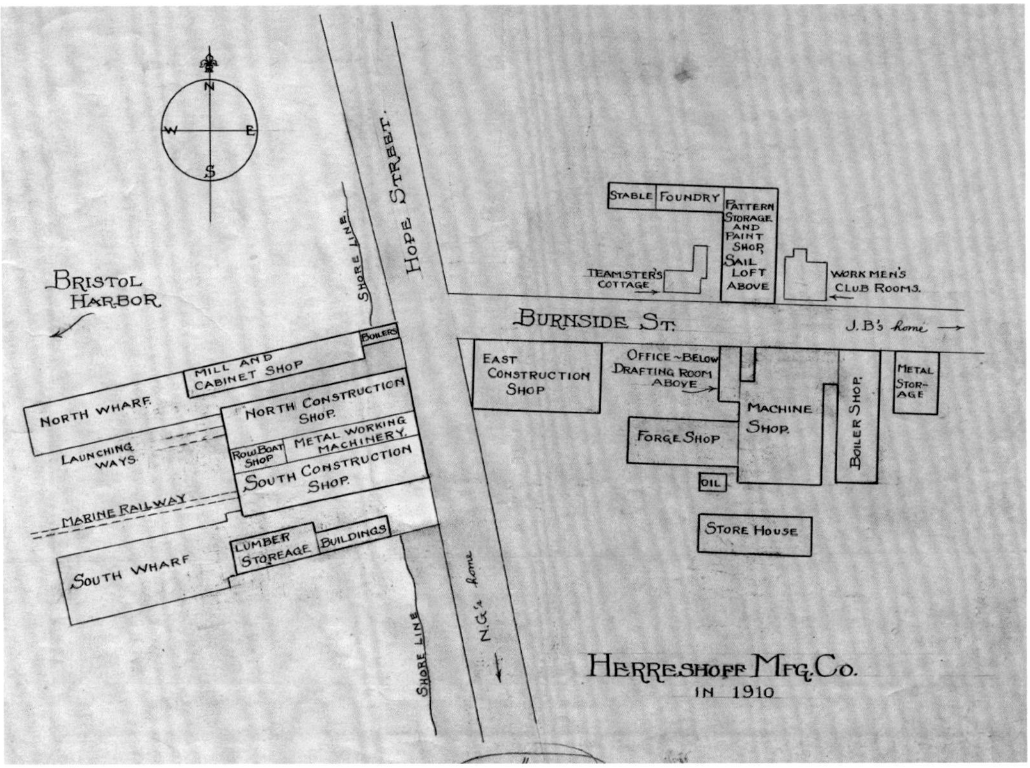

a single, spectacular model, and in many other ways, that he had the skill and patience for the work, and also even the promise of the Herreshoff genius for it. But Nathanael had not been able to acknowledge his different son for who he really was. Francis admired his father more than anyone else and longed for his recognition, yet now he felt abandoned by him.[3]

The decision had been made, and Francis abided by it. He would say later that he hated agricultural school and hated running The Farm, but he did apply himself enough to perform satisfactorily at both places, and he was proud of his ability to succeed in a line of work that was not to his taste. At Rhode Island College, he enrolled in the "Short Course in Agriculture," a two-year curriculum "To meet the needs of those who find it inexpedient to undertake a four-years' college course, but who, nevertheless, desire to increase their efficiency on the farm." As well as basic courses in English and arithmetic, Francis studied Plant Life, Elementary Zoology, Animal Husbandry, Stock Judging, Soils and Fertilizers, and Vegetable Gardening.[4]

He also took a basic woodworking course, in which, as a veteran of the Herreshoff Row Boat Shop, he perhaps taught the instructor more than he learned from him. Francis loved wood, and he had learned much about the properties and uses of many kinds of wood. At Rhode Island College, he studied the scientific details of how a tree grows and of the peculiarities of its structure. Now he discovered the why of what he had learned about using wood for boatbuilding. Francis would write: "Sometimes I am glad I went to an agricultural college."[5]

SCHOOL at Kingston was not total exile. Francis returned home to Love Rocks whenever he could and, inevitably, involved himself with boats. In the winter, there was iceboating. In the harsh winters of the early 1900s, Francis and his brothers could sail iceboats on Bristol Harbor, but their favorite sheet of ice was on the big, brackish pond formed just inside the narrow mouth of the Kickamuit River on the northeast side of Bristol Neck. Sometime before his fifteenth birthday, Francis had designed and built his first small iceboat, rigged with a leg o'mutton sail. At fifteen, he was sailing a bigger boat he had built, the *Grey Gull*, with a large lateen sail set on an A-frame mast. By the time he was at college in Kingston, he had made himself a still larger gaff-rigged sloop, the *Cyrus P. Brown*, a boat big enough to carry a passenger whipping across the ice.

During summer vacations from agricultural school, Francis was afloat in Herreshoff boats of all types, and he joined the family cruises in the *Roamer*. In the summer of 1909, when Francis was eighteen, Captain Joshua Slocum sailed into Bristol Harbor in the vessel in which he had been first to sail around the world single-handed. Francis had a sail in the *Spray* and discovered that because of her full bows, she was well named. He was among the last to have a gam with Slocum on board the yawl before the captain sailed off for Cuba, alone as usual, and he and his little ship went missing.[6]

That same summer, in contrast to joining Captain Joshua Slocum in the *Spray*, Francis joined Captain Charley Barr in the *Avenger*. She was a lovely cutter, 53 feet long on the waterline, as fine a sailing yacht as Nathanael G. Herreshoff created. Francis had raced in her during her first two seasons with her owner, Robert W. Emmons, and now he helped put her in commission and take her down the Bay to Newport to await the New York Yacht Club cruise and the Astor Cup Race. Emmons had hired Barr to run the boat.

Francis wrote later:

> *Capt. Barr had invited me along principally because he wanted someone to talk to in the evenings and thought I would be an appreciative listener, in which assumption he was quite right. The next several evenings were spent by Capt. Barr in describing in great detail some of the famous races he had participated in. He had a most remarkable memory. He could tell just what sails his competitors had*

LEFT TOP: **Francis's plan of the Herreshoff Manufacturing Company in 1910, drawn for his biography of his father, *Capt. Nat Herreshoff*. Francis worked, at one time or another, in most of these buildings, even though, in 1910, he had to concentrate on farming.** (Collection 138, Box 16, Folder 17, G. W. Blunt White Library, Mystic Seaport) LEFT BOTTOM: **Francis catching a gust on the *Grey Gull*, February 17, 1906.** (Herreshoff Marine Museum, Bristol, Rhode Island)

carried in the races, who was on board each yacht, just what tactical mistakes he or they made in each leg of the race, although the race being recounted may have been ten or fifteen years before.

Those evenings on board the Avenger *with Capt. Barr were about the pleasantest of my whole life. If it were a pleasant warm evening, we sat in the cockpit and had the whole fleet of yachts at Newport as our subject of conversation. Each yacht of any consequence (either steam or sail) was described one after another in the most interesting way that could be imagined. The abilities of her designer and builder were reviewed, the peculiarities of her original owner were related, and then a general review of her life was narrated, including her outstanding cruises and races, for Capt. Barr seemed to have the whole history of each yacht stored away in the archives of his memory.*[7]

Francis stayed on board the *Avenger* long enough to help her win the Astor Cup Race, but what he described as the most pleasant evenings of his whole life, listening to Charley Barr's yarns, were, perhaps, an even more important part of his yachting education. In the *Avenger*, Francis was far away from his "Short Course in Agriculture."

And for Francis, as a member of a prominent Bristol family, summer included social life; he remembered going to extravagant parties in Newport. At one, he recalled that everything was pink: the flowers, the linens, the lights, the fountain, even the hostess. He professed to think it all nonsense, but said he enjoyed himself.[8]

Although studying to become a farmer, Francis was allowed to do work for the Herreshoff Manufacturing Company. A scow-like racing class named the Sonder boat, was becoming fashionable among American yachtsmen who were interested in international racing competition. The Sonders, designed to a measurement rule that resulted in a boat of about 18 feet on the waterline and 30 feet overall, with very light scantlings, had been developed in Germany. When German yacht clubs proposed international competition in Sonder boats in 1906, the Herreshoff Manufacturing Company built the first of these boats for Massachusetts yachtsmen. In February 1910, Francis carved a model of one that had been contracted for at the yard. He thus was the designer, presumably under the watchful eye of his father, of Herreshoff Manufacturing Company hull No. 695, Galen L. Stone's *Peg*. Out of sixteen American Sonder boats competing to be among the three sent to Kiel, Germany, in 1911 to race against the European Sonders, *Peg* finished fourth, just behind Nathanael's *Bibelot* (the eventual winner at Kiel).[9]

In addition, Francis was given the responsibility for conducting the trial runs of some of the company's newly built gasoline launches, and he delivered new yachts, both power and sail, to their owners. These delivery trips were an important part of Francis's experience afloat. He had cruised as a passenger in his father's steam yachts and had sailed in many Herreshoff boats, including trials, races, and local cruises, but when he delivered a new boat from the yard, he had the full responsibility, not for a pleasant day's run to an attractive harbor, but rather for reaching the owner's homeport as soon as possible without putting the slightest blemish on a brand-new Herreshoff boat. He later wrote that he "had spent many nights afloat singlehanded." Among the boats he delivered, when they came out a few years later, were the popular 12-1/2-footers and their 16-foot (waterline lengths) sisters, the Fish-class boats. "I have sailed these 12-1/2s in very strong breezes," he wrote.[10]

The month before Francis finished his agricultural studies, he accompanied his father on the trial sail of the great steel schooner *Westward*, 96 feet on the waterline, built for Alexander S. Cochran. The trip was in early April, 1910, and the wind blew very hard and gusty from the northwest. In describing the sail to Francis in a letter nearly twenty years afterward, Nathanael used a rare exclamation point: "She was going some!" He went on to tell of a great, breaking wave she pulled up when her 17-foot draft felt the bottom in twenty feet of water. In his reply, Francis had to remind his father that he had been along on that day: "I went on the trial trip of the *Westward* and remember how fast she went and how cold it was." Then he chided his father a little with a memory his father had omitted, but added an admiring comment: "I remember about missing the mooring and dragging down near Walker's Island when she came in. The *Westward* certainly was a fast and able boat."[11]

AFTER COMPLETING the short course in agriculture at Rhode Island State College in the spring of 1910, Francis moved to The Farm and took over its management. At age twenty, his formal education was finished. His mother had been dead for five years; now The Farm that she had inherited was no longer primarily the Herreshoff family's summer home. The main purpose of this beloved property had shifted from pleasure to profit. The Farm was officially known as "The Captain John DeWolf Farm" after its original owner, Francis's maternal great-grandfather. He had operated it as a gentleman's farm and had passed it on to his son, Algernon Sidney DeWolf (for whom Francis's oldest brother was named). When Algernon died in 1879, The Farm was mortgaged with interest overdue. Algernon's widow, Francis's grandmother Clara, was powerless to save it, but her daughters—Francis's mother Clara and his aunt Florence—together with Nathanael's brother Lewis, tried to run it as a dairy farm to pay off the debt. They, too, were unable to keep up with the interest. After 1883, Nathanael kept The Farm in his new wife's family by staving off the bank with loans to his mother-in-law. Now, in 1910, it was up to Francis to make The Farm pay.[12]

Francis had many happy memories of barefoot summers on The Farm, in its fields and woods, on its ponds and bay shore. Now, as its manager, he would live in the 200-year-old farmhouse, a well-proportioned, two-and-a-half-story building with twelve-pane-over-twelve-pane windows and a walk atop its steep roof. From the house, there were views of Mount Hope Bay to the east and Bristol Harbor to the west.[13]

Francis had charge of The Farm's 140 acres of beautiful, varied land, with hayfields, cornfields, a barn, and all of the accoutrements to care for some thirty head of dairy cattle, raise their feed, and bottle and sell their milk. He was fortunate not to be thrown on his own with this responsibility: Luther Little was employed at The Farm, and he knew all about the details of running the place.[14]

There was much that Francis liked about life on The Farm and much that he disliked. His chief dislike was the cows themselves. He would recall going out every day into the barn to find it filthy. Why, he wondered, would anyone want to spend his life trying to take care of such unclean beasts? He did not. Yet he loved the quiet land with its seasonal rhythms. He was a keen observer of nature (at age thirteen, he had joined the Audubon Society of Rhode Island), and his curiosity, as well as his father's decree, led him to an interest in agrarian matters. Forty-five years later, he could write to a friend who was thinking of moving to a farm: "There is nothing like living on a farm, and if you take an interest in farming you can soon learn all of the principal things about agriculture which are nothing but common sense."[15]

On balance, however, it must have been tedious for Francis to have to direct most of his energy toward the production of milk instead of boats. It must have been frustrating to know that while he was dealing with cow flops, Sid was making a construction drawing of the latest design from their father's model room.

THE TEDIUM and frustration were relieved for Francis the farmer as they had been for Francis the student of farming: he was able to work on a few projects at the Herreshoff Manufacturing Company. In January 1911, he carved a model for the company's hull No. 707, an open (as opposed to one-design) class, 21 feet on the waterline, that raced in Buzzard's Bay. He shaped a model similar to Nathanael's Buzzard's Bay 15-foot class of a dozen years earlier, but made the keel-centerboard hull slightly deeper in proportion, compared to his father's model.[16]

And there was the iceboating on the *Cyrus P. Brown*, with its exhilarating, dangerous speed. On the cold Saturday afternoon of January 20, 1912, Francis took out with him a visitor from Philadelphia, a young lady three years his senior. She was a member of the Howe family, summer

ABOVE: **Among the elements of farming that Francis managed were these great heaps of cow manure.** (Herreshoff Marine Museum, Bristol, Rhode Island) RIGHT: **Readers of the Sunday *New York Times* on January 21, 1912, were treated to the story of a spectacular iceboat accident that occurred the previous day in Bristol, Rhode Island.**

residents of Bristol with connections going back for generations, including connections to his mother's DeWolf family. We don't know the depth of Francis's friendship for Miss Christine Howe.

The pair was enjoying being part of the scene on the ice of Bristol Harbor that day, joining other iceboats and skaters zooming in and out of Walker's Cove. The space for maneuvering was somewhat restricted, because steamers, going about their business, had broken a path up the middle of the harbor. But Francis had no trouble circling round the few mooring buoys that were frozen in at Walker's, until that last run of the day, when the light started to fail as the sun set. The *Brown* reached fast into the Cove, then Francis rounded her up and shot into the wind. Christine began to get up to disembark "when one of the runners smashed against the buoy with a bang, loud enough to attract the attention of many persons on the ice. Next the rudder struck the buoy at an angle, Mr. Herreshoff lost control of the tiller, and the boat broke into pieces, parts of the rudder, runners, backbone, and spars flying into the air and the craft overturning."

Both Christine's forearms were broken, her face was cut and bleeding, and she was badly bruised. Francis had only bumps and scratches. He ran to Christine's assistance, and she was taken to the nearby shelter of Love Rocks, the Herreshoff home, where a doctor attended to her fractures and wounds. Her parents, in Philadelphia, were notified of the accident by wire, and her mother headed for Bristol. She must have been appalled, but, apparently, there were no hard feelings between the families; two years later, Mrs. Frank P. Howe was among the first to order one of the new 12-1/2-foot, one-design sailboats from the Herreshoff Manufacturing Company.

Whether or not he was romantically inclined toward Christine, Francis must have felt terribly guilty and sorry for the accident he had caused. Whatever romance there may have been was evidently ended. Handling a boat, even an iceboat, was an art form for him, a skill and pleasure that he cared deeply about. He must have replayed his horrendous maneuver many times in mind, but he was never known to speak of the accident.

For Francis, there was no escape from the aftermath. Christine was recovering at Love Rocks. Nathanael would have considered the accident to be a blow against his own reputation and would have been furious with Francis. Surely the demise of the *Cyrus P. Brown* increased the tension between father and son. And it was not enough that all Bristol would be talking about Francis's crackup. Because of the prominence of the Herreshoff and Howe names, the "Iceboat Smash" was covered in detail next day in the *New York Times*. Francis could retreat to The Farm and hole up, but he couldn't get the terrible experience out of his head. He was twenty-one when the accident happened; it would be another twenty-one years before he allowed himself to become enamored with a woman. The

GIRL'S ARMS BROKEN IN ICEBOAT SMASH

Miss Christine Howe Badly Hurt in Francis Herreshoff's Craft at Bristol.

STRUCK BUOY IN THE ICE

Helmsman Escapes Serious Injury in Spectacular Accident That Tore Boat to Pieces.

Special to The New York Times.

BRISTOL, R. I., Jan. 20.—An iceboat, Cyrus P. Brown, owned and sailed by Francis Herreshoff, son of Nat Herreshoff, crashed into a mooring buoy

accident with Christine Howe surely contributed to his fear of romantic involvement, as well as complicating his relationship with his father.[17]

A YEAR LATER, in February 1913, Francis got a break from The Farm when Nathanael asked Francis to accompany him to Bermuda. At age sixty-five, Nathanael was seeking respite from overwork and relief from rheumatism. He had first wintered at Bermuda two years earlier and had sailed often in a boat he had shipped down. Now, he was taking a new boat to the island, a lovely, able, 26-foot sloop, the *Alerion III*, that he had designed specifically for sailing conditions that he found more boisterous than he had expected, and he wanted Francis to help him rig her on arrival. Father, son, and the *Alerion* traveled from New York to Bermuda by steamer, a forty-eight-hour passage across the Gulf Stream. Doubtless, both men spent time on the bridge and in the boiler and engine rooms. At Bermuda, a ship's crane eased the *Alerion* overside into the water of Hamilton Harbor and lifted the mast into place. The two experts set up her headstay and single shrouds, rove off the running backstay tackles, put the boom in place, secured throat and peak halyards to the gaff, and bent the mainsail and jib. Then, they would have gone for a trial sail before Francis returned by ship and train to his duties at The Farm.[18]

IN BRISTOL in the evenings, Francis often went to spend time with his cousin Bertie Chesebrough. Albert Stanton Chesebrough, the only child of Francis's Aunt Caroline and Ebenezer Stanton Chesebrough, was twenty-two years older than Francis. As Nathanael's oldest nephew, Bertie had started a career in yacht design at the Herreshoff Manufacturing Company. Nathanael apparently did not welcome his nephew's ideas, and, in four years, they fell out. Bertie left Bristol in 1892, and uncle and nephew never spoke to each other again. For the next eight years, Bertie worked on the design of large steel vessels at Harlan and Hollingsworth in Wilmington, Delaware, and at the Maryland Steel Company. He returned to

LEFT: **Nathanael's third *Alerion* sailing in Bermuda.** (Herreshoff Marine Museum, Bristol, Rhode Island) RIGHT: **An outboard profile drawing of the steam yacht *Cassandra*, designed by Francis's cousin and sometime mentor, Bertie Chesebrough. Bertie's name is misspelled in this drawing made by Ronald R. Moore for Erik Hofman's book, *The Steam Yachts: An Era of Elegance*. Moore sent Francis a print, which he saved.** (© Mystic Seaport, Daniel S. Gregory Ships Plans Library, SP38.314.1)

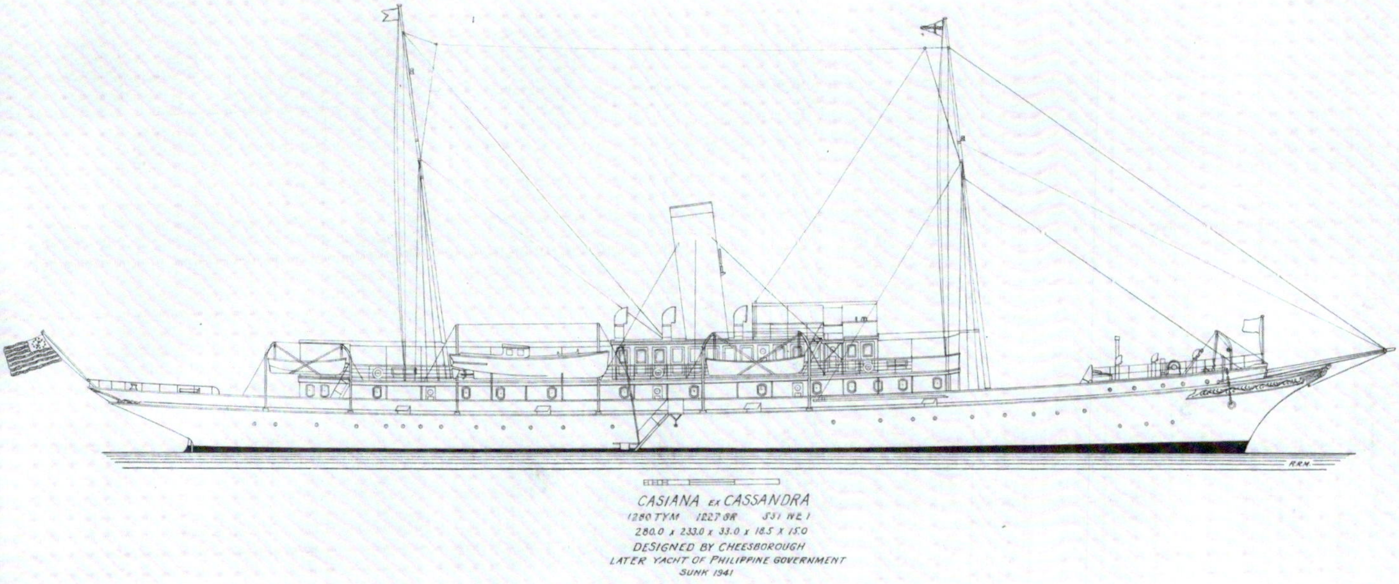

Bristol in 1900 to design yachts on his own. After Bertie's mother was widowed in 1875, she built a three-story house, No. 140 Hope Street, just south of the old Herreshoff homestead. Bertie lived with his mother and had his drafting room on the third floor. Francis would come to the house and, after a brief social visit with his aunt Caroline, would disappear upstairs to join Bertie at the drafting table for a discussion of yacht design. Francis could ask Bertie a great many questions he never dared ask his father; it is probable that Bertie Chesebrough filled in gaps in Francis's knowledge of basic yacht design, especially of the method of creating hull shape in two-dimensional drawings on paper as opposed to the three dimensions of a wooden half-model (Nathanael's method). Bertie Chesebrough demonstrated to the world, if not to Nathanael Herreshoff, that he had the family genius. He designed large, successful, and famous yachts, such as the steel schooner *Hildegarde*, 105 feet on the waterline, launched at Harlan and Hollingsworth in 1897; the 130-foot steel schooner *Invader*, launched at Lawley's in 1905, holder of the course record in the Transpacific Race for fifty years; and the 287-foot steam yacht *Cassandra* that came out in 1908. With these vessels, Bertie Chesebrough was ahead of his famous uncle. Francis had found himself a good teacher.[19]

Francis had little contact with another cousin who had the Herreshoff talent for designing yachts, James's son, Charles Frederick Herreshoff II. Charles worked for the Herreshoff Manufacturing Company briefly when Francis was ten years old, but, as with Bertie Chesebrough, Nathanael didn't want him in his drafting room. Charles went to Glasgow, Scotland, to continue his education in naval architecture. While abroad, he designed the successful 65-foot (waterline) racing cutter *Nevada*. Later designs, after he returned to the United States, included an 18-foot one-design racer and the 25-foot (again, waterline lengths) sloop *Vega* of 1903. Both these sloops were long-ended, low-sided, and fast.[20]

Nathanael chose Sidney, his eldest son, to work in his drafting room. Unlike Bertie Chesebrough, Charles Herreshoff, and Francis Herreshoff,

Sidney had shown no flashes of originality, flashes that looked dangerous to Nathanael's control of all design work at the Herreshoff Manufacturing Company. Bertie Chesebrough and Charles Herreshoff could make their exits from Bristol, but Francis felt he had to stay and do his father's bidding. After four years of enforced farming, his frustration apparently became overwhelming. By March of 1914, Caroline was writing to Nathanael, once again in Bermuda for the winter: "No one hears anything from Francis, but poor fellow, he has had so much trouble he must be excused."[21]

It is not known just what Francis's "trouble" was, but he must have been unhappy with his lot and must have felt trapped, hurt, and depressed. The year 1914 was a big one for the Herreshoff Manufacturing Company. The yard produced its largest yacht ever in the 115-foot-waterline steel schooner *Katoura* for Robert E. Tod; the Cup Defender *Resolute*; and three wonderful one-design classes, the Newport 29-footers, Buzzards Bay 25-footers, and the famous, little 12-1/2-footers. Francis did get a break when he delivered two of the lovely Buzzards Bay 25s—"Special Boats," as the Company listed them—to their owners. But, when he was holed up at The Farm with his unremitting, unsought, unliked chores, he was largely barred from the interest and excitement at the yard: trouble enough, surely, for an aspiring yacht designer, and for a son who couldn't get near the father whose work he admired and wanted to emulate. Francis must have felt that life was passing him by.

THE FOLLOWING year, 1915, brought critical changes to the Herreshoff family. On July 20, Francis's Uncle John died unexpectedly of angina pectoris. Although he was 74, there was no one in the family to take his place as manager of the Herreshoff Manufacturing Company. The long, successful partnership of John and Nathanael had come to an end. John's death meant the loss of his invaluable experience, in judging the cost of building yachts of widely varying size and type, of purchasing materials, of equipping the yard with efficient tools and machinery, of personally dealing with a large number and variety of customers. John's loss started a decline in the fortunes of the Herreshoff Manufacturing Company that efforts at rejuvenation could slow but not reverse. Nathanael, in semi-retirement, could keep designing (at age sixty-seven he was about to produce a model and design for a racing class that would be one of his most famous, the New York 40), but he had neither the interest nor the ability to run the business side of the company. Within two years of John's death, wealthy Herreshoff customers had bought his stock in the company, and Nathanael took the opportunity to sell his own shares. A group of owners headed by August Hecksher and Robert Emmons made Nathanael president of the company as a courtesy; he continued to function as chief designer. They brought in James Swan from the New York Shipbuilding Company as business manager and A. Loring Swasey—a gifted marine executive and designer of power craft—from his own Boston firm of Swasey, Raymond, and Page as vice president for sales, hoping that two experienced men could do the work John had carried on for so long. These changes didn't affect Francis directly, but it must have been unsettling for him to realize that his father no longer had a real say in what course the Herreshoff Manufacturing Company would steer.[22]

Sometime between 1910 and 1915, Nathanael changed the spelling of his first name. The exact date is not known, for, with rare exceptions, he signed his name with the initials "N.G." or with the abbreviation "Nathl." His parents had named him for Nathanael Greene, son of the Revolutionary War general of the same name, who had been his father's classmate at Brown and had remained a close friend; yet, unaccountably, they had spelled his name Nathaniel. He didn't discover the spelling error until he was in his sixties (during a visit to his namesake's grave), and thereafter he spelled his name Nathanael.[23]

The Herreshoffs suffered the mispronunciation of their name. There is no "sh" combination in a German word, so Herres/hoff should be pronounced with a syllabic break between the s and the h, or, at least, with the second h silent. The family pronounced it correctly, of course, but no one else did. The Herreshoffs didn't bother to correct people.[24]

Three months after John's death, Nathanael remarried. Ann Roebuck had been Clara's nurse during her illness and had stayed on for ten years after her death to help run the household and to help Nathanael cope with his rheumatism. She also cared for Clara's mother, who outlived her daughter by eight years and died at the age of eighty-five in 1913. Ann and Nathanael were married in October of 1915. Ann made a real effort to reach out to Nathanael's children. She could never replace their mother, but she was well liked by all of them.[25]

Sidney had continued at the Herreshoff Manufacturing Company doing design work. He had the Herreshoff genius, but his conservative nature kept it hidden. He was a perfectionist for whom everything about a yacht design had to be proven beforehand. Sidney did not take risks, for Nathanael did not take mistakes lightly. Nat Jr. had completed two years at MIT and had spent a year practicing electrical engineering at the General Electric Company in Lynn, Massachusetts. By 1915, he had been working at the Herreshoff Manufacturing Company for five years, designing and supervising the installation of the electrical systems in the vessels. Like his sister Agnes, he was interested in photography. He had a dark room at the company and produced fine pictures of many of the yachts under construction. Griswold, after studying at MIT, had left home and started a career in mechanical engineering at a small company in New Jersey. Griswold most effectively escaped the influence of Nathanael's narcissism. He had the self-confidence to leave the family scene as soon as he was out of college, applied the Herreshoff talent for design and science to mechanical and, later, automotive engineering, and made a successful life for himself, separated from Nathanael. Clarence had left Milton without graduating, had studied engineering briefly at Brown College, and, in 1915, came home and started working in the drafting room of the Herreshoff Manufacturing Company.[26]

THE HERRESHOFFS, with their interest in engineering, were enthusiasts of the automobile. Francis's cousin Charles turned from yacht design to automotive design in about 1905, went to Detroit, and produced the Herreshoff car. The auto had no particular advantage over its competitors and was only manufactured for about two years. In 1916, Sidney designed a fast roadster, using a Scripps-Booth motor and transmission, and oversaw the construction, at his disapproving father's yard, of a prototype with a yacht-like wooden body. The idea was to produce the Novarra, as it was called, at the Herreshoff Manufacturing Company, but production never started.[27]

Francis was allowed to drive a Stanley Steamer at the age of thirteen and a gas-powered car at sixteen. He had a Harley-Davidson motorcycle, but when he fell off in a minor accident, Nathanael chastised him and bought him a Baby Blitzen Benz, a miniature of the famous record-setting racing car, as a substitute vehicle. Francis, seeking to make the car faster by decreasing its weight, designed and built a new open body for it, a modification that made it only marginally less dangerous than the Harley. When Francis sped about in the little car, he chose to wear a Sherlock Holmes deerstalker hat that wouldn't blow off. Francis loved the Baby Blitzen Benz; long after the car was gone, he kept its radiator shroud and honeycomb grill and turned away eager, would-be buyers of these relics.[28]

There were still Herreshoff family cruises,

now in the *Helianthus*, a 64-foot, gasoline-driven cruiser that Nathanael had designed in 1912 as a smaller, simpler replacement for the *Roamer*. In 1915 and 1916, Francis watched the Harvard-Yale boat races in June on the Thames River at New London, Connecticut, from the *Helianthus*, as well as the Astor Cup Races off Newport in August. On these trips, Block Island was a favorite place to visit. During the summer of 1917, Francis would spend a lot more time cruising in the waters around Block Island, but in entirely different circumstances.[29]

ON APRIL 6, 1917, the United States finally joined the Allies and declared war on Germany. Since its outbreak in August 1914, the Great War had claimed millions of young men. Now it would provide Francis Herreshoff with his escape route from The Farm: he volunteered for the US Navy. It is not known whether Nathanael was consulted in the matter, or what his reaction was, but Francis saw his chance and took it. Undoubtedly, patriotism and an affinity for things military also played their parts. The town of Bristol exuded patriotism. Bristolians were prominent in the *Gaspee* Affair of 1772, in which citizens burned one of the King's revenue cutters. Even today, the town, of which Francis's nephew, Halsey C. Herreshoff, has been a longtime mayor, keeps throughout the year the red, white, and blue road stripes that mark the Fourth of July parade route. Francis volunteered for military training at Rhode Island State College and earned medals for sharpshooting. On May 28, the commandant of the Second Naval District at Newport enrolled him in the Naval Coast Defense Reserve, United States Naval Reserve Force, with the provisional rank of ensign. Francis reported for duty in Newport three days later.[30]

An important part of the build-up of the coast defense force was the acceptance of yacht donations for patrol craft. Francis was assigned as junior member and recorder on the board of inspection that examined the condition and inventory of each yacht in the district that was turned over to the government. His duties on the board of inspection quickly became collateral, for, on June

25, he was given command of the *Enaj III* (SP-578), a steam patrol boat that had been launched in 1909 as Thomas G. Bennett's 89-foot Herreshoff steam yacht. Francis reported to Lieutenant (Junior Grade) Harold S. Vanderbilt.[31]

Francis's new orders thrust him into a position of leadership that he had not experienced. He would have felt confident of his seamanship, but the responsibility for a naval vessel and her crew, even on a small scale, must have been a challenge. The United States had vacillated and only entered the war when it was three years old, but Germany and her allies were still far from defeated. The threat of U-boats along the Atlantic coast required naval protection. Francis navigated the waters around Block Island, patrolling either toward Montauk Point on the end of Long Island to the westward, or toward Point Judith on the mainland to the north, thus protecting the eastern approaches to Long Island Sound and New York. The *Enaj* did not miss a patrol for nine months. In the worst weather, Francis would take his vessel to shelter in the landlocked harbor of Great Salt Pond, Block Island. Anchored in its confines in the fall, he rode out the tail end of a hurricane; the weather station ashore recorded a maximum wind of 84 mph. Francis's experience of being responsible for a small vessel underway through the next

LEFT: **Francis (in the stern) and Clarence canoeing in Bristol Harbor, June 5, 1914. Being afloat with a paddle would always help Francis get out of the doldrums.** (Herreshoff Marine Museum, Bristol, Rhode Island) ABOVE: **Ensign Herreshoff and his crew on the bow of the *Enaj III*, summer 1917.** (Herreshoff Marine Museum, Bristol, Rhode Island)

winter in the exposed waters around Block Island was invaluable to his training for yacht design; it was the only time he would observe wave conditions in heavy weather at sea and see how a boat can cope. Years later, he wrote to an aspiring yacht designer: "Your time in the Navy, I am sure, will not be wasted for you will have lots of opportunities for making good observations."[32]

In December, Francis's "opportunities for making good observations" were doubled, for he was given command of SP-56 without being relieved of command of the *Enaj*. "After coming in from patrol on one [I] would go out on the other." The SP-56, built by Murray and Tregurtha in 1916, was a smaller vessel than the *Enaj*, at 70 feet long, and instead of a steam plant, she had a pair of Liberty V-12, 400-horsepower gasoline engines. On patrol, there was much idling of the engines and slow running, not a problem with steam propulsion, but leading to fouling of spark plugs on a big Liberty. Francis devised a system of having a man stand a spark-plug watch on the engines. He taught his engineers how to change plugs without stopping an idling engine: unscrew the plug almost out, wait for the induction stroke, quickly pull the plug and screw in a clean replacement. Then clean the removed plug with gas, ready for the next switch. Another difference with no steam plant was that the only source of heat was the galley stove. Years later, Francis would remember: "[I] have been out forty-eight hours at a time with the thermometer below zero. . . . I have seen times [in the SP-56] when the motion would throw the stove covers off of a coal burning stove so that we had to slow down for this reason if no other." In late January 1918, Francis brought his two charges to Bristol, where, for a time, they were iced in at the Herreshoff company's docks. The purpose of the visit is not known; perhaps the boats needed repairs.[33]

After nine months of sea duty, the last three patrolling constantly in his two vessels, Francis was relieved of both his commands on March 11, 1918. He reported for shore duty in Newport as a member of a board to inspect the condition of the naval vessels of the second district and also of all merchant vessels being constructed in the district. He would write years later that he was pretty well fed up with going to sea after his intense stint, "so that I wanted to stay ashore for several years afterward." Eight years after his naval duty, Francis acquired and kept for the rest of his life a large-scale chart of the waters around Block Island that he had patrolled. He felt that in that part of his naval service in particular, he was doing something important for his country.[34]

On July 13, Francis was ordered to temporary duty at New London, Connecticut, at the Experimental Station, which was a separate part of the Submarine Base. He designed and made streamlined devices to be towed underwater, carrying microphones equipped with the new Pierce compensator to detect the sound of a submerged submarine and indicate its bearing. While in New London, Francis had the experience of diving in a submarine and flying in an airplane on the same day.[35]

The Armistice ending World War I was signed on Francis's twenty-eighth birthday. Still at New London, he was assigned to a "board to find peacetime uses for some of the things that were developed" at the Experimental Station. He suggested a fathometer using the sound of a ship's propellers reflected from the bottom and a colli-

---

LEFT: Francis makes sure the helmsman has the *Enaj* on course. With the coming of fall 1917, Francis has shifted his uniform from whites to blues, and he has grown a mustache, an adornment he would retain for the rest of his life. (Herreshoff Marine Museum, Bristol, Rhode Island)

sion-avoidance system in which each vessel would send by underwater sound a Morse Code signal indicating her course, and each vessel would listen for such signals, giving not only a contact's course, but also its bearing.[36]

Francis's orders releasing him "from all active duty" are dated March 14, 1919, but it took until April 4 to complete the separation process at the Naval Training Station at Newport.[37]

WHILE IN the navy, Francis had been appointed by Rhode Island Governor R. Livingston Beekman to the State Board of Agriculture, to complete the term of a deceased member, from February 18, 1918, to January 31, 1919. He was then appointed for a further two-year term. When he returned to Bristol after his naval service, however, he did not go back to The Farm, but rather to Love Rocks, to tasks at the Herreshoff Manufacturing Company, and to making a start on designing boats on his own. It is not known whether his father desired Francis to return to management of The Farm. Perhaps he did, but perhaps he realized that he could not simply send a twenty-eight-year-old naval officer, an officer who had brought two vessels under his command to the docks of the Herreshoff Manufacturing Company, back to the cow barn. Francis was beginning to consolidate his gains in the struggle for independence from his powerful father.[38]

Despite the potential for building wartime naval vessels, the Herreshoff yard had declined. Although the new management, James Swan and Loring Swasey, started off well at the beginning of 1917, bringing in contracts for a couple of dozen patrol craft, Swasey left within two months to join the Navy Bureau of Construction and Repair in Washington, and his departure effectively reduced to a trickle the company's government contracts and profits. By the end of the year, a good many of the boatbuilders at Herreshoff's had moved to other yards that were expanding.[39]

After the war, Loring Swasey returned as vice president at the company, and one of Francis's tasks was to loft Swasey's lines of a 140-foot steel steam yacht, the *Alert*, built for Charles A. Stone of Boston. He made his big drawings of the vessel's

ABOVE: **Francis at the Experimental Station at New London, Connecticut, in 1918. He is holding one of the shapes he designed and made to be towed underwater to carry a submarine locator device. Note his new-fangled wristwatch.** (*The Common Sense of Yacht Design*, volume 1, figure 93) RIGHT: **Francis after his naval service, all dressed up for target shooting, probably at The Farm. At a younger age, Francis and his friend Nick Potter "used to walk around The Farm with guns under our arms shooting crows."** (Herreshoff Marine Museum, Bristol, Rhode Island; Francis to Nicholas Potter, September 1, 1966, Collection 138, Box 5, Folder 8, G. W. Blunt White Library, Mystic Seaport)

sections on the upstairs floor on the north side of the East Construction Shop on Burnside Street.[40]

Even though Francis was not employed full-time at the Herreshoff yard after his naval service, this was not because the company was not hiring. When his friend Nicholas S. Potter, seven years Francis's junior, came out of the navy, he was put to work in the Herreshoff Manufacturing Company drafting room. Nathanael was wise enough to criticize Potter's work through Sidney; Nick Potter stayed on for five years. Francis and Nick remained friends.[41]

In March 1920, Francis took the train to New York to meet his father's *Alerion III*, arriving by ship from Bermuda. He rigged her and sailed her home to Bristol. It was a memorable trip, sailing the spritely boat through all the vagaries of New England spring weather. Years later, he would record the details of his delivery of the *Alerion* for future generations of appreciative sailors.[42]

Also in the spring of 1920, Francis took the first S-boat, built to his father's design, on her trial sail. This was a one-design class whose sponsors, notably Robert Emmons, had wanted a boat "with short overhangs and full bows and sterns" for racing on Buzzards Bay. The class was designed to rate in the Universal Rule's Class S, at 17 feet, but Class S never proved as popular as the bigger Universal Rule classes. The Herreshoff S-boats, 20 feet, 6 inches long on the waterline, Capt. Nat's last one-design racing class, did prove popular, for the boats are fast, weatherly, and comfortable for day-sailing and overnight cruising, as well as for racing. Beginning in December 1919, the company contracted for twenty-three S-boats through 1920. Francis sailed S-boats to their owners in Marblehead and up Long Island Sound.[43]

At about this same time, Francis, thirty years old, made a sophisticated, complete yacht design, probably his first. The boat is a 15-foot-waterline daysailer for Narragansett Bay. There are certain similarities to the S-boat, and it would be fascinating to know the exact chronology of these two designs by father and son. Perhaps the most likely sequence is that Francis designed his boat with some features of his father's S-boat, notably the curved mast, the first for Nathanael and, of course, for Francis, but without any restriction imposed by prospective owners or the Universal Rule. No boat was built to Francis's design during his lifetime. This first design of Francis's borrows more from his father's Buzzard's Bay 12½-footer than from the S-boat. Like the Herreshoff 12½ of six years earlier, she would be fast and able. But, as a beginner, Francis has not yet achieved the wonderful harmony of his father's 12½-footer.[44]

In 1920, Francis designed a 14-foot sailing skiff as a junior sailors' class for the Bristol Yacht Club. The boats were the first built to a design by L. Francis Herreshoff.[45]

He made a preliminary design for an offshore cruiser, a seaworthy, double-ended, 46-foot ketch. He numbered the design "F-5" (F for Francis?), indicating that he had perhaps made four previous designs designated "F, " but, if so, none have survived. Francis would refine his concept of the seaworthy cruiser with three more preliminary designs before drawing complete plans, twenty-five years later, representing his idea of the best possible vessel for world cruising.[46]

LEFT: Francis's drawing of his sail in the *Alerion.* (*The Rudder* (September 1943): 14) ABOVE: Francis putting the first S-boat through her paces in Bristol Harbor, spring 1920. He's seeing how far a sharp, northerly gust will heel her and has let her go right over to the coaming. The boat is sailing fast even though heeled well down. (Herreshoff Marine Museum, Bristol, Rhode Island)

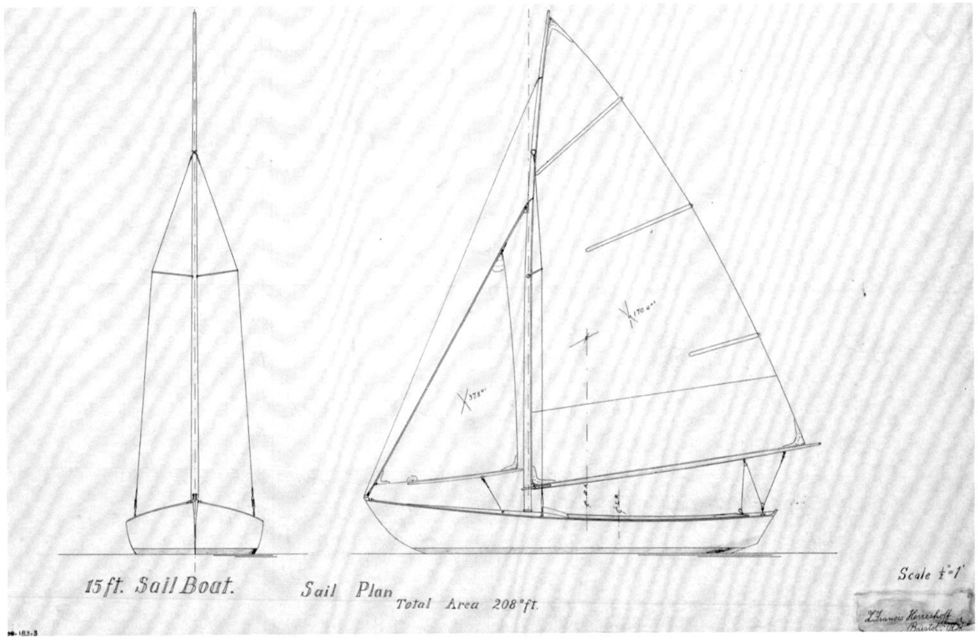

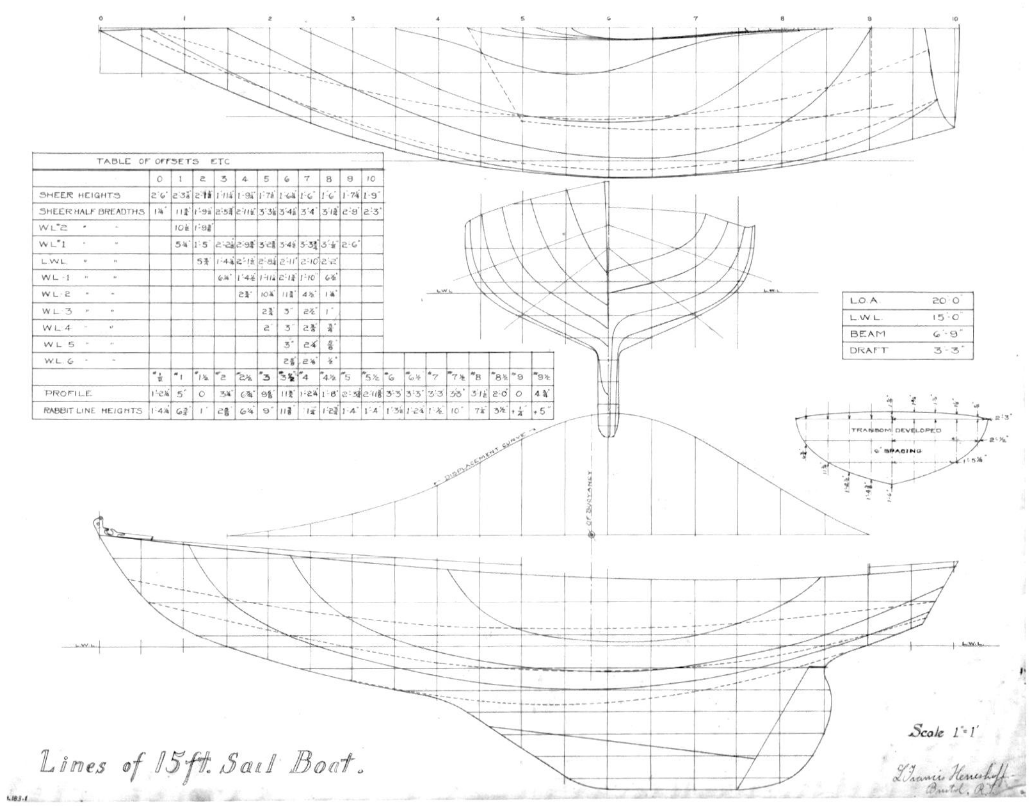

TABLE OF OFFSETS ETC

	0	1	2	3	4	5	6	7	8	9	10
SHEER HEIGHTS	2'6"	2'3⅞"	2'1⅝"	1'11¼"	1'9¾"	1'7⅞"	1'6⅛"	1'6"	1'6"	1'7¾"	1'9"
SHEER HALF BREADTHS	1¼"	11⅝"	1'9½"	2'5⅞"	2'11⅛"	3'3⅜"	3'4⅛"	3'4"	3'1½"	2'9"	2'3"
W.L.#2 " "		10½"	1'9⅜"								
W.L.#1 " "		5¼"	1'5"	2'2⅛"	2'9⅜"	3'2⅛"	3'4½"	3'3¾"	3'½"	2'6"	
L.W.L. " "			5⅜"	1'4¾"	2'1½"	2'8¼"	2'11"	2'10"	2'2"		
W.L.-1 " "				6¼"	1'4½"	1'11¼"	2'1⅛"	1'10"	6½"		
W.L.-2 " "					2¾"	10¼"	11⅜"	4½"	1¼"		
W.L.-3 " "						2¾"	3"	2½"	1"		
W.L.-4 " "						2"	3"	2⅜"	¾"		
W.L.-5 " "							3"	2¼"	⅝"		
W.L.-6 " "							2⅝"	2⅛"	½"		

	#½	#1	#1½	#2	#2½	#3	#3½	#4	#4½	#5	#5½	#6	#6½	#7	#7½	#8	#8½	#9	#9½
PROFILE	1'2¼"	5"	0	3¼"	6¾"	9⅝"	11⅞"	1'2¼"	1'8"	2'3⅜"	2'11⅝"	3'3"	3'3"	3'3"	3'3"	3'1½"	2'0"	0	4¾"
RABBIT LINE HEIGHTS	1'4¼"	6¾"	1"	2⅝"	6¼"	9"	11⅝"	1¼"	1'2⅜"	1'4"	1'4"	1'3⅛"	1'2¼"	1'½"	10"	7¼"	3½"	+¼"	+5"

LEFT TOP: **The sail plan of the Narragansett Bay daysailer that Francis designed at about the time when his father was designing the S-boat. Note the curved mast and long upper battens in the mainsail. With vertical lines, Francis has marked the fore-and-aft positions of the center of lateral resistance of the underwater profile and the center of effort of the sail plan, the "lead," or distance between them, being the critical factor for good steering balance. Both centers are well aft in this design.** (© Mystic Seaport, Daniel S. Gregory Ships Plans Library, SP38.183.3) LEFT BOTTOM: **The lines of the Narragansett Bay boat show the influence of Francis's careful study of his father's models.** (© Mystic Seaport, Daniel S. Gregory Ships Plans Library, SP38.183.1) BELOW: **The construction plan of the Narranganset Bay daysailer. Francis has not followed his father's admirable practice of slanting the cockpit coaming outboard for the comfort of the crew.** (© Mystic Seaport, Daniel S. Gregory Ships Plans Library, SP38.183.1)

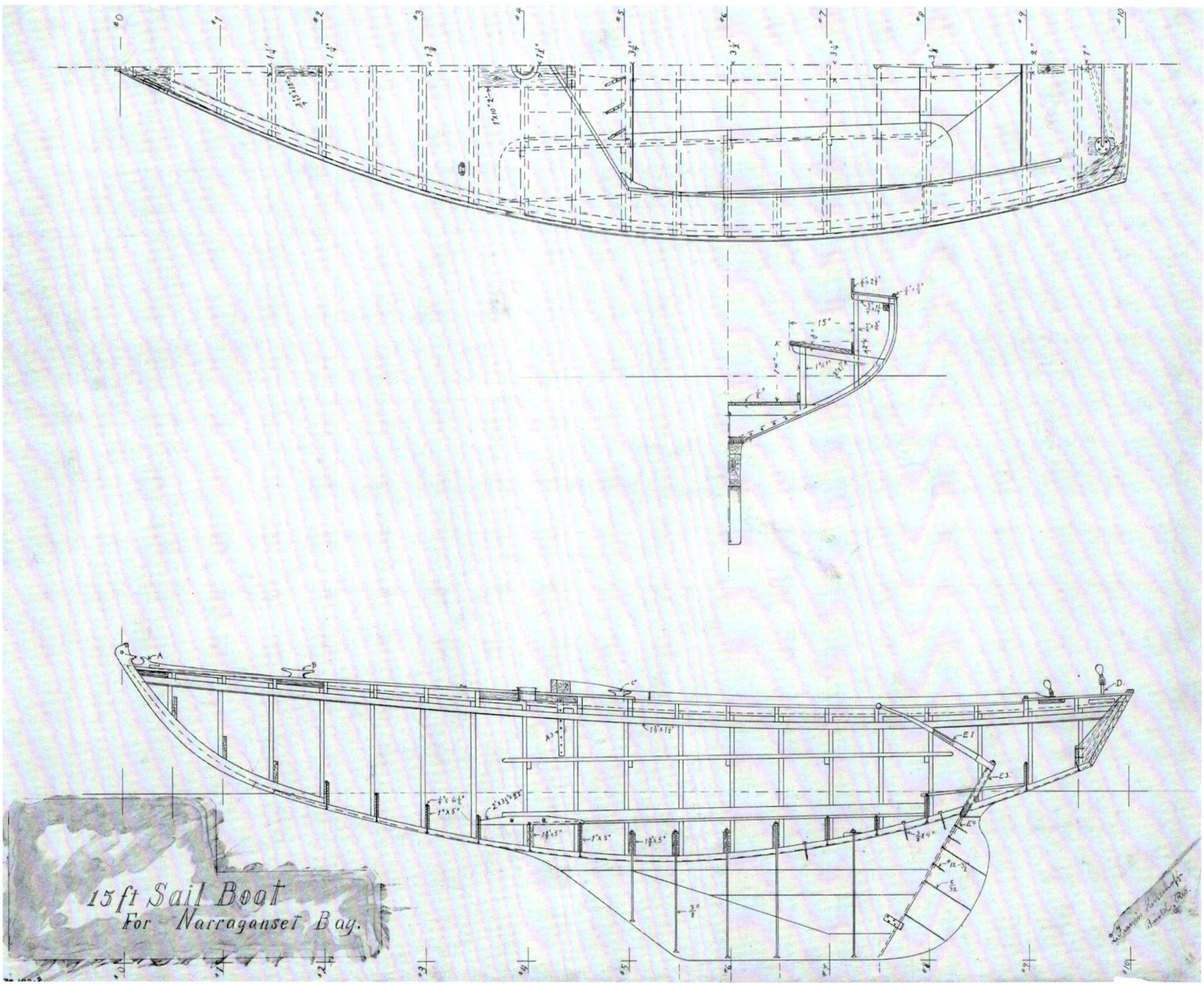

IN THE LATE FALL of 1920, yacht designer W. Starling Burgess came to the Herreshoff Manufacturing Company to try to achieve a first: persuade the Herreshoff yard to build a boat not designed by Nathanael G. Herreshoff. Starling had an order to design a 6-Metre boat, and he wanted his customer, Paul Hammond, to have the best possible construction for his racer.

Starling was well acquainted with the Herreshoffs. His father, Edward Burgess, had been a yachtsman, had summered in Bristol, had sailed his own Herreshoff boats, and had become friendly with the Herreshoff family. Edward used to cross Bristol Harbor from his summer cottage on Poppasquash Point to the Herreshoff works to talk sailboat design with Nathanael. When the Burgess fortune was wiped out in 1883, Edward took up yacht design professionally to support his family and was so successful that yachts he designed defended the America's Cup in 1885, 1886, and 1887. This trio, the *Puritan*, *Mayflower*, and *Volunteer* were clearly influenced by a model for a much smaller boat that Nat Herreshoff had carved in 1880 but had never built to, a model intended to be an improvement on his highly successful *Shadow*, and a model that Burgess, on his summer visits, had often admired as "the perfect model." And in 1889, Burgess designed a Gloucester fishing schooner, the *Fredonia,* that was safer at sea than the then-popular clipper schooners, with their wide, shallow hulls and huge rigs. The *Fredonia* was much copied in the Gloucester fleet. When Edward Burgess died of typhoid in 1891, he was forty-three years old and the leading American designer of large sailing yachts, having in seven years created 137 designs: 83 sailing yachts, 3 America's Cup defenders, 11 fishing schooners, 3 pilot schooners, and 37 steam yachts.[47]

His son, Starling, in the winter of 1896, a few months before he graduated from Milton Academy—a school that seemed to attract boys with boats on their minds—had the Herreshoff Manufacturing Company build him a fast, light, 17-foot sloop. When he went to Bristol from Milton on weekends to examine the construction of his new boat, Starling would stay with "Uncle Nat" and Clara Herreshoff and their six children at Love Rocks. He was treated as a member of the family; Francis was then six years old, and the teenaged Starling would bounce him on his knee. Young Starling had even been allowed into the inner sanctum of Nathanael Herreshoff's model room—until he revealed his ambition to become a professional yacht designer and was banished.[48]

When Starling made the unusual request to have his 6-Metre boat built by the Herreshoff Manufacturing Company in 1920, Nathanael was seventy-two years old, but he was still wary of competitors. His *Resolute* had just won the America's Cup; a key part of her successful campaign had been the defeat of the rejuvenated contender *Vanitie*, designed by William Gardner. Starling had supervised the *Vanitie*'s rig and deck modifications and had sailed in her afterguard. Nathanael might have resisted Starling's request, but, with John gone and his own stock sold, the decision was not his. Loring Swasey was looking for new business and would have wanted to build Starling's 6-Metre. Starling got the answer he wanted. He also got a new draftsman for his yacht design business, L. Francis Herreshoff.[49]

How it came to be that Francis went to work for Starling Burgess is a matter of conjecture. Starling had the opportunity to broach the idea to Francis when they were together at City Island, up Long Island Sound, in the spring of 1920, when Starling was in the *Vanitie*'s afterguard and Francis was sailing the *Alerion* home. And Starling would have made contact with Francis at Bristol, when he came to see about having the 6-Metre *Sheila* built. Yet the idea of Starling's hiring Francis may have come from Loring Swasey. A clever manager of people, Swasey would have realized that there was no place for Francis at the Herreshoff yard.

Starling found Francis working intermittently and without significant responsibility at a Herreshoff Manufacturing Company that was well past its peak. He saw that the child he had bounced on his knee had developed into a young man who had absorbed considerable knowledge of yacht design and construction and had gained experience afloat in a wide variety of craft. Starling saw that Francis was a careful draftsman with plenty of imagination. He saw more potential than accomplishment. He trusted the Herreshoff genes. The Herreshoff Manufacturing Company shut down temporarily on December 8, 1920, giving the employees an unwanted, unpaid Christmas vacation. If Francis needed a signal to leave Bristol, this may have been it. In any event, he would go to work for Starling as a full-time draftsman.[50]

Starling must have appreciated that he was offering Francis much more than a job. Starling was one to share what he had learned and what he believed about the engineering and art of yacht design. He was a humanist who would understand Francis's nature as Nathanael never could. Starling was ready to become Francis's encouraging mentor, and Francis must have been excited at the prospect of helping such a man design yachts.

In what was probably Francis's last design effort before leaving Bristol, he emulated his father with a concept for a catamaran. The drawing, dated November 20, 1920, is futuristic. His craft is as different as can be from his father's *Amaryllis*. Each streamlined hull has its own rig, tipped well inboard. Each quadrilateral sail is complex, with two sheets and two wishbone sprits. Each wing mast rotates, and each sail is double-luffed, hoisting on two mast tracks, so that mast and sail form a streamlined wing whose leading edge can be angled perfectly to the wind direction. It may be just as well that this craft was never built; yet, Francis would later patent her wing-sail idea. If Nathanael Herreshoff saw the drawing, he probably shook his head sadly at its apparent impracticability. Starling Burgess perhaps did see it and, if so, may have been so fascinated as to hire Francis on the spot. The two designers would later discuss the concept and Francis would refine and simplify the design, yet no trial craft ever materialized.[51]

FRANCIS HERRESHOFF had been working around the edges of yacht design. The first thirty years of his life coincided with his father's period of most intense activity, and, despite their great emotional differences, Francis had absorbed much from his father. He had worked at times in every department of the Herreshoff Manufacturing Company from 1910 to 1917, while he was running The Farm, and again in 1919 and 1920, but apparently never as a full-fledged employee. In later writings, he listed the places where he had worked: the row boat shop, pattern shop, foundry, blacksmith shop, machine shop, boiler shop, mold loft, sail loft, rigging loft, steel construction shop, wood construction shop, drafting room, and office. He stated in writing to his commanding officer at the Experimental Station that he had worked "about four years in the drafting room." Those years would have to have been while he was running The Farm, so the work must have been intermittent. It is possible that he may have drawn some of the plans in conjunction with the models he carved for a Sonder boat and the Buzzards Bay 21-footers. It is probable that his work was inking plans that had been drawn in pencil by his father. But until Starling Burgess hired Francis away from Bristol in late 1920, Francis had not had a full-time job working at his chosen profession.[52]

Francis resented that his father had denied him the opportunities given his brothers; yet, with undiagnosed dyslexia, he would probably have had a hard time being admitted to MIT or surviving academically if he had been admitted. And if Nathanael had decreed that Francis come into the Herreshoff Manufacturing Company full-time

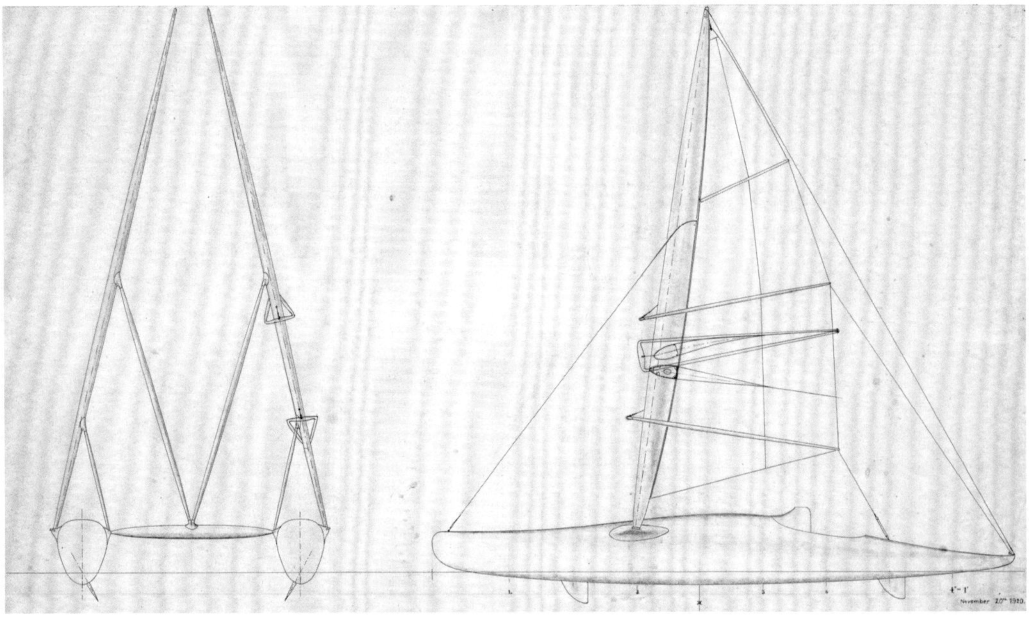

instead of running The Farm, it could have been disastrous; Francis might have followed Bertie Chesebrough and Charles Frederick II into permanent oblivion, as far as Nathanael was concerned. Sidney could operate in his father's shadow, but not Francis. Francis was an artist, different from Nathanael, and the father's inability to recognize his young son's talent was a lifelong emotional wound for Francis.[53]

If there is truth to the theory that an artist must experience the rejection of his art in order to gain the inspiration to make it better, then Francis's father helped him. The obstacles to becoming a yacht designer that Nathanael set up for Francis stimulated him to break away. Nathanael unwittingly spurred Francis to pursue his ambition of designing yachts.

When Francis left his family at Bristol to go to work for Starling Burgess—incidentally, at the same age Nathanael had been when he left Corliss to return to his family and work for John—the family considered him to be a black sheep. Nathanael had a bad opinion of Starling Burgess, although he did respect his design work. He would write later that Starling "has not a good reputation with a good many people. He inherits a bad trait." Nathanael felt that Francis was showing a want of loyalty to the Herreshoffs and to him, in particular. There would be little or no contact between father and son for more than four years.[54]

ABOVE: **Francis's modernistic catamaran. The plan is dated November 20, 1920; Francis had just turned thirty.** (© Mystic Seaport, Daniel S. Gregory Ships Plans Library, SP38. 299.1)

CHAPTER 4

360
843
192
L.R. ₵ ₵ S.A.

A TRUE APPRENTICESHIP

"Starling Burgess's talks with me have always seemed more like poetry than plain conversation."

—L. FRANCIS HERRESHOFF, 1943

When Francis Herreshoff escaped from Bristol in late 1920 and joined W. Starling Burgess in Provincetown, he found in Starling the mentor he wished his father could have been. Starling was twelve years older than Francis, and he became more like an older brother to Francis than his own older brothers ever were. He was of delicate build, six feet tall. His reddish mustache covered a harelip. His face most often wore a kindly, open look. His blue eyes could be mischievous and were so bright and intense that they were not easily forgotten.[1]

Starling had a wide-ranging curiosity. At Milton Academy, he built model boats and tested them in the school pond; he constructed engines; he studied meteorology on a professional level at Abbott Lawrence Rotch's nearby Blue Hill Meteorological Observatory and helped Rotch with his biplane-kite experiments. At Harvard, he learned advanced mathematics, read and wrote romantic poetry, and was introduced to psychology by William James. He became a yacht designer in 1901, and eight years later he went into the new aviation business. On February 28, 1910, seven years after the Wright brothers flew at Kittyhawk, the Burgess Model A was the first aircraft to fly in New England, though the flight was short and not sweet. For a time, his Burgess Company, which sold seaplanes to the US Navy, was Marblehead's largest employer. But he sold his aviation company in 1916 to Glenn L. Curtiss, because the Wright brothers held basic patents that stymied his own design ideas.[2]

In his chosen field of yacht design, Starling took risks; in 1902, he "cheated" a rating rule that measured only waterline length by designing the much-ridiculed *Outlook*, a craft that measured 21 feet long on the waterline and 53 feet long on deck, a craft that won all seven races she entered in her first season and that initiated Starling's reputation as a designer of advanced racing boats. By the time fire put an end to the operations of W. Starling Burgess and Company in Marblehead in 1918, Starling had produced some 250 designs. Francis was working for a man who would become one of the most important yacht designers in the United States.[3]

Starling liked to share his knowledge, his

ideas, his concepts for the future. He fostered a yeasty atmosphere in his design office; it was a place where there was a lot of heady discussion, as well as a lot of hard work. Francis would write later that Starling's "talks with me have always seemed more like poetry than plain conversation." Starling began to give Francis the recognition that he craved. He provided the psychological mirror to show Francis who he was. Starling Burgess brought out the best in Francis Herreshoff; the two would be lifelong friends.[4]

The Burgess family that Francis joined in Provincetown was a divided one; the house on Commercial Street became a bachelor abode for Starling, the boy Frederic, and Francis. Although Burgess had settled in Provincetown at the urging of his wife Rosamund, she and their daughter, whom Starling called Tasha, spent little time there. Guilt over the loss of their firstborn child had contributed to a rift in the Burgesses' marriage. On June 24, 1914, eight-year-old Edward Burgess II had drowned when he fell overboard from the family's small cruising sailboat as she sat on her mooring in Marblehead Harbor, with Starling and Rosamund below in the cabin, unaware. Rosamund, a portrait painter, wanted to seek healing and stimulus in the thriving art colony at Provincetown. She believed that Starling, the poet and philosopher as well as yacht designer and aeronautical engineer, would find the town to his liking. In the end, Starling did thrive in Provincetown, but Rosamund did not, and the emotional strain of their son's death drove a wedge between them.[5]

Starling was gregarious and magnetic; a group often gathered round his fireplace in the evening, the gin would be passed, and Starling would read poetry, his voice casting a spell. The nature of such sociality was all new to Francis, as were the Bohemian ways he saw in Provincetown. Intrigued and attracted, he enjoyed himself, but he was apprehensive about experimenting and strayed little from the conservative behavior that was familiar. He was naturally put off by Starling's least-restrained friends. The social changes he faced in Provincetown must have been unsettling; there may have been times when he wondered if he should even go back to Bristol. Late in life, he would reminisce, not about the social gatherings in Provincetown, but rather of those at Love Rocks, where "New England ladies and gentlemen would often gather in the evenings for civilized discussion on agreed-upon topics."[6]

Francis was more attracted to the place Thoreau had called "the most completely maritime town that we were ever in" than he was to its social activities. Francis liked to walk the Provincetown waterfront, where all manner of vessels were being built and maintained, and was more at ease making friends with the fishermen than with partygoers. And he liked solitary expeditions out among the sand dunes at the end of the Cape. He preferred the dunes in winter and extolled their beauty after a snowfall or when they were frozen after a rainstorm. He wrote, "At these times it seems like walking in some fairyland where the soil is made up of glittering jewels of many colors."[7]

AN IMPORTANT addition to the team working in Starling's Provincetown drafting room was Frank Cabot Paine, who arrived soon after Francis. The son of Charles Jackson Paine, a Civil War general, railroad director, and America's Cup yachtsman, Frank had worked for Starling as purchasing agent in his aviation business during World War I. He was the same age as Francis, and, like Francis, he was dyslexic. In a letter to his father a year after graduating from Middlesex School, he spelled the word "sailing" three different ways. Francis would write: "I am as bad at spelling as Frank was and although neither Frank nor I had dificultys in reading each other's notations or comunications, all other people did." Frank was just starting out in yacht design; as a competitive racing helmsman, he wanted to learn more about the design of the boats he sailed.[8]

At the age of 17, Frank had designed a racing knockabout, the *Owl*, for the 21-foot-waterline class of the Beverly Yacht Club, which raced at the head of Buzzards Bay, Massachusetts. The boat was not successful, so the next year, 1908, Frank asked Starling to design a successor for the class, and he participated in the design, at least as an interested observer. This boat was Frank's first of many *Gypsys*, and the first boat in which he began to make a name for himself in racing. (It was this class for which Francis had modeled Herreshoff hull number 707 in 1911.) By the time Frank Paine joined Starling Burgess in Provincetown, he owned a 95-foot schooner and a summer house on Marblehead Neck, and he was vice commodore of Marblehead's Corinthian Yacht Club.[9]

The Herreshoff, Burgess, and Paine families were connected through yacht racing. The fathers of Starling and his two protégés had, between them, defended the America's Cup against all nine challenges from 1885 through 1920: Edward Burgess as designer and Charles Jackson Paine as an owner and manager for the campaigns of 1885, 1886, and 1887; and Nathanael Herreshoff as designer and builder, and sometimes helmsman, for the campaigns of 1893, 1895, 1899, 1901, 1903, and 1920. And, as we have seen, Starling himself was involved in the campaign of 1920. The three men who came together to design yachts in Provincetown late in 1920 shared a unique heritage for the work. At the outset, Francis and Frank got along well together, and both were happy to soak up Starling's knowledge and skills.

Francis wrote years later about discussing their fathers with Starling: "I have talked with my good friend, Starling Burgess, about our fathers and that is a thing that interests Starling very much for, as he says, his father, Edward, was a pure artist and used mathematics very little while he, Starling, loves mathematics and depends on them a great deal. My father, Captain Nat, he says loved mathematics, but he said that I do things almost entirely by some artistic sense of proportion and this complete reversal of things in the two generations amuses him exceedingly. Strange to say we find this most flattering for above all things Starling would rather be a mathematician (and he is a great one): as for my part, even a small sense of proportion seems a great blessing."[10]

Starling was not sure why the William Gardner design, the *Vanitie*, whose team he had joined, had been narrowly beaten by Herreshoff's *Resolute* in the 1920 America's Cup trials. The three descendants of great men of the America's Cup built 10-foot, rigged models of the two yachts and raced them against each other in Provincetown Harbor, using as tender Starling's son Frederic's pretty little cutter, the *Galena*.This was all doubtless plenty of fun, but it is not known whether or not the *Resolute* upheld her ascendancy over the *Vanitie*.[11]

Norman L. Skene joined the group not long after Francis and Frank. The same age as Starling, he also had worked for the Burgess aviation company. A graduate of the MIT naval architecture program, he had already been a pioneer in the development of the express cruiser, the fast powerboats in which business magnates sometimes commuted to their city offices. His revised edition of *The Elements of Yacht Design* had been out for three years. Originally published by *The Rudder* in 1904, the book would be the standard text on the subject through many editions and for many years; it is still in print, as revised by Francis S. Kinney. Norman was an excellent and speedy draftsman, and a patient calculator. He would be the perfect backup for Burgess and his two tyros, a job for which he was over-qualified.[12]

Starling introduced Francis and Norman to the pleasures of the double-paddle canoe and the sailing canoe, craft he had designed and built in his previous enterprise in Marblehead. Both men were taken with the little boats, especially the double-paddle craft, in which the paddler sat facing forward, so close to the water it was the

6
US4

next thing to swimming. For Francis, the double-paddle canoe would become his favorite sort of personal boat.[13]

THE TEAM'S first challenge, after Francis, Frank, and Norman joined Starling, was to bring out two 6-Metre boats for the rapidly approaching 1921 racing season. Starling designed both, with help from Francis on the *Sheila* and from Frank on the *Jeanie*. Francis made the *Sheila*'s construction plan, according to the Lloyds scantling rule. In anticipation of the *Sheila*'s construction, Starling had come to the Herreshoff Manufacturing Company the previous fall, not only to secure a contract for building her—making her the first Herreshoff-built boat not designed by Nat Herreshoff—and also, in the event, to recruit his son. The *Jeanie* was built at Provincetown by Starling, Francis, and Frank.[14]

These 6-Metres were designed to the second version of the International Rule for measuring yachts and determining their ratings. In 1906, the British Yacht Racing Association had proposed that interested countries adopt a common rating rule to encourage international racing. The result was the First International Measurement Rule, which took effect the following year. Defects were corrected in the second rule, as of January 1, 1920. The International Rule applied to the largest racing yachts, but it also encouraged the creation of smaller racing classes, in particular boats that would rate a maximum of 6 metres and 12 metres. At this time in the United States, the International Rule was only considered by the few yachtsmen who wanted to race abroad. Among them were Paul Hammond, for whom the *Sheila* was built, and Frank Paine, who was to be the owner of the *Jeanie*. Hammond had served in a destroyer based in Queenstown, Ireland, during World War I, had met English yachtsmen, and took the lead in organizing the international racing. He would become an important client to Starling and, later, to Francis.[15]

With Starling's background in aircraft design, he and Francis and Frank discussed and worked on aerodynamics even more than hydrodynamics. Although they designed the new 6-Metres with long waterlines and short ends, it was the light-weight, tall rigs of the new racers that would set the standard for the future. Francis and Frank were learning from a man who would and could take revolutionary leaps forward in yacht design. His leaps were not always successful the first time he tried them.[16]

When the two boats—half of the four-boat American 6-Metre team—were shipped to England on June 15, 1921, Francis was among those who accompanied the boats and their owners; he was to crew for Frank in the *Jeanie*. The boats were rigged at the premier yard of Charles Nicholson at Gosport, and raced off Cowes, home of the Royal Yacht Squadron. Francis stayed at the grand Egypt House in Cowes. Years later, he would write, "I will always recall my visits to Gosport and Cowes as being some of the most pleasant experiences of my life." The pleasure did not derive from racing success in the rough and windy conditions of the Solent, for Starling's first tries at the International Rule fell short. Nor did it derive from racing in pretty boats. Francis would later write: "*Sheila* and

LEFT TOP: **Starling Burgess in one of his double-paddle canoes on Marblehead Harbor.** (Mystic Seaport, 1973-3-509) LEFT BOTTOM: **The Six-Metre *Sheila* on her trial sail at the Herreshoff Manufacturing Company, May 1921. Her short ends and small, round cockpits were innovations. The vessel under cover behind the *Sheila* is the *Alert*, the steam yacht designed by F. Loring Swasey, whose lines Francis had lofted.** (Herreshoff Marine Museum, Bristol, Rhode Island)

Jeanie were strange looking, homely craft." The visit's longest-lasting pleasure for Francis was his meeting the English sailmaker Thomas Ratsey, and the English yacht designer and builder Charles E. Nicholson of the Camper and Nicholsons yard. Already known for the 15-metre *Istria* of 1912, which introduced an early version of the Marconi rig, Nicholson would turn out many large, successful yachts, including the America's Cup challengers *Shamrock IV, Shamrock V*, *Endeavour I*, and *Endeavour II*, as well as the huge, three-masted staysail schooner *Creole*. Nicholson entertained Francis and Frank Paine at his home and gave them a tour of his yacht yard. And Francis had the chance to see the twenty-eight-year-old, 121-foot royal cutter yacht *Britannia* turning to windward in a breeze. She was the masterpiece of the designer whose work he would come to respect most, the great Scottish naval architect George L. Watson. The trip was Francis's first abroad, and it would be his only one.[17]

SOON after Francis and Frank Paine returned to Provincetown, Starling, always looking for working capital for his business, took Frank in as a partner. In October 1921, the Burgess company became Burgess and Paine. The refinanced firm moved from the far end of Cape Cod to the "Hub of the Universe": 131 State Street, Boston, not far from the famous Custom House Tower.[18]

The move doubtless helped the business by bringing it closer to potential customers, but, for Francis, living in Boston meant a city boarding-house instead of the haven he had shared with Starling on the Provincetown waterfront. There were only busy streets and the park-like Boston Common for walks, poor substitutes for Cape Cod dunes. Francis was a bachelor separated from his family. His only friends were his colleagues at the office. When he made more friends they would be Burgess and Paine clients. For Francis in Boston, his life was his work.[19]

Perhaps because Starling's father had designed the great *Fredonia*, a fishing schooner that set a trend for far safer vessels without sacrificing speed, Starling got the job of designing racing fishing

ABOVE: **Francis stares into the official camera for his passport, issued May 28, 1921, so he could go to England for the 6-Metre racing that summer.** (Herreshoff Marine Museum, Bristol, Rhode Island) RIGHT: **Francis's drawing of the *Puritan*. She is 138 feet long and spreads 9,500 square feet of sail. The artist has imagined the scene fully: the vessel is sliding along on the wind, her seven sails set to perfection; the helmsman is steering carefully to get to windward all he can; the derby-hatted skipper is watching her go from the companionway; a hand is tidying things up in the waist; and the boy is looking down the forecastle hatch, maybe mustering the courage to lay below to the galley and tackle a pile of dirty dishes.** (© Mystic Seaport, Daniel S. Gregory Ships Plans Library, SP38.189.1)

schooners to try to beat the Canadian champion *Bluenose,* designed by William J. Roue, in the International Fishermen's Races, which began in 1920. The fishermen scoffed when America's Cup races were cancelled as being too dangerous in a moderate gale, a breeze they thought was just right for racing. They inaugurated their own series between the United States and Canada, which they dubbed "races for real sailors." Starling had designed the controversial *Mayflower* in 1921 at Provincetown for Boston owners. The next year, Gloucester interests commissioned Burgess and Paine to design a new racer, to be named the *Puritan.* Neither vessel would get to try the *Bluenose*. The *Mayflower* had been banned from fishing schooner races for being too yacht-like, mostly because of her weight-saving, chopped-off stern, so Starling drew the lines of the *Puritan* with a more conventional counter stern. On both these vessels—as well as on the famous racing fisherman *Columbia* that Starling would design in 1923—Francis, the ex-naval inspector, was given the job of making sure the vessels' construction and rigging adhered to the plans. He supervised the stepping of the *Puritan*'s masts. And he made a fine drawing of the *Puritan* under full sail to reassure the owners that she would look like a real fishing schooner, not a racing yacht.[20]

Shortly before the *Puritan*'s launching, Francis wrote a detailed discussion of the design differences between the new schooner and her predecessor. This piece of writing is most notable for Francis's using it as a platform from which to launch a diatribe against the poor construction

and maintenance of the New England fishing schooner fleet, vessels he described as "man traps." After blasting away at pinch-penny construction standards on the schooners, he wrote: "Now they are rotten in the bilge and are the nightmares of the insurance companies, who know that if they touch bottom but once, their whole keel will fall out, as most of them are only held together with Portland cement." In his early years, the dyslexic Francis didn't do much writing, but when he did write, he had no trouble expressing his strong opinions. Nor was he shy about putting his quaint style of humor on paper. He began a related piece of writing addressed "To the Knockers of the Schooner *Mayflower*: Oh ye sons of motor-boat-driving landlubbers!" And he went on in like vein to defend his boss's design as that of a true fishing schooner. Banned from racing as being too yacht-like, the *Mayflower* proved to be an able and successful Banks fisherman for two years before her rig was cut down and she was given an auxiliary engine. She ended up as a freighter in the West Indies, as would the *Bluenose.* But the *Puritan,* a bona fide fishing schooner to be sure, was lost three months after she was launched. Sailing at twelve knots in a hard southerly in thick fog after dark, she overran her dead reckoning (Francis thought her dead reckoning was out because she had fore-reached when hove to under foresail) and struck the Northwest Bar of Sable Island. Luckily, only one of her crew of twenty-three was drowned. Francis had a point, particularly about the low maintenance standards of New England fishing schooners, and the *Puritan* did touch bottom but once and much of her keel did fall out, but the *Puritan* was a new vessel, built to a high standard by J. F. James and Son in Essex and inspected by Francis himself according to Starling's design. No wooden schooner could be expected to survive the blow she suffered. The *Columbia* herself was lost with all hands off Sable Island in the Great August Gale of 1927.[21]

Francis may have been skeptical about the standards of construction and maintenance of the American fishing schooners of his day, but he admired them. He would write: "Outside of the clipper ships, the Gloucester fishermen were the handsomest commercial vessels ever built." He put his own ideas of a proper fishing craft into a preliminary design, dated February 5, 1922. She was an 85-foot, handsome, seaworthy-looking vessel, with a flat, transom stern, an outboard rudder, an auxiliary motor, and a tall, Marconi ketch rig. The fishmonger turned naval architect Thomas F. McManus had shaped the form of fishing schooners for twenty years, with yacht-like lines, long overhangs, and tall rigs. But for the sake of safety he had also adapted the knockabout yacht bow, without bowsprit, to fishing vessels, and after 1920 he routinely designed short-ended vessels with reduced rigs and an efficient oil engine. Francis recognized this trend in fishing vessel design but took it to a practical extreme that conservative fishermen would reject. The fishermen races celebrated the features of the extreme, all-sail schooners of the past, while McManus, and Francis, anticipated the more practical powered vessels that fishermen of the future would need. Still, Francis's lofty design had as much chance of being built in 1922 as a codfish has of flying.[22]

TEN WEEKS later, Francis, the draftsman seeking a creative outlet, had finished another preliminary design. His profile drawing, dated April 19, 1922, was inked, partially colored, and decorated with the first of many seahorses he drew on yacht plans. It showed a 100-foot, three-masted schooner, with a hull like a huge lifeboat, his idea of what an ocean cruiser should be. There was no client, and the design was not finished or built to; the craft was a creative doodle that had nothing to do with Burgess and Paine. We will examine this seaworthy vessel in detail in a later chapter, for she was a forerunner of Francis's

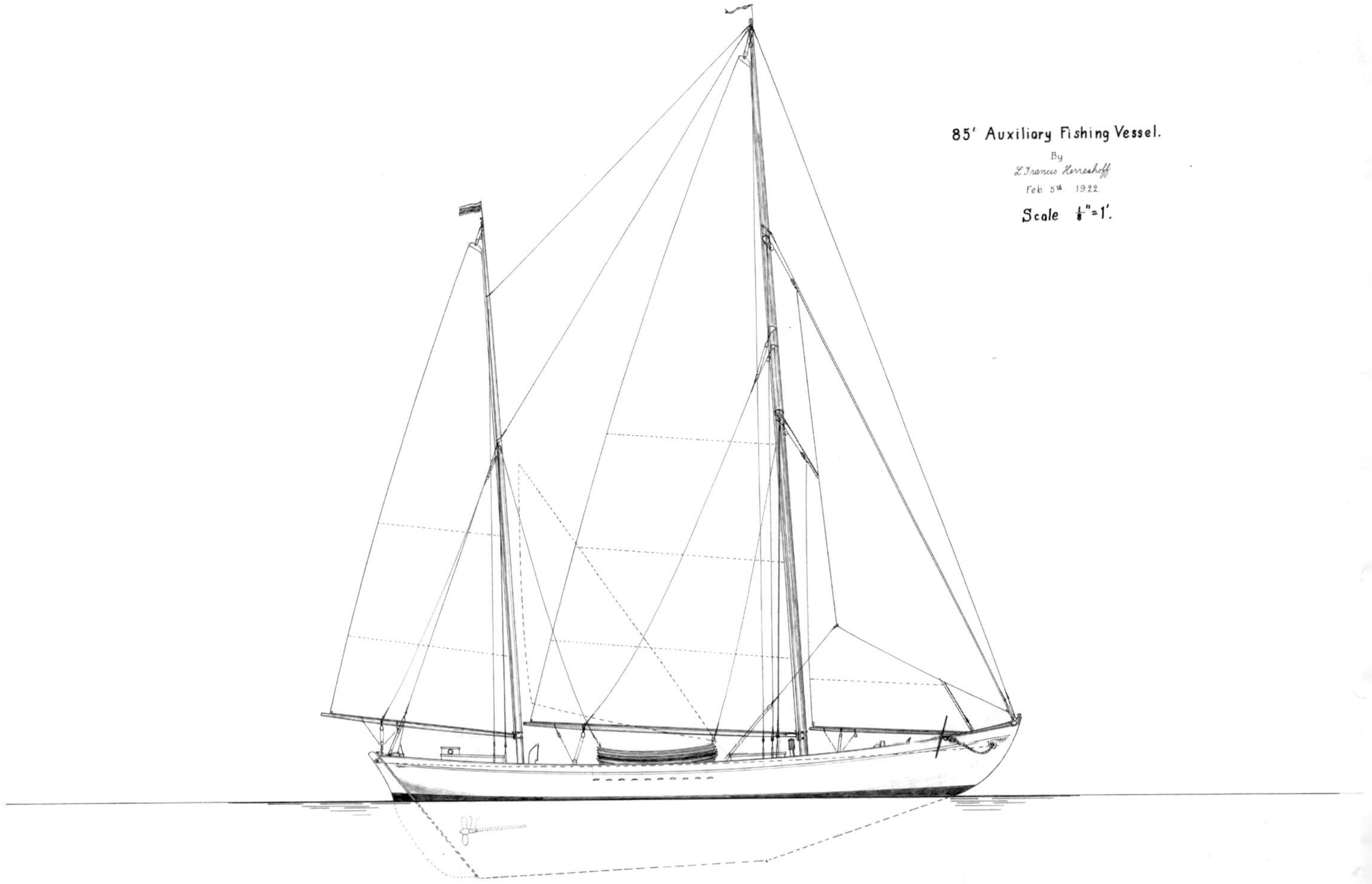

design of his ideal world cruiser twenty years later.

When Francis had been working for Starling for about eighteen months, he began creating original designs for the firm. The first, dated May 17, 1922, was a preliminary design for a 61-foot, shoal-draft cruising ketch. It is not known whether Burgess and Paine had a prospective customer for this design or if Francis drew it on speculation during a slow period. In any event, he did not complete the design. The same year, the Herreshoff Manufacturing Company launched a remarkably similar boat—except for her sloop rig—the *Ventura*, for George F. Baker, a design modeled by Capt. Nat twenty years earlier. The *Ventura* had a modification to the early design, a raised deck forward. Francis's design also had a raised deck forward. Both boats had Capt. Nat's little, rectangular cabin-house windows, all in a row. The Herreshoff genes ran deep.[23]

Francis designed another shoal-draft cruiser for Burgess and Paine, a 62-foot, Marconi-rig schooner for Paul Hammond, "et als." His preliminary plan is dated June 9, 1922. The group probably planned to use the schooner to try their luck at

With her deep reefs and small staysails, Francis's dory fisherman might have worked well on the Grand Banks, but no schoonerman would put to sea with those tall masts. (© Mystic Seaport, Daniel S. Gregory Ships Plans Library, SP38.212.1)

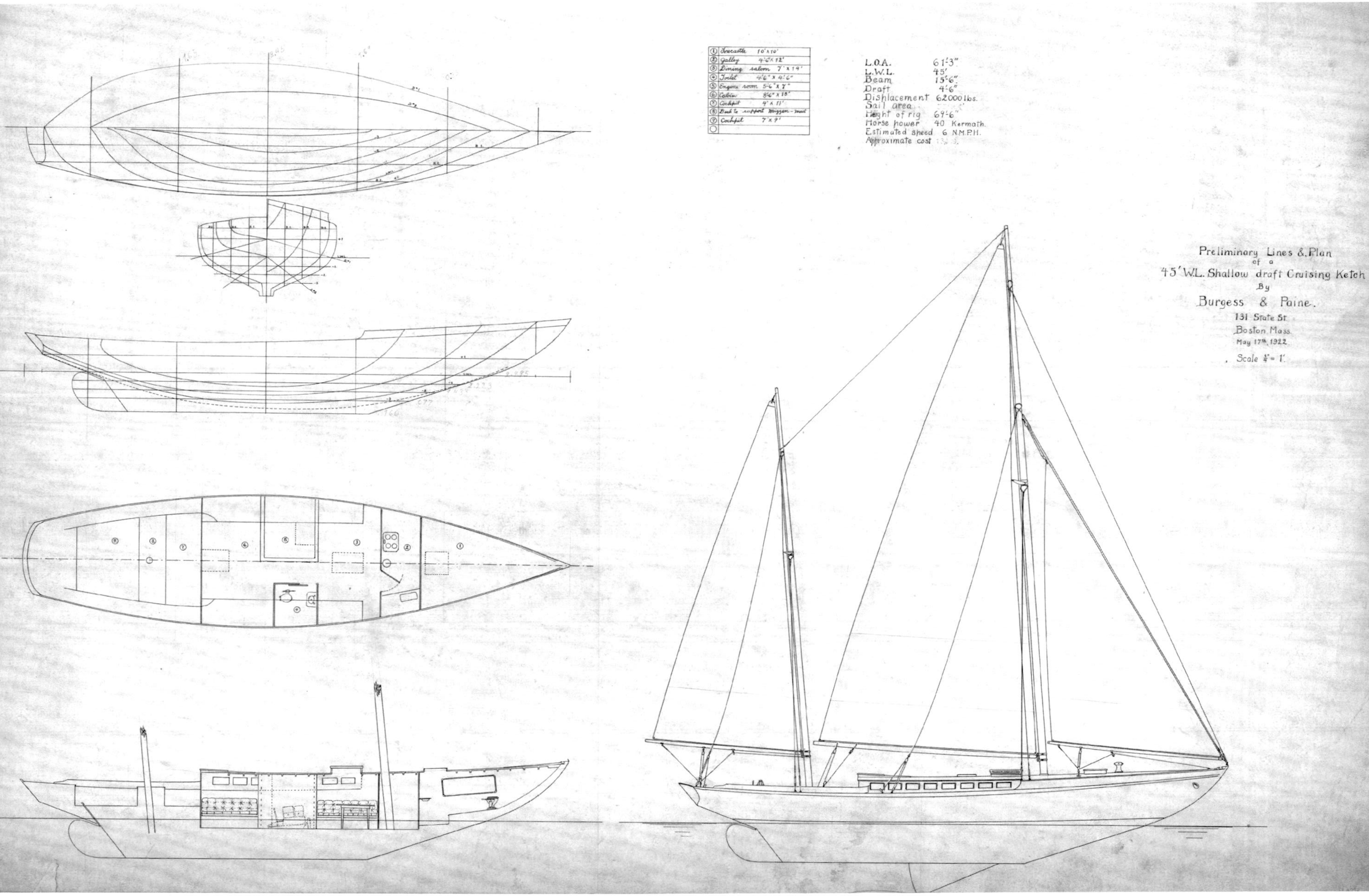

① Forecastle 10'x10'
② Galley 4'6"x12'
③ Dining saloon 7'x14'
④ Toilet 4'6" x 4'6"
⑤ Engine room 5'6" x 7"
⑥ Cabin 8'6" x 15"
⑦ Cockpit 4' x 11'
⑧ Bush to support mizzen-mast
⑨ Cockpit 7'x9'
L.O.A. 61'-3"
L.W.L. 45'
Beam 15'-6"
Draft 4'-6"
Displacement 62000 lbs.
Sail area
Height of rig 69'-6"
Horse power 40 Kermath.
Estimated speed 6 N.M.P.H.
Approximate cost
Preliminary Lines & Plan
of a
45' W.L. Shallow draft Cruising Ketch
By
Burgess & Paine.
131 State St.
Boston Mass.
May 17th 1922.
Scale ¼" = 1'.

wildfowl shooting on the Chesapeake Bay, but the design went no further. She is a good-looking, practical vessel whose most unusual feature is her Marconi foresail. Every cruising schooner had a gaff-rigged foresail, but some months earlier, Francis had written a description of a preliminary design for a cruising schooner in which he explained that her foresail was a Marconi sail in order to do away with the gaff foresail, "which always tends to full [fall] off"; that is, the vertical leech allows the peak of the sail to sag to leeward. Plans for that preliminary design, which Francis numbered F-13, have not survived, but, in early 1922, Francis made what may have been the first drawing of a cruising schooner with a Marconi foresail. His interest in the rig is shown by a photograph in his collection of the Marconi schooner, *Fortune*, designed by B.B. Crowninshield in 1925.[24]

FRANCIS met the Boston yachtsman who would become his best client, when he helped Starling, later in 1922, design a 6-Metre boat for Charles A. Welch 2nd. Welch was a partner in the money-management firm of Welch and

Francis's ketch (LEFT) and his father's sloop *Ventura* (ABOVE) have the same waterline length of 45 feet. The ketch is 8 inches longer on deck, has 1 foot, 6 inches more beam, and 6 inches more draft. Francis wrote the sail area in pencil, so it does not reproduce; unaccountably he gave the figure as 5,520 square feet, whereas the plan shows about 1,310 square feet. (© Mystic Seaport, Daniel S. Gregory Ships Plans Library, SP38.151.1; *Ventura* photo, Herreshoff Marine Museum, Bristol, Rhode Island)

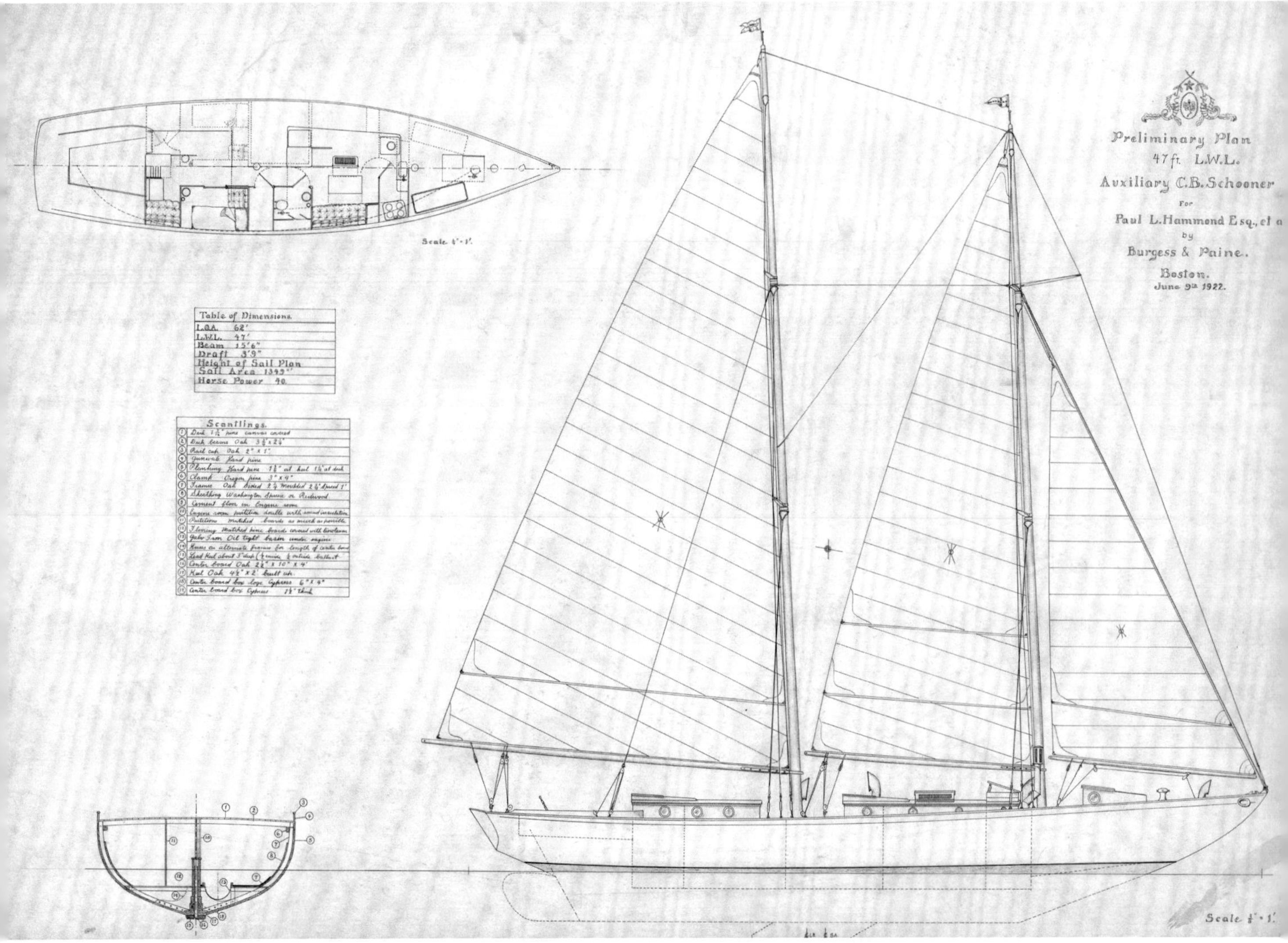

ABOVE: **Francis's preliminary plan of Paul Hammond's schooner is the only drawing of the design that has been found. Her Marconi foresail would obstruct a single, lower springstay between the masts, so Francis shows double springstays attaching to the ends of long spreaders on the foremast, balanced by stays running to the forward end of the jibstay strut. The problem of staying forward the mainmast of a schooner, solved so awkwardly on this design, influenced Francis to favor the ketch rig, in which at least the troublesome after mast is smaller.** (© Mystic Seaport, Daniel S. Gregory Ships Plans Library, SP38.161.1) RIGHT: **Francis's version of a yacht based on the fishing schooner was 49 feet long on deck, with a waterline length of 37 feet, a beam of 12 feet, and a draft of 6 feet. "The rig," *Yachting* commented, "is rather snug, containing only 1,095 sq. feet." The outline of the coal stove may be seen amidships, to starboard; the engine is forward, off-center to starboard.** (*Yachting* (January 1923): 29)

Forbes, but he became disenchanted with the work and could afford, with money inherited from his father, to devote his time to activities that were less onerous to him. Boating took priority. Welch also had America's Cup blood: the uncle for whom he was named had sailed in the afterguard of Charles Paine's Cup defenders. Francis would draw sixteen designs for Charlie Welch, of which thirteen would be built. Welch—eleven years Francis's junior—and Francis became good friends, as well as client-and-designer, for they discovered that they shared deep interests in the history of yachting, in the concept of a small, cruising yacht that could cope with rough weather, and even in iceboats, as well as in the design of sailboats that could win races. The 6-Metre *Undertaker*'s highest attainment was bringing Francis Herreshoff and Charlie Welch together; she did nothing spectacular on the race course.[25]

The first of Francis's designs to be published appeared in the January 1923 issue of *Yachting*, credited to "the board of Burgess and Paine," for it was customary that the firm get the credit, rather than the individual designer. The plans, dated August 31, 1922, show a 49-foot, gaff-rigged cruising schooner. It is not known if this design had a client or if the boat was built. The facts that she has a swordfishing pulpit and a big coal stove amidships for fall cruising suggest that Charlie Welch may have been involved.[26]

She is pretty and well thought out. Francis's first and only attempt at creating a cruising boat in the tradition of the New England fishing schooner is more yacht-like than most of the similar designs that were beginning to emerge from the office of the popular champion of the type, John G. Alden, just down the street at 148 State Street. Alden made most of his schooners closer than was Francis's design to the classic McManus-style fishermen he was emulating, giving them generous displacement, sheer, and freeboard. Francis thought that the Alden office produced yachts that were too heavy and beamy, with too much emphasis on big, comfortable cabins. A happy Alden schooner-owner once admitted that his vessel could make little headway to windward in a four-foot sea, conditions that never stopped an L. Francis Herreshoff design.[27]

Francis would come to scorn the idea of basing a yacht design on a fishing boat, and he would not respect Alden, because Alden, as a broker, did more selling than designing. Francis's negative feelings for Alden were complicated by jealousy, for Alden designs seemed ubiquitous, and he was held in awe by many yachtsmen. Yet Francis considered the products of the Alden office to be lesser art. His disrespect for John Alden was misplaced, however, for Alden gave many young designers a good start, and they did respect him. Designers like Murray Peterson, who would become known for his schooners based on coasters rather than fishermen; Sam Crocker, who became the favorite designer of many cruising sailors; Fenwick Williams, who would be appreciated particularly for his catboats; and K. Aage Nielsen,

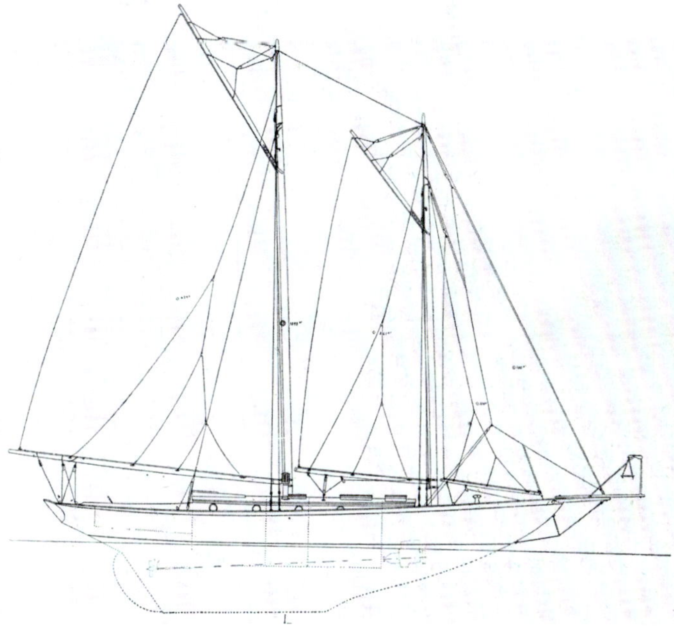

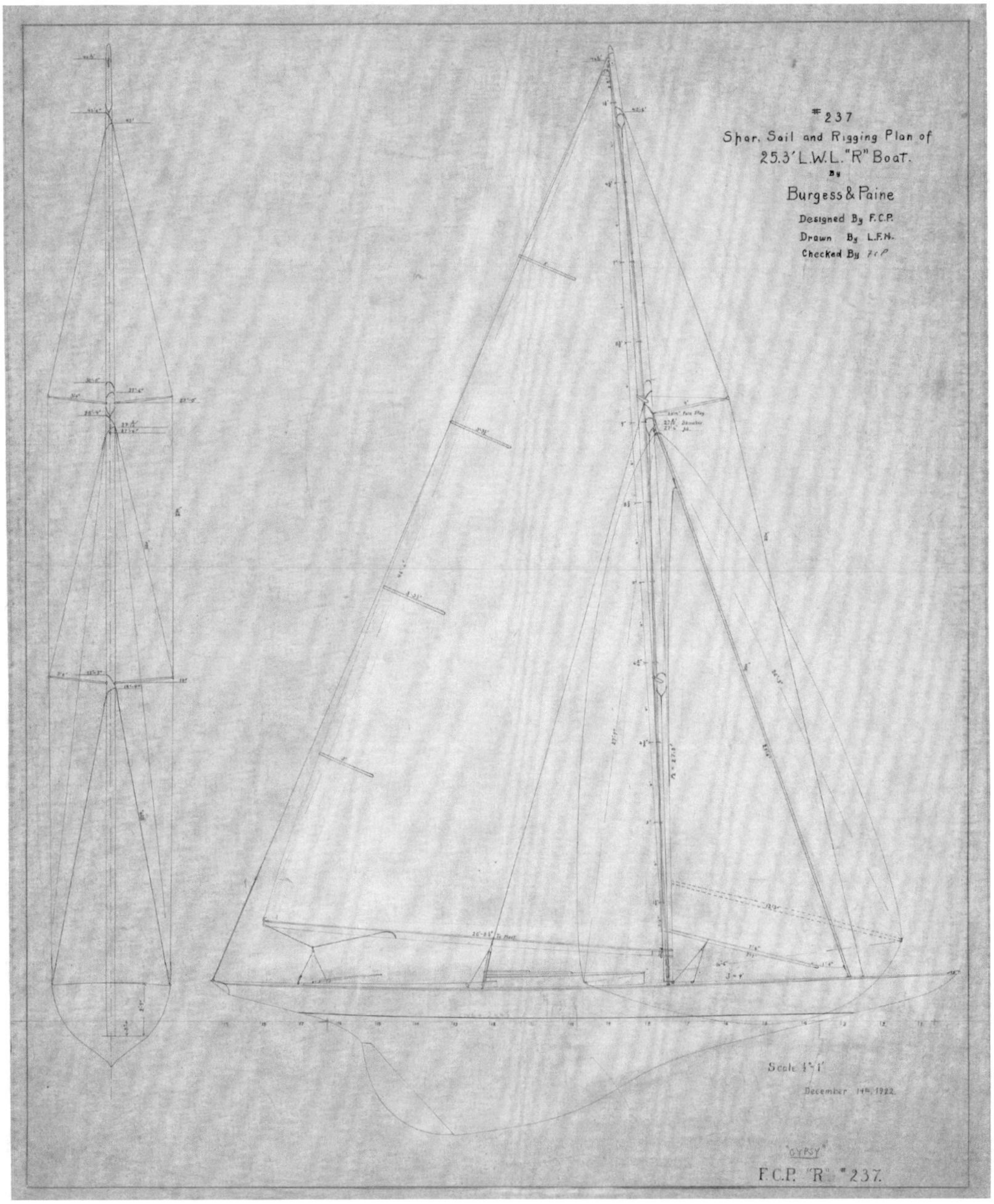

The original sail plan of Frank Paine's R-boat, the *Gypsy*, showing the conventional eye splices around the mast in the upper ends of the wire standing rigging. Francis made the drawing based on Frank's design. She is 38 feet, 5 inches long on deck; 25 feet, 4 inches on the waterline; beam, 5 feet, 10 inches; draft, 5 feet, 7 inches; and sail area, 572 square feet.

(Frank C. Paine Collection, Hart Nautical Collections, MIT Museum, Cambridge, Massachusetts)

whose trademark would be Danish-type, fast, double-ended cruisers; all these men spoke well of their experiences in the Alden office. Francis did respect many of the men who designed Alden boats; years later he would write to a boatbuilder: "If you are building a boat that was designed by [Charles G.] MacGregor she must be pretty good for the various John Alden designs were only as good as the men who made them." Some Burgess and Paine designs were only as good as Francis made them, too, but the difference was that, unlike John Alden, Starling Burgess and Frank Paine were busily turning out their own designs.[28]

IN THE WINTER of 1922-23, Frank Paine designed another racing boat for his own use, this time built to the Universal Rule, an R-boat again named *Gypsy*. He drew the lines of the new boat and designed the sail plan and construction. Francis drew the finished sail and construction plans. He also calculated the weights for the boat, and he noted that she needed an extra 1,500 pounds of inside, lead ballast when she was launched.[29]

Francis's drawing of the sail plan is dated December 14, 1922. It shows a slightly curved mast with the masthead supported by a headstay running over a long strut. This stay has the usual eye splice around the mast at its upper end, as do the other stays and shrouds in the plan.

There must have been further discussion of the sail plan, in which Starling would undoubtedly have been involved, for Francis drew a revised sail plan, dated March 15, 1923. And labeled with the same date, he made a drawing of one of the rig details: "Fittings for Lower Shrouds." Each such fitting was to consist of a triangular plate, held to the mast by nine screws (of five different sizes), and a smaller I-shaped plate. Both plates were to fit over the inboard end of a tubular spreader, and their lower ends were spread three-eighths of an inch apart with holes for a pin to take the upper end of the shroud. (Turnbuckles and swedge fittings were already in use for tensioning the shrouds and securing their lower ends.) Francis would write later that he had thus "developed some sheet metal tangs," a type of fitting used universally to this day, because it will keep far greater tension on wire rigging than can an eye splice. The greater tension means that even a tall mast can be kept straighter in a strong breeze, so the sails don't lose power, and the boat goes faster.[30]

Two years earlier, Francis had designed standing rigging made from metal rods, rather than wire, as a way to avoid rigging stretch. It is not known how he proposed attaching the rod rigging to the mast. Although rod rigging would eventually become common on racing boats, Francis didn't like it. He wrote later, "it is desirable to have a slight amount of spring in the rigging and my opinion is that the 19-strand wire is better than the rod rigging in every way."[31]

So, for Frank Paine's *Gypsy*, Francis designed the first mast tang known to have been used on a sailing craft. This was an adaptation, rather than an invention, for the tang had been used by the Wright brothers to attach wing-support and strut-support wires, and Starling had used the fitting on his flying machines. (It is curious, though, that when Starling designed the advanced staysail schooner *Niña* for the 1928 Transatlantic Race, he used eye splices on the upper ends of the standing rigging, not tangs. Apparently he trusted tangs for day racers, but not for ocean racers.) The mast tang has since been simplified with ever-stronger metals, but no one has improved upon Francis's scientific design. For his original tang, Francis Herreshoff used the remarkable sense of proportion that was an integral part of his growing artistic ability, combined with his exposure to the results of his father's engineering genius, to show that he had his own brand of genius.[32]

But the father could not accept the genius of the son. Four years later, Nathanael wrote to Francis in disparagement of his tangs. Francis wrote back:

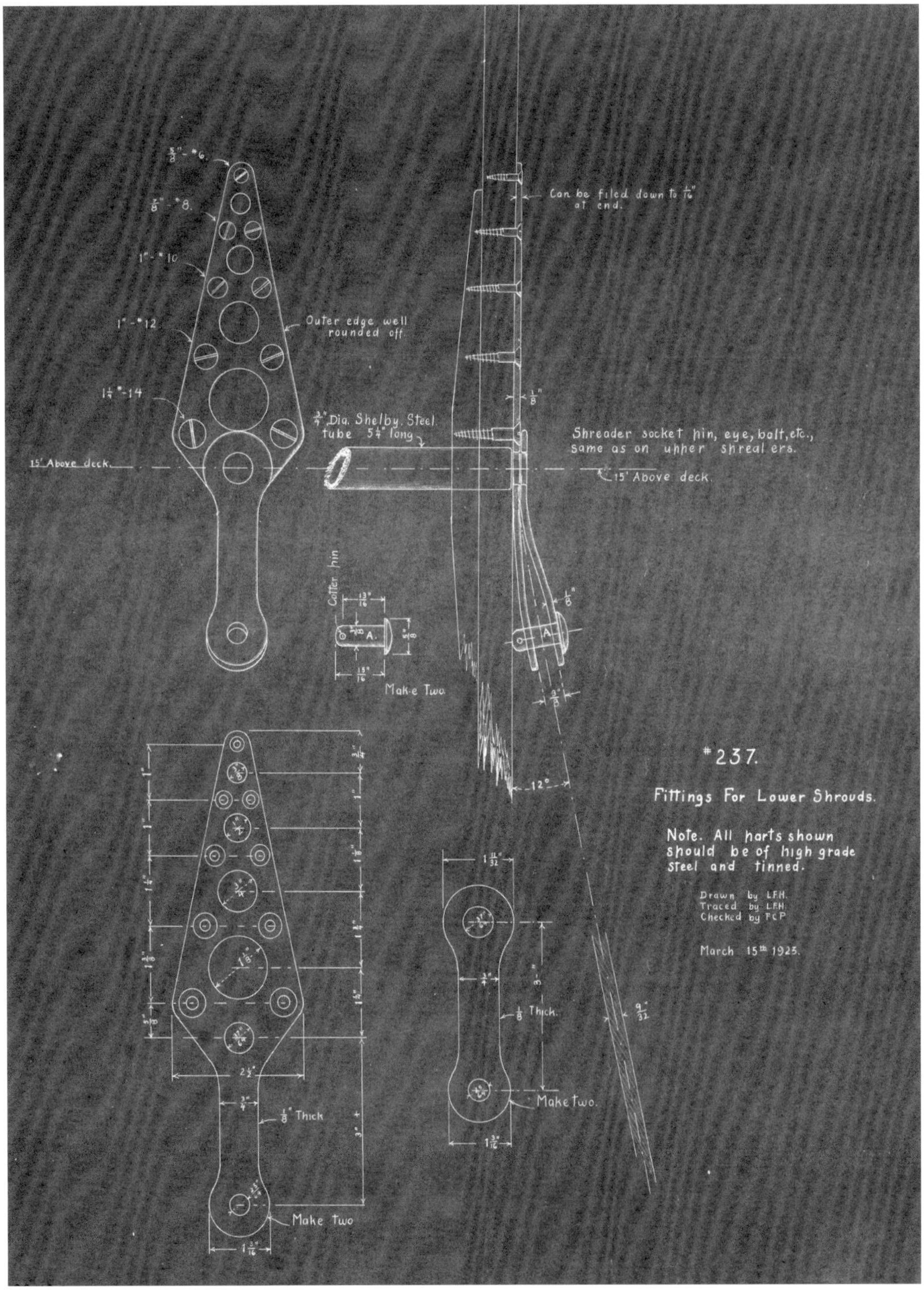
Can be filed down to 1/16" at end.
Outer edge well rounded off.
3/4" Dia. Shelby. Steel. tube 5 1/4" long
Shreader socket hin, eye, bolt, etc., same as on uhher shreal ers.
15' Above deck.
15' Above deck.
Cotter hin
Make Two
1/8" Thick
Make two
1/8" Thick.
Make two.
#237.
Fittings For Lower Shrouds.
Note. All harts shown should be of high grade steel and tinned.
Drawn by LFH.
Traced by LFH.
Checked by FCP
March 15th 1925.

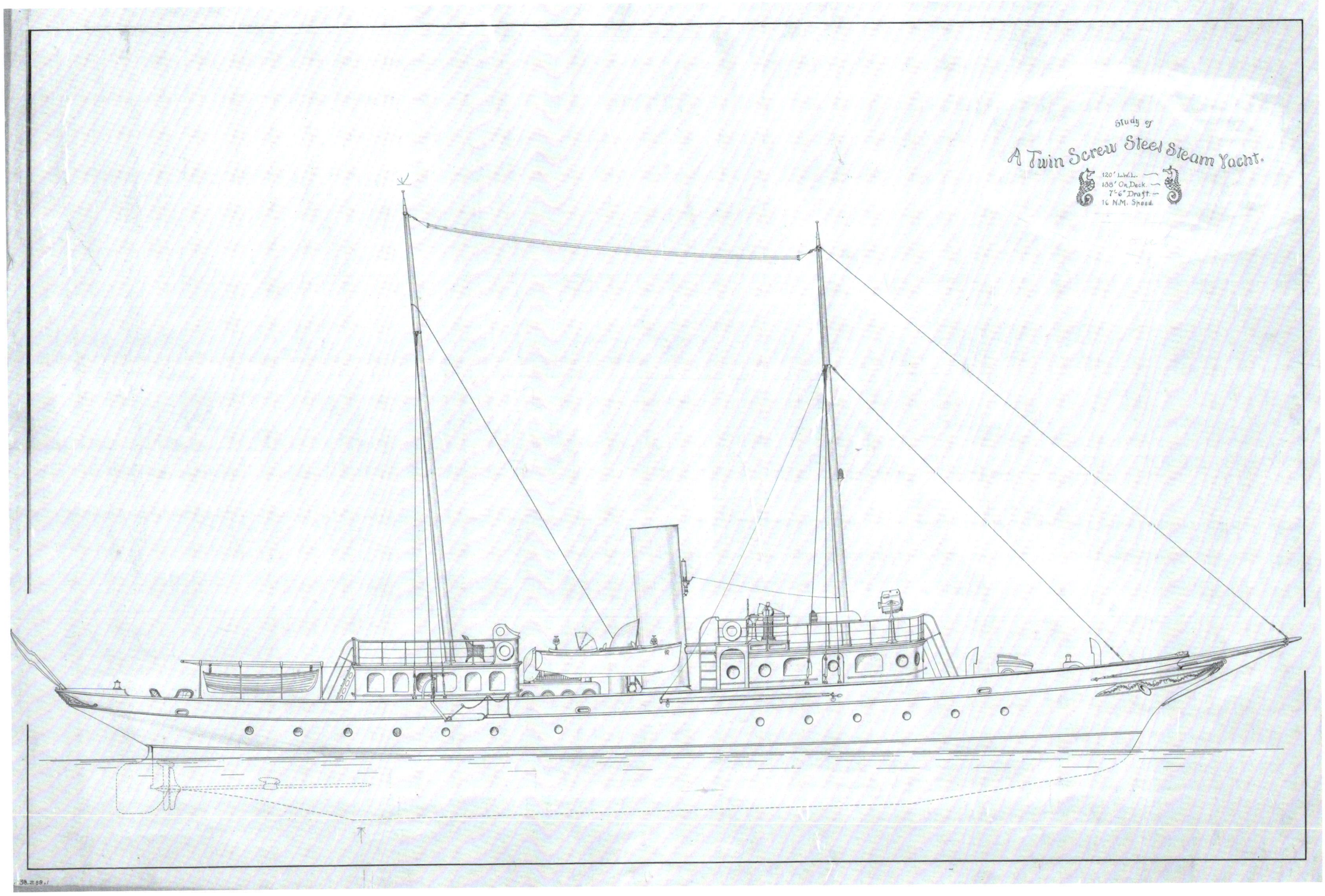

The artistry of L. Francis Herreshoff shines forth in his profile drawing of a 138-foot steam yacht. Many exquisite details are worth study, from the curve of the radio antenna high aloft between the masts, to the scrolls at bow and stern, to the searchlight atop the forward deckhouse, to the deck chairs on the stern. (© Mystic Seaport, Daniel S. Gregory Ships Plans Library, SP38.288.1)

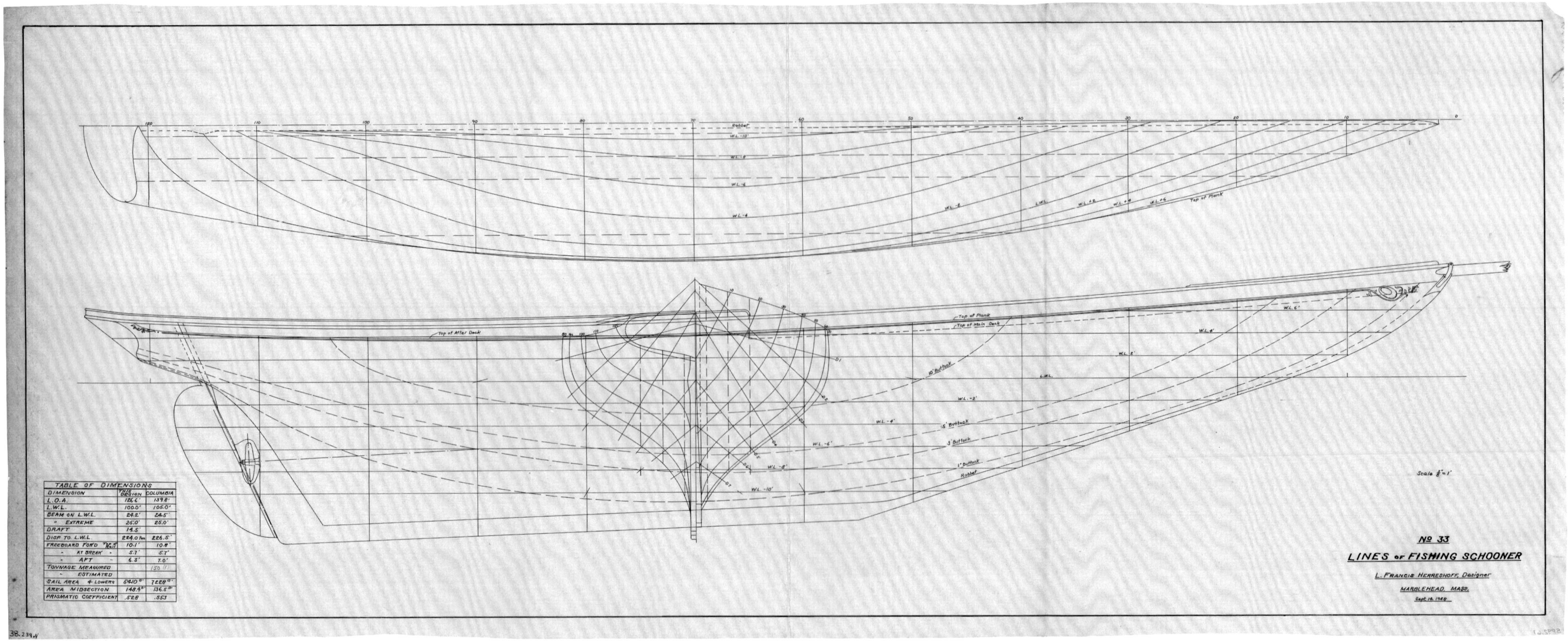

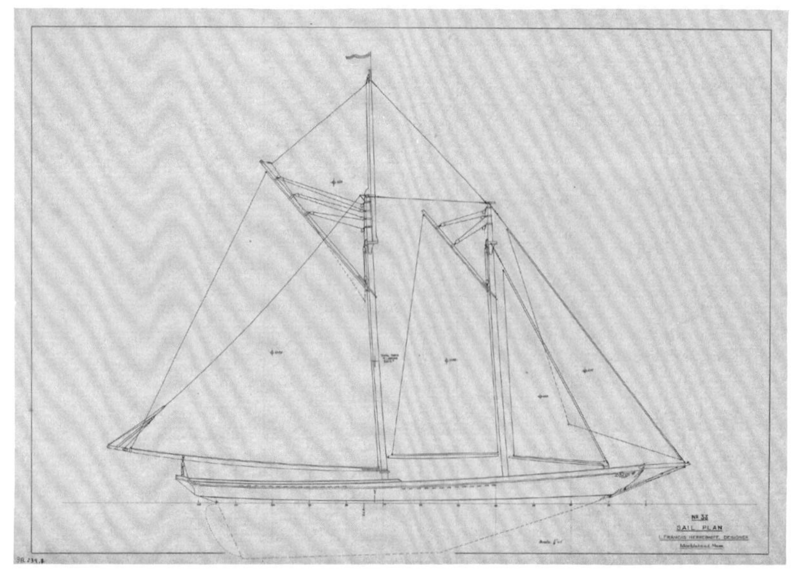

LEFT: Francis's design of the first tangs. He shows five different-sized holes in the triangular plates to make them lighter without sacrificing strength; the lowest of the holes he specifies to be 37/64 inch in diameter. He chose five sizes of screw fastenings, from 1 1/4-inch No. 14s down to 5/8-inch No. 6s. His design staggers the screw positions so that no two line up with the grain of the wood in the mast. This is a good example of Francis's "scientific" designing, as he called it. (© Mystic Seaport, Daniel S. Gregory Ships Plans Library, SP38.118.2) ABOVE and RIGHT: **Francis designed a schooner that any fisherman would have been proud to sail to the Grand Banks out of Gloucester, or even Boston. On the sail plan, he compares her dimensions to those of the *Columbia*, a slightly larger schooner. The design was just an exercise; there was no customer or construction plan. Yet he gave her the No. 33, the number later assigned to the Q-boat *Questa*. Was she, in his imagination, to try the *Bluenose*? Probably not, for he has deliberately refrained from stepping a fore-topmast in the bands he shows at the foremast head, so that she carries no foretopsail, jib topsail, or fisherman staysail. Perhaps he was just demonstrating to himself that he, too, could design an outstanding American fishing schooner. The lines are dated September 14, 1928.** (MSM Plans No. 38.239.1, lines; and 38.239.2, sail plan.)

"I have your letter … and I don't like it very much. In 1925, I brought out the first metal clips [tangs] such as are used on almost all American racing yachts now. They are standard equipment now on Pigeon spars, all Lawley racing yachts and are used on the best racers on the Lakes and Pacific. At least six one-design classes have adopted them as they are the cheapest to make. I understand the *Vanitie*'s new rig will also use them. Before bringing out the original ones on the R boat *Gypsy*, I thought of all the things you mention in your letter, and a great many more." Nathanael replied: "I see you don't accept my criticisms very graciously of flexible ropes and your mast plates for shrouds etc. I only thought I was doing a kindness to you, however, the matter is now closed."[33]

The R-boat *Gypsy*'s new sail plan showed a further significant innovation. The plates of Francis's tangs could have been curved to fit the sectional shape of the masts of the day, but, instead, Francis drew the tangs simply flat, for he "worked out," as he would write later, rectangular-sectioned spars for the *Gypsy.* He believed that a mast "set at the forward edge of a sail or plane has little wind resistance," so that from that point of view, the sectional shape of the mast made little difference. The great advantage of the rectangular mast was that a tapered, hollow spar with straight sides was easier, and thus cheaper, to build than one with curved sides. It was stiff for its weight, yet would bend more than a circular hollow spar before collapsing. A further, less-important advantage was that, as Francis would write, "It is desirable to have a flat surface for attaching shroud and spreader attachments"—his tangs.[34]

Although Francis was not the first person to think up the idea of the rectangular-section, hollow spar (they had been used on airplanes), he was the first to design such spars for yachts. Twenty-two years later, he could write, "This section and construction of spar with slight variations is now quite universally used, and if imitation is the sincerest flattery I should feel highly honored." Although at the time Francis couldn't know that his tang and his rectangular, hollow spar were paramount innovations, it may have dawned on him that in a little more than two years after leaving Bristol, he was proving himself to be his father's own son.[35]

In her first season of racing, 1923, the *Gypsy* won the R-Class championships of both the Eastern and Corinthian Yacht Clubs in Marblehead. William U. Swan wrote in *The Rudder*, "The feature of the R Class this year was undoubtedly the supremacy of *Gypsy* and the leap of her designer, Frank Paine, into the front ranks of yacht architects in one bound." Swan went on to extol the designers of the Burgess firm without mentioning L. Francis Herreshoff.[36]

ONE DESIGNER whom Swan did extol was Albert Loring Swasey, for, early in 1923, Swasey had left the Herreshoff Manufacturing Company and joined forces with Starling. The firm was now Burgess, Swasey, and Paine, and it moved to a larger office space at 585 Boylston Street. Two years older than Starling and a graduate of MIT, Swasey was not only an experienced and successful designer, but also a well-connected and astute salesman. He was gregarious and was good at drawing sketches of large and expensive yachts on the backs of cocktail napkins, sketches that he was capable of expanding into complete, complex designs. He had been the lead designer of the navy's famous 110-foot submarine chasers of World War I. As we have seen, Francis had lofted Swasey's lines of the steam yacht *Alert* at the Herreshoff Manufacturing Company, and Swasey may have been instrumental in Starling's hiring of Francis. Swasey added considerable potential to Starling's business.[37]

Swasey was probably responsible for adding another good designer to Starling's stable, for Nicholas Potter followed Swasey to Boston from

the Herreshoff Manufacturing Company. Francis and Nick thus continued their Bristol friendship. They seem not to have collaborated on Burgess, Swasey, and Paine designs, but Nick, like Francis, added the Burgess influence to his Herreshoff Manufacturing Company training. Francis and Nick were certainly aware of each other's work at 585 Boylston Street.[38]

At about this time, Francis made a "Study of A Twin Screw Steel Steam Yacht," perhaps to prove to himself, possibly even to demonstrate to his colleagues, that he, as well as Loring Swasey, was capable of designing large yachts. Francis admired the elegant steam yachts designed by George L. Watson in Scotland; when he later used this study drawing of a 138-foot, clipper-bowed steamer as an incidental illustration in his *Rudder* series, "The Common Sense of Yacht Design," his caption was, "Small edition of the general type evolved by George Watson." He later called Watson, "the greatest artist of all yacht designers." In an unpublished, written description of the vessel, Francis cites his good fortune to have learned about steam-yacht design both at the Herreshoff Manufacturing Company and with his cousin, Bertie Chesebrough. The study drawing shows Francis at his artistic best; his vessel is more beautiful than any steam yacht designed in Bristol by either his father or his cousin. He even made perspective sketches of the interiors of the yacht's dining saloon, after deckhouse, and owner's stateroom, sketches that show the exquisite detail to which his imagination could go, and that the little ship he envisioned would have been as beautiful inside as out, had she been built.[39]

FOR CHARLIE Welch, the common practice of having a boat in commission from the Fourth of July through Labor Day was not appealing. He wanted a cruising boat that he could use as much of the year as possible. He and Francis talked the idea over, and Francis showed Charlie an outboard profile and sail plan of a 43-foot, 6-inch, gaff-rigged ketch that he had drawn. Francis numbered the design F-18, dated it April 22, 1923, and gave his homeport, so to speak, in the drawing's title block as "Bristol, R. I." He included a lovely little drawing of the ketch close-hauled in light air.[40]

Charlie thought the boat would suit his purpose admirably and asked Francis to complete the design so he could have her built. Working in late 1923, Francis drew lines, made up an offset table, and drew construction, cabin, and deck plans. In December, he designed an alternate sail plan, a Marconi rig with taller masts but less sail area, a plan he carefully labeled, "New Sail Plan with leg o'mutton Rig for Ketch Stoarmy Petrel." But it was the originally drawn gaff rig, with the masts moved aft six inches, that was used on the *Stormy Petrel*, as Charlie had indeed named her. What the Messrs. Burgess, Swasey, and Paine thought of Francis's moonlighting with one of their customers is not known, but there is no evidence of any hard feelings.[41]

Francis included artistic touches in his original

LEFT TOP: **Francis and Starling with the big sailing model of the *Vanitie* in the Boylston Street office.** (Courtesy John N. Brown, Mystic Seaport, 1996-4-10) LEFT MIDDLE: **Starling and Frank with a model of the *Santa Maria*, Boylston Street.** (Courtesy John N. Brown, Mystic Seaport, 1996-4-14) LEFT BOTTOM: **Loring Swasey at his desk, Boylston Street. The photographs of the four leading men of Burgess, Swasey, and Paine at 585 Boylston Street were all made on Friday, November 23, 1923.** (Courtesy John N. Brown, Mystic Seaport, 1996-4-15) RIGHT TOP AND BOTTOM: **Francis carving a half-model of the *Joann*. He has already drawn the lines and is making the model merely to show the schooner's shape in three dimensions. As well as having a workbench at 585 Boylston Street, Francis set up his lathe in the office. These photos were also made on Friday, November 23, 1923. Francis would have had little interest in the diagram on the blackboard. It is a curve of areas, showing the fore-and-aft distribution of volume in a hull shape. The shape has been dictated by mathematics, where the forward part of the curve of areas is determined by versed sines and the after part by a trochoid, supposedly duplicating the shapes of the bow and stern waves of a moving hull. This was the Wave Form Theory, devised independently by Colin Archer and William M. Tileson and based on Scott Russell's Wave Line Theory. Starling Burgess and Norman Skene would have been fascinated by such application of mathematics to yacht design, but not L. Francis Herreshoff.** (Courtesy John N. Brown, Mystic Seaport, 1996-4-11 and 1996-4-9; the model is in the possession of Waldo Brown's son, Paul, at Duxbury, Massachusetts)

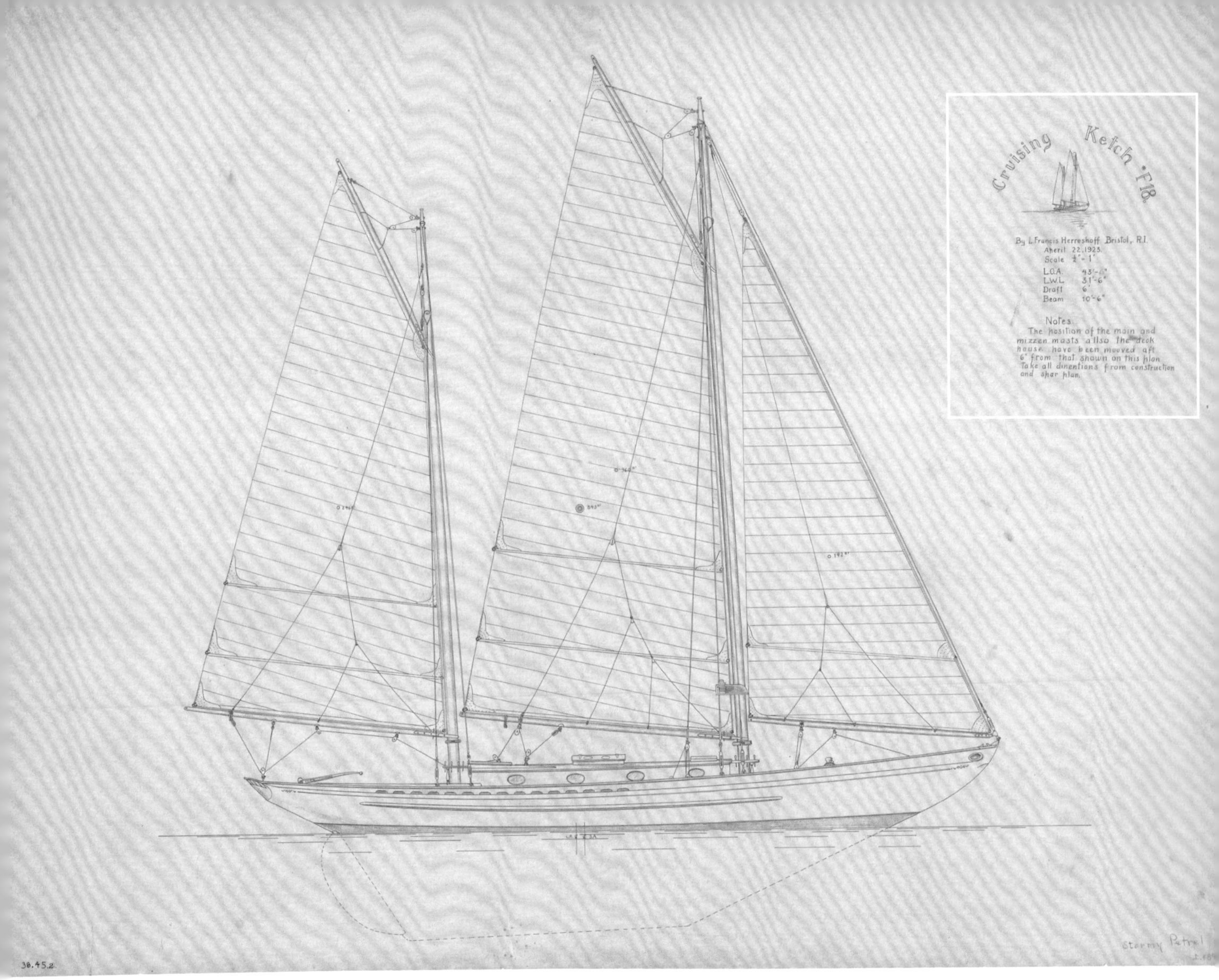

drawing of the *Stormy Petrel.* He made dashed lines to hint that the vessel was actually floating in water, emphasized by his showing the underwater profile in a dotted line. He took the time to draw many details: a nicely sheered boot top; a covestripe ending in scrolls fore and aft; a lovely, curved tiller; a running light; turnbuckles; reinforced tabling in the sails; blocks; all carefully and beautifully drawn. He drew a handsome oval hawsepipe, a fitting he had already adopted, copied from the local fishing schooners. His artist's eye had picked out this detail, and he would use it often to give a design an aura of the traditional.

Francis designed the *Stormy Petrel*'s hull to be straightforward and able. There is but little hollow in the garboards. The bottom of the keel

ABOVE: **Francis's design No. F-18, which became Charlie Welch's *Stormy Petrel.* The sail area is 843 square feet.** (© Mystic Seaport, Daniel S. Gregory Ships Plans Library, SP38.45.2) RIGHT: **A sketch to show what the F-18 would look like underway.** (© Mystic Seaport, Daniel S. Gregory Ships Plans Library, SP38.45.2, detail from title block)

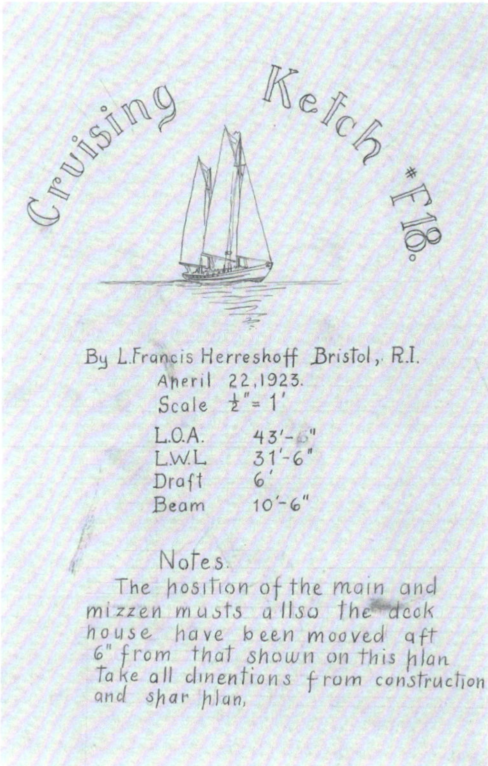

is a straight line, as is the bow profile, all the way from the toe on the ballast keel up to the first waterline he shows above the load waterline. Francis specified light scantlings, for a cruising boat, allowing nearly 50 percent of the displacement to be in the outside ballast. He gave the engine its own separate compartment in the after, port corner of the cabinhouse, with its own entry hatch and full headroom. Francis devised a convenient loading hatch in the cockpit for the icebox, but the cook had to remove the companionway ladder to gain access to cold food.

Francis adopted an excellent way to show clearly the complexities of the yacht's construction details, numbering fifty-nine items on the construction plan and including on the drawing, but not cluttering the construction plan itself, a table giving details on the numbered items. He wrote later, "My experience has been that the men in the shop will not bother to look at specifications but they can find at once the information that they want on the drawings." For seven of the items on the *Stormy Petrel*'s construction plan, he instructed the builder to "See Architect" for further information. The builder was the famous George F. Lawley and Son Company, of Neponset, Massachusetts. Lawley's launched the *Stormy Petrel* the following late March. She was the first of fourteen boats the yard would build to Francis's designs.[42]

The *Stormy Petrel* served Charlie Welch's purpose admirably. The *Boston Globe* reported that she was the first boat on her mooring in Marblehead Harbor in early April and that she had soon made a run across Massachusetts Bay to Provincetown. Two years later, the news in the *Boston Transcript* was that she had been launched for the season on February 20, the first boat in commission in Marblehead for the third year in a row. And the *Boston Herald* told its readers that "Mr. Welch refuses to take his boat out of commission until winter forces him to," and that he had sailed with his wife and young daughter around Halfway Rock on December 6.

When *Yachting* published the plans of the *Stormy Petrel* in the February 1925 issue, the accompanying write-up added the information that "Her owner says she has the most comfortable motion in a sea that a boat could have, and is, in addition, extremely stiff and able." The article went on to quote Charlie: "The ketch rig worked out excellently. *Stormy Petrel* was out several times last year in October and November in hard nor'westers, and laid to under mizzen alone, without helm or sheet requiring any attention all night long. She has been sailed under mizzen and jib, jib and mainsail, or mainsail alone. She will sail herself on any point of sailing, even to running before it, but on this last point it has never been done with the mainsail set." Francis would later draw a diagram of a ketch with two reefs in each of her three sails, showing thirteen different balanced sail combinations for various wind strengths, and he noted, "There are

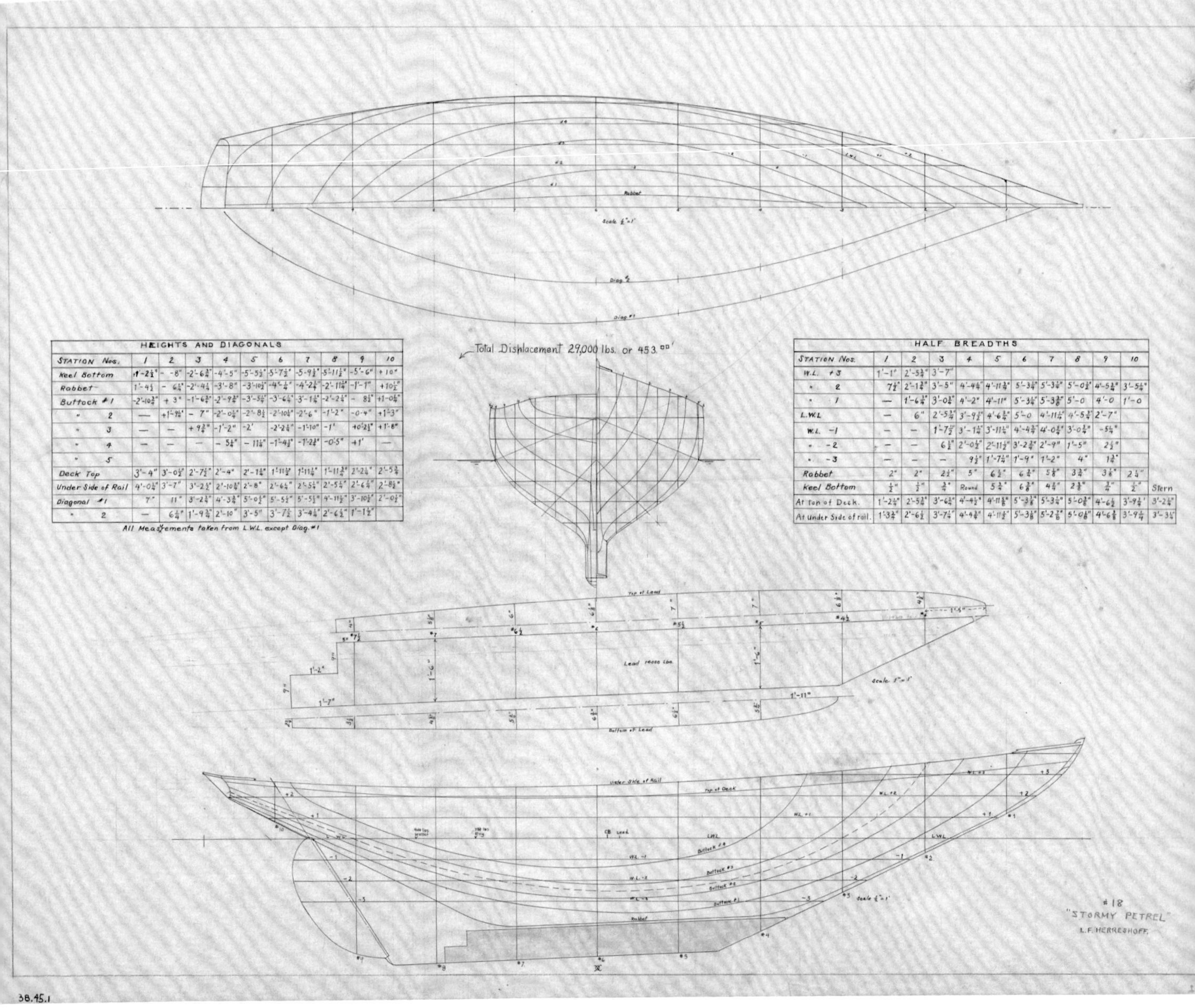

The *Stormy Petrel*'s lines. The ketch's easy motion in a seaway came from her heavy displacement and full sections. She weighed 29,000 pounds, of which 14,000 were in her lead keel ballast. She is 43 feet, 6 inches long on deck; 31 feet, 6 inches on the waterline; beam, 10 feet, 6 inches; draft 6 feet. (© Mystic Seaport, Daniel S. Gregory Ships Plans Library, SP38.45.1)

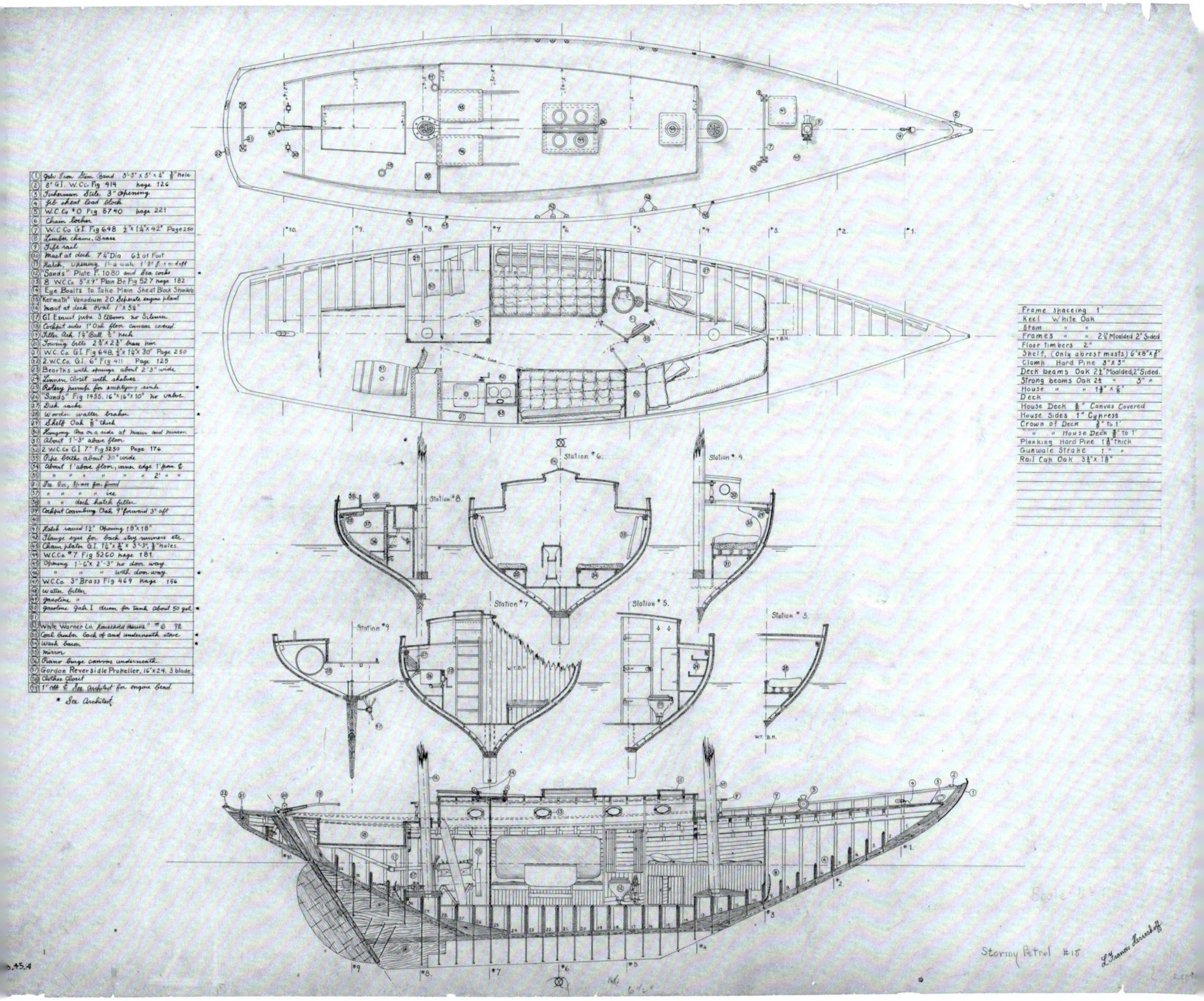

The construction plan shows the masts and cabin house in their changed positions, as built. The tanks are simple enough: a wooden barrel for water and a 50-gallon drum for gas. (© Mystic Seaport, Daniel S. Gregory Ships Plans Library, SP38.45.4)

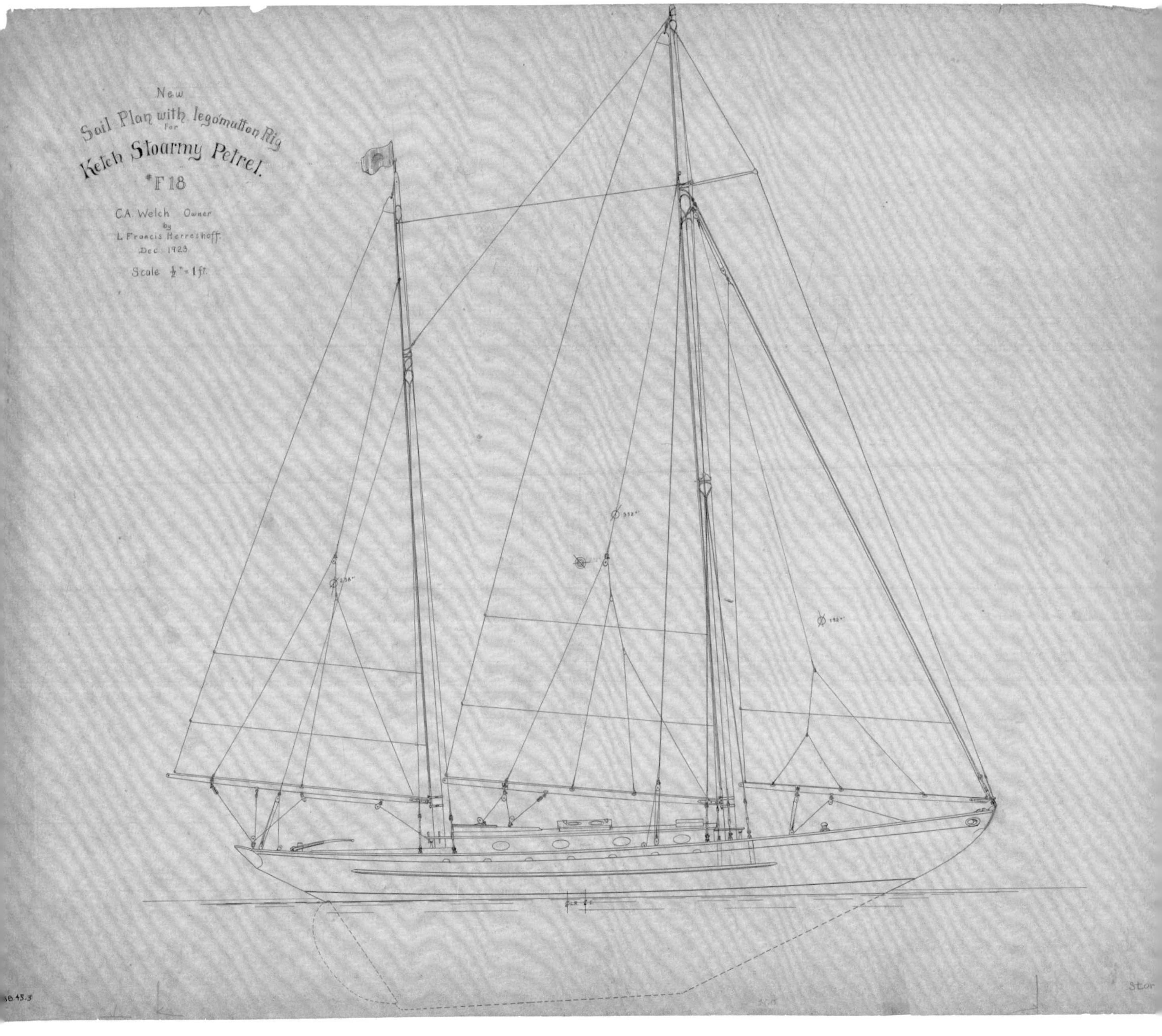

The rejected Marconi rig. Sail area is 782 square feet. (© Mystic Seaport, Daniel S. Gregory Ships Plans Library, SP38.45.3) RIGHT: **Charlie Welch, concentrating on steering his *Stormy Petrel*. There's not much wind, but he doesn't want a stray puff to blow the chart overboard.** (Courtesy Hope Welch Slater, Mystic Seaport, 1996-10-63)

about 14 other combinations of sails which are not balanced but useful in laying-to or running down wind. With a square sail a storm jib and a trysail (that sets on either mast) the combinations are truly manifold."[43]

Francis often accompanied Charlie on his overnight drifts in the *Stormy Petrel*. Later he would write a fictionalized account of a conversation overheard in a yacht club, an account that clearly refers to his trips with Charlie Welch: "I often sailed off to the eastward of a summer or fall night just to lay-to in her. Often ran out at the beginning of a nor'wester when I knew it would be clear. All you had to do was lower her jib and mainsail, sheet the mizzen in about as you do for close-hauled; let her helm go as it pleased. Well, sir, there she would stay as steady as you please, with no way on at all, making a dead set toward the leeward beam. I used to lower a sounding lead over her weather quarter about abreast the cockpit. Used to pay out about ten fathoms. I could tell exactly by the lay of that line how she was drifting. She generally made a dead set sideways of one mile an hour. Yes, those were some of the happiest hours of my life; the stars overhead, and nothing in sight but the whitecaps. Once in a while one of them would roar under her stern. I'd just sit there in the companionway and drink in that sea air. She had a coal-burning stove, kept the whole cabin warm and dry. Yes, those were happy moments." Francis's overheard speaker then went on to explain why the ketch lay-to so well with just the mizzen set and the helm free: "Well, the mizzen on a ketch is well aft of her center of lateral resistance. It is always working her up in the wind and gently pushing ahead just enough to overcome the tendency of the sea and wind that is trying to swing her bow off. No, you can't lay a boat to in a sea and wind unless the area of sail is well aft, and the area of sail set must be just sufficient to kill her sternway, and if you don't believe it, just go out there and try it."[44]

On a blustery, fall night, there wouldn't have

been much traffic off Cape Ann, half a dozen miles southeast of Thatcher Island lights. When Francis got cold, he could duck below, slide the hatch aft, and join his friend Charlie in the warm cabin. There may have been a judicious tot of rum to finish, a pinochle game to play. And there was always a discussion to continue, a discussion of yacht design and specifically of the design of Charlie's next racing boat. Eventually, they'd doubtless take turns catching some sleep in the pipe berths in the main cabin, their angles carefully adjusted to prevent the sleeper from being rolled out, easy motion notwithstanding. Both men greatly enjoyed these escapes to sea. An important result was that their conversations on yacht design, undoubtedly helped along by the

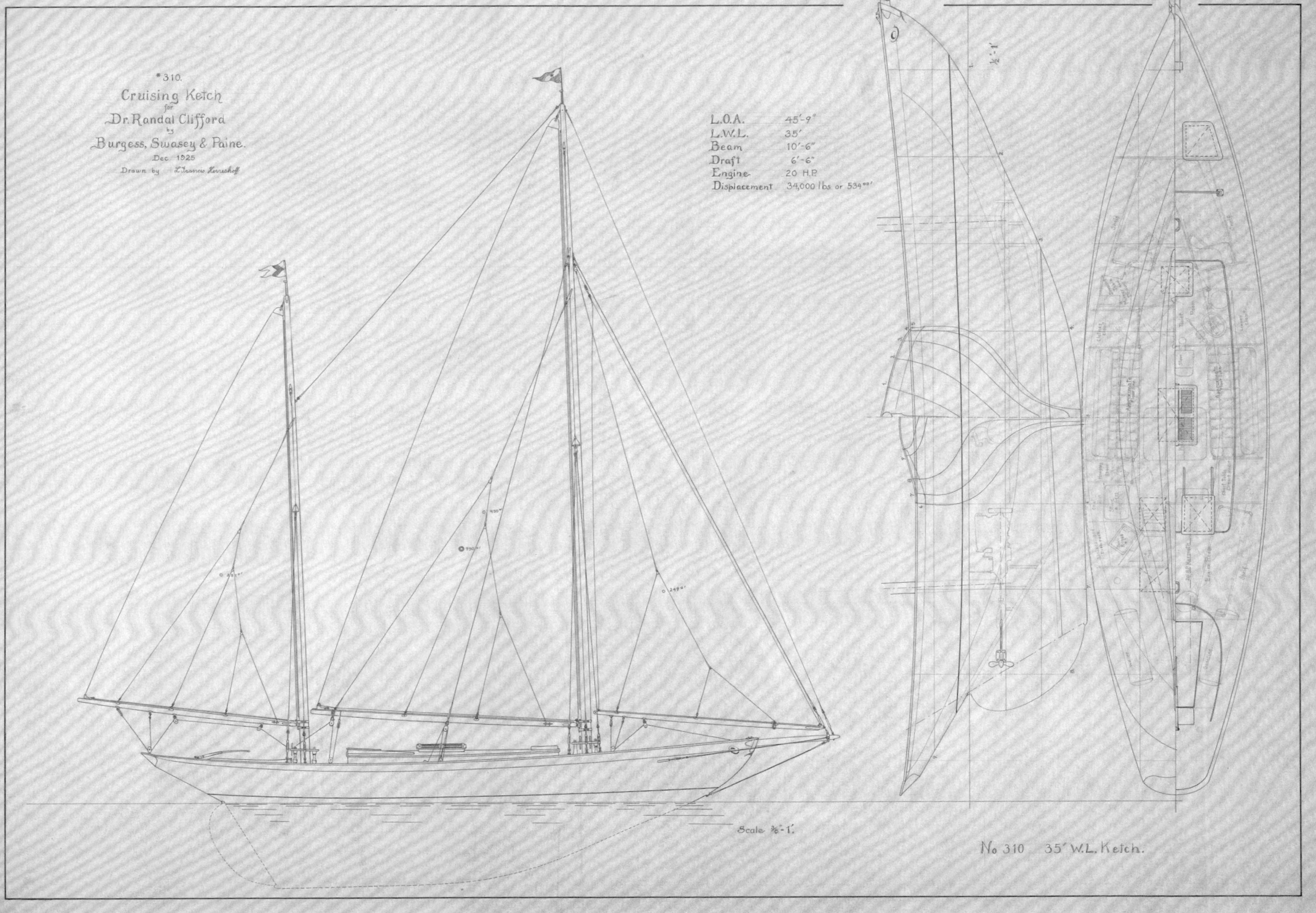

#310.
Cruising Ketch
for
Dr. Randal Clifford
by
Burgess, Swasey & Paine.
Dec 1925
Drawn by L. Francis Herreshoff
L.O.A. 45'-9"
L.W.L. 35'
Beam 10'-6"
Draft 6'-6"
Engine 20 H.P.
Displacement 34,000 lbs or 534 cu ft
Scale 3/8"-1'.
1/2"-1'
No 310 35' W.L. Ketch.

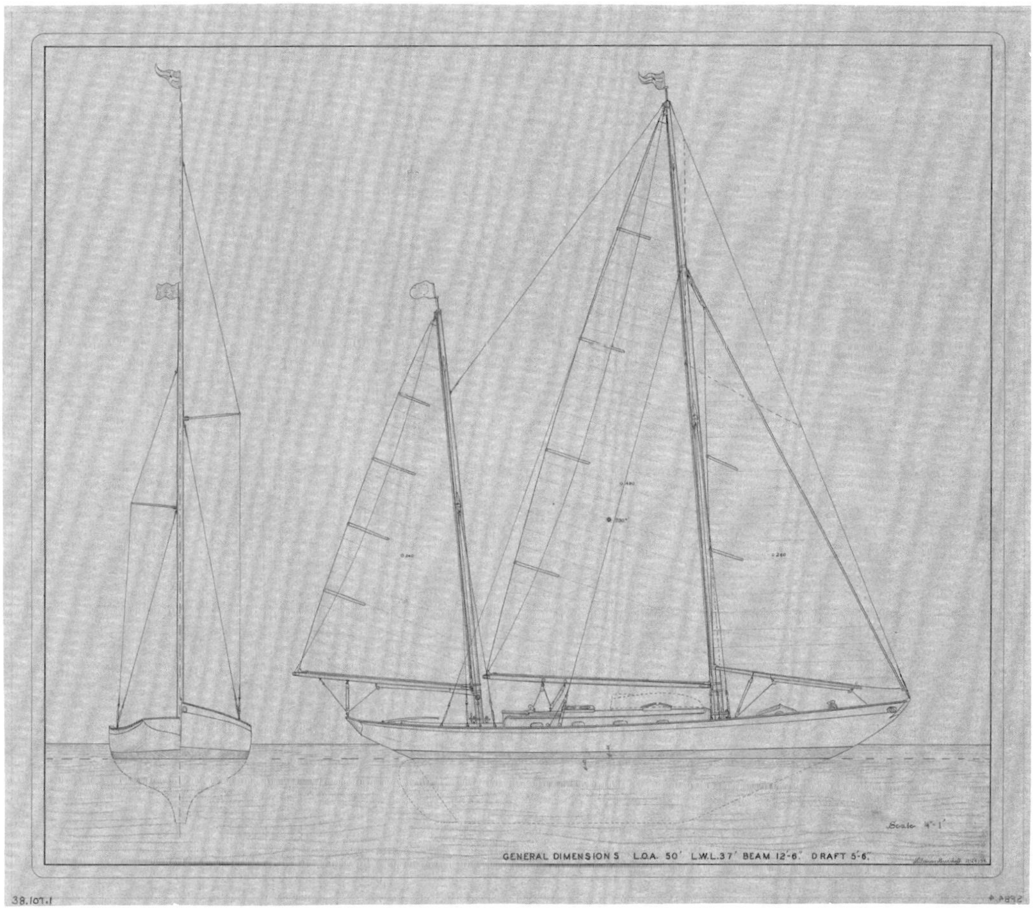

LEFT: **Two years after designing the *Stormy Petrel*, Francis made a preliminary design for a slightly larger ketch for Dr. Randall Clifford. There is no evidence that he completed the design or that a boat was built. She is a prettier boat than the *Stormy Petrel*, with finer lines and a Marconi rig with a bowsprit. Dimensions are: length on deck, 45 feet, 9 inches; waterline, 35 feet; beam, 10 feet, 6 inches; draft, 6 feet, 6 inches. The sail area is 950 square feet; displacement, 34,000 pounds. The plan is dated December 1925. The design is Burgess, Swasey, and Paine No. 310.** (© Mystic Seaport, Daniel S. Gregory Ships Plans Library, SP38.160.1) ABOVE: **Nine years later, in 1934, Francis made a preliminary design for a larger ketch, reminiscent of the *Stormy Petrel*, with relatively lighter displacement and less draft. He has eliminated any drag to the keel. She is 50 feet long on deck; 37 feet on the waterline; 12 feet, 6 inches beam; 5 feet, 6 inches draft. The sail area is 980 square feet without the jib topsail. The plan is dated November 24, 1934. He did not complete the design.** (© Mystic Seaport, Daniel S. Gregory Ships Plans Library, SP38.107.1)

Stormy Petrel's "most comfortable motion in a sea," led to considerable success on the race course for both friends. And when Charlie shifted his abode from Hull to Marblehead, Francis helped him move the furniture; they used the *Stormy Petrel* as a freighter, with the piano as deckload.[45]

The *Stormy Petrel* met well Charlie Welch's objective of a boat capable of stretching the New England cruising season, but her design was ordinary, with none of the outstanding features that would mark later designs of L. Francis Herreshoff. Her design could have been turned out by any of the better men working in John G. Alden's office at the time. Francis had not quite hit his stride.

Charlie Welch was not one

TOP: **Waldo Brown in his naval aviator's uniform.** (Courtesy John N. Brown, Mystic Seaport, 1996-4-17) BOTTOM: **The Salem pilot schooner *Clarence Barclay*, modeled and built in 1856 by Joshua Brown, grandfather of Waldo. This is the vessel that inspired the *Joann*.** (Painting by E. Peterson, courtesy John N. Brown)

to keep a boat long; luckily for Francis, Charlie wanted to keep trying out new designs. He offered the *Stormy Petrel* for sale in the spring of 1925, and she sold the following year.[46]

AT THE SAME time as he was finishing the design of the F-18 for Charlie Welch, Francis made his first design of a yacht with a clipper bow, a shape that would become his artistic favorite. He drew a preliminary outboard profile and sail plan for a 50-foot schooner, Burgess, Swasey, and Paine's design No. 257, in late 1923. The owner was Waldo Hayward Brown. In at least one instance, Waldo Brown claimed sole credit for the design, in writing; in at least two instances, Francis wrote of his making the design, without mentioning any collaboration by Waldo. Both men—they had become good friends—were being disingenuous, for the design of the *Joann*, as she would be called, was certainly a collaborative process.

Waldo Brown was born in Salem, Massachusetts, in 1896, making him six years younger than Francis. His grandfather, Joshua Brown, designed and built more than forty significant commercial vessels and yachts at South Salem between 1856 and 1887.[47]

Waldo was inquisitive and bright, and as a youth he haunted the shipyards of Boston's North Shore. When he was a high school student, prowling the Marblehead waterfront, he visited the Burgess Company, then building airplanes, and he met Starling. After graduating from Phillips Academy, Andover, he studied naval architecture at MIT for a year, and then, in 1917, enlisted in the Naval Reserve Flying Corps. While waiting a month for an opening at the navy's ground school, he worked at the Burgess Company, helping assemble fuselages and wings. He breezed through ground school and was first in his flight school class at Key West, earning a commission as ensign in 1918. Near the end of World War I, Waldo flew coastal patrol in a seaplane out of Chatham, on the elbow of Cape Cod. He took part in the "Battle of Orleans," the only action in the war in which aircraft attacked the enemy on the East Coast, making an unsuccessful bombing attack (the bombs turned out to be duds) on a U-boat.[48]

Waldo left the navy in January 1919, and within two weeks he married Frances M. Gray. His father-in-law, Paul Gray, had, with his brother David and Ora James Mulford, founded the Gray Motor Company in 1905 to build automobile and marine motors in Detroit, as well as its successor, the Gray Marine Motor Company in 1910. Paul and David's father, the Detroit banker John Simpson Gray, had bailed out Henry Ford's then-failing automobile business, on condition that he be allowed to run Ford's business side. The Grays invested heavily in Ford. It was said that Frances Gray's family was worth thirty-nine million dollars in 1912.[49]

After a short time selling bonds in Boston, Waldo went to work for the Gray Marine Motor Company, which began to produce Gray automobiles in 1922. When the first car came off the production line, Waldo drove it from Detroit to Boston, where he was to run the sales agency. "I sold all I could get—at first; was given the whole state of Massachusetts and later all of New England, but in 1924, after having built up a complete wholesale and retail organization with about forty persons on the payroll, the Gray organization in Detroit collapsed and there was nothing to do but pick up the pieces." Actually, the Gray company continued in business for two more years after Waldo left, but they were years of decline.[50]

The first piece Waldo Brown picked up was to see about getting a dream ship built. The first major vessel that his grandfather Joshua had modeled and built, in 1856, was the schooner *Clarence Barclay*, a well-known and successful pilot boat out of Salem. Waldo had inherited a fine painting of the *Barclay*, and he had admired the schooner in the painting all his life. He wondered if a smaller schooner yacht could be designed and built along her lines to make a smart-sailing and able family cruiser. His concept of basing a yacht design on that of a pilot boat was sound, for pilot boats had to be both seaworthy and fast to be successful. To test his idea, he carried the painting into the offices of Burgess, Swasey, and Paine.

Waldo was acquainted with Starling, as we have seen, and he owned the 54-foot powerboat *Boy Scout* that Loring Swasey had designed. He may have previously met Francis, for Waldo and Charlie Welch were friends. In any event, it was Francis who responded with enthusiasm to Waldo's proposal. "Sometime around 1924," Francis would write in a letter years later, "a young man, Waldo Brown, came to me with an oil painting of a boat his grandfather had had built in Salem in about 1850. She was a very nice looking boat that was used for a pilot boat, and he asked me if a modern boat of that type would be practical. I told him that she would not only be practical, but better than the usual boat of that time that was designed to fit some of the measurement rules, and he gave me an order to design that boat which was a schooner named *Joann* 50 feet on deck." Sixteen years later, Francis repeated this account in *Yachting* magazine. What he did not say was that Waldo Brown was an active participant in the design of the *Joann*.[51]

For Waldo's part, when he summarized his career for the US Navy Bureau of Navigation to give his qualifications to justify a promotion to lieutenant in the Naval Reserve, he wrote that he "spent the summer of that year [1926] cruising up and down the coast in the Sch. *Joann*, a vessel of about twenty tons which I designed myself and navigated myself with the aid of just one paid hand—a cook."[52]

The design of the *Joann* would lead Francis Herreshoff—through Waldo Brown and a far more successful car salesman, Harry Noyes—to the great *Tioga* designs of the next decade. The main credit for this wonderful series of yachts must go to Francis; it was he who brought them to artistic and practical perfection. But credit is also due to Joshua Brown, for modeling the *Clarence Barclay,* and to Waldo Brown for his recognition of his grandfather's achievement, his determination to follow it up, and his own contributions to the design of the new schooner.

His signed and dated drawings indicate that Waldo worked with Francis on the design of the *Joann* in the office at 585 Boylston Street, at least from January 1, 1924, through July 2. He was probably not an employee of Burgess, Swasey, and Paine; in his career summary for the navy, he appears to list every company he worked for, even briefly, but there is no mention of Burgess, Swasey, and Paine, nor does his name appear on any of the firm's drawings other than some of those of the *Joann*. Waldo wrote that after his departure from the Gray company, he worked for about two years as assistant to the manager of Wellington, Sears, and Company, a large cotton-goods manufacturer headquartered in Boston. He doesn't state exactly when he started that job, so we don't know whether he made his drawings for the *Joann* as a full-time project before he started work for Wellington, Sears, or whether he squeezed them in as he was starting a new job. In any case, Waldo—because of his acquaintance with Starling and because he had at least some background in naval architecture, and perhaps not least because the prospective vessel, based on a specific forerunner, was his own concept—seems to have made an unusual arrangement to participate in the design of the *Joann* in the Burgess, Swasey, and Paine offices.[53]

Francis's preliminary outboard profile and sail plan established the characteristics of the design. When he drew the lines plan, he eliminated what little drag to the keel he had shown on the preliminary drawing to reduce the draft, and he shortened her overhang a little at both bow and stern. The latter change stole a little of the grace of the preliminary drawing. How much Waldo collaborated on these key drawings is not known,

Francis's preliminary outboard profile drawing of the *Joann.* The slightly longer overhangs and longer main boom and gaff give the design more grace than is shown in the final plans from which the schooner was built. (© Mystic Seaport, Daniel S. Gregory Ships Plans Library, SP38.145.23)

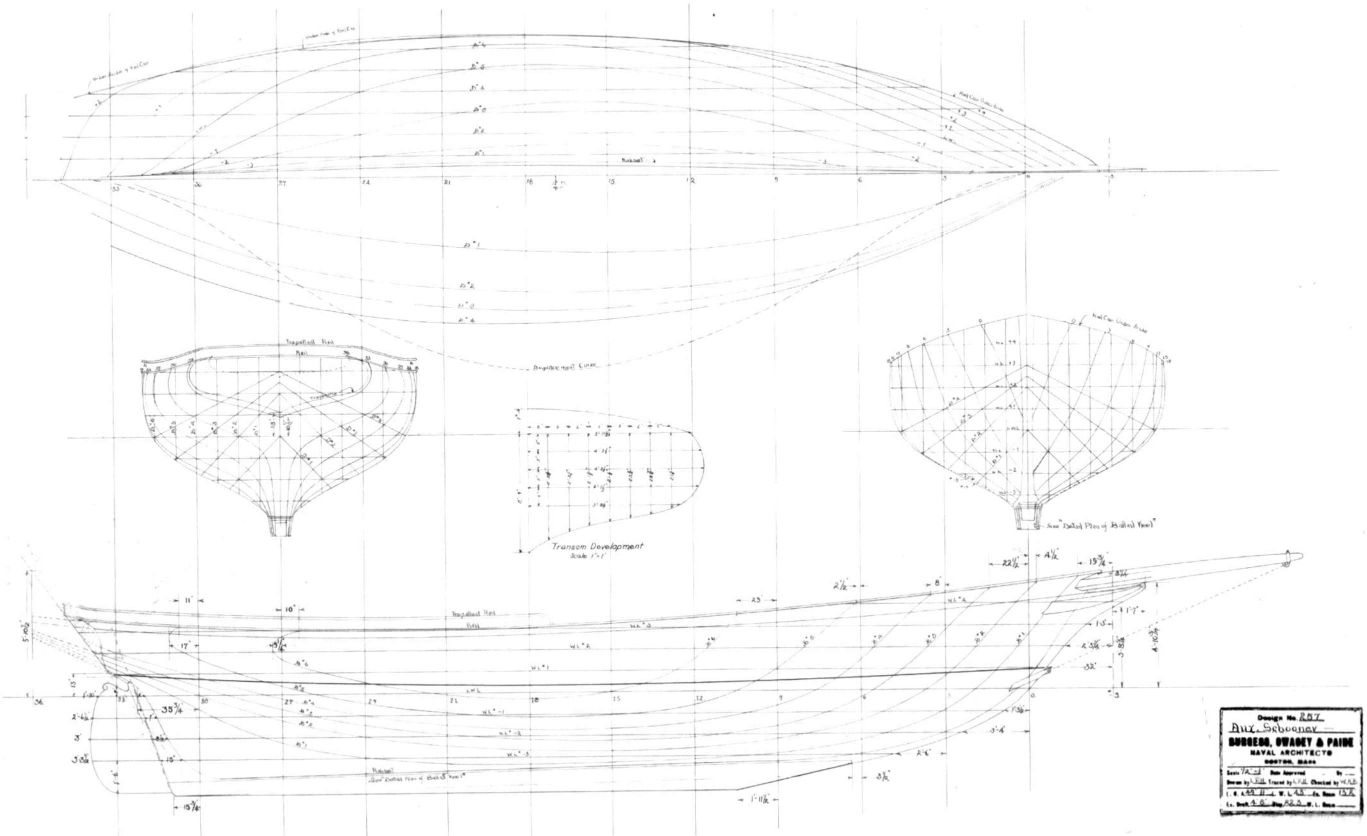

but as the owner—with one eye on the painting of the *Clarence Barclay*—he must have had his say. The standard title block of the lines drawing indicates that it was drawn and traced by Francis and checked by Waldo. The offset table, taken from the lines drawing, purely a measurement-and-recording task, was entirely Waldo's work.[54]

The lines plan shows a relatively shoal-draft hull, drawing only 4 feet, 8 inches. The *Joann*'s home port would be Marblehead, but she was to spend time at Harwich Port, on the south side of Cape Cod, in tiny Wychmere Harbor, where Frances Gray had inherited ten acres of waterfront property that her grandparents bought in

ABOVE: **The lines of the *Joann* were drawn and traced by Francis. Waldo checked them and made up the table of offsets. Dimensions are: length on deck, 49 feet, 11 inches; length on the waterline, 43 feet; beam, 13 feet, 2 inches; and draft, 4 feet, 8 inches. Displacement figured at 44,600 pounds, of which 14,320 pounds would be in an iron, outside ballast keel, giving a ballast-to-displacement ratio of 32 percent.** (© Mystic Seaport, Daniel S. Gregory Ships Plans Library, SP38.145.22) RIGHT: **The *Joann*'s sail plan, as made by Waldo Brown, dated April 5, 1924. With the overlapping foresail, her sail area is 1,422 square feet.** (© Mystic Seaport, Daniel S. Gregory Ships Plans Library, SP38.145.5)

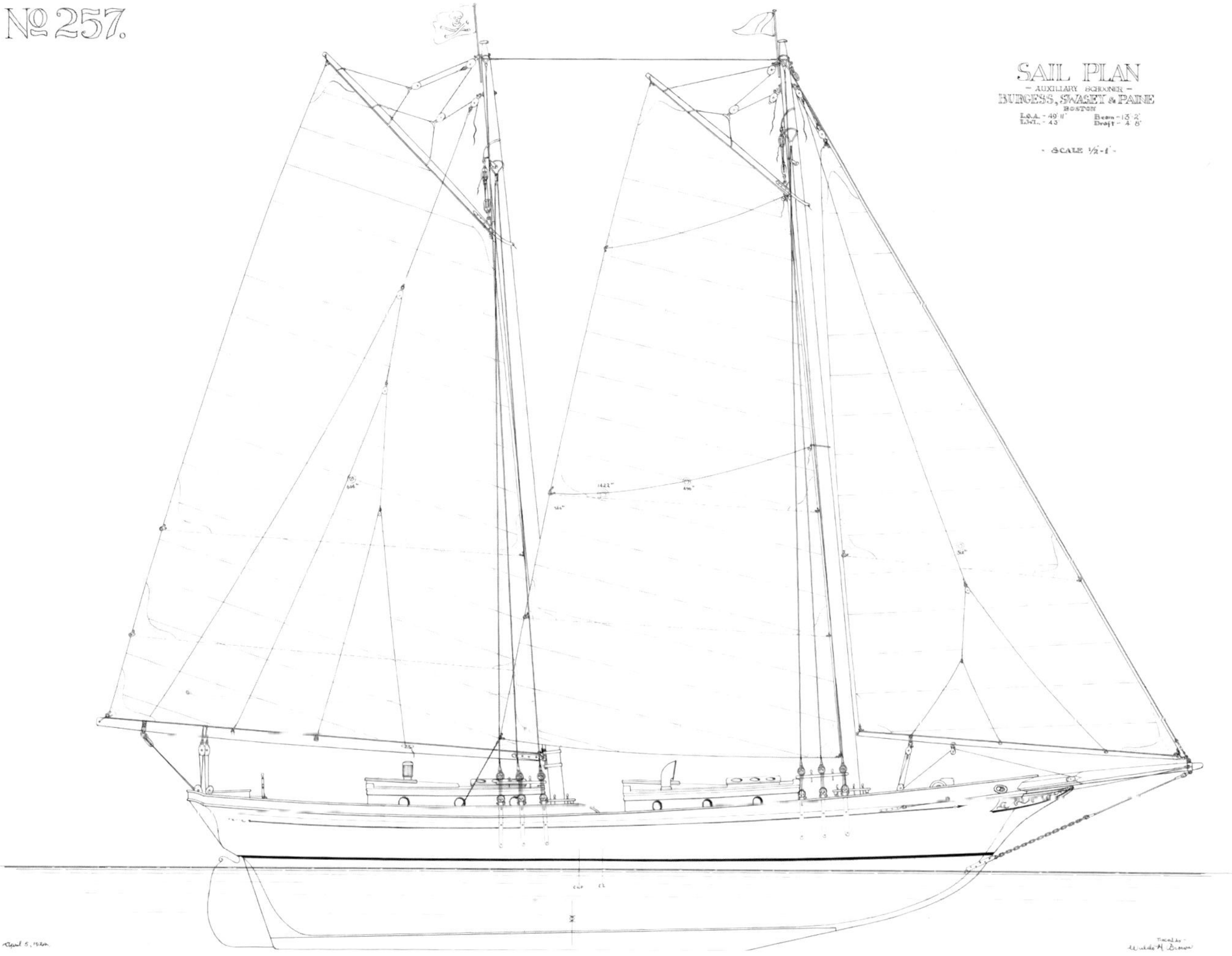

1866 and developed into a family compound. It was the five-foot depth of Wychmere Harbor and its narrow, dredged entrance across the sand flats that governed the *Joann*'s draft. Moreover, Waldo wanted to be able to ground her out, and so her designers specified iron for the keel rather than more easily damaged lead, and they did not give her a centerboard, for the sand and gravel of Cape Cod's shoals could easily jam a centerboard trunk.[55]

"*Joann* is a little shallow for best performance to windward," Francis would write many years later, "but she is a fast, able boat under all other conditions." He would also remark that she made "quite a little leeway," especially "when first coming about."[56]

Waldo drew the sail plan for the *Joann,* dated February 1, 1924, using Francis's lines drawing for the shape of the hull in outboard profile. He made changes to Francis's preliminary sail plan, all of which moved the center of effort forward:

No. 257.

~ SCALE ~
1/2 in. = 1 ft.

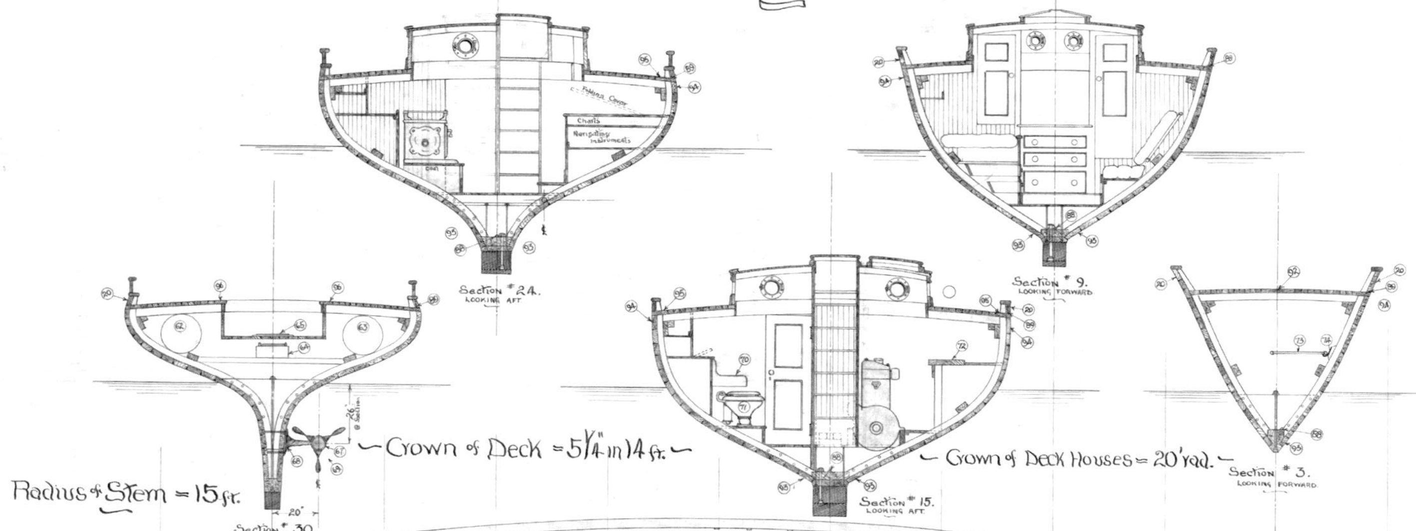

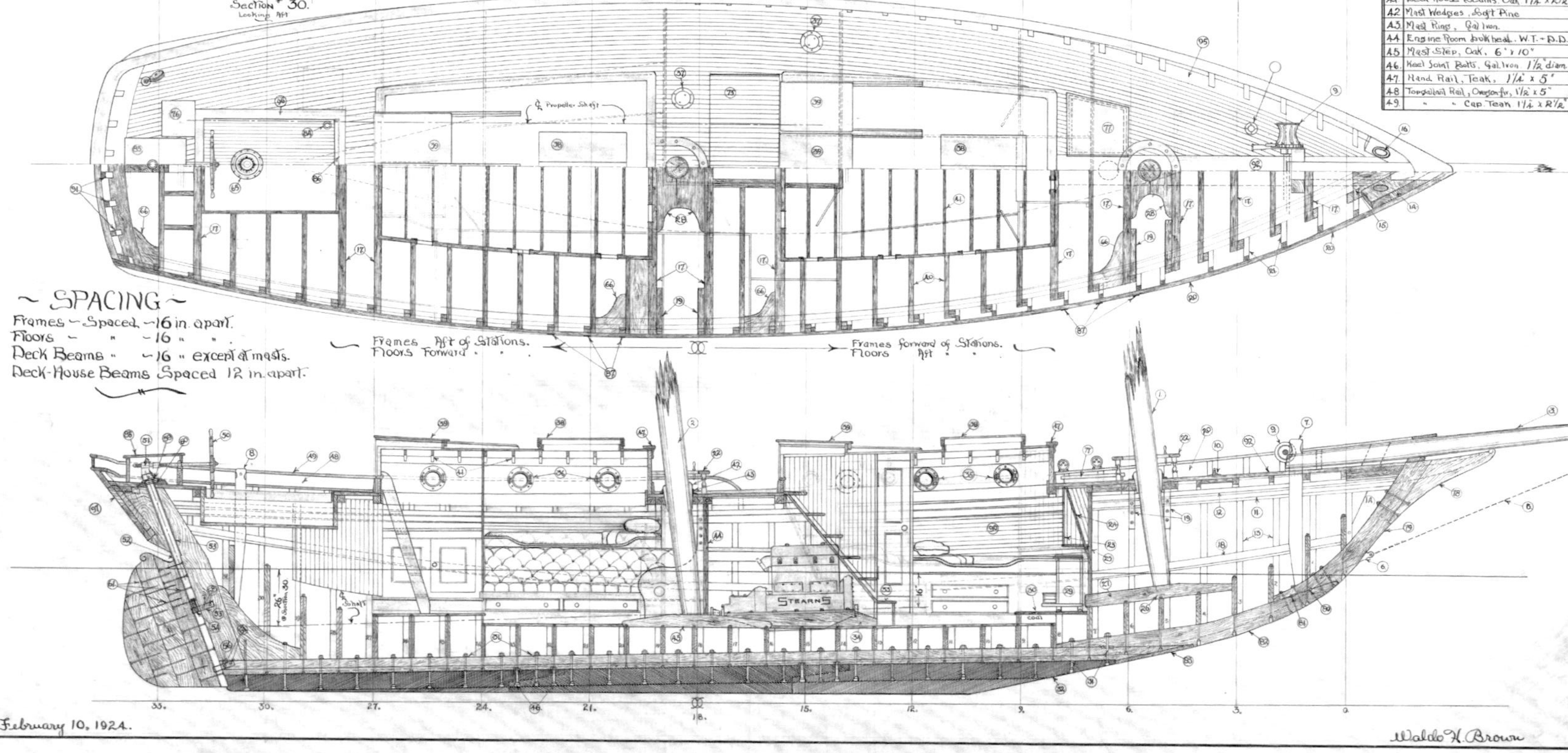

	REFERENCE		NUMBERS
1.	Foremast, Oregon Pine, See Spar Plan.	50.	Steering Wheel. Teak. 32" diam.
2.	Mainmast, " "	51.	Steering Gear. Edson
3.	Bowsprite, " "	52.	Rudder Post. Brass Tube Ex. Heavy 3" (O.D. 3.500 in.)
4.	"	53.	Sleeve, Brass. 3 1/2 Stand Tube (I.D. 3.548 in.)
5.	Bobstay "	54.	Pin. To fit inside Post. (One bolt to pass through this pin)
6.	" , Chain Plate	55.	Rudder Pintle Socket. Cast Brass (2 pc.)
7.	Bowsprite Bits, Oak, 4" x 8"	56.	Strap hinge, brass 2 1/2" x 3/16"
8.	Quarter Bits, " , 4" x 4"	57.	" " Rivets, Copper 3/8" diam.
9.	Windlass.	58.	Pintle Socket Bolts. Brass. Counter sunk heads. Threaded into One Side.
10.	Traveler, Stirsail Sheet.	59.	Rudder Post Ball Bearings.
11.	Clamp, Oregon Pine, 2" x 6"	60.	Flange Threaded to Sleeve
12.	Shelf, " , 2 3/4" x 2 3/4"	61.	Rudder Blade Bolts - Bronze.
13.	Frames, Oak, bent, 2 1/2" x 2 3/4"	62.	Water Tank Cap.
14.	Knightheads, Oak, 2 1/2" Thick.	63.	Fuel Tank Cap.
15.	Breast hook, Oak 3 1/4" Thick.	64.	Compass, 7" Card, Electric Lighted.
16.	Hawser holes, Gal. Iron.	65.	Glass deck Plate over Compass
17.	Strong Beams, 3" x 3 1/4" (Moulded)	66.	Lodging Knees, Hackmatack, 2"
18.	Stringer, Oregon Pine, 2 1/4" x 5"	67.	Gordon Reversible Propeller. Hub #5. 26" diam.
19.	Hanging Knees, Hackmatack, 2"	68.	Strut. Bronze.
20.	Gunwale, Oregon fir, 1 1/2" (Note: 1/4" Crown)	69.	Goodyear "Cutless" Rubber bearing.
21.	Stanchions, Oak, 2 1/2" x 2 1/2"	70.	Basin
22.	Fife rail, Teak.	71.	Toilet.
23.	W.T. Bulkhead. Double Diagonal	72.	Workbench, 12" x 2"
24.	Hatchway Sog. W.T.	73.	Pipe Berth, 6' long 20" Wide
25.	Bookcase (Covering hatchway Sog.)	74.	" " , hooks
26.	Mast Step, Oak, 6" x 10"	75.	Removable deck over Motor - 31" x 50"
27.	Aux. Step for double-headsail Rig -	76.	Lazarette hatch (One on each side.)
28.	Mast Partners, Oak, 3 1/4" thick.	77.	Forecastle hatch. Teak
29.	"Yacht Cabin" Stove, Open Grate - 12"	78.	Billet Head, Oak
30.	Hinged Cover over Coal Bin.	79.	Stem head. Oak. Sided in.
31.	Keel Bolts, Gal. Iron. 1" diam.	80.	Stopwater. Locust.
32.	Cast Iron Ballast Keel. (See detail Plan)	81.	Key. Oak 1" x 2"
33.	Hinged Step over Wood Box.	82.	Stem foot. Oak. Sided in.
34.	Engine Bed Logs, Oak, 3" Thick	83.	Fairing Piece. Oak. 24" x 1 1/2"
35.	Port Lights, brass diam.	84.	Scupper
36.	" " , " "	85.	Steering Gear Box. Cover Teak.
37.	Deck Plates, (for Cowls)	86.	Cockpit Covering Board.
38.	Skylights. See detail Plan. Teak	87.	Chain Plates. Angle to be set by Riggers.
39.	Companionway Hatch. See detail Plan	88.	Limber holes, 1/2"
40.	Deck Beams. Oak. 2" x 3 1/4"	89.	Waterways, Cut on Gunwale before fastening
41.	Deck House Beams. Oak 1 1/4" x 2 1/2"	90.	Sheathing (Ceiling)
42.	Mast Wedges, Soft Pine	91.	Tail Feathers, Oak. 2 1/2" wide.
43.	Mast Rings, Gal. Iron.	92.	King Plank - Teak - 14" x 1 7/8"
44.	Engine Room bulkhead. W.T. - D.D.	93.	Garboards - Hard Pine
45.	Mast Step, Oak, 6" x 10"	94.	Sheer Streak - Oak
46.	Keel Joint Bolts, Gal. Iron 1 1/2" diam.	95.	Covering Boards - Oak
47.	Hand Rail, Teak, 1 1/4" x 5"	96.	" , Teak, 1 5/8" x 5"
48.	Topgallant Rail, Oregon fir, 1 1/2" x 5"	97.	Transome, Oak, 1 3/4"
49.	" " Cap. Teak 1 1/4" x 2 1/2"	98.	

Design No. 257.
CONSTRUCTION PLAN
BURGESS, SWASEY & PAINE
NAVAL ARCHITECTS
BOSTON, MASS.
Scale 1/2" = 1' Date Jan. 1, 24
Drawn by W.H.B. Traced by W.H.B. Checked by
L.O.A. 49' 11" W.L. 43' Ex. Beam 13' 2"
Ex. Draft 4' 8" Disp. 22.3

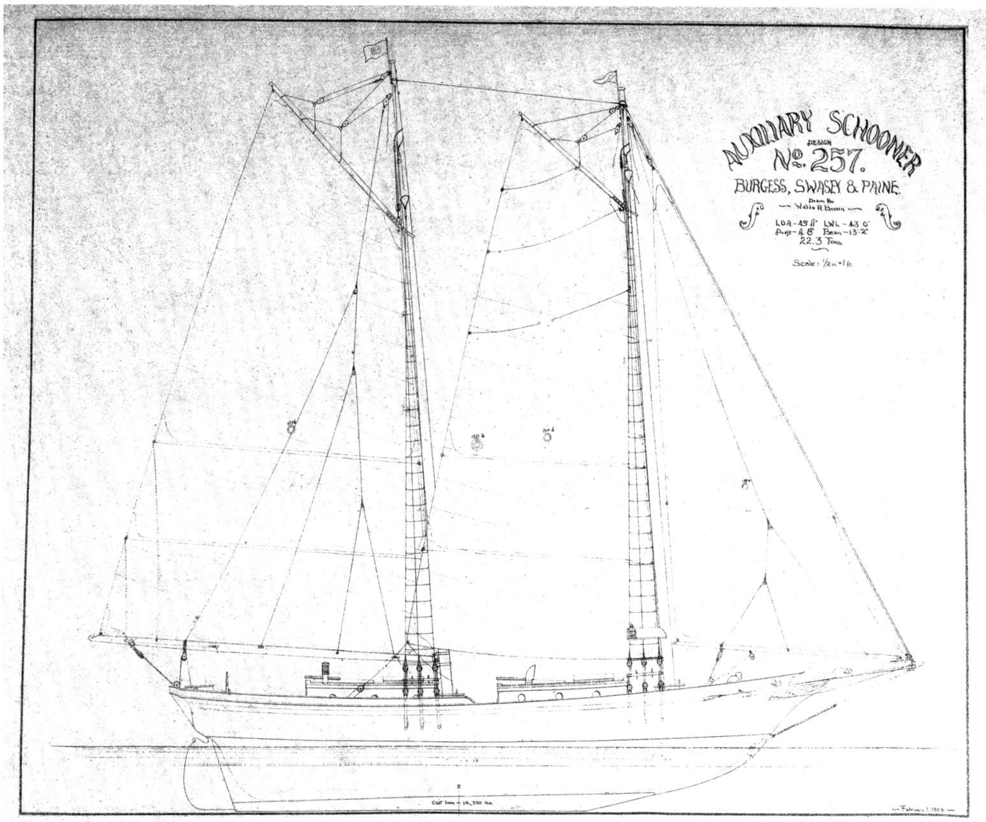

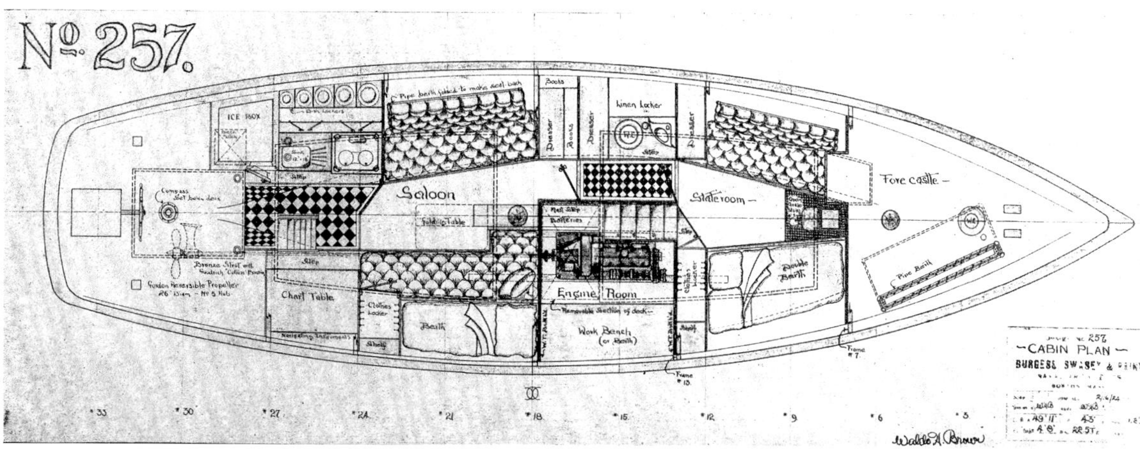

LEFT: **The *Joann*'s construction plan was drawn and traced by Waldo and dated January 1, 1924.** (© Mystic Seaport, Daniel S. Gregory Ships Plans Library, SP38.145.3) ABOVE: **Waldo drew and traced the schooner's outboard profile and cabin plan, dated February 6, 1924.** (Courtesy Paul G. Brown, Mystic Seaport, 1996-10-4)

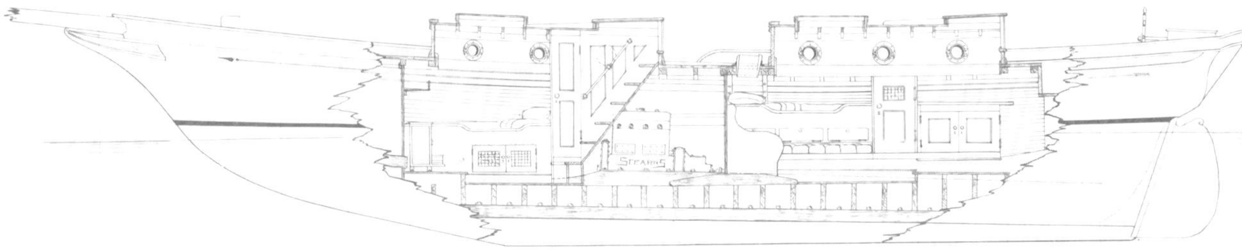

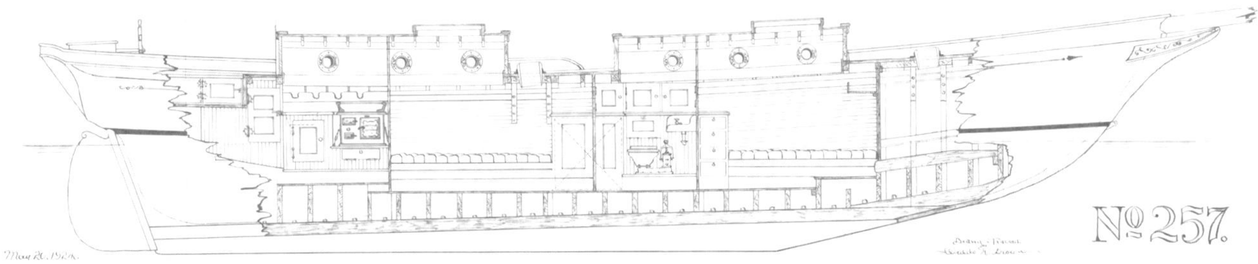

he decreased the rake of the masts, and he shortened the mainmast and the main boom and gaff, removing about 100 square feet of sail area from the mainsail. Presumably, Francis approved of these changes. In any event, the result is a vessel that balances beautifully.[57]

Waldo redrew the sail plan in a drawing dated April 5, 1924. The two sail plans are identical, except for these details: in the second plan, the mainmast, already kept short, has been shortened a little more, the reefs in the mainsail are shallower, and the main lazyjacks and foresail brails are led a little differently. In the lower, right-hand corner of the new sail plan, Waldo noted, "Drawn and Traced by Waldo H. Brown." On the copy that Francis saved, the words "Drawn and" have been erased (though they are still barely legible on the original). Apparently, Francis wanted the record to show that the *Joann's* sail plan was essentially his creation, since it was based on his original,

ABOVE: **Waldo made detailed interior profile drawings of his schooner, dated May 20, 1924.** (© Mystic Seaport, Daniel S. Gregory Ships Plans Library, SP138.145.7) RIGHT: **The *Joann* under her original rig, with the overlapping foresail.** (© Mystic Seaport, 1973.3.365)

preliminary sail plan. Francis was Waldo's friend; he was also competitive and proud. Actually, he may have needed a little reining-in by Starling. The circumstances are not known, but in successive advertisements featuring the *Joann* in *The Rudder* by the Stearns Motor Manufacturing Company, of Ludington, Michigan—the *Joann* had a four-cylinder Stearns gasoline engine rather than a Gray—the credit for the schooner's design was changed from L. Francis Herreshoff to Burgess, Swasey, and Paine.[58]

The purpose of the overlapping foresail, the typical arrangement on early pilot schooners, was not only to gain sail area, but also to make the sail set better. The combination of a relatively short gaff and long foot allowed the sheet to draw the leech aft, as well as down, so that the head of the sail could be kept from twisting off so far to leeward, thus losing power. A further advantage of the overlapping foresail was that when the schooner was hove-to under just the foresail, the sail could be trimmed readily to windward of the mainmast and adjusted to control with precision the vessel's headway, or bring her to a complete stop. The drawback of the overlapping sail was the necessity to tend the foresail sheets when tacking, and since the *Joann*'s foresail had an area of almost 500 square feet, the strain on the lee sheet was heavy in a breeze. The sheets were single-part to avoid blocks crashing against the mainmast (or somebody's head) when going about. They led through turning blocks on deck and forward to a two-part tackle, still a hard pull. After a season of coping with this gear, Waldo cut down his foresail

ABOVE: **The *Joann* shows her speed in a gentle breeze, even after being re-rigged with a smaller boomed foresail.** (Courtesy John N. Brown, Mystic Seaport, 1996-2-92) RIGHT: **Waldo Brown, busy on board his schooner, tied off at the Eastern Yacht Club, Marblehead.** (Courtesy Paul G. Brown, Mystic Seaport, 1996-10-2)

and put a boom on it, so it would be self-tending.

In a spar plan that Waldo drew and traced, dated April 2, 1924, he included an unusual stern view of the schooner with her mainsail trimmed for a close reach. On her stern, he lettered the name *Joan,* evidently a name modification that he decided against. He named his schooner with a combination of the names of his two children at the time, John and Ann.[59]

Francis drew and Waldo traced the construction drawing of the midships section of the *Joann*. This drawing was approved by Loring Swasey. Waldo drew and traced the main construction plan, adopting the system that Francis used of putting only circled numbers on the drawing and including a table of remarks keyed to the numerals, which avoided cluttering the drawing with labels.[60]

Waldo drew and traced the cabin plan, dated February 6, 1924, and he changed the schooner's arrangements below considerably from a preliminary cabin plan that Francis had sketched. He did keep the main saloon about where Francis had placed it, and he retained the idea of a separate engine room amidships, though he moved it from port to starboard. In a beautifully detailed drawing dated May 20, 1924, Waldo showed interior profiles of the cabin from both sides.[61]

In all, Waldo Brown made eight carefully drafted plans showing the design of the *Joann* in great detail. He was obviously enjoying the process of putting his visions of the *Clarence Barclay*'s successor on paper. In later years, Francis sold the *Joann*'s plans as a set of ten for between $75 and $105.[62]

The builder that the design firm selected for the *Joann* was Britt Brothers at West Lynn, Massachusetts. Chester and Andrew Britt, both in their fifties, had migrated south from Harpswell, Maine, and had worked as carpenters until 1902, when they opened a boatshop at 24 Raddin Street, on the Saugus River. Besides a number of small craft, they had built sixty-four powerboats up to a length of 68 feet, many of their own design, and twenty-three to designs by Loring Swasey. They had never built a sailing yacht, and the *Joann* was not a simple one, but Swasey must have had confidence

in them. For their part, the brothers may have been intrigued by the *Joann*'s hull shape, particularly her clipper bow. She may have reminded them of handsome schooners built in Maine. Chester, Andrew, and their fifteen employed boatbuilders built the schooner well. They would build ten more boats to Francis's designs.[63]

Francis sailed in the *Joann* with Waldo and his wife, Frances. Years later, to emphasize his belief in keeping the cabin and accoutrements of a cruising boat simple, he wrote a droll description of a hard chance he had experienced in the schooner. He and the Browns, and "a young man from the city who had done most of his cruising

ABOVE: **The *Joann* frozen into the Charles River, looking toward Cambridge. Francis lived on board during the winter of 1924-25. Note the tall chimney for the coal stove.** (Courtesy Hope Welch Slater, Mystic Seaport, 1996-10-65) RIGHT: **Francis at his drafting board at Burgess, Swasey, and Paine, February 9, 1925. This photograph was published in the *Boston Globe*, February 10, 1925, and became the catalyst for Francis's reconciliation with his father.** (Mystic Seaport 1997-2-12)

in books," were caught off Gloucester in a sudden squall that heralded the onslaught of a northeaster. Francis's enthusiasm for the schooner rig was as an artist, not as a sailor. He would write, "If the Gentle Reader loves the looks of a schooner as I do, my advice to him is to buy a fine painting of one and let it go at that." And he wrote: "I wish more were done in U. S. A. to encourage yawls and ketches for with high rigs they certainly are efficient for their sail area and much better than the schooner which I think is the invention of the Devil." But that day, in the *Joann*, the schooner rig came into its own. While Waldo and his "brave little soul" of a wife were below trying unsuccessfully to cope with "the best part of a four course meal . . . scattered over the floor together with a lot of broken china and most of the pots and pans off the galley" (Francis's object lesson in simplicity), Francis and the city slicker had the schooner scudding for harbor at eight knots, safely under foresail alone.[64]

The *Joann* was indeed a fine yacht-version of the pilot schooner *Clarence Barclay*; Waldo Brown got just the vessel he wanted. She turned out to be the forerunner of nine further clipper-bowed designs by Francis. As we shall see, once the constraint was removed of designing with the image of a working pilot schooner in mind, Francis gave his yachts with clipper bows a grace and beauty that is missing in the *Joann*. But Waldo Brown's idea of a boat was the vital catalyst for some of Francis's greatest designs.

The *Joann* is still sailing, now named the *Brigadoon*. Sterling Hayden had her trucked to the West Coast. He wanted a more conventional schooner rig, with a taller mainmast. He got the top team of Murray Peterson and Aage Nielsen to design such a rig, and the old *Joann* still carries it. She is now owned by Terry Klaus, who sails her out of Alameda.[65]

IN THE FALL of 1924, after three years of boarding-house living, Francis accepted Waldo Brown's offer to move on board the *Joann* for the winter. The vessel was moored in the Charles River near the Boston end of the West Boston or Cambridge Bridge (soon to be renamed the Longfellow Bridge). Francis lived alone in the schooner until Waldo commissioned her the following spring. He reveled in the privacy and coziness of the schooner's cabin. "I remember the winter I spent on the Charles River at Boston in a small vessel," he wrote twenty years later.

> *In a few minutes after leaving the city streets one could easily imagine oneself safely in the islands of the blessed. It was a cold winter and when the northwest gales screeched across the city and the big dwellings were drafty I lay back on the transom, propped up with cushions, and read by the kerosene light. She had a good size coal burning stove and as the hot water kettle chortled on the back of the stove and the cabin clock ticked off the time I am sure I was more comfortable in body and soul than the owner of the best house on Beacon Street. I read some pretty good books that*

> *winter and am sure I got more out of them than I would have in some other surroundings. We had company at times, and on a winter evening as we sat around the cabin or lay out in the shadow of a berth the talk usually took an interesting turn. One could speak slowly and think, and the spirit of the cabin seemed to enter into the conversation and made it a thing worth listening to and remembering.*[66]

Some years before painting that delightful word picture, he had admitted that he didn't think much of the Charles River, except that it was better to be on a boat than on shore. A luxury he had was the services of a housekeeper, who would come on board the *Joann* to do such chores as emptying the ashes from the big Household Marine Company stove.[67]

By February, Leonard Fowle, the yachting writer for the *Boston Globe*, had discovered that a son of Nathanael G. Herreshoff was living on board a boat in Boston that winter. Here was a good story at a season when yachting reporters were hard up for copy. Fowle interviewed Francis and had him photographed at work at 585 Boylston Street. Francis told Fowle, "Living in a boat is very fascinating. It is a life of constant change. The wind and weather affect a boat in a way they do not affect a house. A house just does not lend its personality to the elements the way a boat does. Being a bachelor made it possible for me to live as I pleased and I decided in favor of the boat. There is nothing remarkable about it."[68]

Fowle felt the story was remarkable enough to present to his readers, and his interview, with a photograph of Francis and one of the *Joann*, was published on February 10, 1925. Francis's brother Griswold spotted the article as reprinted in the *Providence Sunday Journal* on the twenty-second, and he sent a clipping of it to their father. Nathanael and Ann were spending the first of many winters in Florida. As Griswold would have known, there had been little or no contact between Francis and Nathanael for the more than four years since Francis had left Bristol. There is no evidence that Francis even went home for Christmas. In any event, about a month after he received the clipping about Francis, Nathanael wrote him a letter on March 19, 1925.[69]

CHAPTER 5

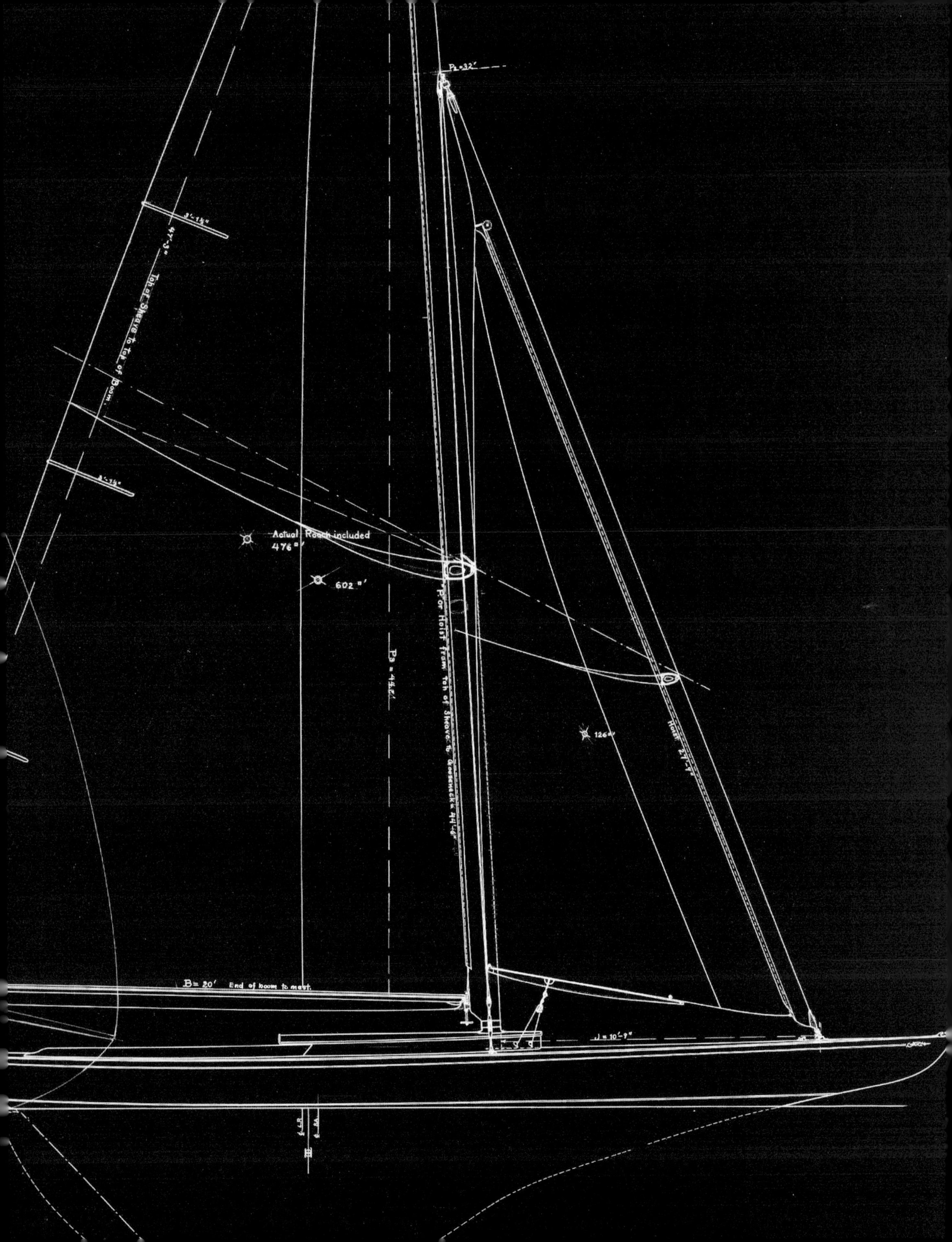

P₂=32'
Top of Sheave to top of Boom.
Actual Roach included
602
P₃=44.5'
"P" or Hoist from top of Sheave to Gooseneck 44'-6"
Hoist 27'-7"
B=20' End of boom to mast.
J=10'-9"

THE R-BOAT YANKEE

"I congratulate you on the victory of the "Yankee"

—NATHANAEL G. HERRESHOFF TO L. FRANCIS HERRESHOFF, SEPTEMBER 17, 1926

In the four years since he had separated himself from his family, Francis had been learning yacht design from his mentor, Starling Burgess. He was doing outstanding, original, and innovative design work of his own. He had met associates and customers who would be lifelong friends. He had, at last, made a running start on his chosen profession. In Bristol, Nathanael, at age 76, had officially retired from designing for the Herreshoff Manufacturing Company. On August 21 and 22, 1924, the company had been sold at auction; Rudolph F. Haffenreffer had acquired most of the physical plant and would keep the yard going. Nathanael had found a fast friend in Commodore Ralph Middleton Munroe and a congenial winter retreat in Florida at Munroe's place in Coconut Grove, on Biscayne Bay. But overriding these important happenings, there lay between Francis and Nathanael a separation and, farther back, a father's misdirection of his son's vocation. They had a lot to sort out.[1]

Yet, rather than deal with things past, Francis and Nathanael picked up as if there had been no hiatus, as if there had been no long detour to a farm. There was no reference in their ensuing, regular correspondence to any parting or misassignment, no talk of missing each other, no hint, even, of any family awkwardness. Francis expressed no anger. Nathanael expressed no remorse. They did not write about the sadness of separation or the joy of reconnecting. These feelings were there for both son and father, but we can discern them only between the lines of their letters. As was the custom of the time, Francis and Nathanael hid their pain and their joy behind a facade of mere propriety.

Nathanael referred to the newspaper account of Francis's living on board the *Joann* and commented, "all of which is interesting and novel." He signed the letter, "Your affect. father, Nathl. G. Herreshoff." "P. S.," he added, "I would be pleased to have a letter from you." Francis obliged promptly.[2]

Even if Francis and Nathanael weren't addressing their real conflicts, it was a huge boon to Francis to be back in touch with his father. He harbored hurts from his father, but there was no one he respected and admired more. Francis was

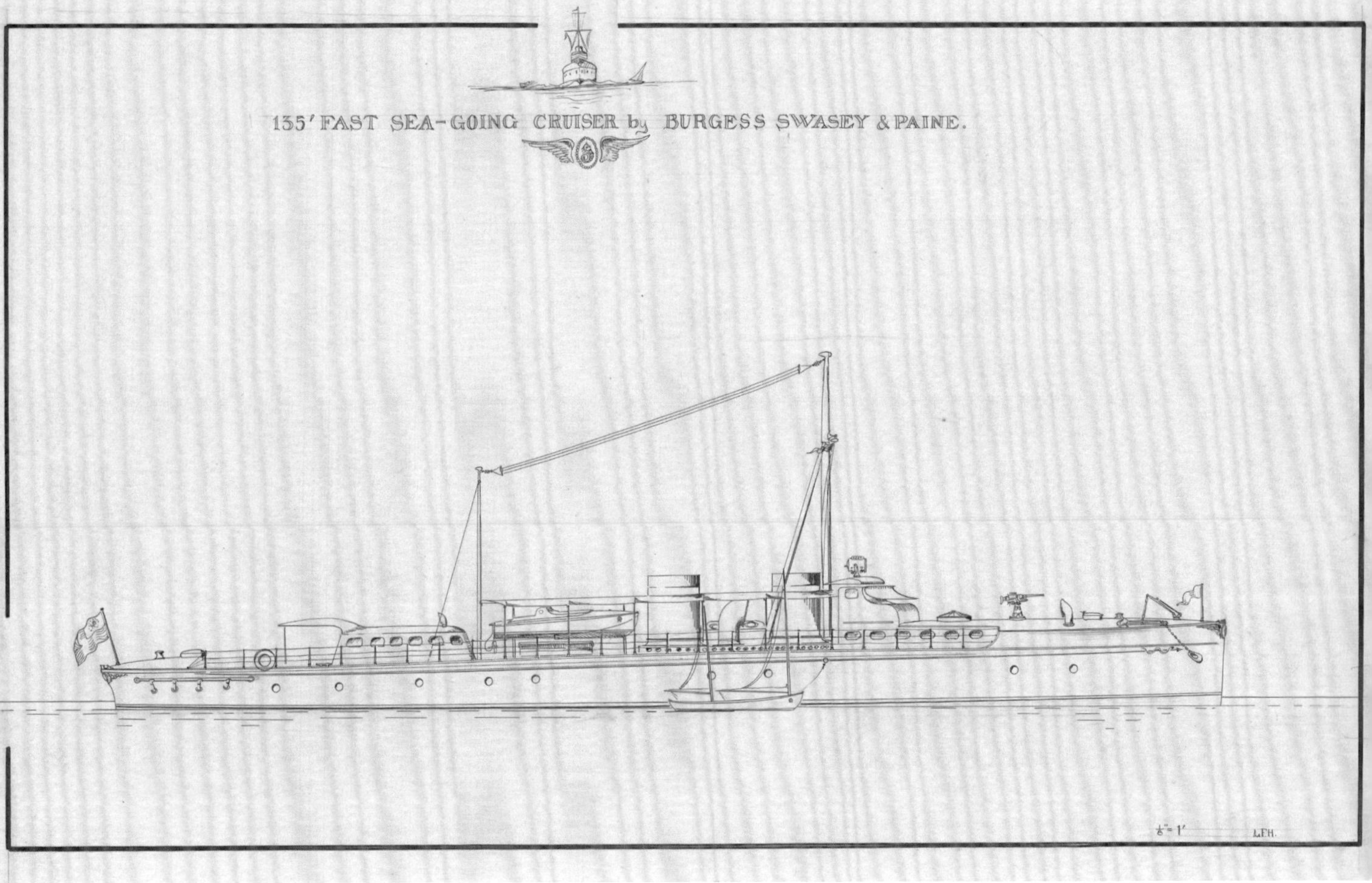

ABOVE: Francis's concept for a 135-foot, fast, seagoing cruiser. Double-ended, with whalebacks fore and aft, a deck gun, and a sizeable searchlight, she has a naval look about her. For tenders she has a lovely cat-ketch (also a double-ender) and a streamlined speedboat. Every detail of the design contributes to the overall impression of exactly what the vessel is—fast and able. (© Mystic Seaport, Daniel S. Gregory Ships Plans Library, SP38. 287.1) RIGHT: The beautiful 104-foot brigantine that Francis drew in 1924. The design was evidently a self-indulgent exercise, without a client. It is a pity that the design was not completed and a vessel built to it. The drawing shows the extent to which Francis had paid attention to the details of traditional craft and their rigs. (© Mystic Seaport, Daniel S. Gregory Ships Plans Library, SP38.286.2)

always proud to be his father's son. Little more than a month later, he would have enough confidence in their renewed contact and in his own work to be able to send a blueprint of his most important design to the man he considered to be the world's most gifted and accomplished yacht designer.

While Francis and Waldo were working on the design for the *Joann*, Francis was also designing other boats. Two were forerunners of his most popular design of all, the H-28, so we will examine them later: a 33-foot ketch, preliminary plan dated January 2, 1924; and the 33-foot, 6-inch sloop *Santee*, designed in March and April. With regard to the *Santee*, it may be noted that there was another erasure. In the title block on the lines plan, "Drawn By" was filled in FCP, for Frank Paine. The "FCP" has been rubbed out on the plan Francis saved, but is just visible. Again, Francis is apparently jealous that a friend might get credit for his design. It is probable that Frank drew the lines from a preliminary plan by Francis. Francis drew the rest of the plans for the boat.[3]

During this period, Francis made a preliminary drawing for a 135-foot "Fast Sea-going Cruiser," a vessel that evoked the memory of the steam torpedo boats of the Herreshoff Manufacturing Company. The drawing is labeled "by Burgess Swasey & Paine"; presumably there was a prospective client, but the design did not proceed beyond the initial concept. Shorn of its title, the drawing was used twenty-three years later merely as a tailpiece, without comment, in Francis's series of articles for *The Rudder*, "The Common Sense of Yacht Design."[4]

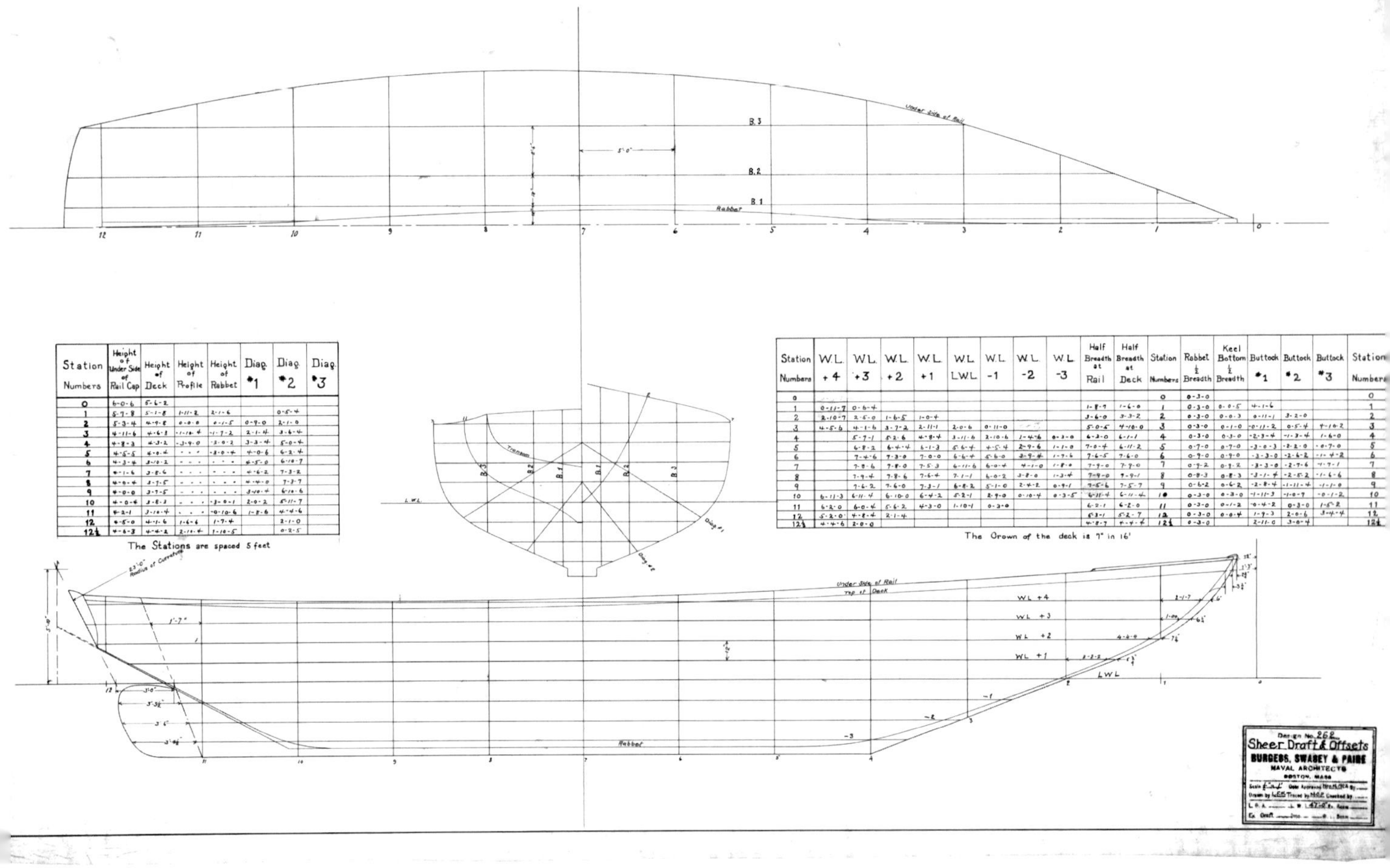

ABOVE: Francis's Sheer Draft and Offsets plan for the *Mañana*, Burgess, Swasey, and Paine Design No. 262, the plan dated November 14, 1923. She is 61 feet long on deck; 47 feet on the waterline; beam, 15 feet, 6 inches; and draft, 3 feet, 9 inches with the centerboard up. Displacement is 64,000 pounds. (© Mystic Seaport, Daniel S. Gregory Ships Plans Library, SP38.79.1)
RIGHT: The *Mañana*'s outboard profile and sail plan, March 1, 1924. The sail area is 1,391 square feet. In dotted lines, Francis has drawn in the outline of her double-reefed foresail, as well as a main trysail and a storm jib. With those three sails set, her sail area would be reduced to 661 square feet. (© Mystic Seaport, Daniel S. Gregory Ships Plans Library, SP38.79.4)

Also in 1924, Francis demonstrated, probably just to himself rather than to a customer, that he was able to design a large sailing yacht with a complex traditional rig. He drew a preliminary, but detailed, plan for a 103-foot brigantine, without reference to Burgess, Swasey, and Paine. He loved to study old-fashioned rigs and ways of handling vessels. As a youngster, he had been excited when an old commodore demonstrated what a square-rigger could do by sailing the naval training brigantine *Boxer* around Gould Island, in Narragansett Bay, stern first. His own brigantine design was of more than passing interest to Francis; nine years later, when he learned that Henry Gruber, an outstanding yacht designer from Germany working at Megargel and Gruber in New York, had made a design for a similar, larger vessel, he obtained the plans to study and save.[5]

Concurrently with his design work with Waldo Brown on the *Joann*, Francis designed another schooner, a 61-footer, a shoal-draft cruiser that her owner would use primarily as a base for bird-shooting in the Chesapeake Bay. The owner was George Upton, of Marblehead, who was descended from a major owner of Boston clipper ships. He named his vessel *Mañana*. She was Burgess, Swasey, and Paine's design No. 262.[6]

It appears that the *Mañana* is the only yacht whose hull shape Francis designed by making a model, other than the two models he made earlier at his father's company. When he made the model of the *Joann*, he checked its shape with templates made from the lines drawing. The lines drawing was the medium by which he determined the shape of the hull. But there is no lines drawing for the *Mañana*. Francis made a drawing showing the outline of the schooner's shape in profile, plan, and section, but other than three curved sections, there are no lines to show the hull shape, no bowlines, buttocks, or waterlines. Yet the drawing includes the table of offsets, which must have been compiled by taking measurements off a model.[7]

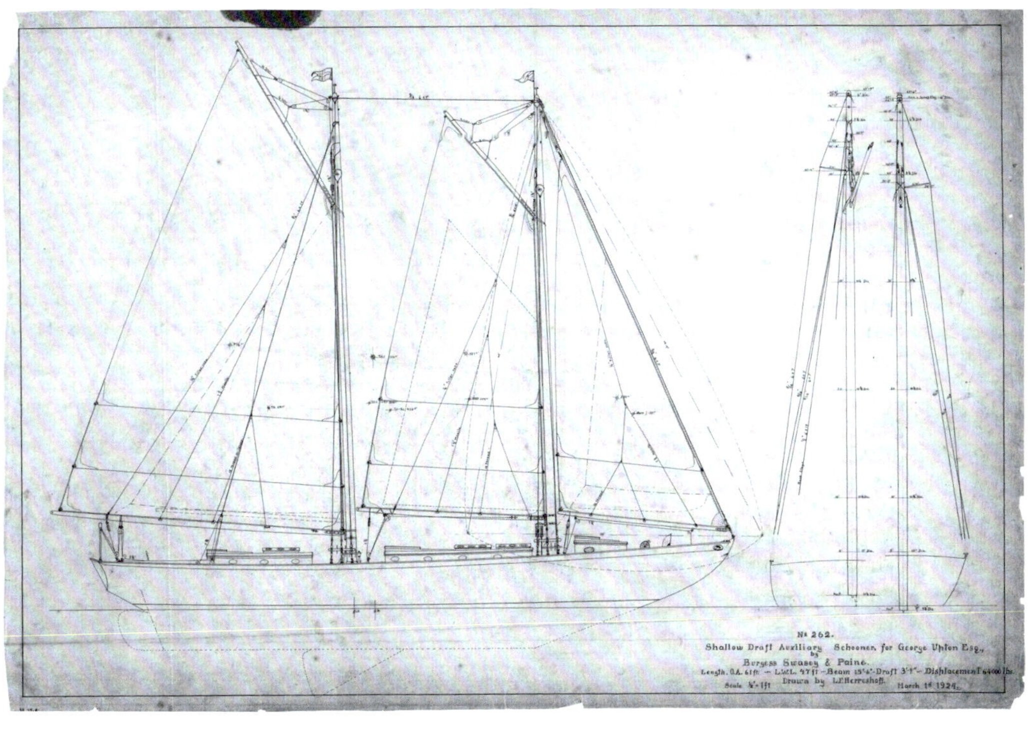

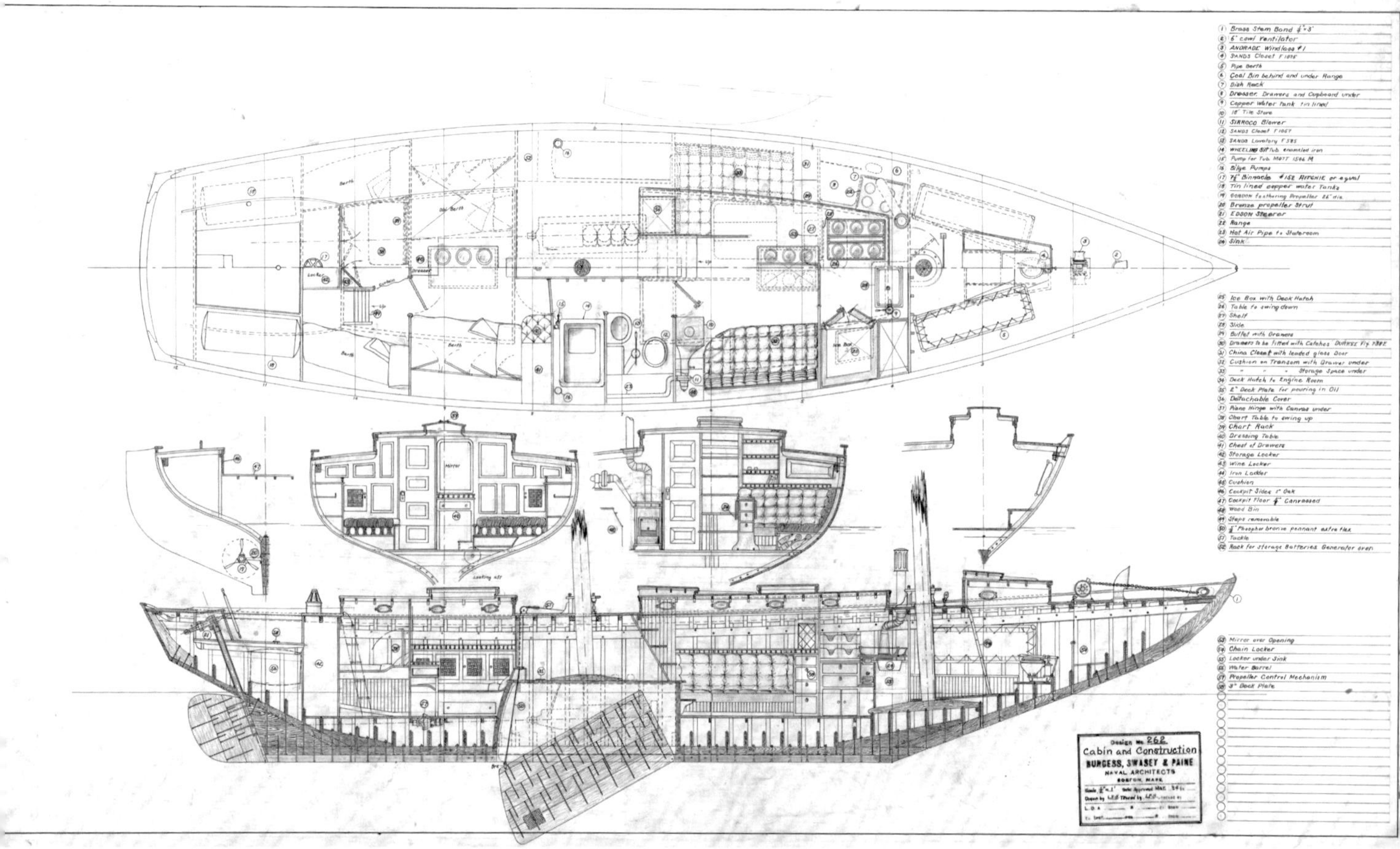

Francis's later writing implies that he designed more yachts than just the *Mañana* by starting with a model. He would write that he "designed boats both ways [by lines and models] and can say from actual experience that the model making method is the quickest and most natural way to design a shape," and that "a model always gives me a much better idea of the shape than a lines drawing." He certainly made a great many models during his lifetime—we remember the exquisite one he carved at age sixteen—but they were not models leading to a full-sized yacht. Later on, he would sit by his fireside with a friend in the evening and would whittle out a hull shape as a doodle, but a very well-formed doodle. When he was finished, he would toss it to the friend, asking "Here, what do you think of this?" It may be that some of these doodles inspired the shapes of later yachts he designed and led to his comment about designing "both ways," but for every design of Francis's that was built to, excepting the *Mañana*, there is a lines drawing. It is surprising that Francis didn't do more of his designing of hull shapes using models, for he had grown up observing his father carving models for his designs. On the other hand, N. G. Herreshoff was among the last designers to create hull shapes in a model-maker's vice. Francis's later writings extolled the art of model making. To cite two examples, he wrote, "in art as in design the schools of planographic art and sculpture have usually been in separate hands. In speaking of design this way I, of course, refer to the schools of developing shapes with line drawings as planographic art, and of model making as sculpture, and in my opinion sculpture is not only the most exacting of all arts but it is by far the most expressive." And he wrote, "For if the lines can be compared to music the model can be compared to sculpture, and sculpture is all things."[8]

We do not have the *Mañana*'s model, and there is no lines drawing, but we can see from the outboard profile and sail plan drawing that she was the crudest looking vessel Francis designed, with her unbalanced ends, short stern, and flattish sheerline. He must have realized, at some point, that the design lacked beauty, and perhaps this model-making experience was enough to discourage him from further use of models to determine hull shape. In the opinion of one of Francis's later friends, an artist, he had "outgrown modeling hulls," and his years of observing his father's modeling had educated his eye for form to the point where he could visualize the hull shape he wanted and merely had to get it down on paper so a builder could fashion what he had in mind.[9]

While Francis was developing his artistic ideas and applying them to his designs, he was also increasing his technical knowledge of yacht design. As we have seen, he had gained considerable understanding of what went into the design and construction of an efficient yacht by observing his father's work and by performing tasks in many of the shops at the Herreshoff Manufacturing Company. Now, Starling Burgess, ever at the cutting edge of the application of science and mathematics to yacht design, was teaching Francis much on the technical side of the profession. Albert Einstein once remarked that the only mathematician he had met in America was Starling Burgess. Francis was no advanced mathematician, and he later belittled naval architects, like Norman Skene, who depended on numbers, but he respected Starling's ability to use mathematics, because he knew that Starling could always check numerical solutions

LEFT: The construction plan of March 1924 that Francis drew for the *Mañana* is colored so that the viewer's eye could be drawn immediately to, for example, brown, wooden, structural members, or blue upholstery. We may start our examination by noticing the use of the centerboard trunk as a girder to take the thrust of the mainmast. There is much else to admire, whether the grain of the wood; the tufts of the upholstery; the bottles of wine, carefully stowed under a settee in the main cabin; the Sirroco blower, to send hot air from the 18-inch, tile stove back to the after stateroom; or perhaps the Wheeling enameled-iron, sit-tub in the head. (© Mystic Seaport, Daniel S. Gregory Ships Plans Library, SP38.79.2) RIGHT: The *Mañana* on the wind in a gentle breeze and, judging by her bow wave, footing fast. She was built by the Cumberland Shipbuilding Company, South Portland, Maine. (© Mystic Seaport, 1990.37.925)

REDWOOD
FIR
George L. Dunning
PACIFIC COAST LUMBER
BOSTON · MASS.
EASTERN PINE

to problems in yacht design against his excellent intuition for what did and did not make sense.[10]

Francis was about to demonstrate his own ability to apply the engineering he had absorbed from his father and learned from Starling to a design for a new racing boat for Charlie Welch. By the fall of 1924, Charlie had decided he wanted a boat to race in the R Class, a boat doubtless discussed at length with Francis on those cold, blustery evenings in the snug, gently rolling cabin of the *Stormy Petrel*, lying-to overnight in Massachusetts Bay. Charlie wanted a boat that would be different from her competitors, hopefully to her advantage. He was willing to take a risk with his friend, Francis Herreshoff. And for Francis, the artist whose engineering was chiefly by eye from experience, there was the constant need to take a chance in order to find out how his vision of a boat would work in practice.

Francis would later describe his yacht designs as "scientific." He did not mean by this that he conducted experiments with models in towing tanks or wind tunnels, for he did not trust that the results of such tests would translate accurately to full-sized vessels. Nor did he mean that he used mathematical formulas to determine the characteristics of his designs. What he did mean was that he used his artistic sense of proportion, together with his own design experience, to work out every detail of a yacht, including all of its construction members and all spars, fittings, and hardware, to exact specifications that would maximize strength, durability, and lightness. He emphasized lightness, as had his father, to increase the ballast-to-displacement ratio of sailboats and the power-to-displacement ratio of powerboats, for best performance. He was justifiably proud of his "scientific" approach to yacht design, for he did have extremely high aptitudes and abilities on both the artistic and engineering sides of his designing, even though his engineering was not based on the usual curricula, such as were taught at MIT. In any event, Charlie Welch's new R-boat would be the vehicle that would demonstrate that L. Francis Herreshoff was a top yacht designer.

The R Class was one of the Universal Rule classes, the 20-raters. For sloops, there were thirteen designated classes under the Rule, each with a letter for a given rating in feet. To race in the class, a yacht had to rate, according to a formula, no more than the designated rating in feet. The most popular classes were: S, 17 feet; R, 20 feet; Q, 25 feet; P, 31 feet; M, 46 feet; and J, 76 feet. The length of the boats was always considerably more than the rating produced by the formula; a typical R-boat, for example, was at least 35 feet long on deck. To quote from the Universal Rule itself, "The rating shall be the product of the length multiplied by the square root of the sail area divided by the cube root of the displacement." To discourage extreme overhangs, the length measurement, in feet, combined the normal waterline length with "quarter beam length," a measurement of length that included half the overhangs at a point a quarter of the beam out from the centerline, thus approximating effective waterline length with the boat heeled. Sail area was in square feet, and displacement was in cubic feet. The resulting figure was then multiplied by a constant of 18 percent to give the rating. Thus the formula is .18 (L x square root SA) ÷ cube root D.[11]

The Universal Rule for rating racing yachts

LEFT: A composite view of Nathanael's model room from five photographs made by Francis in May 1938, shortly after his father's death. The six America's Cup defenders are above the fireplace. Having grown up sleeping in the next room to this one, Francis was well steeped in his father's method of creating hull shapes with models; yet, the ugly *Mañana* was the only boat he designed via a model. (Photos by L. Francis Herreshoff, Herreshoff Marine Museum)

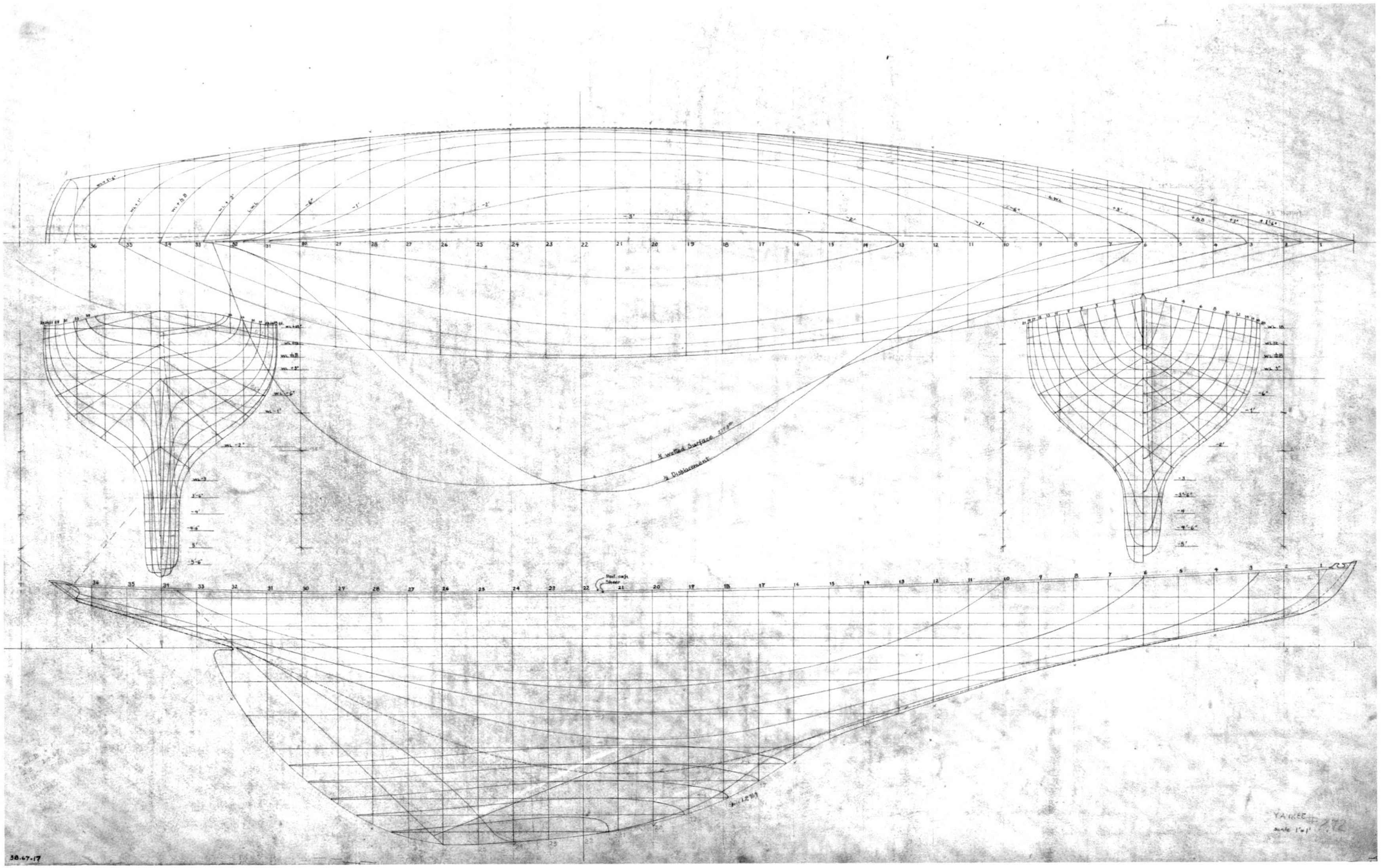

½ Wetted Surface
½ Displacement
YANKEE
scale 1"=1'
38.47.17

was a radical departure from the rule it replaced, the Seawanhaka Rule, which had been adopted first by the Seawanhaka Corinthian Yacht Club at Oyster Bay, Long Island, in 1883, and soon after was in general use. Under the Seawanhaka Rule, only the speed-giving elements of waterline length and sail area were measured. The formula was .5 LWL + .5 √ SA. Designers, seeking the form of yacht that would sail fastest with the lowest rating under the rule, produced specialized "racing machines" that were good for little else. We have seen that Starling Burgess, designing to a rule that measured only waterline length, created the freakish scow *Outlook*, a boat well over twice as long on deck as on the waterline. To encourage the design of more wholesome, generally useful boats, the New York Yacht Club, in 1902, determined to explore a new rating rule. The club invited comments from the leading yacht designers. Nathanael G. Herreshoff took the opportunity to propose a rule based on concepts that he had been considering for a decade, a rule that would not only thwart a boat like the *Outlook*, but also would restrain extreme examples of his own highly successful fin-keelers. Nathanael had in mind a rule that would counterbalance the speed-giving factors of length and sail area with the speed-reducing factor of displacement. The New York Yacht Club adopted Francis's father's rating formula at its annual meeting in December 1902, rewarding its author with an honorary membership in the club for his creation of what would come to be called the Universal Rule. The New York Yacht Club, as holder of the America's Cup and with a long tradition of racing, was accepted as the authority on rating rules, so that when it adopted a new rule, other clubs fell into line. With modifications, the Universal Rule remained popular for about thirty-five years. By 1940, it ran to twenty-five pages.[12]

Francis started to design Charlie Welch's R-boat, to be named the *Yankee* (Burgess, Swasey, and Paine design No. 272), in late 1924, after a summer of crewing in every race in an R-boat. His lines drawing of the hull was traced in ink by Norman Skene and dated October 22, 1924. There is nothing radical about the shape of her pretty hull, the only unusual feature being the shape of the bow. The bow lines reach forward, low to the water, to increase sailing waterline length, then, when they are too high to reach the water even with the boat heeled, they rise quickly in a snub nose. The practical reason for the bow shape was to reduce the on-deck portion of the quarter-beam-length measurement in the rating formula; the aesthetic result was a distinct knuckle-shape in the stem profile. Francis liked the looks of the knuckle, accentuating the ever-changing curve, and he reproduced it in a number of future designs that had nothing to do with the Universal Rule.[13]

In the title lettering on the drawing of the *Yankee*'s sail plan, dated October 27, under Burgess, Swasey, and Paine for the design firm and C. A. Welch, Esq., for the client, Francis lettered, "Designed and Drawn by," and then, instead of the usual initials, wrote his signature, "L. Francis Herreshoff." He wanted there to be no possible question of who created the design; in reporting on the new design in January, the *Boston Globe* credited Francis as the designer, rather than Burgess, Swasey, and Paine.[14]

LEFT: **The *Yankee*'s lines drawing shows Francis's first knuckle bow, a profile shape induced by the Universal Rule and one that would become a recognizable feature of some of his future designs of both racing and non-racing boats. The 20-rater is 37 feet, 1 inch long on deck; 26 feet on the waterline; with a beam of 6 feet, 9 inches; and a draft of 5 feet, 11 inches. Displacement is 11,900 pounds, including 8,900 pounds of lead ballast on the keel, for a ballast-to-displacement ratio of 75 percent.** (© Mystic Seaport, Daniel S. Gregory Ships Plans Library, SP38.67.1 and 38.67.17)

The *Yankee*'s sail plan showed an important evolutionary step in the design of the Marconi sloop rig for racing: the enlargement of the fore triangle, particularly its height. On Frank Paine's R-boat *Gypsy*, of two years earlier, the height of the fore triangle was measured at just under 28 feet, and the length of its base at 9 feet; comparable measurements for Francis's *Yankee* were 36 feet and 10 feet. The *Yankee*'s jib was more than half again as large as the jib of the *Gypsy*. While the *Gypsy* had 17 percent of her sail area in the jib, the *Yankee* had 26 percent. In an evolutionary trend that would continue, Francis had taken a giant step. How much Starling or Charlie Welch may have been involved in the decision to give the *Yankee* her big fore triangle is not known, but there is no recorded argument against Francis's taking credit for it. Yet, at the least, since Starling was applying his knowledge of aerodynamics to the relatively new Marconi rig, was watching what his designers at 585 Bolyston Street were doing, and was prone to engaging them in discussions of the work, then he must have been an important influence on Francis's enlargement of the fore triangle.[15]

Concurrently with the design of the *Yankee*'s evolutionary R-boat rig, Francis was assigned the task of designing a revolutionary R-boat rig for Charles Henry Wheelwright Foster, a founder of the Corinthian Yacht Club. A yachtsman with a half century of racing experience and "a keen interest in experimentation," Foster had owned as many as seventy yachts, including, for four years, the *America*, which he rescued from becoming a Cape Verdes Islands packet in 1917; the former America's Cup defender *Puritan*, converted to a schooner; and a 147-foot, three-masted, ex-coasting schooner, the *Lillian Woodruff*, converted to a sailing houseboat by the addition of a huge deckhouse and a crew of ten. Foster wanted to try to beat the rule by putting a schooner rig on his R-boat. Francis drew him a tall rig with a Marconi mainsail, and a narrow, gaff foresail that was really part of the fore triangle, despite the fact that the height of the foremast kept the stay that ran from stem to foremasthead to mainmasthead from being quite a straight line. Foster did sail his Crowninshield-designed R-boat, the *Mary*, with Francis's schooner rig, but he was not allowed to race her in the R Class. Perhaps the exercise of drawing the schooner rig, with its huge "fore triangle," including the foresail, influenced Francis's decision to give the *Yankee* her large jib.[16]

To support the *Yankee*'s long forestay and keep it as straight as possible, Francis led the running backstays much farther aft than was normal practice, an innovation of his that would be much copied. Moreover, to help keep the forestay straight, he "left off the headstay [an outer stay leading to the masthead]," he would write later, " in order that all of the aft tending strains would come on the forestay, and this necessitated a spanstay to support the masthead." Besides helping keep the forestay straight, this novel staying arrangement made a significant reduction in windage; there was no long, separate headstay from bow to masthead to drag through clear air. Designers also copied Francis's use of spanstays, or jumper stays, as they would come to be called, an arrangement that had less wind resistance than the much longer headstay that they replaced. Later, Francis would write ambivalently about a further advantage of jumper stays over masthead stays: eliminating the headstay removed a major interference with the spinnaker and allowed the development of

RIGHT: **The *Yankee*'s sail plan shows her high fore triangle, backstays led well aft, and self-censored main-boom strut. Her sail area is 633 square feet, with 479 square feet in the mainsail (including roach) and 154 in the jib.** (© Mystic Seaport, Daniel S. Gregory Ships Plans Library, SP38.67.4)

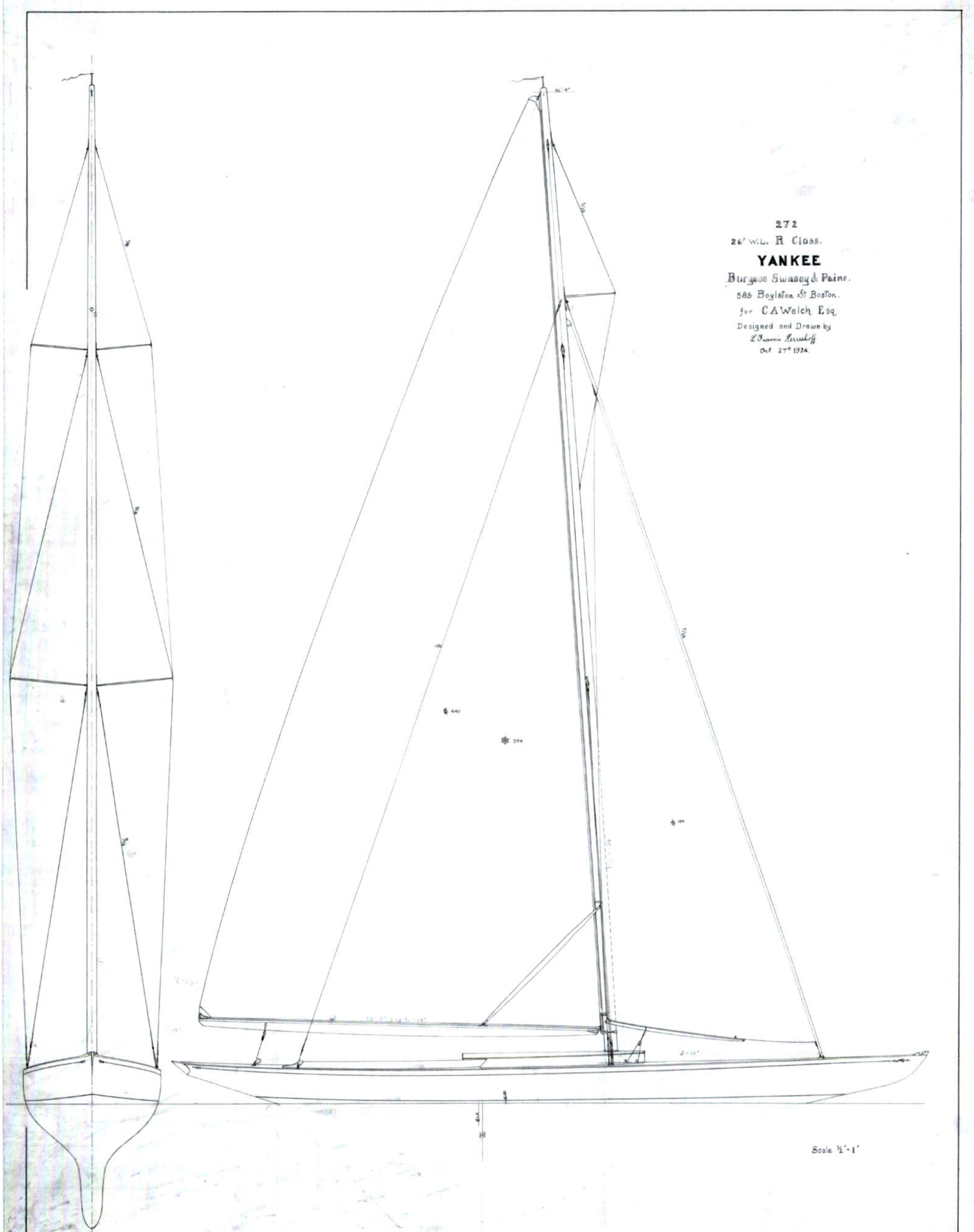
272
26' W.L. R Class.
YANKEE
Burgess Swasey & Paine.
585 Boylston St Boston.
for C A Welch Esq
Designed and Drawn by
L Francis Herreshoff
Oct 27th 1924.
Scale ½" - 1'

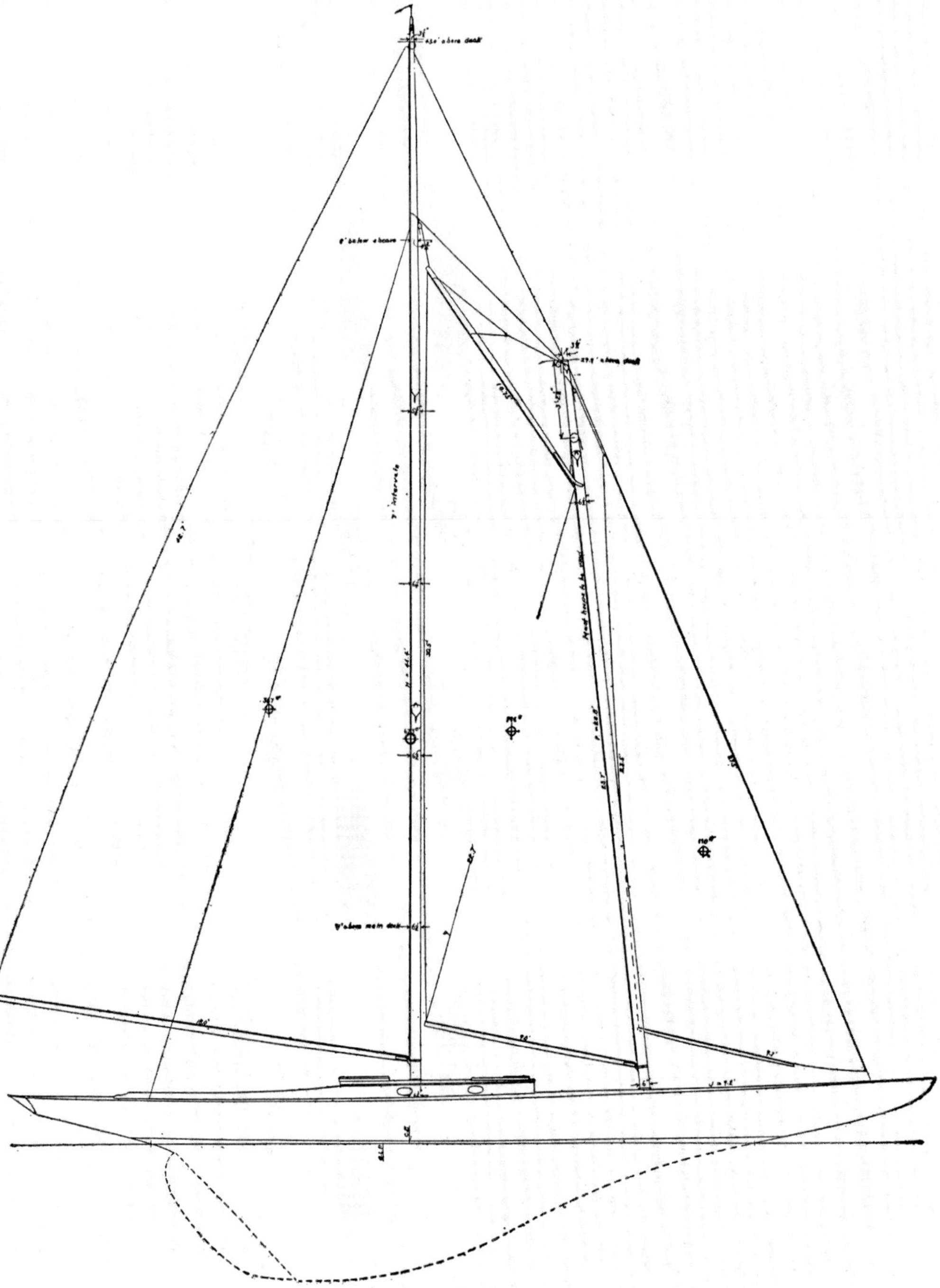

the double-luff, or parachute, spinnaker, once the rules were changed to allow such sails. Francis would be at once proud of his part in such an important change and scornful of the huge sails, which he thought emphasized the power of money and muscle over sailing skill.[17]

Francis used the tangs and box-section mast that he had developed for Frank Paine's *Gypsy* on Charlie Welch's *Yankee*. Without his tangs, the standing rigging could not have been set up taut enough to keep the long jibstay from sagging. The hollow, rectangular mast facilitated another innovation he made to reduce the wind resistance of the rig even more: running the hauling parts of the main and jib halyards down inside the mast, instead of outside. This was yet another of Francis's ideas that would become common practice. Again, Starling's influence may be felt. Francis would write, "In 1925 I was much interested in schemes for reducing the wind resistance of rigs when close-hauled. I was working for Starling Burgess at the time, and perhaps because he had been an aeroplane designer we were over wind-resistance conscious." Nor was water resistance ignored; the *Yankee* was first with chainplates—which anchored the lower ends of the shrouds—fastened inside the planking, rather than outside, where they would have created a bit of resistance when the boat heeled.[18]

For the main boom, Francis designed a T-section spar. The purpose was to provide an endplate at the foot of the mainsail to force the downdraft off the sail to go aft and provide driving power. Other designers would also copy this idea, but we should note that at about this time, Dr. Manfred Curry, in Germany, was also experimenting with the T-boom. Marine hardware manufacturers would copy Francis's design for a block that could take a shackle either parallel or perpendicular to the sheave, a great convenience when rigging halyards and sheets.[19]

And he drew in one more new scheme, a strut to hold down the main boom when the sheet was eased. It was decided, however, that the rules did not allow such an unusual (and efficient) way of keeping the sail from twisting and losing power, so the *Yankee* never sailed with such a strut. Years later, mechanical boom vangs using the same concept would become common.

Francis redesigned the *Yankee*'s sail plan, in a drawing dated March 12, 1925, to give her a slightly curved mast. The idea of curving the top of the mast aft was not new; as we have seen, it was a feature of Nathanael's S-boat and Francis's design for a daysailer, his first complete design, five years earlier. The purpose of curving the mast was similar to that of the T-shaped boom, to force air leaving the top of the mainsail to go aft, rather than up, thus helping to drive the boat ahead. On the new rig, Francis kept the masthead from bending aft with both a forward strut and spanstay and by leading the hauling part of the main halyard over a sheave on the end of a second, higher, shorter strut before it entered the lower, straight part of the mast.[20]

Part of the revision of the rig was to reduce the size of the giant step he was taking with the much-enlarged fore triangle. On the new rig, he lowered the height of the fore triangle by 1 foot, 3 inches, so although the *Yankee* would sail with a bigger jib than those of her competitors, the difference would not be quite as much as Francis had originally envisioned.

He didn't trust even such a great sailmaking

LEFT: **The schooner rig that Francis designed, while he was working on the *Yankee*'s plans, for Charles H. W. Foster's R-boat. The rig was never tested in competition.** (*Yachting* (June 1925): 61)

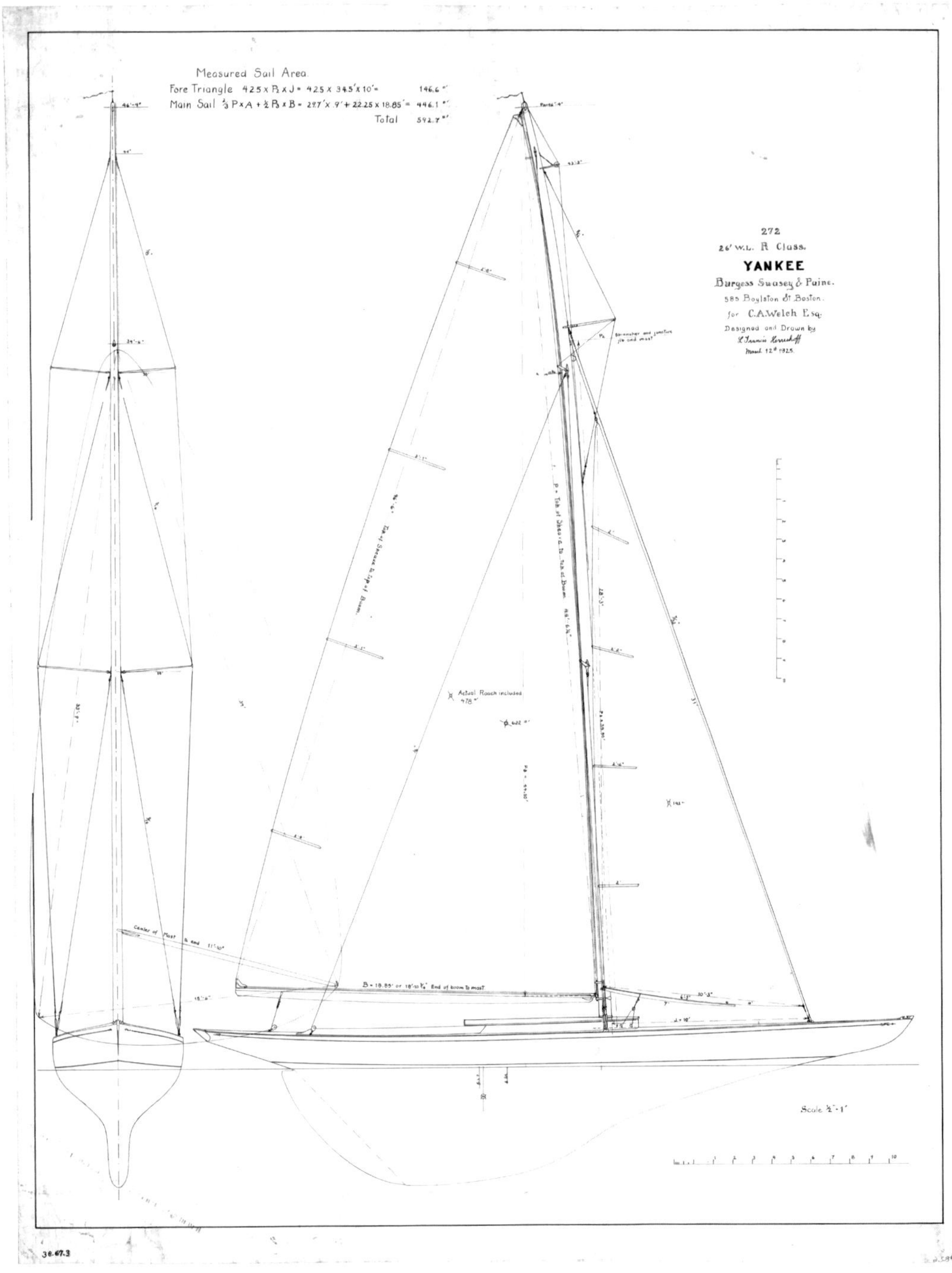

Measured Sail Area
Fore Triangle .425 x P₂ x J = .425 x 34.5' x 10' = 146.6 □'
Main Sail ⅔ P x A + ½ P₃ x B = 29.7' x 9' + 22.25 x 18.85' = 446.1 □'
Total 592.7 □'
272
26' W.L. R Class.
YANKEE
Burgess Swasey & Paine.
585 Boylston St Boston.
for C.A.Welch Esq.
Designed and Drawn by
L. Francis Herreshoff
March 12th 1925.
Actual Roach included
B = 18.85' or 18'10¼" End of boom to mast
Scale ½" = 1'
36.67.3

firm as Ratsey and Lapthorn, in Cowes, England, with the shape of the *Yankee*'s curved-luff mainsail: in a drawing dated April 12, he laid out the precise curvatures of all three edges of the sail. Francis later praised both the shape and the longevity of the *Yankee*'s "wonderful" mainsail, and wrote, "a well cut one [sail] will take a shape seldom equaled for beauty by any man-made thing." It was the first and last sail he designed in such detail. Thomas White Ratsey wrote him that he would scale the size and shape of the sails from the plan and that he "did not want confusing dimensions on the sail plan."[21]

The *Yankee*'s rig was evolutionary, but her hull construction was revolutionary. With the *Yankee*, Francis designed the first wooden yacht built with longitudinal construction; that is, with a framework that depended equally for its strength on lengthwise stringers and athwartship frames, rather than on athwartship frames alone, with perhaps a longitudinal stringer or two added. Her competitors had some forty frames per side, perhaps 1-1/2 inches square in section. The *Yankee* had eleven web frames, 1 inch in section fore-and-aft, but varying from 5 inches to 8-3/8 inches athwartships, each designed "as a separate engineering problem." Each frame was continuous, from the keel, up one side of the boat, across under the deck, and back down to the keel on the other side. The five frames in way of the deckhouse and cockpit had to be interrupted by those structures. The smallest frames, in the bow and stern, were almost solid. And instead of a stringer on each side, added almost as an afterthought, she had nine on each side, including one under the deck. The sectional shape of the stringers was like a capital I, 2-1/2 inches high, with 1-inch-wide serifs. Francis's description of the construction was "longitudinal frames like stringers let into deep web frames widely spaced." In March 1926 he listed the advantages of longitudinal construction for the readers of *Yachting* as rigidity, longevity, economy, and lightness above the waterline. Ten months earlier, *Yachting* had editorialized against allowing longitudinal construction in racing yachts, and Norman Skene had defended the concept in a letter to the editor. Longitudinal construction was never outlawed for racing boats.[22]

Nathanael G. Herreshoff had been the first to conceive of and use longitudinal construction. He had "studied" it in 1899 and applied it to his America's Cup defender *Constitution* the following year. Ten-year-old Francis doubtless watched the frames and stringers of the 132-foot steel vessel being fashioned and assembled. That he applied his father's concept for metal construction to wood with the *Yankee*, may well have been due to Starling's influence, for wooden marine longitudinal construction is very similar to the aircraft construction Starling had used, both with the same objective: strength with lightness.[23]

In designing the first longitudinal construction for a wooden yacht, Francis had no experience of his own or of anyone else to go on. He may have been able to borrow some of Starling's experience with aircraft construction; nevertheless, the *Yankee*'s construction drawing (page 137-38), showing the shapes and dimensions of an entirely new structure, is a stunning indication that Francis had a superb sense of proportion. In later designs, he made only minor refinements to his first try at the revolutionary method.

LEFT: **The revised sail plan with the curved mast, the rig used on the *Yankee*. It has a slightly taller, narrower mainsail of the same 633 square feet, but Francis has lowered the forestay a little, taking away 11 square feet from the big jib. The mast is nearly 50 feet long, with a section 7 inches fore-and-aft and 5-1/2 inches athwartships, and an average wall thickness of 5/8 inch.** (© Mystic Seaport, Daniel S. Gregory Ships Plans Library, SP38.67.3)

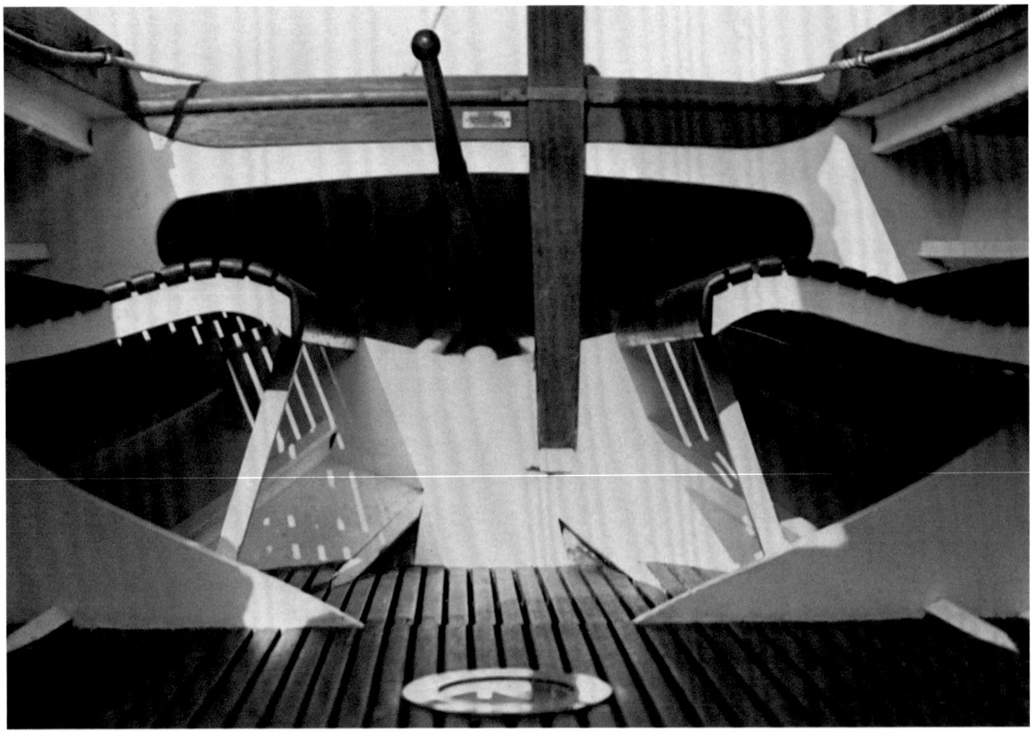

Francis specified double planking for the *Yankee*. The outer planking was horizontal; the inner ran at about a 35-degree angle from the waterline. The two layers were glued together, and the outer layer had tongue-and-groove edges. In designing the *Yankee*'s construction, Francis adopted another idea of his father's, the elimination of the usual wooden keelson, which then necessitated fastening the garboard plank directly to the lead ballast keel. Nathanael had conceived this method two years before and first used it on the 30-foot-waterline racing sloop *Grayling*, a boat he hoped would replace the New York 30s. It is not known how Francis learned of this innovation in construction at the Herreshoff Manufacturing Company, but it was evidently not directly from his father. Francis would use this construction often in the future. Five years later, he wrote to his father, "the several boats I designed with planking overlapping the lead never showed any working at all and this seam [at the lead] stayed as smooth as any seams in the planking." The method eliminated the Achilles heel of a large wooden structural member prone to deterioration and expensive to replace, and one that could damage the garboard plank by its swelling when the boat was afloat and shrinking when she was hauled out.[24]

Being well satisfied with the way the Britt brothers built the schooner *Joann*, Francis and Burgess, Swasey, and Paine chose them for the

ABOVE: This view of the *Yankee*'s cockpit shows what her web-frame construction looked like. (Mystic Seaport, 1973-3-45C)

exacting task of building the Yankee to his unusual construction ideas. She would be their first racing boat. Francis's later evaluation of the Britts would be that they built yachts to about the same quality as the Herreshoff and Lawley yards, but at 25 percent less cost.[25]

He wrote in his notebook, and presumably copied for the Britts: "These Specifications are for the Reference and guidence of the builder and as the boat is to be built by the time and materials basis it must be understood by the builder that all of architect's instructions must be carried out to the best of the ability of the builder even if the architect's instructions are in variance with previous practices of the builder. The Architect will at all times be responsible for the work done according to his instructions and ready to give any information required by the builder." Francis's care, the Britt brothers' skill, and the ingenious design of the *Yankee*'s construction produced a boat that held up remarkably well through years of racing that included being shipped to the Great Lakes.[26]

On May 6, 1925, Francis sent a copy of the blueprints for his design of the *Yankee* to his father. There could be no greater evidence that Francis was finding his way with a growing sureness and confidence than the fact that he, the fledgling yacht designer, had the courage to send his work to the man he thought was the world's greatest yacht designer, the father who had banished him to The Farm. Francis was proud of his work and doubtless wanted to show his father what he could do, but he must also have been anxious about Nathanael's reaction. Nathanael was favorably impressed, but his praise was lukewarm. He congratulated his son on his draftsmanship and for the design itself. He promised to keep the blueprints "strictly private." Carefully reconnecting, son and father were tiptoeing around the possibilities of discussing the great subject that fascinated them both.[27]

By the season of 1925, the R Class on the East Coast had grown to twenty-two boats. R-boats were raced as well from six harbors on the Great Lakes, where the class had originated, and three on the West Coast. Of the East Coast fleet, Burgess, Swasey, and Paine had designed the most, seven boats, including Francis's *Yankee*. Designs of the Norwegian, Johan Anker; of John Alden's office; and of Charles D. Mower were also prominent, and four designers had produced one R-boat each, including Nathanael G. Herreshoff. Charlie Welch and the *Yankee* would be up against serious competition.

Francis's father designed the R-boat *Game Cock* for the 1925 season. The *Yankee* beat her whenever they met on a racecourse. Francis wrote later, "Captain Nat did not know whether to be mad or glad at this result but he never spoke to me of these races." Nor, evidently, did Francis mention them to his father, but he must have cherished these victories as evidence that he could live up to the Herreshoff name. After the 1925 racing season, Nathanael wrote to Francis, "I was pleased to hear how well you came out with the *Yankee* up [Long Island] Sound" (where the *Game Cock* didn't race). His father's expression of pleasure at Francis's success may have been his greatest reward for the *Yankee*'s superlative racing record.[28]

And superlative it was. In reporting on the Eastern Yacht Club's series in early August, the *New York Times* man wrote: "the Boston productions were always to be reckoned with, especially the *Gypsy*, designed in 1923 by Frank C. Paine and sailed with great skill to victory in two races today, and the *Yankee*, designed by L. Francis Herreshoff, a son of the master naval architect, with which her owner, Charles A. Welch, won two races not only against such an able skipper as Charles Francis Adams in his new *Dandelion*, but also against Commodore Johan Anker in one of his own boats. The accomplishment of Captain Welch in the *Yankee* was perhaps the feature of the day."

In her first season, the *Yankee*, won two major East Coast racing cups, as well as Marblehead Race Week. She won the Manhasset Bay Yacht Club Challenge Cup and the Greenwich Cup at

The *Yankee* slicing along on the wind. She has a big jib for an R-boat of the time, and a curved mast. Instead of a headstay, she has a strut and spanstay; her main halyard leads over a smaller, higher strut before it goes down inside the hollow box mast, along with the jib halyard. Thus, Francis has reduced the wind resistance of the rig and has cleared the area forward of the jib for the introduction of the double-luff spinnaker. (Photo 47-9, Charles H. W. Foster Collection, Hart Nautical Collections, MIT Museum, Cambridge, Massachusetts)

the Indian Harbor Yacht Club, both sailed on Long Island Sound. At Marblehead, she beat nine other R-boats. The *Yankee* was proving to be a fast boat, and Charlie Welch, the youngest of the R-boat skippers, was proving himself to be an excellent racing sailor. Charlie had a fine crew, including for at least some of these races, the boat's designer.[29]

The racing for the Greenwich Cup resulted in a tie between the *Yankee* and P. R. Mallory's *Quiver*. They were supposed to have a match race to decide the victor, but the *Quiver* had to bow out, because she was scheduled to be shipped right out to the Great Lakes for more racing. There must have been some possibility of a match race, however, for, while Charlie Welch went back to Boston on business, Francis stayed with the *Yankee* and her tender, Charlie's ketch *Stormy Petrel*. When no race materialized, Francis and a paid hand towed the *Yankee* back to Marblehead with the *Stormy Petrel*, arriving to a warm reception at the Corinthian Yacht Club.[30]

At some point during the 1925 racing season, the *Yankee* was hauled out at the Herreshoff Manufacturing Company, probably to have her bottom scrubbed for a race off Newport. Nathanael took the opportunity to inspect his son's creation. He "noticed a very neat arrangement to prevent eddies" around the rudderpost and "suppose it was your device," as he wrote Francis in November. This was a metal fairing that slid inside the deadwood as the rudder turned. Nathanael wanted to know if Francis would have any objection if he copied it on his own new R-boat design, another *Grayling*. Francis had no objection and sent his father a blueprint of the sliding fairing. In April, Nathanael wrote him that one like it had been made for the *Grayling*. Francis must have been delighted. Nor could it have hurt his feelings that the fairing did not enable the *Grayling* to beat the *Yankee*.[31]

Evidently, other designers were watching the *Yankee* with close interest. The sail plan of an R-boat from the Alden office, published in the November 1925 issue of *Yachting*, showed a fore triangle with almost exactly the same proportion of area as the enlarged one that Francis had given the *Yankee*. This boat was to have raced on Lake Ontario, but she was not built.[32]

After the season of 1925, Francis designed a radical, streamlined racing rig. He shows the rig on the hull of an advanced, double-ended R-boat, with sharp knuckles at both bow and stern. This drawing is numbered "303," which fits the Burgess, Swasey, and Paine numbering system for that time, though 303 was also used for a smaller, one-design class that Starling designed. Francis showed his ultra-modern R-boat design to the prominent racing sailor Henry L. Maxwell, but it "scared him," Francis thought, and the boat was not built, although Maxwell evidently paid him something for the design, "so I cannot kick." Francis had designed versions of the rig five years earlier on his fanciful catamaran and the previous winter on an iceboat for Charlie Welch. And sometime after December 11, Francis drew the new rig concept for the *Yankee*.[33]

Francis, Charlie Welch, and Starling probably discussed how to continue to reduce wind resistance in the rig of a racing sailboat, but it was Francis who patented the new concept as his own invention. He wrote to his father, "This to me seems a very interesting experiment but no one else likes it and it is going to be hard for me to put it over as every one seems sore because they didn't originate it." Francis was reacting to detraction with a sense of being isolated and even victimized, an attitude that would sometimes mar his enjoyment of his achievements in the future.[34]

Francis's idea for the new rig was to beef up the mast so much that very little standing rigging would be needed, and to set the jib on a luff spar instead of a stay. He stepped the mast on deck in a bearing, so the spar could rotate in order to achieve the optimum angle of attack of the mainsail's leading edge. The jib spar could also rotate. In addition, he smoothed out the airflow between spars and sails. In section, the mast and jib spar

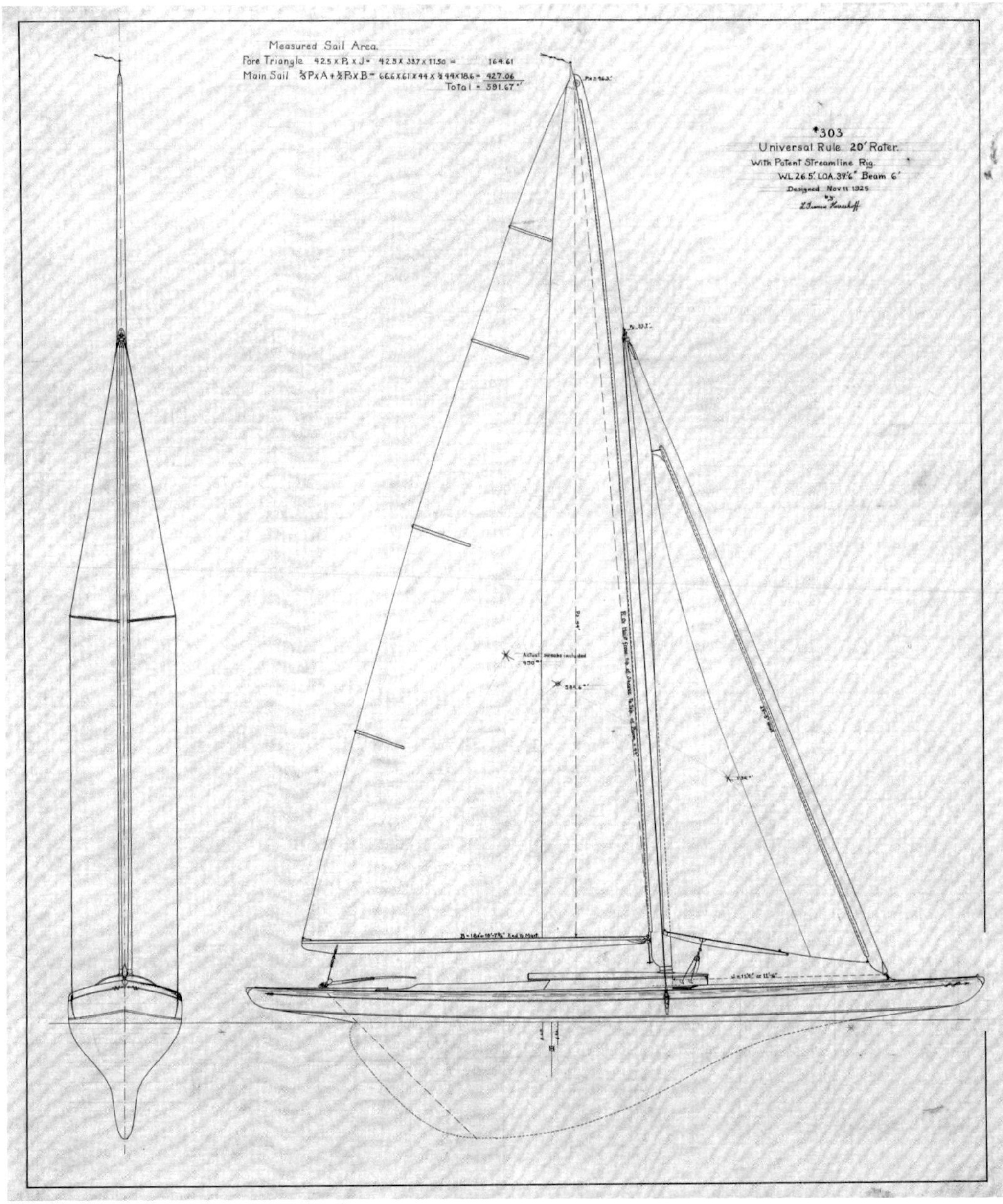

Francis's design for an advanced R-boat is dated November 11, 1925, his thirty-fifth birthday. This is his first drawing of his "Patent Streamline Rig." The jib sets on a luff spar instead of a stay. Each sail has two leading edges, each edge being attached to the corresponding side of its supporting spar. The mast and jib spar rotate to present the optimum angle of the luffs of the sails to the wind. The pivot point is where shrouds and jib-luff spar attach to the mast, so the strain on them will remain constant as the mast turns. Measured sail area is 592 square feet. (© Mystic Seaport, Daniel S. Gregory Ships Plans Library, SP38.68.1)

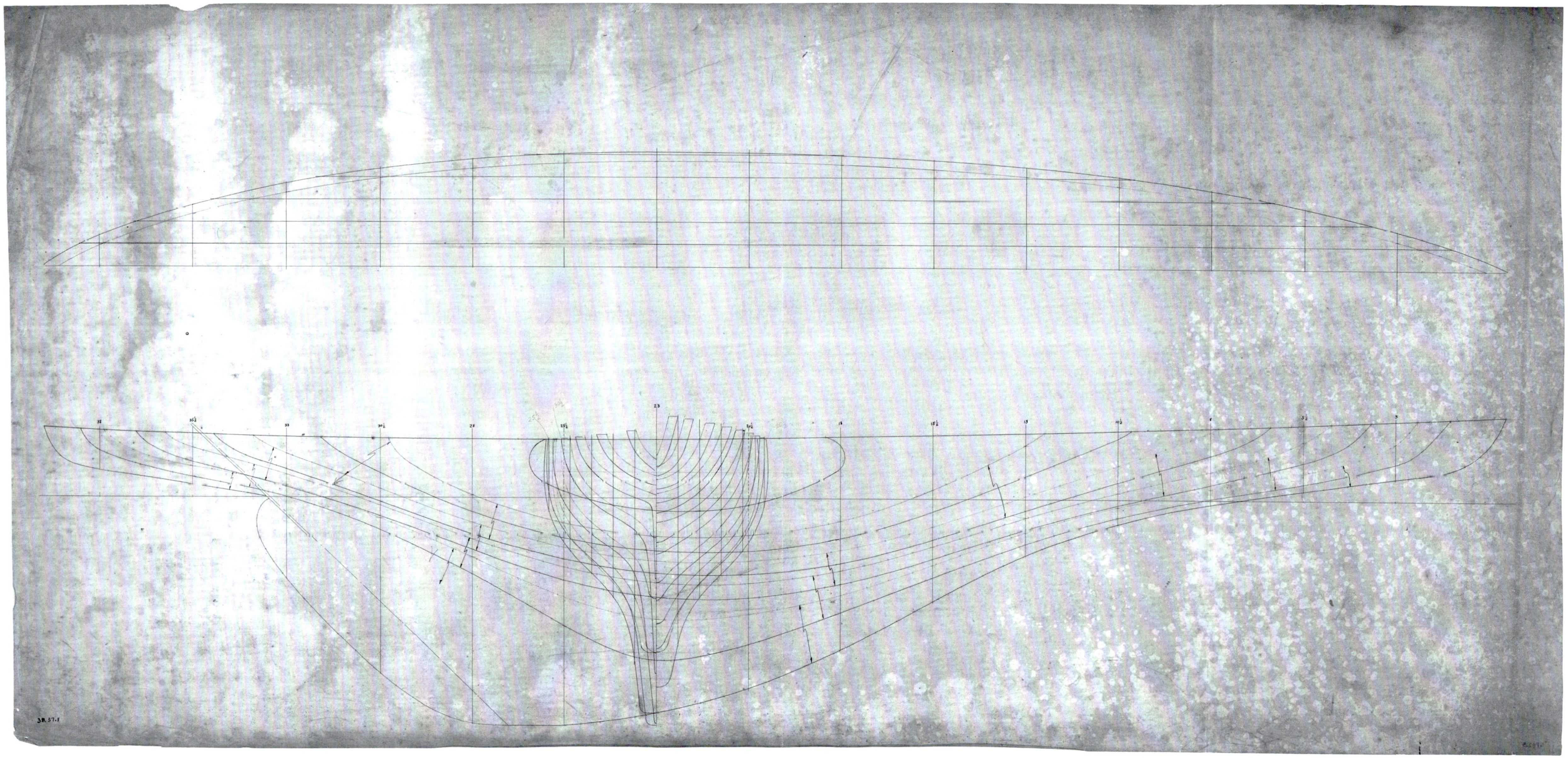

The lines of the double-ended R-boat. Her sharply knuckled bow and stern reduce the quarter-beam-length measurement of the Universal Rule. She is 39 feet, 6 inches long on deck; 26 feet, 6 inches on the waterline; with beam and draft both 6 feet. It is a shame no boat was built to this design, which is certainly advanced for 1925. (© Mystic Seaport, Daniel S. Gregory Ships Plans Library, SP38.57.1)

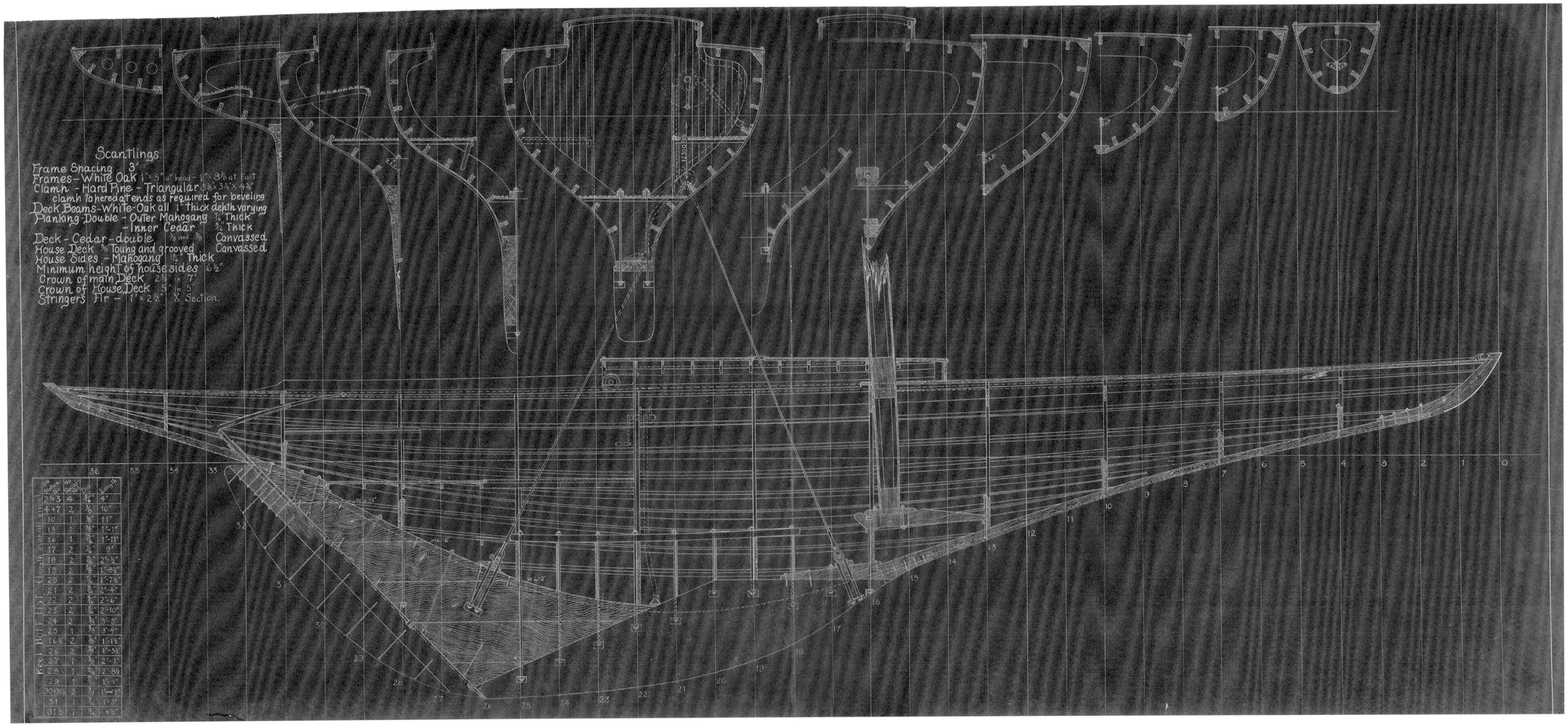

The *Yankee*'s revolutionary construction plan, in which Francis adapted for wooden construction the longitudinal method his father had devised for metal vessels and that Starling and others had used for aircraft. This method, with its long, light stringers running fore-and-aft and its widely spaced web frames, saved considerable weight without sacrificing strength. Francis has saved further weight by replacing the conventional L-shaped sheer-clamp-and-shelf structure under the deck edge with a simple triangular-section shelf. The longitudinal construction was the major factor in giving the *Yankee* her advantageously high ballast-to-displacement ratio. (© Mystic Seaport, Daniel S. Gregory Ships Plans Library, SP38.67.14)

RIGHT: This sectional drawing of Francis's streamlined rig, made for the later R-boat *Live Yankee*, shows the shape of the mast, the two luff ropes in their grooves, and the two luffs of the sail, converging to meet further aft. The narrow slots between mast and luff ropes were to be further streamlined by "Tape fairing Strips furnished by C. A. W." (Charlie Welch). (© Mystic Seaport, Daniel S. Gregory Ships Plans Library, SP38.6.25)

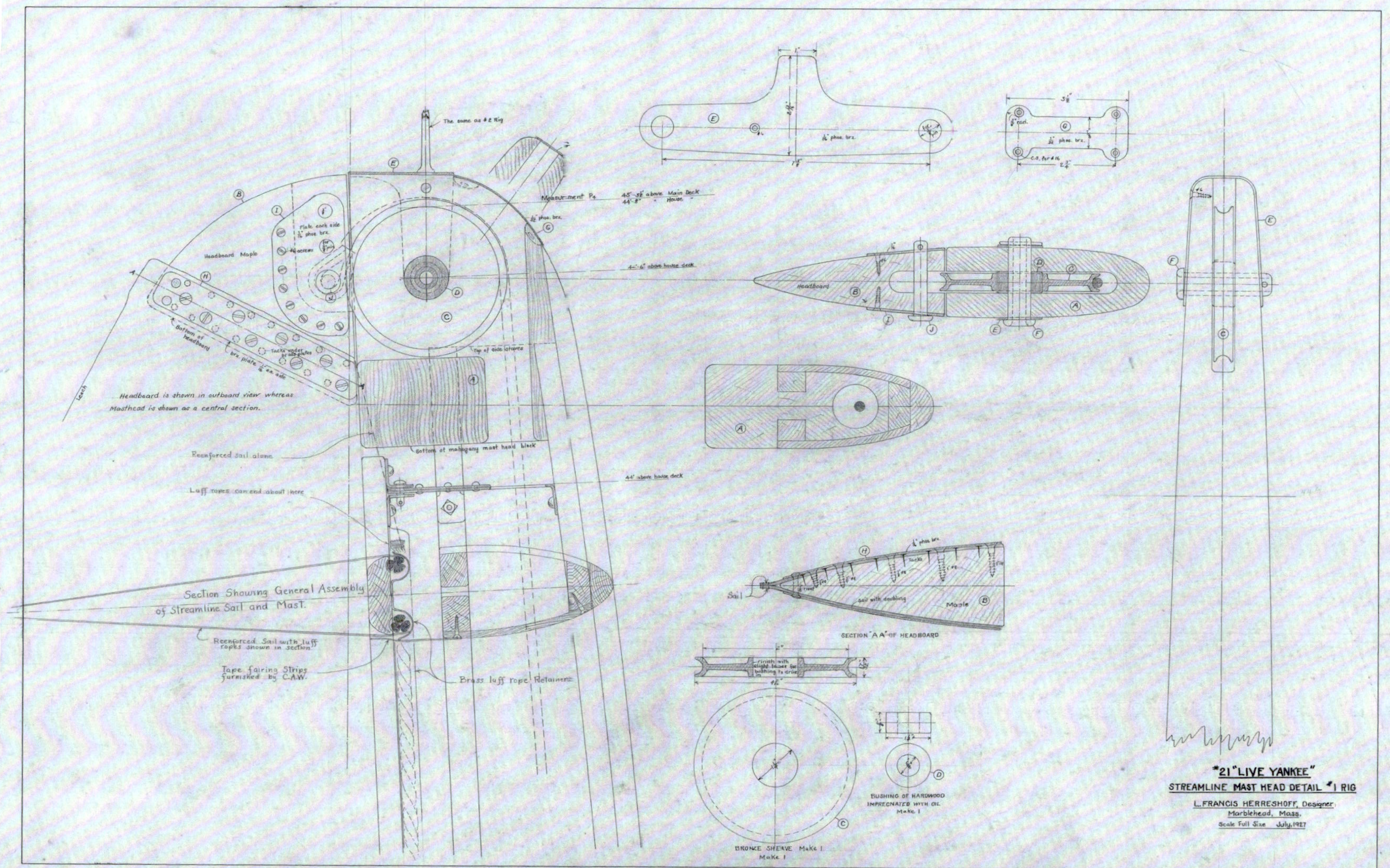

#21 "LIVE YANKEE"

STREAMLINE MAST HEAD DETAIL #1 RIG

L. FRANCIS HERRESHOFF, Designer.
Marblehead, Mass.
Scale Full Size   July, 1927

38.6.25

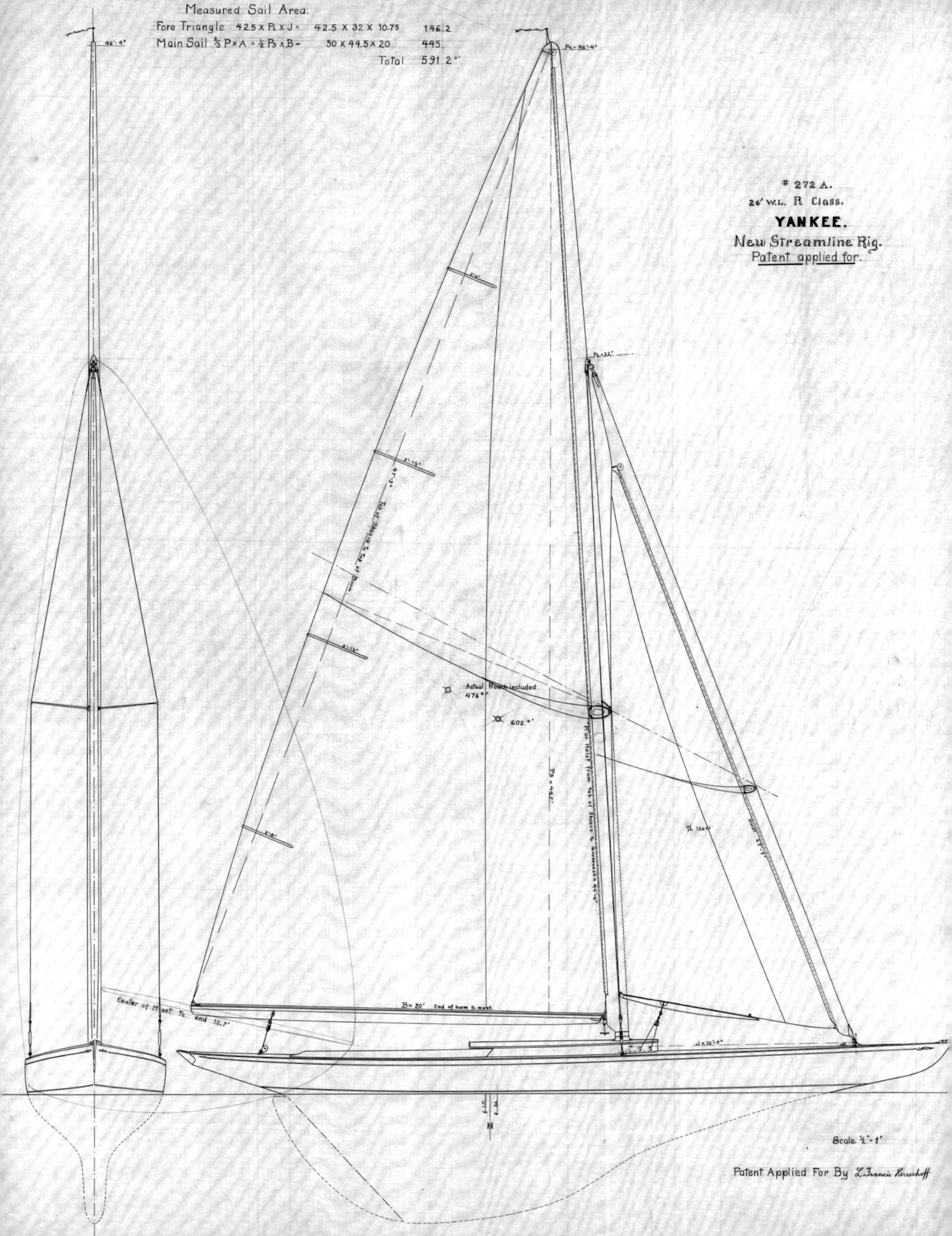
Measured Sail Area.
Fore Triangle 42.5 x P2 x J = 42.5 x 32 x 10.75 146.2
Main Sail 2/3 P x A + 1/2 P3 x B = 50 x 44.5 x 20 445
Total 591.2 □'
272 A.
26' W.L. R Class.
YANKEE.
New Streamline Rig.
Patent applied for.
Actual Roach included
476 □'
602 □'
B = 20' End of boom to mast.
Center of Mast to end 12.7'
Top of Sheave to Top of Boom 47'-3"
P2 = 32'
Scale 1/2" = 1'
Patent Applied For By L. Francis Herreshoff

were to be about the normal width of conventional spars, but of about twice the normal dimension fore-and-aft, for strength. Whereas the *Yankee*'s curved mast was supported by ten pieces of wire standing rigging, including running backstays (plus the partly exposed main halyard)—all of this, in turn, supported by two pairs of spreaders and two struts—the new rig would be supported by just two shrouds and one pair of spreaders. The forward sides of the hollow mast and jib spar were rounded off, but their after sides were left nearly square. The sails did not have a simple luff hoisting on a single, central track; rather, each sail had two luffs that hoisted together on a single halyard, each luff on a rope in its own groove, let into the after corners of the squared-off spar. The two luffs extended aft for about a quarter of the width of the sails and then joined to form a single layer of sail the rest of the way to the leech. By joining spar and sail in this way, Francis created an almost entirely smooth airfoil. He applied for a patent on the new rig on December 11, 1925; Patent No. 1,613,890, for seventeen years, was granted him exactly thirteen months later.[35]

By the following spring of 1926, as we shall see, Francis and his father had begun discussing the details of their profession. Francis sent Nathanael a drawing of the "New Streamline Rig;" Nathanael wondered exactly how the sails hoisted and lowered; Francis sent him a sketch showing the double luffs in more detail. Nathanael saw as a drawback that the fore-and-aft sides of the spars would be measured as sail area, since they were, in effect, joined to the sails. Francis replied that the measurer had said that only the sails themselves would be measured, unless the new rig caused a change in the measurement rule. Francis told his father that he wasn't trying to cheat the rule by using the mast as unmeasured sail area, but was simply making a streamlined luff connection. And he reported that the *Yankee* would sail under her old rig in 1926, for "we could not get anyone to build [the streamlined rig] for a reasonable price."[36]

Despite not having a new streamlined rig, the *Yankee* had another successful racing season in 1926. She won her first race of the season at Marblehead on June 27, skippered as usual by Charlie Welch and with Francis in the crew, beating six other R-boats. Charles Francis Adams's *Gossoon* was second, nearly three minutes back. And she won her last race of the season, on August 29, and did well enough in between to capture the R-Class season trophy of the Eastern Yacht Club.[37]

One of her wins came on August 15, with Ruth Welch at the helm in her husband's absence. Charlie and Ruth each claimed the honor of being a better sailor than the other and threatened a match race to settle the question. Such a race evidently never happened, but in one race, Ruth was skipper and Charlie was crew, and he fell overboard. Ruth yelled, "Swim to that buoy and hang on and I'll come back and pick you up." Charlie yelled back, "You can't do that. You have to finish with the same number you started with." Thus reminded of the rule, Ruth had no choice but to reverse course. Francis believed that most women have a greater sensitivity to a boat's motion than do most men, so that female skippers—though rare in 1925—could be, in his opinion, superlative at the tiller. He thought that Ruth was even better

LEFT: Francis's design for the "New Streamline Rig" for the *Yankee*, a rig that he patented but that was outlawed for racing. The drawing shows a big advance in decreasing wind resistance, for the mast and jib spar are strong enough to require almost no wire standing rigging, and the luffs of the sails are attached to the spars in a way that forms a smooth airfoil. The solid, vertical lines from leech to foot, about a quarter of the sails' widths aft from their luffs, show where the double luffs end and the single layers of the sails begin. (© Mystic Seaport, Daniel S. Gregory Ships Plans Library, SP38.67.5)

than Charlie at steering a small racing yacht.[38]

In September, the *Yankee* added another major trophy to her collection, the New York Yacht Club Cup for Class R. Nine R-boats competed for the cup off Newport. The races were sailed in breezes from light to fresh, with a big ground swell. William U. Swan reported in the *New York Times* that "the *Yankee* breezed up to windward faster than any boat in the fleet. Indeed, her speed was so great relatively that her skipper did not have to worry about covering this or that yacht but sailed his own course and usually reached the weather mark with the race well in hand." After four races, the *Yankee*, sailed by Charlie Welch with Francis in the crew, had the most points. The race committee eliminated the last five boats (including Nathanael's *Grayling*), and the four leaders sailed two more races. Again, the *Yankee* triumphed to win the cup (Nathanael's *Game Cock* coming in last).[39]

Francis was showing his father that he had been wrong to believe him incapable of designing yachts; Nathanael may have admitted that error in judgment to himself, but he didn't admit it to Francis. However, he wrote to Francis: "I congratulate you on the victory of *Yankee* in the races at Newport this week. And in fact, all your work in the last year or two stands for a good deal of credit."[40]

The following spring, further congratulations came to Francis and Charlie when George Nichols, Commodore of the New York Yacht Club, hosted a dinner at the clubhouse in their honor. Francis had a rare chance to bask: "The men at the dinner were about the nicest, intelligent, high grade men I have ever seen together. We had a very pleasant meeting," he wrote his father. And Charlie was recognized for the outstanding racing skipper that he was, deserving credit for getting the most speed out of the *Yankee* in all conditions.[41]

Charlie Welch sold the *Yankee* after the 1926 season to make way for a new R-boat. The *Yankee* raced successfully on Long Island Sound for the next ten years and on Lake Michigan for another nine years. *Lloyd's Register of American Yachts* listed her through 1974, her longitudinal construction serving her well. Francis sold a set of her plans for forty-five dollars in 1969, nearly forty-five years after he had drawn them, not to a boatbuilder, but to a collector of works of art.[42]

The R-boat *Yankee* was a fabulous design that any yacht designer could be proud of. It is remarkable that Francis could make such a design a mere five years after his first, the Narragansett Bay daysailer, but he was nearly thirty-five years old, and even though he had spent a decade on the farm and in the navy, he had prepared himself to design a boat like the *Yankee* in many ways for many years. With the *Yankee*, Francis experienced the intense pleasure of seeing a complicated racing yacht he had designed, with evolutionary and revolutionary concepts, take shape at the hands of builders; had enjoyed sailing in the boat, sensing her speed and motion; and had participated in some of her wins on the racecourse at the highest levels of competition. The *Yankee* showed Francis and the world that L. Francis Herreshoff was his father's own son. For Francis's psyche, nothing could have been more important.

CHAPTER 6

532.
P = 83'
P_2 = 82'
P = 64'
Total, JT. FS. MTS. MS. + M.
3349.
Actual Roach Included
350.
416.
341.
D = 19'
J = 28'
Scale 1/4" = 1'
34
32
30
28
26
24
22
20
18
16
14
12
10
8
6
4
2
0

THE CHOSEN SON

"Let me congratulate you on the fine appearance of the drawings and particularly on the care and thoughtfulness of the details worked out in all of them."

—NATHANAEL G. HERRESHOFF TO L. FRANCIS HERRESHOFF, MAY 2, 1926

At the same time Francis and Charlie Welch were mounting a serious campaign in the R Class, they were having fun with boat design ideas that had nothing to do with racing. Francis told Charlie tales of zipping across the ice under sail, and Charlie had to have an iceboat. In January 1925, Francis signed the sail plan drawing of the "Ice Yacht *Slipper*" (Burgess, Swasey, and Paine design No. 285). He wrote his name and that same date across the construction plan and all but two of the seven additional sheets he used to show the details of hull, runner plank, runners, steering arrangement, and rig of this sophisticated design.[1]

The *Slipper* was 26 feet long and 13 feet, 6 inches wide. The hull was flat-bottomed with nine longitudinal stringers. The original intent was merely to stretch canvas over the stringers in the cockpit to save weight, but the canvas was quickly replaced by bone-protecting ply-board. Francis noted on the construction drawing, "Light weight and strength are verry important." Francis and Starling built the *Slipper* themselves that winter.[2]

The leg-o'-mutton-sloop rig had 197-1/2 square feet of sail area and was, as mentioned, Francis's first experiment with the streamlined, double-luff rig originally conceived for his catamaran in 1920. Francis designed the mainsail with its two luffs forming a sleeve around the mast, and he designed the mast so that it could rotate with the pull of the sail to present the optimum angle to the wind. Francis later reported to his father that "the mast revolved just the right amount, as well as one could see by eye." He would also write, "The few [double-luff sails] I have tried are most satisfactory." The luff sleeve of the mainsail joined the single-layer sail at a distance abaft the mast varying from a little less than a foot to a little less than two feet, thus forming a smooth surface from spar to sail. The luff sleeve was set to the desired tension on the mast by a seizing at the masthead before the rig was raised into position. The main sheet was rigged to be hauled from either its forward or its after end, and it had a separate swaying bridle amidships to bend the boom down to flatten the sail in a breeze. The jib was merely set flying on its own luff wire. Both sails were fully battened from luff to leech. All this was quite a handful to raise and lower, particularly if it was blowing hard.[3]

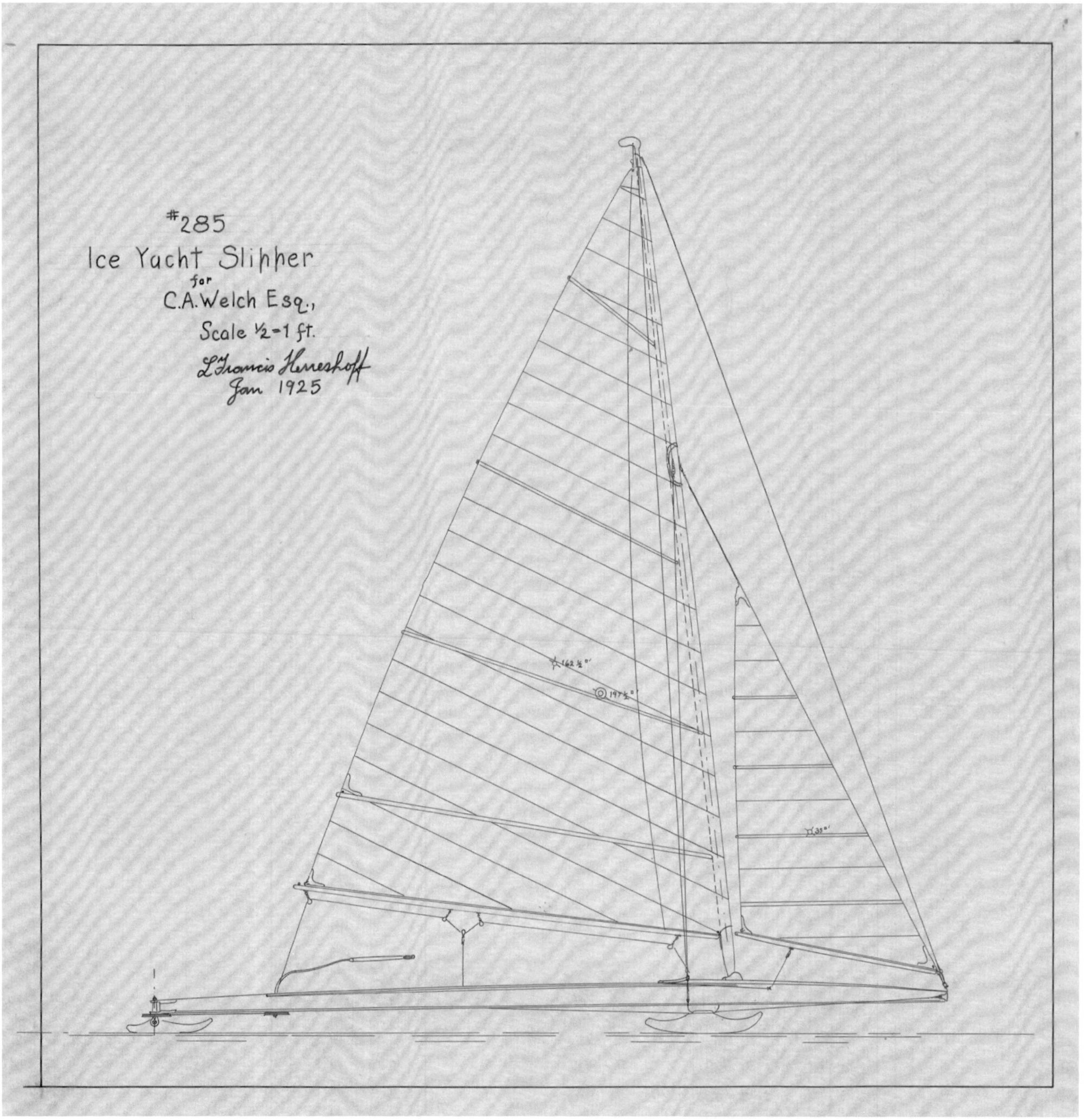

ABOVE: **The sail plan of the iceboat *Slipper*, one of the craft that gave Francis and Charlie Welch a change of pace from serious yacht racing. Her double-luff mainsail, forming a sleeve around the mast, is an experiment that influenced Francis's patented streamlined rig.** (© Mystic Seaport, Daniel S. Gregory Ships Plans Library, SP138.125.1) RIGHT: **The *Slipper*'s construction plan. Francis was proud of his work at Burgess, Swasey, and Paine, and he wanted credit for his new ideas; he wrote his signature, with the date, across most of his drawings for the iceboat design.** (© Mystic Seaport, Daniel S. Gregory Ships Plans Library, SP138.125.2)

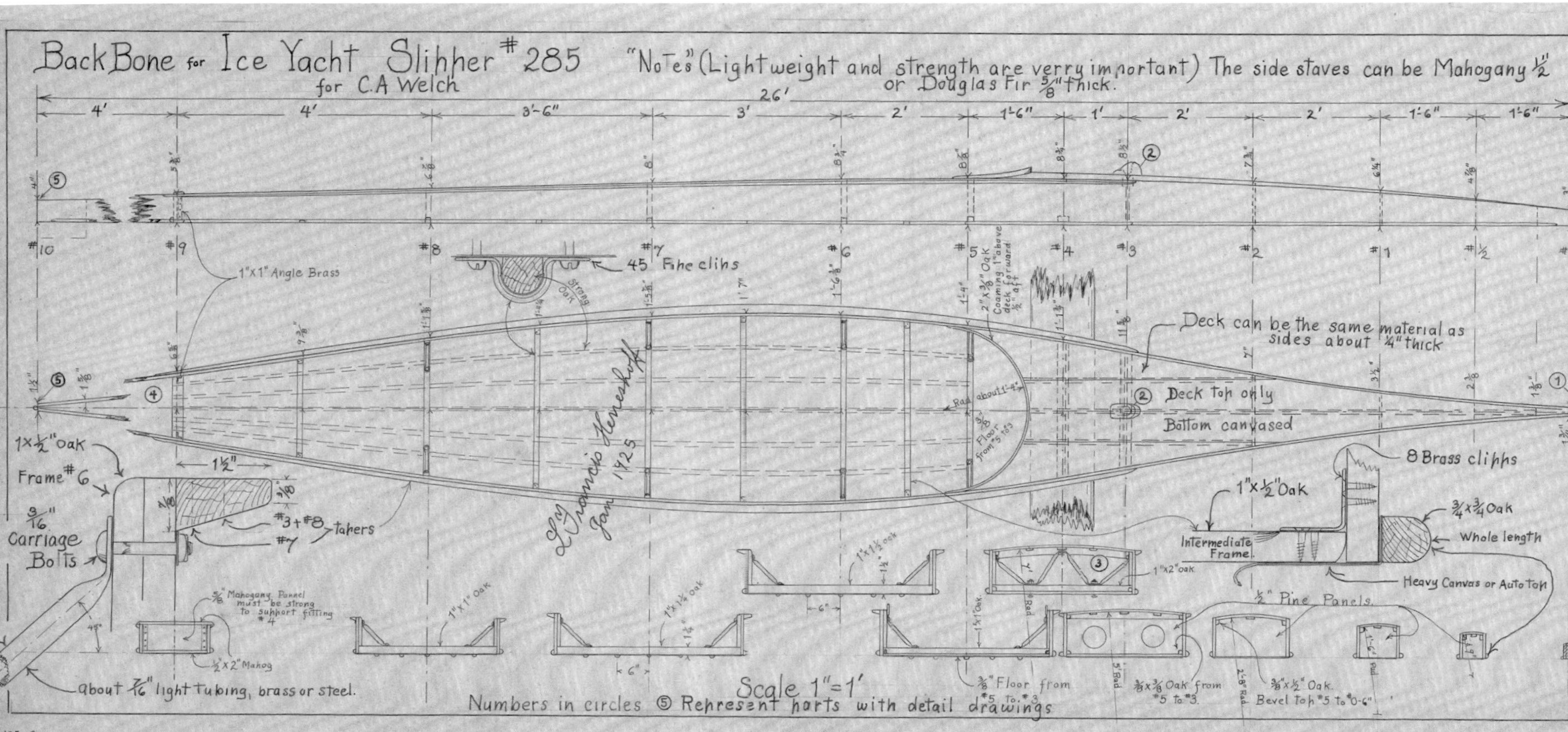

BackBone for Ice Yacht Slipper #285
for C.A Welch
"Notes" (Lightweight and strength are verry important) The side staves can be Mahogany 1/2" or Douglas Fir 5/8" thick.
26'
4'
4'
3'-6"
3'
2'
1'-6"
1'
2'
2'
1'-6"
1'-6"
#10
#9
#8
#7
#6
#5
#4
#3
#2
#1
#1/2
#0.
1"x1" Angle Brass
45 Pipe clips
Strong Oak
2"x3/8" Oak Coaming 1" above deck forward 1/2" aft
Deck can be the same material as sides about 1/4" thick
Deck top only
Bottom canvased
Rad about 1'-4"
3/8" Floor from #5 to #3
1x1/2" Oak
Frame #6
9/16" Carriage Bolts
#3+#8 tapers
#7
8 Brass clipps
1"x1/2" Oak
3/4x3/4 Oak
Whole length
Intermediate Frame.
Heavy Canvas or Auto top
1/2" Pine Panels.
5/8" Mahogany Pannel must be strong to support fitting #4
1/2x2" Mahog
1"x1" Oak
1"x1 1/4" oak
1"x1 1/2" oak
1"x2" oak
3/8" Floor from #5 to #3
3/8x3/8 Oak from #5 to #3.
3/8"x1/2" Oak. Bevel top #5 to #0-6"
about 7/16" light tubing, brass or steel.
Scale 1"=1'
Numbers in circles ⑤ Represent parts with detail drawings
L. Francis Herreshoff Jan 1925

Charlie and Ruth Welch both sailed the *Slipper* in such boisterous, even dangerous, conditions. The craft had sprocket-and-chain steering that required great care, for a small movement of the tiller had a big effect. As a lark, Charlie once sailed his iceboat, heeled over on one runner, over the head of a movie photographer. On another occasion, the *Slipper*, at speed, ejected Ruth onto the ice, unhurt. The *Slipper* is still giving excitement, having been restored by Mark Mason and Nat Wilson, a maker of traditional sails, both enthusiasts of L. Francis Herreshoff. And she is now back in the Welch family, owned by Josh Welch of Stonington, Connecticut.[4]

The *Slipper* came near the end of the era of the stern-steering iceboat. While stern-steerers were prone to spinning out of control when the steering runner lost its grip on the ice—"flickering" is the word iceboat sailors use for the mishap—later bow-steerers were easier to manage. Nonetheless, veteran iceboater Lloyd Roberts has reported: "*Slipper* steers very nicely with neutral helm and

only a modest feeling of wanting to oversteer in turns. She is very manageable with a definite feeling of being in solid control." Yet, Ruth Welch was probably the victim of a flicker.[5]

ALTHOUGH THE *Stormy Petrel* had served Charlie Welch well as an off-season cruiser, he and Francis talked of designing a vessel that would be more specially suited for safety in heavy weather. When Charlie asked Francis to proceed with such a design, he turned naturally to the lifeboat, a type of craft that intrigued him. As we have seen, he had made a preliminary design of his idea of an extremely seaworthy ocean cruiser three years earlier, his F-16, a 100-foot, three-masted lifeboat. Now, he scaled down the concept to a much smaller lifeboat-cruiser for Charlie.

Francis must have expected that Charlie would build the lifeboat-cruiser, for he completed the lines and offsets five weeks before the outboard profile drawing. Usually, he started with the outboard profile, to show the general appearance of the yacht, and then, once the decision had been made to proceed with the design, he would draw the lines, and when building was contemplated, figure the offsets. For the "Twin Screw Launch," as Francis called Charlie's new 44-foot boat, the lines-and-offsets drawing is dated February 2,

LEFT TOP: **Charlie Welch showing off in the *Slipper*.** (*The Common Sense of Yacht Design*, figure 39) LEFT BOTTOM: **Details of the main-sheet arrangement and of the sprocket-and-chain steering can be seen in this view of the *Slipper* at rest.** (Courtesy Hope Welch Slater, Mystic Seaport, 1996-10-62) ABOVE: **Charlie Welch (center), with his wife Ruth and his brother Sohier, on board the *Stormy Petrel*. All three were fine sailors.** (Courtesy Hope Welch Slater, Mystic Seaport, 1996-10-60))

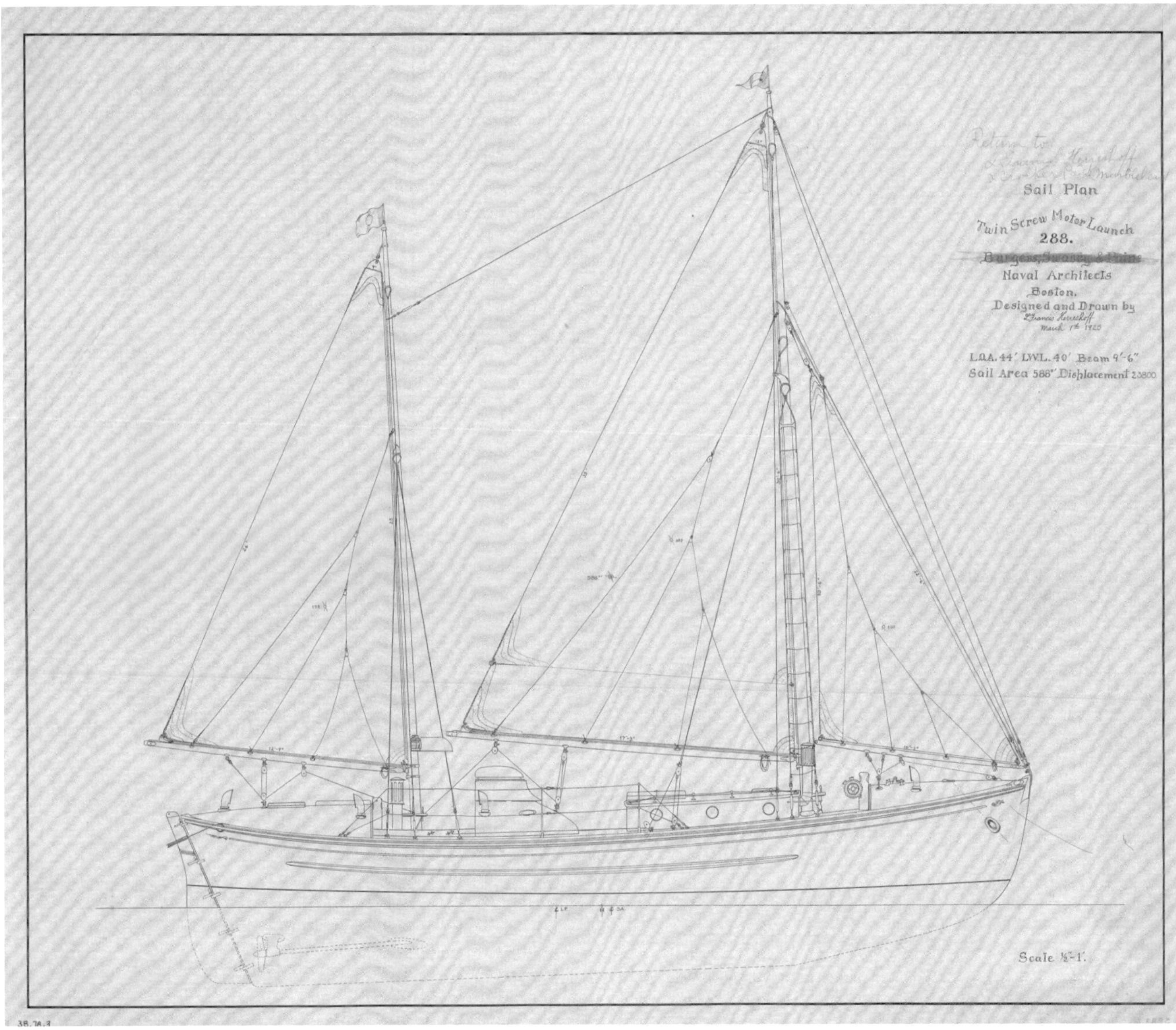

ABOVE: **Francis's design for a 44-foot lifeboat-cruiser was never built for Charlie Welch. She would have been 40 feet long on the waterline, with a beam of 9 feet, 6 inches, and a draft of 3 feet, 7 inches. Francis figured the displacement at 23,800 pounds, of which 4,000 pounds was in an iron ballast keel. The sail area was a modest 588 square feet. Power was to be two 30-horsepower Lathrops. She was to have a water closet under the turtleback in the bow; a double stateroom under the trunk cabin; the engine room amidships, beneath the conning tower; the galley in way of the mizzenmast; and the wardroom under the turtleback at the stern.** (© Mystic Seaport, Daniel S. Gregory Ships Plans Library, SP38.78.3) RIGHT: **The lines and offsets of the lifeboat-cruiser. Francis, looking back, believed that this was one of his best designs.** (© Mystic Seaport, Daniel S. Gregory Ships Plans Library, SP38.78.1)

1925; the outboard profile, March 9. The design was given Burgess, Swasey, and Paine No. 288. Francis started a construction plan, but he didn't finish it. Charlie had changed his mind. He apparently decided that the boat was too big. Burgess, Swasey, and Paine design No. 293 is Francis's design for a 33-foot lifeboat-type launch, but this design was also aborted, with less work on it than for the 44-footer. What Charlie really wanted, he thought, was a more conventional motor sailer, so Francis began thinking about that project and made eight pencil drawings, to scale, showing his ideas for full-powered ketches from 36 to 55 feet in length. This time, Charlie brought Francis to a halt before he had made any finished drawings. All this backing and filling wasn't wasted, as we shall see, for three years later Francis designed a fine motor sailer, the 50-foot *Walrus,* that was built for Charlie Welch. And forty-three years later, Francis sold a set of plans for the 44-foot lifeboat cruiser (he scratched out in pencil "Burgess, Swasey, and Paine") with the comment: "I am ashamed that this design is not more complete for I think it is one of the best I ever made." This "one of the best" of Francis's designs would indeed have made Charlie Welch a good boat for rough weather; but, alas, no boat was ever built to this design.[6]

IN 1924 AND 1925, Francis had the opportunity to perfect his skill at sailing a type of boat at the opposite end of the spectrum from a lifeboat: the sliding-seat sailing canoe, to which Starling had introduced him at Provincetown. This type of fast, narrow boat with a large sail area could only be kept from capsizing by the acrobatics of its sailor, who actively balanced the changing force of the wind against the sails by shifting his weight back and forth on the sliding seat, often hanging

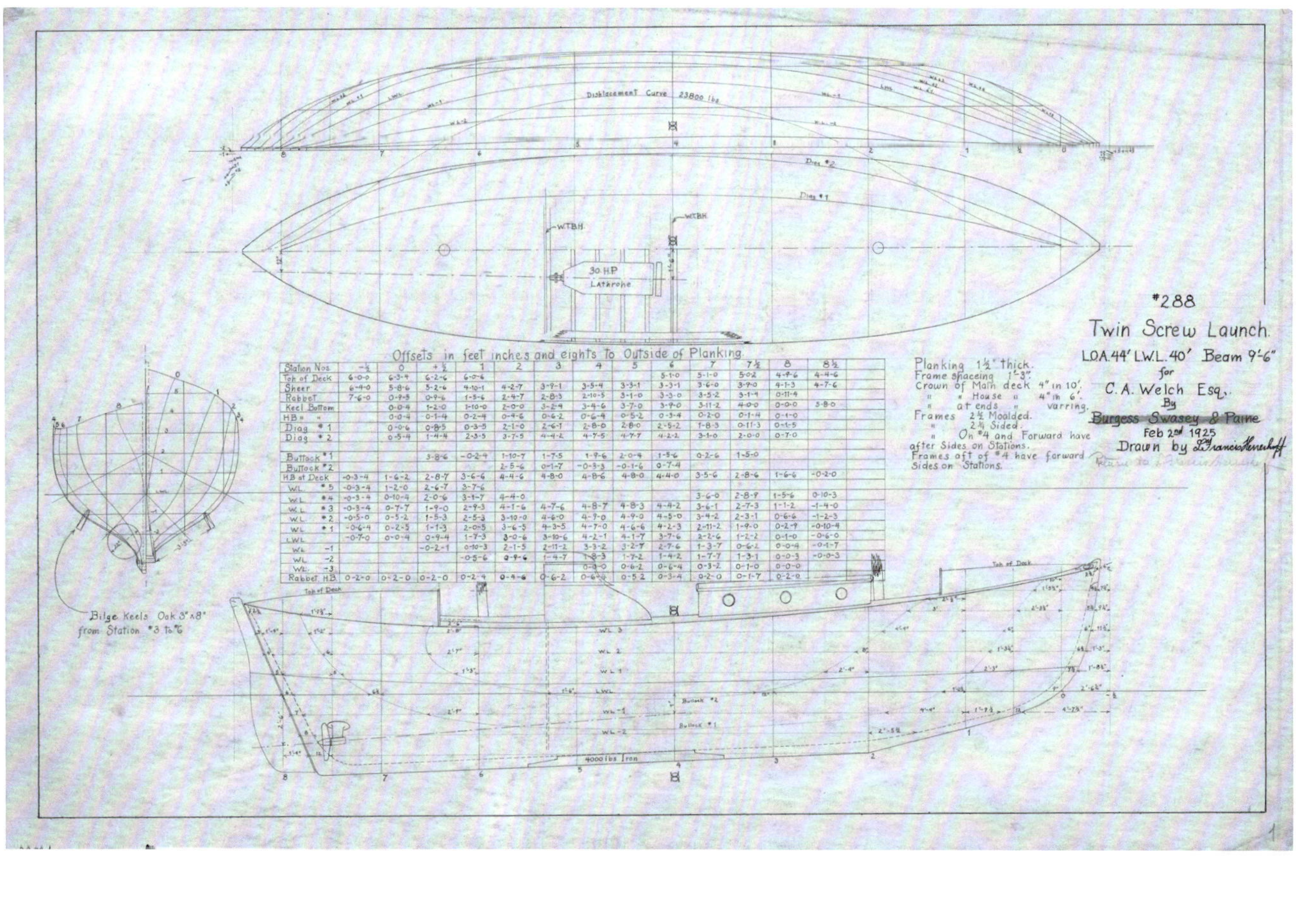

far out over the windward side in a gust, ready to jump back in when it subsided. Probably because of his employers' good connections in Boston's high society, Francis had the use of such a canoe, the *Wasp*, owned in the Butler family, who had also owned the famous schooner *America* herself. The *Wasp* had been the late Paul Butler's last canoe, and it was he who had invented the athwartships sliding seat in 1886 and had done the most to develop the sailing canoe as a highly sophisticated racing craft. Francis became adept enough at the art of sailing these tricky boats to be able to report to his father that he had raced them on the Charles River "with good success on several occasions."[7]

Although Francis did not continue sailing in canoes, he loved the experience, as evidenced by his later writing about them:

> *The sailing canoe has more beauty, longevity, and, we might say, verve than any of the manmade objects. . . . I use the word "verve" because almost nothing else will express the lively movements of a sailing canoe when she is sailing in a good breeze and a chop of a sea. On the usual sailboat one cannot see her in action even if he can feel her movements, but when one is out on the sliding seat of a sailing canoe he has a picture before him that is most thrilling. He sees the stem of the canoe as it knifes its way through the water, often . . . throwing up a halo of spray which takes on rainbow hues. Now she pitches slightly till her stem head is under water, now she raises her forefoot and planes out three or four feet, always changing her wave formation, always dancing, always jumping forward, and all the while under the sliding seat the water whizzes by. It seems to move like lightning, which is because the sailor is in such close proximity to the moving water. At times his seat just clears it, and at times it dips into it. He sees before him the centerboard and the rudder clearly silhouetted in the moving tide. In fact when the sun is opposite him, if the water is clear, he sees the whole outboard profile of the bottom. At these times his sensations of speed are more pronounced even than in flying.*[8]

Later he would write, "to me the pleasure of sailing is almost in direct proportion to the speed." As we shall see, Francis would later add to the development and design of sailing canoes.[9]

IN THE SUMMER of 1925, as the *Yankee* was starting to build her reputation as an unbeatable R-boat, Francis made two preliminary designs for a proposed one-design racing class at Marblehead. The first was a full-keel boat with a waterline length of 14 feet, his outboard profile and sail plan dated July 30. Two weeks later, he had drawn a 15-foot waterline version with a centerboard adding lateral plane to a keel that was one foot, three inches shallower. The rigs of both designs had span stays instead of a headstay and running backstays that led well aft, features of the *Yankee*'s rig. But Starling took over the design

One of Francis's preliminary designs for the Marblehead T-Class (RIGHT), and Norman Skene's drawing of Starling's design for the class, as built (PAGE 154). Starling has shortened the hull a little and moved the rig aft. Skene's drawing, dated August 28, 1925, shows an overlapping (Genoa) jib that Francis claimed to have invented in early 1927. (Frank C. Paine Collection, Hart Nautical Collections, MIT Museum, Cambridge, Massachusetts)

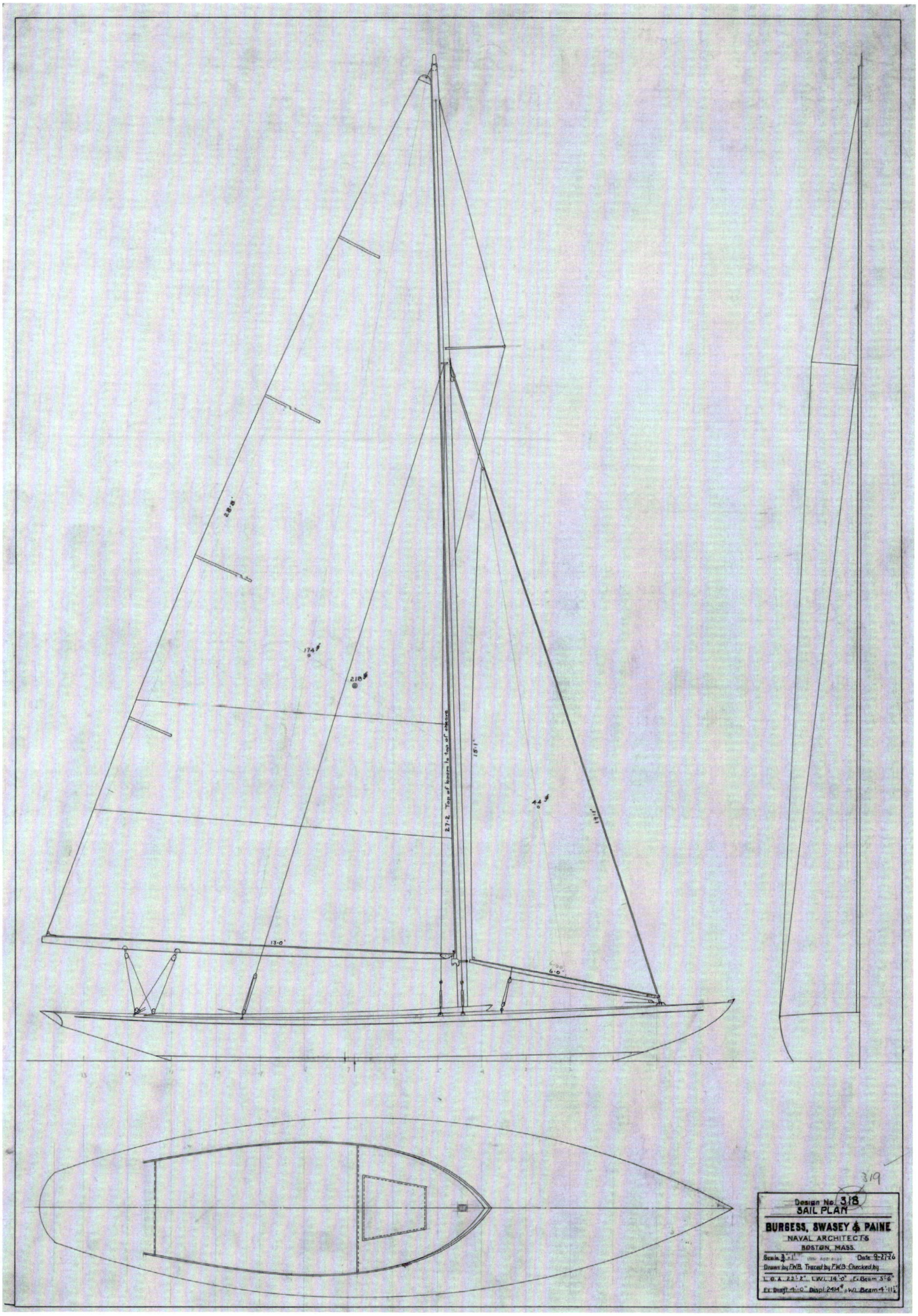

319
Design No. 318
SAIL PLAN
BURGESS, SWASEY & PAINE
NAVAL ARCHITECTS
BOSTON, MASS.
Scale 3/4" = 1' Date 9-27-26
Drawn by F.W.B. Traced by F.W.B. Checked by
L.O.A. 22'-2" L.W.L. 14'-0" Ex. Beam 5'-6"
Ex. Draft 4'-0" Displ. 2414# W.L. Beam 4'-11½"
28'-8"
174#
218#
Top of boom to top of sheave 27'-2
18'-1"
44#
19'-1"
13'-0"
6'-0"

Design No. 295
SAIL PLAN
BURGESS, SWASEY & PAI
NAVAL ARCHITECTS
BOSTON, MASS.
Scale $\frac{3}{4}$" = 1' Date Aug. 28, 1925
Drawn by N.L.S. Traced by N.L.S.
L.O.A. 22'-2" L.W.L. 14'-0" Ex. Beam
Ex. Draft 3'-10½" Disp. 2575#

of what was to become the Marblehead T Class, Burgess, Swasey, and Paine design No. 295.[10]

In his lines for the 15-foot design, Starling changed the hull shape considerably, apparently with the object of making the boat cheaper to build by giving her a plank keel, a shorter counter, and a flat transom. In the end, however, Starling chose the 14-footer to be built, and he completed her design with a set of lines that changed Francis's knuckle bow and long counter stern just enough to reduce beauty to mere handsomeness. The construction drawing was made by Nick Potter. Starling modified Francis's rig, moving the whole sail plan aft a few inches and leading the backstays farther forward. The T-Class sail plan was both drawn and traced in ink by Norman Skene, but Skene was probably working from Starling's ideas, either verbal or sketched. This sail plan, dated August 28, 1925, shows a flat-cut, overlapping jib as an extra sail for a light breeze, a sail that would later be called a Genoa jib, and, as we shall see, a sail that Francis would claim he invented about two years later.[11]

FRANK PAINE, who was brought up in most comfortable surroundings, felt that Francis deserved better than the cabin of a schooner in cold weather, and invited him to spend the winter of 1925-1926 with his family in the elegant old house on Boston's exclusive Beacon Hill that he had inherited, 87 Mount Vernon Street. Francis had often been an overnight visitor "in the large, rather somber bedroom over the starboard side of the front door." When he accepted Frank's offer, he asked Frank's wife, Virginia, if there wasn't a smaller room where he could stay, and she installed him on the third floor. Each morning before heading off for 585 Boylston Street, Francis and Frank had breakfast together. Sometimes, in the evening, they would work on projects on Frank's lathe, which was set up downstairs in the billiard room. Francis had spotted a pair of abandoned lathes two years earlier at the George Lawley yard, and Frank had agreed to buy them if Francis would put them in working order. Then each would take one. The design and fabrication of machinery was an interest the two yacht designers shared all their lives.[12]

Francis had been able to set up his lathe in the Burgess, Swasey, and Paine office. "I am very busy but get time once in awhile to do some turning on my lathe," he wrote to his father, "which gives me as much pleasure as ever. I do not make anything on it of value but have a good time just the same. The lathe gives me more pleasure and satisfaction than anything I have ever had."[13]

AT THE OFFICE, Francis was designing powerboats as well as sailing yachts. He would write: "It is my opinion that the powerboat (when properly designed) is capable of giving as much pleasure as the sailboat. Her model can be made to have as much grace and character as the sailboat, and for those who really want to go places she is the moving home par excellence." Between August 1925 and April 1926 he drew three designs for 40-foot "launches," as he called them, all three for fishing and cruising. None proceeded beyond an outboard profile with a small cabin plan in the upper right-hand corner of the drawing.[14]

The first is a swordfisherman, with a steering wheel up the mast, reached by ratlines, and a pulpit for the harpooneer on the bowsprit. Her mast is set well aft, which allows a big headsail amidships to steady her and save fuel. She has a very small pilothouse for the helmsman, a fish well under the cockpit, a good-sized engine room, and bunks for three fishermen. She was to make 10 knots with a 40-horsepower Lathrop. There was no named client for this design. The title block credited Burgess, Swasey, and Paine for it; Francis merely initialed the drawing beside its date, August 4, 1925.[15]

The third of these powerboat designs was

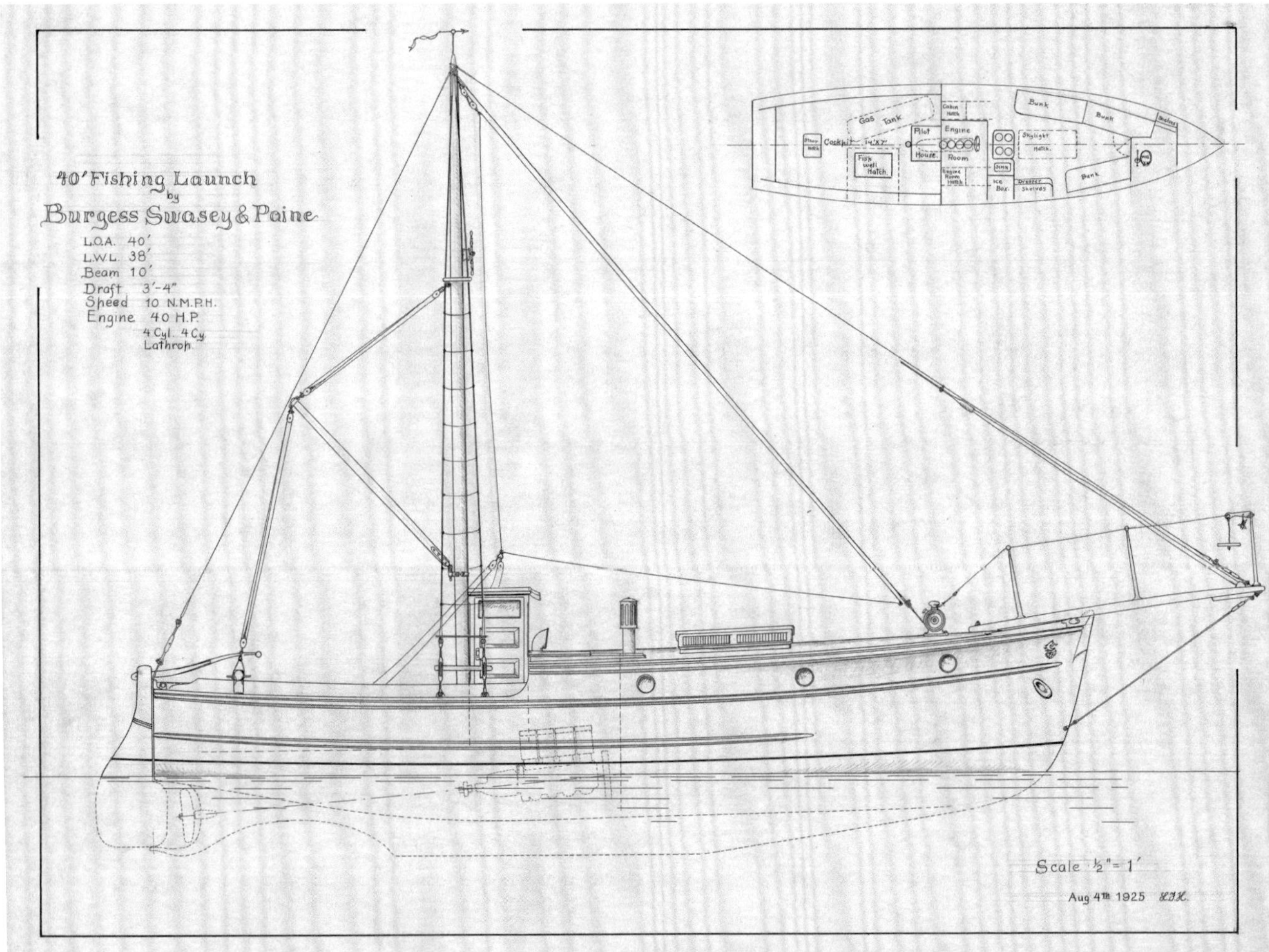

ABOVE: **Francis's design for a 40-foot swordfisherman. She was to be 38 feet on the waterline, with a beam of 10 feet, and a draft of 3 feet, 4 inches. This is a fine drawing with many nice details to notice. Unfortunately, no one who saw the drawing decided to build.** (© Mystic Seaport, Daniel S. Gregory Ships Plans Library, SP38.213.1) RIGHT: **A cruising launch designed by Francis in early 1926, perhaps with George Upton in mind as client. This 40-footer was to have a beam of 12 feet, 6 inches; a draft of 3 feet, 3 inches; a displacement of 10 tons; and a speed of 9 knots with a 40-horsepower Lathrop.** (© Mystic Seaport, Daniel S. Gregory Ships Plans Library, SP38.244.1)

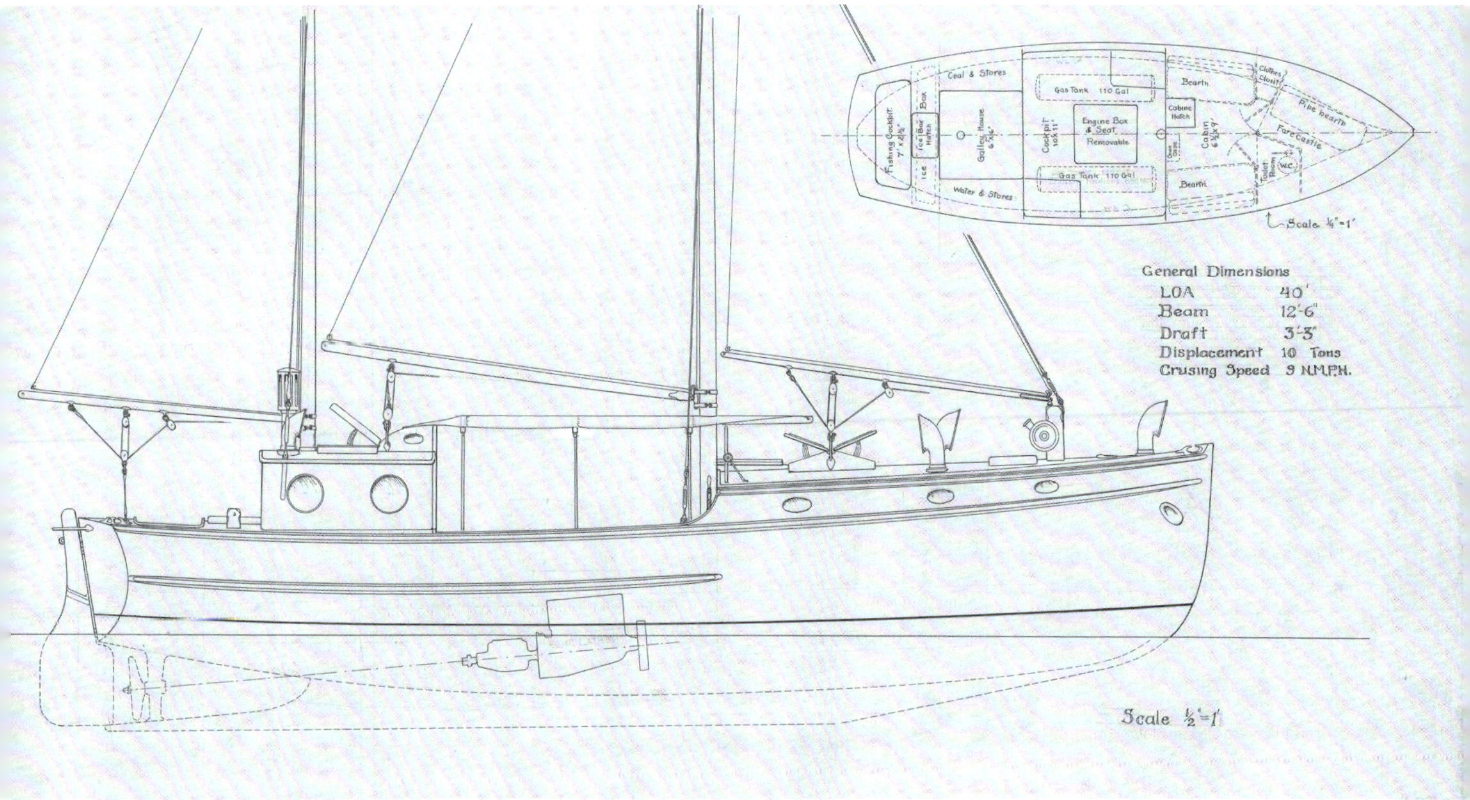

to be for George Upton, owner of the schooner *Mañana*; the second may have been a preliminary design for Upton's boat, for the two craft are quite similar. But Upton did not decide to have either design built. The preliminary design has a short, ketch rig, a midships cockpit, and the galley in a separate house aft. The later, somewhat more finished design, dated April 29, 1926, has Upton's name in the title block and Francis's signature as the designer, at Burgess, Swasey, and Paine. She is more conventional, with a big cockpit aft and the galley arranged as an integral part of the cabin. She has a small gaff-sloop rig, with both sails loose-footed. On each boat, the helmsman was to steer from the forward end of the cockpit, behind a glass windshield and under an awning that was open at the sides.[16]

These three designs for powerboats, especially in the context of the three very different designs Francis was producing for Charlie Welch at the time—and taken with his preliminary designs for large power craft, lifeboat cruisers, and a brigantine—show Francis's versatility as a yacht designer early in his career. It is unfortunate that these diverse designs weren't built. All were drawings of remarkable vessels that would have served their various purposes well.

IN THE SPRING of 1926, Francis was experiencing the inevitable setbacks of a yacht designer working for clients who could be capricious. Charlie Welch backed away from

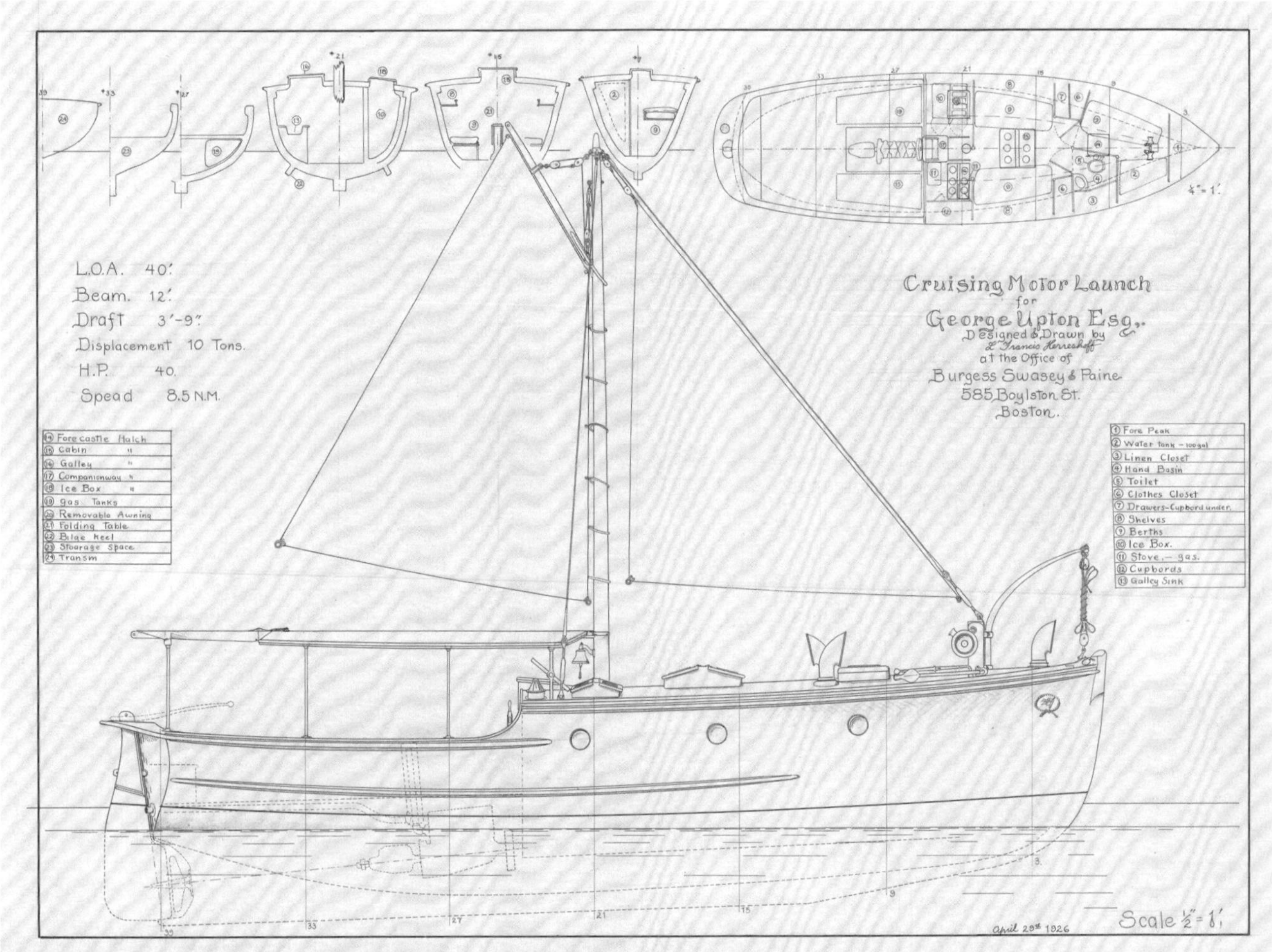

committing to Francis's new, streamlined rig for the *Yankee*; he decided not to build either a lifeboat cruiser or a motor sailer; George Upton did not proceed with Francis's design for a cruising motor launch. These were disappointments to Francis in Boston, but, in Bristol, a tragedy was unfolding.

Nathanael Jr., two years older than Francis, had caught pneumonia and was not recovering. Nat's employment at the Herreshoff Manufacturing Company had been interrupted by service in both the army and the navy in World War I and had been ended when the yard was auctioned off in 1924. After leaving the company, he had gone to work for the Cranston Worsted Mills in Bristol.[17]

Nathanael Jr. died on April 8, 1926, at age thirty-eight, leaving his wife, Helen Warren Herreshoff, and their daughters, Clara and Natalie, five and two years old. Nathanael and Ann were still in Florida and did not make the journey north for Nat Jr.'s funeral, because they did not trust Nathanael's frail health, at age 78, to the cold New England spring. All Nat Jr.'s siblings were there, however, experiencing the irony of a reunion caused by a death in the family. It was only a little more than a year since Nathanael and Francis had reconnected, yet it was to Francis whom Nathanael wrote for a report on the funeral. But first, he inquired about "how Sidney appeared to be."[18]

Sidney had stayed on at the Herreshoff Manufacturing Company through thick and thin. His father had encouraged him to take on more responsibility for managing the yard, but Sidney, shy and quiet by nature, had not responded. He was content to limit himself to the technical side of the business and had taken over much of the design work when his father retired. As the yard's new owner, Rudolph F. Haffenreffer, and his two sons struggled to bring the Herreshoff Manufacturing Company back from the dead, Sidney was feeling the stress of an increased load. He still lived at Love Rocks, but, when Nathanael and Ann went to Coconut Grove for the winter, he had stayed with Nat Jr. and Helen and was living with them when his brother died.[19]

Griswold did not work for the family yacht business. He returned to Bristol for the funeral from Plainfield, New Jersey, where he worked as an engineer for the Rushmore Company. Clarence had worked briefly for the Herreshoff Manufacturing Company and was now a draftsman at the Fall River Shipyard. He came to Bristol from his house in East Braintree, Massachusetts, where he had his own troubles. The woman he had recently married had proved to be disturbed and reclusive and had left him.[20]

The Herreshoff brothers were self-conscious and shy. They had little contact with each other. They learned of major changes in each other's lives indirectly, from their father, who sometimes gently encouraged contact between his sons without much success. At Nat Jr.'s funeral, there was doubtless politeness among the brothers, but probably little or no expression of grief or discussion of the subjects of design and engineering in which they all were interested. Mention of Clarence's marital separation would have been taboo.

For Francis, Nat Jr.'s death broke the ice with his father. Responding to his father's request, Francis wrote to Nathanael expressing his thoughts and concerns and trying to ally himself with his father. He reported briefly on the funeral and then turned to his father's question about Sidney. Francis wrote:

> *Sidney appeared better at the funeral but I am rather worried at his general condition. I think he is generally run down and seamed to have taken the sorrow very hard. He is back to work today I have heard by telephone from Tom Brightman [superintendent at the yard].*
>
> *There is something rong with Sidney's relations with every day life. He realy hasent any thing to work for. You must realize that you and I have the spirit of competition which makes thought and work along creative lines as interesting as a game and at times a pleasure. Poor Sidney has not had the chance on account of his retiaring nature to be in competative creative work and he has never come in contact with people who understood or appreciated his work so that his efforts must seam fruitless. He also has been in a position of considerable responsibility for*

LEFT: **Francis designed this 40-footer for George Upton, but she remained a dreamship. She was to have a beam of 12 feet; a draft of 3 feet, 9 inches; a displacement of 10 tons; and a speed of 8.5 knots with the usual 40-horsepower Lathrop that Francis liked.** (© Mystic Seaport, Daniel S. Gregory Ships Plans Library, SP38.245.1)

several years and feels the failure of some things at Bristol which are not his falt. He has gotten considerable blame and no glory for his efforts. All of the workmen at the shop come to him for information and he is the only one now at Bristol who can direct any new construction. I doubt if you realize how much of the actual laying out of work during your absence is dun by him. He is the only one who can answer the many questions that arise every day. Thare is now a large Office force at Bristol, They all with the exception of Tom Brightman run around like chickens with their heads off. Sidney's position with no authority and no efficiant superintendants must be verry trying.

Sidney takes good care of himself physically (exercise etc.). But he should have some object in life to encourage him. He should have some interest or hobby besides his work. You and I must say some words of encouragement to him.[21]

These good intentions of Francis came to naught. Nathanael did not allow himself to be allied with Francis. He replied: "Your observations on Sidney's relation to everyday life are interesting, but hardly correct in that he has not had a chance due to his retiring nature. I did everything possible to give him a good education, and may I say I also did for all my boys—and he was the only one who went thru the course and graduated [*sic*], the others, either thru their inability or want of interest, or personal determination or pigheadedness, failed to go thru the course intended, and that other boys do." Nathanael then listed his attempts to encourage Sidney to get more training and to take more interest in managing the Herreshoff yard, his giving Sidney one-fifth of his stock in the company, his enlisting the aid of the men who took over the business to try to get Sidney to assume managerial responsibility, all to no avail. Nathanael was past "saying some words of encouragement" to Sidney. "After your Uncle John died," Nathanael wrote, "it was very obvious to me that not one of my boys had the ability to run the shops—I might have continued to superintend the work, but could not find any one to take your Uncle John's place, so, as opportunity offered decided to sell out and retire."[22]

Nathanael's disappointment in his sons is understandable, given the extraordinary level of achievement that he was accustomed to in himself and his brothers. His expectations of the next generation of Herreshoffs, his own children, were unnaturally high and proved impossible for them to live up to. None of his sons had the rare combination of talents and single-mindedness that had enabled him to be both a prolific yacht designer and a superintendent of yacht construction of the highest order, but neither did any of them want to emulate their father's total devotion to the Herreshoff Manufacturing Company. None of them wanted to follow their father's example in which "their entire efforts would be given to business," as Nathanael had agreed with his brother John. Sidney resisted all the pressure to take on the responsibility of trying to save his father's declining company in addition to the design work that he liked and excelled at; though, as Francis noted, circumstances forced him into a supervisory role. Nat Jr. and Clarence had left the yacht yard without having taken on significant responsibility. Griswold had gone his own way from the start. And Francis, whose "good education" had been agricultural school, whose determination to design yachts had survived his father's exiling him to The Farm, and who had never been offered full-time employment in his father's yacht yard, was pursuing his art, not in Bristol, but under a man whom Nathanael considered to be a rival. Nathanael had been disappointed to be sure, and seeing no possibility of keeping his company in the family, had sold his stock to outsiders. He had done the best he could with his sons, but he could be narcissistic, capable of thinking of his world as an extension of himself, a mind-set that blocked his recognition of the potential abilities of others.

Nathanael continued his letter to Francis with brief praise and then with criticism that ended in a sarcastic comment. He wrote: "It is very nice and I am well pleased Francis that you are so much interested in your work and show so much inventive talant." "But," he wrote, and then advised Francis to be more practical, and gave, by example, his opinion that Francis's streamlined rig would "kill the spirit of racing to many that cannot afford it." Then Nathanael threw in, "It would hardly due for a Bank fisherman."[23]

Nathanael displayed a reaction to his talented son's work that would continue: praise, guarded or faint, followed by detailed negative criticism, in this case capped by sarcasm. Nathanael's lifelong habit of being competitive did not lapse when he dealt with his son. Nathanael was not empathetic. That Francis could treat such reaction from his father—the great N. G. Herreshoff—with objectivity, sometimes agreeing with the criticism, sometimes disagreeing and giving his reasons, and could keep coming back for more, is a sure mark of his strength of character and growing self-confidence. In such interchanges, he at least had his father's attention.

Francis wrote a strong retort to his father. He over-reacted in saying he hoped Nathanael wouldn't try to get his streamlined rig outlawed for racing. Then he wrote:

> *History shows that almost all improvements in mechanical devices have been condemned by people who are imbibed with tradition. Note, the steam railways, screw propellers, automobile, and aeroplane. In spite of these things being condemned, the progress of improvement has been continual. The things man will be using in the next 1,000 years are beyond our conception. I consider any improvement in anything very desirable, and anyone who attempts to stop the wheels of progress is doing harm. I expect to bring out several new things in the next few years, and am not going to be discouraged by criticisms.*[24]

Nathanael replied, "I hardly know what you mean by hoping I will not start any legislation against your rig. Why should I? Can't you stand a little criticism? That is the best thing to bring out anyone's ability." And Nathanael had more criticism for Francis, who had made another trip to Bristol—probably to get plans of the New York 50 Class, for one of which he was designing a staysail schooner rig—without making contact with Sidney or Helen and her little girls. Nathanael wrote: "It seems strange that you would go to Bristol and not take the trouble to see any of the family, particularly after the disaster [Nat Jr.'s death] and the sorrow it has caused. It seems a want of good feeling toward your kin that perhaps someday you will feel sorry for." Francis had been thoughtless not to visit members of his grieving family in Bristol, no matter how rushed he may have been to do his errand and get back to his work. Nathanael reminded him fairly of a basic responsibility, but the truth was that Francis had little affection for his brothers. He had seen a need to encourage Sidney, but he could not or would not do it himself.[25]

Nathanael had written encouraging words to Francis, but he had also written hurtful words. The important thing for Francis, however, was that the ice was truly broken with his father, and they now could and would write more candidly to each other about family concerns and especially about the science and art of yacht design. If Nathanael was not emotionally allied with Francis, at least Francis could count on him for criticism of his work based on long and outstanding experience, and at last son and father could begin to express, ever so cautiously, their mutual respect.

Each signed these two letters, "Affectionately." Gradually, Francis began moving toward the position of being his father's chosen son.

ONE DESIGN assignment that Francis described to his father was the new rig he was designing for the New York Yacht Club 50-footer (waterline length) *Pleione*. Nathanael had given this big, one-design class the gaff-sloop rig of the day in 1913. Starling Burgess had designed a large racing boat, John Lawrence's *Advance,* with what came to be known as the staysail schooner rig, in 1925. He had filled the space between the schooner's masts with an array of staysails, in effect converting the schooner into a cutter that would have the advantage of rating as a schooner. The staysail schooner rig had become all the rage, and Joseph V. Santry, the owner of the *Pleione*, had to have one. Francis did "not at all approve of these racing freek schooners," but he agreed to do the job for Santry and for Burgess, Swasey, and Paine, "for if I did not do it some one might even do a worse job of it." Nathanael thought Francis had done a fine job of it. Perhaps influenced by his son's strong reaction to previous criticism, his praise was unstinting: "Let me congratulate you on the fine appearance of the drawings and particularly the care and thoughtfulness of the details worked out in all of them." L. Francis Herreshoff was the best draftsman at Burgess, Swasey, and Paine; the recognition of his skill could have come from no more rewarding source than his father.[26]

Francis first tried to sell Santry on the idea of an actual cutter with a fore triangle from mainmast head to bowsprit end. He drew a foremast raked aft within the triangle and setting a Marconi foresail, to make the *Pleione* technically a schooner. But Santry was set on the idea of a more conventional staysail schooner, so Francis obliged with such a sail plan. Over the next twenty-four years, despite his basic disapproval, Francis would supply this valuable client with seven modified staysail-schooner rigs for his New York 50. Santry raced the *Pleione* using Francis's rig in 1926 with great success, winning a number of prizes, including the Astor Cup, and he continued to win with his beloved boat for many years with Francis's later rigs.[27]

FRANK PAINE, like many wealthy men, had other sporting interests than yachting. He missed the entire racing season of 1926 to go big-game hunting in Africa. Francis wrote to Nathanael, "I will miss him very much as he is my most intimate friend in Boston." Starling missed him too; he had come to feel that Frank was not pulling his weight at Burgess, Swasey, and Paine. And a fundamental difference had arisen between the two partners in their approaches to yacht design. While Francis readily took to Starling's way of trying methodically to master a problem, and applying innovative solutions, Frank did not. Frank would get an idea, quickly draw it, and want to get on to something else without necessarily reaching solutions. The different approaches contributed to the tension between Starling and Frank.[28]

By the time Frank Paine returned from Africa in the fall of 1926, there was no more Burgess, Swasey, and Paine. Starling had shut down the firm in August and was soon doing business as Burgess and Morgan at 11 Broadway, New York, with Jasper Morgan as his new partner. The Jamaica-born yacht broker J. Linton Rigg would soon join them to form Burgess, Rigg, and Morgan.[29]

Starling's move to New York brought him closer to the big market for designs of new yachts to be raced on Long Island Sound, but, together with the rift between him and Frank, it left Francis high and dry. Francis took Starling's side and had minimal contact with "his most intimate friend" for the next twenty years, until their mutual interest in machinery design and

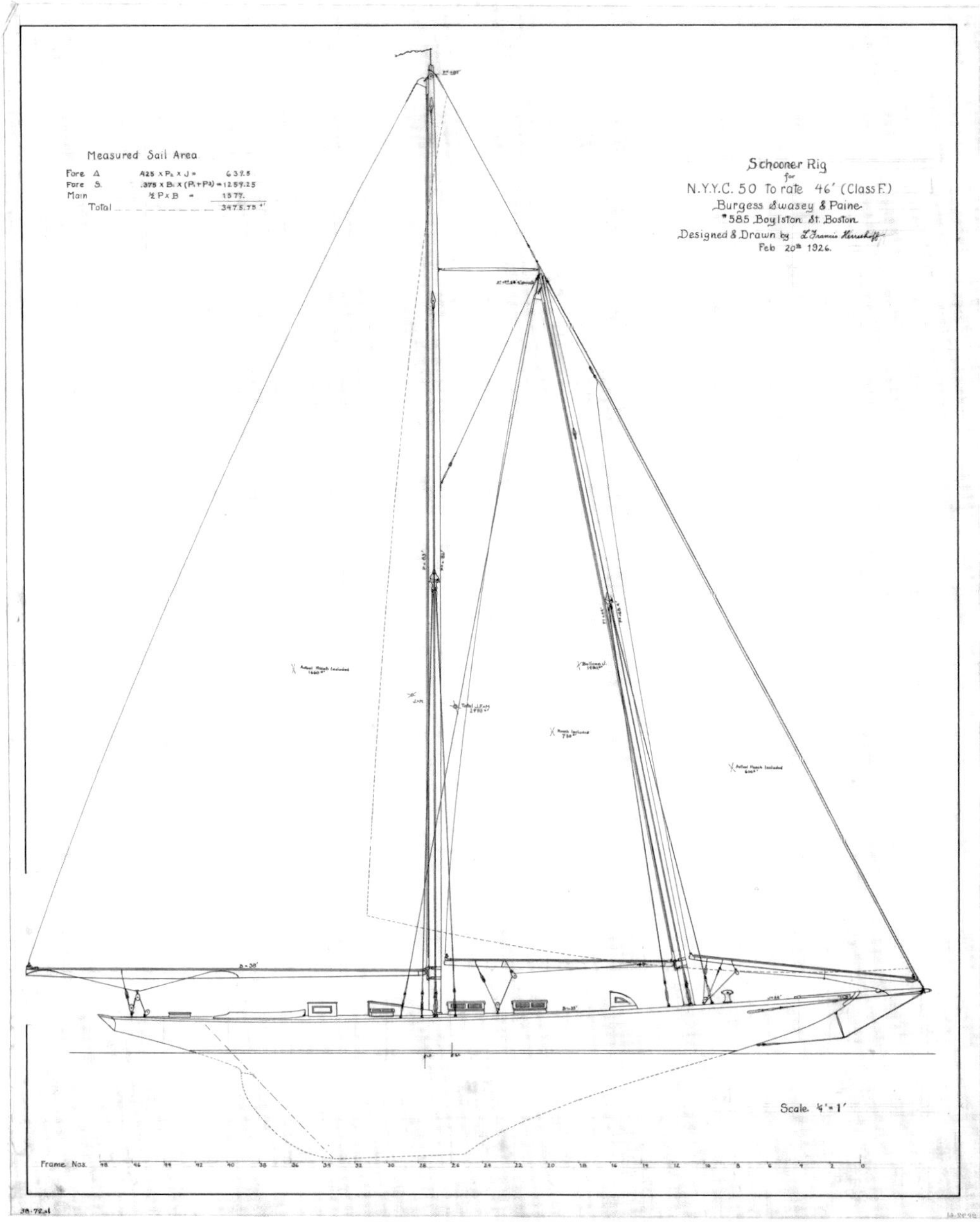

Francis's first new rig for Joseph V. Santry's New York 50 *Pleione*, dated February 20, 1926, was technically a schooner, but actually a cutter. The rig had the advantages that all three working sails were self-tending and there were no running backstays, so she could be tacked by simply turning the rudder, but Santry rejected this plan. The measured sail area was 3,475.75 square feet. The actual working sail area was 2,990 square feet, but she could add a huge balloon jib, set from bowsprit end to mainmast head. (© Mystic Seaport, Daniel S. Gregory Ships Plans Library, SP38.72.1)

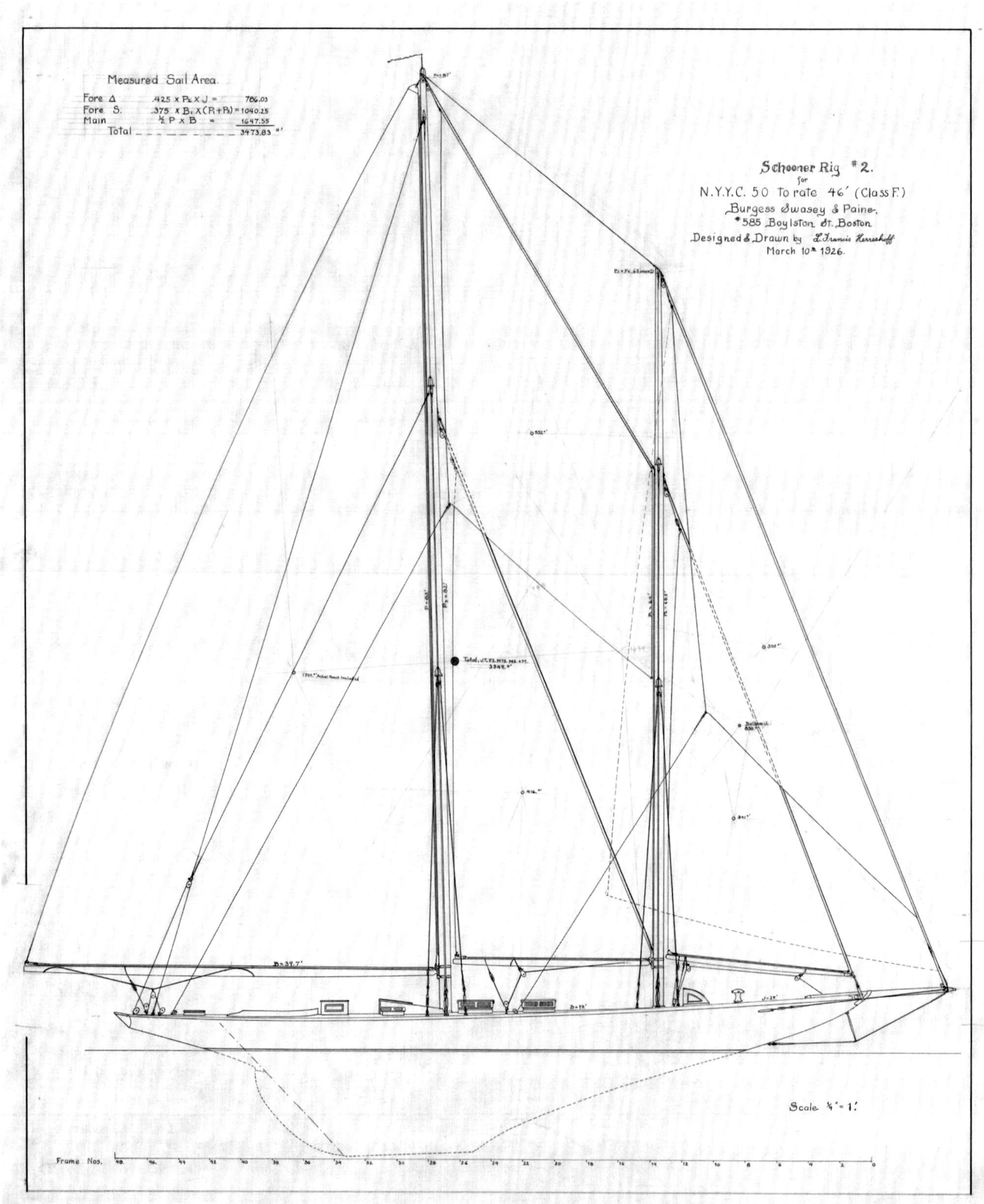

Measured Sail Area.
Fore Δ .425 x P2 x J = 786.03
Fore S. .375 x B1 x (P1 + P3) = 1040.25
Main ½ P x B = 1647.55
Total 3473.83 □'
Schooner Rig #2.
for
N.Y.Y.C. 50 To rate 46' (Class F.)
Burgess Swasey & Paine.
#585 Boylston St. Boston
Designed & Drawn by L. Francis Herreshoff
March 10th 1926.
B = 37.7'
Scale ¼" = 1'.
Frame Nos.

LEFT: **Francis's staysail schooner rig under which the *Pleione* raced with great success in 1926. When tacking under working sail, there are both jib and upper main staysail sheets to tend, as well as the double running backstays at the stern. The measured sail area is 3,473.83 square feet. The area of the five working sails is 3,349 square feet, 12 percent more than Francis's more-simple rig. The plan is dated March 10, 1926.** (© Mystic Seaport, Daniel S. Gregory Ships Plans Library, SP38.72.3)
ABOVE: **The New York Yacht Club 50-footer *Pleione* in August 1926, showing off the first of the several staysail schooner rigs that Francis designed for her.** (© Mystic Seaport, Rosenfeld Collection, 1984.187.20090F)

lathe work brought them back together. Frank Paine continued to design yachts in Boston, at first in partnership with Francis W. Belknap at 11 Beacon Street. Loring Swasey also went to New York, but to work for Henry J. Gielow, Inc., not Starling. Gielow had died the year before, but the firm continued under his name and was a better fit for Swasey, for it concentrated on the big power yachts that Swasey was good at sketching for a rich customer and then designing. Francis's friend, Nick Potter, went to California, where he would become known as the "Herreshoff of the west," perhaps because both designers would come to favor long, pointed sterns on racing boats. In any event, Francis did respect Nick Potter as a designer.[30]

It is not known if Starling offered Francis a job in New York, but even if he did, Francis had other ideas. He stayed behind, and, though their friendship never suffered from the separation, Francis's "talks . . . more like poetry than plain conversation" with Starling were ended, until Starling returned to New England in the mid 1930s.

With Francis distanced from his two best friends, reconnecting with his father was vital. He was proud of his father, proud of his Herreshoff heritage, and proud to still call Bristol, Rhode Island, his home. During his five-and-a-half years with Starling, Francis had made only thirteen designs of his own, and only six of these were built; yet he was proud of what he had accomplished while apprenticing with Starling Burgess. Before the door was finally locked at Burgess, Swasey, and Paine, Francis made sure to lay his hands on the drawings he had made and on photographs of yachts he had designed. As we have seen, he did some erasing and crossing out of the name of the design firm that had benefited from his work and signed his own name to the Burgess, Swasey, and Paine plans that he had created.[31]

The greatest benefit from Francis's work under Starling Burgess came to Francis himself, however his drawings were labeled. By the time he was left on his own, he had gained the confidence to be on his own. Starling Burgess's shutting down his business in Boston was probably the best thing that could have happened to Francis Herreshoff at the time. He was ready to start his own yacht design business. He was approaching his thirty-sixth birthday. His technical development was complete; his prodigious artistry was just starting to show.

CHAPTER 7

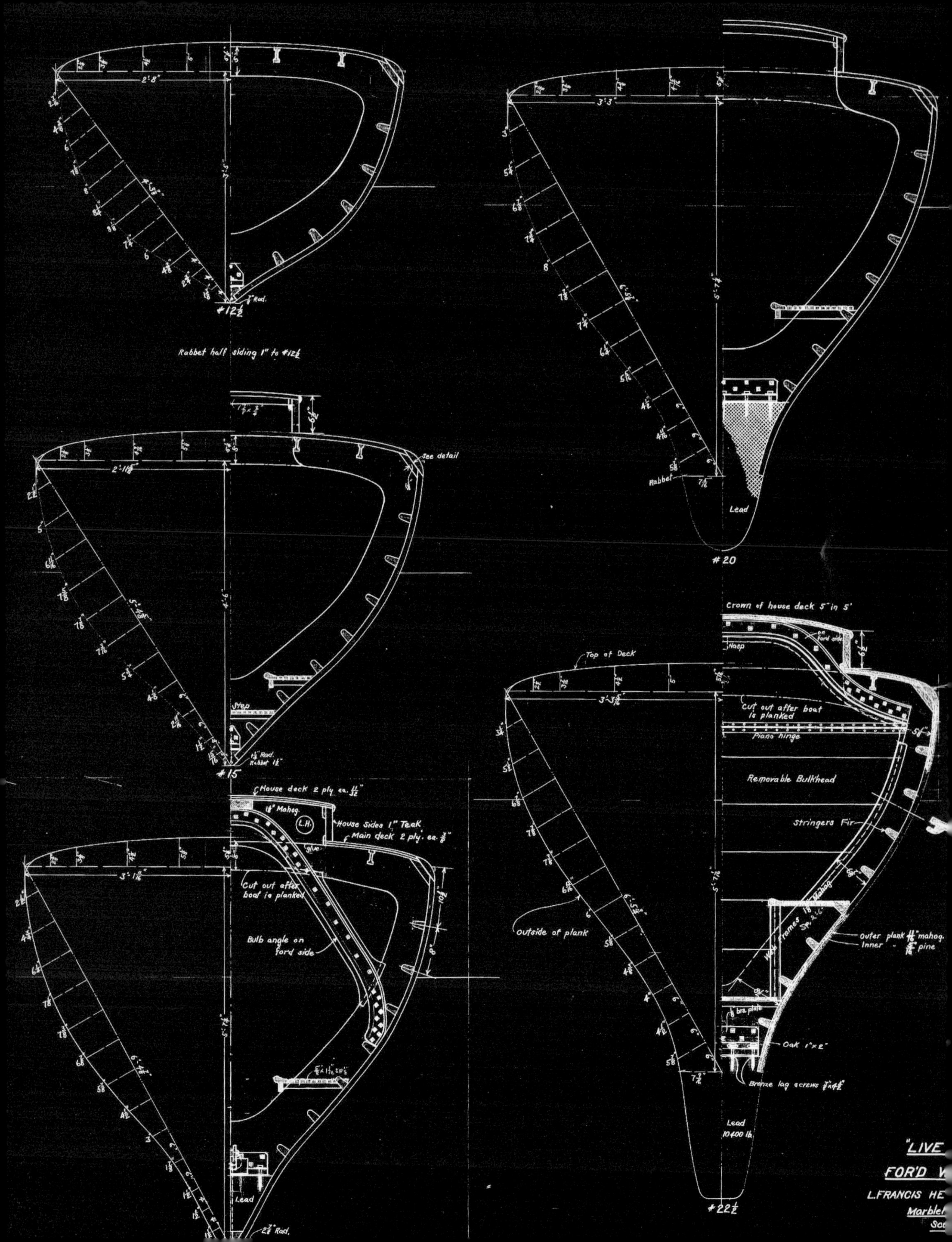

#12½
Rabbet half siding 1" to #12½
See detail
Step
#15
Rabbet
Lead
#20
Crown of house deck 5" in 5'
Hasp
Top of Deck
Cut out after boat is planked
Piano hinge
Removable Bulkhead
Stringers Fir
Outside of plank
Oak 1"x2"
Lead
10400 lb.
#22½
House deck 2 ply ea. 11/32"
House Sides 1" Teak
Main deck 2 ply
glue
L.H.
Cut out after boat is planked
Bulb angle on ford side
Lead
L.FRANCIS

TO MARBLEHEAD

L. FRANCIS HERRESHOFF
Racing Yachts
20 Lee Street
Marblehead, Mass.

—ADVERTISEMENT IN YACHTING, JULY 1927

For a designer who wanted to establish himself with racing boats, there were only two yachting centers to choose between on the East Coast: Marblehead or the west end of Long Island Sound. The latter venue would likely mean setting up shop in New York City, so as to be available to yachtsmen with offices in Manhattan, memberships in the New York Yacht Club, and moorings at, say, the Larchmont Yacht Club or the Seawanhaka Corinthian, at Oyster Bay, on Long Island. Marblehead, on the other hand, was merely a New England town of 7,000, eighteen miles up the North Shore from Boston, but one with three prominent yacht clubs: the Boston (Marblehead Station), the Eastern, and the Corinthian. Francis had already made successful designs for three members of these clubs, George Upton, Waldo Brown, and Charlie Welch, and the latter two had become his good friends.[1]

Despite its small size, Marblehead claimed to be the "Yachting Capital of the World." That was a fair claim considering its commodious, if not perfectly protected, harbor, its socially prominent yacht clubs, its fleet of yachts owned by the wealthy and the not-so-wealthy of the Boston area, and its large squadrons of racing boats skippered by top sailors. Since 1889, the sailing season had culminated in Marblehead Race Week. In 1925 there were more than 1,500 starters, who came from as far as Long Island Sound to compete in up to thirty classes. The starting line was only a half mile from the lighthouse on Marblehead Neck, and large crowds assembled on the rocks, armed with binoculars and the *Boston Transcript*'s free program for the day's racing, which gave the racing number, name, and owner of each competing yacht. Next day, the spectators could check their own observations against detailed, sometimes even knowledgeable, press accounts.[2]

Moreover, Marblehead was a "Yankee" place whose inhabitants took pride in a history of making both war and money at sea. Francis could find working watermen to talk to at boatyards and fishing wharves, as he had at Provincetown. For Francis Herreshoff, Marblehead was an easy choice; after all, as a town, it resembled Bristol.

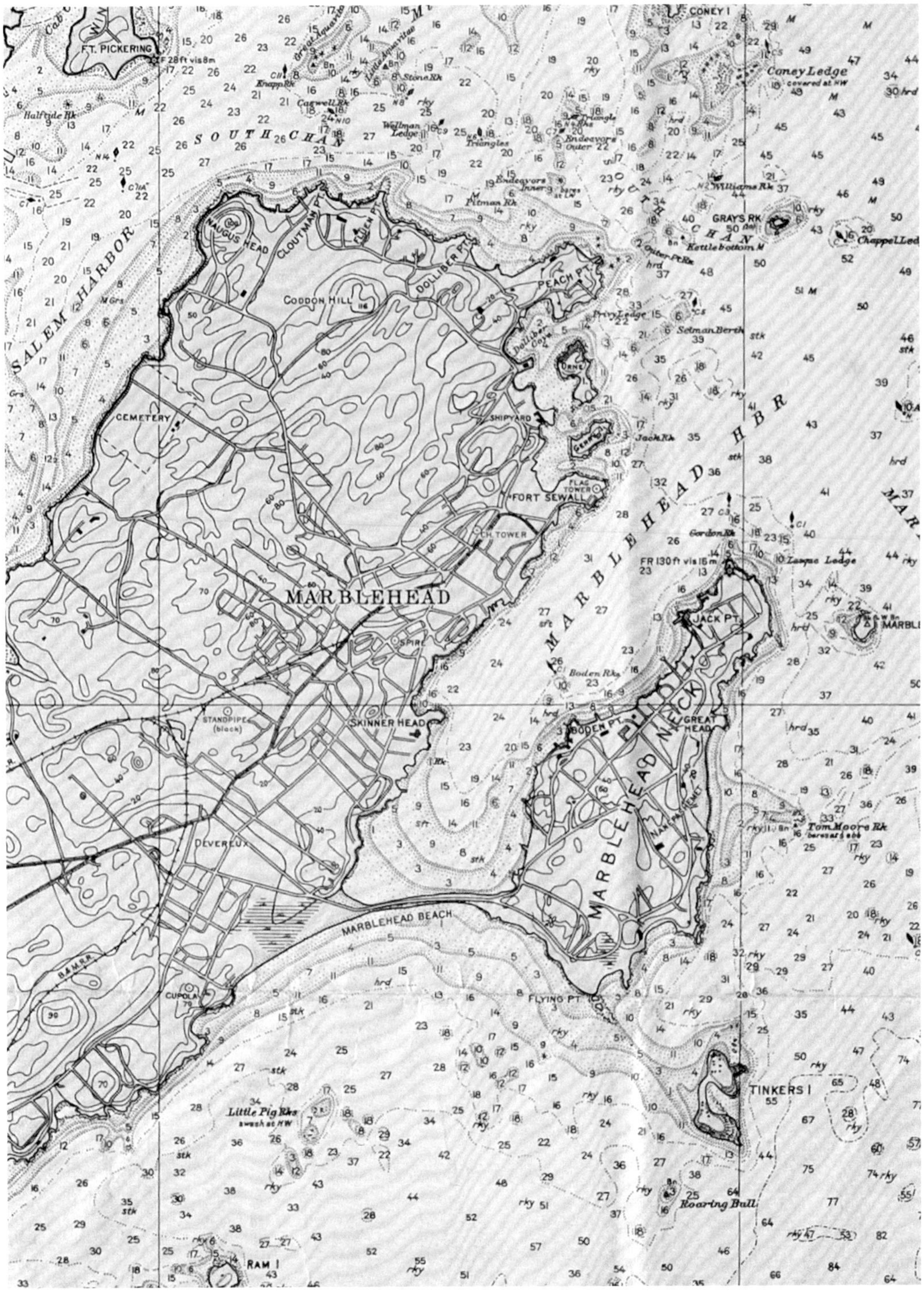
FT. PICKERING
SOUTH CHAN
SALEM HARBOR
NAUGUS HEAD
CODDON HILL
PEACH PT
CEMETERY
SHIPYARD
FORT SEWALL
MARBLEHEAD HBR
MARBLEHEAD
SKINNER HEAD
JACK PT
MARBLEHEAD NECK
DEVEREUX
MARBLEHEAD BEACH
FLYING PT
TINKERS I
Little Pig Rks
Roaring Bull
RAM I
Coney Ledge
GRAY'S RK
Tom Moore Rk

He would feel comfortable and free in Marblehead and would live and work near its harbor for the rest of his life.

FOR THE first ten years, from 1926 to 1936, Francis rented at 20 Lee Street, just down from the famous "Five Corners," where the Lafayette House stood, with one of its own corners taken off so its namesake, on a visit to the town in 1824, could make the sharp turn in his carriage. Lee Street had been part of the King's Highway before Independence; most of its houses were built before the name was changed and had been occupied by the families of sea captains, shipowners, and merchants. Skipper Ireson's route doubtless included Lee Street when, accused of failing to stand by a foundering fishing schooner from his own village, he was, in John Greenleaf Whittier's poem, "Tarred and feathered and carried in a cart by the women of Marblehead."[3]

Francis's building, a small, three-story, brick structure of nice proportion, was 200 years old and had been built as a customhouse. Facing the water, it had a view of the harbor, obstructed on the right by "Frazier's Yacht Yard & Railway," as John H. Frazier's sign proclaimed. In winter, Francis could see the water from his second and third floors only, for Frazier stored boats right out front. Within months of his moving in, the water view would be further restricted on the left, when Charles Foster—he of the schooner-rigged R-boat—built, at the west end of Front Street, a three-storey,

LEFT: **Chart of Marblehead Harbor.** (US Hydrographic Office, Salem & Lynn, Chart 240, 1933, G. W. Blunt White Library, Mystic Seaport)
ABOVE: **The Corinthian Yacht Club on Marblehead Neck, founded in 1885 as an antidote to the Eastern, which required boats to be a minimum of 30 feet long on the waterline to race. The limit at the Corinthian was 16 feet. Charlie Welch became the club's commodore in 1929.** (© Mystic Seaport, 1990.37.1093)

square hotel, primarily for his friends to use when they picked up moorings in the harbor and found their yachts' quarters too cramped. Foster called it "The Ship's Cabin." The old customhouse backed into a low, but steep hill. "At my place, under the lee of the higher part of the town," Francis wrote his father, "we hardly feel the northwest wind at all." By the time Francis rented the customhouse, it also backed into and abutted a larger wooden residence that had been built on his protecting hill. The postman had to sort mail addressed to 20 Lee Street into that to be delivered to the more recent residence with the actual address up on the street, and that to go to "L. Francis Herreshoff, Yacht Designer," as he billed himself on his new letterhead, down the hill at the old customhouse. Francis

---

ABOVE: **The lounge of the Corinthian. With its models, books, paintings, and fireplace, the room must have appealed to Francis, but his membership in the Corinthian was brief.** (C. M. Knight Orinth drawing, *Yachting* (October 1928): 46) RIGHT: **Francis's first home of his own, the former customhouse at 20 Lee Street that he rented from 1926 to 1936. A second-floor, hillside front door is out of sight on the far side of the building, and the entrance to the ground floor on the near side is all but hidden in this view. The rear side of the newer residence, built on the rise behind the building and against its back, just shows in the upper left corner; Francis's roof is covered by the back porch of this abutting residence. Francis made this photograph with a 1A Speed Folmer Graflex that he obtained about 1910.** (Mystic Seaport, 1973-3-343; Francis to Nathanael, June 26, 1931, Collection 138, Box 17, Folder 7, G. W. Blunt White Library, Mystic Seaport)

made friends with the mail carrier; and, anyway, everybody knew everybody in Marblehead.[4]

The house was well suited to Francis's needs. The layout of the building was simple, with one big room occupying most of the space on each of the three floors. Francis set up his workshop in the ground-floor room. Its entrance door, facing the harbor, was rough-hewn and painted a dark red that gave the place an aura of mystery and romance, at least to a child passing by. It was as if the door could lead to a fairy tale. The second floor room served as drafting room and living room, for it had a fireplace. The third floor contained sleeping quarters and simple eating facilities. The dining area and kitchen were small, and Francis took many of his meals at one or another of the local restaurants.[5]

The rooms began to reflect Francis's personality, profession, and interests as he settled into the first home that was his own. He already had a fine collection of tools, and his big, new shop gave him plenty of space to add more and to install his new Hjorth lathe, as good a machine of its type as money could buy. The only trouble was that the shop, with its back wall under the hill, was damp, so Francis, who liked to keep his tools in perfect condition, had to fight "the ravages of rust." He would hang pictures of all manner of handsome vessels on the brick walls of the drafting-living room: photographs and plans of his own designs; photos of his father's designs; and the beginnings of what would become an extensive collection of prints and paintings of yachts of the previous century and of square-riggers of long ago, pictures he found offered at low prices in antique shops. At a local auction, he bought a large old ship's half model that nobody else wanted and installed it as a mantelpiece over his fireplace. Eventually, he had brass andirons cast as graceful, playful dolphins of his own design. He put up a large piece of India-print fabric on the bricks behind the couch in the living part of the drafting room to add color and warmth, and he draped smaller such prints over his desks to lend them elegance. A friend who became thoroughly familiar with Francis's quarters at 20 Lee Street described them as "extremely cozy and home-like." To be sure, the decor was cluttered, for Francis the artist crowded many beautiful things into his modest quarters; yet there was always a neatness to his arrangements.[6]

Francis took these four views of his drafting-living room at 20 Lee Street sometime after 1930. Visible on the walls are a plan and photo of the motor yacht *Siva* that Francis designed in 1927; a small photo of the *Resolute* that his father designed in 1914 and that defended the America's Cup in 1920; and a large photo of the *Whirlwind*, the Cup contender that Francis designed in 1930. Next to the window, Francis has also framed and propped up a drawing by Waldo Brown of a fishing schooner smashing into a head sea. The front door shows in the third picture. (Mystic Seaport, 1973-3-344; 1973-3-345; 1973-3-341; and 1973-3-342)

Francis was neat in his person, as well. He spent little on clothes, but he dressed carefully. His move from city to small town allowed him to replace the white shirt with starched collar with a wool plaid, at least in cool weather, but there was still a necktie in the drafting room and a jacket in public. And when he wasn't working, the Provincetown influence could be seen in his attire, for there was often a beret or a sailor's neckerchief over an open-collared shirt. He was fastidious, keeping his hair combed and his fingernails carefully trimmed. His hands were those of a craftsman, with long, dexterous fingers. His eyes were bright, shiny, and piercing. He was not outgoing with strangers, but was warm with his friends, bestowing his quiet little smile.[7]

The hearth at 20 Lee Street was often an evening gathering place for boatbuilders like Bror Tamm of Lawley's, other designers like Fenwick Williams, or yachtsmen like Charlie Welch, watermen without affectation, conversationalists who would listen to Francis, as well as talk themselves without boasting. A friend remembered that "there were always people coming and going at 20 Lee Street."[8]

WHEN FRANCIS let his father know that Burgess, Swasey, and Paine was no more and that he was setting up his own business to design yachts, Nathanael came as close as he ever would to admitting that he had been wrong to send his fourth son into farming. After wishing Francis "the best of success," he wrote, "I know you have the ability for it." In Francis's work for Starling Burgess, Nathanael had seen that Francis could design yachts all right. By 1926, Francis was sure of his own ability. But finally to have it recognized, clearly and simply, by his father must have been a redemption for him. Those words, "I

ABOVE: **Francis photographed his fireplace at 20 Lee Street. The ship-model mantelpiece and dolphin andirons are clearly visible. Less obvious at the top of the picture are various nautical decorations: a log line and rotor for measuring distance run through the water, a set of one-hand dividers, a sextant. The ship model was unidentified; Francis guessed (in 1933) that it "was one of the small barks or brigs built at Newburyport around seventy-five years ago." The andirons heard many an evening conversation among a wide range of yacht designers, builders, and owners; perhaps the dolphins agreed with their creator that "those who know most speak least, and those who know nothing can carry on an endless conversation."** ("The Common Sense of Yacht Design," *The Rudder* (March 1947): 83; Francis to Nathanael, August 4, 1933, Collection 138, Box 17, Folder 9, G. W. Blunt White Library, Mystic Seaport) RIGHT: **Helen Bamford at work at Starling Burgess's aircraft plant in Marblehead in 1915. Eleven years later, she went to work for Francis as Mrs. Helen Bolster.** (Courtesy Anne Bondy)

know you have the ability for it"—perhaps written almost casually by his father—must have leaped off the page to gladden Francis's heart, a gladness that may have been tempered with regret that the recognition hadn't come twenty years earlier. And Nathanael couldn't resist adding a practical warning, probably recalling his business agreement with his brother John: "Do be careful with the business transactions and accounts involved. Have all agreements in 'black and white'—and be prompt in paying all bills, and in making out bills for work done and collecting payments due." Nathanael was worried that his different son would not be able to translate his ability to design yachts into cash; his advice would sometimes prove elusive for Francis, an artist at heart, to follow.[9]

Francis, the dyslexic speller, knew that he would need help with correspondence and record-keeping in his new business. He hired Mrs. Helen Bolster, whose Marblehead roots went back nearly three centuries; she would be his secretary until illness forced her to retire forty-one years later. Francis knew of "Mrs.," as he called her, or, sometimes, "Mrs. B," omitting both her names, for she had worked at the Burgess aircraft plant as a secretary and as assistant to General Manager Frank Russell. She set up an italic typewriter—a style found in such offices as Burgess, Swasey, and Paine and the George Lawley yard—in a corner space off the drafting room on the second floor at 20 Lee Street and began typing specifications for boats and business letters that would eventually fill 162 folders. She made carbon copies of Francis's replies on the backs of incoming letters to save paper. Mrs. B worked from Francis's penciled composition, correcting his spelling and any obvious grammatical errors, but otherwise doing no editing. She could also take dictation using shorthand, her always-sharp pencil quickly forming graceful calligraphy.[10]

The closing of Burgess, Swasey, and Paine had left Norman Skene jobless, as well as Francis. The two had worked for Starling for nearly six years. They were different: Francis, the artistic experimenter; Skene, the by-the-numbers naval architect. Francis offered Skene the chance of working for him, perhaps with some trepidation, and Skene accepted, perhaps with an equal measure of doubt. Nevertheless, their temperaments and skills complemented each other well enough so that Skene did drafting and design calculations for Francis for about two years. Francis would hire other draftsmen; but none, he believed, could turn out finished, inked drawings faster than Skene.[11]

Norman Skene was engaged in one of the many revisions of his book, *Elements of Yacht Design*, while he worked for Francis, and they "discussed many points in it." One point they disagreed on was the distribution of strain on a triangular mainsail. Twenty years later, Francis wrote in his own book on the subject: "Mr. Skene . . . assumes that the sail pulls on the mast somewhat in proportion to its widths at various elevations parallel with the boom. Well, that is

about as close as a mathematician would come to the matter, but if you have someone hoist you up in a bo'sun's chair while the yacht is under way you will find that the sail pulls very little, if at all, on the lower mast slides, but as you go further aloft the strains increase even more rapidly than you are elevated and you will find almost all the strain concentrated on the upper slides and the halliard." Francis delighted in citing examples of how practical, hands-on experience could show certain mathematical concepts to be ridiculous. Skene, he wrote, "loved mathematics and had to depend on them because he had no artistic ability or sense of proportion." Francis included Skene among mathematicians who, he would write, had "confused and confounded the sailor." Yet, with his own book on the subject still in the future, he recognized Skene's *Elements of Yacht Design* as "about the best book of its kind ever written." Norman Skene would calculate the displacement, wetted-surface area, weight of materials, and racing rating, where appropriate, for each of the first eleven designs that Francis turned out. Francis needed Norman's skill.[12]

FRANCIS could afford to hire Helen Bolster and Norman Skene because he had commissions. Charlie Welch was anxious for Francis to start work on a new R-boat design for the 1927 season, and he wanted Francis to complete a design that he had started for him at Burgess, Swasey, and Paine, for an innovative, high-speed cruising launch. Moreover, Francis would soon be asked to design new rigs for five Marblehead racing boats, and he would be asked to propose a design for a big Universal Rule racer for one of the country's foremost yachtsmen, all for the 1927 racing season.

For the first time, Francis would be totally responsible for new design work. When Starling Burgess had seen what Francis could do, he had allowed Francis independence; but Francis had

TOP LEFT: **Norman Locke Skene in about 1931.** (*The Rudder* (September 1932): 51) TOP RIGHT: **Charles Alfred Welch in about 1929.** (*Yachting* (June 1929): 85)

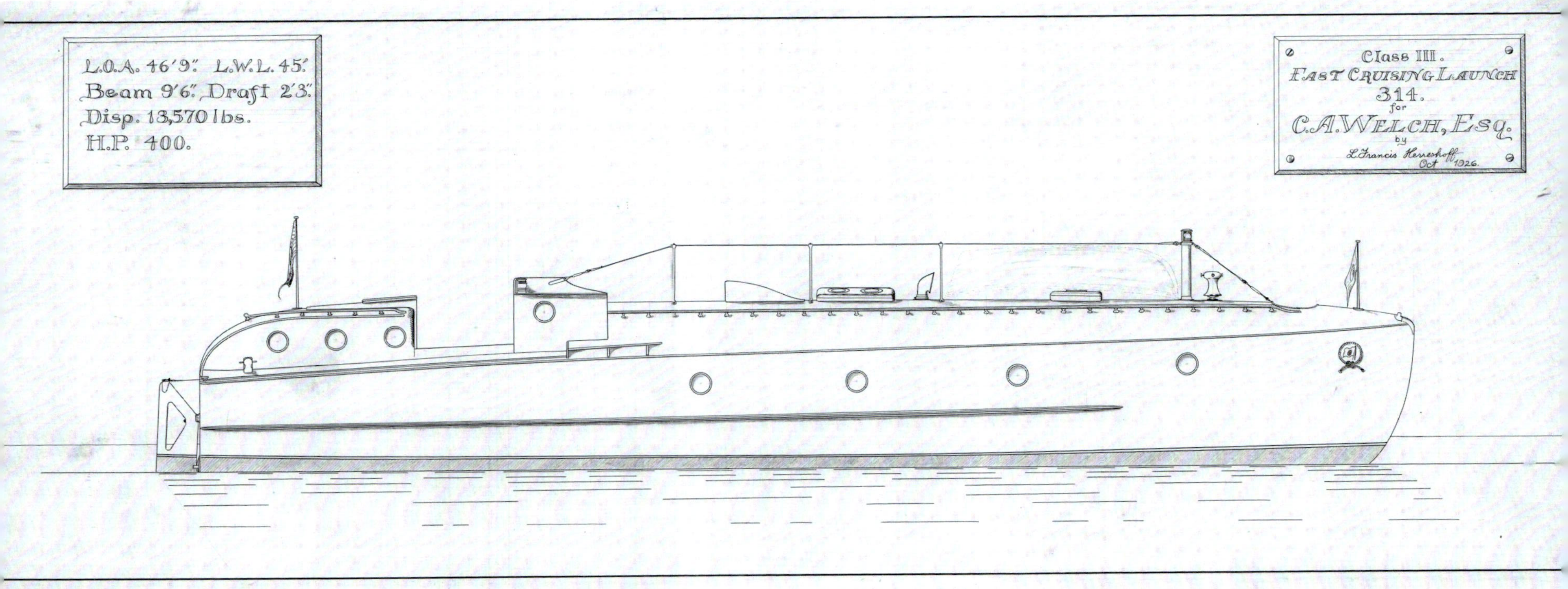

Charlie Welch's fast cruising launch, the *Dispatch*. She is a boat with many innovations, starting with a turtleback hull and almost no superstructure to cause wind resistance. She could plane at about 25 knots. (© Mystic Seaport, Daniel S. Gregory Ships Plans Library, SP38.91.3)

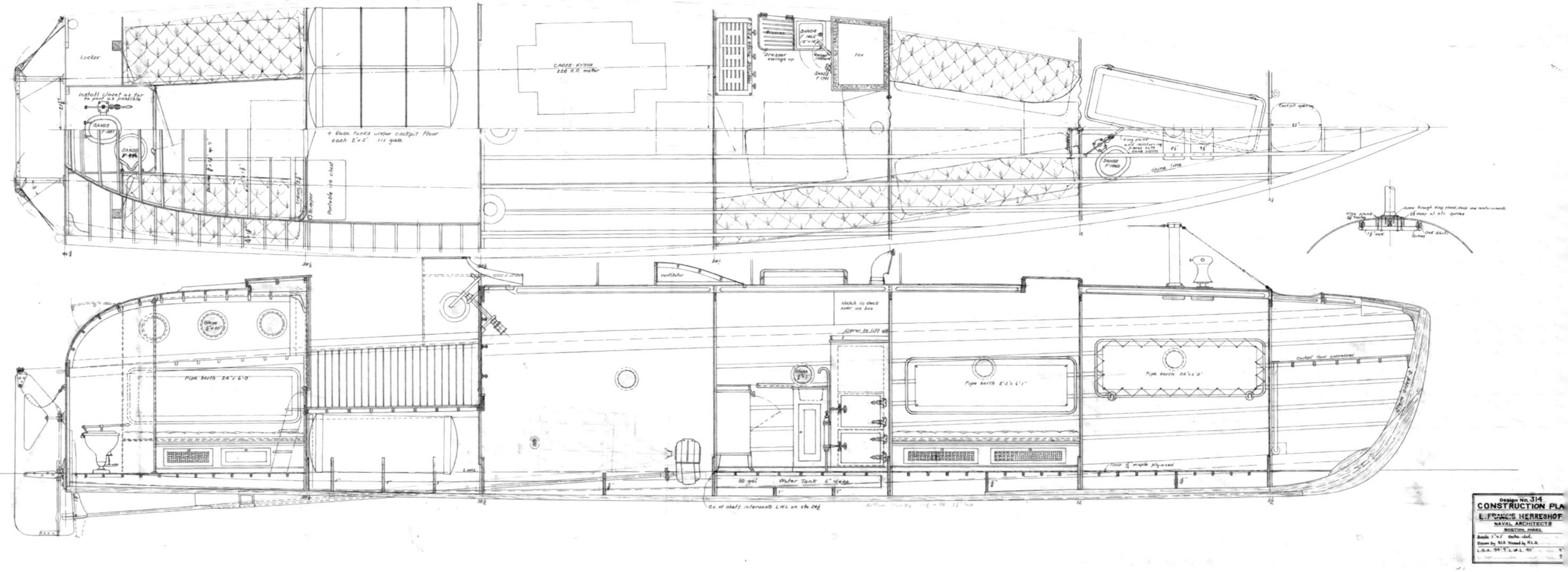
Design No. 314
CONSTRUCTION PLA
L. FRANCIS HERRESHOF
NAVAL ARCHITECTS
BOSTON, MASS.
Drawn by N.L.S. Traced by N.L.S.
Pipe berth
Water Tank
Portable ice chest
Locker

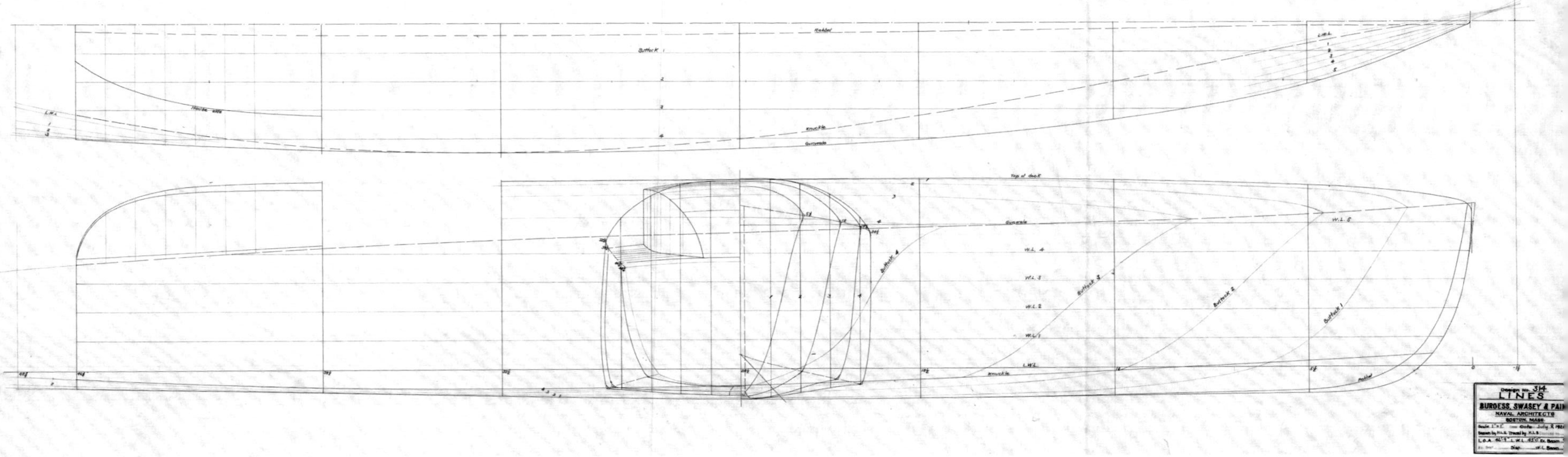
Design No. 314
LINES
BURGESS, SWASEY & PAI
NAVAL ARCHITECTS
BOSTON, MASS.
Drawn by N.L.S. Traced by N.L.S.
Disp. W.L. Beam
Buttock 1
Buttock 2
Buttock 3
Buttock 4
W.L. 1
W.L. 2
W.L. 3
W.L. 4
L.W.L.
knuckle
Top of deck

always known that Starling was there to back him up, perhaps to forestall elements of a yacht design that could cause trouble. Francis could now count on the vast experience of his father for the critiquing of his work, if he wanted it, but he almost always sent Nathanael finished designs rather than seeking his advice during the process. His apprenticeship with Starling had given him confidence in his "ability for it." Francis was ready to take on the responsibility for his own yacht designs, and he must have been excited to have established creative independence by starting his own business. It was a condition of his life that he would never relinquish.

As he started out on his own, Francis was beholden to his friend Charlie Welch, for without Charlie's commissions Francis would have been hard pressed to print his name on new stationery, much less hire employees. He had no bankroll or trust fund, but had to earn his way. Charlie Welch was a friend and a customer; he was also a patron and a near neighbor. He lived on Gregory Street, which ran along the water right into the section of Lee Street where Francis lived. The Welch place, number 12, was a gambrel-roofed house with a stone front on the ground floor, a porch on the back side overlooking Timmy Lane's Cove and the harbor, and a dock with a float for dinghies. Francis and Charlie lived no more than 200 yards apart, and they spent a lot of time in each other's houses, talking boats. Nathanael, Starling Burgess, and Frank Paine were all at varying distances from Francis, geographically and psychologically, so Charlie Welch, close on both counts, became even more of a vital sounding board for Francis than he had been in *Stormy Petrel* times.[13]

FRANCIS AND Norman Skene went to work on the plans for both of Charlie's boats. The design of the *Dispatch*, as Charlie's fast launch would be called, had been started at 585 Boylston Street as Burgess, Swasey, and Paine design No. 314, and Francis continued using that number, only later incorporating the design into his own system as No. 20. This advanced design for a powerboat, "full of distinctive features," required no less than twenty-five drawings to show Chester and Andrew Britt and their boatbuilders how to construct the unusual craft. Nevertheless, designer and draftsman had completed their work by November of 1926.[14]

One of the distinctive features of the *Dispatch* was her hull itself. At Burgess, Swasey, and Paine, Francis had streamlined sailing rigs; now he streamlined the hull of a powerboat. He gave Charlie's fast cruising launch a full-length turtle-back deck and minimal superstructure. With her lightweight, longitudinal construction, planing hull, streamlining, and big engines, the *Dispatch* could make almost twenty-five knots. Despite her light displacement and shallow draft, "she was a good sea boat and steered well in a following sea," Francis claimed. Her steering was helped by twin screws and rudders.[15]

Looking back on her design years later, however, Francis was not happy with the *Dispatch*.

OPPOSITE PAGE, LEFT: **The lines of the *Dispatch*. She is 46 feet, 9 inches long on deck; with a beam of 9 feet, 6 inches; and a draft of 2 feet, 3 inches. Norman Skene calculated her displacement at 13,570 pounds.** (© Mystic Seaport, Daniel S. Gregory Ships Plans Library, SP38.91.1) OPPOSITE PAGE, RIGHT: **The *Dispatch*'s construction and cabin drawing. Francis has used the longitudinal construction that he pioneered with Charlie's R-boat *Yankee* to reduce displacement (for speed) without sacrificing strength. The engines and fuel tanks necessarily take up most of the vessel aft of amidships, but there are accommodations for five or six.** (© Mystic Seaport, Daniel S. Gregory Ships Plans Library, SP38.91.4)

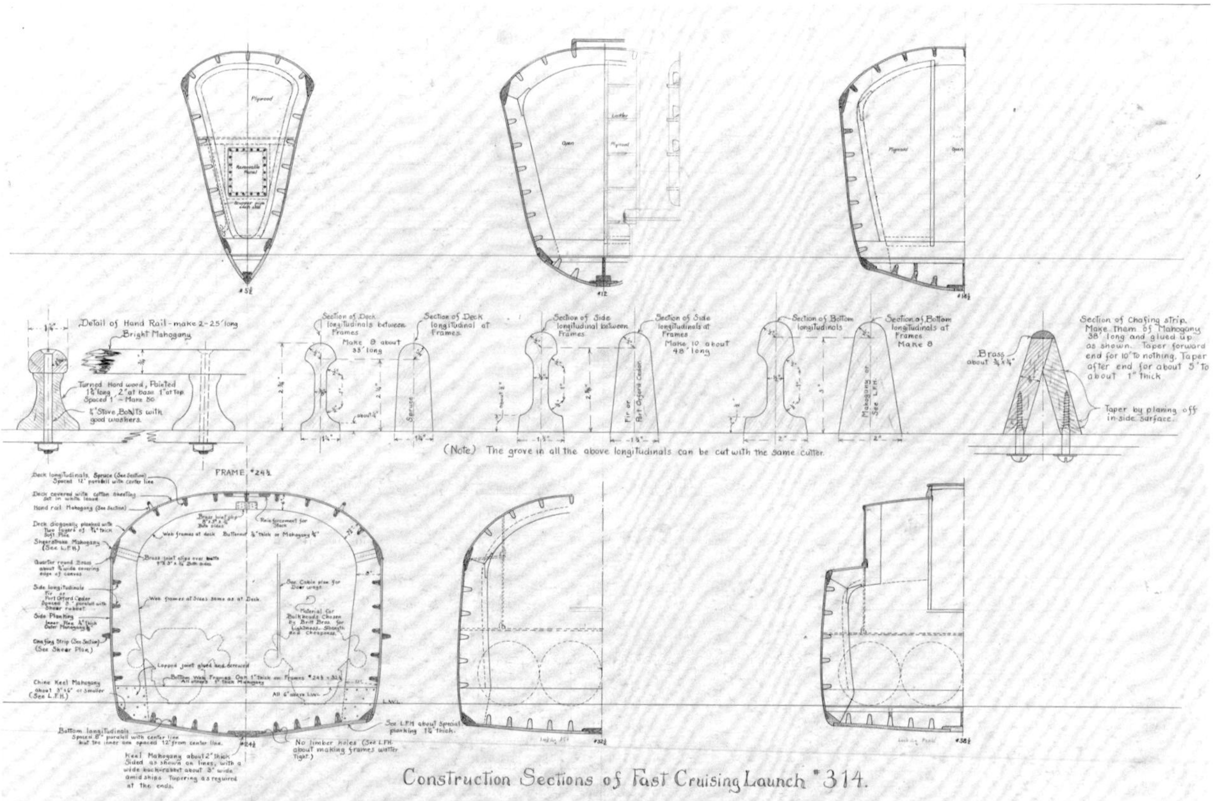
Detail of Hand Rail - make 2-25' long
Bright Mahogany
Section of Deck longitudinals between Frames
Make 8 about 35' long
Section of Deck longitudinal at Frames
Section of Side longitudinal between Frames
Section of Side longitudinals at Frames
Make 10 about 48' long
Section of Bottom longitudinals
Section of Bottom longitudinals at Frames
Make 8
Section of Chafing strip. Make them of Mahogany 38' long and glued up as shown. Taper forward end for 10' to nothing. Taper after end for about 5' to about 1" thick
Brass
Taper by planing off inside surface.
(Note) The grove in all the above longitudinals can be cut with the same cutter.
FRAME #24½
Construction Sections of Fast Cruising Launch #314.

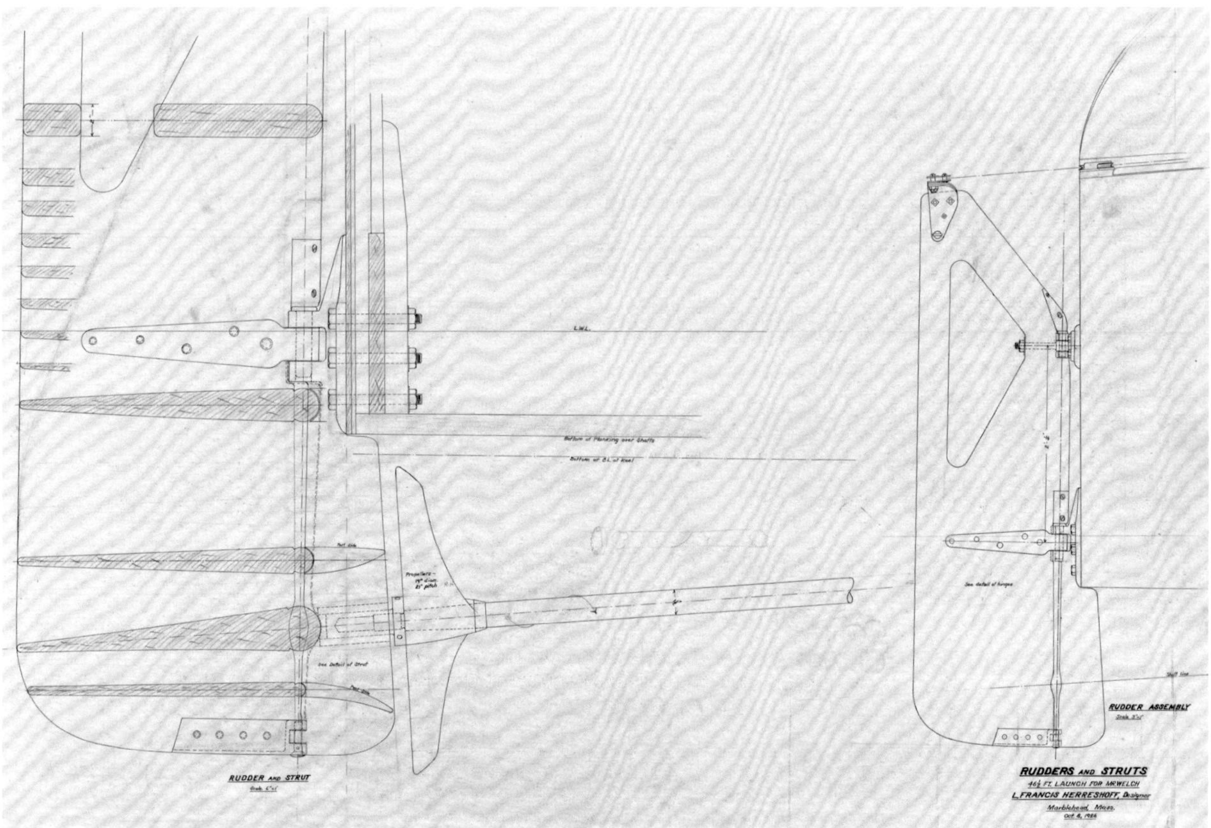
RUDDER AND STRUT
RUDDER ASSEMBLY
RUDDERS AND STRUTS
46½ FT. LAUNCH FOR MR WELCH
L. FRANCIS HERRESHOFF, Designer
Marblehead, Mass.

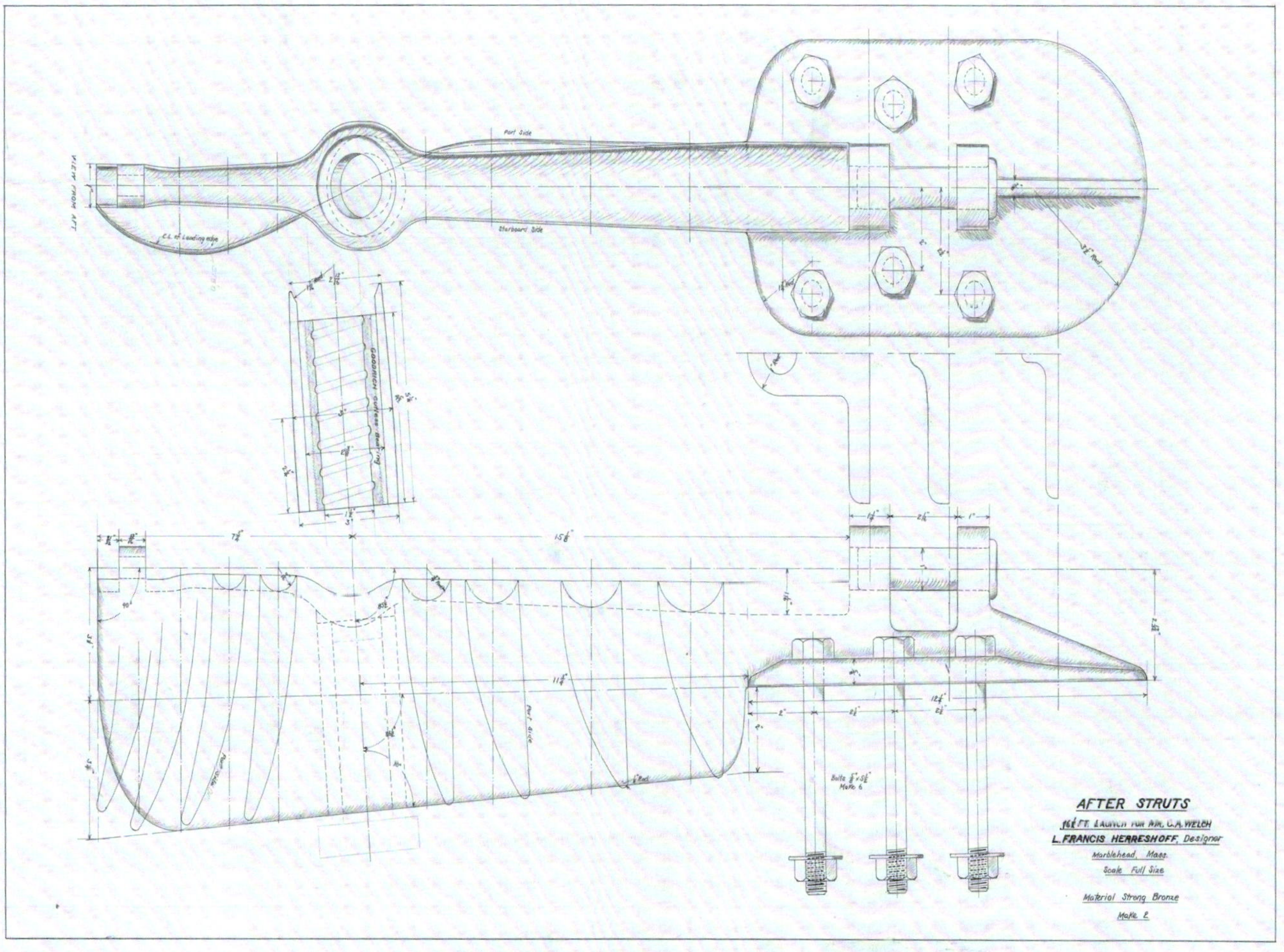

LEFT TOP: **Francis's drawing of the construction sections, showing the shapes of the web frames and the differing sectional shapes of the longitudinal stringers, solid where they intersected with frames and I-shaped between frames to save weight. The 5/8-inch side planking was double, with an inner layer of 1/4-inch pine and an outer of 3/8-inch mahogany. For the 1-1/8-inch bottom, Francis noted on the plan, "See LFH about special planking," presumably also multi-layer.** (© Mystic Seaport, Daniel S. Gregory Ships Plans Library, SP38.91.5) LEFT BOTTOM and ABOVE: **Construction drawings showing details of the *Dispatch*'s twin rudders and the tall, narrow, spirally curved struts that supported the after ends of the propeller shafts. Francis called such a strut a "contra propeller." Its purpose was to change the direction of the propeller wash from angled to straight astern to increase thrust. It was one of Francis's inventions that he would not pursue, though he did use it on a later fast launch that he designed for Charlie Welch.** (© Mystic Seaport, Daniel S. Gregory Ships Plans Library, SP38.91.19 and SP38.91.21)

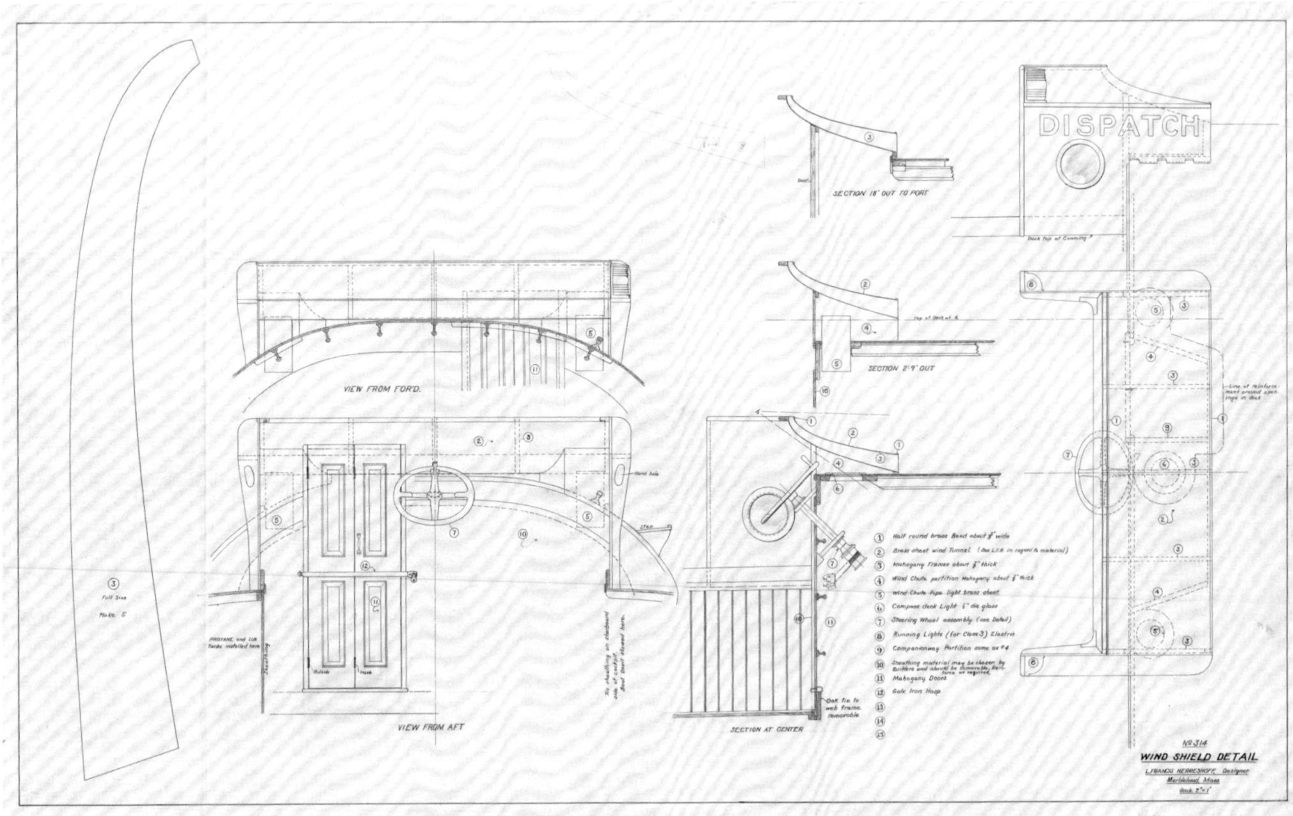
DISPATCH
SECTION 18" OUT TO PORT
SECTION 2'9" OUT
VIEW FROM FOR'D.
VIEW FROM AFT
SECTION AT CENTER
NO 314
WIND SHIELD DETAIL
L. FRANCIS HERRESHOFF Designer
Marblehead, Mass.

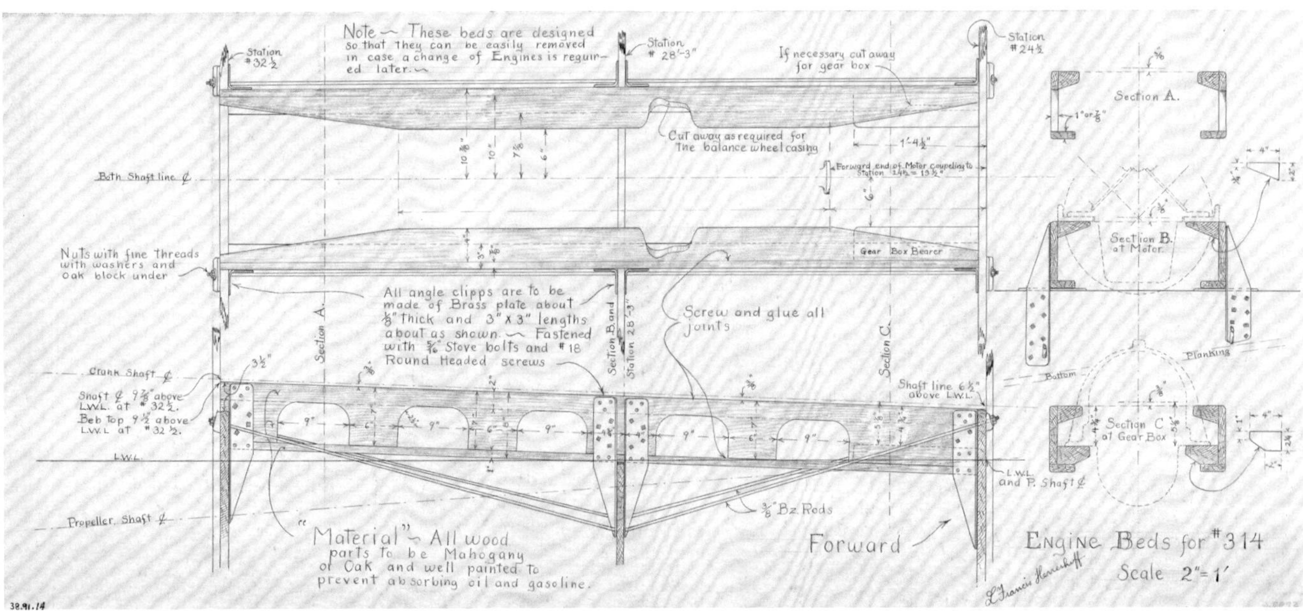
Note — These beds are designed so that they can be easily removed in case a change of Engines is required later.
Station #32½
Station #28'-3"
Station #24½
If necessary cut away for gear box
Cut away as required for the balance wheel casing
Both Shaft line ℄
Nuts with fine threads with washers and oak block under
Gear Box Bearer
All angle clipps are to be made of Brass plate about ⅛" thick and 3" x 3" lengths about as shown. Fastened with 5/16" Stove bolts and #18 Round Headed screws
Screw and glue all joints
Section A.
Section B and Station 28'-3"
Section C.
Section B. at Motor
Section C at Gear Box
Planking
Bottom
Crank Shaft ℄
Shaft line 6½" above L.W.L.
L.W.L. and P. Shaft ℄
Propeller Shaft ℄
⅜" Bz Rods
"Material" — All wood parts to be Mahogany or Oak and well painted to prevent absorbing oil and gasoline.
Forward
Engine Beds for #314
Scale 2" = 1'
L. Francis Herreshoff

LEFT TOP: Details of the steering station, drawn by Norman Skene. The helmsman could see over the wind deflector without his fedora blowing overboard. The shield was hollow, made up of brass sheets separated by mahogany frames, so it not only deflected a headwind upward off its top surface, but also produced, through its tapered tunnel, an upward wind of increased speed (due to the Bernoulli effect) for further deflection. (© Mystic Seaport, Daniel S. Gregory Ships Plans Library, SP38.91.12) LEFT BOTTOM: Francis's drawing of the engine beds. He notes, "These beds are designed so that they can be easily removed in case a change of Engines is required later." The engines were a pair of Hispano-Suizas, delivering 440 horsepower (though Francis noted their horsepower on the profile drawing as the rounded-off "400"). (© Mystic Seaport, Daniel S. Gregory Ships Plans Library, SP38.91.14) ABOVE: The *Dispatch* under construction at the Britt Brothers yard. (Mystic Seaport, 1973-3-458)

Although he was ahead of his time with the streamlining of the design, he would write, "Football bows and rounded off sheer lines are quite impractical," claiming he designed the *Dispatch* "before I knew any better." Nor did this speedy, ultra-modern lightweight seem to be Charlie Welch's type of boat; she was no boat for the off-season cruising he loved. He tried her for a summer and then sold her to Frank Paine. Despite Francis's claim for the seaworthiness of the flat-bottomed *Dispatch*, the vee-bottomed launches designed by William Hand in New Bedford, for example, were doubtless more comfortable in rough water, and some of them were just as fast.[16]

YET CHARLIE'S next Francis Herreshoff design would also be speedy and ultra-modern and "full of distinctive features," although the speed would be far less, hopefully just enough to win sailboat races. Charlie named the R-boat *Yankee*'s successor the *Live Yankee*. Father Edward Thompson Taylor, the preacher at the Seamen's Bethel in Boston, made famous as Father Mapple in Melville's *Moby-Dick*, liked to say, "Catch a real green live Yankee and you always caught a man who could say a song, especially on the sea-coast." This *Live Yankee* would be Francis's design No. 21.[17]

ABOVE: The *Dispatch* on a mooring in Marblehead Harbor. Francis used this photo in a full-page advertisement he took out in *Yachting*, as a broker, to try to sell the boat for Charlie Welch. (*The Common Sense of Yacht Design*, figure 124) RIGHT: The original rig designed for the *Live Yankee* was Francis's patented rig, similar to the one he had designed for the *Yankee*'s second season, but that had proved too expensive. It has a jib-luff spar, double-luff sails back as far as the curved, vertical line about a third of the way aft to the leech, and just one pair of shrouds for standing rigging. In dotted lines, Francis has drawn a curved strut to hold the boom down when sailing off the wind, but it was not tried. The streamlining of both rig and hull gave the design a strange, ultra-modern look in 1927. The measured sail area under the Universal Rule was 586 square feet, but the actual area, including roaches, was 615 square feet. The drawing is dated January 1, 1927, ten days prior to the date of Francis's patent for the rig ideas. This rig, too, would die on Francis's drawing board, stopped, not this time by expense, but by the rule-makers. (© Mystic Seaport, Daniel S. Gregory Ships Plans Library, SP38.6.2)

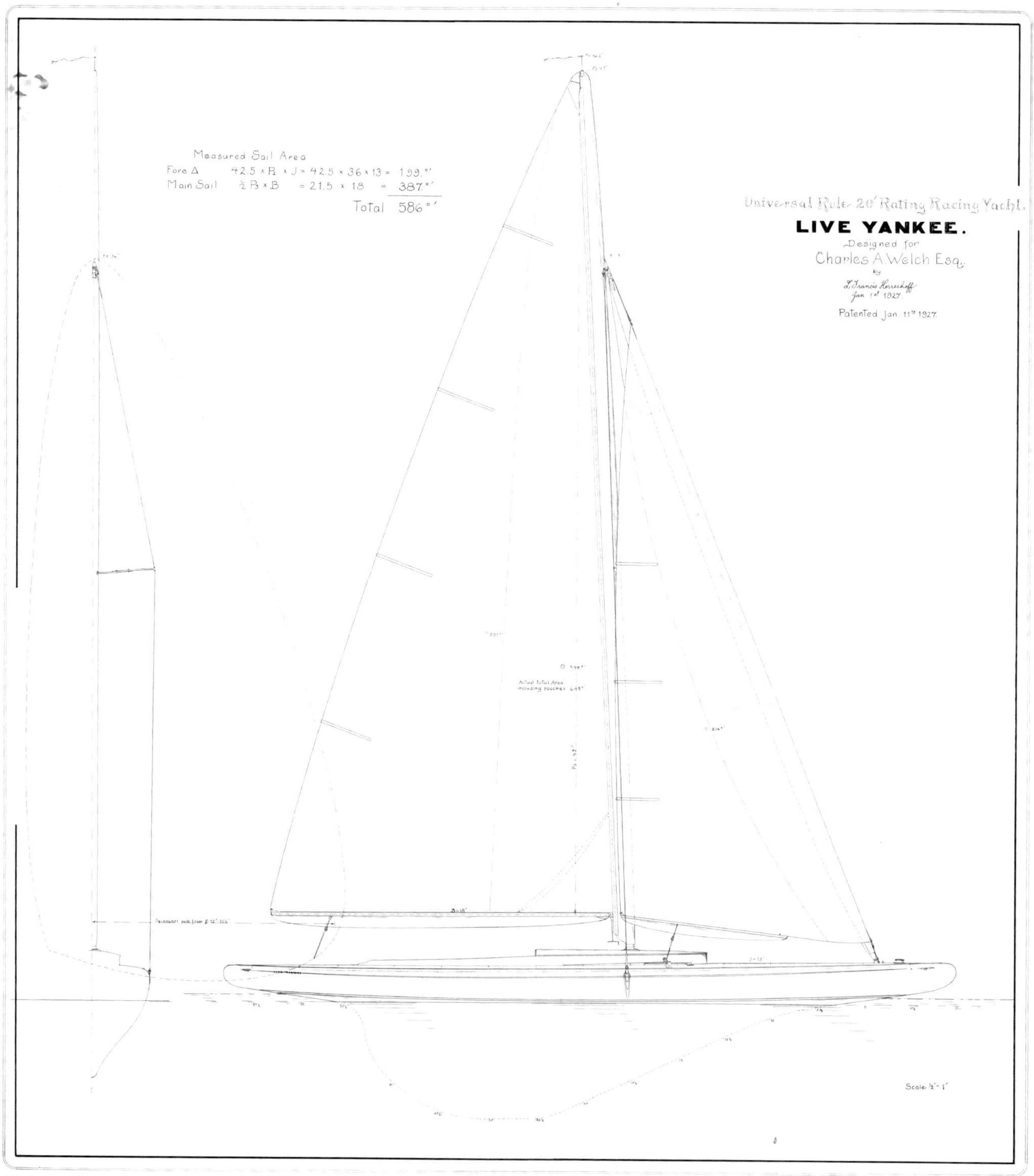
Measured Sail Area
Fore Δ 42.5 × P̶ × J = 42.5 × 36 × 13 = 199.°'
Main Sail ½ P̶ × B = 21.5 × 18 = 387.°'
Total 586°'
Universal Rule 20' Rating Racing Yacht.
LIVE YANKEE.
Designed for
Charles A. Welch Esq.
by
L. Francis Herreshoff
Jan 1st 1927.
Patented Jan 11th 1927.
Actual Total Area including roaches 645°
Scale ½" = 1'

58.6.2

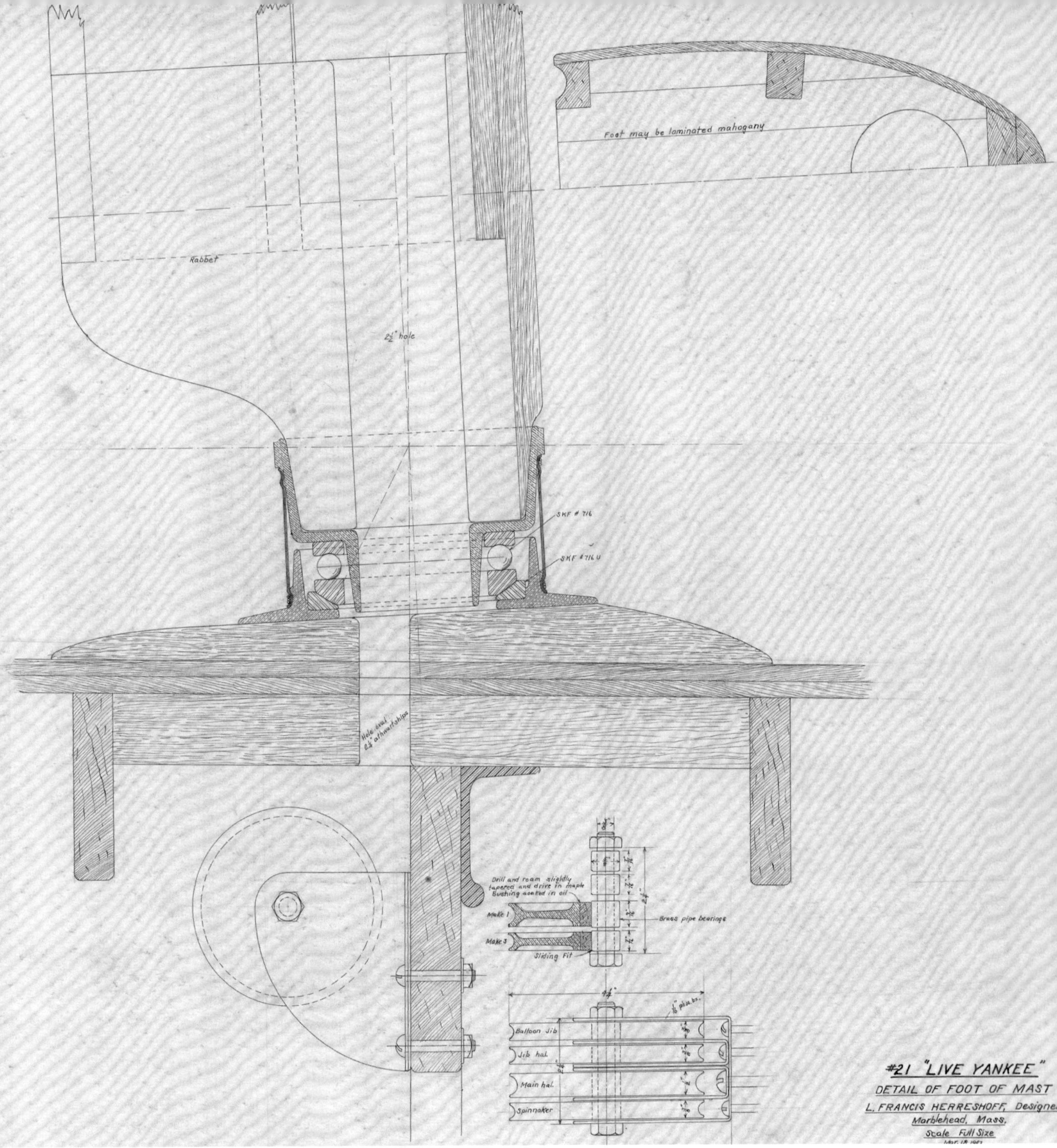

One of Francis's patented ideas was a rotating mast that allowed the luffs of the mainsail to swing to leeward on either tack, so as to present the optimum sail angle to the wind. "Detail of Foot of Mast" shows the construction looking athwartships from the starboard side. The mast is stepped atop the low deckhouse on ball bearings. The four sheaves down inside the boat are to lead aft the running rigging coming down inside the mast. On the design for the *Live Yankee*, Francis threw caution to the winds and drew plans for many intricate—"scientific," as he would have said—new ways of making a sailing boat. (© Mystic Seaport, Daniel S. Gregory Ships Plans Library, SP38.6.27)

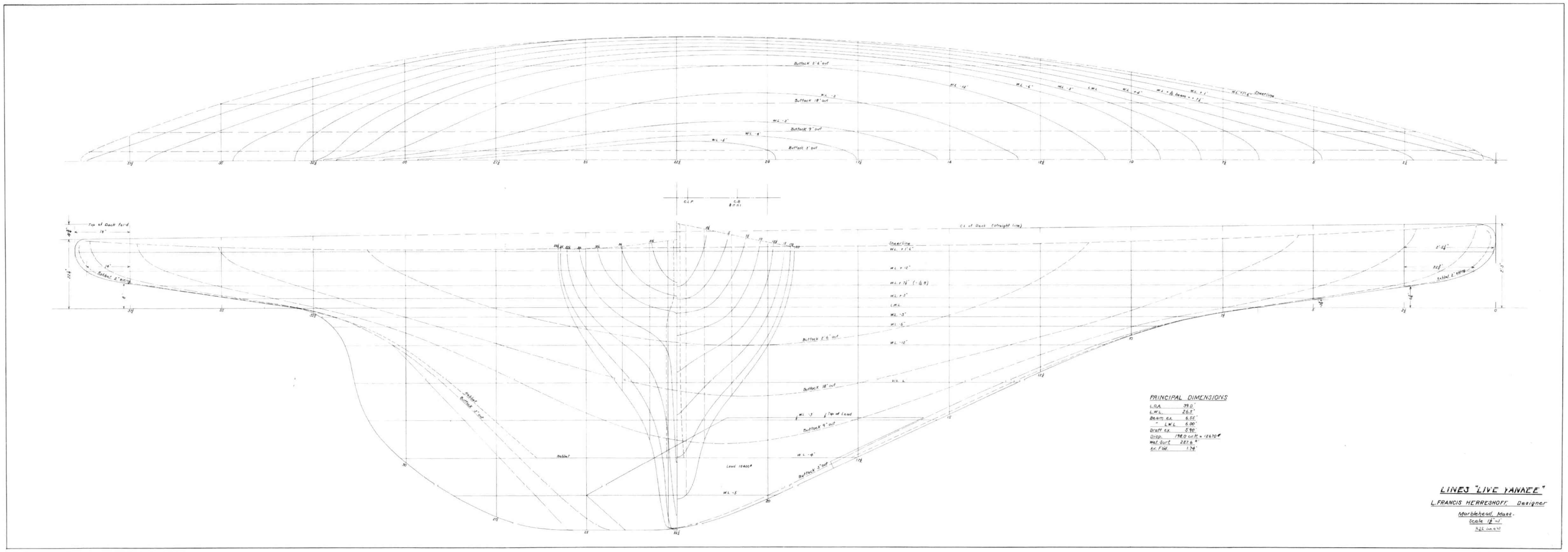

38.6.1

The *Live Yankee*'s lines, drawn by Francis and traced by Norman Skene. Dimensions are: hull length, 39 feet; waterline length, 26 feet, 6 inches; beam, 6 feet, 6 inches; and draft, 5 feet, 11 inches. Francis kept wetted surface, with its attendant resistance, low with a deep, V-shaped hull, rather than the wine-glass-shaped hull he had given the *Yankee*. The *Live Yankee* is a little longer and narrower than her predecessor, with the same draft; to achieve the longer, slimmer hull, he had to give up a little sail area under the Universal Rule. By making both ends of the boat pointed, with low overhangs ending in sharp knuckles, Francis has maximized speed-giving waterline length when heeled, while minimizing the Universal Rule's quarter-beam-length measurement. The *Live Yankee* has a gentle sheerline at her streamlined deck-edge, but the boat's deck at the centerline is dead straight fore-and-aft.

Francis and Charlie were an unusual combination. Most designers and owners of such a successful and innovative racing boat as was the *Yankee* would have designed and sought successor craft that duplicated the *Yankee*, with minor improvements. That would be the safe, logical course. (It was the course Nathanael steered when he followed his innovative, successful *Gloriana* with her near sister ship, the *Wasp*.) But Francis and Charlie were stimulated by the *Yankee's* success, rather than satisfied with it. Charlie had great respect for Francis and gave him free reign with the *Live Yankee*.

Charlie was intrigued by Francis's streamlined rig; he had flirted with trying it on the *Yankee*. Francis's initial drawing of the rig a year before, on the streamlined, double-ended R-boat that he had numbered 303 at Burgess, Swasey, and Paine, may have scared Harry Maxwell, but it didn't scare Charlie Welch. For the *Live Yankee*, Charlie encouraged Francis to make the most advanced R-boat design possible.

In 1927, most sailboat racing was in one-design classes. The year before, Charles D. Mower had designed the Long Island Sound Interclub Class and the Alden office had produced the Triangle Class, both of which proved popular. In these classes the boats were sister ships, so winning races depended on the skills of skipper and crew; the designer of the boats in the class had no influence on which boat won. But under the Universal Rule, the boats, though squeezed into similar molds by the measurement formulas, were not alike; the Universal Rule gave designers a chance to show their stuff. Designing the *Live Yankee* was a dream come true for Francis. With Charlie Welch's new R-boat, Francis could try any of his ideas for making a sailboat go faster, all at the financial risk of his friend and patron. With the *Live Yankee*, Francis pulled out all the stops. To get his schemes on paper took thirty-two sheets of plans.[18]

Francis based the design of the *Live Yankee* closely on his drawing of No. 303, but when he designed the streamlined rig for the *Live Yankee*, he used the straight mast he had proposed for the *Yankee*, rather than the curved mast of No. 303. He increased further the size of the fore triangle. He used the ideas that he was patenting: double-luffs on both mainsail and jib, a rotating mast, and a rotating jib-luff spar. Both these spars were complicated designs for hollow, lightweight structures. The mast was to have thin walls of 3/16-inch Spanish cedar laid over twenty-two metal web frames, the upper eleven of which were all different because of the mast's taper. The jib-luff spar was to be constructed in a similar manner; Francis described it to his father as being like a rowing

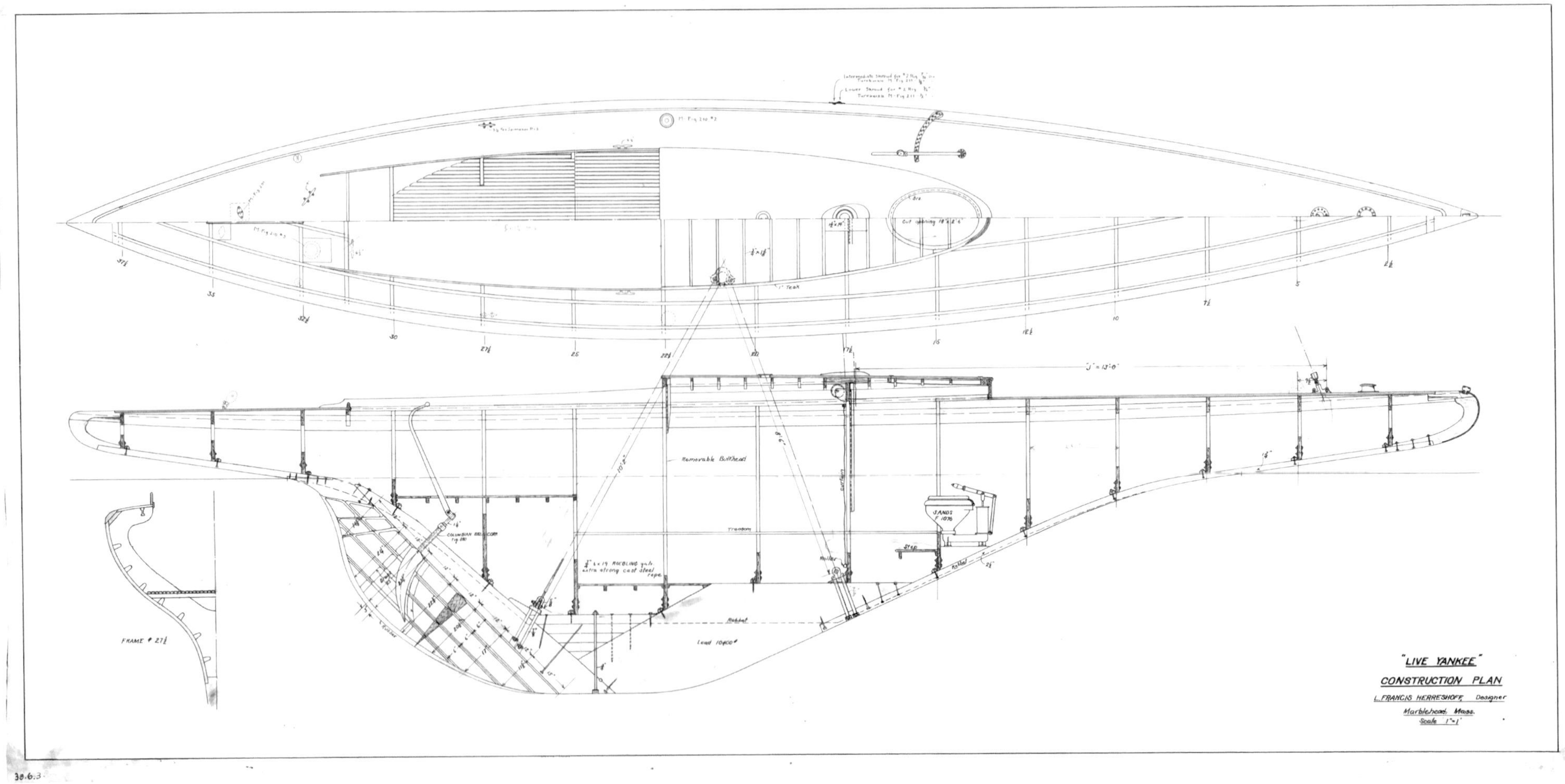

The construction plan of the *Live Yankee*. Francis has used the longitudinal construction he devised for the *Yankee*. Comparing the two boats, he has increased the number of web frames from 11 to 14, thus decreasing their spacing from 3 feet to 2 feet, 6 inches. He has kept the same number of fore-and-aft stringers, changing their sectional shape from the capital I to a simple oval, 2-1/4 inches high and 1-1/2 inches wide at the base. Planking was double, with an inner layer of 5/16-inch pine and an outer layer of 11/16-inch mahogany, with the garboard fastened directly to the lead ballast. Running the light stem piece and the heavy sternpost down over the ends of the lead ballast to help hold it on was the Britts' idea. To help keep hull shape when sailing, Francis designed a seven-board, removable bulkhead to be installed at the after end of the cabin house; there would still be access to the required toilet, a Sands, through the oval hatch in the forward end of the house. This drawing shows the support for the mast, provision of hoisting eyes, and the very deep forward end of the cockpit. It also shows Francis's innovative fish-tail rudder, made up of tapered, rubber strips connected by piano hinges. It was controlled by a vertical tiller. The idea was to reduce the rudder's drag, but nobody, including its designer, copied this innovation. Note also, in the deck plan at the top, the fully adjustable jib sheet lead; the attachment for the sheet block can slide on an arm that can swing. (© Mystic Seaport, Daniel S. Gregory Ships Plans Library, SP38.6.3)

shell. On the drawing that showed his fittings for the "Juncture of Forestay Strut to Mast," made in late March, Francis scrawled, "Patented Jan. 11th 1927," and underlined the word "patented" twice. Although he was able to include his design for the jib-luff spar as part of his patent for the streamlined rig, he had first seen the idea of a racing boat's jib set on a luff-spar in the German magazine, *Die Yacht*.[19]

For the new R boat, Francis used the same double-ended hull design that he had conceived for No. 303. A double-ender takes advantage of the Universal Rule by reducing the quarter-beam on-deck length at the stern without reducing waterline length proportionately, so that rating is reduced with no adverse effect on speed. He streamlined the deck edges even more than on the 303, especially at the bow and stern, thus giving the boat the feature that did most to make her look modernistic, or, as *The Rudder* put it, when the editors got around to recognizing the design after she'd raced for a summer, "startling." *Yachting* was less kind, describing the *Live Yankee* as a "sensational, not to say freakish, so-called R-boat." The "startling," "freakish" *Live Yankee* branded L. Francis Herreshoff, in some circles, as a crackpot. Although Francis was willing to risk much in order to try out his ideas, he was sensitive to criticism. He could be hurt and driven inward, but his confidence in his design concepts didn't waver.[20]

It may be significant, however, that the *Live Yankee* was the only one of Francis's racing boats that was given black topsides. Francis would say that there are only two colors to paint a yacht, white or black, and that only a fool would paint a boat black. He believed in white because it brought out best the contours of hull shape. We don't know his influence, if any, on the decision to paint the *Live Yankee* black; could he have suggested it as a way to veil her strange, new shape?

Francis used the same underwater shape he had been thinking of for No. 303, one different from that of the *Yankee*. The *Live Yankee* is a little longer and narrower than the *Yankee*, but the chief difference between the boats may be seen by comparing their midsections. The new boat is less cut away, with slack bilges extending down in a nearly straight line to a thick keel. This deep, almost triangular sectional shape increases speed-reducing displacement, but decreases the speed-reducing area of wetted surface, hopefully an advantageous trade-off. With the *Live Yankee*, Francis went far down the road of reducing wetted surface, much farther than he had with the *Yankee*, and farther than he would with any future boat he designed to the Universal Rule.

Francis drew the *Live Yankee*'s bold new hull shape in January 1927, and Norman Skene traced his penciled lines in ink and figured the boat's displacement, based on Francis's lines. When designing to a rating rule, like the Universal Rule, displacement is a key factor in the rating formula and so must be determined in advance, along with the rule's way of measuring length and sail area, in order to produce a boat with the designer's concept of the optimum relationship between the three factors that will not exceed the maximum allowed rating. Thus, in drawing the lines for an R-boat, Francis had to "hit" his desired displacement, as well as his desired length measurements. Many a designer took the guesswork out of the procedure by drawing a curve of areas of the sections, representing the exact desired displacement and how it would be distributed from bow to stern. Then he would draw cross-sections, showing the shape of the hull, with areas corresponding to the displacement curve, perhaps adjusting the shapes of the sections in revised drawings, but knowing that as long as he drew sections that conformed to his displacement curve of areas, he would create a boat with the exact displacement he wanted. Francis preferred to draw his lines without the guidance—and restrictions—of a displacement curve, trusting that his sense of proportion and his growing experience would enable him to draw a shape based on his artistic sense of what was right and that would

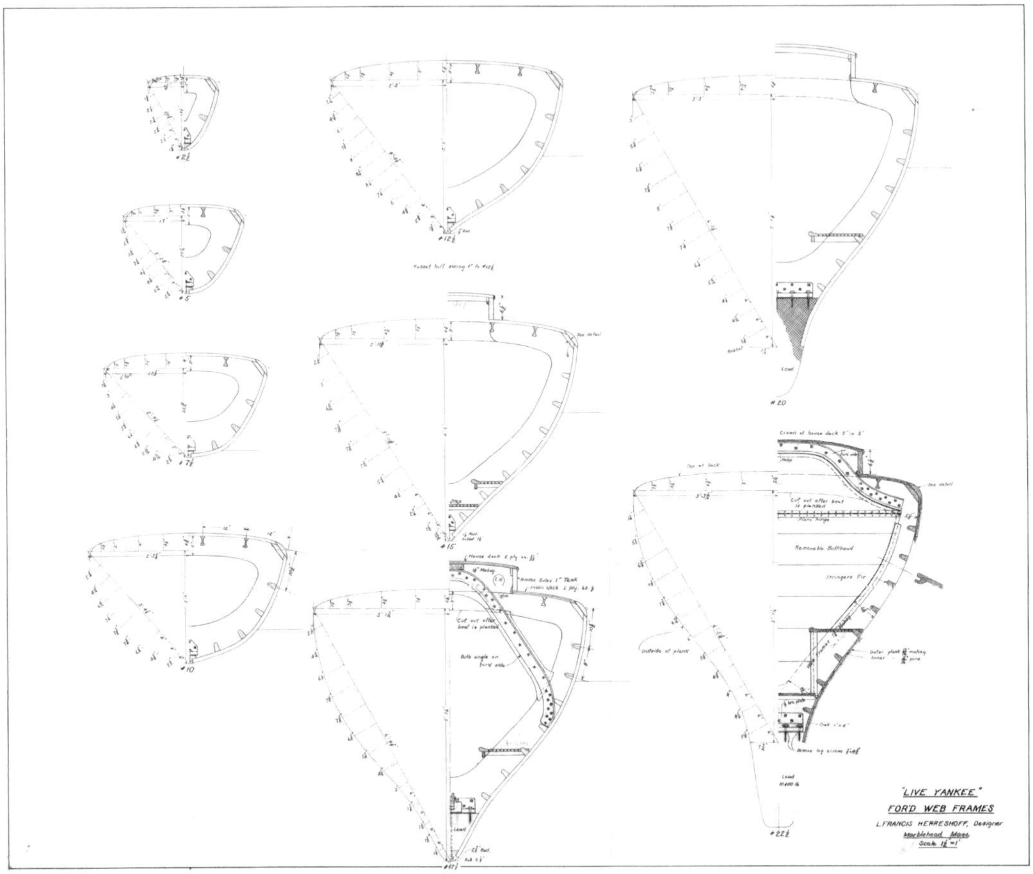

come very close to his desired displacement.[21]

In the case of the *Live Yankee*, when Norman Skene figured the boat's displacement (by measuring the areas of the underwater sections Francis had drawn, multiplying by the distance between them to get the underwater volume of the boat in cubic feet, and then multiplying by the weight of a cubic foot of salt water, 64 pounds) he got 12,670 pounds. And that was exactly the maximum displacement allowed by a provision of the Universal Rule that limited displacement in proportion to waterline length! Francis had hit it, all right.[22]

The next step was to decide how much of the *Live Yankee*'s displacement could be ballast. The more stability for a given displacement, the faster the boat, so the more ballast the better. Norman

---

The *Live Yankee*'s forward construction sections. At the mast (bottom center) and at the after end of the cabin house (bottom right). Francis has added strength with metal overhead web frames, metal to help take the strain of the mast on the cabin top and the combination to make up for the weakening of the deck structure by the interruption of the cabin house. The lower right-hand drawing shows details of the removable bulkhead that gave the boat a solid structure amidships. (© Mystic Seaport, Daniel S. Gregory Ships Plans Library, SP38.6.4

Skene figured the weight of the materials he had dimensioned according to Francis's longitudinal construction scheme at just over a ton, so all the rest of the 12,670 pounds of total displacement could be ballast. Francis approved giving the new racer the advantage of 10,400 pounds of outside lead on her keel, a ballast-to-displacement ratio of a whopping 82 percent. The moment of truth for all these drawings and calculations comes when the boat is launched. Thus, launchings produce not only the excitement of the birth of a new, promising racing yacht, but also the tension—especially for the designer—surrounding the discovery of just how the newborn will float.[23]

The *Live Yankee* floated low. Francis didn't quite hit it this time. He had been optimistic about the ballast, and 750 pounds of the lead had to be removed, reducing the ballast-displacement ratio to 76.2 percent, still the highest of any R-boat. Somehow, the discrepancy wasn't discovered until the racing season was about to begin and the boat was officially measured. Her waterline was a little longer than designed, so, according to the Universal Rule, she measured just over the maximum rating of 20 for the R Class; in her first race, before her rating could be corrected by removing ballast, she had to sail hopelessly against the 25-raters in the Q Class.[24]

It has been said that the *Live Yankee* was the most expensive R-boat ever built. That is probably true; she was certainly the most complicated. Perhaps influenced by Starling, Francis was keeping an eye on aircraft construction (Nathanael thought too much so), but he wasn't copying, he was adapting. He had to design each of her fourteen web frames as a separate problem, trusting to his sense of proportion to make each as light as possible (any weight saved could be added to the all-important ballast) and as strong as necessary. The Britt Brothers, again as builder, had to fabricate them all and put together their third longitudinal skeleton and cover it with a double skin of planking. And they had to replicate in wood Francis's streamlined curves at the deck edges and tops of the stem and sternpost. At least the *Live Yankee*'s pointed stern was easier to construct than had been the *Yankee*'s counter stern. Francis went often to the Britts' yard, nearby in West Lynn, and talked over the details with Chester and Andrew, but still, building to his complex, different design was a challenge. That the brothers built the *Live Yankee* to perfection was due not only to their great skill, but also to their respect for L. Francis Herreshoff.[25]

When he had studied the plans Francis sent him, Nathanael wrote, "The blueprint of *Live Yankee* is certainly very interesting and bristles all over with new and original ideas which you have applied." Just one of the "new and original" ideas was the boat's steering: she had a flexible rudder controlled by a vertical tiller. Nathanael made no comment on what he thought of all these ideas, but later he wrote, "I am afraid your inventions will be the cause of changing the rules." Francis's reply to the great designer of racing yachts, his father, was, essentially, "So what?" But he wrote it with tact: "It will be natural if there is some rewording of rules next year as I imagine there will have to be from time to time as new developments come out."[26]

In the midst of designing the *Live Yankee*, Francis made a trip to New York City. He went to the Motorboat Show and attended a dinner at the New York Yacht Club where Junius S. Morgan Jr., grandson of J. Pierpont Morgan, hosted a discussion on the future of the R Class. "We had a very pleasant evening," Francis wrote his father. The tendency was to add restrictions to the Universal Rule to plug loopholes so that there could be no "cheating" the rule with freakish designs, but Francis resisted such lawyering as preventing improvements in future designs. Not one to speak up in public, he would doubtless have remained silent about all the new ideas he had for the *Live Yankee*.[27]

But Charlie Welch realized that the New York Yacht Club would have to have its say about the

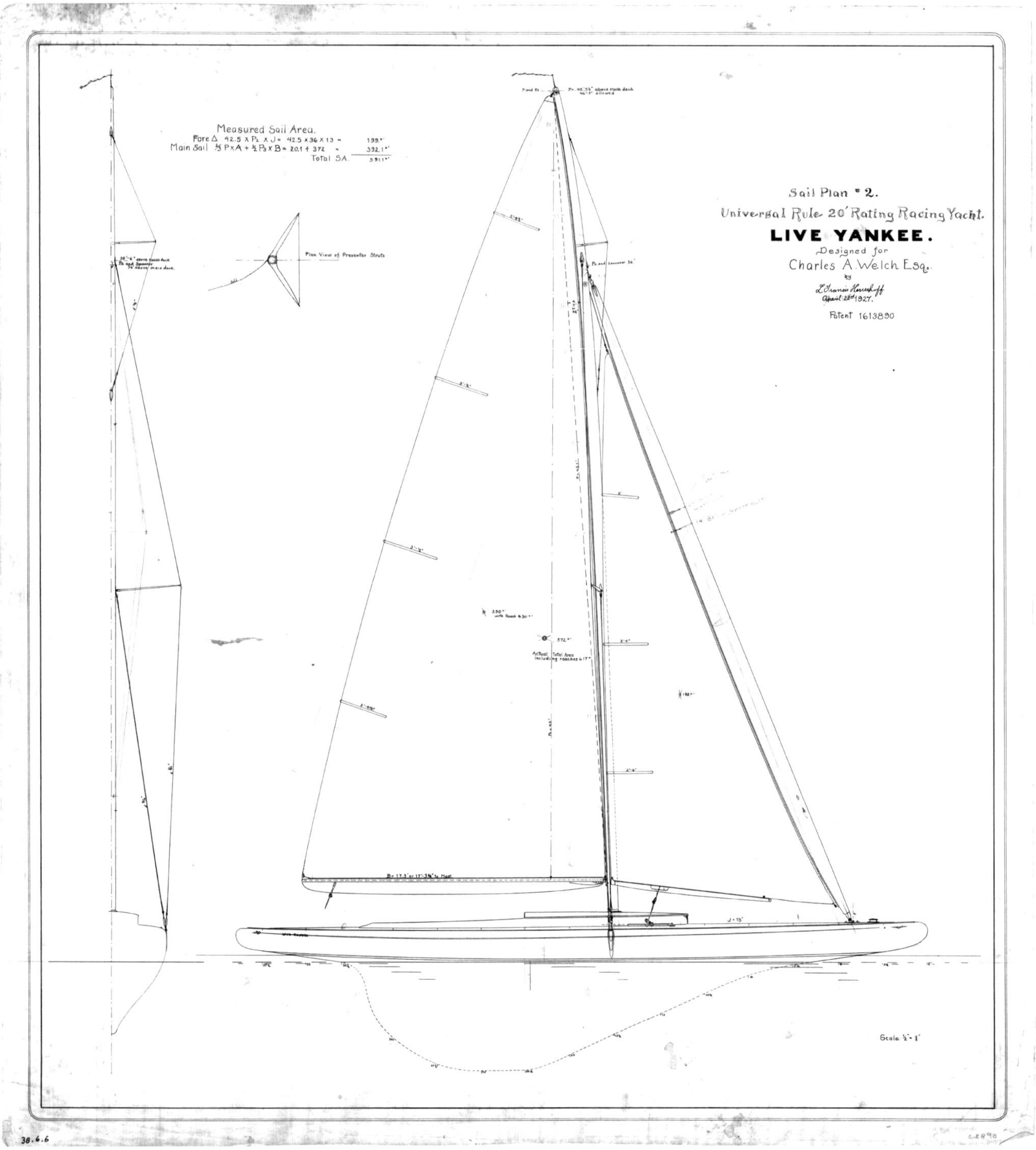
Measured Sail Area.
Fore Δ 42.5 x P2 x J = 42.5 x 36 x 13 = 199.□'
Main Sail ⅔ P x A + ½ P3 x B = 20.1 + 372 = 392.1□'
Total SA. 591.1□'
Plan View of Preventer Struts
Sail Plan # 2.
Universal Rule 20' Rating Racing Yacht.
LIVE YANKEE.
Designed for
Charles A. Welch Esq.
by
L. Francis Herreshoff
April 28th 1927.
Patent 1613890
J = 13'
Scale ½" = 1'
38.6.6

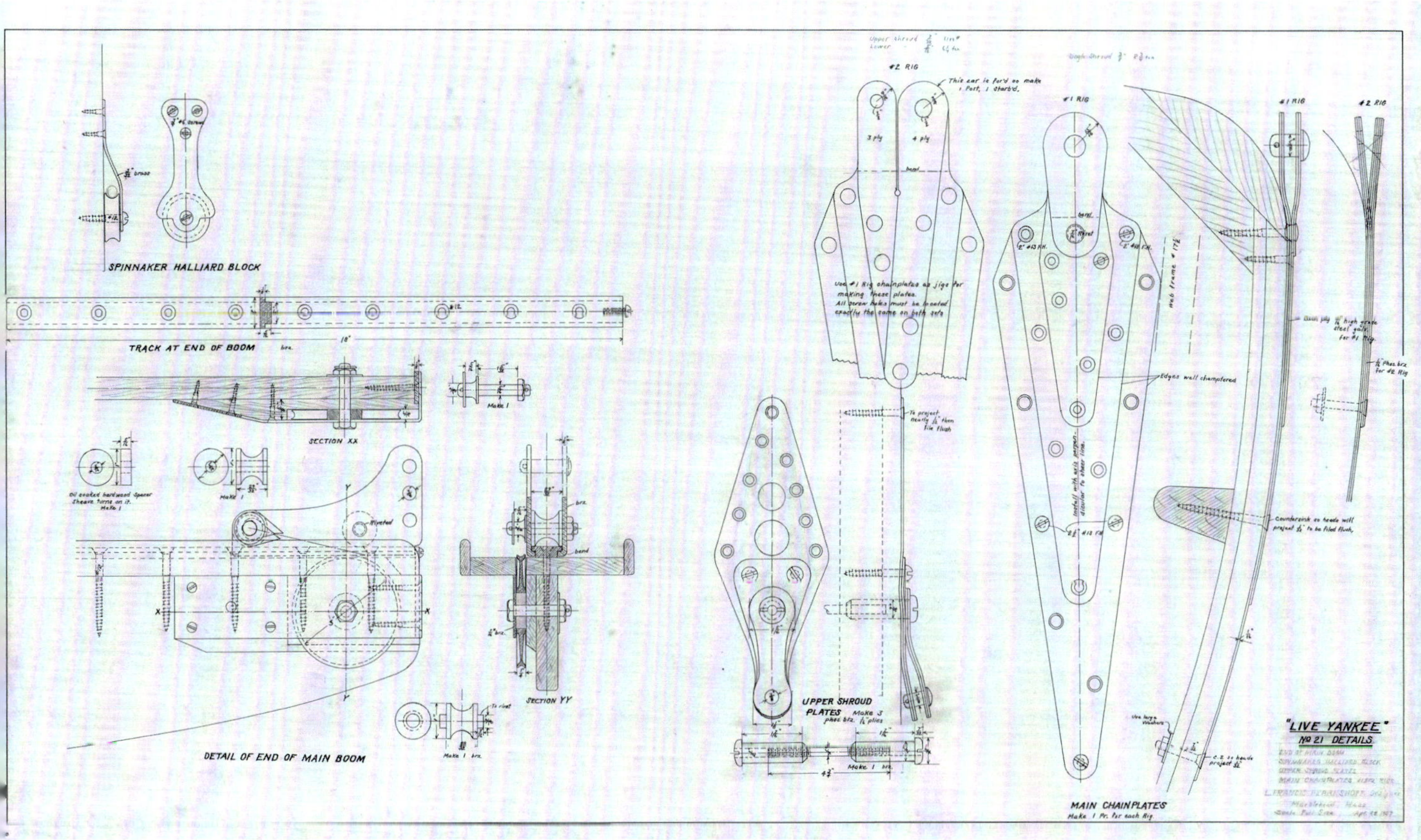

LEFT: **When the patented rig was outlawed, Francis drew this sail plan for the *Live Yankee*, dated April 22, 1927. Gone are the streamlined double-luffs, but there was no objection to the jib-luff spar, so Francis kept it to eliminate running backstays. To support the curved masthead, he designed two struts instead of one, placed at an angle so that their stays would pull sideways as well as forward. This V-shaped arrangement of jumper stays, as they would come to be called, became standard practice.** (© Mystic Seaport, Daniel S. Gregory Ships Plans Library, SP38.6.6) ABOVE: **The *Live Yankee*'s chain plates. In the right half of the plan, the two drawings in the center are for the original rig with one shroud on each side; the two outside drawings show the changed arrangement to take two shrouds on each side to support the new, slimmer mast. These are the chain plates that Francis developed to be light and strong with minimum resistance to water flowing by them when the boat is heeled. The wide, overlapping plates are only 1/16-inch thick; Francis specified "high-grade" galvanized steel for the original chain plates, but changed to "phosphor bronze" for the new rig. It is surprising that he didn't repeat the *Yankee*'s inside chain plates on the *Live Yankee*. The right-hand drawings show how the *Live Yankee*'s deck edge was curved to reduce water resistance when the "rail" went under, and to reduce wind resistance of the hull when beating to windward. In the left half of the plan, we see details of the after end of the T-shaped boom.** (© Mystic Seaport, Daniel S. Gregory Ships Plans Library, SP38.6.10)

new and different features of his R-boat, so one day he rolled up the plans and took them off to New York. When he showed the *Live Yankee*'s plans to the members of the committee who were responsible for interpreting the provisions and intent of the Universal Rule, they commented on one of Francis's "new and original ideas." A couple of months before the boat was to be launched, they outlawed Francis's double-luff sails and rotating mast (fulfilling Nathanael's prophecy).[28]

Francis felt betrayed by Charlie's action. He was vulnerable and could misinterpret people's motives as being against him. Fortunately, his friendship with Charlie Welch was strong enough to withstand this imagined assault.[29]

But Francis had to design a new rig in a hurry. There was no objection to the jib-luff spar, so he kept it. He couldn't keep the rotating mast, but he left the new mast stepped on deck, because there wasn't time to design and build a new mast step down inside the boat. Thus, the *Live Yankee* became the first racing sailboat with a deck-stepped mast, though the next year, and for the rest of her life, she had a conventional mast step below deck.[30]

The jib-luff spar turned out to be a problem; it slatted violently when the boat was moored in a strong breeze. Moreover, in the early racing of the boat, Charlie felt that the jib spar's windage was detrimental. So Francis drew a third sail plan, with a mere forestay, held straight by running backstays led well aft, as on the *Yankee*. He added a permanent backstay from masthead to stern and another pair of shrouds. Making these between-races changes to the *Live Yankee*'s rig became a race against time, and Francis helped by turning out a few fittings, such as turnbuckles, on his Hjorth lathe.

When the jib-luff spar was replaced by a forestay, backstays, and additional shrouds, Francis had also intended that the mast be beefed up, but the *Live Yankee* raced again before that could be accomplished, with the result that ten minutes before the start of the Fourth of July race, in a fresh northwester, the mast "crumpled into what seemed 50 pieces." This description of the dismasting was telling, in terms of Francis's engineering by eye, instead of by mathematics. His sense of proportion for the related sizes of the different parts of a rig was so good that when there was a failure, there was general disintegration, rather than the more typical single break. Two other R-boats were dismasted as well that day. Francis, who was crewing in another boat, reported that the wind was "the hardest in which I have ever raced an R-boat in Marblehead." Northwesters in New England being what they are, a fresh one will have brief gusts of gale force. Francis raced often in R-boats, noting the performance of boats of other designers as well as his own.[31]

In her early races, the startling-looking *Live Yankee* didn't startle anyone with her speed. In her first three races in the R Class, she was seventh out of eight, seventh of nine, and eighth of nine. True, she was racing with a new rig that Charlie Welch hadn't had time to test and tune, but she was also a different sort of boat to sail, with her flexible rudder and vertical tiller. A later owner wrote to Francis that "It took some time to become acquainted with her peculiarities." And Francis agreed, replying, "She was a very difficult boat indeed to get going," and he added, "and always was very erratic."[32]

One of the *Live Yankee*'s idiosyncrasies, with her deep triangular hull form, low freeboard, and rounded off ends and deck-edges, might have been to throw spray at her crew, sailing her to windward

---

RIGHT: **The *Live Yankee* working to windward in a gentle breeze off Marblehead. The boat's deep cockpit allows even the crew to be streamlined, down out of the wind.** (Willard. B. Jackson photo 4197, Charles H. W. Foster Collection, Hart Nautical Collections, MIT Museum, Cambridge, Massachusetts)

in a chop. Or, conceivably, such a low, heavy, open boat could dive under a wave and not come back up. Perhaps a boat that looked like a submarine might act like one? The Universal Rule sought to prevent such a catastrophe by prescribing a minimum volume of hull, including reserve buoyancy above the waterline, relative to sail area. Francis did make sure that the boat he had drawn could pass this mathematical safety test. In any event, he wrote that "She was not particularly wet under sail for some reason or other," but that she could be "wet under some conditions," and that "under tow in a sea and wind she was very, very wet."[33]

The *Live Yankee*'s new gadgets and resemblance to a submarine inspired a bit of mocking Marblehead doggerel:

> *Some likes sloops that sail like hell,*
> *though boats ain't what they are*
> *With double luffs and spinnin' masts,*
> *and the jib stay a wooden bar,*
> *But I wants gear that looks like gear,*
> *an' a spar that looks like a spar.*
> *Nor I don't want my boat all lead,*
> *nor a half-tide rock to be, That soaks you*
> *through and drives you home when you*
> *strike a lump of a sea.*
> *So build me a ship as* looks like a
> ship, *and that'll do for me.*[34]

The ditty must have reached Francis, but his reaction is unrecorded, other than his belief that Charlie had succumbed to peer pressure when he removed the *Live Yankee*'s jib-luff spar.[35]

Yet Francis himself was disappointed in the *Live Yankee*. He believed that he had gone too far with his triangular mid-section and wrote his father that the boat was "too thick at the top of the lead," and that she carried "a large combing sea" on the weather quarter when driven hard. Howard Chapelle believed that the problem was inherent in the Universal Rule. He wrote: "The tendency of the rule to produce a faulty type can be verified by

the disturbed wake when driven hard, evident in all boats designed under the rule." But there are degrees of disturbed wake, and while it is true that the Universal Rule's quarter-beam length measurement encouraged a pot-bellied effect, which would increase the disturbance of the water particularly as the boat approached hull speed, each designer could minimize that effect if he so chose. The *Live Yankee* had more of a paunch than did her predecessor. Francis eventually grew to disdain Universal Rule racers because of this characteristic.[36]

Another factor in how much a racing boat disturbs the water is how hard the skipper is willing to drive his boat for best speed. Charlie Welch could drive the *Live Yankee*—almost "all lead," as the ditty had it—all he wanted to; she had plenty of stability. Francis wrote, "the R-boats are capable of carrying their full sail plan in very heavy weather; in fact they practically never reef at all."[37] Maybe they should have.

The denigrations of Marblehead wits and the disappointment of her designer notwithstanding,

ABOVE: The start of a match race between the *Yankee* (left) and *Live Yankee* in Marblehead Harbor. The Corinthian Yacht Club may be seen between the boats. On the *Live Yankee*, the jib luff-spar has been eliminated and the height of the fore triangle has been lowered by 18 inches, much as was done on the *Yankee*. Still, Francis has continued the evolutionary trend he started: the *Yankee*'s jib is a quarter of her sail area; the *Live Yankee*'s is a third. (Willard B. Jackson photo 4235, Mystic Seaport, 1973-3-455) RIGHT: It is not known who won the match race between the two R-boats, but by the time photographer Willard. B. Jackson clicked his shutter two more times after filming the start, the *Yankee* had worked out a nice lead on the *Live Yankee*'s weather bow. With the shedding of the jib-luff spar, the latter is now wearing both running backstays and a permanent one from masthead to stern. Her beautifully setting sails were made by Ratsey of Cowes, England, considered by many yachtsmen to be the best in the business. Inspection with a magnifying glass suggests that Charlie Welch is steering his new boat with his wife, Ruth, and a newcomer to Marblehead, the Norwegian sailor O. Lie-Nielsen, huddled down in the cockpit, and another crew member standing aft. Perhaps Francis is sailing the *Yankee*. (Willard B. Jackson photo 4237, Charles H. W. Foster Collection, Hart Nautical Collections, MIT Museum, Cambridge, Massachusetts; e-mail from O. Lie-Nielsen to Andrew W. Britt, April 25, 1999)

the *Live Yankee* began to win races as the season of 1927 progressed and Charlie Welch got used to sailing her. In August she won her class in Marblehead Race Week, and in September she won the New York Yacht Club Cup for R-boats off Newport, coming in first in each of the three races in light, fresh, and strong breezes. Charlie was encouraged to see what he could do against West Coast R-boats. Wouldn't it be great if he, the new rear commodore of the Corinthian Yacht Club, could capture the Don Lee challenge trophy in Los Angeles and bring it home to the club? But before putting her on the deck of a steamer to go through the Panama Canal, he made some changes.[38]

In January 1928, Leonard M. Fowle reported in the *Boston Globe* that the *Live Yankee* had been hauled at Lawley's yard, that her hull had been filled out at the waterline forward, her mast moved aft "a few inches," and her rubber rudder replaced by a conventional one. These modifications to Francis's design were probably initiated and carried through, with the expert help available at Lawley's, by Charlie Welch. Francis exhibited little interest in tinkering with a completed design to try to make small improvements. There is no evidence that he was involved in the changes to the *Live Yankee*, and, by winter, he was busy on other designs. Charlie Welch's outstanding feel for a boat would make the discarding of Francis's flexible rudder hard to dispute. The changes to hull and rig are less understandable, for the *Live Yankee* already had full waterlines forward and a large fore triangle.[39]

In late January, a truck hauled the stream-

lined R-boat from Lawley's in Neponset to Commonwealth Pier, Boston, where she was loaded on board the SS *Minnesota* of the American-Hawaiian Line for the trip to Los Angeles. The ship sailed at noon on January 30, Leonard Fowle told *Globe* readers, with the *Live Yankee* buckled into a cradle on deck. She was to arrive less than a month later, on February 25. From March 10 through the eighteenth, Charlie, Ruth, and their friend Dr. John H. Cunningham, a Marblehead surgeon and sailor, raced the *Live Yankee* in the international R-boat regatta for a perpetual challenge trophy—a $500 gold cup—named for its donor, prominent southern California yachtsman Don Lee. Sixteen boats were to compete, but only eight showed up for the five races. The West Coast boat to beat was L. E. "Ted" Geary's *Sir Tom,* representing the Seattle Yacht Club, an older boat that Geary had designed and raced successfully for years, starting with a gaff rig and modernizing her with Marconi rigs. Charlie, Ruth, and Jack Cunningham won three of the races and won the series by 2-1/2 points. Charlie Welch and the *Live Yankee* did bring the Don Lee Cup to Marblehead.[40]

Francis must have been pleased, but he seemed more proud of the boat's construction than of her racing record. He wrote Nathanael: "The *Live Yankee* . . . is the strongest boat of her size I have ever seen. She has just returned to Marblehead after two trips through the Panama Canal and the tropics and does not show a seam anywhere." This is all the more remarkable because her topsides were finished in "a beautiful black Japanese lacquer," which was especially vulnerable to showing seams.[41]

Nathanael was near his eightieth birthday,

The *Live Yankee*, still with her jib-luff spar, having her streamlined hull furbished. (Mystic Seaport, 1973-3-456)

but his competitive spirit was alive and well. He replied that some of his racers, like the Buzzards Bay 21-footers and the Newport 30-footers, had raced hard for ten years and were still sailing after twenty-five years. Then he added, "I wonder if the *Live Yankee* will be afloat after that time." Nathanael forgot that the Buzzards Bay 21-footers had been out only seventeen years, and he probably also forgot that it was Francis who had carved their model (though, to be sure, it was Nathanael who was responsible for their lasting construction). These details aside, Nathanael could still wound Francis with his barbs. He still couldn't bring himself to congratulate Francis on his obvious achievement with the *Live Yankee*'s innovative design. He still would not fully affirm the Herreshoff genius in his fourth son.[42]

Charlie Welch continued to race the *Live Yankee* through two more summer seasons. In 1928, she won her class at Marblehead Race Week and was the national R-boat champion. On August 14, 1929, she won the Manhasset Bay Cup, beating a new Frank Paine-designed *Gypsy* by one point. And Ruth Welch won three more Lady's Plate trophies in the *Live Yankee* to go with two she had won with the *Yankee*.[43]

After the 1929 season, Charlie sold the *Live Yankee* to Jessie P. Morton, who won the season R-boat championship in Marblehead in 1930. The next winter, Morton shipped her back to Los Angeles and recaptured the Don Lee Cup. Under the ownership of Schuyler W. Gillespie, she raced through the 1933 season on Long Island Sound, winning the Manhasset Bay Cup again, as well as the William H. Childs Cup, the Dalley Cup, and the R Class at Larchmont Race Week. By 1935, the *Live Yankee* was owned in Seattle by Cully Stimson and was raced to victory in that year's Pacific International R-Class Championship, by Ted Geary. She was bested, though, in another race, by Geary's old *Sir Tom*. In 1944, she went to the Chesapeake Bay, and her owner, John Graham Jr.—the one who took "some time to become acquainted with her peculiarities"— wrote to her designer, "I think her to be the finest boat of her type I have ever sailed." He went on to say that once he had mastered those peculiarities, "she was unbeatable." Arthur J. Atkinson took the *Live Yankee* to Chicago in 1947 and had to remove more lead, about 360 pounds, or 3 percent of her displacement, for the shift to fresh water. She sailed on the Great Lakes at least until 1966, when she disappears from *Lloyds Register of Yachts*.[44]

So the *Live Yankee* met Nathanael's criterion for longevity and then some. And she met Charlie Welch's and Francis's criteria for an R-boat that was different and innovative. That she won races for so long with such a variety of hands on the tiller shows that her distinctive features gave her an advantage. The *Live Yankee*, like her predecessor, was a landmark design. It is puzzling that neither Francis nor any other designer copied her. Perhaps her reputation as a weird-looking "lead mine" was simply too powerful. In 1946, Francis sold a set of her lines and sail plan to an admirer of the design for six dollars.[45]

WHILE HE was finishing the design of the *Dispatch* and designing the *Live Yankee* for Charlie Welch, Francis was also working on new rigs for an R-boat and four Q-boats, the Universal Rule 25-raters. Marblehead yachtsmen had decided they wanted rigs from the drawing board of the Herreshoff who had given Charlie Welch such an edge with the *Yankee*. In October 1926, Francis drew a new sail plan for the *Scapa II*, an R-boat designed by the Norwegian, Johan Anker. The owner, Richard P. Jenks, didn't want to pay for a new, rectangular-section mast, so Francis specified eye splices for the upper ends of the shrouds, rather than his tangs. Nathanael had never come to believe that tangs were an improvement over eye splices, but Francis knew better.[46]

Early in 1927, Francis received commissions

for new rigs for the Q-boats *Hawk, Leonore, Hayseed VIII,* and *Nor'easter IV.* Norman Skene had designed the *Hawk* at Burgess, Swasey, and Paine; now, he traced Francis's new sail plan for her. The *Hawk*'s mast was moved aft and the upper end of her jibstay raised to give her the *Yankee*'s enlarged jib, and the rig was stiffened up with tangs and running backstays led well aft. Much the same was done with Robert Amory's *Leonore*, another Anker design, increasing the area of the jib from 189 square feet to 231. The *Hayseed VIII*, another Skene design at Burgess, Swasey, and Paine, simply got a new rectangular-section mast and a T-section main boom; spars were made from this design for the Q-boat *Dawn* as well. When it came to Grafton Smith's *Nor'easter IV*, a design from the office of John G. Alden, Francis gave her a bigger jib with a jib-luff spar, a rectangular-section mast with tangs, his wide, thin chainplates, and a T-section main boom. J. V. Santry bought this Q-boat for the season of 1929, renamed her *Taygeta*, and—as he did with his New York 50 *Pleione*—had Francis design a series of modified rigs, starting with eliminating the jib-luff spar. From 1931 to 1952, Francis would draw five more rigs for Santry's *Taygeta*, gradually moving the mast aft and the jibstay up the mast. All these small jobs, particularly those that had come in the first winter of Francis's new business, brought in welcome money.[47]

BUSY AS Francis was, establishing a reputation as a designer of racing boats and making ends meet, he still found time for a design job that he knew would earn him nothing. Marblehead was not only a center for the racing of R-boats, Q-boats, and other classes, but also a center for the racing of model yachts. On Sunday afternoons, a couple of dozen racers, every bit as keen as any R-boat skipper, would carry their three- or four-foot-long model yachts to the east end of town, where Pond Street curved up Old Burial Hill to Redd's Pond. This calm sheet of water, 500 feet by 200 feet, had provided racecourses since the turn of the century for many a hard-fought contest. To this day, Redd's Pond is used for model yacht racing.

When Francis moved to Marblehead, he couldn't resist being drawn into the fun. He remembered racing model boats across one of the ponds at The Farm. He had drawn a sail plan for an R-boat-like model for a 500-square-inch-sail-area class racer back in 1923, when he was working for Starling Burgess. He had clipped plans of sailing models from the German magazine, *Die Yacht*. For him, just as with full-sized boats, the fun was more in the design of the models than in the racing of them.

Now, in late 1926, Francis made a major contribution to the sport of model yacht racing. He inaugurated the 450-square-inch-sail-area class in Marblehead, a class that would dominate the racing for the next six years and that is still associated with his name. L. Francis Herreshoff, the new resident of Marblehead, helped keep Redd's Pond famous.[48]

NONE OF the new racing boat rigs that Francis designed for the 1927 season included an overlapping jib for beating to windward in a light or gentle breeze. Overlapping jibs had been used for centuries on working craft, and, more recently on yachts; but on yachts these balloon jibs were always conceived as lightweight, full-cut sails, to be used only for reaching. Around 1900, some of the big English racing cutters had set overlapping forestaysails cut flat enough to stand when close-hauled. Schooners, both working vessels and yachts, had used overlapping foresails for beating to windward. Francis would have been familiar with the overlapping foresails of the double-enders used to fish and carry at Block Island, and with such sails on early pilot schooners, one of which Waldo Brown had tried on his *Joann*.

But making an overlapping jib of the heavier weight of a working jib so that it could be set in more than a gentle breeze, and cutting it flat so that it could be kept full close on the wind, was a new idea in the mid-1920s.[49]

The three purposes of designing an overlapping jib for the windward work of a racing boat were: first, to increase sail area without increasing rating, since the Universal Rule (and the later International Rule) measured only the area of the fore triangle; second, to improve the set of the sail by pulling more aft on the leech, thus keeping the upper part of the leech from sagging off to leeward; and, third, to take advantage of Bernoulli's principle, an advantage that we will examine because it was accepted by almost every designer and racing sailor except L. Francis Herreshoff. Francis came to dislike the big jibs. In 1932, he wrote, "I think the large jibs now allowed are the greatest danger and nuisance on the modern yacht." Yet Francis would claim that he had been the first to design an overlapping jib for windward work.[50]

We have seen that the earliest known drawing of the new sail in the United States was Norman Skene's sail plan of the Marblehead T Class, dated August 28, 1925, Burgess, Swasey, and Paine design No. 295. This is curious, because the design of the Marblehead T-boat was for a one-design class, in which all boats would be the same, so that there was no advantage to be gained from unmeasured sail area. In any event, we surmise that the concept of the big jib for the T Class came from that innovative and experienced student of aerodynamics, and Skene's boss, W. Starling Burgess. As we have seen, Francis had been involved with the T-Class design himself, having produced a preliminary drawing that was modified by Starling, so he must have seen Skene's drawing of the big jib. He makes no mention of the Marblehead T-boat in his claims of being the originator of the sail.

What Francis did claim, in a letter to his father in 1933, when his memory of the events was relatively fresh, was: "in 1927 I designed some large lapping jibs for an 'R' boat that Mr. Welch had at that time and some other boat that I had

Standing near the shore of Redd's Pond, Marblehead Model Yacht Club member Dexter Goodwin shows off his 1926 Herreshoff 450 Class model yacht. The only measurement was the 450-square-inch sail area, for Francis's design for the class was inspired by the Swedish Square Metre Rule, which at that time measured only sail area. This model is 40 inches long and weighs 9 pounds. Note the curved mast, large fore triangle, and swept-back fin keel. She has "Marblehead steering," a self-steering arrangement with an aft-facing tiller guided by tension on the mainsheet, such that the harder the sheet pulls in a puff, the more weather helm is applied to keep the model on course. (Courtesy of Marblehead Model Yacht Club Archives/James Dolan)

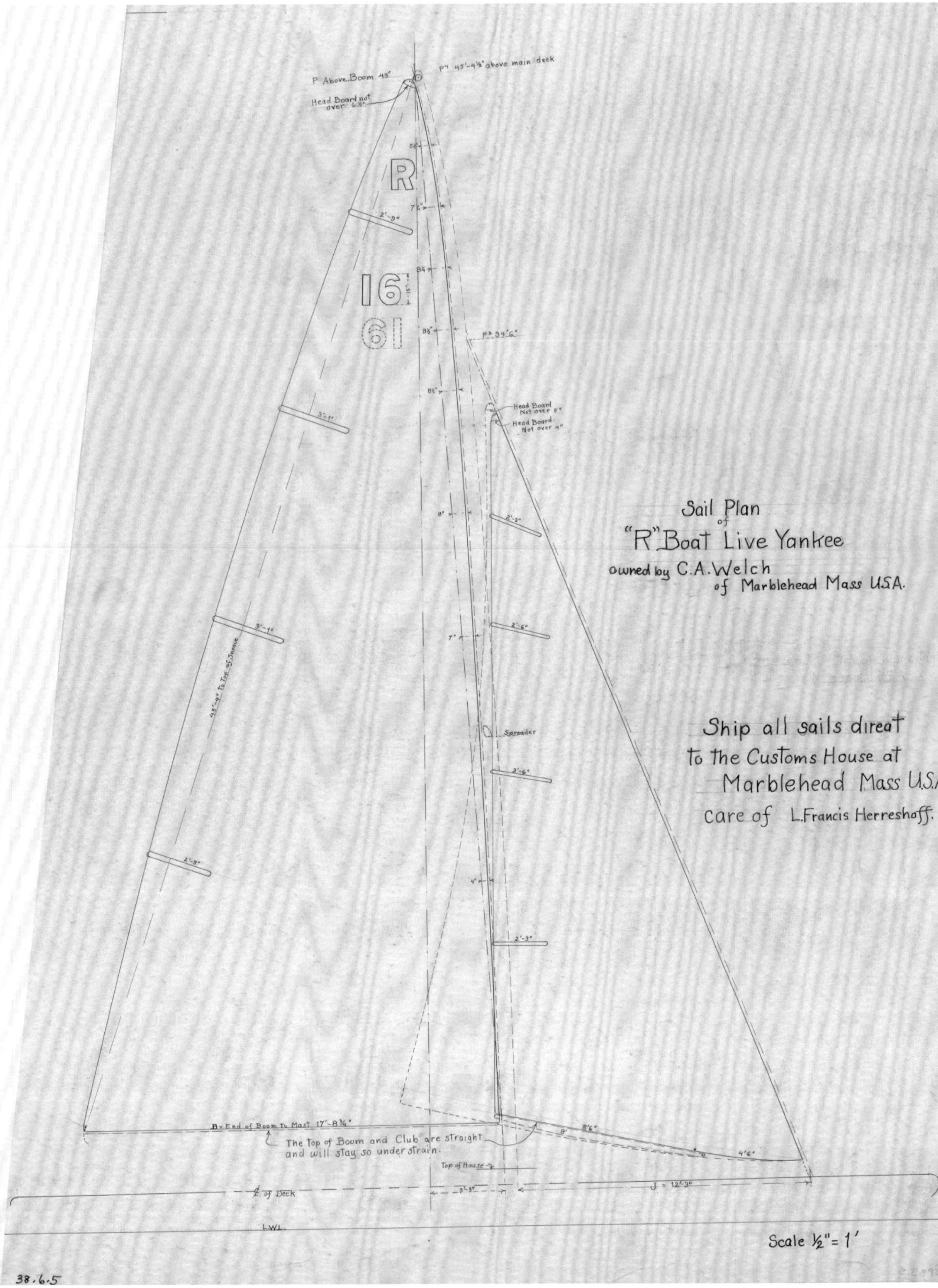

P Above Boom 43'
P+ 45'-4½" above main deck.
Head Board not over 6½"
R
16
61
P³ 34'-6"
Head Board Not over 5"
Head Board Not over 4"
Spreader
B = End of Boom to Mast 17'-8¾"
The Top of Boom and Club are straight and will stay so under strain.
Top of House
℄ of Deck
J = 12'-3"
L.W.L.
Sail Plan of "R" Boat Live Yankee
owned by C.A. Welch of Marblehead Mass U.S.A.
Ship all sails direct to the Customs House at Marblehead Mass U.S.A. care of L. Francis Herreshoff.
Scale ½" = 1'

38.6.5

in construction. They were made by the great Ratsey and Lapthorn sail loft in England. He rather liked the idea of these big jibs as they helped to hold the leach up aloft so that he made some for several 6-meter boats [from Sweden] that were to race at Genoa that winter. English Ratsey has told me himself that he made the first ones for me so that I prefer to call them lapping jibs instead of Genoa jibs or Swedish jibs, or Curry jibs, or any other places in which these jibs were used later on." Francis would retell this story, with variations, including changing the year to 1926, many times.[51]

Francis's story of his invention of the overlapping jib for windward work is borne out by an undated drawing he made sometime in the spring of 1927 of the new sail plan for the *Live Yankee*, to go with her third rig, the one Francis designed after Charlie Welch had had enough of the jib-luff spar. This sail plan was for Ratsey in England and is marked, "Ship all sails direct to the Customs House at Marblehead Mass U.S.A. care of L. Francis Herreshoff." It shows a flat-cut, overlapping jib. Presumably Ratsey made the big jib at his sail loft in Cowes and shipped it, though no evidence has come to light of Charlie's using the sail during the season of 1927.[52]

Several months later, in a drawing dated October 2, 1927, Francis showed a similar "lapping jib" on a new sail plan for the 1928 season for Charles Foster's R-boat *Mary*. The *Mary* was probably "some other boat that I had in construction," even though he was only designing a new rig for her. In 1931, he would draw a bigger jib for the *Mary*—then owned in Portland, Maine, by C. D. Alexander—a jib whose foot was nearly twice the length of the fore triangle, for the trend with these sails was for ever-greater overlap.[53]

With the above evidence in mind, we can credit Francis's claim to be the first, in 1927, at least in the United States, to design the flat-cut, overlapping jib as a way to gain unmeasured sail area, but we need to remember Starling Burgess's prior idea for the sail. The new type of sail would not be called a Burgess jib or a Herreshoff jib, but rather a Genoa jib.

The first place the Genoa jib was used in the United States was Long Island Sound. The Swedish sailor Sven Salen, in his 6-Metre *Maybe*, and other Scandinavian 6s, appeared with the sail during the Scandinavian Gold Cup races at Oyster Bay, Long Island, in September 1927. The *Maybe* and the other 6s got their big jibs from Ratsey in England, who said he got the idea from Francis. The Scandinavian 6s trounced the Americans, doubtless with help from their Genoa jibs. As noted, in 1927 Charlie Welch seems to have refrained from using his "lapping jib," as Francis called his design, perhaps because he thought the unmeasured sail area would be outlawed and cause disqualification in a race, or perhaps simply because, as a gentleman, he eschewed what he considered to be an unfair advantage.[54]

But all of this discussion of who was first with the overlapping jib in the United States in 1927 is less important than earlier developments in Europe. While there is no reason to doubt that "English Ratsey" made his first flat-cut, overlapping jib for L. Francis Herreshoff, or that he then copied the sail for Swedish sailors to use at Genoa and on Long Island Sound, we need to consider Francis's deprecating reference to "Curry jibs." Dr. Manfred Curry had been experimenting in

Francis's sail plan for the *Live Yankee*'s third rig, made in the spring of 1927, shows a flat-cut, overlapping jib for windward work. Francis claimed it was the first such sail and that its maker, Thomas Ratsey of Cowes, England, liked it so much that he copied it for boats that were to race in Genoa, Italy. Flat-cut, overlapping jibs have been called Genoa jibs ever since. (© Mystic Seaport, Daniel S. Gregory Ships Plans Library, SP38.6.5)

Germany since the end of the First World War with ways to make monohull sailboats go faster. In his book, *Yacht Racing: The Aerodynamics of Sails*, published in German in 1925 and in English in 1928, he claimed to have been the first to suggest the use of the Marconi rig, the parachute spinnaker, the T-section boom—and the overlapping jib for windward work. Curry wrote in the fifth edition of his book, in 1948, "It seemed impossible to convince yacht[s]men of the value of the overlapping jib for beating to windward through the publication of articles until I beat the six meter boats on the Mediterranean by using the first overlapping jibs at Genoa (Italy) and until the Swedish boat *Maybe* beat the American six meters [at the Gold Cup races in 1927] by using these large jibs." The "large jib" was certainly used in Europe before 1927, particularly in Sweden on the Skerry cruisers built to the Square-Metre Rule, and had been described and analyzed in *Die Yacht* by Curry. In March of 1927, before he drew an overlapping jib for the *Live Yankee* (probably in June), Francis wrote to his father that he made a practice of reading foreign yachting journals, particularly the German *Die Yacht*. "It might be a great revelation to some American yachtsmen," he wrote, "if they saw the rapid progress the Germans, Swedes, Norwegians, and French are making in racing sailing yachts and particularly with experiments in sail plans derived from aeronautical knowledge." So Francis must have seen what Curry and others in Europe were doing with the overlapping jib before 1927. Moreover, Curry made his ideas on the overlapping jib available in English with an article in the July 1927 issue of *Yachting*.[55]

From the foregoing evidence, we can conclude that Francis got his idea for the flat-cut, overlapping jib in 1927 from Dr. Manfred Curry, if not from Starling Burgess, and it is possible that Burgess got the idea from Curry in 1925. Why, then, did Francis claim the credit for himself? It does not seem likely that when Francis first wrote the claim to his father in 1933 he had forgotten "the rapid progress . . . particularly with experiments in sail plans" that he had read about six years before. The answer probably is that Francis thought Curry was all wrong with his theories about *why* the overlapping jib worked. Francis loved to ridicule those whom he thought applied scientific theory to yacht design at the expense of common sense and practical experience. He had no respect for Curry. At some point, Curry visited Francis in Marblehead and was a member of an evening's group conversing about yacht design at his hearth. Francis rated Curry on the bottom rung of his guests, writing that Curry "had done nearly all of his yachting in the sphere of his imagination." Francis was overlooking the fact that by the time he was twenty-nine, Dr. Manfred Curry had come in first in 810 sailboat races, mostly in boats of his own experimental design. And Francis treated Curry shabbily as his guest. He drove Curry to the Marblehead station and left him there to figure out the local, American trains for himself.[56]

Dr. Curry, the theorist, was enamored with what the aeronautical engineers called "lift." Because of the designed cross-sectional shape of an airplane wing, air deflected by the cambered

Dr. Manfred R. Curry in about 1929. Despite Francis's claim, Curry deserves credit for the first experiments with the Genoa jib. (*Yachting* (February 1930): 80)

upper surface of the wing travels across the wing faster than the air passing the flat, lower surface. The result is less pressure on the top surface of the wing than on the bottom surface, hence lift. Francis must have understood the truth of this cause of lift, but he pointed out that common sense decreed that this form of lift is minor compared to the pressure gained by a positive angle of attack of the lower surface of the wing, simply angling the wing upward so that the pressure of air on its lower surface is greatly increased, the air striking the wing is deflected downward, and the wing is forced upward. A modern jetliner pilot demonstrates this phenomenon each time he lands, putting his wing flaps down and deflecting so much air downward, even at landing speed, that the whole aircraft shudders.

When we shift our attention from the cambered sectional shape of the wing to the similarly cambered shape of the sail, the upper, curved surface of the wing corresponds to the leeward side of the sail, and the lower, flat surface of the wing corresponds to the windward side of the sail. But the sail cannot be flat on its windward side, for it is not rigid. Thus both sides of the sail are cambered, with the result that the difference in wind speed across leeward and windward sides of the sail is far less than the differences across a wing, so that the aeronautical engineer's "lift" is far more significant than that of the naval architect. Francis would demonstrate his familiarity with all of this theory by designing a futuristic catamaran with rigid, wing sails that could be "oscillated" around a fore-and-aft axis when tacking, so as always to present their flat sides to the wind and bring their cambered sides to leeward. But again, all of this cambered lift is dwarfed by angle of attack, which increases pressure on the lower surface of a wing or on the windward side of a sail by angling or trimming it to maximum advantage. This is where Francis disagreed, if we may use such a mild word, with Curry.[57]

Curry wrote: "The new theory of sailing has revealed the fact that the suction in the lee of the sail is from two to three times as great as the pressure on the windward side. Thus we sail with suction rather than with pressure."[58]

Francis wrote: "It has become stylish of late years to say the leeward side of a sail or the upper side of an aeroplane's wing did two-thirds of the work and the pressure side did but a paltry one-third. . . . To hear some people talk you might think a vacuum was composed of some sort of magnetism, mucilage or fish hooks, or had a magical power of attaching itself to things so it could pull on them. But it is not so: nor is there anything in the realm of physics, with the exception of electricity or gravity, which has any such action. All other things are moved, held together or supported by pressure, or something pushing on them." And he added, "leave the leeward side of the sail to Dr. Curry and some other myth lovers."[59]

In the 1730s, mathematician Daniel Bernoulli discovered that fluid flowing through a constricted area speeds up, with a corresponding reduction in pressure. This principle applies to airflow as well. Thus, the third advantage of the Genoa jib: by creating a narrow "slot" between its leech and the mainsail's luff, air flowing through the slot between the two sails is accelerated, decreasing the pressure on the leeward side of the mainsail. This increases the pressure differential between the windward and leeward sides of the mainsail, in effect increasing the pressure on the windward side. Thus, the driving force is greater, and the boat goes faster. Francis understood Bernoulli's principle, for, as we have seen, he designed the *Dispatch*'s windscreen in accordance with it; the device not only deflected the wind upward off its front surface, but also provided a constriction to increase the speed of upward flowing air. To be sure, in this case, it was only the increased velocity that was useful, not the decreased pressure, but still the designer of that windscreen had to be cognizant of Bernoulli's work.

Yet Francis wrote: "I would like to discuss...

what is generally spoken of as the jib feeding the partial vacuum on the leeward side of the mainsail. Some people seem to think this partial vacuum is some sort of a draft animal, like a horse or an ox, and must be fed. There is evidently some confusion in their logic, for if a partial vacuum to leeward is good, then to feed it a stream of air from the jib which at once kills the vacuum seems queer logic." Francis is writing this colorful argument in 1944 to carry the readers of *The Common Sense of Yacht Design* along with him in his debunking of the theoretical side of yacht design, but he is getting carried away, and is being disingenuous. He certainly realized that the air being fed through the slot between jib and mainsail exited the slot as well as entering it, so that the partial vacuum was maintained, not "killed." Curry and many others have overrated the suction of the "slot effect," but Francis denied it entirely.[60]

The story of Francis Herreshoff and the Genoa jib sheds light on some unattractive sides of his character. Pride, harsh judgment of the work of competitors, manipulation of facts to meet the requirements of the story he wished to tell: the Genoa jib lays these personal flaws at Francis's doorstep. He was capable at times of altering facts in order to have them agree with the impression he wished to make.

Where Francis was right about the Genoa jib was to point out that the sail would be more effective if it were moved out from overlapping the mainsail so that the wind could reach its entire windward side unimpeded. No one would argue with this; but, given the rules, which would then have measured the entire sail, thus increasing the boat's rating, it was beside the point for a racing boat. Francis would argue in vain for a change in the rules to measure the full area of any jib carried. "We hope and expect the large [partially unmeasured] jibs will be ruled out in the future," he wrote in 1945, but they were not ruled out.[61]

And his belief that the Genoa jib is "the greatest danger and nuisance on the modern yacht" is valid. If the extra area of the Genoa jib were incorporated into the working sail area of the yacht, the rig would be safer and easier to handle, because the elimination of the Genoa jib would remove a dangerous blind spot for sailors steering and keeping a lookout and would replace the potentially dangerous strain on the single-part Genoa sheet with a much tamer, multi-part sheet. Francis believed that racers should not be forced by the measurement rules to use, and that other sailors should not accept, the Genoa jib he claimed to have invented. The premier Marblehead racing helmsman and Secretary of the Navy Charles Francis Adams III agreed with him. He wrote Francis: "I cordially agree with your belief that we ought to do something to protect yachting from the abuse of big jibs and spinnakers. They increase the expense, make large and expensive crews necessary, and do not add to the pleasure. More than all, they are likely to distort sail plans in a most unfortunate way. I shall be personally glad if something could be done." But by the mid-1930s, just about every serious racing boat had a Genoa jib in her sail inventory. And today, strange to say, the sail is taken for granted and appears more frequently than a working jib on cruising boats, where its unmeasured overlap is irrelevant.[62]

WHEN Francis specified a particular sailmaker to make the sails for one of his complete new designs or new rig designs, he, like other designers, received a commission from the sailmaker of 10 percent of the cost of the sails. His commissions on all the sails he drew over the years for the various staysail-schooner rigs of Joseph V. Santry's *Pleione,* for example, amounted to a worthwhile sum. He counted on this ancillary business to help pay the bills. Francis's favorite sailmakers—and the favorite of every sailor who could afford them—were at the Ratsey and Lapthorn loft. And Francis felt that "English" Ratsey, the old, original firm in Cowes,

Isle of Wight, was more thoroughly reliable than the recent branch of the firm established at City Island, at the west end of Long Island Sound.[63]

Also, like other designers, he engaged in the sideline activity of yacht brokerage. A large design firm like the John G. Alden Company may have had years in which they made more money from selling yachts than from designing them. Not L. Francis Herreshoff. He was no salesman, and he minimized any activity that took him away from his drawing board. He would try, without much success, to sell boats for his design clients, like Charlie Welch. We have noted his full-page advertisement in *Yachting* for the *Dispatch*. In October 1928, Francis took out another full-page ad in *Yachting*, offering the *Live Yankee* for sale, but no buyer came forward; as we have seen, Charlie raced her for another season. In February 1927, Francis responded to a request from his father to try to sell his 30-foot yawl, the *Pleasure*. But he cautioned Nathanael, "I am a poor salesman and generally have to wait till I find a man who wants just the size of boat I have for sale. My market, of course, is very local." Thus warned, Nathanael listed the *Pleasure* also with Burgess, Rigg, and Morgan in New York, since Starling had yacht broker J. Linton Rigg as a partner in his business, and the firm served a much larger market. While Francis relied on word-of-mouth to sell the *Pleasure,* Burgess, Rigg, and Morgan advertised her in *Yachting*, along with an 83-foot schooner and a 219-foot steam yacht. But Starling couldn't resist the *Pleasure*; he bought her himself and kept her in Bristol, so that Nathanael was able to keep sailing her. Francis didn't pay many bills with yacht brokerage commissions.[64]

AT HIS drawing board, Francis designed another radical new sailing rig. In a plan dated February 16, 1927, he drew another new rig for the R-boat *Mary*, owned by Charles Foster, he of the "keen interest in experimentation." Foster's interest was so keen that in a long lifetime of sailing—he was actively afloat at age ninety-five—he owned seventy yachts. Having designed a schooner rig for the *Mary* two years before, Francis now devised a "swing rig," for her, in which the mainsail and jib were both attached to a single boom that pivoted on the mast. The perceived advantage was two-fold: first, on a reach or run, when the main sheet was eased, the boom swung the jib out to windward into clear air, undisturbed by the mainsail; second, with the boom positioned so that the sails were close-hauled, the hull of the boat could be steered independently of the rig slightly closer to the wind.[65]

Francis never wrote about this interesting concept. He did write of Foster: "He certainly is a most enthusiastic yachtsman but it is very difficult for me to talk with him about mechanical matters or about the action of wind on sails for his type of mind and mine seem to work in opposite directions and I cannot follow what he is talking about." It is not known if the swing rig was tried on the *Mary*. By October 2, as we have seen, Francis had drawn another new sail plan for her 1928 season, showing a conventional sail plan with an overlapping jib.[66]

The designer who did write about the swing rig was Dr. Manfred Curry. And by the end of 1927, he had shipped a boat with the rig to the United States for demonstration. In January 1928, *Yachting* published Curry's article on the swing rig. Perhaps the swing rig for the *Mary* was Francis's idea; perhaps it was Foster's. Probably either one first saw the swing rig in Curry's earlier articles in *Die Yacht*. Although promising experiments using the swing rig were carried out in England a half century after Curry's work, the swing rig has never become popular.[67]

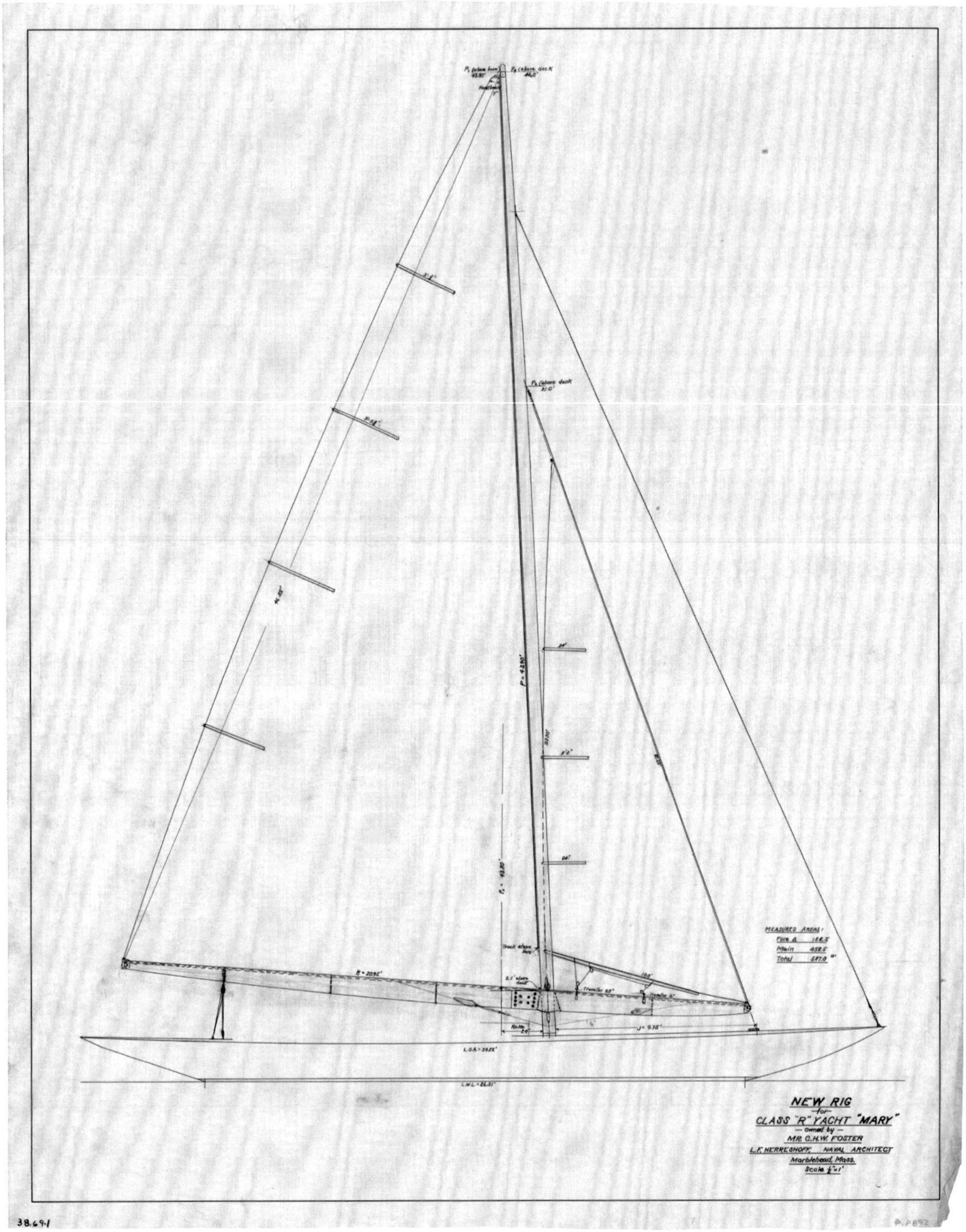

The swing rig that Francis designed for Charles H. W. Foster's R-boat *Mary* in February 1927. The idea probably came from the experimental work of Dr. Manfred Curry. (© Mystic Seaport, Daniel S. Gregory Ships Plans Library, SP38.69.1)

CHAPTER 8

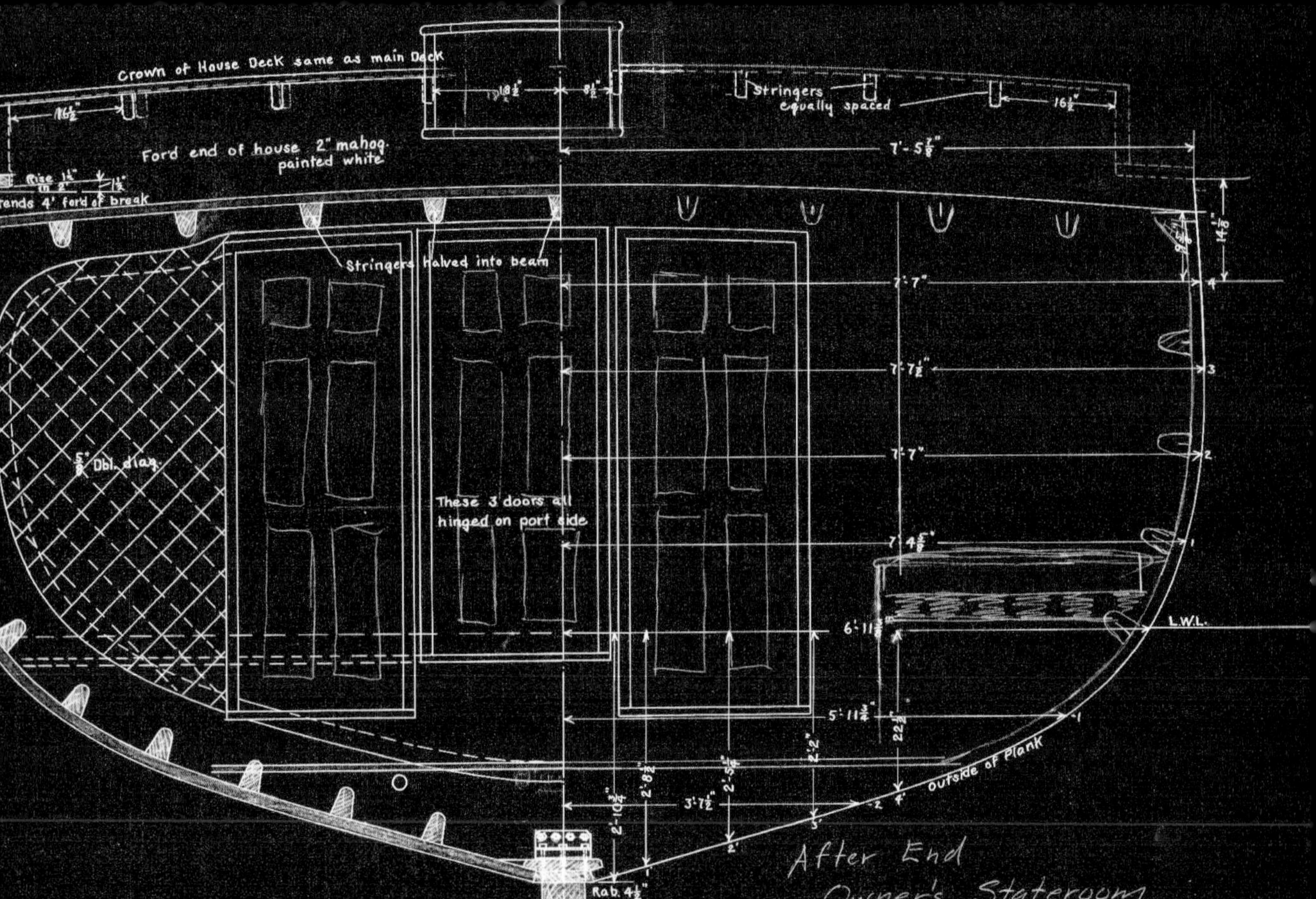

No 54
Looking Aft

After End
Owner's Stateroom

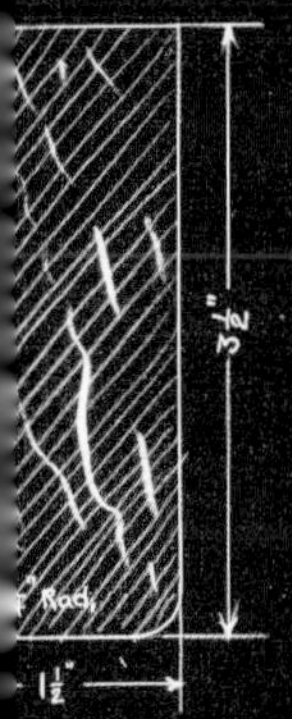

DECK STRINGERS
Full Size

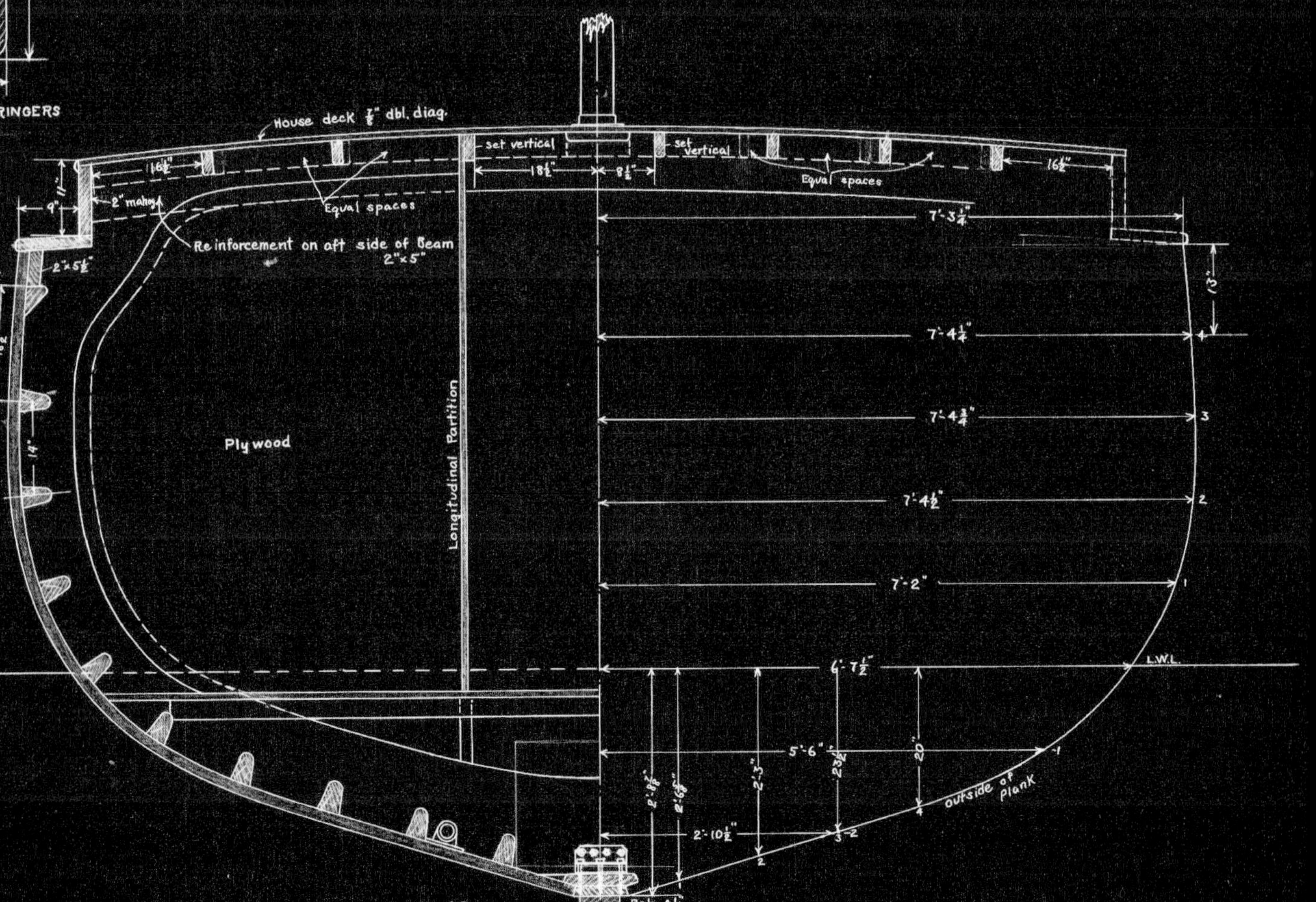

No 60

FROM FRUSTRATION TO FUN

"Vanderbilt apparently did not have much confidence in me..."

—L. FRANCIS HERRESHOFF, 1927

"These little boats are the most fun to sail of any I have ever tried..."

—L. FRANCIS HERRESHOFF, 1946

In early 1927, Francis conceived and drew plans for the most spectacular racing boat he would ever design. His design No. 22, for the Universal Rule's Class M, was gorgeous and ultramodern. She had the potential to become a landmark racing yacht. Alas, it was not to be. Francis was too far ahead of his time. The wealthy yachtsman for whom the design was made, so eager to make his mark with a fast boat, didn't dare try Francis's advanced concepts; his father showed little enthusiasm for the design; the amazing vessel never went beyond her two-dimensional drawings.

This is how it happened: A designer of racing yachts whose work Francis respected was Clinton H. Crane, and Crane recognized the Herreshoff genius in Francis's designs. Twenty years older than Francis, Crane had studied engineering at Harvard and the University of Glasgow. In 1900 he opened his yacht design office in New York, producing some very influential and competitive sailing and power yachts. But in 1912, Crane had changed professions. Upon his father's death, he took over the family mining business, the St. Joseph Lead Company, in Missouri. He continued designing boats for his own use and for close friends, but he didn't want to deprive full-time designers of work. When a yachtsman came to him seeking the design for a winning racing yacht, he would offer to pass along the commission, on a subcontract basis, to a designer in whom he was confident, particularly to L. Francis Herreshoff, in his new business in Marblehead, and later, to a young designer in New York, Olin J. Stephens II.[1]

When the experienced racing skipper, Harold S. Vanderbilt, asked Crane to design him a boat to race in the Universal Rule's Class M, the big 46-raters, 85 feet long, for the 1927 season, Crane passed the commission along to Francis. It was a great opportunity, and Francis drew the most remarkable racing boat of his career. His design No. 22 is a wonderful example of his ability to blend his artistry with his own brand of scientific

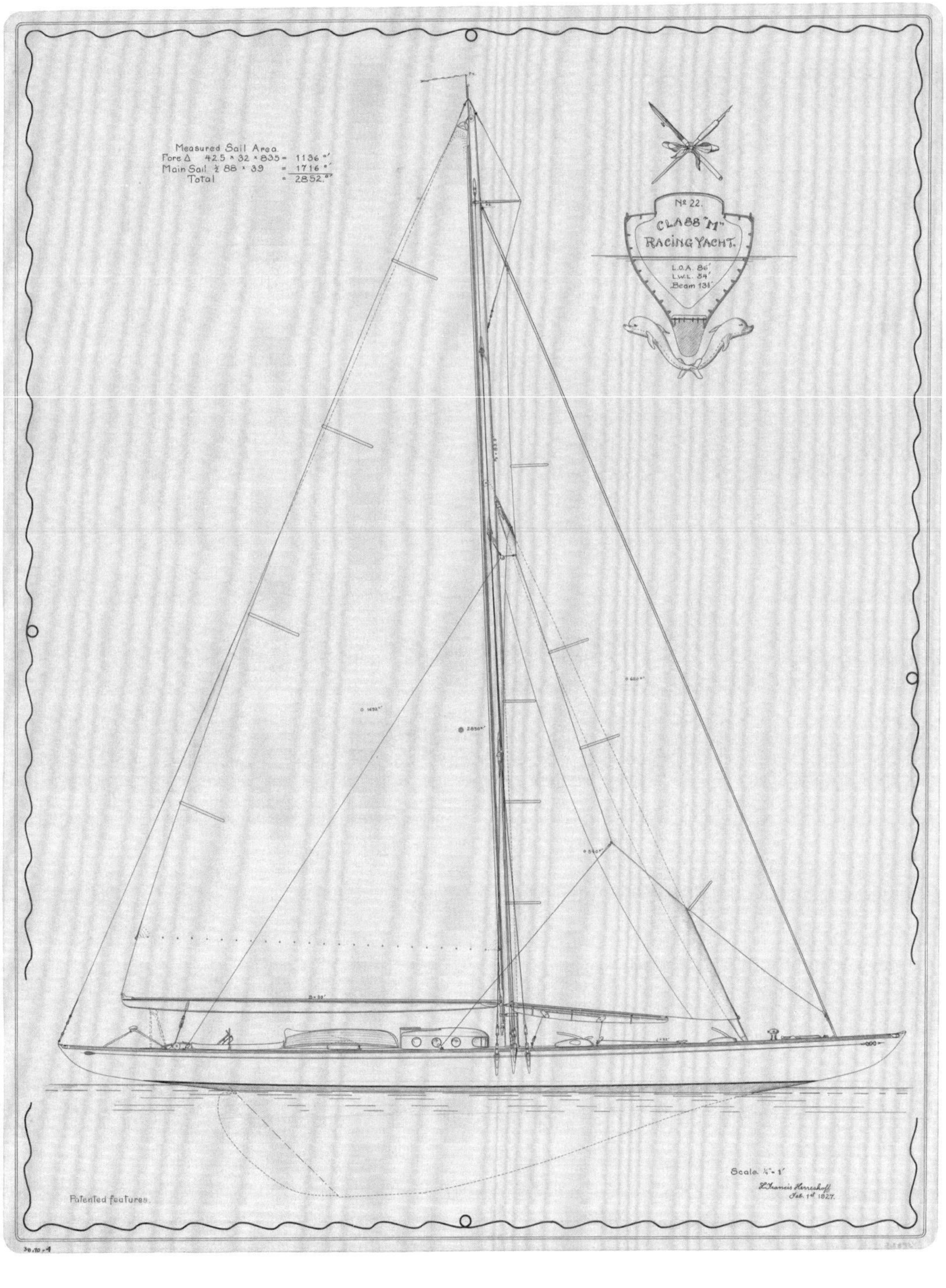
Measured Sail Area.
Fore Δ 42.5 × 32 × .835 = 1136 □'
Main Sail ½ 88 × 39 = 1716 □'
Total = 2852 □'
Nº 22.
CLASS "M" RACING YACHT.
L.O.A. 86'
L.W.L. 54'
Beam 13½'
Patented features.
Scale ¼" = 1'
L. Francis Herreshoff
Feb. 1st 1927.

innovation. The design has many new ideas, ideas that he tried neither to prove with numbers nor to justify with theories, but ideas whose value he hoped would be tested on the water.

Francis wrote to Nathanael of Crane's commission and reported that he had taken the sail plan and lines of No. 22 to New York to show to Vanderbilt, his former naval superior. "He apparently did not have much confidence in me, and so is having Starling Burgess design him a boat of exactly the dimensions I offered. This yacht is to be built at Bristol for use this summer. I imagine the Herreshoff Manufacturing Company is quite pleased that I am not making the designs as I might be nearly as particular as you used to be and require that the owner get something for his money." Vanderbilt's Herreshoff-built Burgess design was the successful *Prestige*. This yacht began a ten-year, propitious, designer-client tie between Burgess and Vanderbilt. Francis took hard and personally the disappointment of having his beautiful, advanced design overridden by Vanderbilt and Starling. Later, Francis would disparage Vanderbilt, the inventor of contract bridge, in a thinly veiled, published diatribe: "The sailor wants to sail, and says to hell with the wealthy, bridge playing sea lawyers who win their races traveling at a rate slower than their ancestors."[2]

Yet, Clinton Crane was impressed by Francis's M-boat design and persuaded him to continue with construction drawings. Before he did, Francis sent the sail plan and lines to his father and asked for his criticism. Some of the energy and imagination that Francis put into these drawings must have been fueled by his need to show his father that he did indeed have the Herreshoff genius for designing yachts. And when Nathanael unrolled the plans of his son's design No. 22 for the first time, he must have recognized that they could only have been drawn by a genius. While his praise of the design was ample, he still did not react to Francis's work as if he gladly welcomed another first-class Herreshoff yacht designer on the scene. Perhaps doing so would have been tantamount to admitting the error of his previous denial of Francis's talent for yacht designing; perhaps he simply didn't want his son to think he could equal his father. Nathanael replied to Francis: "You have worked up the thing wonderfully well and [the design] certainly has merit enough to be built from."[3]

Nathanael made no comment on one element of Francis's spectacular drawing of an M-boat that probably made him frown: the whimsical decorations with which Francis adorned it. One cannot imagine Nathanael, or Sidney for that matter, embellishing drawings with such unprofessional decoration. They were too formal to allow lightheartedness to enter their working world. Francis would write: "My father was not a very finished draftsman and did not like fancy drawings." Perhaps Francis's fancy title block, with its dolphins, had some negative effect on Vanderbilt's confidence in him; maybe Vanderbilt thought the whimsy trivialized the design. Clinton Crane didn't seem to be put off.[4]

Francis's spectacular drawing of a proposed Universal Rule M-Class racer, his design No. 22, dated February 1, 1927. The 86-foot hull is simply elegant. The streamlined deck structures give the yacht something of an Art Deco look. She has a huge fore triangle and the first double head rig with parallel stays. The forestaysail is set on Francis's patented luff spar, the sail being double-luffed for a smooth air foil, since this advance had not yet been ruled out for racing. The staysail luff spar and high fore triangle with jumper stays and a permanent backstay eliminate the need for running backstays. We see the first quadrilateral jib, with upper and lower clews, each with its own pair of sheets. The sail area is 2,852 square feet. Note the folding boom crutch, slanted steering wheel with perpendicular handle for high-speed turning, and the wrap-around windshield in the companionway deckhouse. (© Mystic Seaport, Daniel S. Gregory Ships Plans Library, SP38.70.4)

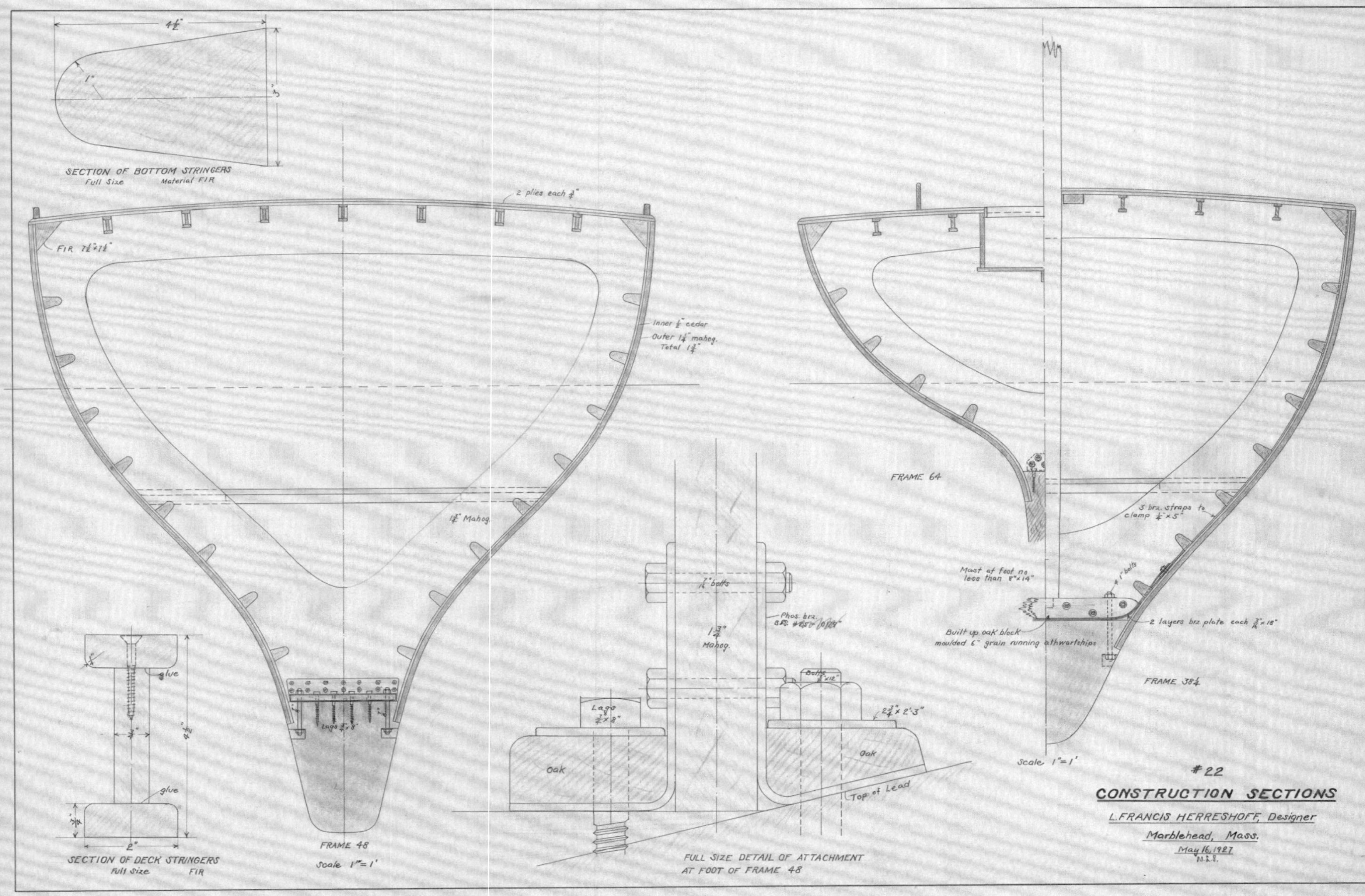
SECTION OF BOTTOM STRINGERS
Full Size Material FIR
2 plies each ⅜"
FIR
Inner ½" cedar
Outer 1¼" mahog.
Total 1¾"
Mahog.
FRAME 48
Scale 1" = 1'
SECTION OF DECK STRINGERS
Full Size FIR
glue
glue
bolts
Phos. brz.
Mahog.
Lags
Oak
Oak
Top of Lead
FULL SIZE DETAIL OF ATTACHMENT
AT FOOT OF FRAME 48
FRAME 64
3 brz. straps to clamp ⅛" x 5"
Mast at foot no less than 8" x 14"
Built up oak block moulded 6" grain running athwartships
2 layers brz. plate each
FRAME 38½
Scale 1" = 1'
#22
CONSTRUCTION SECTIONS
L. FRANCIS HERRESHOFF, Designer
Marblehead, Mass.
May 16, 1927

It is interesting to speculate on whether or not Nathanael showed any of the plans that Francis sent him to Sidney. Probably not, for Nathanael was obsessed by secrecy when it came to yacht design. There is no evidence that the brothers ever communicated to each other their ideas about their lifework.

Francis also sent to his father a written summary of his ideas for the construction of the M-boat. Nathanael wrote: "You ask me to criticize your description of the M Class Design, I think it a very able document and I congratulate you on it. There is little I can say for I am too 'Old fashoned' for the doings of this age of new developments. . . . You mention several times your improvements as compared to the 'old fashon way.' Please bear in mind the old saw 'There is nothing new under the sun.'" He went on to tell Francis that "before you were born" he had designed a very similar steering wheel to the one that Francis contemplated for the M-boat. And Nathanael wrote: "The longitudinal and web frame construction I developed for 'Constitution' in fall of 1900,—and afterwards cribbed and patented by the englishman Isherwood,—you have modified and developed for wood construction, using the diagonal inner skin planking we used in many yachts in the early 80s. . . . Without intermediate floor timbers on Keel-Knees [between the web frames] I am afraid you will have trouble in holding the lead keel to the planking properly, Think it over. I am a little skeptical of your reasons for long life in your construction. . . . Construction that is correct for an airship will not do at all in salt water." Francis may have been irritated by his father's recital of his own past accomplishments and by his intimation that he, Francis, had designed an "airship" rather than a spectacular racing boat, but, even so, he was probably glad to get his father's thinking on "holding the lead keel to the planking properly."[5]

Although Francis's design No. 22 would never be built, it was an important forerunner to his most successful large racing boat design. He was proud of the design and "sent the sail plan to a number of his clients and friends." He also used it as an illustration in his book on yacht design. But he must have been extremely frustrated when his design for what could have been a brilliant racing yacht came to naught.[6]

A year later, Francis would repeat this unfortunate sequence of events, designing another splendid M-boat with, as the potential client, Junius Morgan. Design No. 31 was another double-ender, and Francis cut away the midsection more than he had on No. 22, continuing to back away from the *Live Yankee*'s being "too thick at the lead," as he had concluded. He eliminated the forestaysail-luff strut, so he shows preventer backstays, led well aft from the forestay. Gone is the art deco companionway house. On the lines plan, Francis drew a conventional counter stern in dotted lines, perhaps fearing that the long, overhanging, pointed stern would put Morgan off. Something did, and Morgan went to Charles D. Mower, a designer of proven ability, for the design of the more conventional M-boat *Windward*. At least Francis was becoming thoroughly familiar with designing a racing boat to rate in Class M, experience that would prove valuable.

LEFT: **The construction sections for No. 22. The garboard planking was to be attached directly to the lead ballast, as were two of the amidships web frames, as shown by the detail in the center, lower portion of the drawing. As he often did with unusual construction details, Francis showed at full size the exact structure he envisioned for attaching the feet of the frames to the lead. Norman Skene traced this drawing in ink and initialed it on May 16, 1927. For lines and construction plans see foldout following page 224.** (© Mystic Seaport, Daniel S. Gregory Ships Plans Library, SP38.70.3)

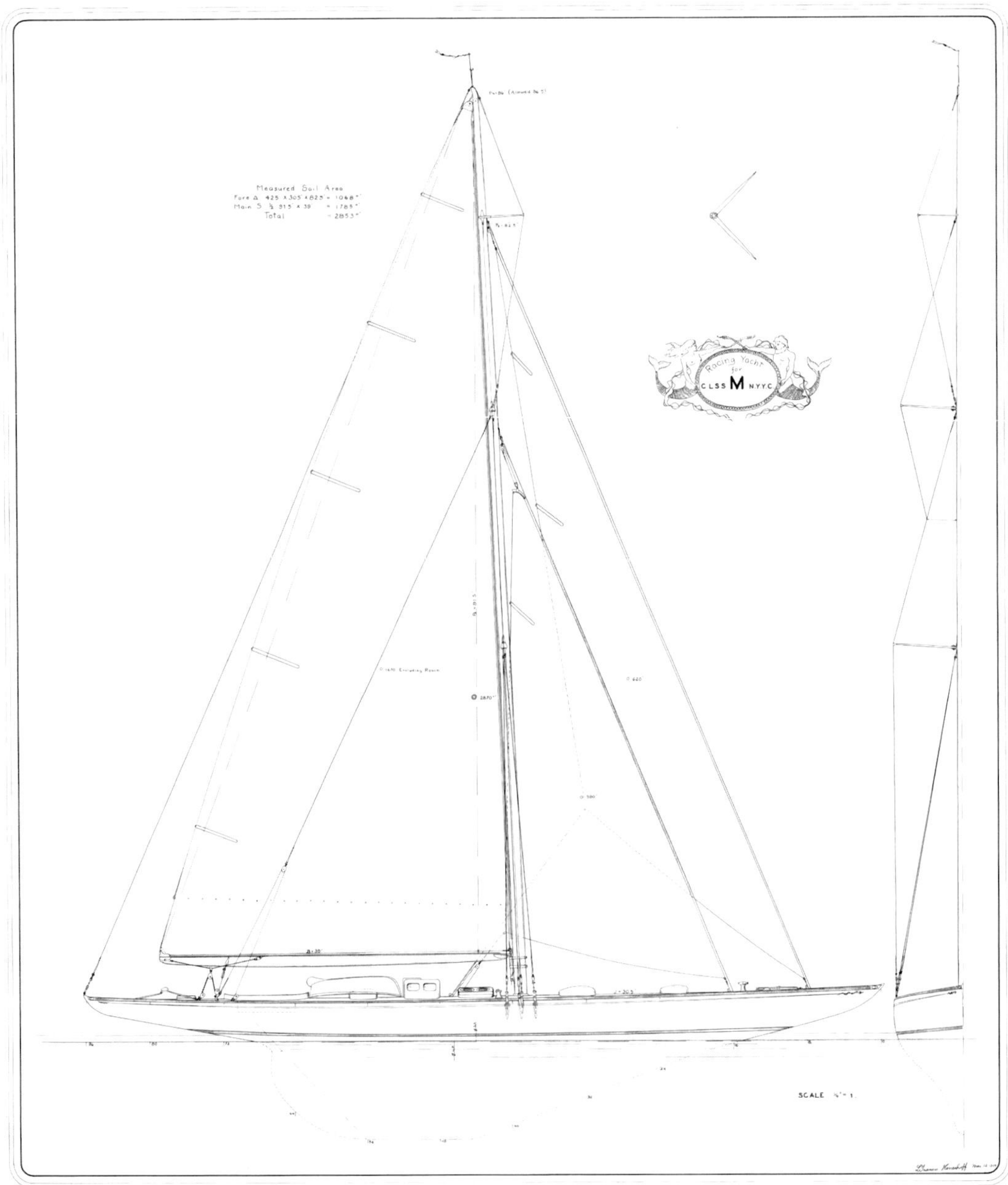

38.71.2

Francis's design No. 31 was for a Universal Rule M-boat, another double-ender similar to No. 22, but with a conventional triangular jib. Measured sail area was 2,853 square feet; actual area, including roaches, was 2,870 square feet. Note the dotted line at lower right, showing a deep, triangular mid-section. The title block is held by Francis's mermaid and merman. He signed the drawing on March 12, 1928. (© Mystic Seaport, Daniel S. Gregory Ships Plans Library, SP38.71.2)

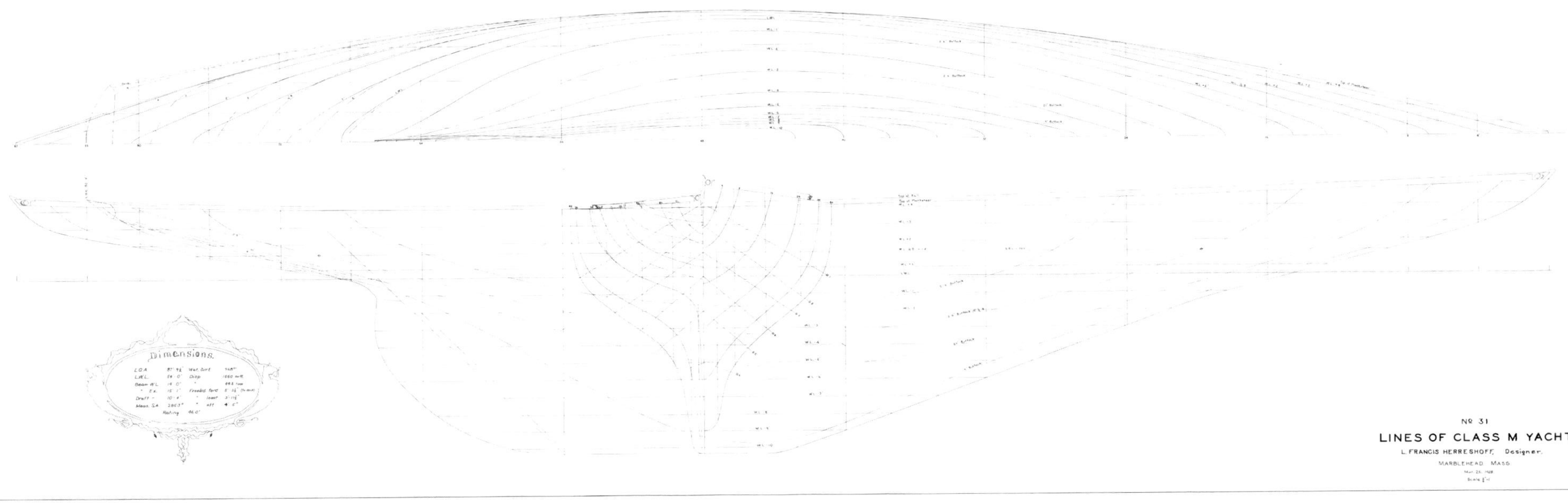

When Francis drew the lines of No. 31, he cut away the mid-section considerably from his initial concept of the hull shape shown in dotted lines on the sail plan. On the lines drawing, the dotted lines show a conventional counter stern as an alternative to the longer, pointed stern. This nod toward conservatism was not enough for the prospective client, Junius S. Morgan Jr., who chose, instead, an altogether more conservative design from Charles D. Mower. Francis's design No. 31 was never built. She would have been 87 feet, 10 inches long on deck; 54 feet long on the waterline; beam, 15 feet, 1 inch; and draft, 10 feet, 4 inches. Displacement was figured at 44.3 tons. This plan is dated March 26, 1928.

BY 1927, with Francis only a few months into his new business at 20 Lee Street, Marblehead, he was already feeling its restrictions. "Now-a-days," he wrote to his father, "I am so tied down with my work that I never can get off for any length of time. Starting up in business for myself without any capital, of course keeps me very busy and I expect I shall be tied down for some years to come as I am a very slow worker and it takes all my time to make ends meet."[7]

Yet, the late winter and spring of 1927 was an exciting time for Francis. There were all the new racing-boat rigs taking shape on his and Norman Skene's drawing boards; and the drawings needed against stringent deadlines to keep up with the changes to the innovative *Live Yankee* required by the New York Yacht Club authorities and by Charlie Welch; and the thrill, and then the disappointment, of designing a big, Class-M racer that would sail only in Francis's daydreams, in imaginary races. And the spring brought two more disappointments, but also the genesis of a large, successful design that would earn a substantial fee.

Joseph V. Santry, the *Pleione's* owner, wanted Francis to design him a day launch with minimal shelter and accommodations. Remembering the handsome 35-foot gigs he had seen carrying navy captains to and from their ships on moorings off Newport, Francis made a preliminary design for a refined version of the type. Santry liked the boat, so Francis proceeded with a complete construction drawing, using his longitudinal system. He replaced

ABOVE: **Francis's design No. 23 was for a 35-foot day launch for Joseph V. Santry. She was a finer-lined version of the US Navy's captain's gig. His handsome drawing is dated March 22, 1927.** (© Mystic Seaport, Daniel S. Gregory Ships Plans Library, SP38.215.1) RIGHT: **The construction plan of No. 23. Long and slim, the launch would have been fast, even though Francis has decreased his proposed horsepower from the 220 of the preliminary proposal to a 150-horsepower Sterling Petrel engine. There are two pipe berths and a small galley for crew in the forward engine room, and wash and toilet rooms in the enclosed forward end of the cockpit shelter for guests. These minimal arrangements would not be tried, for Santry decided against building to the design. This plan, traced by Norman Skene, is dated May 6, 1927. On his hand-printed list of his designs, Francis wrote that he had destroyed the drawings for No. 23, but he did save these two plans.** (© Mystic Seaport, Daniel S. Gregory Ships Plans Library, SP38.41.1)

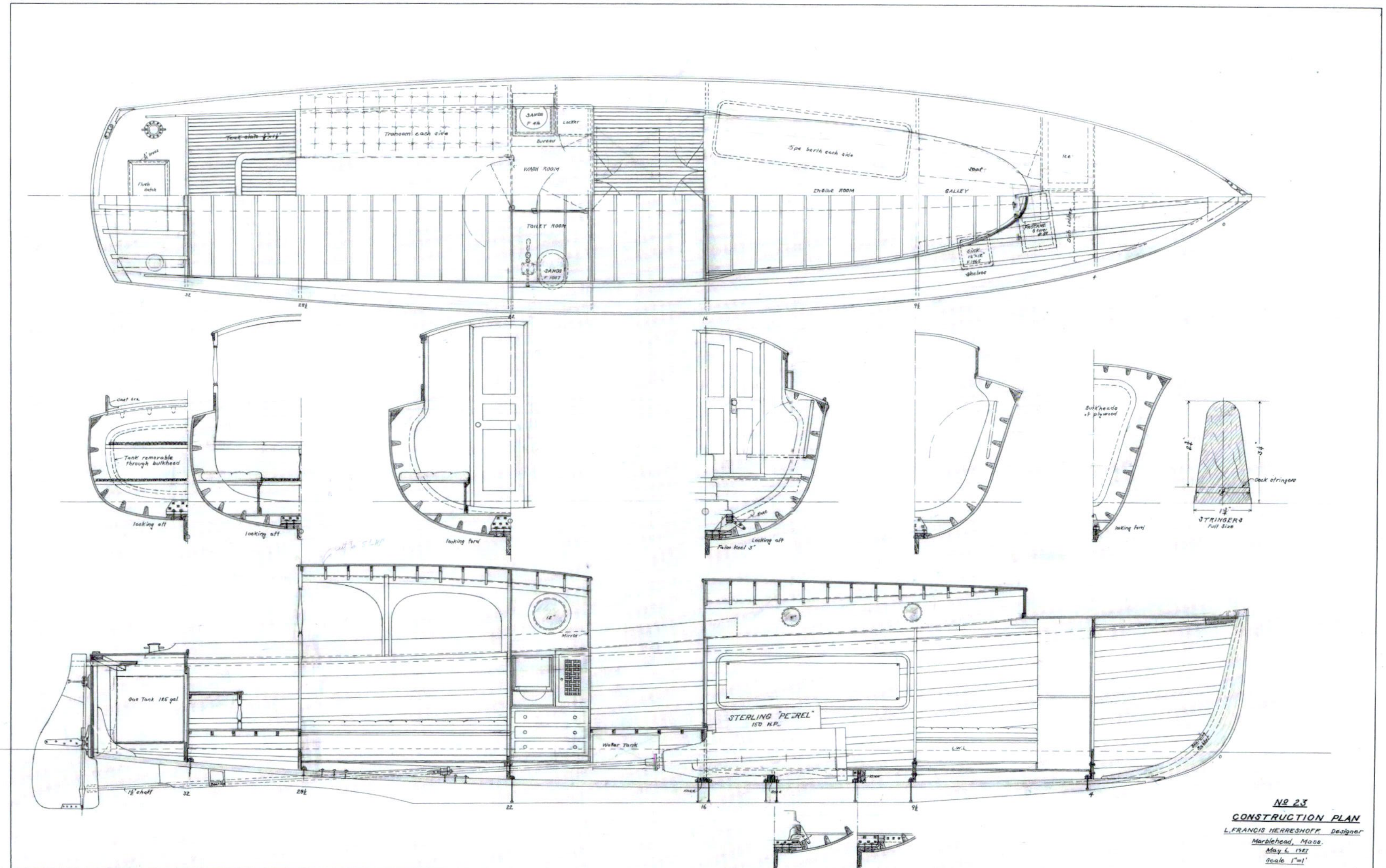
Trahoom each side
Sando F 46
Locker
Bureau
Wash Room
Toilet Room
Sando F 1007
7pe berth each side
Engine Room
Galley
Flush hatch
Tank removable through bulkhead
looking aft
looking aft
looking ford
looking aft
looking ford
Bulkheads of plywood
Oak stringers
STRINGERS Full Size
Gas Tank 125 gal.
Mirror
12"
STERLING "PETREL" 150 H.P.
Water Tank
1¼" shaft
No 23
CONSTRUCTION PLAN
L. FRANCIS HERRESHOFF Designer
Marblehead, Mass.
May 6, 1951
Scale 1"=1'

The outboard profile and sail plan of the *Albacore,* Francis's Design No. 36, actually designed by his new draftsman, Samuel H. Brown. She has a conventional, Alden look to her, though Sam Brown never worked for Alden. The mizzenmast is stayed forward to the mainmast head, with running backstays pulling in opposition to that stay. There's also a permanent backstay on the mainmast. She has the cruising boat's lazy jacks on all three sails, to gather them on their booms when they are lowered. The sail area is 832 square feet. (© Mystic Seaport, Daniel S. Gregory Ships Plans Library, SP38.207.5)

RIGHT: The *Albacore*'s lines. Owner George N. Gregory required shoal draft, so she is a centerboarder with a long, shallow keel. She has a little hollow in the waterline at the bow and lots of buoyancy in her short, wide, counter stern; she might get a little down-angle when heeled, and she might root a bit in a big, following sea. The *Albacore* is 40 feet, 8 inches long on deck; 32 feet, 3 inches on the waterline; with a beam of 12 feet; and a draft of 4 feet, 2 inches. (© Mystic Seaport, Daniel S. Gregory Ships Plans Library, SP38.207.1)

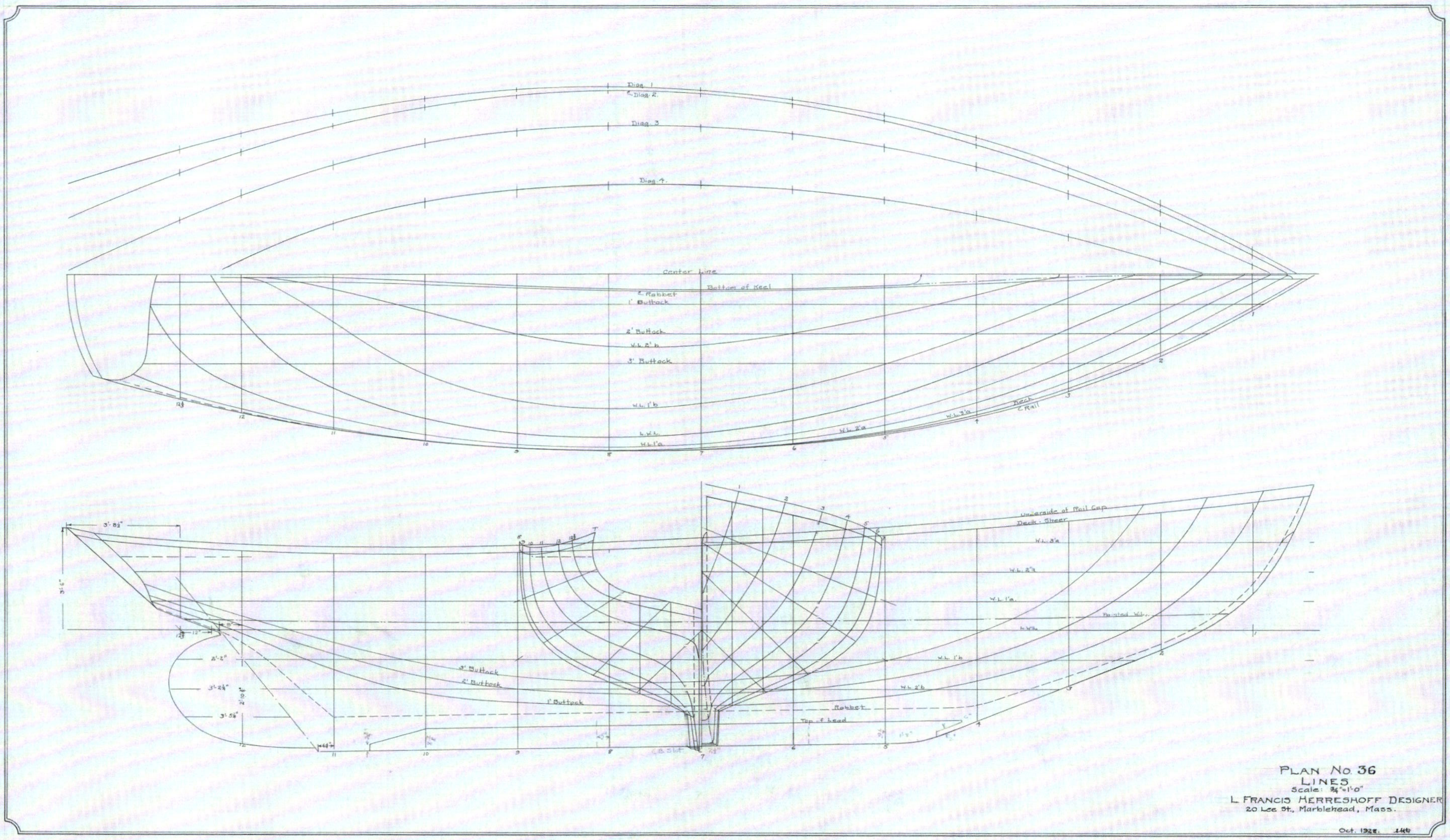
PLAN NO. 36
LINES
Scale: 3/4"=1'0"
L FRANCIS HERRESHOFF DESIGNER
20 Lee St., Marblehead, Mass.
Oct. 1928. 148
Diag. 1
Diag. 2
Diag. 3
Diag. 4
Center Line
Bottom of Keel
Rabbet
1' Buttock
2' Buttock
3' Buttock
Deck
Rail
Underside of Rail Cap
Deck Sheer
Painted W.L.
L.W.L.
Rabbet
Top of Lead
B-207.1

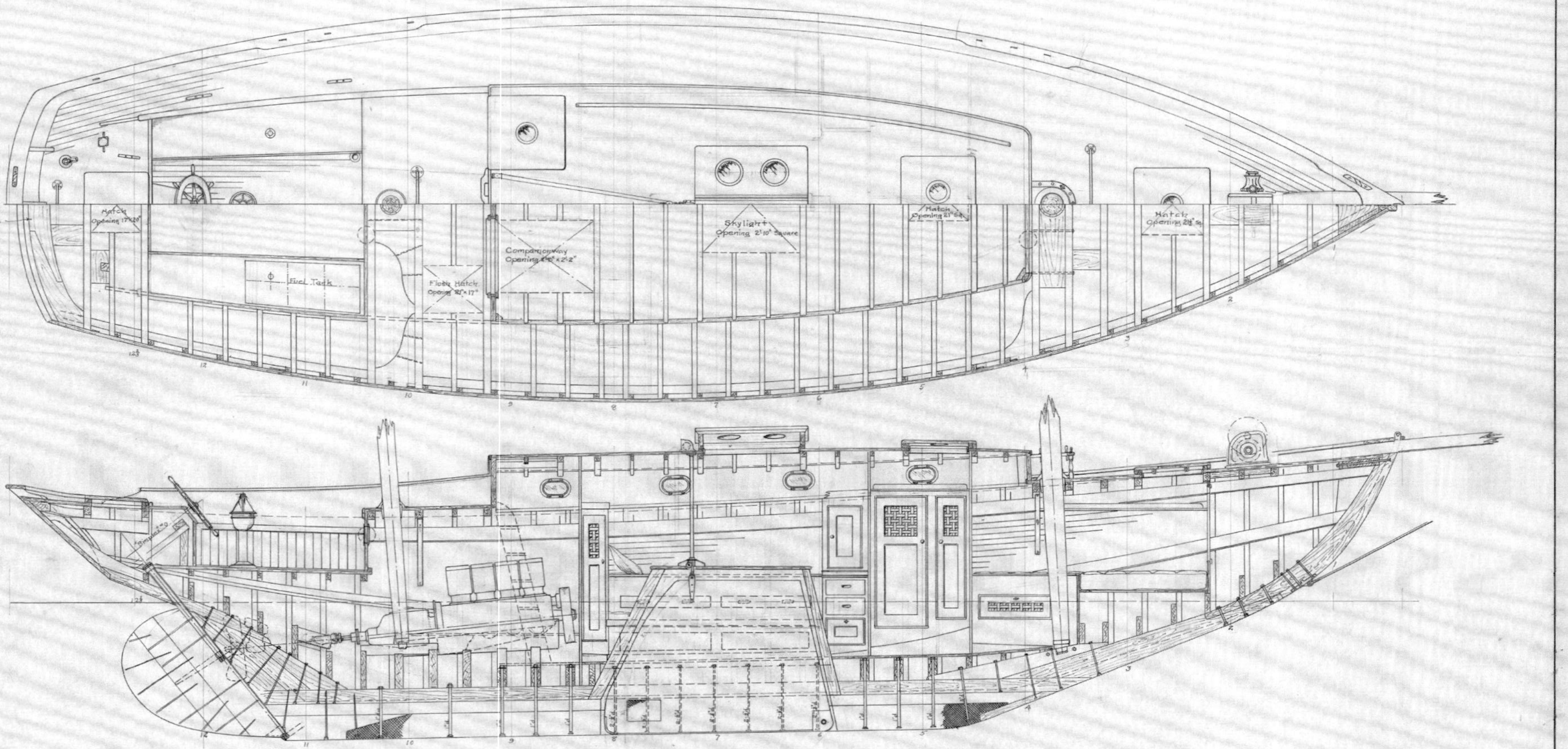

— No. 36 —

— CONSTRUCTION PLAN —

Scale: ¾" = 1'-0"

L. FRANCIS HERRESHOFF DESIGNER

Marblehead, Mass.

Oct. 1928

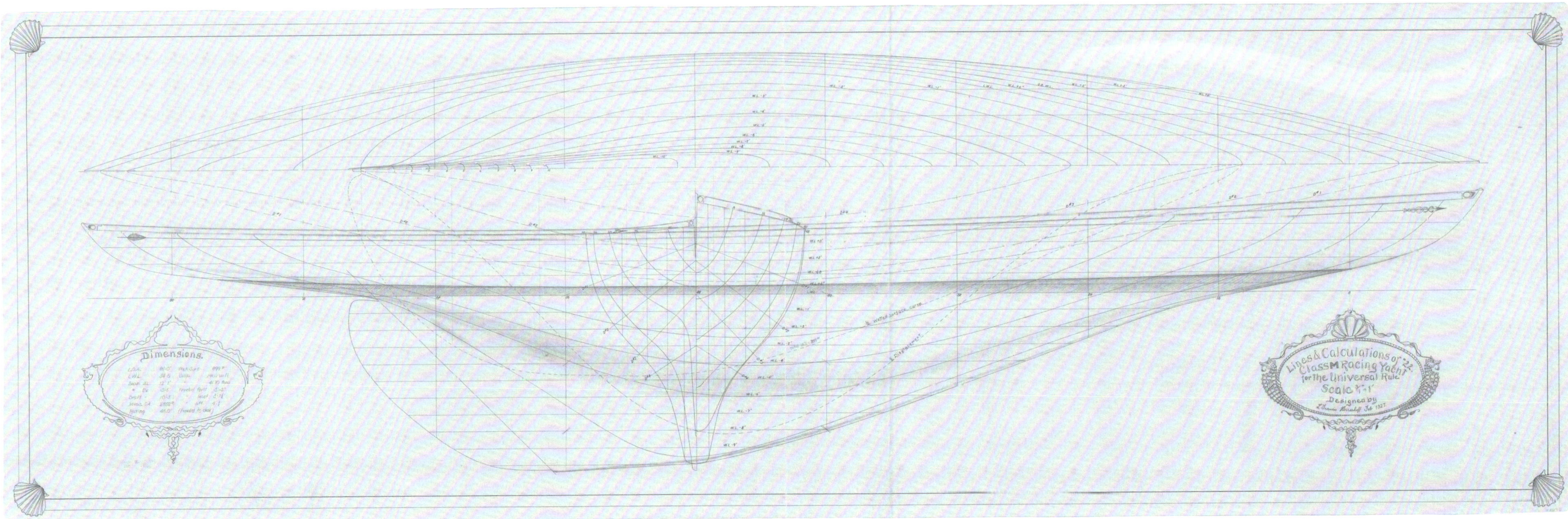

The lines of No. 22. Her hull shape emphasizes low wetted surface, but is not so extreme in that respect as is the *Live Yankee*. The double-ended hull is traditional, rather than streamlined. The maximum rating of the M-class under the Universal Rule was 46 feet. Besides her on-deck length of 86 feet, her other dimensions are: length on the waterline, 54 feet; beam, 13 feet, 6 inches; and draft, 10 feet, 5 inches. Displacement is 41.7 tons, with 30.8 tons of ballast, giving a ballast-to-displacement ratio of 73.9 percent. (© Mystic Seaport, Daniel S. Gregory Ships Plans Library, SP38.70.1)

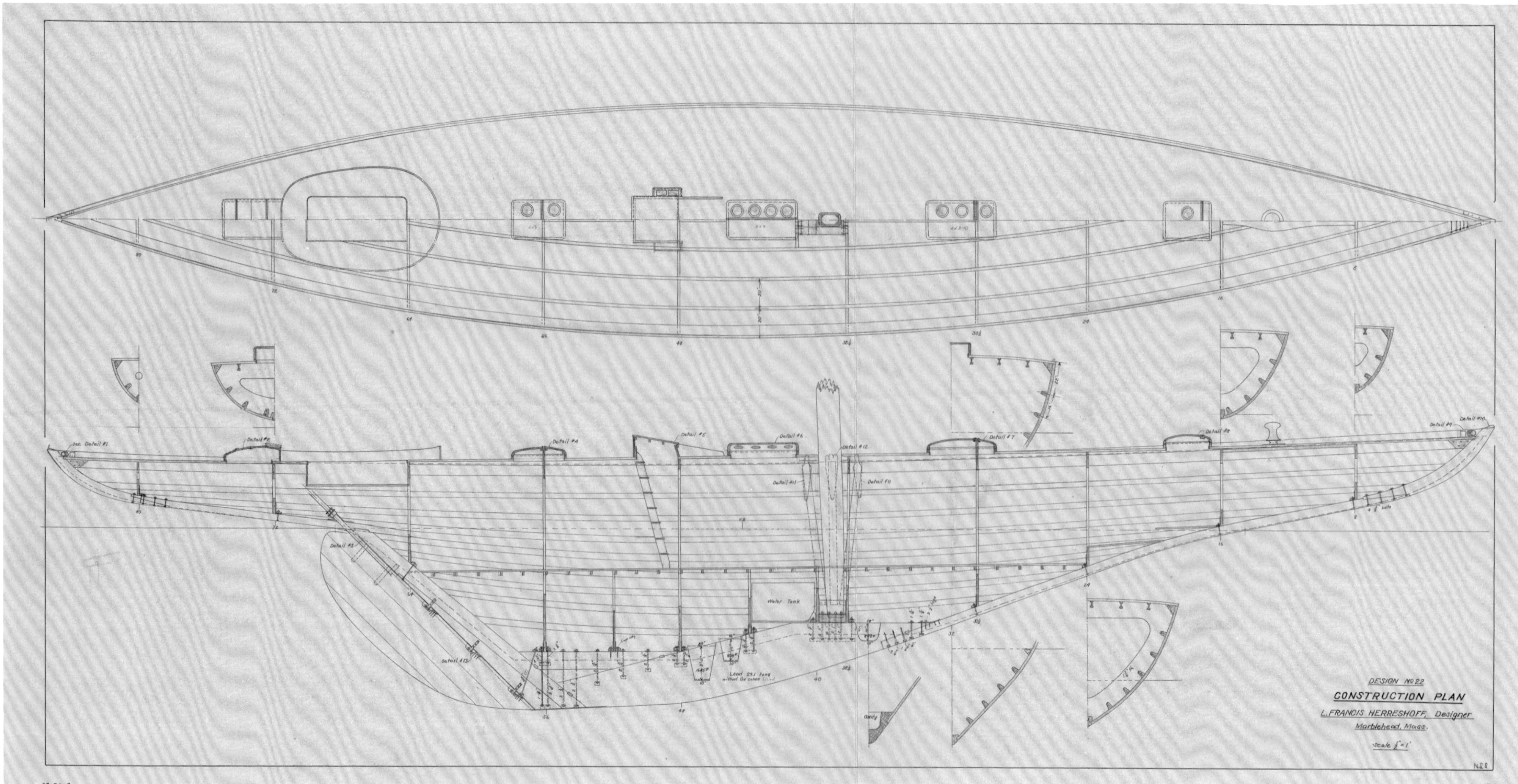

LEFT: The *Albacore*'s construction plan. The weight of her 8,000-pound lead ballast keel is well spread fore-and-aft to dampen her pitching motion. The off-center propeller shaft allows the mizzenmast to have a good step, resting on three floor timbers. Brown specified extra-heavy floors under the big 40-horsepower Lathrop. The limber holes at the bottom of the floor timbers, to drain bilge water fore-and-aft, had a brass chain running through them for clearing debris. She has teak rails, cabin house sides, and cockpit coamings. The cove stripe just below the rail is picked out in gold leaf. The hatch in the after, port corner of the cabin house leads down into the engine room. Not shown in this drawing is a square, flush, bronze hatch in the cockpit sole for access to the lazarette (and propeller shaft stuffing box) below. The George Lawley and Son Corporation did a smooth job on her 1¼-inch Oregon pine planking. (© Mystic Seaport, Daniel S. Gregory Ships Plans Library, SP38.207.3)

the rounded, naval superstucture with more conventional, yacht-like structures and moved the engine forward a bit. He may have sensed that this design wasn't going anywhere, for he has omitted a propeller and a steering station. Sure enough, Santry decided not to build such a craft.[8]

Perhaps Francis was paid something for his hours of design work, and for Skene's tracing of the construction plan, but perhaps not. Francis would normally receive, as a design fee, 10 percent of the cost of building the yacht he had designed. If he completed the design to the point where a boat could be built from his plans, but then the prospective owner changed his mind about spending the money to build the boat, Francis had to negotiate for recompense for his skill and time, and he was far from aggressive in such matters.

Richard P. Jenks, for whose R-boat, the *Scapa II*, Francis had drawn a new rig the previous fall, wanted him to design what Francis called a "Cruising R-boat," design No. 24 on his list of designs. Nothing more than that is known about this concept, for Francis destroyed whatever plans he drew for it. Could he have thought the design to be so bad he was ashamed of it? Probably not. Is it possible he fell out with Jenks to the point where he didn't want his drawings to remind him of an unpleasant situation with a client? This, too, seems improbable, because two years later he designed a small cruising boat for Jenks (bearing no resemblance to an R-boat), and Francis's nature was not forgiving once he had a falling out. Perhaps he simply felt that the idea of trying to make a Universal Rule racing boat into a cruiser simply made no sense. In any event, No. 24 was another design to be chalked up merely to experience.

IN MARCH 1927, Francis made a preliminary drawing showing the outboard profile of a large power yacht for financier Donald F. Tripp of New York City. Compared to the designs being turned out by Lawley's, Consolidated, or the New York Yacht, Launch, and Engine Company, Francis's motor craft had a simple, clean, seaworthy appearance. This prospective owner liked what he saw and, though it took him several months to decide to go ahead, he didn't change his mind.[9]

Tripp was Francis's first client from New York. His reputation was just beginning to break through that invisible yet palpable barrier that separated the yachtsmen of New England waters from those of Long Island Sound. The breakthrough was for a power yacht, but it would soon be followed by a chance to make designs of racing sailboats for New Yorkers.

By August, Francis was busy with Tripp's involved design, a project that would occupy him through the following fall and winter. He would also get commissions to design three more racing boats for the 1928 season. Francis needed more help. He hired as draftsman Samuel H. Brown Jr., a Marbleheader, who, like Norman Skene, was already an experienced yacht designer.

Sam Brown and Francis got on well together.

LEFT: The construction plan of No. 22. Francis has adapted his longitudinal construction to a much larger structure than before attempted. Note the three separate cones in the top of the lead ballast. Francis was hedging his bet on how much ballast she could carry; he has provided himself an easy way to remove up to 3,411 pounds of lead, should she float lower than her designed waterline. Neither the expanded longitudinal construction nor the necessity to remove ballast were tested, for the potential owner, Harold S. Vanderbilt, shied away from Francis's advanced design and chose, instead, a more conventional M-boat from the drawing board of Starling Burgess. (© Mystic Seaport, Daniel S. Gregory Ships Plans Library, SP38.70.2)

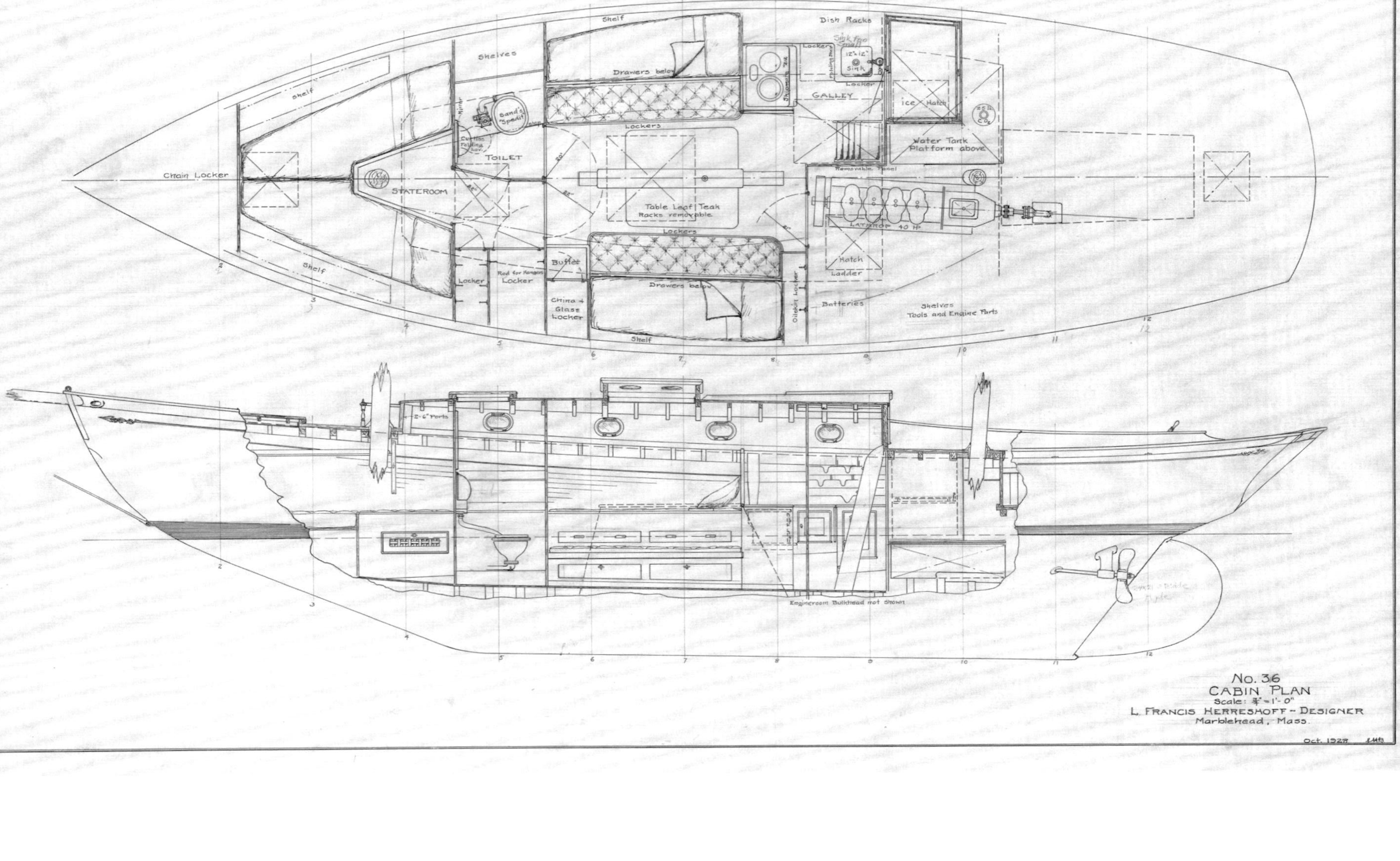

No. 36
CABIN PLAN
Scale: ⅜" = 1'-0"
L. FRANCIS HERRESHOFF - DESIGNER
Marblehead, Mass.

Oct. 1927 LFH

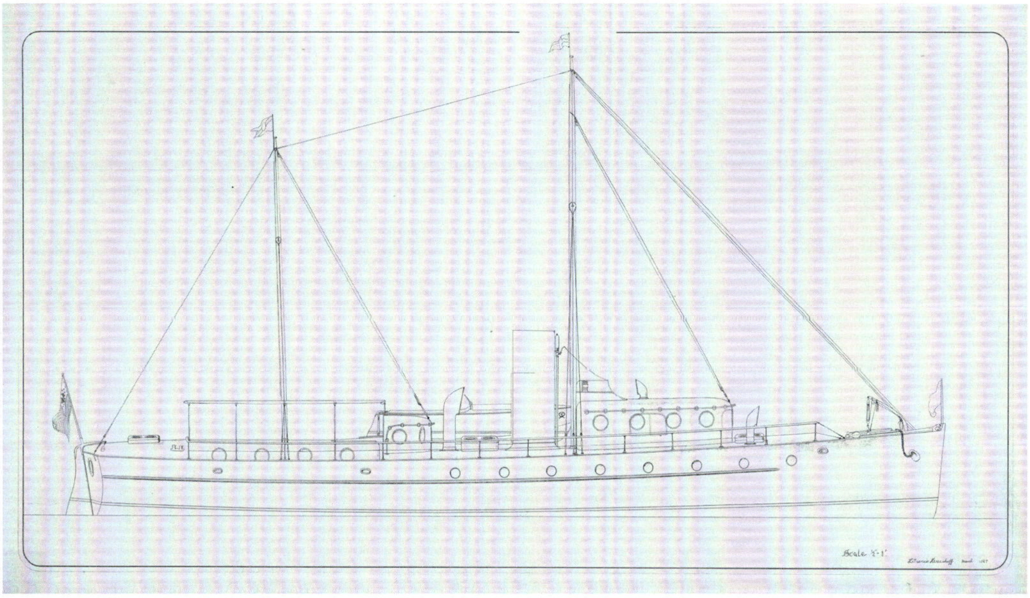

Sam admired Francis's work and seemed to be happier making finished ink drawings from Francis's penciled designs than he was originating his own yacht designs. He had been designing boats since 1920 and had turned out handsome sailing cruisers, as well as fast power cruisers, straightforward designs without quirks. He had been the in-house designer for the Cumberland Shipbuilding Company at South Portland, Maine, in 1924, at the time when Cumberland built the schooner *Mañana* to Francis's design. Shortly before joining Francis, he designed a class of 18-foot racing dories for Cape Ann waters. And he designed a 21-foot Beachcomber dory, the *Outlaw*, that was so fast she broke up that racing class. Sam Brown was a connection for Francis to the Marblehead and Salem watermen who raced dories. These were working-class sailors, not yachtsmen; men, like those of the Provincetown waterfront, with whom Francis felt most comfortable.[10]

And Sam brought a client to Francis who was looking specifically for a Samuel H. Brown design. By October 1928, Sam had completed the plans for a 41-foot cruising ketch for George N. Gregory, to

LEFT: **The cabin plan of the *Albacore*. There is access to the engine room from the cabin, as well as from the deck. In the snug galley, the cook has just enough room to dodge companionway traffic. There is a hatch in the bridge deck so that ice may be lowered directly into its box. The obstruction of the big centerboard trunk is almost hidden under the cabin table. A later owner complained about the narrowness of the berths in the main cabin. On this drawing, someone penciled: "Sink too small." It was a foot square.** (© Mystic Seaport, Daniel S. Gregory Ships Plans Library, SP38.207.6) ABOVE: **Francis's first preliminary drawing of the motor yacht *Siva*, for Donald F. Tripp, made in March 1927. She has provision for considerable auxiliary sail area in her two-masted rig; a tall stack, complete with whistle, even though she will be powered by gasoline engines, not steam; and a well-rounded transom stern with outboard rudder. A fast motor launch shows on deck to port. She has a handsome, businesslike, naval look.** (© Mystic Seaport, Daniel S. Gregory Ships Plans Library, SP 38.76.47)

be named the *Albacore*. Her plans are all labeled, "L. Francis Herreshoff—Designer." Francis was doing what Alden and other designers did, putting his own name on a design by an employee. He would surely have gone over the plans and approved them, but he made no attempt to put his own ideas into the design. The *Albacore* is the only L. Francis Herreshoff yacht that wasn't born in his mind.

Nathanael was not aware of the situation, and, when he saw the *Albacore*'s plans published in William Atkin's magazine, *Fore an' Aft,* he gave Francis a detailed review of the design, softening his remarks with, "Excuse my criticism." Francis replied: "I think very little of her, but she is exactly what her owner wanted. She was designed almost entirely by Mr. Sam Brown, who works for me and is almost exactly like a boat Mr. Brown designed before he worked for me, and which the owner saw and wanted one built like." Gregory required less draft than that of the Brown ketch he admired, so Sam drew a centerboard version, cutting down the draft by 1 foot, 7 inches, and adding 1 foot, 2 inches to her beam.[11]

Francis remarked to his father that he thought that the *Albacore*'s mizzen was too big. He had evidently been playing with the ketch rig in his mind for the last five years since designing the *Stormy Petrel* for Charlie Welch. He surely remembered those starry nights in that ketch, lying-to off Cape Ann under just the mizzen. The *Stormy Petrel*'s mizzen, in proportion to her mainsail, was at least as big as that of the *Albacore*. But when Francis returned to the ketch rig in later designs, he would give them smaller mizzens.

The *Albacore* was to be built at the Lawley yard. The contract named Francis as the "Architect," and specified that the boat was to be built "under the direction and to the satisfaction of said Architect." She was to be delivered by April 1, 1929, at a price of $12,500. The owner had to provide the sails, but the contract price included such items as anchors and rodes, binnacle, brass bell, windlass, bilge pump, running lights, and even fenders. Francis's commission was $1,250. There is no record of whether or not he passed any of it along to Sam Brown, who would have been getting a modest weekly paycheck from Francis.[12]

Lawley's launched the *Albacore* on schedule, but George Gregory was only to enjoy her for one summer. October of 1929 brought the stock-market crash. Gregory was one of those so devastated by his losses that he took his own life. It was years before the *Albacore* found a new owner. We leave her now, to languish in the back corner of a Marblehead boatyard, but she will come back into Francis's story.

Sam Brown continued his own design work independent of Francis's business, turning out a few designs under his own name during the years he worked for Francis. Sam had designed and built a 24-foot cruising sloop for his own use, the *Har*, and Francis thought enough of the design to include it as an example in a published study he made of an evaluation of different types of cruising boats. In 1931, Sam enlarged the design to a length of 30 feet. In 1933, Charles Foster came to Sam, rather than to Francis, to design another experimental rig for a big cruising boat he had bought, the "backstaysail rig," in which the mizzen of a ketch was set on a backstay from the mainmast head, rather than on its own mast. Two years later, Sam tried rigging the mizzen of a yawl that way on one of his own designs, but the backstaysail rig was not successful. Sam would stay working as a draftsman for Francis until 1936, when the effects of the Great Depression would force Francis to lay off all his help. Sam Brown kept designing good, small cruising boats at least until 1945.[13]

For Donald Tripp's motor yacht, Francis made a second preliminary drawing, dated August 22, 1927, changing the stern from a transom with outboard rudder to a longer, pointed stern. Francis convinced Tripp that the double-ended hull would have less resistance than the one with a transom stern, perhaps explaining that this difference had been demonstrated by his father's model experi-

ments of nearly fifty years before. Nathanael had towed models from a launch running in smooth water, two models of differing hull shape side-by-side on a yoke, so that it was obvious which of the two had greater resistance, and he had found that the double-ended hull had the least resistance of any hull form that he tried. Tripp asked Francis to go ahead with the design of the double-ended version of his preliminary drawings. The design became Francis's No. 25. Tripp named his motor yacht the *Siva*, after the Hindu god of energy.[14]

In the fall of 1927, Francis and his two draftsmen went to work on the *Siva*'s plans. In the big, second-floor drafting room in the old custom-house at 20 Lee Street, there were now five drafting boards set up, one for Norman Skene, one for Sam Brown, and three for Francis. Norman and Sam worked on one drawing at a time, making finished, inked copies of Francis's penciled work, but Francis had to coordinate the different elements of the multiple designs he was working on, going back and forth among overall appearance, hull shape, rig or space for machinery, cabin fixtures, and construction details, while keeping ahead of his draftsmen.[15]

Although the only copy of the *Siva*'s lines plan that has come to light is not reproducible, we can see the general shape of the hull, with its shallow, vee-bottom and well-rounded, easy bilges, from the construction-section drawings and

---

The second preliminary plan of the *Siva* that Francis drew in August was the one followed for the design, which would be Francis's No. 25. The stern has been lengthened by nine feet, coming to a point, and there are less-important changes to the superstructure. The original lines drawing for this design has not come to light, and the only copy is not sharp enough to reproduce. The vessel's dimensions are: length on deck, 91 feet; length on the waterline, 88 feet, 6 inches; beam, 15 feet, 6 inches; draft, 4 feet, 10 inches. (© Mystic Seaport, Daniel S. Gregory Ships Plans Library, SP38.76.3) **For the *Siva*'s inboard profile, cabin, deck, and deck construction plans, see foldout opposite page 244.**

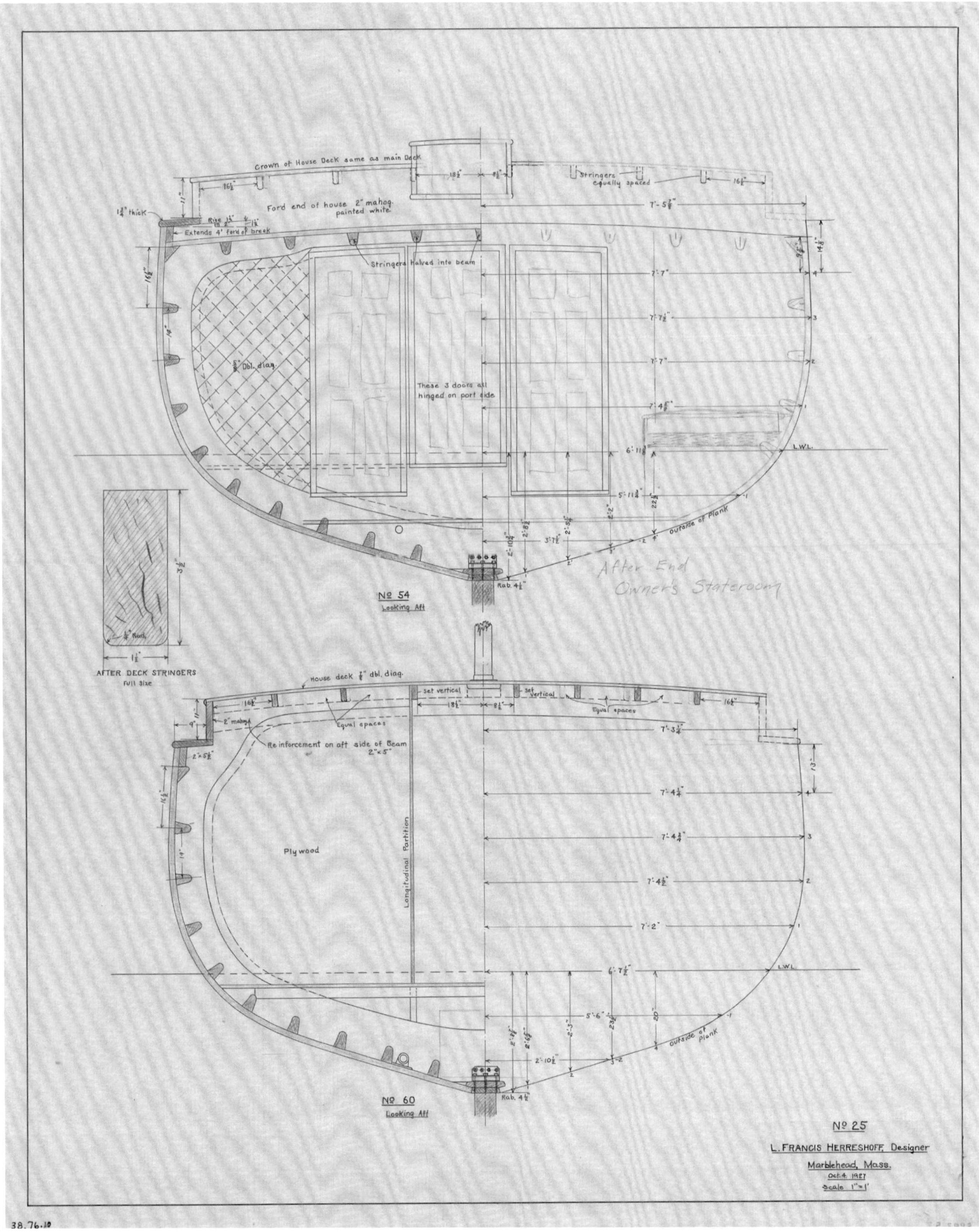
Crown of House Deck same as main Deck
Stringers equally spaced
Ford end of house 2" mahog. painted white
Extends 4" ford of break
Stringers halved into beam
Dbl. diag.
These 3 doors all hinged on port side
LWL.
outside of plank
After End Owner's Stateroom
Rab. 4½"
№ 54
Looking Aft
AFTER DECK STRINGERS
full size
House deck ⅞" dbl. diag.
set vertical
set vertical
Equal spaces
Equal spaces
Reinforcement on aft side of Beam 2"×5"
Plywood
Longitudinal Partition
outside of plank
Rab. 4½
№ 60
Looking Aft
№ 25
L. FRANCIS HERRESHOFF, Designer
Marblehead, Mass.
Oct. 4 1927
Scale 1"=1'
38.76.10

the inboard profile drawing. As he had with the *Dispatch*, Francis used his longitudinal construction system, so that the vessel would be strong and relatively light. Still, the *Siva* had to be built with heavier scantlings than those of a sailing yacht of comparable size, for her hull would have to be able to support powerful engines and large tanks full of gasoline and water, while negotiating waves at twice the speed of a sailing yacht. Francis achieved a displacement for this 90-footer of just under 43 tons, of which 2-1/2 tons was iron ballast on the keel to add stability for standing up to her auxiliary sail. He sought high cruising speed with low power by designing a long, narrow, light hull, and one with the shape that his father had shown to be of least resistance. Francis again entrusted Chester and Andrew Britt to follow his construction drawings and build the largest wooden longitudinal hull yet. As with the other boats he designed this way, Francis specified double planking, the inner layer laid diagonally, the outer, of mahogany, laid fore-and-aft and set in glue.[16]

LEFT: **The *Siva*'s construction sections, showing her web frames and twenty-six longitudinals. Norman Skene drafted these drawings and dated them October 7, 1927.** (© Mystic Seaport, Daniel S. Gregory Ships Plans Library, SP38.76.10) ABOVE: **The *Siva* running smoothly at 16 knots.** (Edwin Levick photo 97928, The Mariners' Museum, Newport News, Virginia)

The Rudder reported that the *Siva* was the largest wooden yacht built east of Cape Cod in 1928. Francis, Norman Skene, and Sam Brown turned out fifty drawings describing the design for the Britts to follow, including detailed plans of the deckhouse windows, life-rail stanchions, skylights, launch and anchor davits with special winches, hawsepipes, and bulkhead stuffing boxes (so watertight integrity would not be compromised by piping and wiring running through the bulkheads). He left as little as possible to chance, by thinking through all these details and putting his ideas on paper. For cabin partitions, Francis specified plywood, for lightness. The *Siva* was a big, complicated vessel that required many hours of skilled work at the Britt Brothers' yard. Her cost was given variously at $75,000 and $80,000. The design commission, at 10 percent, was welcome

ABOVE: **Looking forward in the *Siva*'s owner's stateroom. Francis designed the door leading to the tank space to be watertight, with naval-style dogs to tighten it down against its gasket.** (Edwin Levick photo 97853, The Mariners' Museum, Newport News, Virginia) RIGHT: **Sam Brown's drawing showing how the *Siva*'s two Winton 106-A, six-cylinder gasoline engines and the Winton W-17, 5-kilowatt generator were to be installed in the engine room.** (© Mystic Seaport, Daniel S. Gregory Ships Plans Library, SP38.76.34)

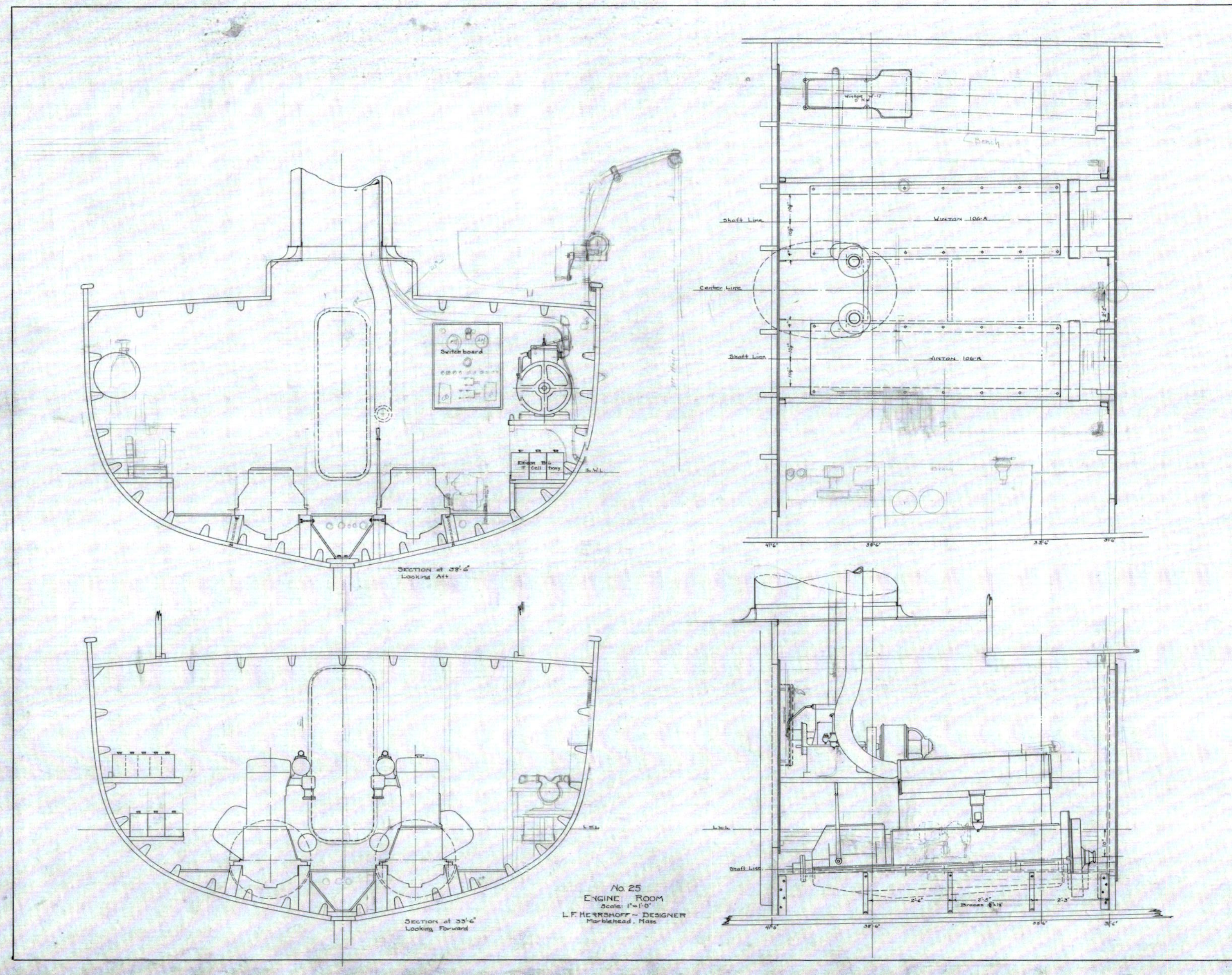
Switchboard
Looking Aft
Shaft Line
Center Line
Shaft Line
Winton 106-A
Winton 106-A
Bench
Section at 33'-6"
Looking Forward
No. 25
Engine Room
Scale: 1"=1'-0"
L.F. Herreshoff – Designer
Marblehead, Mass.

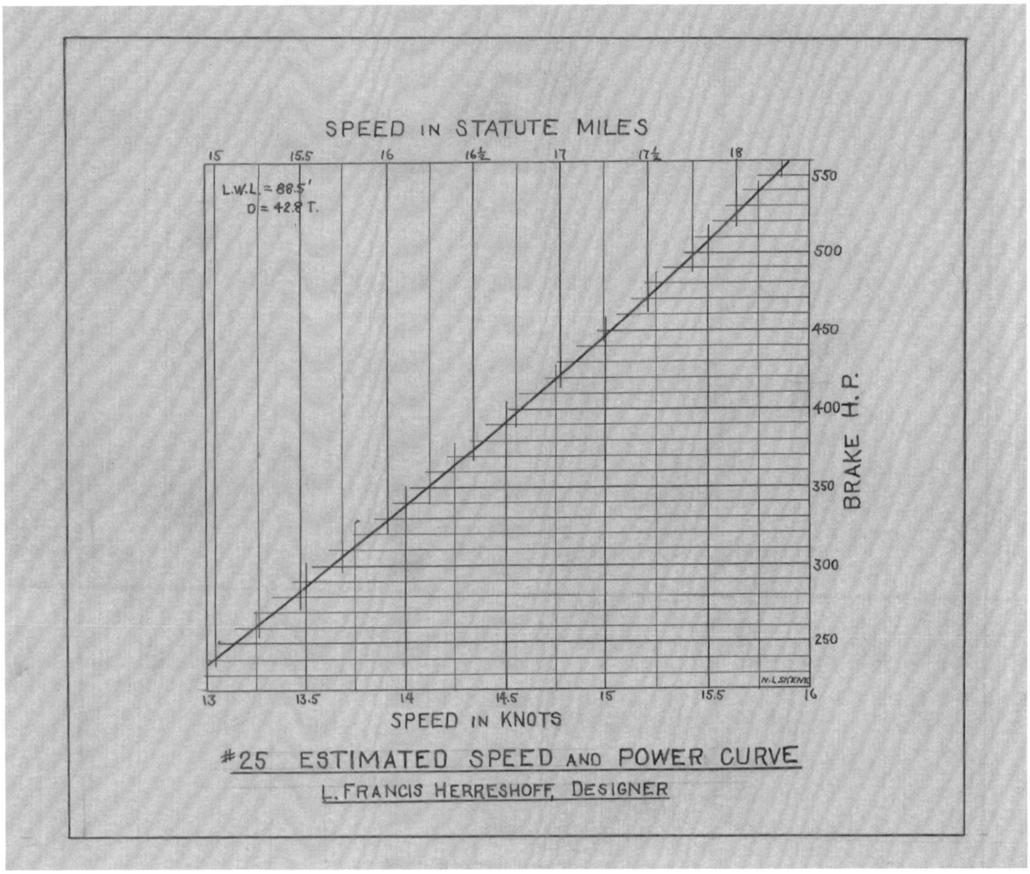

income indeed to Francis's fledgling business.[17]

The editors at *MoToR Boating* were impressed. In a spread on the *Siva*, they concluded, "The boat is ultra-modern in its conception and construction, and a result has been obtained with no compromises as to speed, comfort or sea quality as she exceeds in these points anything of her size. The *Siva* is the forerunner of a new type cruiser of marked distinction." They assumed that L. Francis Herreshoff, having produced a new and different

ABOVE: The estimated-speed and power curve that Norman Skene drew for the *Siva*. Her two Wintons developed 530 horsepower, which showed as 15.7 knots. Francis gave her speed at different times as 16 mph and 16 knots (18.4 mph). (© Mystic Seaport, Daniel S. Gregory Ships Plans Library, SP38.76.41) RIGHT: The *Siva*'s power tender. She is 15 feet long, with a beam of 4 feet, 4-1/2 inches, and a draft of 1 foot, 5 inches. The gasoline engine is a Gray, with four cylinders developing 30 horsepower, giving a speed of 15 mph. Since the boat was to be hoisted out on davits, Francis kept her weight down to 900 pounds (440 pounds for the engine) with his longitudinal construction. Sam Brown made this drawing in October 1927. The penciled-in spray hood and windshield resulted from a telegram with a last-minute thought from the owner the following June 25th: "Please suggest to Britt some provision for rain and spray cover for launch." (© Mystic Seaport, Daniel S. Gregory Ships Plans Library, SP38.76A.1; Collection 138, Box 16, Folder 9, G. W. Blunt White Library, Mystic Seaport)

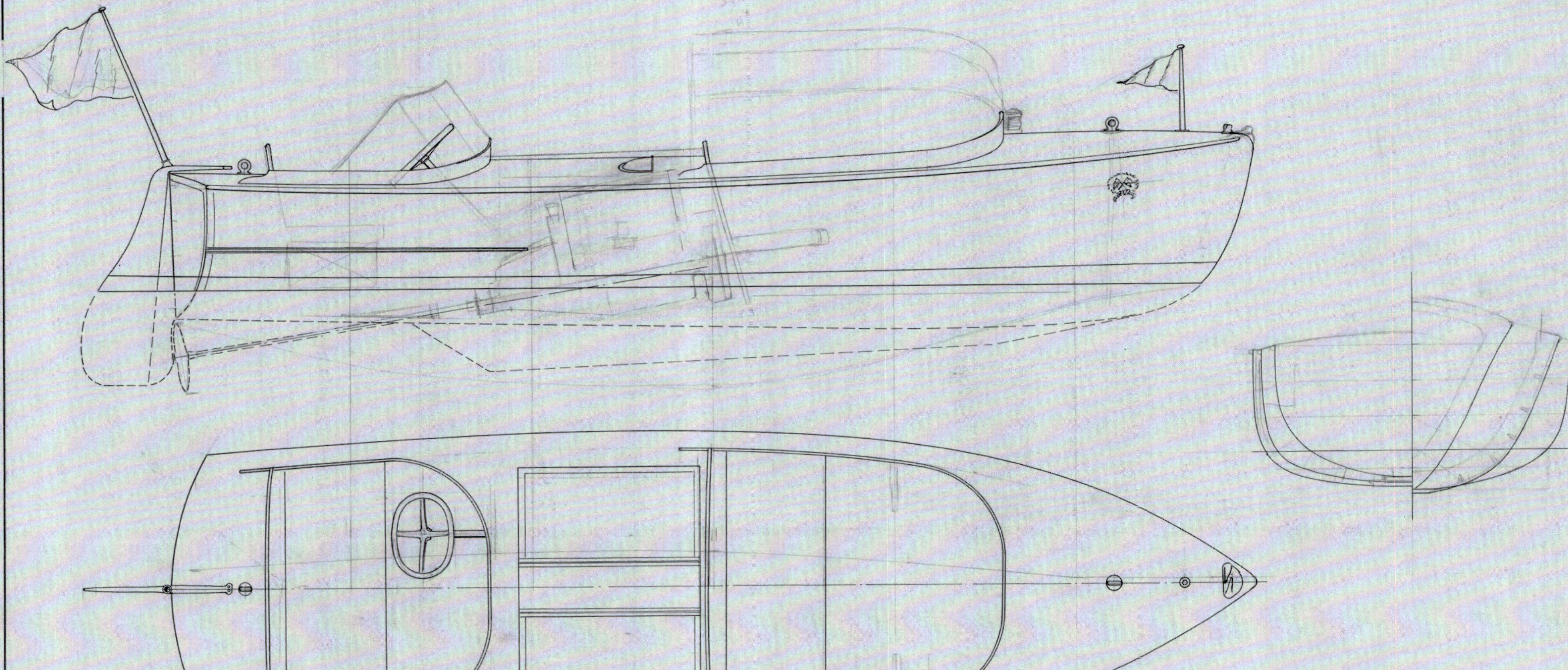

No. 25

POWER TENDER

Scale: 1" = 1'-0"

L.F. HERRESHOFF DESIGNER

Marblehead, Mass

October 1927

S.H.B.

design for a large power yacht with advantages over current designs, would capitalize on his concept and follow the *Siva* with, perhaps, a family of gradually improved near sister ships that would become popular. Not Francis. *MoToR Boating* had used the word "Unique" in its headline on the *Siva*, and it was that word, rather than "forerunner," that would be operative. Francis's primary interest was in the design of racing sailboats, and he had no time or entrepreneurial interest or energy for trying to create a business around the designing of a series of large power yachts. His personality simply wasn't suited for business. He did not see himself as a man of financial success, and, unlike his father, he had no partner who did.[18]

It was, perhaps, just as well. Editorial opinion notwithstanding, Tripp didn't keep the *Siva* long, and she had a succession of owners in the thirties. She was certainly different from other motor yachts of her day, and her owners may have been jealous of their friends' bigger engines (fuel was cheap to anyone who could afford such a craft), to say nothing of their large, plate-glass windows. Boats with those features were the bread and butter of designers working for companies like Elco or Consolidated, and were also typical of a power-boat designed by Sam Brown, but Francis never followed the crowd. Still, the design commission for the *Siva*, even though it didn't lead to others, must have been a great relief to Francis as he sought to "make ends meet."

And Francis liked the *Siva*. She was renamed, coincidentally, the *Roamer*, a name with which he had grown up. He wrote to the new owner of the *Roamer:* "You will find her a very fine sea boat and particularly steady. I am quite sure she is one of the safest, strongest boats of her type around, and when her engines are in condition, her bottom cleaned, and proper propellers on she will go sixteen miles per hour." The *Roamer* saw service as a patrol boat during World War II. With her double-ended hull, strong construction, small windows well out of reach of all but the biggest waves, and watertight compartmentation, she was a more seaworthy vessel than many owners needed, but she was one of the most suitable yachts for war service. Whether Tripp and others wanted it or not, Francis's wartime experience off Rhode Island's exposed coast in winter showed in the design. The *Siva* was the only large power yacht built to a design by L. Francis Herreshoff. In looks and performance, she was a superior vessel. The *Roamer* was still running as a yacht at least until 1956.[19]

AS INTERESTING and successful a commission as was that of the *Siva*, it was the request for the design of a new racing sailboat that Francis wanted most. When a racing sailor was contemplating a new boat and choosing a designer for it, he naturally sought as many opinions as possible on which designer was likely to give him the edge on the racecourse. The most valuable tips came from fellow yachtsmen discussing, or maybe just gossiping about, who was getting a new design from whom. At yacht club bars, in many a cockpit after the day's race, and on the lawns or around the fireplaces of yachtsmen, there was lots of talk about the details of racing sailboat design. It was in those places, as well as on the water, where the reputations of yacht designers flowed and ebbed. When the *Live Yankee* joined the Marblehead R-boat fleet, the yachtsmen's grapevine must have shaken with polemics ranging from "Herreshoff is a genius, like his father" to "Herreshoff has gone round the bend." Some designers, like Loring Swasey and John Alden, participated purposefully in the give-and-take, seeking to sell themselves or enhance their reputations. Francis, socially shy, proud, and disdainful of such doings, was not among them. The men who gathered round his hearth of an evening to talk boats rarely included a prospective customer.

Another way yachtsmen had of keeping abreast of developments and judging the work of

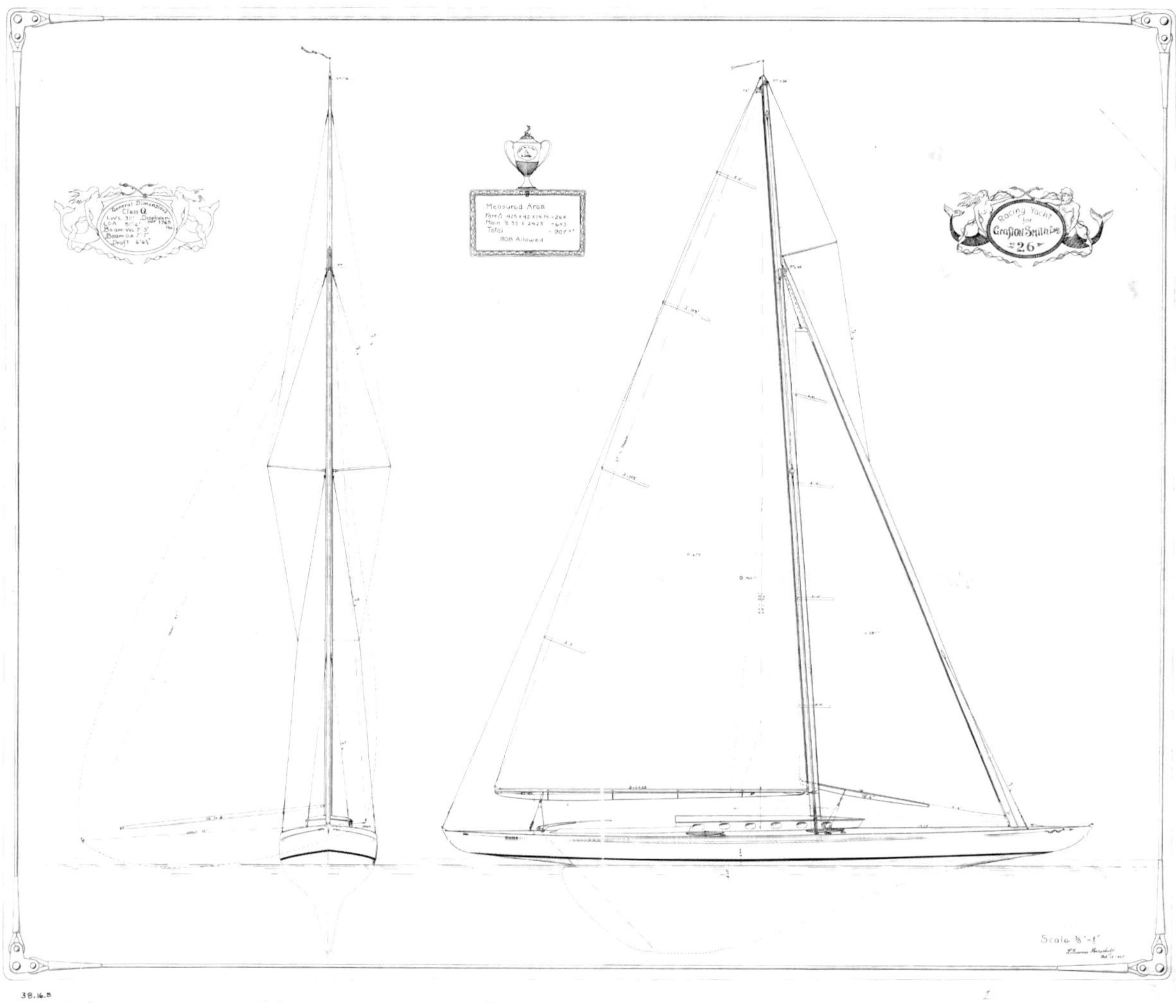

Francis's outboard profile and sail plan for his first Q-boat design, the *Nor'easter V* for Grafton Smith, his design No. 26. The measured sail area is 907 square feet. The jib sets on a luff spar, eliminating the need for running backstays, and has a slightly overlapping, partial club. In dotted lines, Francis shows a Genoa jib, an overlapping, reaching jib, and a single-luff spinnaker; the latter all that was allowed by the rules. He uses a single strut with its stay led to the jib-luff spar to support the masthead. The upper and intermediate shrouds lead all the way to the deck, but he has bowsed them in to the lower shrouds to keep them clear of the lower leech of the Genoa jib. Chain plates are inside the planking, as introduced on the *Yankee*. Francis shows the boat floating at her waterline, with the outline of her underbody in dotted lines. He has given her a high, sheered boot top and an embellished-arrow cove stripe for grace and to reduce the apparent height of her topsides. He has decorated his drawing with a rod-rigging border, mermaids and a merman holding his oval title blocks, and, atop the picture frame around the sail-area figures, a racing trophy inscribed, "Won by the Best." Francis is a proud artist, having fun. He dated the drawing October 15, 1927. (© Mystic Seaport, Daniel S. Gregory Ships Plans Library, SP 38.16.8)

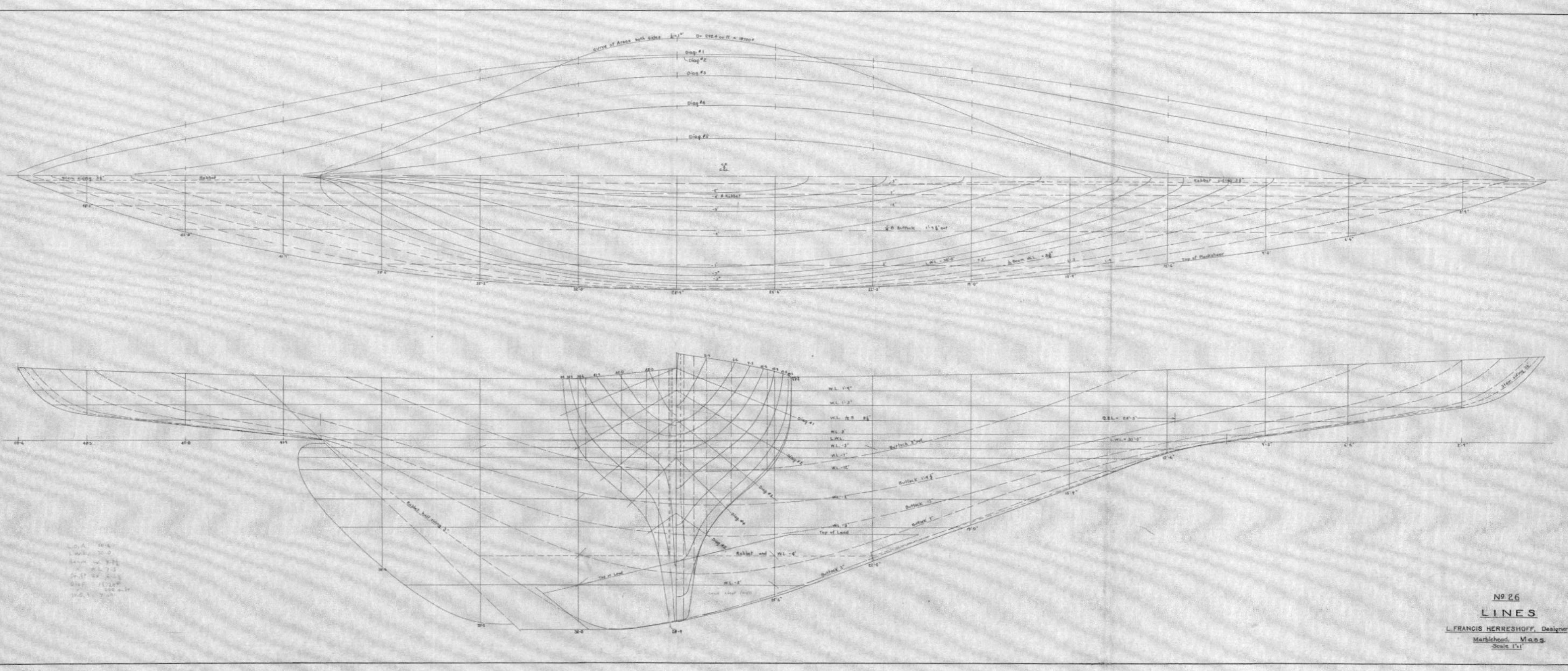

Nº 26

LINES

L. FRANCIS HERRESHOFF, Designer

Marblehead, Mass.

Scale 1" = 1'

designers was to read the daily newspapers and the boating magazines. Big city papers, like the *Boston Globe* or *New York Times*, had their yachting writers, like Leonard M. Fowle of the *Globe* or William U. Swan of the Associated Press, who were more or less expert at covering the racing scene. In the twenties and thirties, many column inches were devoted to the subject. Francis mentioned to his father that he kept friendly with Swan, whom he thought well-meaning but inaccurate, "for fear of the harm he might do me." The leading magazines were *Yachting* and *The Rudder*, both published in New York. We have seen how they treated the *Live Yankee*; there was some reason for Francis's press paranoia. A standard feature of both magazines was a page or so of calling-card-type advertisements of yacht designers. Francis's first one appeared in the July 1927 issue of *Yachting*. Besides his name and address, his card gave, as his specialty, "Racing Yachts."[20]

Francis's self-promotion was low-key; but, after all, he was a Herreshoff, and he had shown what he could do with the R-boat *Yankee*. He did well in Marblehead with the racing community. In the first four years of his yacht design business, he could count as customers, for boat and rig designs, ten of the town's dozen leading racing sailors. The two top sailors who never came to him for a design were Charles Francis Adams and B. Devereux Barker. Francis did have a talk with Adams about the many boats he had raced; maybe the *Live Yankee* scared Adams off. Francis's record of designing winning racing boats undoubtedly would have been enhanced had he designed for Adams, for he was the racing skipper to beat in Marblehead. For seven of the ten who did seek his designs, Francis produced complete designs for racing boats; he drew new rigs for the others. Only one of the seven, however, his good friend Charlie Welch, was a repeat customer, and even Charlie would try other designers. Many yachtsmen of the day wanted to seek a hoped-for advantage on the racecourse nearly every season with a new designer.

THE WINTER of 1927-1928 was a busy one for Francis and his draftsmen, Norman Skene and Sam Brown. Concurrent with work on the *Siva*, Francis designed new racing boats for Grafton Smith, the boating partners W. A. W. Stewart and Harry M. Curtis, and Dr. Morton Prince. Each design was for a different class. Smith wanted a new Universal Rule, 25-rater, Q-boat in Marblehead to replace his *Nor'easter IV*, for which Francis had designed a new rig. Stewart and Curtis wanted a 6-Metre sloop, designed to the

The lines of the *Nor'easter V*. When he determined the details of her hull shape in his penciled lines drawing, Francis cut away the mid-section he had shown in dotted lines on the sail plan. That mid-section was close to the *Live Yankee*'s; the one he used for the *Nor'easter V* was close to that of No. 22, the unbuilt M-boat, whose lines he had drawn eight months earlier. The penciled lines drawing, here inked by Norman Skene, shows how Francis worked. For the profile lines drawing, he started with an inked outline of the boat's profile: sheerline, stem, keel, rudder and rudderpost, and stern; together with inked waterlines, the straight, horizontal lines in the profile view. He used these inked lines as a framework on which to superimpose the curved pencil lines showing hull shape: the fore-and-aft bow and buttock lines and the athwartships sections. He did the same for the half-breadth lines drawing, with the centerline and deck-edge inked, along with the straight buttock lines, as the framework for his penciled, curved waterlines. With his artistic ability to visualize and then put on paper a beautiful and functional hull shape, Francis was able to draw these three sets of coordinated curves, buttock lines, sections, and waterlines, as a single exercise; the *Nor'easter V*'s penciled lines drawing shows only minor erasing and reworking. Dimensions are: length on deck, 50 feet, 6 inches; waterline length, 30 feet; beam, 7 feet, 8 1/2 inches; and draft, 6 feet, 6 1/2 inches. (© Mystic Seaport, Daniel S. Gregory Ships Plans Library, SP38.16.1)

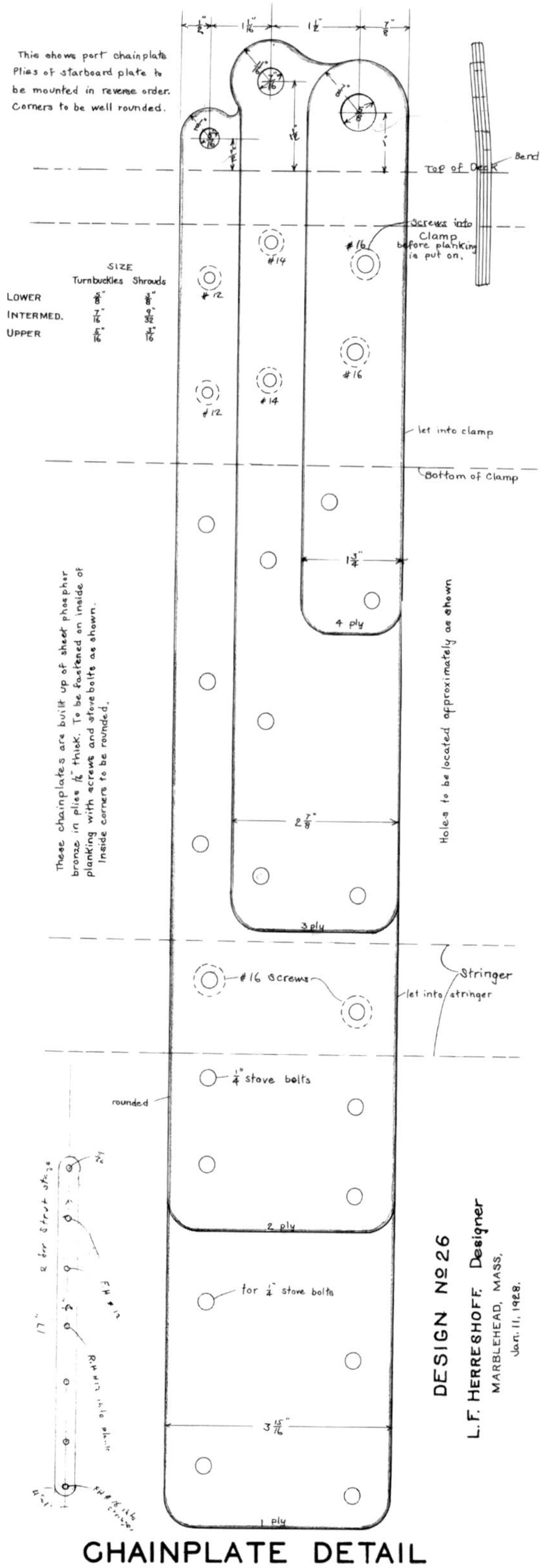

International Rule, for Long Island Sound. Prince wanted a new R-boat in Marblehead.

This was a stressful time for Francis. He wanted to build on his success with the *Yankee*, and he was encouraged by getting orders for more racing boats, but, unlike John Alden, he would not delegate. He cared deeply about his work, about his drawings. He was a proud artist. He would not suffer his draftsmen making any "improvements"

LEFT: The *Nor'easter V*'s inside chain plates are a good example of Francis's scientific design. The four plates, each of 1/16-inch-thick phosphor bronze, overlap. The hole at the upper right (forward on the boat, since the drawing shows the port chain plate viewed from inside the boat) takes the turnbuckle pin for the lower shroud. This pin would go through all four plies, giving maximum strength for the shroud with the most strain. The intermediate shroud, with less strain, would be fitted to the middle hole, through three plies, and the upper shroud, with the least strain, through two plies. The shapes and sizes of each ply, with its fastenings into the various parts of the boat's wood structure (clamp, stringer, and planking) were proportioned to the varying strains of the shrouds. To achieve this scientific design, Francis used his sense of proportion, not mathematics. This is one of Francis's fittings that, had it failed, would perhaps have had all its parts disintegrate simultaneously. (© Mystic Seaport, Daniel S. Gregory Ships Plans Library, SP38.16.22) RIGHT: The *Nor'easter V*'s cabin plan. There wasn't much room for accommodations in a narrow racing boat, and Francis's longitudinal construction, with its web frames extending into the cabin from almost 7 inches at their upper ends to almost a foot at the cabin floor, didn't help. He could squeeze the galley, with its propane stove and sink, and the toilet room, with its folding wash basin, in between frames, but the four bunks had to span frames, so he cut those frames back and reinforced them on the sides. She does have a large icebox under the forward end of the cockpit, accessible by removing the companionway ladder. Francis specified plywood for the fore-and-aft partition of the toilet room to save weight. (© Mystic Seaport, Daniel S. Gregory Ships Plans Library, SP38.16.5)

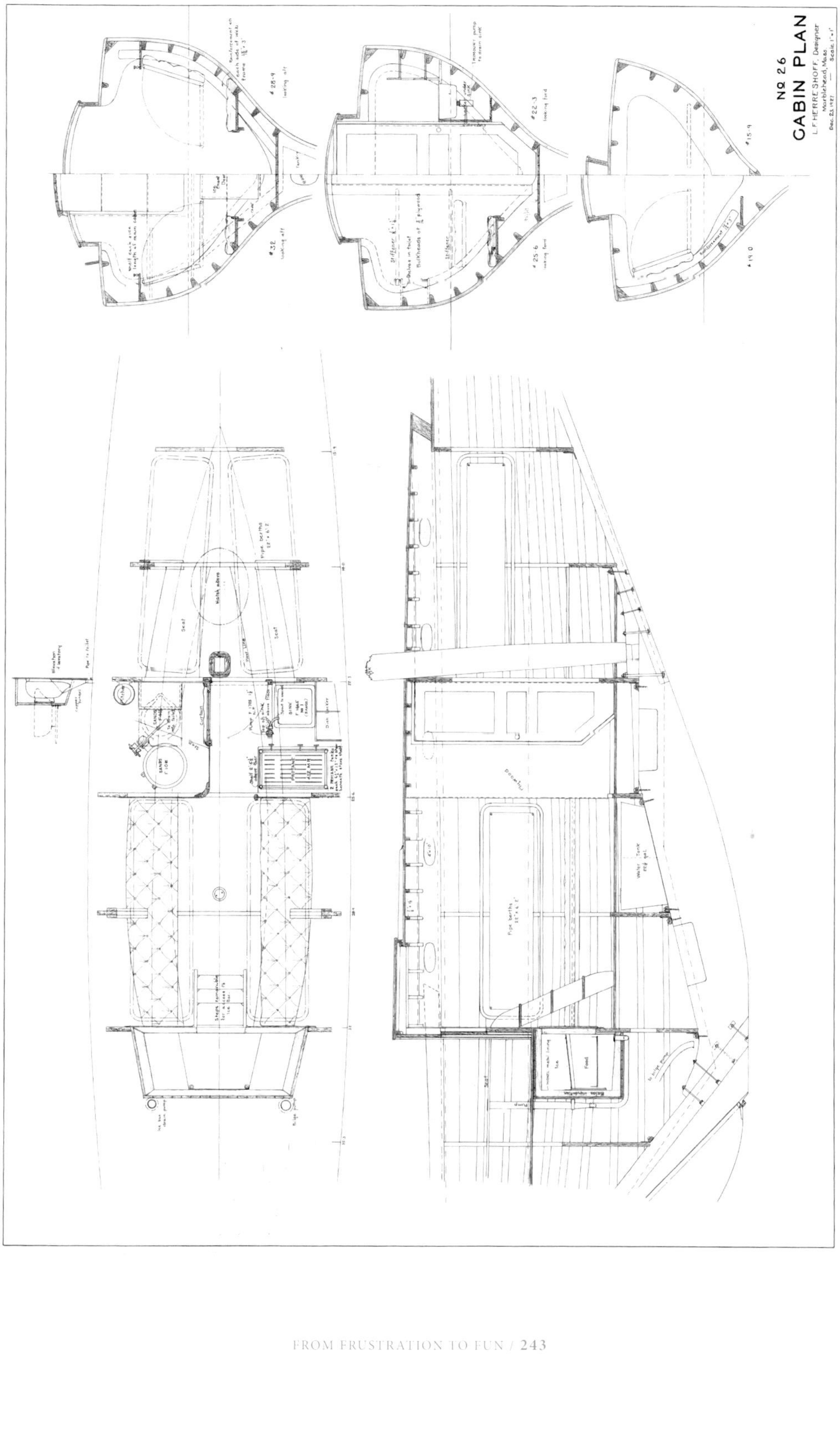
Nº 26
CABIN PLAN
L.F. HERRESHOFF, Designer
Marblehead, Mass.

to his designs. He had to work out every detail for himself.

Francis drew an outboard profile and sail plan for Smith's Q-boat, his design No. 26 to be named the *Nor'easter V*, and dated it October 18, 1927. Then he and Skene and Brown went to work to complete the design. The Q Class was gaining in popularity, in Marblehead in particular, as several owners of R-boats decided to move up to the larger class. A typical Q-boat was 50 feet long on deck and was big enough for a real cabin, cramped for four to be sure, but with a small galley and an enclosed toilet room. Compared to an R-boat, the Q, with her longer waterline, would have a hull speed of something like nine knots, instead of eight. The first Q-boat came out in 1904; by the season of 1928, over sixty had been built. The Marblehead fleet for 1928 numbered sixteen boats, of which thirteen were raced. Three of them, besides the *Nor'easter V*, were new boats designed by Starling Burgess, Frank Paine, and the John Alden office.[21]

For the design of the *Nor'easter V*, Francis's first Q-boat, he drew another double-ender. This hull-form for racing boats was becoming a trademark for him. It would also become a trademark for his old Bristol friend, Nick Potter, who designed double-ended racing boats on the West Coast, like the 8-Metre *Angelita*, which also came out in 1928. Francis cited four reasons for using the pointed stern. First, this form of stern allowed for a longer waterline aft without increasing the quarter-beam length measurement proportionately. Second, the longer, pointed stern made a good attachment point for a permanent backstay. Third, the pointed stern was easier to build, lighter, and less prone to rot than the counter stern. And fourth, the double-ended hull made for a more seaworthy boat.[22]

Nathanael had shown that the double-ender had least resistance and had designed many power-driven boats with pointed sterns, but he believed that a sailboat was best designed with a broader stern to add stability to stand up to her sail. Francis was willing to give up stability from a broader stern and add stability through greater sailing waterline length. His designs show much influence from his father's work, but in designing double-ended sailboats, he broke away entirely.

Another reason for his choosing the double-ended hull form, which Francis did not cite, was his long-standing appreciation of the simple, functional shape of a pointed stern. L. Francis Herreshoff loved the looks of a double-ender.

Grafton Smith wanted his Q-boat designed to be especially fast in light weather, believing that many races in Marblehead waters would be sailed in such conditions. Smith suggested a short waterline to reduce resistance with the boat sailing nearly upright and because the higher potential speed of a long waterline would only come into play as the wind increased. Compared to the one other Q-boat that Francis would design, the *Nor'easter V* was the same length on deck, but a full two feet shorter on the waterline. Francis wrote: "I think her very best point of sailing is close hauled in light weather and a choppy sea," just the conditions that often stymie an otherwise fast boat. But he wrote that "in a strong wind," any Q-boat longer than the *Nor'easter V* on the waterline would be faster.[23]

The George Lawley yard in Neponset built the *Nor'easter V* in the spring of 1928, and the loftsman made a mistake that Francis didn't catch until it was too late. Francis had, as usual, drawn the lines in pencil, making his own small corrections, as evidenced by a little minor erasing on the drawing. Norman Skene traced Francis's drawing accurately in ink. But when the lines were laid out full-size on the lofting floor, the waterlines below the load waterline, just forward of the rudder, were drawn fuller than shown on the lines drawing. Francis probably would have caught such a mistake at Britt Brothers, but at Lawley's he didn't yet have the close relationship with the builders that he enjoyed with Chester and Andrew Britt. Francis was friendly with Bror Tamm, the Danish boatbuilder who had come over to work at Lawley's, but Tamm was involved with spars and rigging. At any rate,

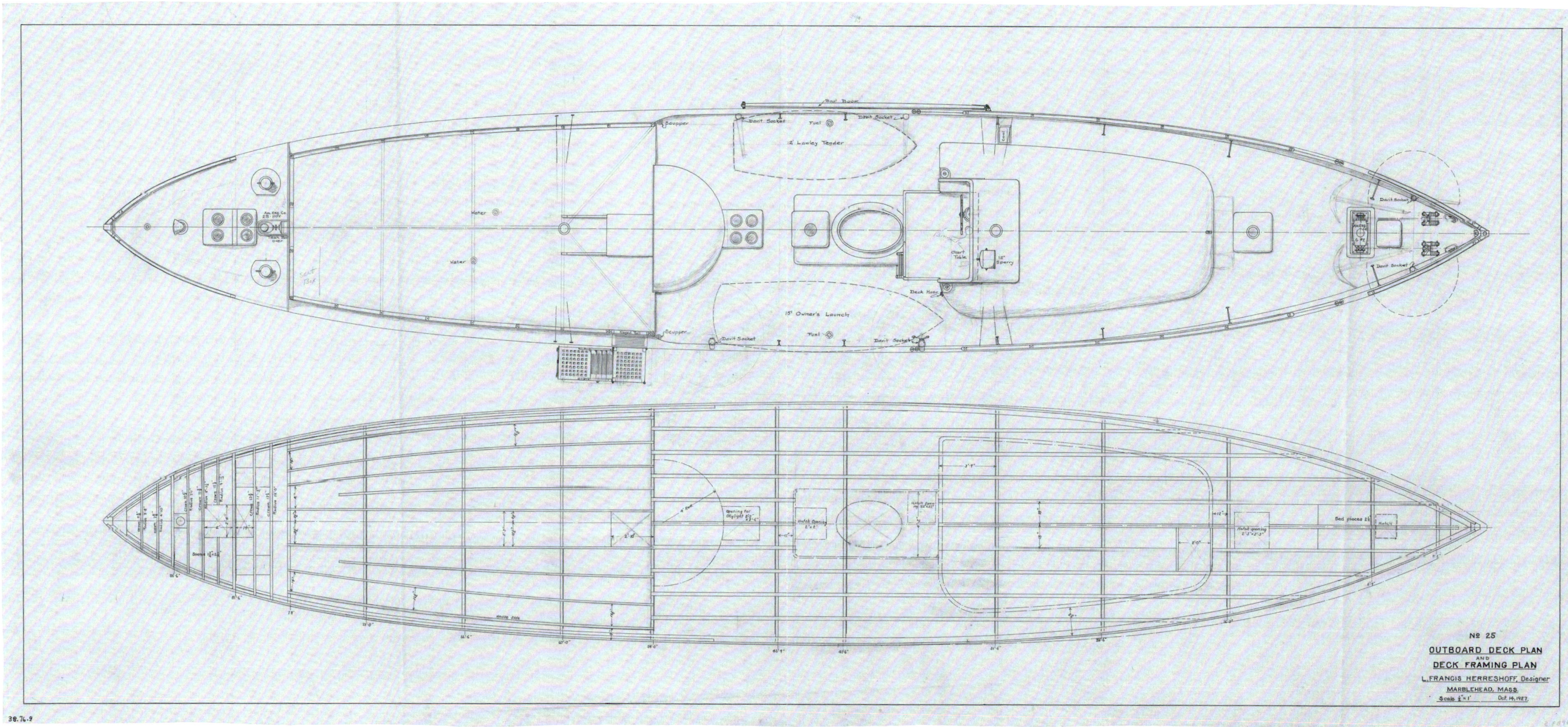

The deck plan and deck construction drawing for the *Siva*. Amidships, in dotted lines, Francis shows the yacht's two tenders, a 15-foot power launch he would design and a standard 12-foot Lawley yacht tender. These boats could rest on deck, as shown in the drawing, or remain hoisted out over the side on the davits Francis designed for them. Norman Skene made this drawing, dated October 14, 1927. (© Mystic Seaport, Daniel S. Gregory Ships Plans Library, SP38.76.9)

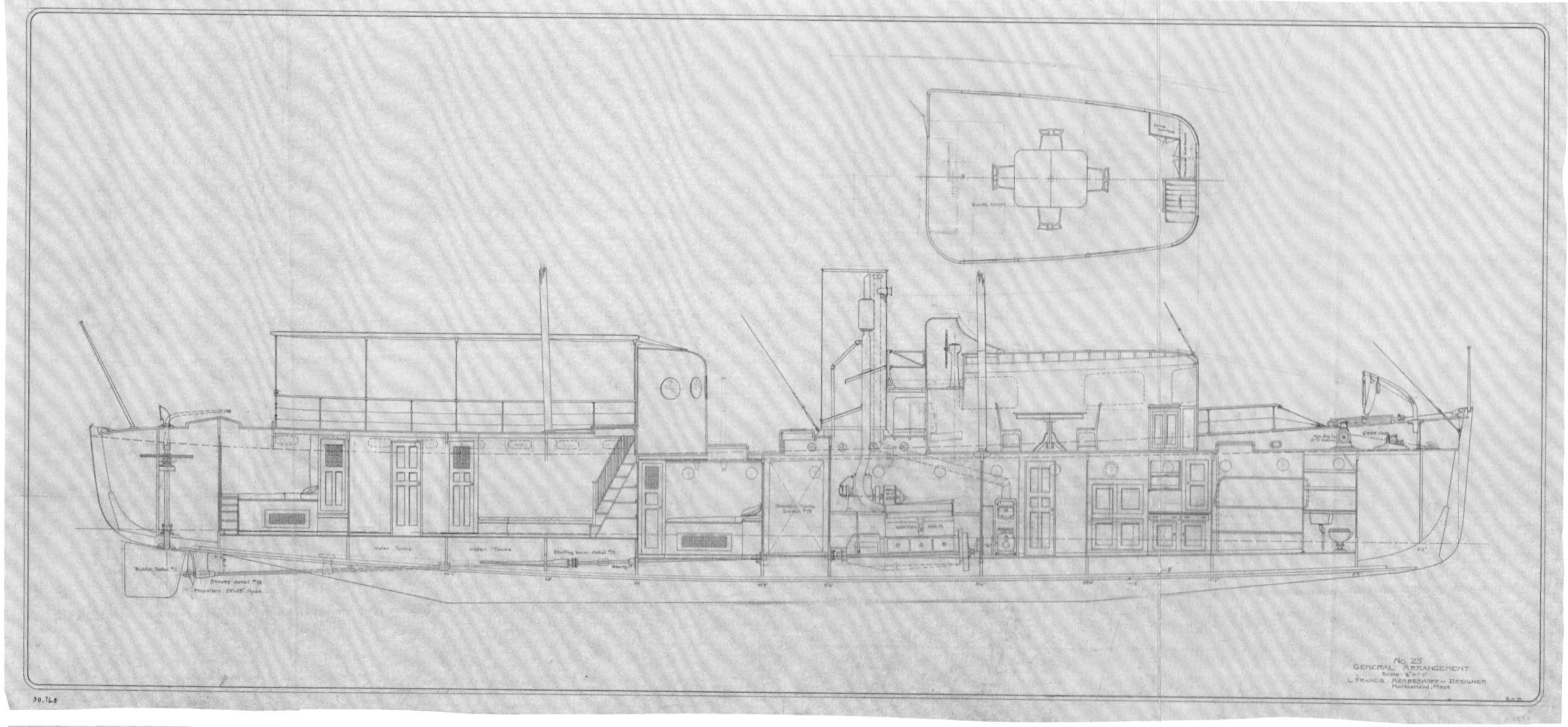

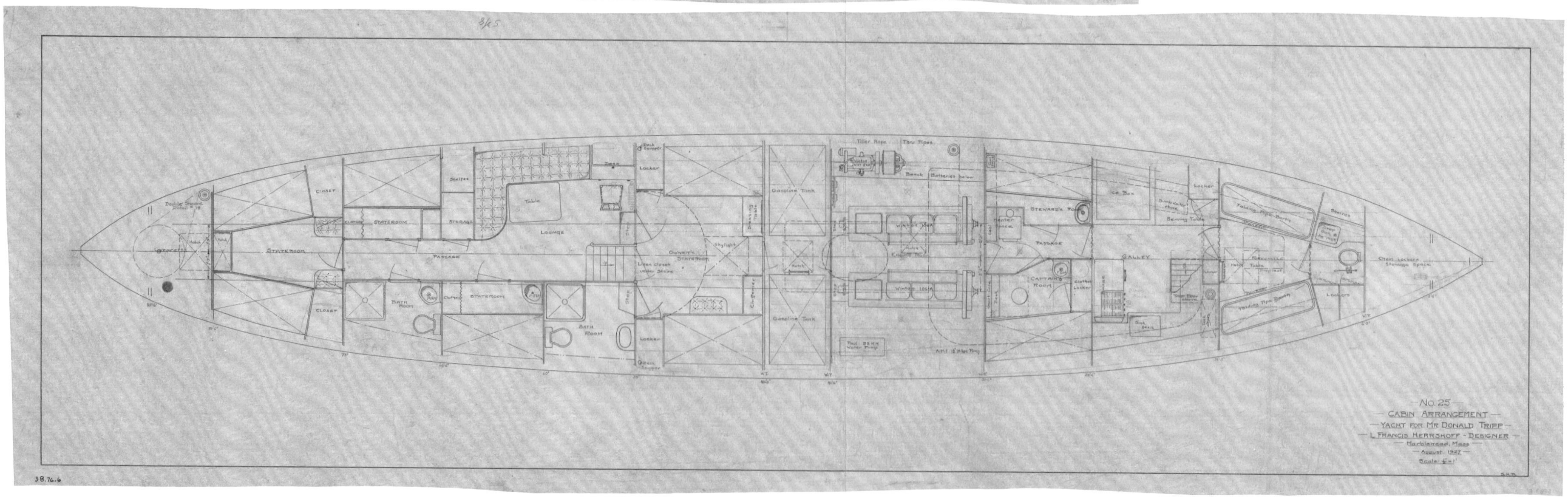

LEFT: Samuel H. Brown's first drafting job for Francis, in August 1927, was to make some of the finished drawings for the *Siva*, including this inboard profile. We can see that the forward deckhouse is to be used for the dining saloon. Note the steps, forward, down to the galley. But the steward need not balance the gravy as he climbs, for Francis has provided him with a dumbwaiter in the forward, port corner, rising directly from the serving counter below. There is a settee in the alcove under the steering station. The latter is out in the open, but it has a Bernoulli windscreen, similar to the one Francis designed for the *Dispatch*. The stack houses the exhausts for the two main engines, an auxiliary generator, and an Arcola heating furnace. The fuel tanks amidships hold 1,690 gallons of gasoline; water tanks under the after accommodation hold 550 gallons. The main companionway to the owner's quarters has a curved shelter reminiscent of a naval launch. The freestanding rudder is "balanced" for easier turning; that is, it has a small percentage of its area forward of its pivot point. Note the removable emergency tiller. (© Mystic Seaport, Daniel S. Gregory Ships Plans Library, SP38.76.5)

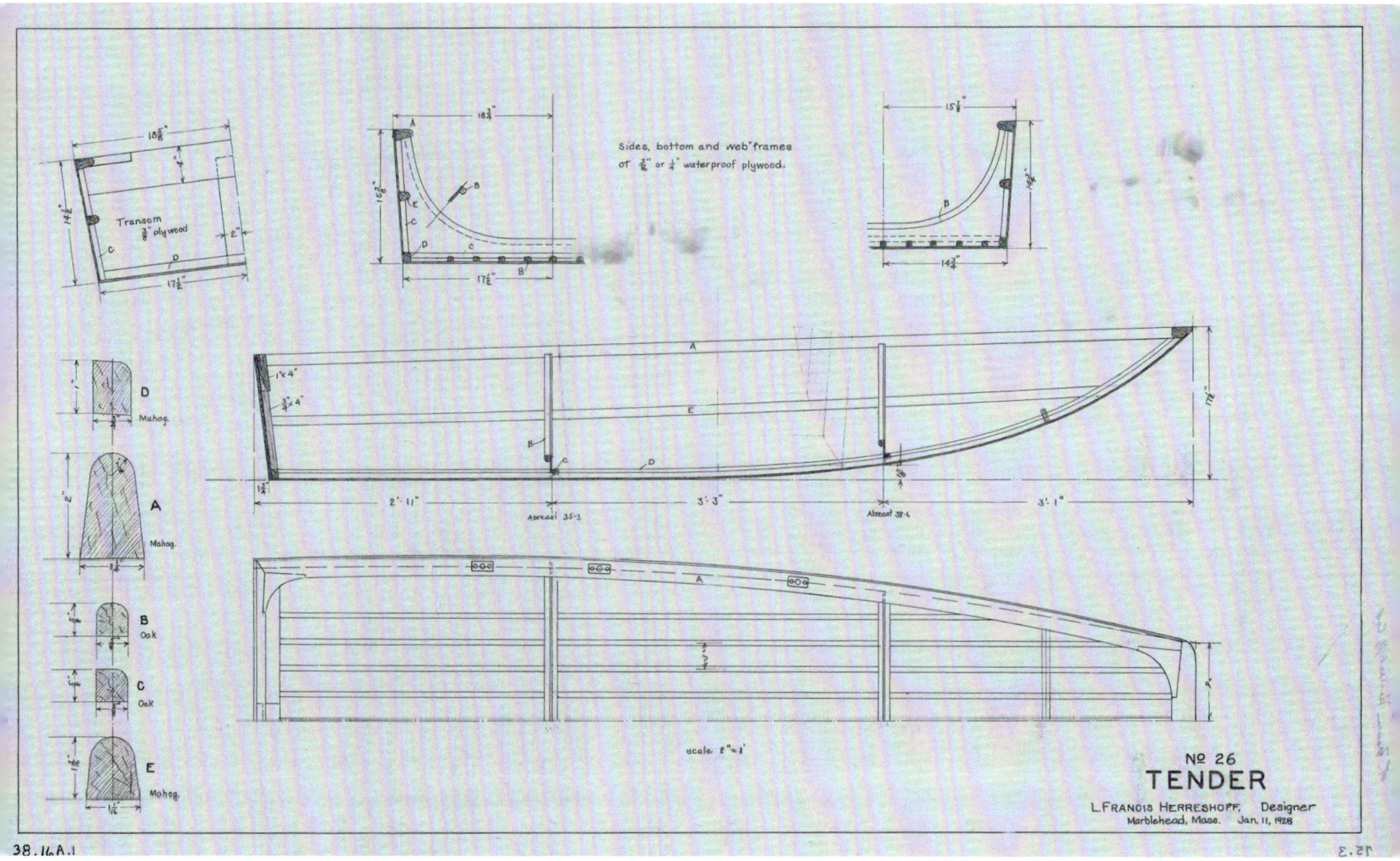

OPPOSITE PAGE, BOTTOM: The *Siva*'s cabin plan shows a large owner's stateroom amidships with its own bathroom, a lounge, two single staterooms, a double stateroom, and a bathroom for guests. Forward are the galley, cabins for the captain and steward, forecastle for two crewmen, and a washroom. The engine room and fuel tanks separate the accommodations for the owner's party and the crew. Francis provided deck access for the crew on vertical ladders through two hatches, one between the fuel tanks and one in the forecastle. The vessel's naval appearance is borne out in her below-decks arrangement. The *Siva* has six watertight compartments. She has solid collision bulkheads separating both fore and after peaks from the accommodations. And there are three watertight bulkheads, with watertight doors, making watertight compartments of the forward accommodations, engine room, tank space, and after accommodations, yet allowing access fore-and-aft throughout. Sam Brown made the drawing. (© Mystic Seaport, Daniel S. Gregory Ships Plans Library, SP38.76.6)

ABOVE: The construction plan of the special tender that Francis designed for the *Nor'easter V*. Grafton Smith had the idea of making a dinghy whose hull shape would conform to the inside of the mother ship's cockpit. Francis obliged his client with this contraption, which did, indeed, become a sort of lining for the Q-boat's cockpit, her shovel bow facing aft. The 9-foot, 3-inch pram, built on longitudinal framing for lightness, has three rowing positions for different combinations of passengers, but Smith intended to use her primarily as an outboard-motor boat. Besides having a unique, onboard stowage arrangement, the tender gave a measure of watertight integrity to the *Nor'easter V*'s otherwise open cockpit. (© Mystic Seaport, Daniel S. Gregory Ships Plans Library, SP38.16A.1)

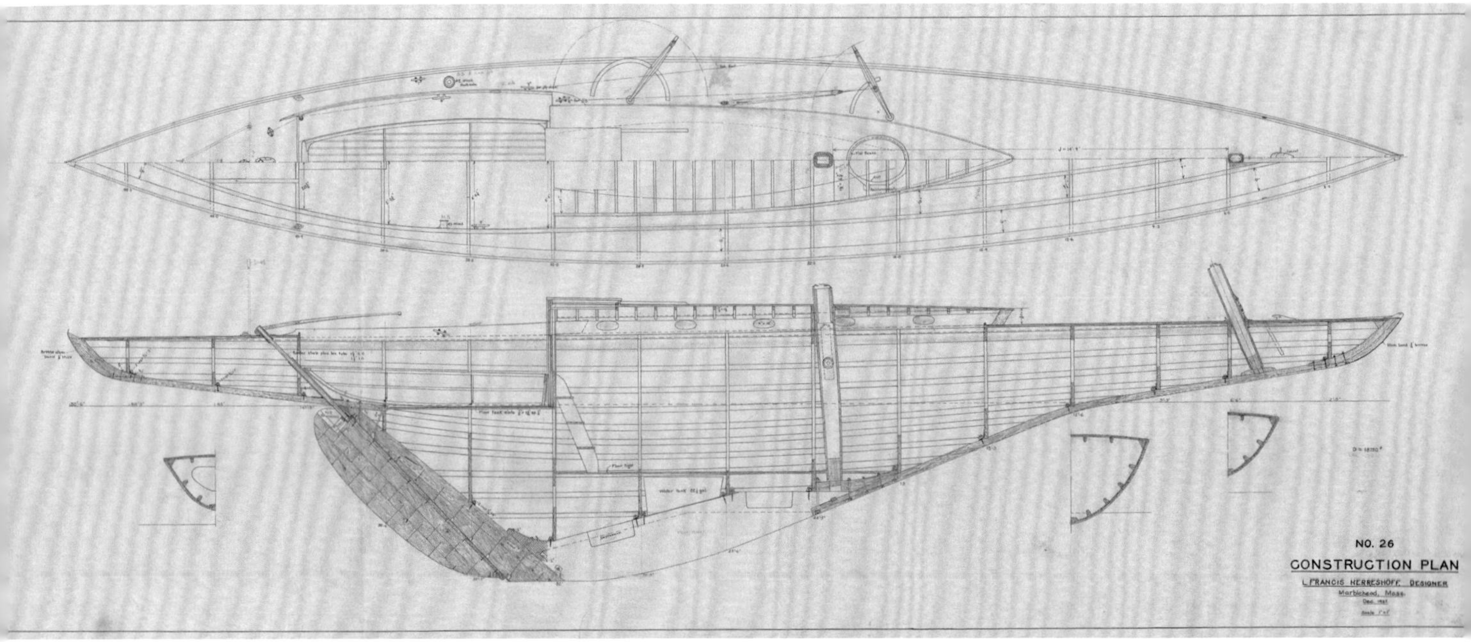

ABOVE: The *Nor'easter V*'s construction plan. The Q-boat has many of the features with which Francis was stamping his designs for "Racing Yachts": long, sharp ends for maximum sailing waterline length compared to the measured quarter-beam length; longitudinal construction for strength with lightness; a jib-luff spar, this one stepped below deck on the bow timber; halyards hauled down inside the mast; cut-out sections in the top of the lead ballast for easy adjustment of the weight. He also shows his adjustable arms for the sheet leads of the working and Genoa jibs, with a four-part tackle for hauling them aft. These arms allow the sheet to be trimmed to a point outboard of the rail, an idea that Manfred Curry had published in Germany (and in *Yachting* in July 1927) but that would soon be outlawed by the rules. Note the carefully streamlined, locust mooring and towing bitt on the foredeck, a refined version of a Nova Scotian fitting whose simple practicality Francis admired. The *Nor'easter V*'s displacement was 18, 720 pounds. Ballast was 13,000 pounds with keel cavities filled, or 12,100 pounds if they had to be left empty. Thus the ballast-to-displacement ratio might vary from 64.6 percent to 69.4 percent. Norman Skene made this drawing for "L. Francis Herreshoff, Designer" and dated it December 1927. When he did the math to be sure the boat met the rating of 25, he got 25.06. That may be the reason why, when the boat was built, the topsides were raised a mite. (© Mystic Seaport, Daniel S. Gregory Ships Plans Library, SP38.16.2)
RIGHT: The *Nor'easter V* nearly rail down in a fresh breeze. The rig Francis designed has been changed. Like Charlie Welch, Grafton Smith eschewed Francis's jib-luff spar. Perhaps it is missed on this day: both the jib stay and the jib halyard are sagging. The span stay from the masthead now comes all the way down to the deck. The upper and intermediate shrouds are not bowsed in. Running backstays have been added. She is pulling up a noticeable quarter wave along the lee side by the cockpit, even though she cannot be approaching hull speed when sailing almost close-hauled. The helmsman is standing up to his work, and, judging by the angle of his tiller (not the upward angle, but the angle to windward), his boat is carrying a healthy amount of weather helm. (CF-19-019, Charles H. W. Foster Collection, Hart Nautical Collections, MIT Museum, Cambridge, Massachusetts)

the *Nor'easter V* was built with an unwanted bustle. "For this reason," Francis wrote, "she carries a very pronounced quarter wave when reaching and this retards her speed so that she is a hopeless boat in strong breezes on a reach and will steer hard."[24]

But Grafton Smith was evidently onto something; he raced his new Q-boat with great success during the season of 1928. On July 9, she won the sloop class on the Eastern Yacht Club cruise and "showed her remarkable light weather qualities." Leonard M. Fowle, reporting in *Yachting* on "The Season of 1928 at Marblehead," described the usual Marblehead conditions as being "soft winds from the southeast and south." When it came to the Q Class, he wrote: "The smartest 25-rater of the season, in the usual Marblehead conditions, was Grafton Smith's double-ender *Nor'easter V*, designed by L. Francis Herreshoff.

Had her owner been able to have the *Nor'easter V* in the right racing trim before Midsummer [Marblehead Race] Week, the [class] championship would have gone easily to the Smith craft. As it is, the *Nor'easter* has the largest number of races [wins] to her credit, a half dozen in the class racing, all the trophies of Midsummer Week, along with the Eastern [Yacht Club] championship."[25]

Francis never raced in the *Nor'easter V*, and he "only sailed on her once or twice." His writing that she was "hopeless" on a reach in a strong breeze—doubtless an overstatement—was probably based on wise supposition rather than any trial of the boat. Francis only tried out half the racing boats he designed. He knew instinctively how they would sail, and he didn't care for the interaction with many owners that a trial sail would involve. Nathanael had always tested his designs and he advised Francis to do likewise, but Francis didn't have his father's ideal situation, as builder, of control of the boat before it was delivered.[26]

Yet Francis was an experienced, consummate sailor and helmsman and could instruct a later owner of the *Nor'easter V* exactly how to take advantage of her "remarkable light weather qualities." For working to windward in a light breeze and left-over bobble of sea, Francis advised as follows:

> *I should be sure to bear in mind that the main sheet will have to be worked in and out carefully. As the boat gains speed, it can be flattened down, sometimes very flat indeed, but as soon as she begins to get a little logy, or if she has been stopped because of a series of big seas, or on account of coming about, it will be necessary to slack her sheets out until she gets going again. . . . If you do not take advantage of this you cannot head her as high as you could otherwise. Also always remember that when the wind lets up the sail shrinks and the main sheet holds the sail in very flat. Then it must be let out. When a breeze comes again it will have to be hauled in. One of the most important things with this boat is to develop the sense of judging the amount the mainsail should be sheeted in various weathers. If I were you in steering this boat I should concentrate mostly on the mainsail and have a good man constantly working it in and out under your direction, as indicated by the feeling of the helm and the speed of the boat. This can be done with the winch provided for the same. Then I would have a reliable man working the jib sheet so that the jib is kept in proportion with the mainsail.*[27]

Grafton Smith must have known how to sail the *Nor'easter V* much as Francis described.

For the season of 1935, Francis designed a new, higher fore triangle for the Q-boat, by then named the *Spindle* and owned by E. W. Preston. The following year, A. M. Herrmann bought her, changed her name to *Gloriant*, and took her to the Great Lakes. Apparently, no lead was removed for the change to fresh water, and at first the boat raced with her waterline five inches longer than designed. While this might have been seen as an advantage to the short-waterline *Gloriant,* it didn't help her against the Alden Q-boat *Hope*, which beat her in five straight races, even though the *Nor'easter V* had usually bested the *Hope* when they raced in Marblehead. It is not known whether or not Herrmann needed or heeded Francis's sailing lesson for light weather.[28]

Between 1939 and 1951, Francis's short-waterline Q-boat, designed for round-the-buoys racing, enjoyed success in Great Lakes long-distance racing. Francis tried to discourage Herrmann from sailing the *Gloriant* in the Chicago-Mackinac Race, but Herrmann entered and won the race in 1939. The boat repeated in 1943 under the ownership of Vitas S. Thomas. In 1946, Thomas, having renamed her *Spindle*, won the Universal Rule Class in the Chicago-Mackinac. In 1949, international Star Class champion Harry G. Nye Jr. bought the boat. He named her *Gale* and sailed her to victory in that year's Detroit-Mackinac Race. Nye won the Universal Class in the Chicago Mackinac in 1950 and the overall Mackinac Cup in 1951. The *Rudder*'s observer of the 1950 race recorded: "The wind is light. The lake is sloppy. Type of water the *Gale* slithers through."[29]

The design of the *Nor'easter V* met its objective. The boat was certainly fast in light weather and achieved all-around success in racing even though her disturbance of the water at high speed was accentuated.

By 1953, her racing days over, the *Nor'easter V*, boat of many names, had a cutter rig and an engine. Later, she became a hard-luck boat. In 1971, her crib collapsed while she was being shipped by rail to Puget Sound. It might have been much worse; part of her stem and mast step were shattered. Francis supplied a construction plan to aid repairs. In Puget Sound, she had her stern demolished by a collision with a freighter. And even when her rescuer arrived on the scene in Seattle in 1991, she didn't make it onto his trailer without being dropped by the crane operator.[30]

The rescuer was Doug Averill, proprietor of a deluxe dude ranch in Big Fork, Montana, the Flathead Lake Lodge. Flathead Lake is a 200-square-mile body of water near Glacier National Park that is a rare mountain lake, in that it often provides fairly steady reaching breezes. The Lodge, started by Doug's father, Les, in 1945, has always provided boats, as well as horses, for its guests. When the *Nor'easter V* arrived, she joined another Q-boat designed by L. Francis Herreshoff, the *Questa*, a slightly later design, that Averill had acquired in 1983. Woodworkers at the Lodge's shop had added boatbuilding skills to their carriage-making talents, and, led initially by Jon Derry, a graduate of the Rockport, Maine, Apprenticeshop, they repaired and have maintained the two Qs to the continuing delight of many equestrians.[31]

WHEN CLINTON Crane heard that Francis Herreshoff had a commission to design a 6-Metre, he realized that the younger designer had no experience with the International Rule and so offered to share what he had learned from designing several 6-Metres himself. Francis would have none of it. He scorned any yacht designer whom he thought was copying the work of another. He was proud of his own work and of his own name and wanted no help, even from a designer he respected. Crane couldn't understand Francis's rejection of his offer.[32]

W. A. W. Stewart and Harry H. Curtis, who had ordered the 6-Metre from Francis, were experienced yachting partners. They had big plans for the 1928 racing season. They intended to ship the *Wasp*, as their new boat would be called, to Europe to race in Scotland and on the Continent, including for the Scandinavian Gold Cup race off Stockholm. Stewart already had a 6-Metre, the *Priscilla*, designed by Clinton Crane, that was being raced successfully for him by Ralph Ellis on the West Coast. And he and Curtis had ordered a 12-Metre to be designed by Starling Burgess and to be built at Henry Rasmussen's yard in Germany, Stewart selling his 10-Metre to make room for the new Twelve in his racing stable.[33]

As may be seen by his choice of racing boats, W.A.W. Stewart was an enthusiast of the International Rule. Along with Clinton Crane, he was a representative of the North American Yacht Racing Union at the 1928 conference on the rule in London. NAYRU had been formed in 1925 "To encourage and promote the racing of sailing yachts, and to unify the rules." The organization's representatives at the London conference sought modifications to the International Rule that they believed would make it more suitable for the generally lighter winds on the windward side of the Atlantic. They succeeded in selling a few changes to the rule's limits on hull shape and rig. As well

as influencing the International Rule, Stewart was also chairman of the selection committee to choose the five 6-Metres that would be shipped to Scotland on June 23.[34]

Stewart and Curtis were not the only yachtsmen flocking to the International Rule. Although the Marbleheaders would stick to their R-boats and Q-boats for a few more years, William H. Taylor of *Yachting* estimated that for the 1928 season on Long Island Sound there would be from twenty to thirty new racing boats built to the International Rule, and not one to the Universal Rule. When he mentioned the *Wasp* as one of the boats in the big, new fleet, he wrote, "As this one is to be designed by Francis Herreshoff, who turned out the *Live Yankee* last season, its advent is awaited with fear and trembling. We'll see how the heir to the Herreshoff traditions goes to work to beat the International Rule."[35]

Bill Taylor needn't have trembled. Francis Herreshoff didn't think of designing to a rating rule in terms of "beating" the rule. Of course he juggled the elements of a design to aim for the fastest boat possible within the limitations imposed by the rule, but the unusual features of the *Live Yankee* that caused Taylor such feigned alarm were aimed at speed, not rule-beating.

What Francis had done, the previous winter, was try to influence Mr. Stewart to see some of the drawbacks of the International Rule, as compared to the Universal Rule. His correspondence with Stewart is not among his collection of letters; he sent it to Nathanael and evidently didn't keep copies. Francis sounded off to his father, referring to "the men in the NAYRU who are trying to scuttle the Universal Rule [he refers to it as "our rule"] will only work with designers who prostrate themselves before them in carrying out their selfish work of deceiving the public to attain their ends." As Alfred F. Loomis reported in *The Sportsman*, "Francis Herreshoff, by the way, is a staunch upholder of the Universal Rule, and in the contest now raging against proponents of the International Rule is a most outspoken partisan. It is said that when his letter on the subject was delivered before the last gathering of the American Yacht Racing Union his spokesman deleted fifty 'damns' and a hundred and fifty 'God damns.' But not even this unpardonable emasculation weakened the face of his arguments."[36]

Nathanael saw that his son was sailing into dangerous waters with such strong negative feelings about his customers and competitors. He advised Francis: "You must bear in mind you are

LEFT: The outboard profile and sail plan of the *Wasp*, Francis's only design for a 6-Metre, his No. 27. His first design to the International Rule, she was about the same length on deck as a Universal Rule R-boat, but had much less displacement, waterline length, draft, and sail area. The *Wasp* was 38 feet long on deck; only 22 feet on the waterline; with a beam of 6 feet, 4½ inches; and a draft of 5 feet, 1 inch. She displaced 7,880 pounds and had 436 square feet of measured sail area. The International Rule limited the height of the mast for 6-Metres to 42.65 feet above the deck; the *Wasp*'s mast stood at 42.6 feet. As well as a working jib, Francis shows a smaller jib for a strong breeze and a lapping jib for moderate and light-wind conditions, all setting on a luff spar. Note the jumper stay and the "baby" stays to either bow. These three to support the jib luff spar to stop it from slatting in the wind when the boat is on her mooring. The lower ends of the upper shrouds attach to the intermediate shrouds rather than to the mast at the lower spreader, an unusual way to save windage that Francis did not repeat. The helmsman has his own cockpit. All sheets lead to the crew's cockpit. Francis has drawn the mainsheet with only two hauling parts and a winch, so that the sail could be trimmed rapidly in a light and shifty breeze and could also be strapped down hard in a fresh breeze, using the winch. But the boat was rigged with double blocks on the boom, giving four parts. The swinging arm to allow the lapping jib to be trimmed outboard of the rail could not be used, for it was outlawed. (© Mystic Seaport, Daniel S. Gregory Ships Plans Library, SP38.11.4)

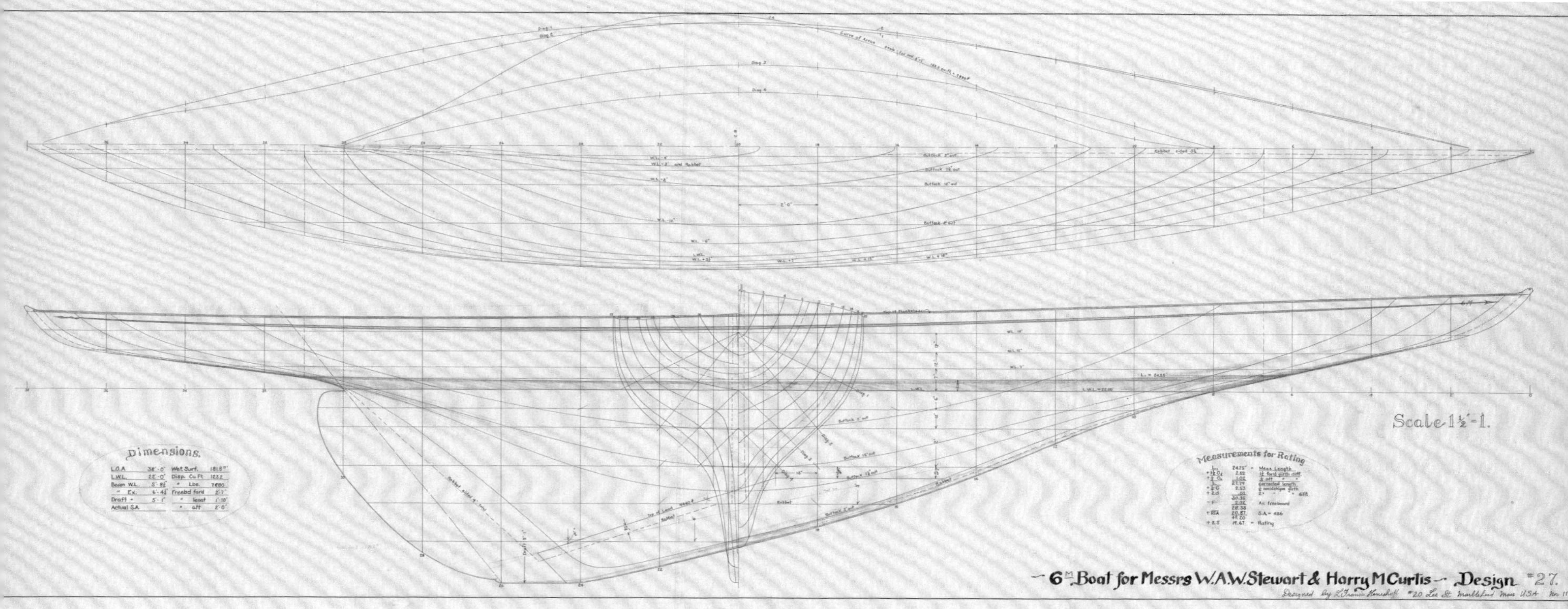
Dimensions.
L.O.A 38'-0"
L.W.L. 22'-0"
Beam W.L. 5'-8½"
" Ex. 6'-4½"
Draft " 5'-1"
Actual S.A.
Wet Surf. 181.8 □'
Disp. Cu.Ft 123.2
" Lbs. 7880
Freebd ford 2'-7"
" least 1'-10"
" aft 2'-0"
Measurements for Rating
L₁ 24.25' = Meas. Length
+1½ D₁ 2.82 1½ ford girth diff.
+½ D₂ 1.02 ½ aft " "
L 27.79 corrected length
+½ G 2.53 ½ amidships girth
+2d .03 2× " " diff.
30.35
−F 2.02 Av. freeboard
28.33
+√SA 20.87 S.A. = 486
49.20
÷2.5 19.67 = Rating
Scale 1½"=1.
6 M. Boat for Messrs W.A.W. Stewart & Harry M Curtis — Design #27.
Designed by L. Francis Herreshoff #20 Lee St Marblehead Mass USA

LEFT: The lines of the *Wasp*. With her long overhangs, the *Wasp* is one of the most graceful and elegant of Francis's double-ended racers. But besides giving the boat her beautiful hull shape, he had to balance the complexities of the International Rule to make the boat fast within her rating. He came within 355 pounds of giving her the minimum displacement allowed by the Rule, and he gave her the maximum draft permitted, still, less than the Universal Rule encouraged. He resisted the temptation to reduce the rating by giving her the maximum freeboard allowed by the Rule; he kept her sides 4 inches lower than the Rule's limit, knowing that the resulting reduced wind resistance would make her faster to windward, and that there is nothing that detracts from a boat's beauty more than high sides. He hollowed the garboards a bit more than is shown in the preliminary midsection on the outboard profile drawing in order to decrease displacement, but thereby increased the girth measurement slightly, a worthwhile trade-off. The inked lines drawing is dated November 11, 1927, Francis's thirty-seventh birthday. (© Mystic Seaport, Daniel S. Gregory Ships Plans Library, SP38.11.1)

BELOW: Norman Skene's drawing to explain the basics of the International Rule. It shows that the length measurement was taken about 3-1/2 inches above the boat's waterline and that length also took into account girth measurements at the bow and stern. "G" is a girth measurement at a specified point nearly amidships, reduced by freeboard at that point; "d" is a girth-difference measurement that penalizes the amount of curvature in the midsection from the rail to the top of the ballast keel; "SA" is measured sail area; and "F" is average freeboard. By subtracting freeboard twice from the rating, the Rule encouraged high-sided boats, though it did put a maximum limit on freeboard. Notice Skene's "NOTE," referring the designer to further multiple complexities. The full text of the International Rule took more than twice as many pages as that for the Universal Rule. (© Mystic Seaport, Daniel S. Gregory Ships Plans Library, SP38.446.2)

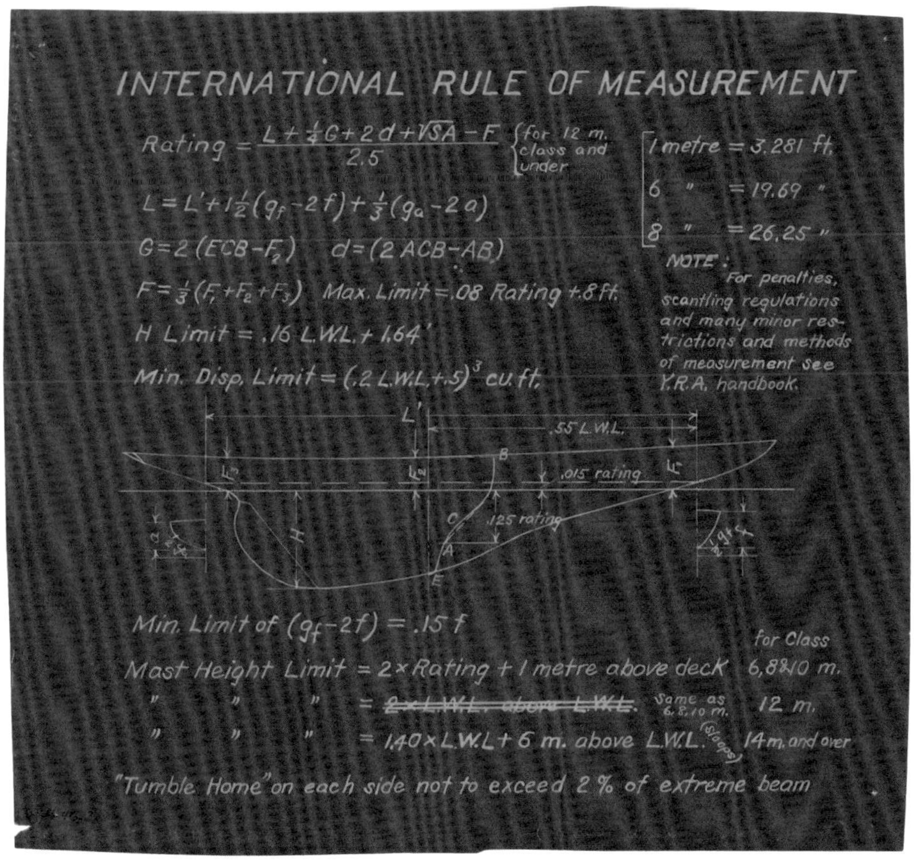

working for that class who have the money and order yachts, and use them for *their* pleasure, and it is not policy to thwart their wishes or ideas. It is better to first accept their ideas and then later, at the proper time, explain to them wherein they are wrong, and how they should be improved. It is better to lead than to drive." Yet, Francis knew that his father had sometimes been stubborn and had refused to change a design to meet an owner's whim. He replied: "I will try to profit by your advice in dealing with people like Mr. Stewart, but I am not a sucker and would rather not have their business than become one." Francis was judgmental, and, often, his reaction to someone he judged negatively was simply to flee. But in the case of Stewart, he must have taken at least some of his father's advice, for Stewart did order a yacht from him.[37]

The *Wasp* had unusual features for a 6-Metre of 1928, but she was a more conservative design than that of the *Live Yankee*. She was a double-ender with long, low overhangs to gain sailing length. She had the unusually large fore triangle that Francis had pioneered under the Universal Rule. She had the jib-luff spar that he still believed in. She had inboard chainplates, with the shrouds led through the deck, seven inches inside the rail. But the *Wasp* was to be built by the conventional plank-on-frame method, not with Francis's longitudinal construction, and her garboard planks were fastened to a conventional wood keelson, not directly to the lead ballast, as Francis had found advantageous.

Perhaps the conventional construction was due to the fact that under the International Rule the construction plan had to be approved by Lloyd's Bureau of Shipping, and any changes the Lloyd's men decreed had to be made. The *Wasp*'s conventional construction plan came back from Lloyd's New York office with eighteen modifications. Each of the changes added to the boat's weight. Lloyd's wanted various structural members and fastenings beefed up, and the Bureau disapproved of Francis's wider spacing of frames in the ends of the boat. Francis's sense of proportion that enabled him to design a structure that would be no heavier than necessary went for naught. This was the beginning of Francis's scornful relationship with Lloyd's. And the necessity of dealing with Lloyd's was one reason why Francis grew to hate the International Rule. Another reason was purely artistic: the rule prohibited concavity above the waterline, and so, in Francis's opinion, barred the most beautiful hull shapes, particularly the hollow bow, an elegant feature of naval architecture with a long tradition. He would design only one other boat to the International Rule, and that was as a favor to a friend.[38]

Adding weight to the *Wasp*'s hull structure meant that the lead outside ballast on the keel had to be reduced. As late as April 26, with the selection of Sixes to go to Scotland fast approaching, Norman Skene was figuring various sizes of lead keel that might be used to ballast the new, Lloyd's version of the *Wasp*. He had figured the lead at 5,910 pounds (giving a ballast-to-displacement ratio of 75 percent) back in November, but now he was figuring weights of lead from 5,350 pounds to 5,605 pounds. His note at the bottom of his sheet of calculations of the weights of various-sized keels reads: "Abandoned. Final keel much less put in by eye when keel was dropped and straightened. Not figured yet." Francis and his draftsmen had run out of time. Their frustration must have been great.

RIGHT: Francis designed a special mooring and towing eye for the *Wasp*. A big shackle set flush into the deck for streamlining (and to remove a tripping hazard), it could be raised to do its work. He thought about every detail of a design and spared no effort to bring his own brand of science into play. (© Mystic Seaport, Daniel S. Gregory Ships Plans Library, SP38.11.8)

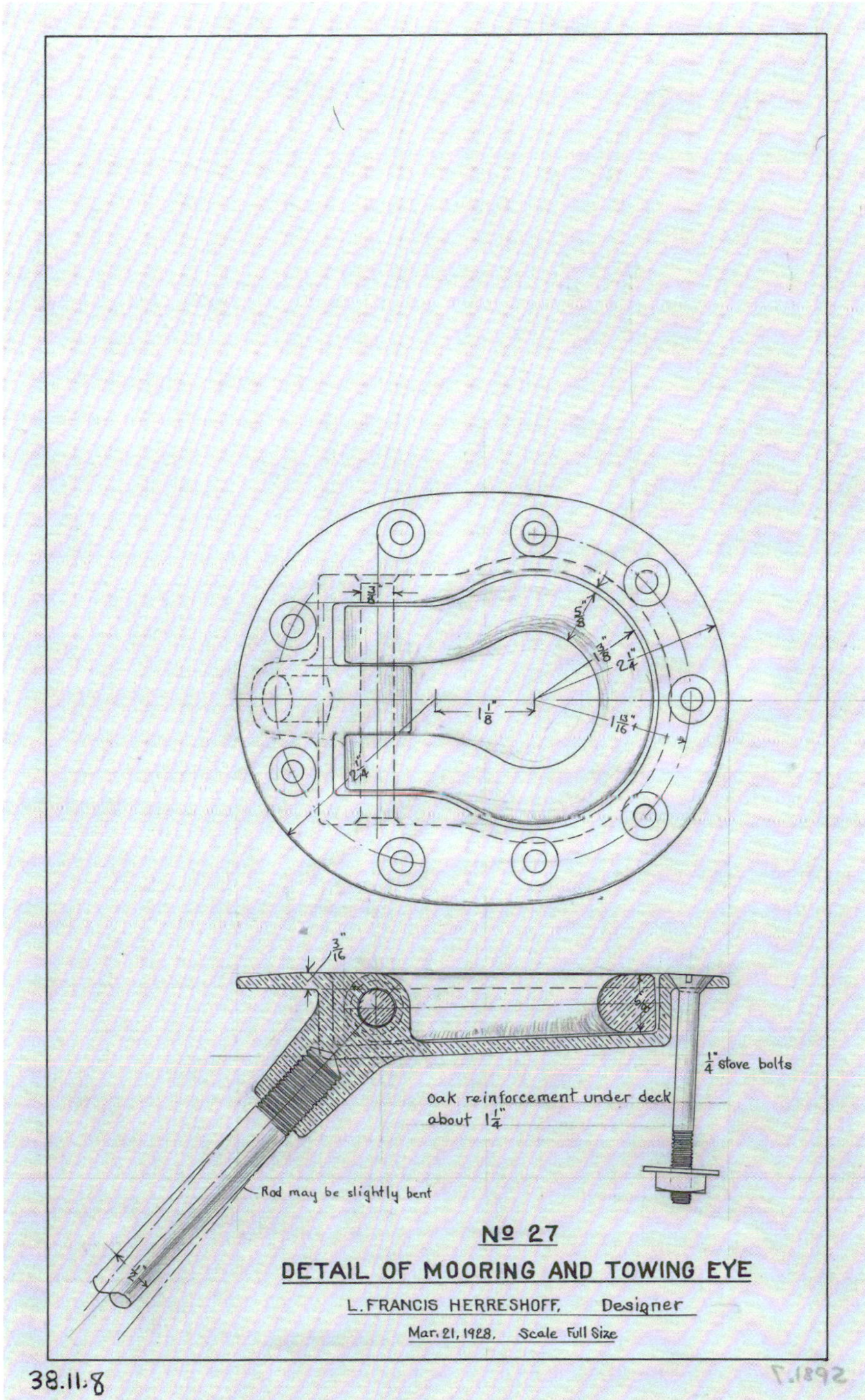

1 1/8"
1 13/16"
2 1/4"
3/16"
1/4" stove bolts
Oak reinforcement under deck about 1 1/4"
Rod may be slightly bent
Nº 27
DETAIL OF MOORING AND TOWING EYE
L. FRANCIS HERRESHOFF, Designer
Mar. 21, 1928. Scale Full Size
38.11.8

The *Wasp* was launched at the George Lawley yard with an outside ballast keel weighing only 4,000 pounds and was then given 1,160 pounds of lead inside ballast, for a ballast-to-displacement ratio of only 65 percent and with the weight of lead abnormally high. Inexplicably, when Francis made a comparative table of displacements, weight of ballast, and ballast-to-displacement ratios for five of his racers, though he states displacement and weight of ballast as above for the *Wasp*, he gives her ballast-to-displacement ratio as the originally intended 75 percent. At any rate, this new racing boat for highly motivated owners took the water with appreciably less stability than her designer had intended.[39]

But did Francis take out his frustration on the *Wasp*? Faced with the problem presented by Lloyd's, Skene was calculating different sizes of lead keel that would reduce the ballast by from 305 pounds to 560 pounds. Why does he suddenly abandon this task with the result that the ballast keel is arbitrarily reduced by 1,910 pounds? It sounds as if his boss threw up his hands and said, in effect, "They won't let me build the boat as I designed her, so rather than design to their standards, let's just cut the ballast keel way back, add as much inside ballast as we can, and be done with it." Francis was capable of such a reaction, something akin to the exit strategy he sometimes used to escape personal situations he didn't like.

Stewart displayed the gentlemanly attitude of the day. Despite his being chairman of the committee that chose the 6-Metres to go to Scotland, his *Wasp* was not selected. Clinton Crane's *Akaba* won the Gold Cup in Sweden. The decision not to send the *Wasp* proved to be sound, for her racing record was mediocre. In the 1928 season of strong winds, she was fast reaching and running, but slow on the windward legs, when stability was a big factor. But when Francis wrote to Nathanael about the *Wasp*'s performance, he blamed her bad showing to windward on poor sails and faulty helmsmanship. For the 1929 season, W. A. W. Stewart turned to his Crane 6-Metre, the *Priscilla*.

Francis wasn't the only one dissatisfied with Lloyd's ideas of how a 6-Metre should be built. At the same time that the Bureau was telling him to increase the scantlings of the *Wasp*'s structure, "some younger yachtsmen," as he wrote to his father, asked Francis to make up a scantling rule for 6-Metres to replace the Lloyd's requirements, which they thought too complicated. Francis liked the idea and sought advice from others, including his father.[40]

By May 1, Helen Bolster had typed up "A Suggested Rule to Take the Place of Scantling

Eyes shaded by their fedoras, the designer and owners of the *Wasp* pose at her after cockpit. Francis (right) looks away from the camera; W.A.W Stewart is in the cockpit; his partner, H. M. Curtis, is on deck. (*Yachting* (June 1928): 78)

Rules for Racing Yachts of Under 20,000 Pounds Displacement." The rule that Francis came up with has only seven statements and takes up less than one page. As its title indicates, it is not a scantling rule that would legislate the sizes of each structural part of a yacht, but instead is a statement of general principles of structural proportion that would limit excesses in designing a yacht's construction, thus rendering a scantling rule unnecessary. For example, he writes: "The weight of deck per square foot shall be at least 75 per cent of the weight of the planking per square foot." His "Suggested Rule" is surprising coming from L. Francis Herreshoff, for under it, he could not have designed a racing boat with a ballast-to-displacement ratio as high as 75 percent, nor could he have used his strong, lightweight, longitudinal construction. He suggested limiting ballast to 60 percent of displacement and limiting the molded dimension of framing to 1/25th of beam, a limit that his web frames in his longitudinal construction exceeded.[41]

Francis explained to Nathanael that his "Suggested Rule" was "intended for small racing boats only, where it is desired that each of the competitors is allowed the same percentages of hull structure weight and approximately the same means of securing strength and stability." Francis seems to be denying a yacht designer the freedom to design a new and different and better-constructed yacht, in terms of strength, durability, and lightness—an accomplishment of his own on which he placed a high value. And when he defended his "Suggested Rule" to Nathanael, who had urged him to "read carefully" his own "Construction Rules for Wood Yachts," Francis seems paradoxically to be arguing against himself. He wrote to his father: "They [Nathanael's rules] are very fine if it is desired to compel all designers in the future to stick to certain methods of construction as developed by one builder but which might not be as efficient as some other methods of construction for other builders in the future." While it is true that any rule that legislates minimum scantlings for a yacht's structure puts the designer in a straightjacket, so does Francis's "Suggested Rule" by limiting the proportions of structural parts.[42]

In the event, Francis never had to wear this particular straightjacket. It is not known what, if anything, "some younger yachtsmen" did with Francis's "Suggested Rule"; there is no indication that it was submitted to anyone with decision-making power. Francis included it in a short article he wrote for *Yachting* about the 30-Square-Metre Rule and sent a copy to the German arbiters of that rule, but neither airing of his ideas had effect. Francis was still stuck with Lloyd's.[43]

THE THIRD racer that Francis designed in the winter of 1927-28 was a new R-boat, the *Bonnie Lassie*, for Dr. Morton Prince. The project was relatively straightforward: Francis was settling in to a hull design for Universal Rule boats. He had tried to improve on the successful *Yankee* by filling out the midsection, changing it from a wineglass to a narrower, fuller shape to reduce wetted surface and hence resistance. He felt he had gone too far in that direction with the *Live Yankee* and had come back to a compromise between the midsections of the two *Yankees*, a shape with which he was comfortable. He used the compromise midsection on No. 22, the M-boat that wasn't built, on the Q-boat *Nor'easter V*, and on the *Bonnie Lassie*. And on these three designs, he lengthened the ends close above the waterline and drew pointed sterns.

It was on the rig where Francis continued to experiment. He knew the advantage of "endplates" along the top and bottom edges of a sail to get a little drive from air that otherwise would simply spill. He continued to use his T-section boom as an endplate for the foot of the mainsail. He had tried the curved masthead as an endplate for the head, but was not convinced of its effectiveness. For the *Bonnie Lassie*, he tried a curved, oversize

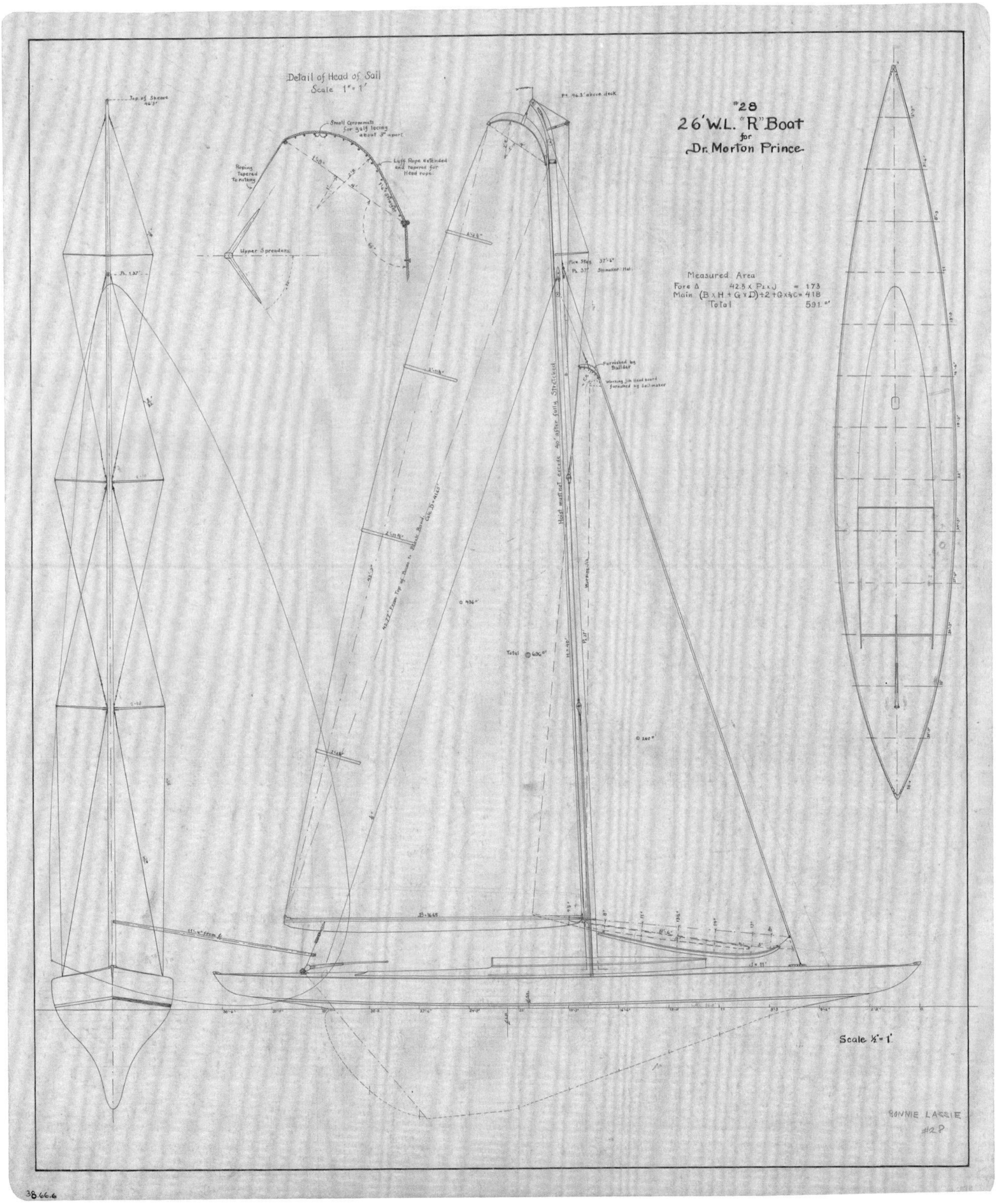
#28
26' W.L. "R" Boat
for
Dr. Morton Prince
Detail of Head of Sail
Scale 1" = 1'
Measured Area
Scale ½" = 1'
BONNIE LASSIE
#28

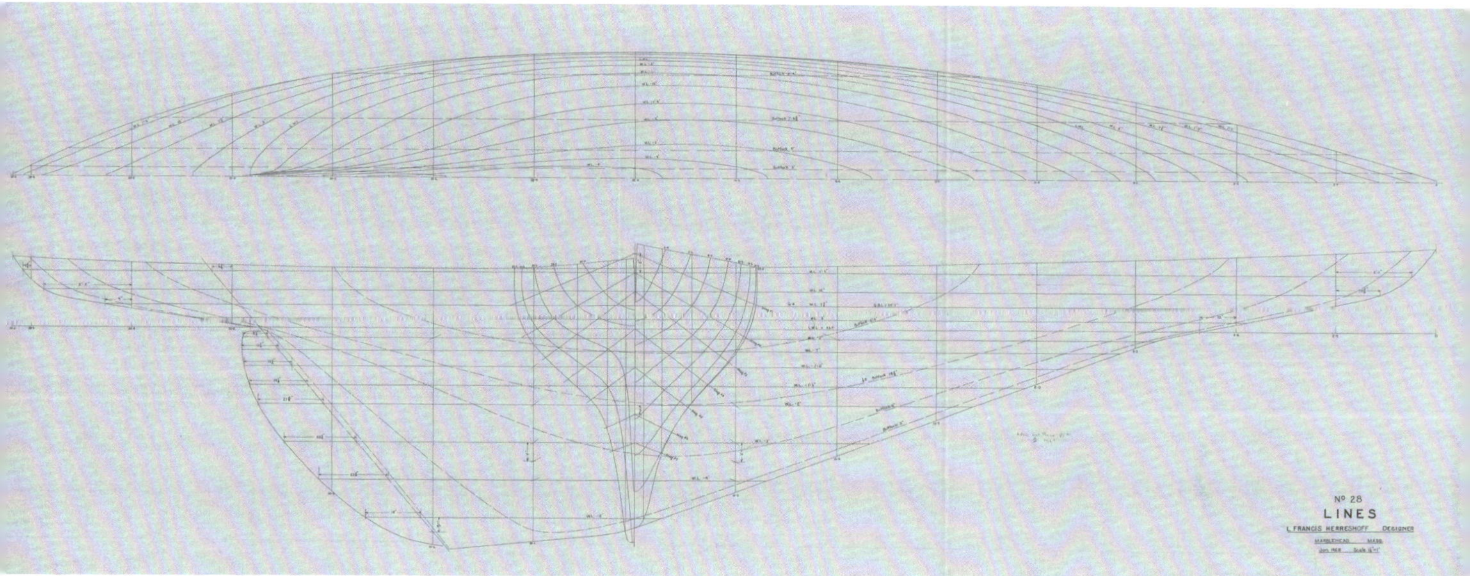

headboard supported by a halyard leading from the top of a curved mast. It was not an experiment he repeated.

Being well pleased with his longitudinal construction design, and without Lloyd's to contend with on the Universal Rule, he used it for the *Bonnie Lassie.* He wrote to Nathanael: "I have now had nine boats built to the same construction as *Yankee* and they have all turned out lighter, stronger, and cheaper than I had expected."[44]

Racing in Marblehead was becoming ever more popular, and so, ever more competitive. For the 1928 season, between the Corinthian Yacht Club and the Eastern, seventy races were sailed, each with an average of fifty-five starters in all classes. The competition in Marblehead's Class R was improving. Frank Paine's newest *Gypsy* dominated. The *Bonnie Lassie*'s season record showed her beating only one boat in the class of twelve. She did better in later years and went on to win the Manhasset Bay Challenge Cup, but under a new owner and with a borrowed rig, the slightly

---

LEFT: **The outboard profile and sail plan for the R-boat *Bonnie Lassie*, Francis's design No. 28 and the third double-ended racing boat he designed for the 1928 season. He has used a large, curved headboard on the mainsail (reminiscent of a traditional Dutch gaff), hoisted by a single halyard led internally over two sheaves in the curved masthead. The purpose of the big headboard was to get forward drive from air going up the sail. Francis designed a similar headboard for an overlapping jib; the working (measured) jib had a normal headboard. He shows a curved, partial club on the foot of the lapping jib to get unmeasured roach, with a straight club for the working jib. The *Bonnie Lassie*'s measured sail area was 591 square feet. She has a T-section main boom and running backstays led well aft.** (© Mystic Seaport, Daniel S. Gregory Ships Plans Library, SP38.66.60) ABOVE: **The lines of the *Bonnie Lassie* are similar to those of the bigger Q-boat *Nor'easter V*; Francis worked up both sets of lines during the busy winter of 1927-28. The *Bonnie Lassie* was 39 feet long on deck; 26 feet on the waterline; with a beam of 6 feet, 2 inches; and a draft of 5 feet, 10 inches. Displacement was 11,980 pounds.** (© Mystic Seaport, Daniel S. Gregory Ships Plans Library, SP38.66.1)

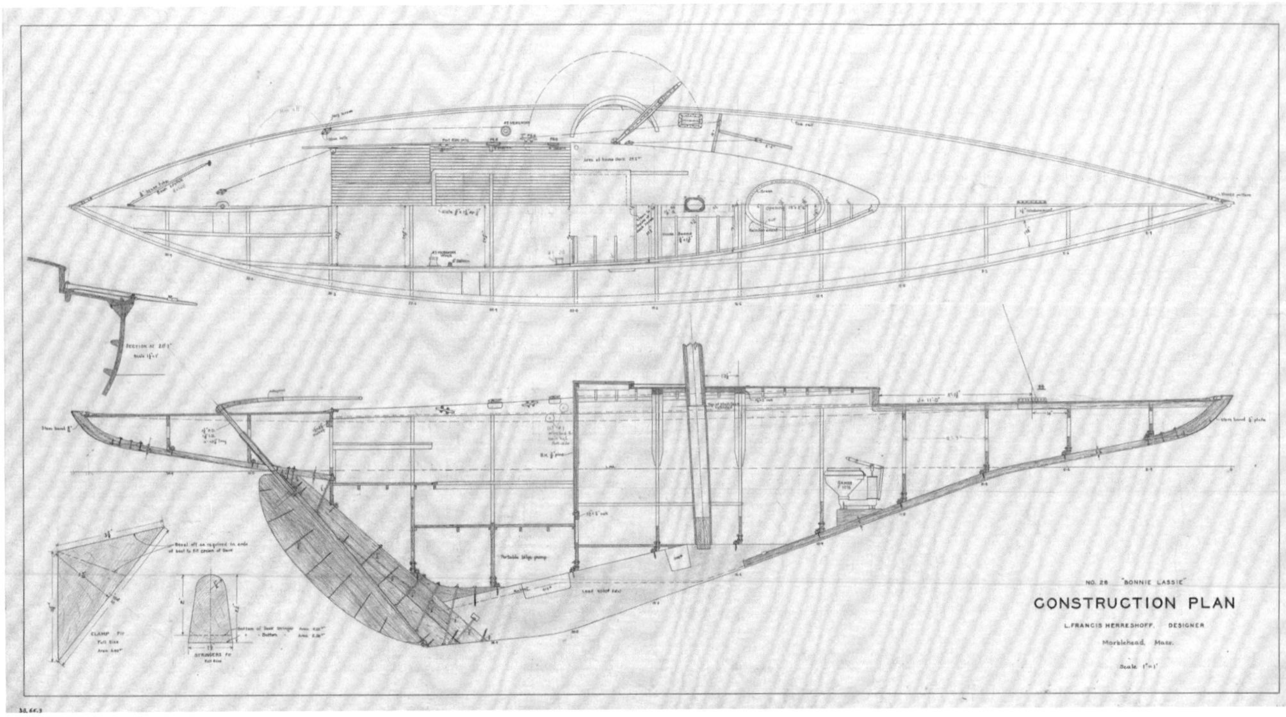

ABOVE: The *Bonnie Lassie*'s construction plan shows Francis's longitudinal method. The boat was built in Marblehead by the James E. Graves yard, so both Francis and the owner, Marblehead doctor Morton Prince, could keep an eye on progress; this was the Graves yard's first experience building with Francis's individually designed web frames and multiple stringers. The lead keel weighed 9,000 pounds, giving a ballast-to-displacement ratio of 75 percent. There was provision to add another 750 pounds in two pockets in the top of the lead keel if she floated a little high when Graves launched her. There is neither a wooden keelson nor a wooden mast step; the garboard planks are fastened directly to the lead keel, and the mast steps directly on the lead keel. As with the *Wasp*, the design of the outlawed outriggers for the overlapping jib sheets was superfluous. (© Mystic Seaport, Daniel S. Gregory Ships Plans Library, SP38.66.3) RIGHT: The *Bonnie Lassie* close-hauled. Despite the head of the jib luffing, she is going well, judging by the way she is spitting off that little sea on her lee bow. (*The Common Sense of Yacht Design*, figure 32)

curved mast of the *Live Yankee*. For Charlie Welch bought the *Lassie* in 1930, and with his touch at the tiller and the discarding of the big headboard, she became a successful racing boat. She went to the Great Lakes from 1941 to at least 1971, when she was last listed in *Lloyd's Register*.[45]

The change of skippers in the *Bonnie Lassie* highlights the question of why sailboats win races. How much is due to the skill and knowledge of the designer, and how much is due to the skill and knowledge of the skipper? Both are, of course, important. The importance of the skipper can be shown by the fact that in one-design classes, where the boats are all the same, certain skippers rise to the top, while others stay at the bottom. While design is of obvious importance in an open class, where the boats are different, the flat statement can be made that for a racing boat design to be successful, the boat must be sailed by a competent, competitive skipper. Howard I. Chapelle, in discussing this subject relative to fishing schooners, wrote: "in fact, a very good skipper was usually the deciding factor in establishing the reputation of a vessel for fast sailing." Francis was lucky to have Charlie Welch to race the two *Yankees*, and lucky that Charlie showed that the *Bonnie Lassie* was not a bad design. Francis was not always so lucky. He was frustrated with many of his racing boat designs, because he had no control over how the boat was raced. That frustration was to drive him out of designing racing boats.[46]

BUT, FOR FRANCIS, the busy spring of 1928 was more exciting than frustrating. Even if Junius Morgan was too hesitant to build to his elegant M-boat design, three new racing boats and a big new power yacht were being built at Lawley's, Graves', and Britts', each boat to his careful, detailed, innovative, and scientific design. And Francis's favorite client, Charlie Welch, had

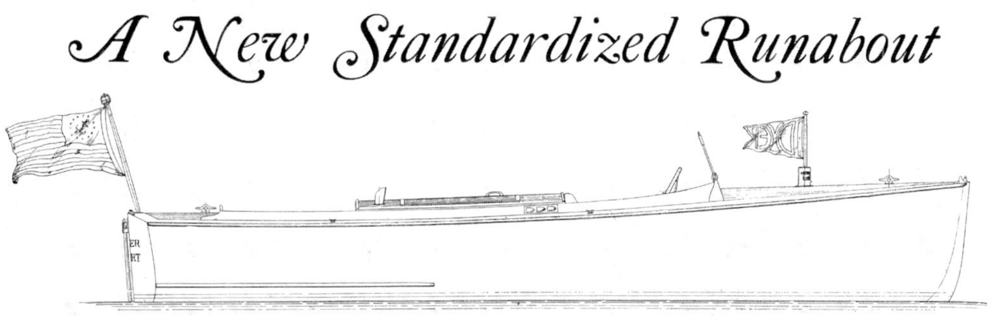

Francis designed this 21-foot fast launch in 1928 for the Dyer Motorcraft Corporation of Providence, Rhode Island. It was the only boat he designed for this or any other corporation. He destroyed her plans, but William J. H. Dyer saw that this outboard profile drawing appeared in both *Yachting* and *The Rudder*. The launch's beam was 5 feet, 9-1/2 inches, and her draft was 1 foot, 10 inches. Cost varied from $1,875 to $2,995, as horsepower varied from 45 to 120. (*The Rudder* (January 1929): 146)

finally made up his mind about what he wanted in the powerboat line: a good-sized motor sailer *and* a fast launch, so plans for these two boats were on his drawing boards. He even received praise for his work from his father. Nathanael wrote: "I want to compliment you on the fine appearance and completeness of the prints you put out." Francis must have noted, however, that his father was praising technique rather than design concepts, and that much of the praise was thus due Norman Skene and Sam Brown.[47]

While all this was going on, Francis made an attempt to expand further his growing business: he had a fling at working for a corporation. He surrendered his independence to the point of allowing his name to appear on a full-page advertisement in the April 1928 issue of *Yachting* as Designing Engineer for the Dyer Motorcraft Corporation. William J. H. Dyer, an experienced yachtsman with plenty of entrepreneurial drive, had the idea of building, in his plant at East Greenwich, Rhode Island, on Narragansett Bay, a series of fast, seaworthy motorboats. He wanted boats that could take a pounding. He wondered whether L. Francis Herreshoff's longitudinal construction might be the answer, and, in any event, he thought it would do his project no harm to associate it with the name Herreshoff.[48]

We don't know much about Francis's business arrangements with Dyer, but, on April 11, 1928, Francis filed for a patent on the construction that he proposed for Dyer's motorboats. Its précis read: "This invention relates to an improved boat construction; and has for its object to provide a boat construction that is very strong and durable and yet light in weight and one that will not weave, wring or twist but will retain its original shape even when subjected to the great strains of being driven at high speed thru a heavy seaway." Soon after getting the patent in early 1929, Francis sold it to Dyer. His career in the corporate world was brief. He designed a 21-foot launch for Dyer and that was all. Bill Dyer based additional boats in his series on Francis's initial design, but Francis was no longer listed as Designing Engineer, and he got no credit for the later boats, undoubtedly to his relief. Francis destroyed the plans he had drawn of the Dyer motor launch.[49]

Francis's launch met Dyer's objectives. The boat was deemed fast and seaworthy, even if we subtract a bit from *The Rudder's* wide-eyed account of her trials: "this new model opened up at 35 m.p.h. in a wintry sea, took the waves at every angle at various speeds, made circles in a forty-foot radius and then throttled down suddenly to prove that she would not bury her nose when cut down in a following sea. All through this test no water was taken in and she was as safe as though she was being maneuvered on calm summer seas."[50]

In any event, sales of the boats were satisfactory. Two were built in Marblehead by William H. Brown for display at the Boston Boat Show in February 1928. Dyer built twenty-five of the 21-footers for the 1929 season. In 1930, the Dyer Motorcraft Corporation became the Dyer Motorcraft Division of the Herreshoff Manufacturing Company.[51]

Soon after designing the fast 21-footer for Dyer, Francis drew the plans for a fast 28-footer for Charlie Welch. Charlie continued to be Francis's best customer to the point of being something of a patron. He liked and admired Francis. The two sustained their friendship, spending much time together in one or the other of their neighboring

RIGHT: **The illustrations for Francis's patent for the longitudinal construction of the Dyer launch, US Patent 1,698,304, issued January 8, 1929.** (Collection 138, Box 16, folder 3, G. W. Blunt White Library, Mystic Seaport)

Jan. 8, 1929. | L. F. HERRESHOFF | 1,698,304

BOAT

Filed April 11, 1928

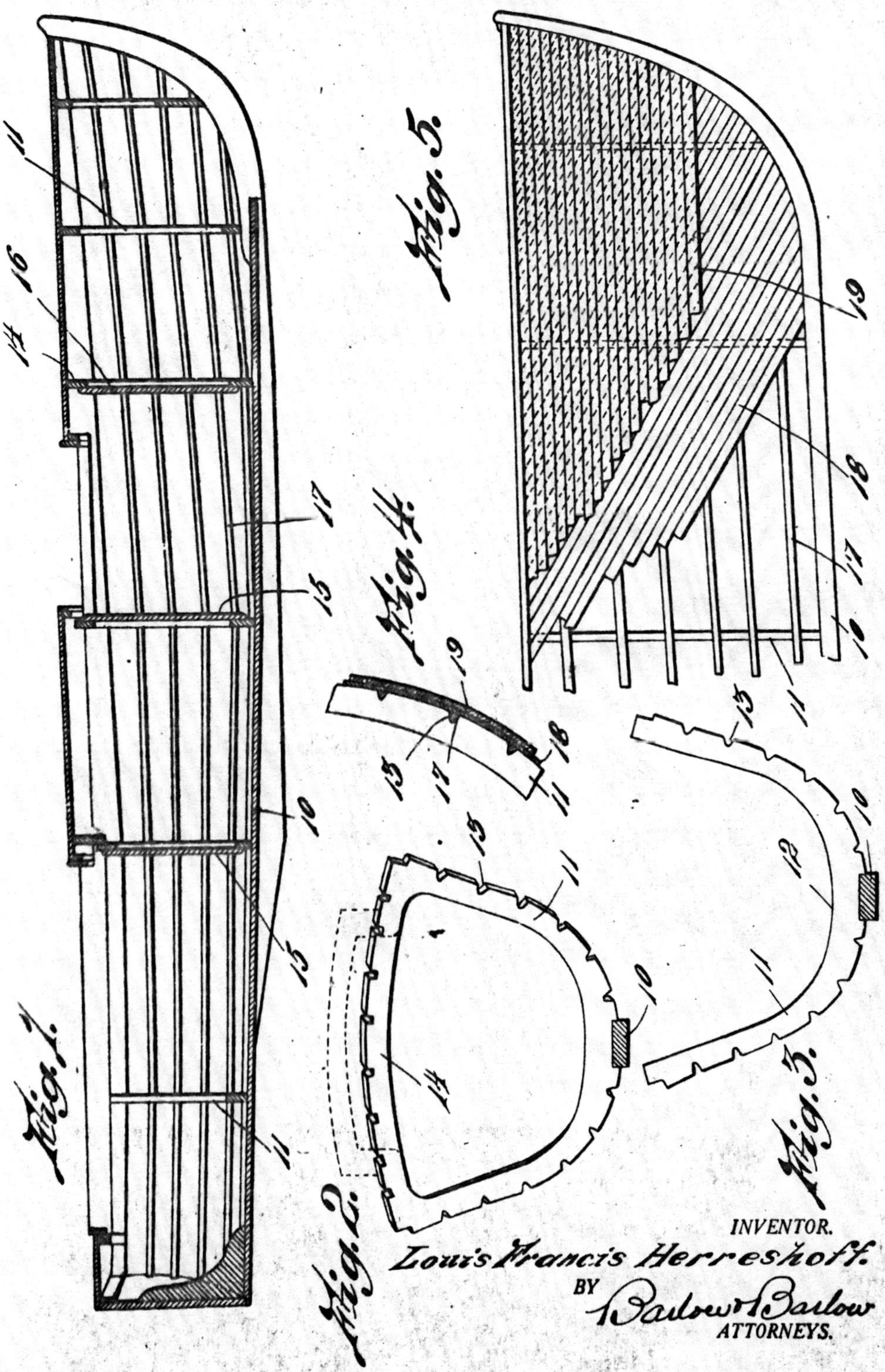

INVENTOR.

Louis Francis Herreshoff.

BY *Barlow & Barlow*

ATTORNEYS.

houses discussing boat design. Charlie loved to go on the water under sail and power in all seasons, and he trusted Francis's experience and genius to provide him with the best possible boats in which to do so.

The *Retriever*, as Charlie called his new launch, gave him a fast, open boat in which to zip out to watch a race that he wasn't sailing in, or run alongshore for an island picnic or a visit to a neighboring harbor, like Manchester or Gloucester. Her name and towing bitt suggest that he intended also to have a boat to bring home one of his racing boats that might have lost her breeze. In any event, the *Retriever* was fast. Francis would write: "Over our measured course here in the ocean she made a little over 26 statute miles an hour, but strange to say she could pass a well-known stock motor launch stained bright red (built in Michigan) which was sold to go 35 m.p.h."[52]

FOR A DESIGNER primarily of racing boats, summer came as something of a relief; it was then up to the skippers to see what they could do with Francis's brain children. In the summer of 1928, Francis had some fun. Down in Huntington, Long Island, William J. Atkin, a designer of attractive cruising boats, both sail and power, was trying out a simple way of racing small sailing boats in order to experiment with hulls and rigs at low cost. In the previous summer, his idea had attracted enough designers and builders, both professional and amateur, so that his Development Class numbered ten sailboats, about 17 feet long, each with a different hull and rig. The top designer in the class, besides Atkin himself, was Charles D. Mower. In an attempt to widen the field, Atkin wrote to both Francis and Charlie Welch to see if that interesting combination of designer and racing skipper might want to join in the experimentation. They would indeed.[53]

ABOVE: The Dyer launch being driven at 30 mph (Dyer's advertisements claimed 35) by her 8-cylinder, 120-horsepower Universal motor. (*The Rudder* (July 1929): 100) RIGHT TOP: The outboard profile and deck plan of Charlie Welch's *Retriever*, Francis's design No. 30. Length on deck is 28 feet; beam, 5 feet, 10 inches; draft of hull, 1 foot, 4 inches; draft at propeller struts and rudders, 1 foot, 11 inches. The dotted line over the after cockpit indicates that thought was given to shelter. Steering was from behind the windshield. Francis inked the plan himself and dated it January 29, 1928. (© Mystic Seaport, Daniel S. Gregory Ships Plans Library, SP38.84.6.) RIGHT BOTTOM: The *Retriever*'s construction plan for the builders at the George Lawley Company to follow. Francis has used his longitudinal system. She has twin Universal Victory six-cylinder motors of 60 horsepower each, twin screws and propeller struts of Francis's contra-propeller type, as used on Welch's *Dispatch*, and twin rudders. Speed was 26.5 mph. Francis designed the running gear, but all the boat's hardware, even to the Lawley windshield, was off the shelf. Fuel tanks are under the athwartships seats. She has a 'midships towing bitt, but, with her small propellers, she wouldn't have made an ideal towboat. Francis made a drawing of an adjustable, horizontal stern plane to fit between the struts (its after corners cut away so as not to interfere with the rudders), evidently to ensure that the boat ran level, but it is not known whether this device was needed or installed. Sam Brown traced this drawing in ink in March 1928. (© Mystic Seaport, Daniel S. Gregory Ships Plans Library, SP38.84.1)

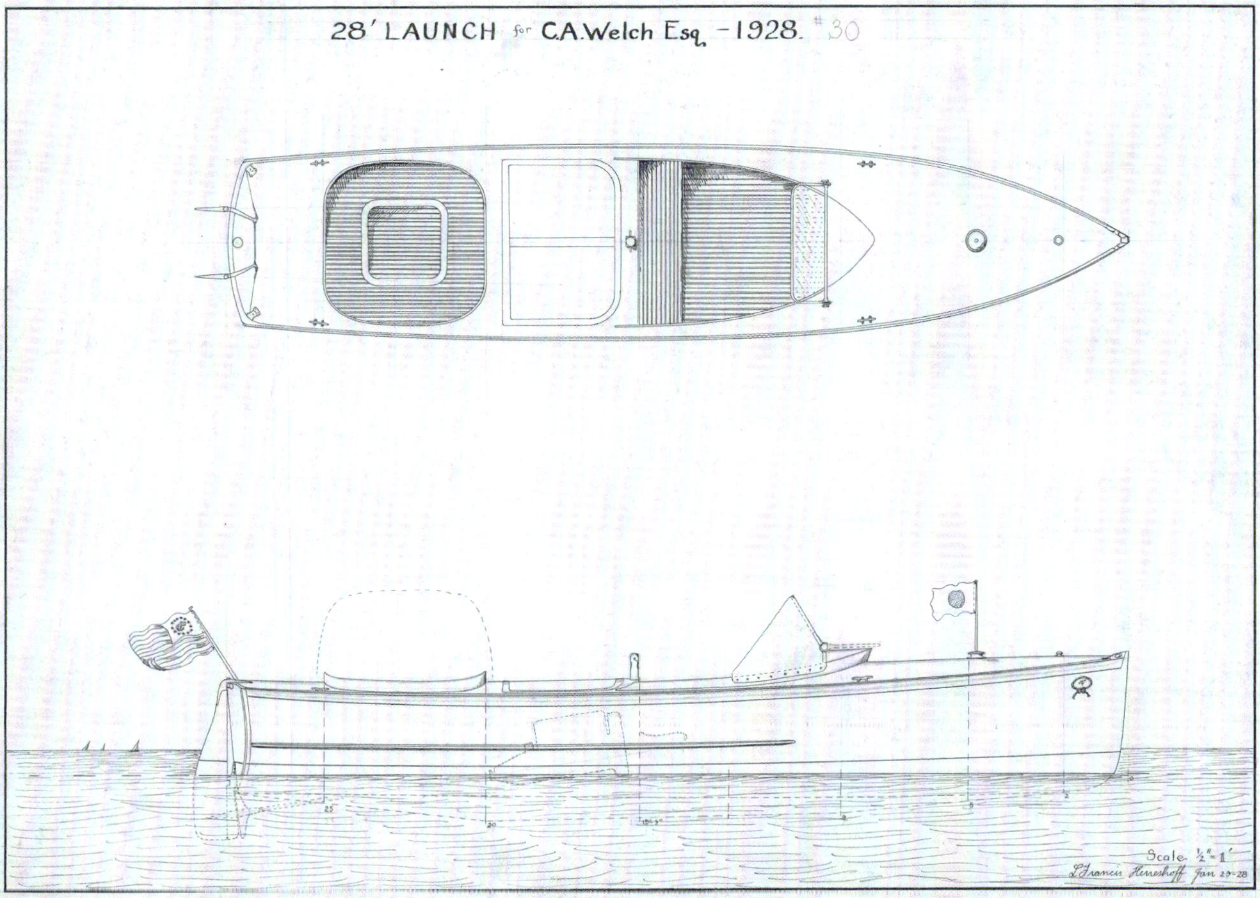
28' LAUNCH for C.A.Welch Esq. -1928. #30
Scale ½" = 1'
L.Francis Herreshoff Jan 29-28

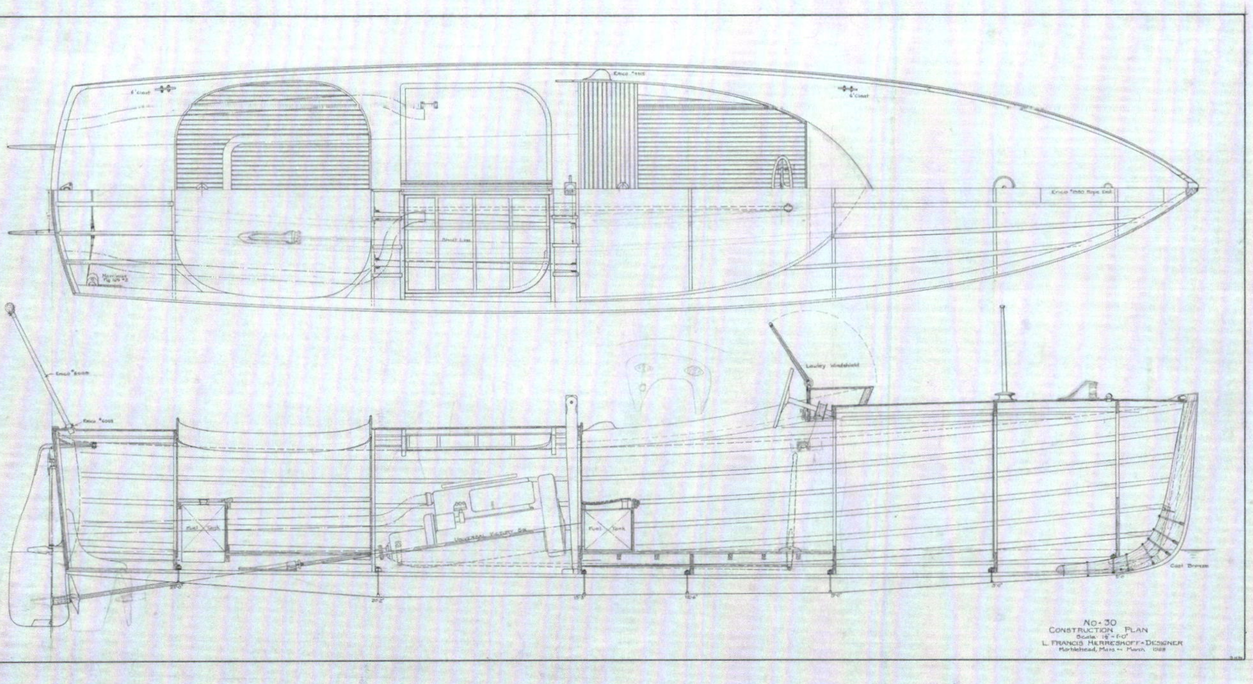
Cast Bronze
NO-30
CONSTRUCTION PLAN
Scale: 1½" = 1'-0"
L. FRANCIS HERRESHOFF - DESIGNER
Marblehead, Mass. -- March 1928

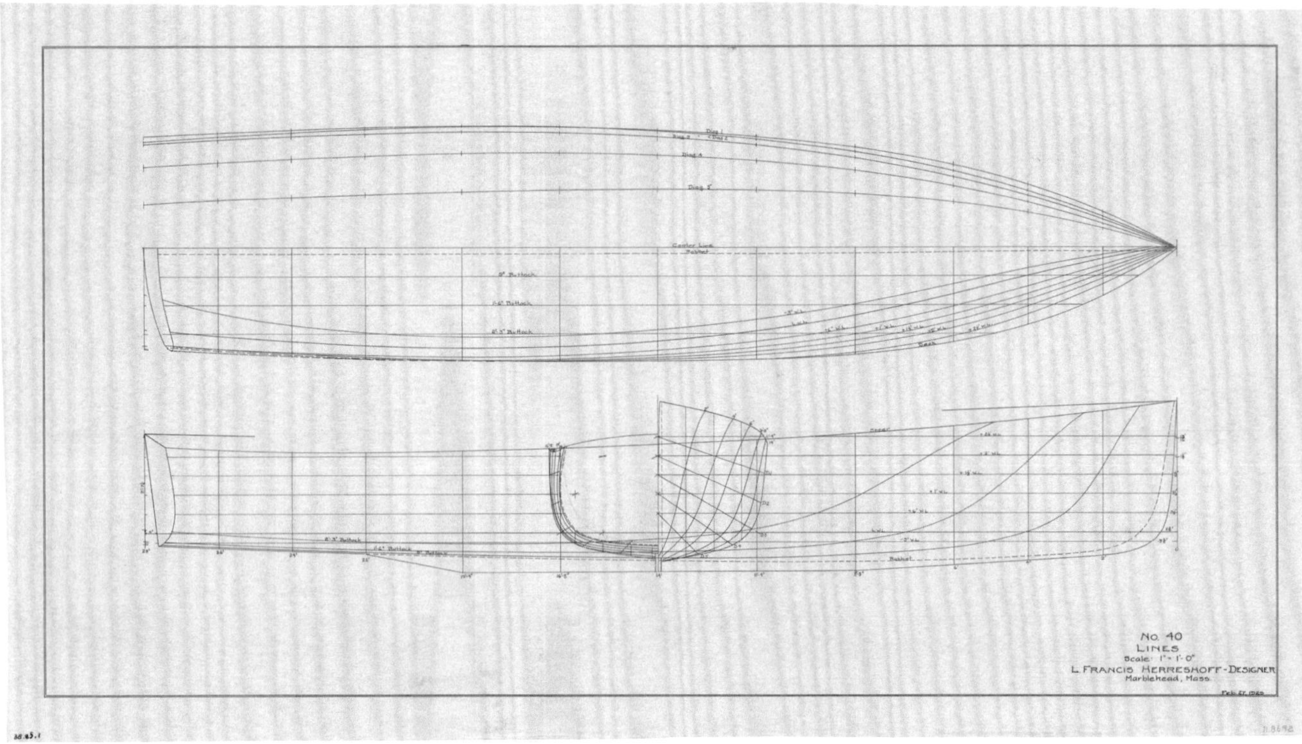
No. 40
LINES
Scale: 1" = 1'-0"
L. FRANCIS HERRESHOFF-DESIGNER
Marblehead, Mass.

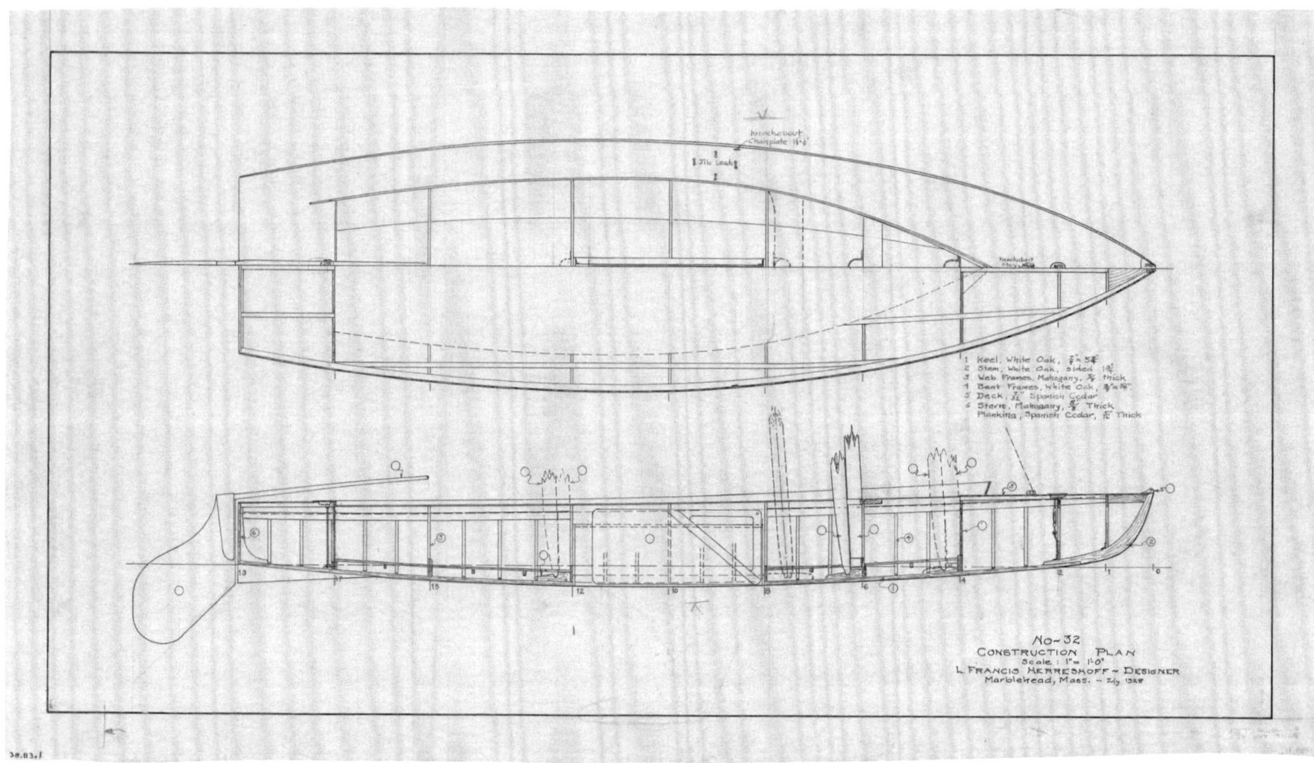
1 Keel, White Oak
2 Stem, White Oak, sided
3 Web Frames, Mahogany, thick
4 Bent Frames, White Oak
5 Deck, Spanish Cedar
6 Stern, Mahogany, Thick
Planking, Spanish Cedar, Thick
No-32
CONSTRUCTION PLAN
Scale: 1" = 1'-0"
L. FRANCIS HERRESHOFF - DESIGNER
Marblehead, Mass.

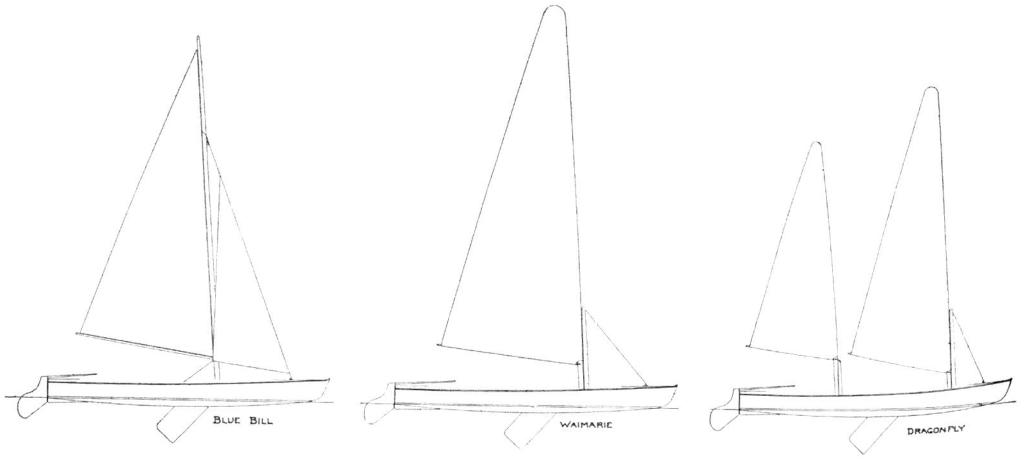

Francis drew a design for the Development Class, and he and Charlie built three boats to it in the ground-floor workshop of 20 Lee Street, one for each of them, and one for Commodore Lawrence F. Percival Jr. of the Corinthian Yacht Club. Francis and his friends wanted the experiment to be scientific, with one variable, not two, so, unlike the Huntington boats, these three were built with identical hulls, and each owner chose the rig he thought would be fastest. Percival wanted the sloop rig on his *Blue Bill*; Charlie Welch, the cat for the *Waimarie*; and Francis chose a cat-ketch for the *Dragon Fly*. Francis wrote: "almost everyone laughed at the cat-yawl [ketch] rig. Many people lately have been laboring under some popular theory that an efficient sail plan must have an

LEFT TOP: **The lines of the *Manatee*, Francis's design No. 40, a runabout for Marblehead yachtsman Lawrence F. Percival, drawn a year after those of the *Retriever*. The two boats are similar: length is the same, with the *Manatee* having 2 inches more beam and 4 inches less draft. The *Manatee* had a single-screw, driven by a Sterling Petrel motor.** (© Mystic Seaport, Daniel S. Gregory Ships Plans Library, SP38.85.1) LEFT BOTTOM: **The construction plan for Francis's Development Class boats. No lines plan has survived, but photographs show that the boats had lots of flare amidships and hollow sections forward. Length on deck is 19 feet; length on the waterline, 17 feet, 2 inches; beam, 5 feet, 1 inch; and draft, light, 3 inches. Francis has used a combination of seventeen conventional bent frames with nine built-up web frames and four longitudinal stringers. Only on this small craft did he mix conventional and longitudinal construction. Keel, stem, and bent frames were of white oak; web frames and transom were mahogany; and planking and deck were Spanish cedar. Francis and Charlie Welch built the boats carefully, planking them like rowing shells. In this drawing, Francis shows the different mast positions for all three boats. The narrow decks were an important feature of the design, keeping the water out when the boats were well heeled over.** (© Mystic Seaport, Daniel S. Gregory Ships Plans Library, SP38.113.1) ABOVE: **Francis drew the three different sail plans given the identical hulls of his Development Class boats in July 1928, his design No. 32. The cat-ketch *Dragon Fly* was Francis's own boat; the cat *Waimarie* belonged to Charlie Welch; and the sloop *Blue Bill* was the boat of Lawrence F. Percival Jr. The first two had double-luff sails in sleeves around tall clubs mounted in a bearing on very short masts so that the clubs could revolve to present the smooth airfoil at the best angle to the wind. The sails' booms were also in sleeves. The sail area of the Development Class was limited to 125 square feet.** (*Yachting* (February 1929): 74)

overlapping jib." This was in an article he wrote on the Development Class for *Yachting* at the request of Editor Herbert L. Stone, an article in which he admitted that his *Dragon Fly* had the best racing record of any of the boats. Presumably, the laughter subsided.[54]

Everyone who wrote about the Development Class expressed regret that it had become known as the Suicide Class, perhaps implying that the boats were dangerous. They were not. Francis wrote: "unfortunately, this class was nicknamed the Suicide Class simply because some of the first boats had reckless names." *Hell, No!, Hooch,* and *Spook* were three of them. The Huntington boats used, as a sail emblem for the class, a skull-and-crossbones.[55]

Francis enjoyed the contact with Billy Atkin that the little boats brought him. Atkin was down-to-earth, friendly, and open, and he designed sensible, appealing cruising boats. He

---

ABOVE LEFT: **Francis, in a suit jacket and his fedora, sailing the *Dragon Fly* in Marblehead Harbor. His more casually dressed crew is Sam Brown. Keeping her going just right on the wind by the feel of her tiller and the sense of the wind's direction on the back of his neck, he is watching the water go by the lee quarter to judge her speed; in a moment, he'll be glancing at the luffs of her sails and then at the exact motion of the tiny ripples just to windward and will make a slight movement of the tiller in response to what these vital indicators tell him.** (Robert L. Morton photo, *Fore an' Aft* (November 1928): 7) ABOVE RIGHT: **Charlie Welch sailing the *Waimarie*. This view gives a good indication of the hull shape of Francis's Development Boats and shows how the revolving, double-luff sail works. Marblehead Harbor was a good place to try out the little, low-sided Development Boats, even though it was so busy that fifteen Marbleheaders petitioned the Massachusetts Legislature to regulate the speed and noisiness of motorboats.** (Robert L. Morton photo, *Fore an' Aft* (November 1928): 10) RIGHT: **Francis designed a bigger version of the Development Boats for William L. Taggart, but he backed out, so no more than a preliminary plan was drawn, and the boat was not built. She was to be 25 feet long, with a beam of 5 feet, 10 inches. Sail area in the gunter rig was 202 square feet. This boat would have been a flyer. Sam Brown traced Francis's drawing in ink and dated it September 1928.** (© Mystic Seaport, Daniel S. Gregory Ships Plans Library, SP38.169.1)

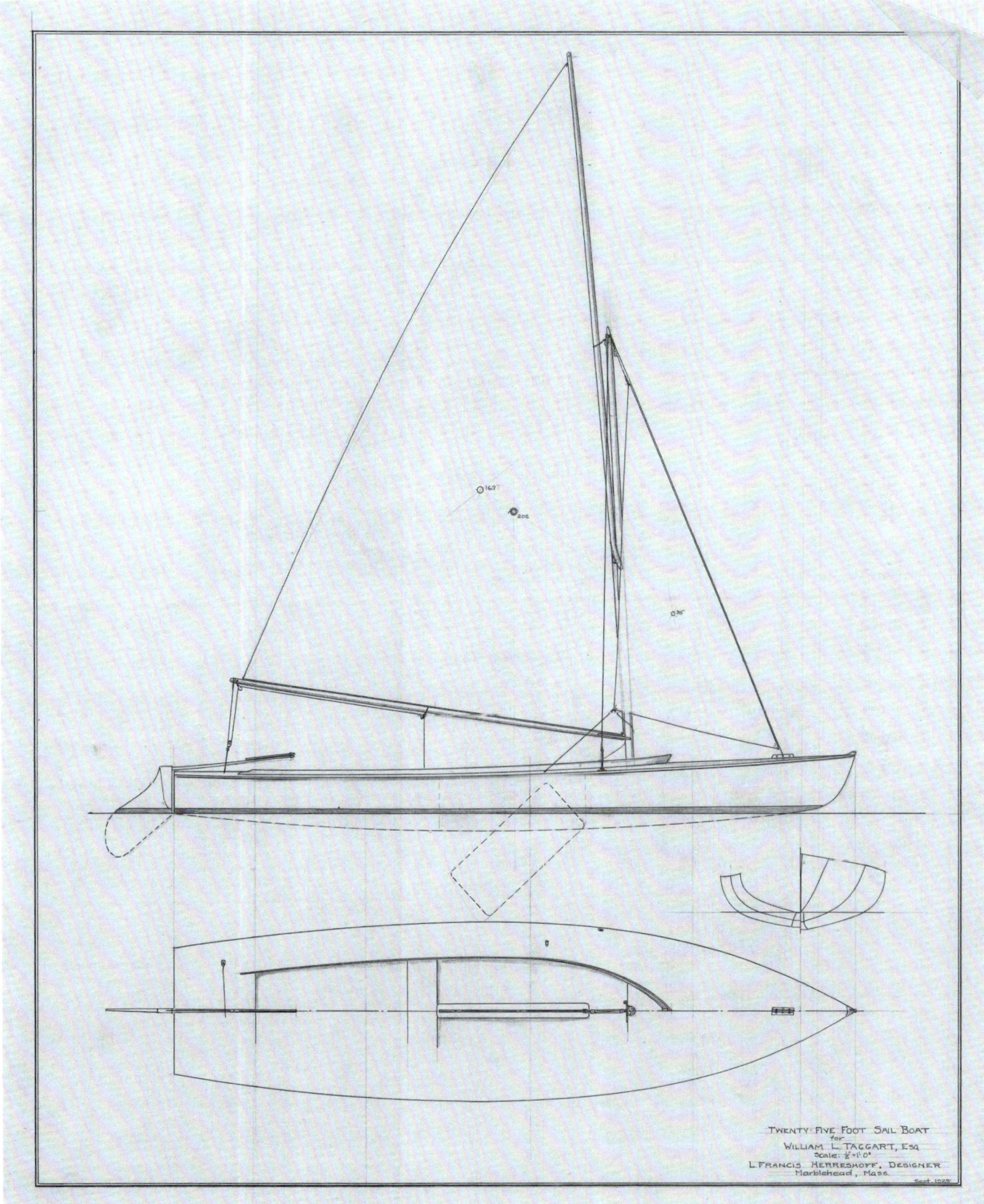
TWENTY-FIVE FOOT SAIL BOAT
for
WILLIAM L. TAGGART, ESQ
Scale: ½" = 1' 0"
L. FRANCIS HERRESHOFF, DESIGNER
Marblehead, Mass.
Sept. 1925

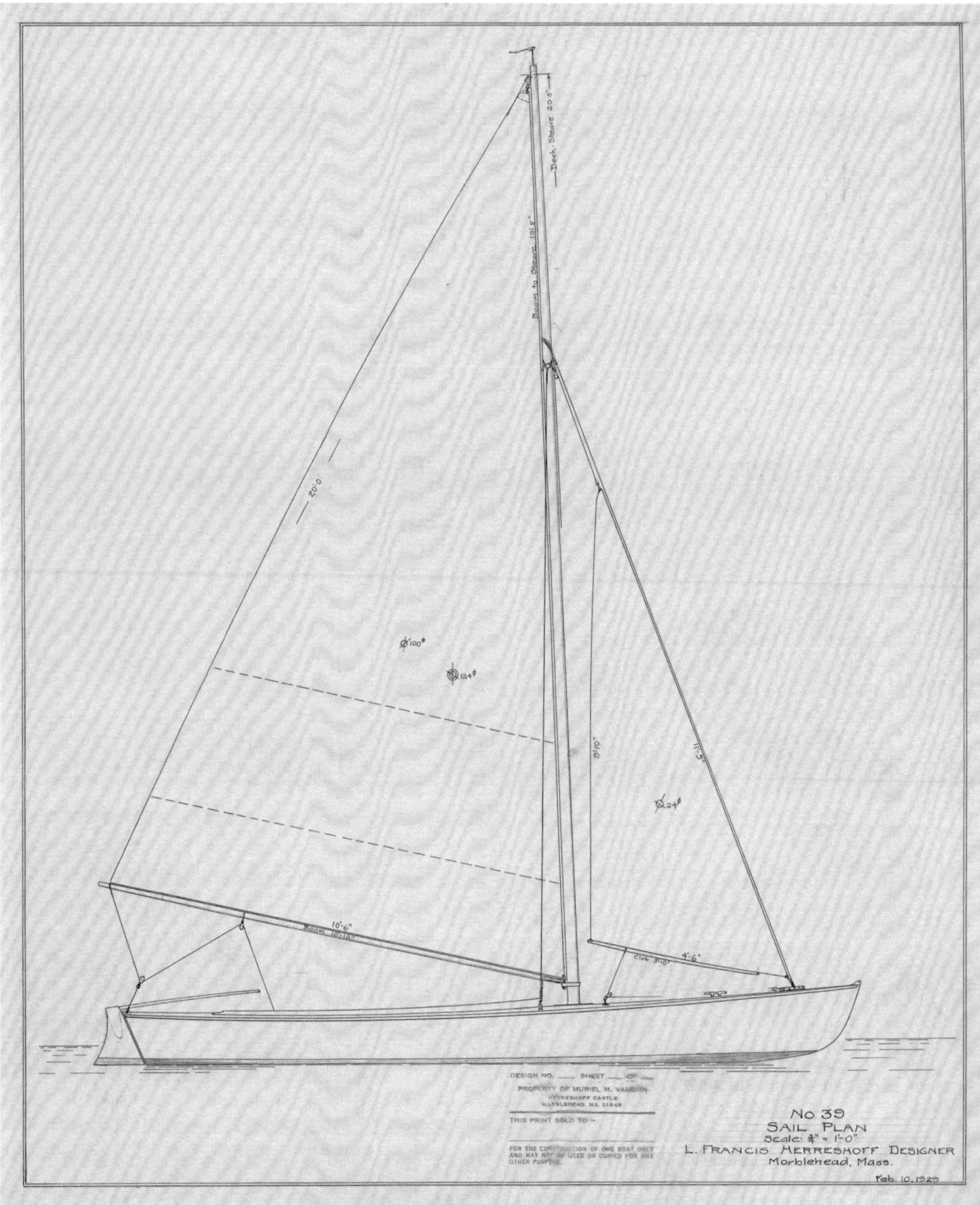
20'-0
10'-6"
4'-6"
DESIGN NO. ____ SHEET ____ OF ____
THIS PRINT SOLD TO –
No. 39
SAIL PLAN
Scale: ¾" = 1'-0"
L. FRANCIS HERRESHOFF DESIGNER
Marblehead, Mass.
Feb. 10, 1929

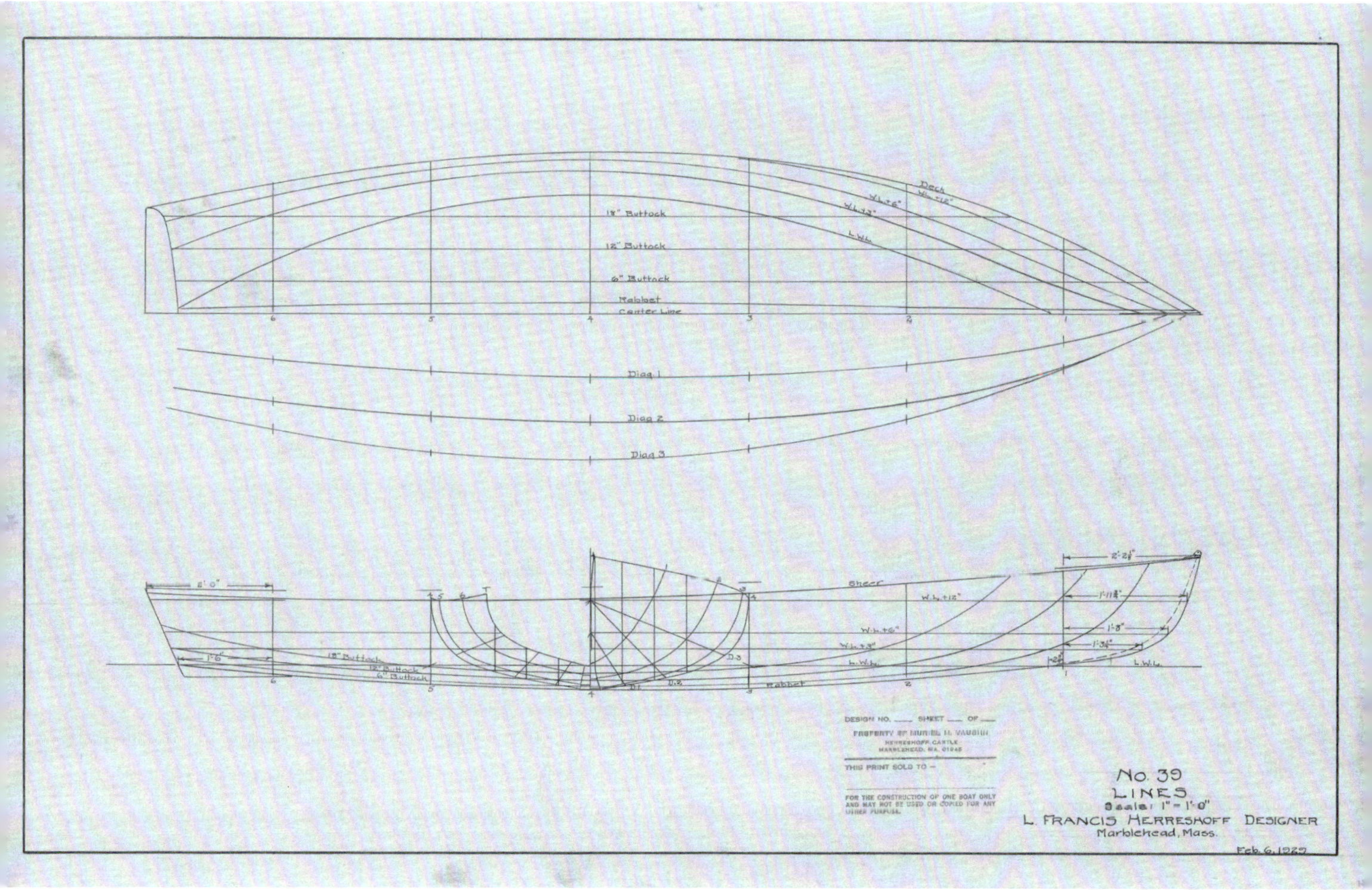

LEFT: **Francis's design No. 39, for a junior racer based on the 1928 Development Boats. For a small, simple boat, he has gone back to eye splices rather than tangs to hold the standing rigging to the mast. The three plans shown were inked by Sam Brown from February 6 to 10, 1929. The sail area is 124 square feet.** (© Mystic Seaport, Daniel S. Gregory Ships Plans Library, SP38.178.4) ABOVE: **The lines of No. 39. She is 16 feet, 10 inches long on deck; 14 feet on the waterline; 5 feet, 2 inches beam; and 5 inches draft, light. She could plane under ideal conditions.** (© Mystic Seaport, Daniel S. Gregory Ships Plans Library, SP38.178.1)

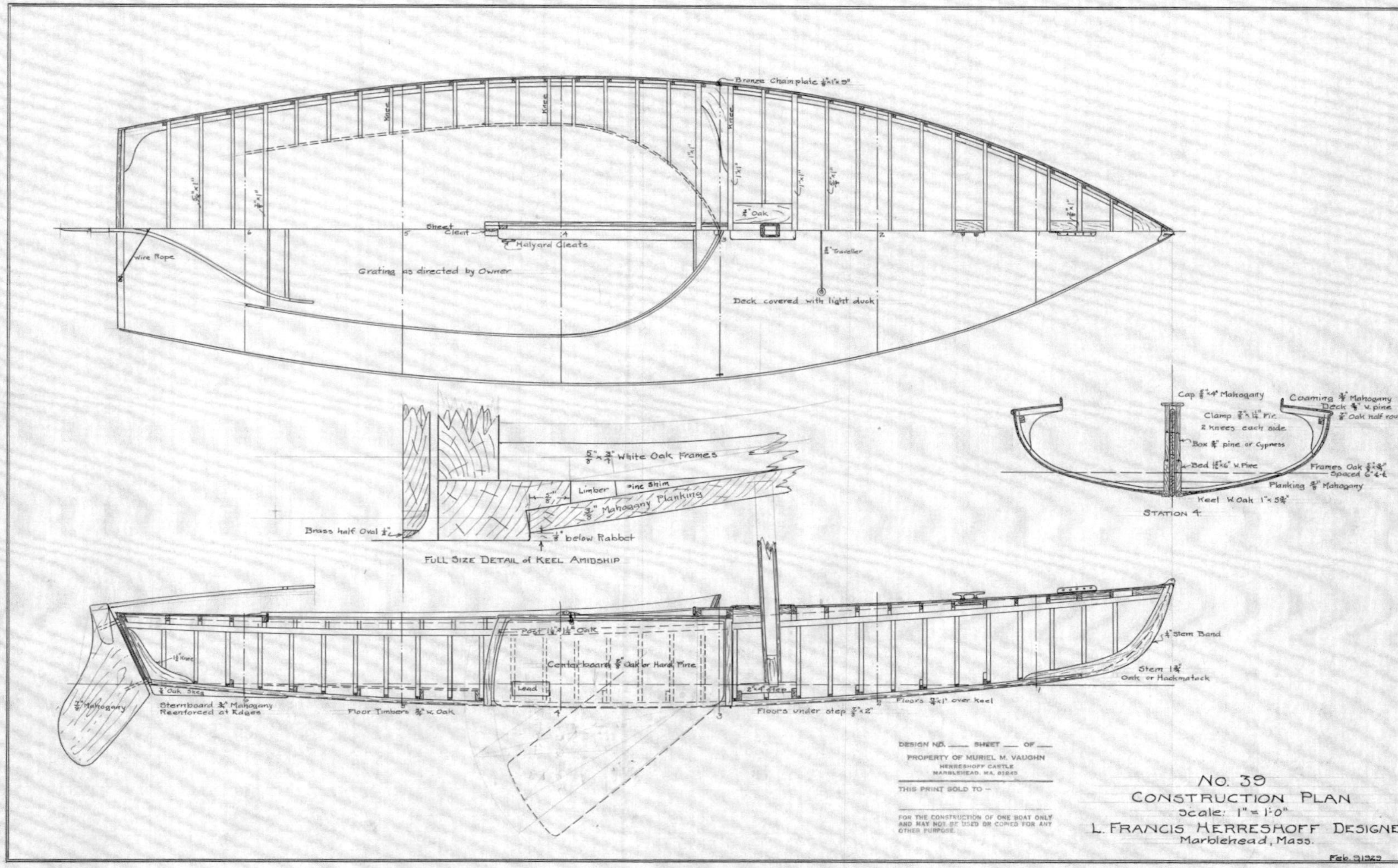
Bronze Chainplate
Knee
Knee
Knee
Wire Rope
Sheet
Cleat
Halyard Cleats
Grating as directed by Owner
Oak
Traveller
Deck covered with light duck
White Oak Frames
Limber
Pine Shim
Mahogany Planking
Brass half Oval
below Rabbet
FULL SIZE DETAIL of KEEL AMIDSHIP
Cap Mahogany
Coaming Mahogany
Deck W. pine
Oak half round
Clamp
2 knees each side
Box pine or Cypress
Bed W. Pine
Frames Oak
Planking Mahogany
Keel W. Oak
STATION 4
Mahogany
Sternboard Mahogany
Reenforced at Edges
Oak Skeg
Knee
Floor Timbers W. Oak
Lead
Centerboard Oak or Hard Pine
Step
Floors under step
Floors over keel
Stem Band
Stem
Oak or Hackmatack
DESIGN NO. ____ SHEET ___ OF ___
PROPERTY OF MURIEL M. VAUGHN
HERRESHOFF CASTLE
MARBLEHEAD, MA. 01945
THIS PRINT SOLD TO –
FOR THE CONSTRUCTION OF ONE BOAT ONLY AND MAY NOT BE USED OR COPIED FOR ANY OTHER PURPOSE.
NO. 39
CONSTRUCTION PLAN
Scale: 1" = 1'-0"
L. FRANCIS HERRESHOFF DESIGNER
Marblehead, Mass.

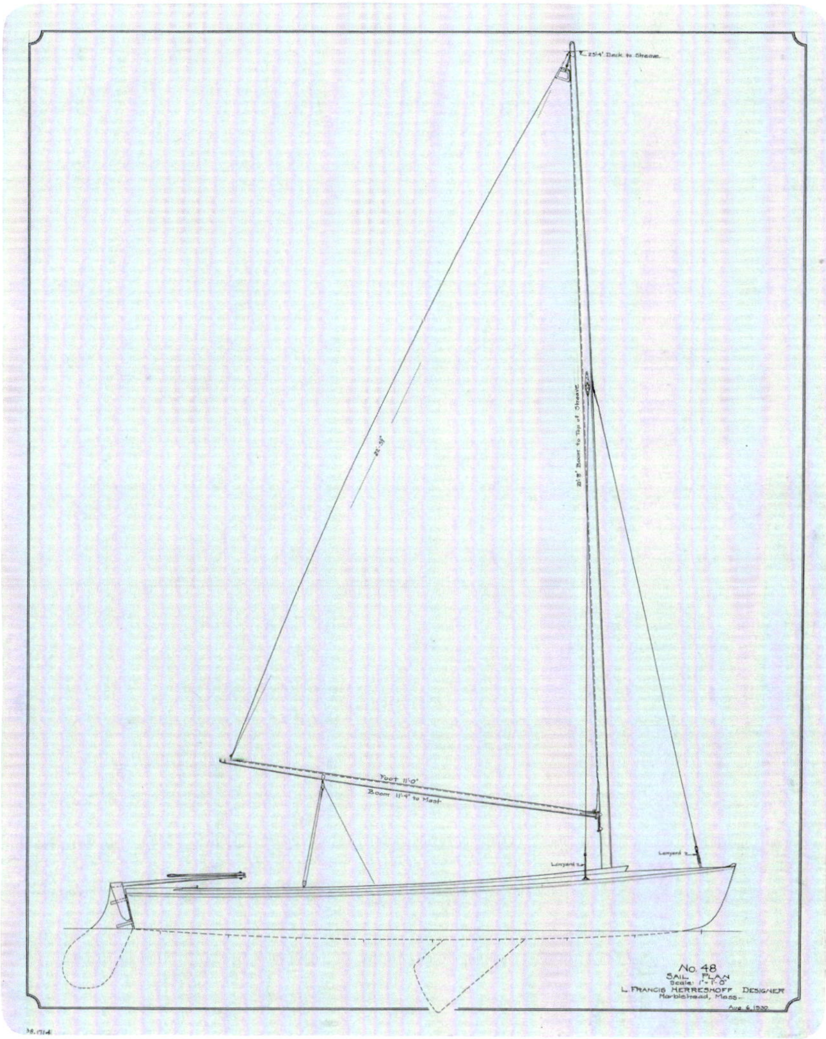

LEFT: **The centerboard knockabout's construction was conventional plank-on-frame. She was heavier than the Development Boats. Francis specified 7/8-inch oak or hard pine for the centerboard, rather than bronze. Note the nicely curved double tiller, designed so the helmsman can reach it easily when sitting out on deck to help keep the boat on her feet in a breeze.** (© Mystic Seaport, Daniel S. Gregory Ships Plans Library, SP38.178.3) ABOVE: **The outboard profile and sail plan of Francis's Development Boats of 1930, design No. 48, his own *Butterfly,* and Charlie Welch's *Flutterby.* The rig is conventional and simple, with a 121-square-foot sail, well within the 125-square-foot limit of Billy Atkin's rule. The sail is held to the mast by a luff-rope in a groove. The centerboard is ¼-inch bronze plate for stability; it was hung in the trunk in such a way that its position could be adjusted fore and aft to change the boat's steering balance. Francis thought later that the board should have been a little bigger. Note the deep rudder, and the hiking-stick on the tiller. The plan is dated August 6, 1930, but the other plans for these Development Boats were drawn in June; Francis chose the Marconi cat rig as the final element of the design.** (© Mystic Seaport, Daniel S. Gregory Ships Plans Library, SP38.171.4)

praised Francis in his magazine, *Fore an' Aft*, writing, "I feel I, as a designer of small craft, should pay a tribute to Mr. Herreshoff in the matter of all his designs, and I do. Not only are his boats original; but they reflect his experience in craft that are practical, handsome and at the same time accomplish the purpose for which they are built." In later letters, Francis would write that he had liked Atkin ever since meeting him in connection with the Development Class (Francis never used the Suicide name) and that he had had pleasant talks with him.[56]

The most important stipulation in Atkin's rule for the Development Class was the limitation of sail area to 125 square feet. All the boats had to have the same horsepower, so to speak. Beam of the hulls had to be between 3 feet, 6 inches and 5 feet, 6 inches. Minimum freeboard was 6 inches; minimum thickness of planking, 5/16ths inch. Each boat had to have a centerboard, maximum weight fifty pounds, that could be housed completely in its trunk, so that the boat could be hauled out on a float. Nothing else on the boats needed to be measured. There was no restriction on length, no artificial advantage to any particular hull shape through a complicated measurement rule, and no way to set unmeasured sail area. No Lloyd's. L. Francis Herreshoff was having fun all right.[57]

In the summer of 1928, Francis, Charlie, and Commodore Percival raced their Development boats in Marblehead Harbor, sometimes venturing outside in settled weather. They wouldn't have raced at all on the Fourth of July, when it gusted to 70 knots out of the west, and nine of the bigger racing boats capsized. The Development Class racing was not competitive; the point was not to win the race, but to see which rig had an advantage. Usually the skippers took along a crew, for these boats needed live ballast. Francis often had his draftsman and friend, Sam Brown, go with him to tend the mainsheet in his cat-ketch. This was the kind of racing Francis liked, where the emphasis was on learning something new about boat design, rather than on trying to get ahead of the other fellow, maybe through some tricky tactic or by catching a wind-shift just right. And Francis liked to sail the *Dragon Fly* just for fun. Sometimes friends would go with him or he'd go off sailing by himself, just to feel his small vessel dance over the waves, pushed along by the quiet wind. He would write: "These little boats are the most fun to sail of any I have ever tried, not barring sailing canoes."[58]

Trying the three boats against each other showed that the cat rig was best in a light breeze, the sloop in moderate, and the cat-ketch in fresh or strong. Francis observed that the tall yards on short masts of the cat and cat-ketch slatted around some when the water was choppy, giving the sloop an advantage. (In the interest of science, it would have been advantageous to see how the cat and cat-ketch would have done with normal masts.) Francis saw that on his cat-ketch, both sails worked in relatively undisturbed air (as on the cat, but not on the sloop) and that his rig presented the greatest total length of entering edges (luffs) of sail. He noted that his *Dragon Fly* seemed to point the highest of the three and that, with her low center of effort, she was the stiffest and so the fastest in fresh and strong winds, especially to windward.[59]

The Development Class racing did become competitive in the fall, when three of the Huntington boats came to Marblehead to see what they could do against Francis's boats. The *Spook* was sailed by her amateur designer and builder, Charles Young. *Hell, No!* had been designed by Mower and *Daiquiri* by Atkin. Two races were sailed on Saturday, September 29, the first in a dying northwest breeze, the second in a light southerly. Next day, the sailors braved a strong, dry northeaster. The Marbleheaders swept. Francis and Charlie Welch were first or second in all three races, Francis winning two and Charlie, one. Percival took two thirds and a fourth. Of the Huntington boats, Young's *Spook* did best, with a third and two fourths. Francis noted that his boats had an advantage because of their light, careful construction compared to the Huntington boats. They were also sailing in their home waters, and, as with any racing, we must take into account the skill of the sailors.[60]

Francis and Nathanael had corresponded about the Development Class. There were Development Boats in Coconut Grove, where Nathanael wintered, and he had watched their performance with his usual professional interest. He was fascinated with what his son was doing, though he never told Francis that in so many words. He also needed to show Francis that, at age eighty, he could still compete. After some initial defensiveness on both their parts, father and son worked together on Development Class ideas, each trying to improve on the concepts of the other. Nathanael had designed successful cat-yawls and liked Francis's cat-ketch. He took Francis's design a step farther with a three-masted rig. He also tried the wishbone boom around a sail to allow it to keep its curvature at the foot. One of the pleasures experienced by Francis, Norman Skene, and Sam Brown in Francis's design office was discussing plans, models, and letters of and about Development Boats sent by Nathanael G. Herreshoff. Francis wrote to his father: "We are never tired of hearing about the Development boats and your letters are read with great interest and cause much interesting conversation."[61]

Early in 1929, Francis designed a racer for juniors in the Beverly Yacht Club at Marion on Buzzards Bay. He based the design, his No. 39, on the Development Boats that he had found were so much fun to sail. At first glance, this boat looks like a normal, half-decked, centerboard knockabout, but although she wasn't designed as a Development Boat (she had twice the minimum planking thickness allowed by Atkin's rule), she could have raced in the class, with her 124-square-foot sail area. The prototype was for H. Nelson Emmons, Commodore of the Beverly Yacht Club in Marion, Massachusetts, whose Boston firm dealt in real estate on the shores of Buzzards Bay. He named her the *Suicide,* presumably as a nod toward her heritage. Two of the club's juniors capsized her one day with an audience, so the powers that be decided she was too tender for youngsters, and the class died aborning.

Waldo Brown (he of the *Joann*) bought the *Suicide* and brought her to Harwich Port, giving her to his daughter. Ann Brown found the knockabout a handful; the *Suicide* became her brother's boat. John raced her in the Stone Horse Yacht Club's handicap class, where he could beat everybody but the Walker sisters in their old gaff-rigger, the *Bay Bird*, designed by Starling Burgess. John Brown kept the *Suicide* for twenty years. He said: "It went like Hell."[62]

By the summer of 1930, Francis was sending Nathanael prints of a new Development Class design, his No. 48. He and Charlie Welch had sold the *Dragon Fly* and *Waimarie* to Huntington sailors that spring (where the *Dragon Fly* took second in the fall championships) and Francis had designed a stiffer, simpler boat, better for afternoon sailing around Marblehead Harbor and environs in a variety of wind conditions. He and Charlie had Lawley's build two boats to the design, one for each of them. Francis designed the boats to Atkin's simple rule, but they were identical in both hull and rig, and he and Charlie would use them more for enjoyment than to further the progress of yacht design. Years later, Francis would agree with a suggestion that there should be two development classes, one with identical hulls and different rigs, and one with identical rigs and different hulls, but this sensible idea for improving both rigs and hulls scientifically was not put into practice.[63]

At 18 feet, the 1930 boats were a foot longer than the 1928 boats, with the same beam on deck but considerably more at the waterline to increase stability, and with 3 inches more freeboard at the bow for dryness. Francis specified lapstrake construction, and the George Lawley Company built the boats like big dinghies. Hull weight was

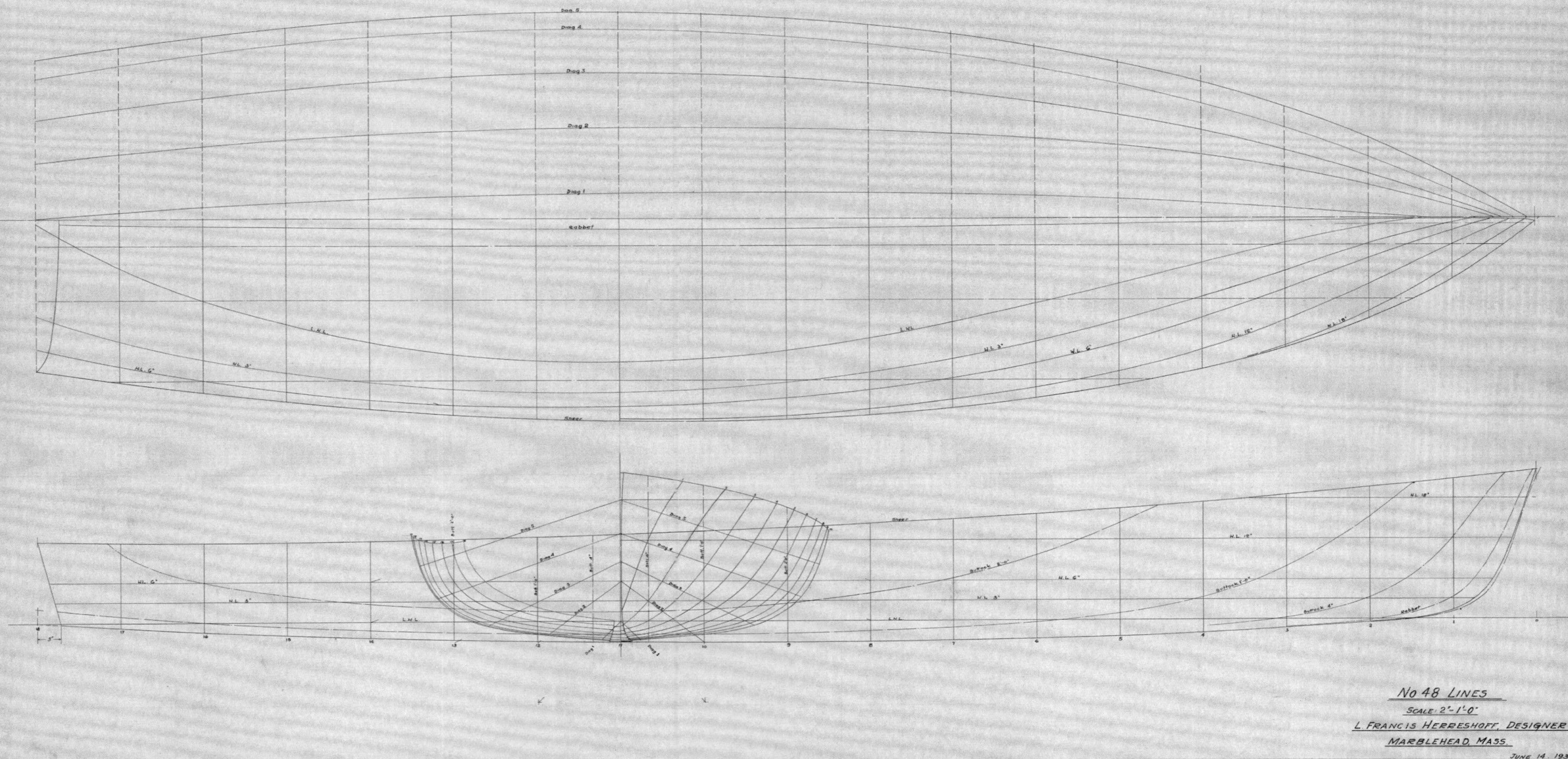
Diag 5
Diag 4
Diag 3
Diag 2
Diag 1
Rabbet
Sheer
L.W.L.
W.L. 3"
W.L. 6"
W.L. 12"
W.L. 18"
No 48 LINES
SCALE 2"-1'-0"
L. FRANCIS HERRESHOFF, DESIGNER
MARBLEHEAD, MASS.
JUNE 14. 1930.

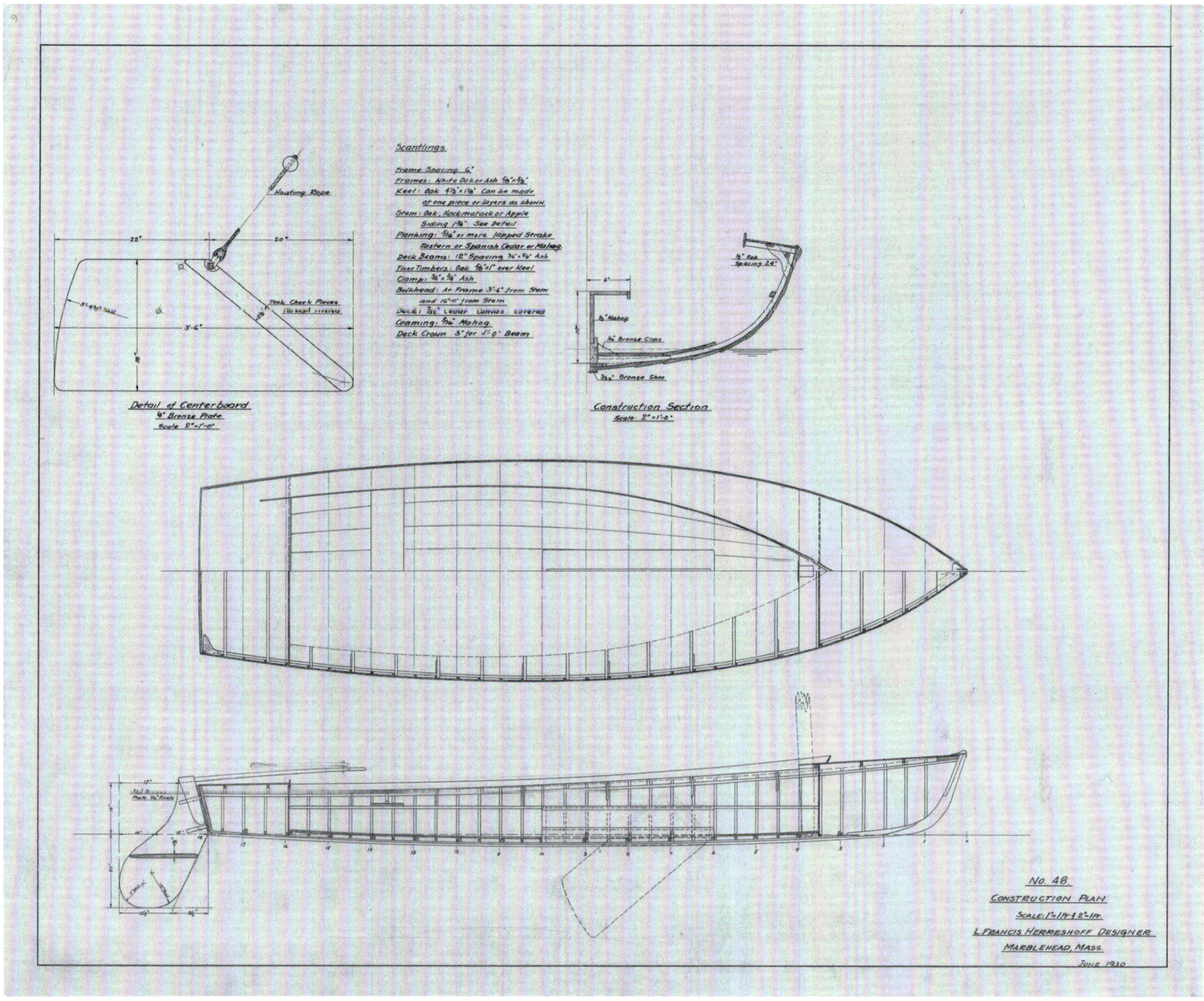

LEFT: The lines of the *Butterfly*. She is 18 feet long; 17 feet, 3 inches on the waterline; with a beam of 5 feet. Her draft of 3 inches with the waterline shown would, of course, vary with load. Her bottom has little deadrise, so that she would plane off the wind in a breeze. She has considerable flare at the bow to keep her dry. (© Mystic Seaport, Daniel S. Gregory Ships Plans Library, SP38.171.1) ABOVE: The *Butterfly*'s construction plan shows a conventional lapstrake-dinghy layout. The two boats were to be built by Lawley's, and Francis gave the small-craft workers latitude in choice of materials. The stems could be of oak, hackmatack, or apple; planking could be eastern or Spanish cedar or mahogany, 5/16-inches "or more." All that mattered was that the two boats be built alike. (© Mystic Seaport, Daniel S. Gregory Ships Plans Library, SP138.171.3)

less than 250 pounds. But the 1930 Development boats proved expensive, costing over $1,000 each. No more boats were built to the design.

Surmounting his praise of the 1928 boats, Francis wrote to Nathanael that the new boats were "much more pleasant to sail than [the] previous ones," and he later wrote that "they proved to be very fast." Francis named his new Development Boat the *Butterfly*; to his slight annoyance, Charlie named his *Flutterby.* L. Francis Herreshoff didn't like cute names for boats.[64]

Francis promoted his new Development Class boats over the popular Frostbite dinghies and, later, over the even more popular International 14-foot dinghies, but his preaching was only to the choir, his father. The *Butterfly* and *Flutterby*, in comparison to the Frostbites and International 14s were, he told Nathanael, much faster, dryer, and safer, and they would take three people comfortably, whereas the dinghies were limited to two. But comparing 18-foot boats to 14-footers and 11 ½-footers was unfair; Francis's disingenuous side was coming out. His design for the Development Class was outstanding; it didn't need a specious argument. It needed a promoter (and perhaps cheaper construction) to become popular, but Francis was not one to preach beyond the choir. He apparently sold only a couple of sets of plans of No. 48 in later years, from which only one known boat was built. Francis could complain about the lack of popularity of some of his designs and would put the blame on the public's lack of taste or common sense, and he had a point. But the fact is that promotion was simply not in his nature; he wanted and expected his designs to speak for themselves.[65]

The Development or Suicide Class did achieve modest popularity as a continuing way to experiment. Nathanael reported to Francis on Development boats sailed at Coconut Grove in the winter. Wirth M. Munroe was cleaning up in the early 1930s with long, lean, sharpie hulls and wishbone sprits instead of booms. At the same time, Seth Persson, a Brooklyn boatbuilder, was designing and building Suicides; he put a swing rig on one.[66]

The *Butterfly* was Francis's favorite sailing boat; he kept her for many years and sailed her often in the summer and fall. A correspondent reported to Francis that he had sailed in a Development boat at fourteen miles per hour, and Francis replied that he thought he had too, "for a short distance (maybe an eighth of a mile) with a very strong wind on the quarter."[67]

In 1939, one of Francis's important clients, William J. Strawbridge, would design a Development boat. One of Strawbridge's many interests was yacht design, and, perhaps with Francis looking over his shoulder, for they were friends, he drew the outboard profile and sail plan and the lines of a new *Flutterby.* Francis's comments when he saw the lettering of the name on Strawbridge's drawings are unrecorded. The design has a plumb bow and transom, a skimming-dish midsection, a deep centerboard, a spade rudder, and Francis's cat-ketch rig, with normal masts and loose-footed sails with sprits instead of booms. Evidently, Marconi and gunter cat rigs were also considered. The boat looks fast.[68]

Francis's *Butterfly* is now in the Small Craft Collection at Mystic Seaport. Charlie Welch's *Flutterby* is still sailing on the West Coast. It is good that these fine, fun little boats are still with us.[69]

CHAPTER 9

AUXILIARY
BEAM
DRAFT
POWER
Pipe Berth
Pipe Berth
Locker
Locker
Hatch
Engine Room
Bureau
Stove
Folding Table
Toilet Room
Fore Peak
Hatch

FROM THE WALRUS TO THE 30-SQUARE-METRES

"I was quite surprised that the boat sailed so fast and tacked to windward and handled so nicely."

—L. FRANCIS HERRESHOFF ON THE WALRUS

"...the class, which I had started in this country, turned out one of the greatest disappointments of my life."

—L. FRANCIS HERRESHOFF ON THE 30-SQUARE-METRE BOATS

Francis used Charlie's float, moored right in front of the Welch house in Timmy Lane's Cove, as a base for his small sailing boats. He was fussy about how he kept a boat and appreciated having a float where he could easily haul out a dinghy when he wasn't using it. He wrote: "dinghys that are left in the water are so logy that they are not much fun to sail."[1]

Charlie was generous with his facilities, and other friends and neighbors also kept dinghies at his waterfront. One was a young girl named Katherine Jones, who lived up on Tucker Street, scarcely more than a hundred yards beyond Francis's house. When Katherine walked down to the Welch's to go sailing, she would walk right by 20 Lee Street, but she didn't meet its customhouse occupant until one day in the summer of 1928. When she arrived at the float and said hello to Mr. Welch that day, he introduced her to another man there tending to his boat, Mr. Francis Herreshoff. It was the beginning of a friendship between a thirty-seven-year-old man and a girl twenty-five years his junior.

Francis was judgmental of children, as he was with adults. If they didn't "behave," he would have nothing to do with them, but if they were quiet around him and watched what he was doing with interest and listened to what he had to say, he was attracted to them. He loved to teach, and he realized that young minds were fertile ground, at least some young minds. He didn't want children underfoot when he was at his drawing board, but he welcomed them to his lathe. He would show a youngster like Katherine what he was making and how he went about it. He taught her to examine a boat fitting that he might be machining and to appreciate its form and how it was made to perform its function. His purpose was to teach an attitude,

a way of looking at things, rather than a specific procedure. To one who watched and listened, his lessons went far beyond boats.

And so some children were attracted to Francis. Some could sense his artistic side, his romanticism. To them, he was like a man out of a fairy tale. They also appreciated an adult who would let them into his world. Francis never talked down to children. Katherine Jones was one who would sense that Mr. Herreshoff was a wonderful romantic. But for now, this twelve-year-old dinghy sailor who liked boats and the water simply became fascinated to get to know the man who had created the *Yankee* and *Live Yankee*, famous racing boats that she could see from her bedroom window. For Francis, he had found a young kindred spirit to mentor, someone with whom he could subconsciously rewrite the history of his own childhood.[2]

FRANCIS WROTE to Nathanael on August 3, 1928, saying that he wanted to come down to Bristol to pick up some books that he had left at The Farm and also to take back to Marblehead a small steam engine that was at The Farm. It would be the first time father and son had been face-to-face since Francis had left Bristol in late 1920. On the couple of times when Francis had gone back to Bristol, Nathanael had been in Florida. They had corresponded with gradually increasing cordiality during the latter half of this seven-year separation, and Francis had sent blueprints of his design work to his father, but they had not seen each other or talked together. Francis had a telephone at 20 Lee Street, but it was only as a necessity for business, and he hated to use it.[3]

Francis made this drawing of a dinghy well snugged down on a float to illustrate a poetical piece called "A Midsummer Night's Sail" that he wrote for *The Rudder* in 1943. This may well be a smaller version of Charlie Welch's float in Timmy Lane's Cove, where Charlie, Francis, and others, including a young girl named Katherine Jones, kept their dinghies. (*An L. Francis Herreshoff Reader*, 311)

We have no way of knowing just what took place when Francis and Nathanael met, but we can guess with some accuracy that there were neither tears nor laughter. Emotions between son and father were to be stifled, or at least hidden. They probably spoke about the Development Class boats in which they were both much interested at the time and which they had discussed in letters. They would not have mentioned anything personal, except, perhaps, their health. The two had traded epistolary remarks about their digestion, or lack of same, and about Francis's pipe smoking, which Nathanael advised him to "leave off," and which Francis did reduce but continued.[4]

The visit continued the process of bringing Francis closer to his father. Soon after it, Francis asked Nathanael to help him out by making models of the *Yankee* and *Live Yankee* that the New York Yacht Club wanted, and, though it would seem impossible to improve on his father's collection of hand tools, Francis sent him some, including a favorite Swedish plane blade. And Francis visited his father again in October, before he and his wife, Ann, went to Florida for the winter, repeating his need to retrieve a book as his justification for making the trip.[5]

In 1928, Francis's business, two years old, was doing all right. Between the big motor yacht *Siva*, the three new racing boats, and keeping up with Charlie Welch's wants for getting afloat, Francis could meet his payroll of two draftsmen and a secretary and pay his bills. That Christmas, he could even send a worthwhile sum of money to his cousin Grace, the daughter of his Uncle Julian, who was trying to repair major damage to her house in Puerto Rico caused by a September hurricane. She wrote him: "I do not know what to make of you, dear, for sending me such a wonderful Christmas present. . . . I have not seen so much money together for a long time and it makes me feel very comfortable."[6]

Francis had no desire to emulate John Alden and build up a large firm of brokers and other designers. He must have lamented that for every design of his being built, there were many "Aldens" under construction, but he wanted to be able to design every yacht credited to his name himself; he wanted every line drawn on his plans to have his personal touch. He did take on the occasional pedestrian job, such as drawing two new rigs for the old Lawley schooner *Mistral* (one of which, had it been used, would have been a rare staysail schooner with a gaff-rigged mainsail), and reducing the sail area for a new owner of the *Speejacks,* a big schooner designed by William H. Hand, of New Bedford, that had sailed around the world. Although Francis didn't want to be distracted by brokerage, he did respond, as we have seen, to requests to sell a few boats. For the first time, in the August 1928 issue of *Yachting*, his advertisement in the Directory of Naval Architects listed L. Francis Herreshoff as "Yacht Designer and Broker." In the same issue, he ran a full-page ad to try to sell the *Live Yankee* for Charlie Welch, as well as two other R-boats not of his own design.[7]

CHARLIE WELCH, as well as getting the launch *Retriever*, finally decided in early 1928 just what he wanted in the way of a sizable boat for out-of-season cruising. All his discussions of such a boat with Francis and the starts and stops of designing and building one (we recall the 44-foot lifeboat ketch design that was never built) finally resulted in a commission for Francis to design a 50-footer with plenty of power and enough sail area and lateral plane to be independent of her engines if necessary. Francis drew preliminary plans that showed an outboard profile, sail plan, and cabin plan of an "Auxiliary Power Cruiser" that were published in the March 1928 issue of *Yachting*.

For the design of the *Walrus*, as Charlie's winter boat would be called, Francis went all the way back to earlier work he had done for Charlie

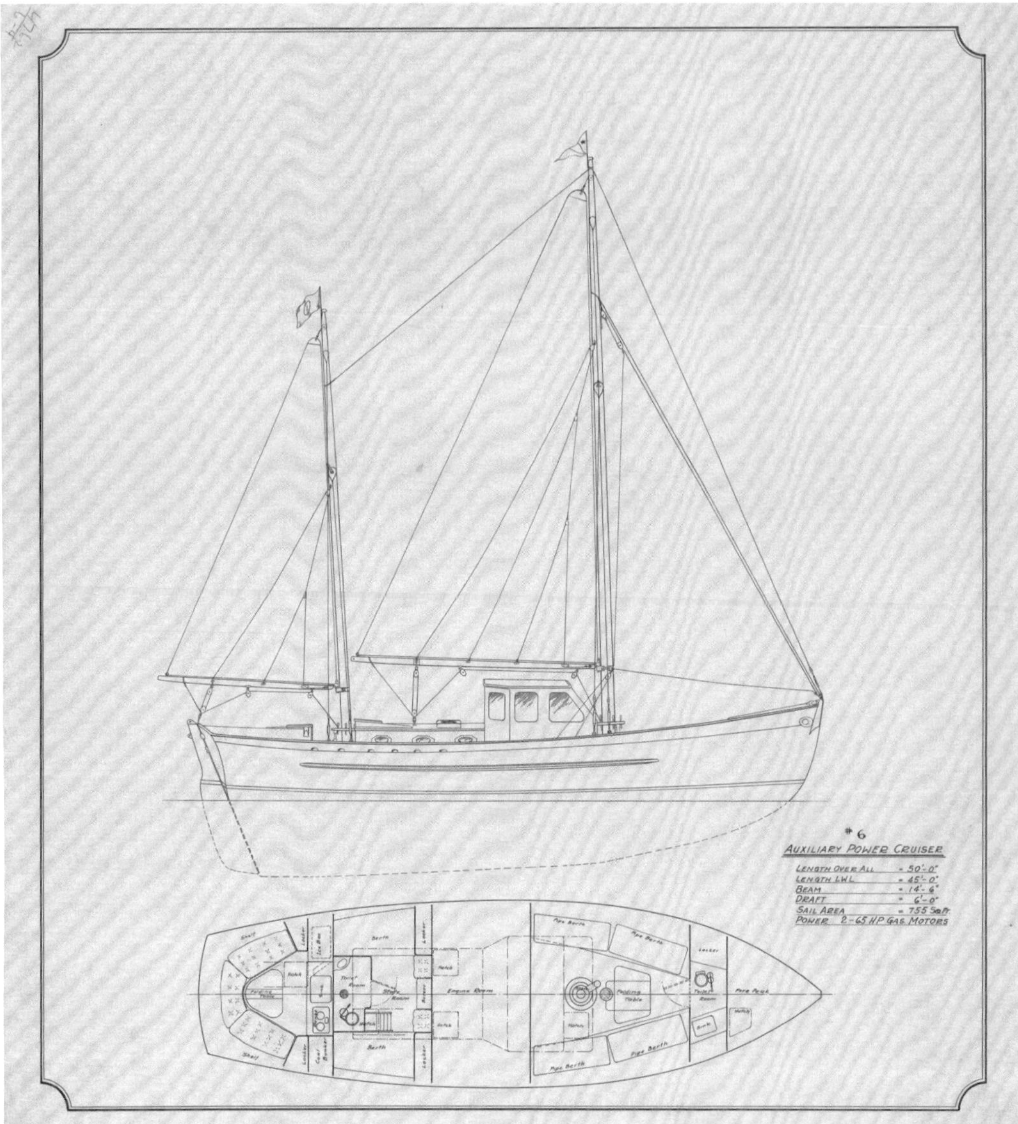

ABOVE: **The outboard profile and sail plan of the *Walrus*, Charlie Welch's winter boat that had been so long in incubation that it was Francis's design No. 19, instead of following consecutively, in August 1928, as No. 32. For power, Francis wanted a pair of 40-horsepower motors, but Charlie insisted on 65s, with which, wide open, she could make 10 knots. Sail area was 755 square feet, enough to make her handle well under sail alone.** (© Mystic Seaport, Daniel S. Gregory Ships Plans Library, SP38.81.5) RIGHT: **Francis's profile drawing of a yacht's stern, with raised quarterdeck and round skylight, stern windows, and portholes to light a great cabin, has neither title block nor date. It might be an alternative, handsome, traditional concept for the stern of the *Walrus*. If so, it was, unfortunately, rejected by Charlie Welch. This drawing could have been inspired by plans of a "Cogge ketch" by Douglas P. and F. Wavell Urry, published in the November 1927 issue of *Yachting*.** (© Mystic Seaport, Daniel S. Gregory Ships Plans Library, SP38.308.1)

on the concept, drawings that he thought would be built to and had given No. 19, which thus became the *Walrus*'s design number. Francis finished his pencil drawings for the design in the summer of 1928; Norman Skene calculated the displacement of the boat and constructed a curve showing estimated speed versus horsepower; and in August, Sam Brown traced Francis's drawings in ink. Completing the design of the *Walrus* must have been a great satisfaction for both Francis and Charlie Welch. They had been discussing the merits of many types of boats that would make good off-season cruisers for the last five years, ever since those November nights lying-to off Marblehead in the ketch *Stormy Petrel.* Now, here were plans that the boatbuilders at the George Lawley Company could follow to bring into existence a 50-foot vessel in which Charlie could put to sea year-round.

Yet there were further delays. Charlie didn't give Lawley's the go-ahead, and Sam Brown was still fussing around with wheelhouse details more than a year later. She finally slid down the builder's ways in January 1930. Francis didn't think Lawley's had done their best on the *Walrus.* Twenty-five years later, when one of his customers was looking at her to buy and found her in bad shape, Francis wrote him: "in fact she never was a really excellent job anyway."[8]

As we have seen, Francis didn't spend time in most of the yachts he was designing, except vicariously, but since Charlie Welch was a good friend, he did get to know the *Walrus* well. He came to agree with Charlie's choice of bigger engines than he, as designer, had first specified. With two 65-horsepower, -six-cylinder, Lathrop Standards (instead of his 40-horsepower models), "when the engines are wide open, she can be driven about ten knots," as he wrote Nathanael. He added that "the engines seem like a pair of nice old steam engines," and he wrote to the Lathrop Engine Company to congratulate them on the performance of their machines. Nathanael thought that the *Walrus*

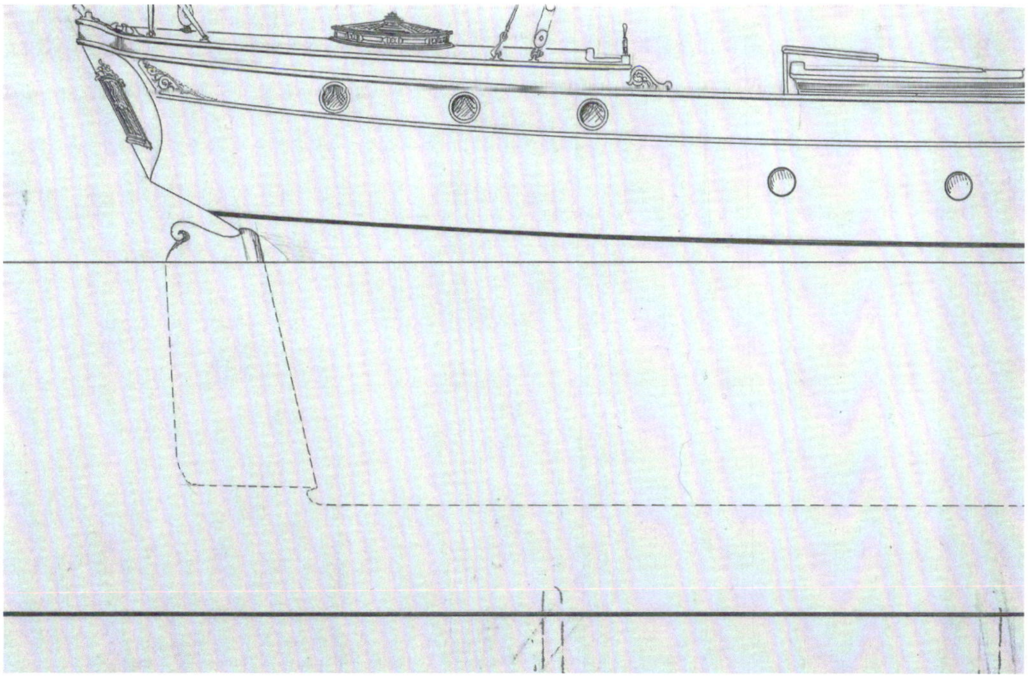

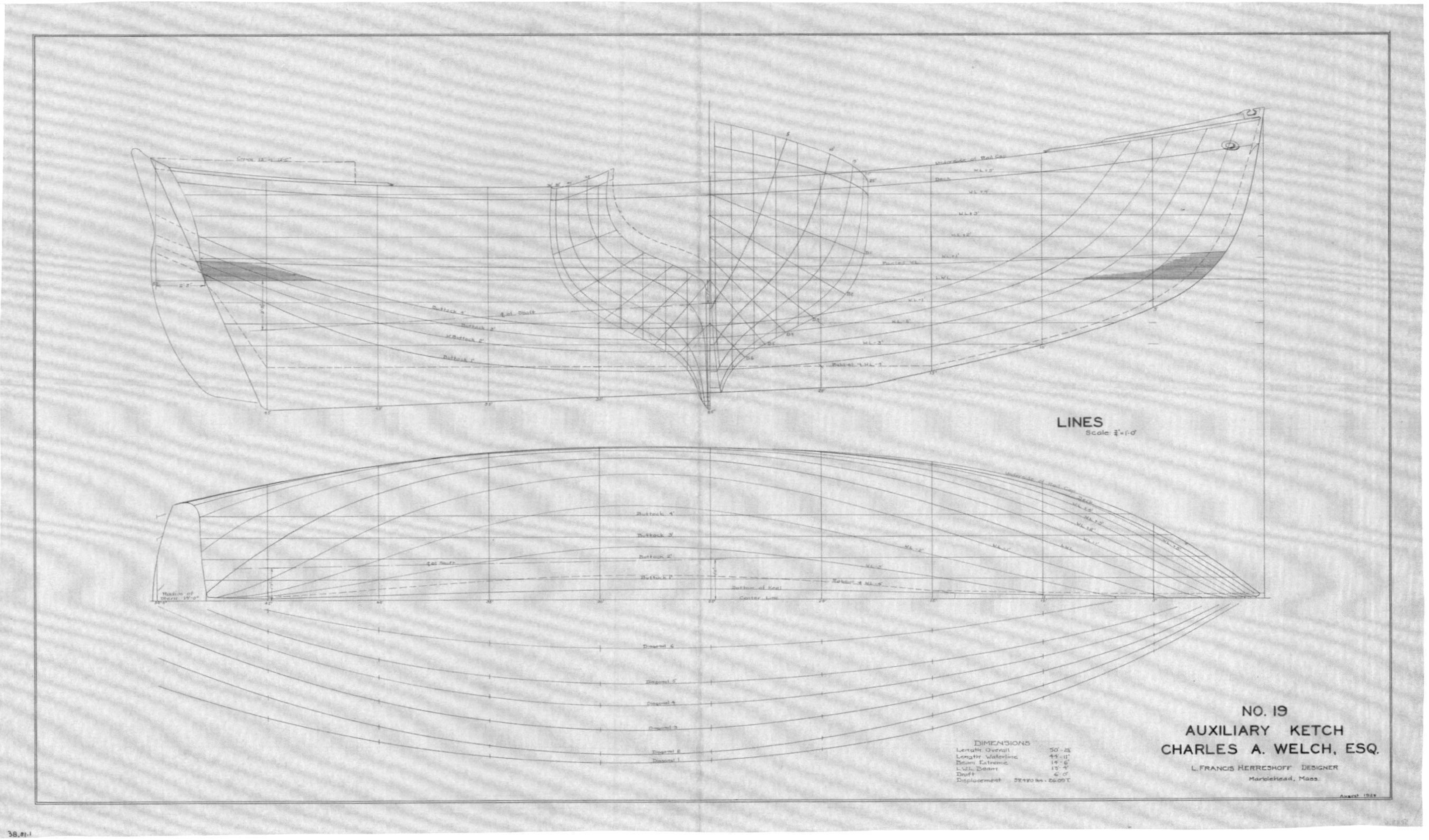
LINES
DIMENSIONS
Length Overall
Length Waterline 44'-11"
Beam Extreme 14'-6"
L.W.L. Beam 13'-4"
Draft 6'-0"
Displacement
NO. 19
AUXILIARY KETCH
CHARLES A. WELCH, ESQ.
L. FRANCIS HERRESHOFF DESIGNER
Marblehead, Mass.

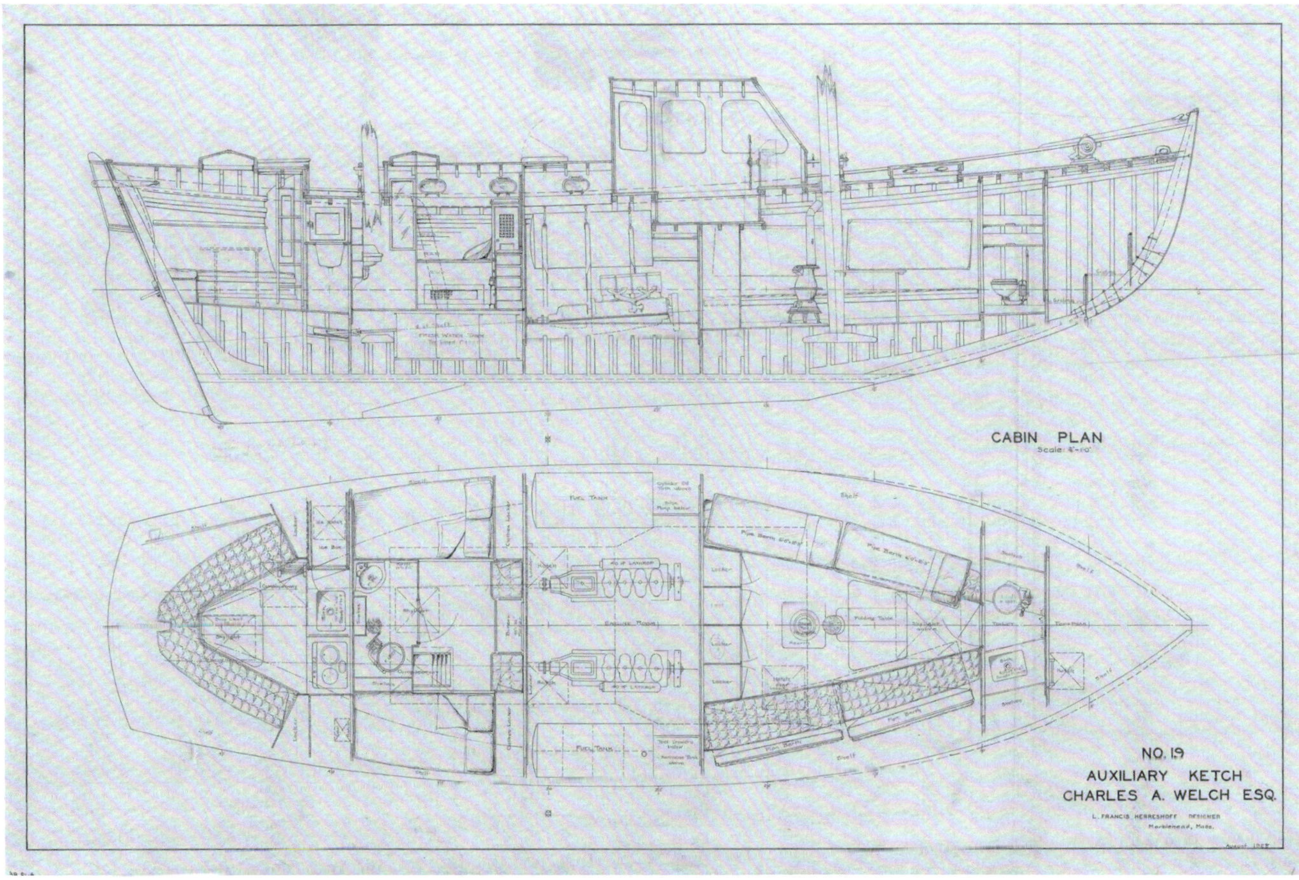

LEFT: **Lines of the *Walrus*. She is 50 feet, 2-1/2 inches long on deck; with a waterline length of 44 feet, 11 inches; a beam of 14 feet, 6 inches; and a draft of 6 feet. Norman Skene figured the displacement as 58,480 pounds, with ballast of 20,900 pounds, for a ballast-displacement ratio of 36 percent. With so much draft and ballast, she could stand up and beat to windward in a breeze exceptionally well for a powerboat with auxiliary sails.** (© Mystic Seaport, Daniel S. Gregory Ships Plans Library, SP 38.81.1) ABOVE: **The cabin plan of the *Walrus*, including an inboard profile. *Yachting*'s reporter wrote: "The accommodations below decks are decidedly interesting." The wheelhouse has a big chart table in the forward, port corner and a settee across its after side. Forward, to starboard, is the ladder down into the big four-berth cabin, with its most memorable feature (at least for a nephew of Charlie Welch), the pot-bellied stove. There's no connection between the after stateroom and the wardroom-and-galley under the turtleback in the stern; to get from one to the other, you have to climb up on deck and then go back down. There would be a lot of climbing on the *Walrus*'s five ladders, four of them vertical, but the advantage to her "decidedly interesting" arrangement is that she has four solid, watertight bulkheads, a valuable safeguard for a winter boat. Her planking at the waterline was sheathed with phosphor bronze for ice protection.** (© Mystic Seaport, Daniel S. Gregory Ships Plans Library, SP38.81.6)

could have gotten along fine with the total of 80 horsepower that Norman Skene had estimated would give her eight and a half knots. But Charlie and Francis liked cruising at that speed with the bigger engines throttled back to reduce noise and vibration.[9]

Charlie moored the *Walrus* right off his Gregory Street house in Marblehead Harbor. The January launching was no problem; the vessel would usually be on her mooring all winter anyway. *The Rudder* reported that she was the first yacht in commission north of Cape Cod in 1930. And on the last day of 1930, Francis reported to his father that the *Walrus* was still in commission, "but is the only boat in the harbor now."[10]

The *Walrus* didn't languish on her mooring for long periods. Charlie Welch kept his winter boat for seven years, a long time for him, and he did get her underway in all seasons. One wintry night, Charlie, Francis, and others were celebrating, and the talk turned to the *Walrus* and her sailing qualities. Someone reminded the group that speculation was unnecessary: the boat was nearby, she was ready for sea, and there was plenty of wind. So, off they went at midnight under sail and rounded the "heaving groaner" off Cape Ann, twenty miles away, before returning and picking up the mooring without ever starting an engine.[11]

Francis reported to Nathanael on a couple of the winter cruises he made with Charlie in the *Walrus*. There was an overnight trip to Rockport on the outside of Cape Ann in February and a

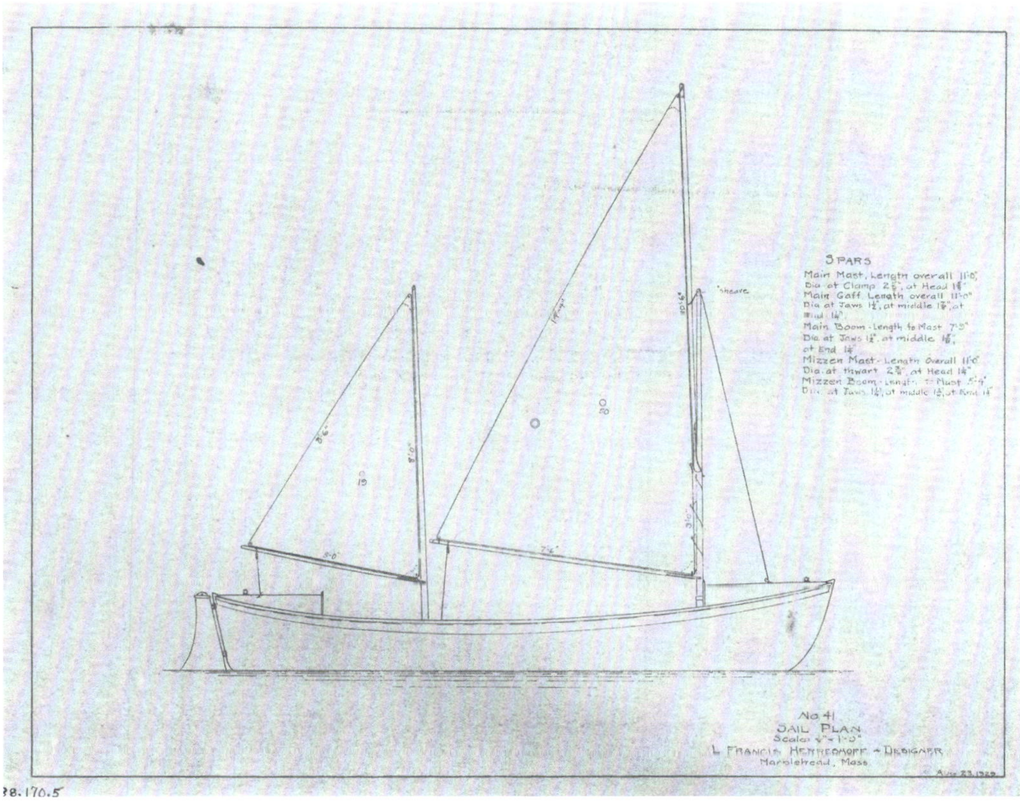

three-day jaunt to the Isles of Shoals and the Portsmouth (New Hampshire) Navy Yard begun on Friday, the thirteenth of March. Of the latter, Francis wrote: "I was quite surprised that the boat sailed so fast and tacked to windward and handled so nicely, showing that even small, leg-o'-mutton sails that have some hoist are very efficient. We were very comfortable on board as the boat has a nice galley and a coal stove in the forecastle, and the pilot house was very comfortable."[12]

The Welch family had a summer place, Pimpneymouse Farm, at Chappaquiddick, on Martha's Vineyard, a hundred acres that captured

LEFT: **The *Walrus* at speed. Although she is rigged for swordfishing, with a harpoon at the ready across the pulpit and the gin pole set up to haul a fish aboard, she is going too fast to get near a dozing swordfish. The white bulwarks appear to diminish the height of her black topsides.** (Courtesy Muriel Vaughn, Mystic Seaport, 1993-3-397) ABOVE: **The outboard profile and sail plan of the *Carpenter*, tender to the *Walrus*. She's an 18-foot surfboat with turtlebacks fore and aft for reserve buoyancy, flotation if swamped, and dry storage space. The gunter mainsail has an area of 50 square feet; the mizzen, 19 square feet. Her short masts need no standing rigging, but the main halyard is led through a block on the foredeck to act as a headstay. None of her five spars is too long to fit inside the boat between the turtlebacks. There's a third mast position, so that she can be sailed as a catboat with either sail.** (© Mystic Seaport, Daniel S. Gregory Ships Plans Library, SP38.170.5)

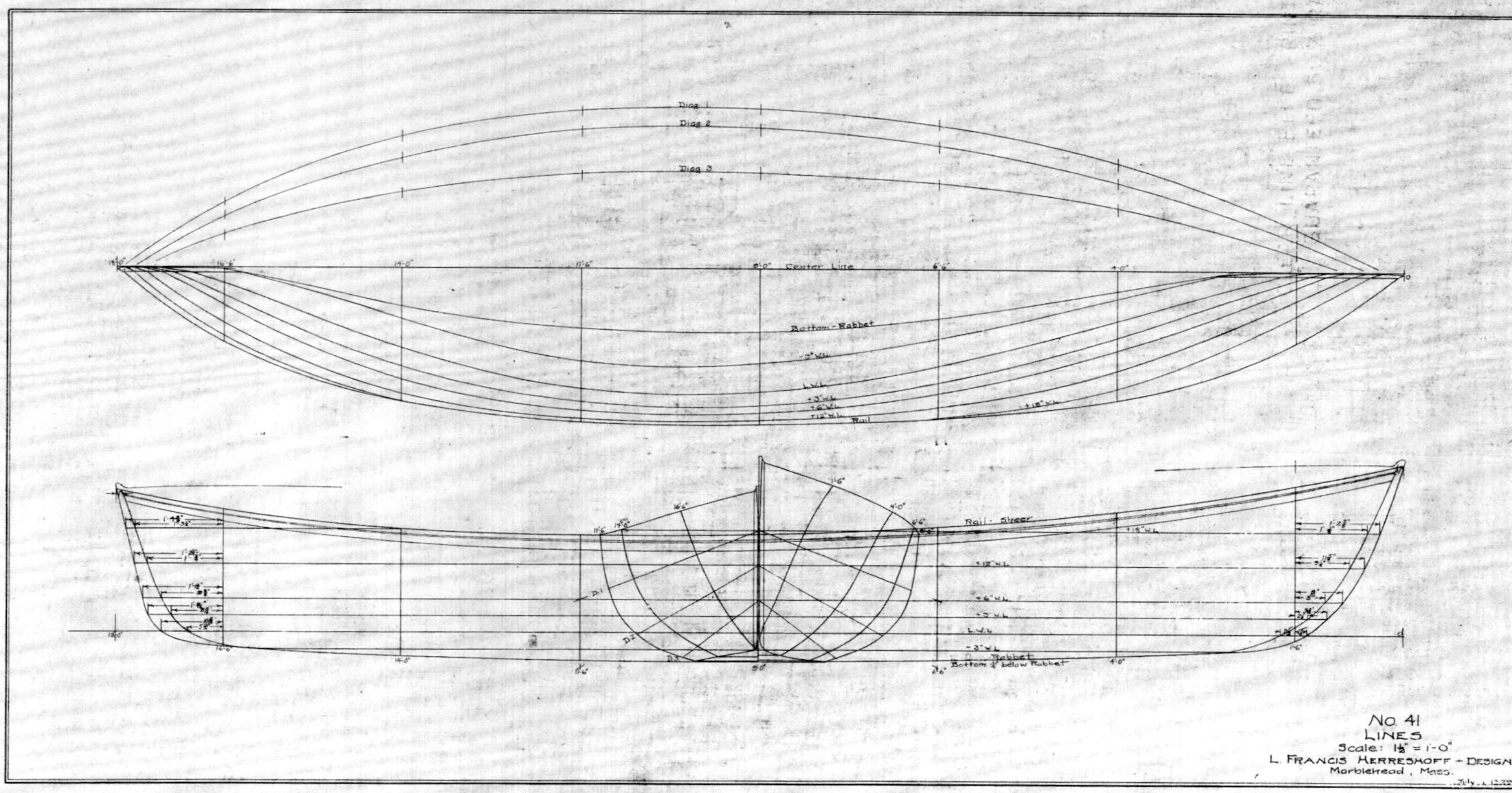
Diag 1
Diag 2
Diag 3
Center Line
Bottom - Rabbet
Rail
Rail · Sheer
Bottom & below Rabbet
No. 41
Lines
Scale: 1½" = 1'-0"
L. Francis Herreshoff - Designer
Marblehead, Mass.

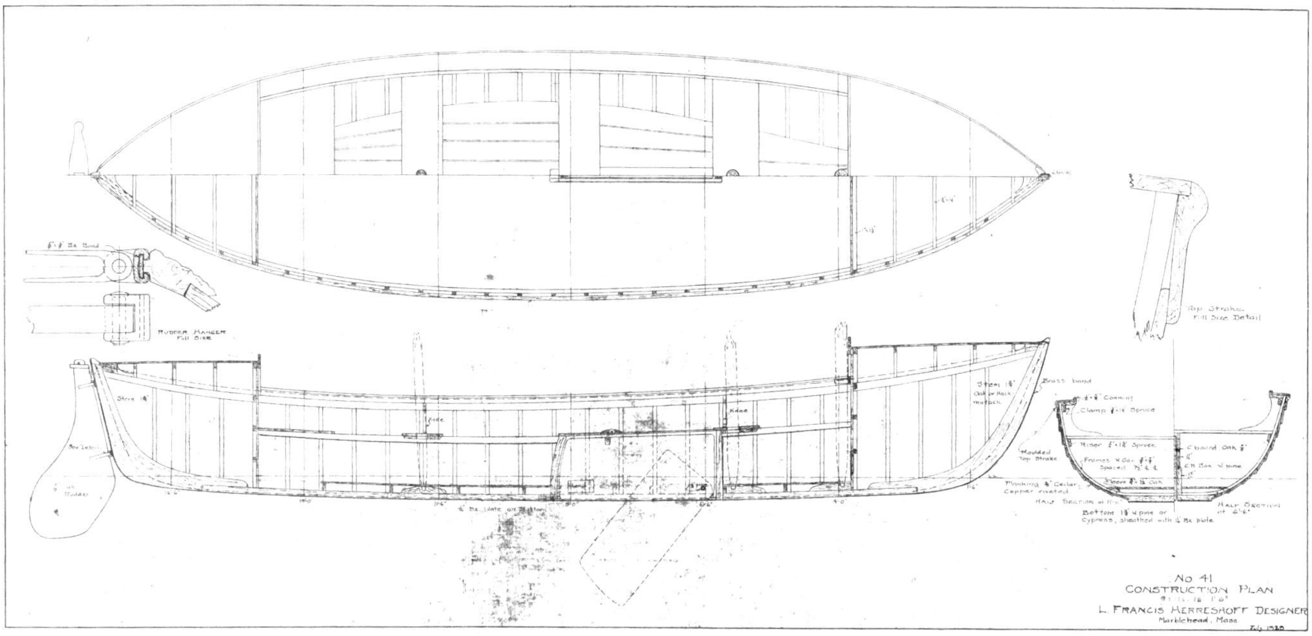

Charlie's interest to the point that he would give up sailboat racing for farming. Charlie used the *Walrus* to commute to his farm from Marblehead, making trips through the Cape Cod Canal in the open winter of 1930-31, as well as in milder seasons. His daughter, Edith, who liked to sail her dinghy, hated the passages in the *Walrus*. She spoke of rolling in the swell to the tune of what to her delicate senses were noisy, smelly engines and nothing to do but just sit there. She and her sister, Hope, preferred the day trips in the *Walrus* from the Vineyard to Tarpaulin Cove, on Naushon Island, or on to Cuttyhunk. Charlie used to get a gang and go swordfishing in the *Walrus*, for which he rigged her with a long bowsprit for the pulpit and masthead hoops for the lookouts. He also took her south to fish a couple of winters, making the passage to Florida outside.[13]

Charlie Welch also intended to use the *Walrus* as an expedition vessel. He envisioned anchoring

---

LEFT: **The lines of the *Carpenter*. Waterline length is 16 feet, 3 inches; beam, 4 feet, 7 inches; and draft, 4½ inches, light. The waterlines are hollow fore and aft, there is flare at the bow, and she has a flat bottom for beaching.** (© Mystic Seaport, Daniel S. Gregory Ships Plans Library, SP38.170.1) ABOVE: **The *Carpenter*'s construction plan, showing her lapstrake planking. The top strake has the extra, rounded thickness that was a trademark of small craft built at the Herreshoff Manufacturing Company, a shape with which Francis had become thoroughly familiar as a child. He kept the *Carpenter*'s scantlings as light as was reasonable for the strength needed for beaching. Despite the flat bottom being sheathed with 1/16-inch bronze plate, the stripped hull weighed only 500 pounds. The third mast position is shown through the thwart at the forward end of the centerboard trunk. The three thwarts give a variety of rowing positions. Note the rudder yoke: the boat was steered with lines leading forward from it. The rudder draws 2 feet, 4 inches with the boat light. She cost $700 at Lawley's, so, presumably, Charlie paid Francis $70 for this sophisticated, well-thought-out design. Sam Brown inked these three drawings of the *Carpenter* in the summer of 1929.** (© Mystic Seaport, Daniel S. Gregory Ships Plans Library, SP38.170.2)

in a harbor that would take her six-foot draft and having a tender big and seaworthy enough to then haul alongside by her towline and set off alongshore, even along an inhospitable shore, where to land might mean going in through surf. He and Francis had discussed this kind of tender, and Francis had doubtless shared his childhood experience in the *Roamer*'s big sailing and rowing cutter. In the summer of 1929, with the building of the *Walrus* hanging fire, Francis designed her a tender for much rougher conditions than the cutter of his memory could have handled.

Charlie, of course, named the *Walrus*'s tender the *Carpenter,* from Lewis Carroll's poem in *Through the Looking Glass,* in which the protagonists ate all the oysters. She was an 18-foot, double-ended surfboat, complete with lifeboat-like turtlebacks in bow and stern, and a bronze-sheathed, flat bottom for beaching. She had a short, versatile, sailing rig and three rowing positions. The tender suited her purpose. Francis considered designing a larger version of the boat "for landing on our rocky New England shores," but nothing came of it.[14]

The *Carpenter* was indeed used in rough conditions. Francis wrote that she was "good to come ashore in on a winter night in bad weather," and that she was surprisingly stiff and fast under sail. One night in December 1930, the *Walrus* was towing the *Carpenter* by the stern home to Marblehead from Martha's Vineyard, punching into a northwesterly gale in Massachusetts Bay. The *Carpenter* iced up, and the weight reduced her freeboard so that she shipped water. In the morning all that was left on the towline was the boat's stern. She was recovered on the beach at Provincetown, undamaged except for the missing stern. Francis repaired her in his ground-floor workshop at 20 Lee Street. He reported to Nathanael that "she now has a hard maple stern faced with large Manganese stern board so we don't think it will pull out again."[15]

Charlie Welch liked getting afloat in the *Walrus* so much that he had grandiose ideas for a much bigger version of the vessel, one that would sail better and, particularly, be more comfortable going offshore to Florida. So, starting in the summer of 1931, Francis made a design for an 83-foot, double-ended, auxiliary power cruiser. This was his design No. 51, named the *Albatross.* She exists only on paper. The depression year of 1931 was not a time for making a big dream-ship a reality, and Charlie continued to run the *Walrus.* It is not known what he paid his friend Francis for the creation of this complete design for the magnificent *Albatross.*

Charlie sold the *Walrus* in 1937. In advertising her in *Yachting,* New York broker Linton Rigg wrote: "This is probably the best boat of this type ever built." In 1944, she was owned by A. W. Laytham of Patterson, New Jersey. By 1954, she had been donated to the Marine Historical Association at Mystic, Connecticut, which sold her to Mystic boatbuilder Ernest F. Post. Post or somebody before him put on a much-enlarged deckhouse. In the 1960s, Jerry and Alva Hefty ran her as a charter boat out of Nassau, renaming her *Leilani.* She was last listed in Lloyd's in 1979 as the *Wind Quest.*[16]

RIGHT: The outboard profile, sail plan, and cabin plan of the dreamship *Albatross*, Francis's design No. 51. The dreamer was Charlie Welch. She is a stretched-out version of the *Walrus*, with proportionately less displacement and more sail area than the *Walrus*, so she would sail better. The sail area is 1,820 square feet. She is rigged for swordfishing and has a large fish hold just forward of the mizzenmast. Other than the hold and a forecastle forward, she has the same interior arrangement as the *Walrus.* (© Mystic Seaport, Daniel S. Gregory Ships Plans Library, SP38.144.13)

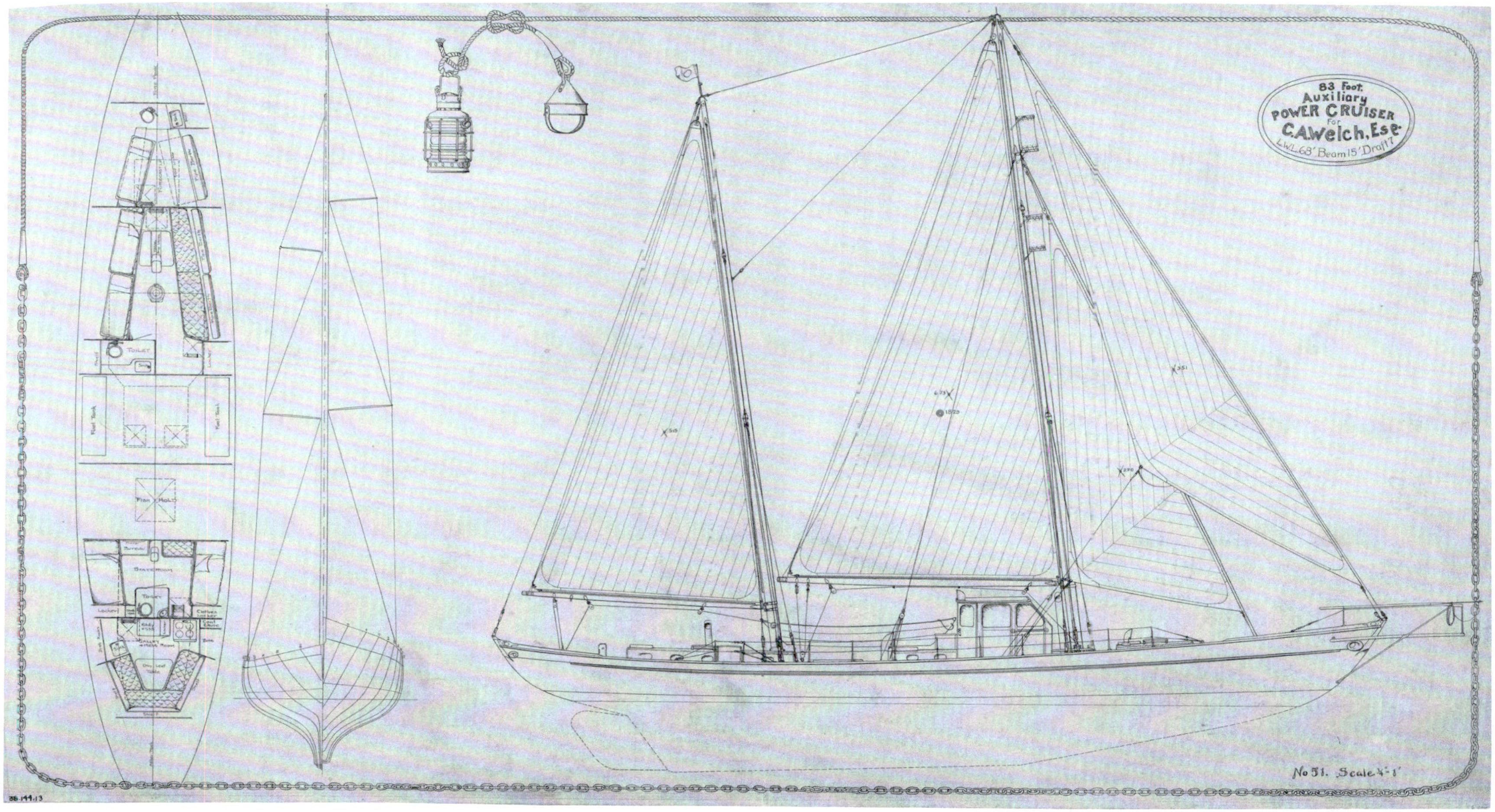
83 Foot.
Auxiliary
POWER CRUISER
For
C.A.Welch, Esq.
L.W.L. 68' Beam 15' Draft 7
No 51. Scale ¼"=1'
86.144.13

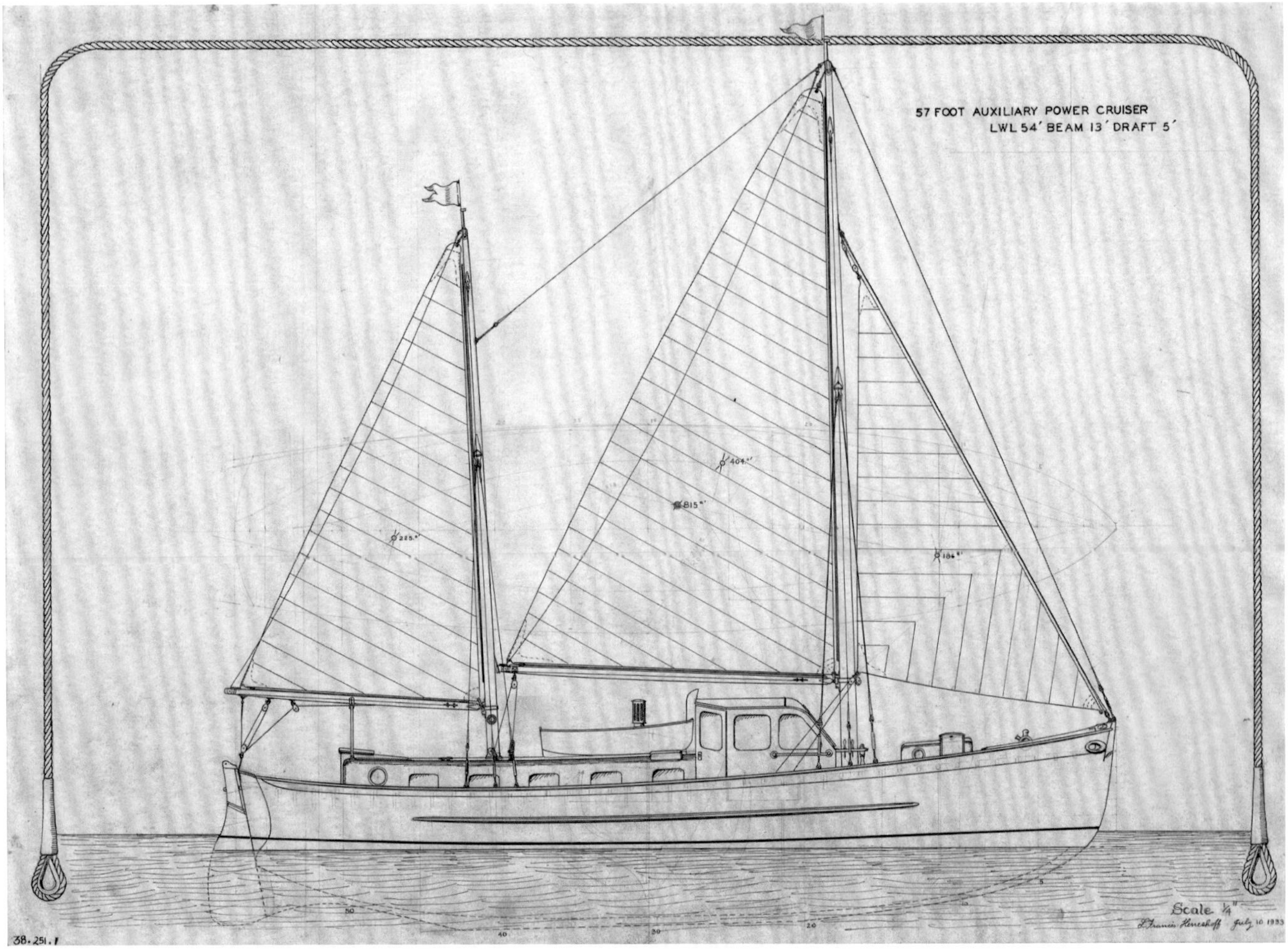

In 1933, Francis designed an "improved *Walrus*." The hull was longer, narrower, and shoaler than that of the *Walrus*, with less freeboard and no turtleback at the stern. She has a cutaway deadwood for maneuverability. She was 57 feet long on deck, 54 feet on the waterline, with a beam of 13 feet, and a draft of 5 feet. The sail area was 815 square feet. Neither client nor design number appear on the outboard profile drawing; the vessel was not built. There is also a preliminary drawing of a 50-foot, 8-inch version of this design. And, in about 1938, Francis made a preliminary drawing of a 45-foot ketch, reminiscent of the *Walrus*, but with more emphasis on sailing qualities. This is a fine design and was initially given the No. 76, though that number was later used for another design. No client is named, but it may have been for William S. Strawbridge. The design was not completed, and, unfortunately, the drawing, in hard pencil, is not reproducible. (© Mystic Seaport, Daniel S. Gregory Ships Plans Library, SP38.251.1; SP38.248.1; and SP38.246.1)

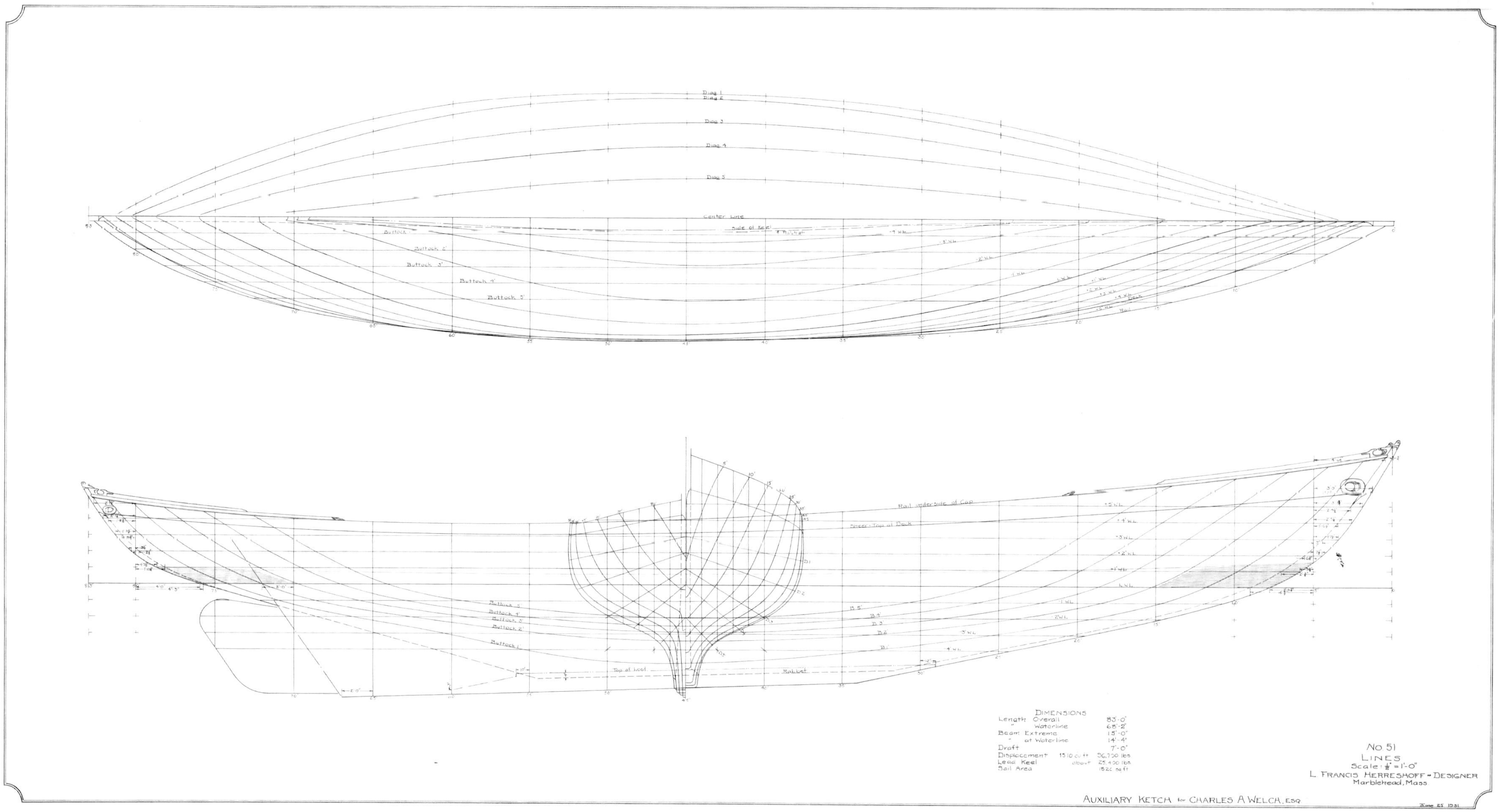

The lines of the *Albatross*. She is 83 feet long on deck; 68 feet, 2 inches on the waterline; with a beam of 15 feet, and a draft of 7 feet. Displacement is 96,700 pounds, with 25,400 pounds of ballast, for a ballast-displacement ratio of 26 percent. Had she been built, she would have been fast for her sail area and an able vessel. (© Mystic Seaport, Daniel S. Gregory Ships Plans Library, SP38.144.1)

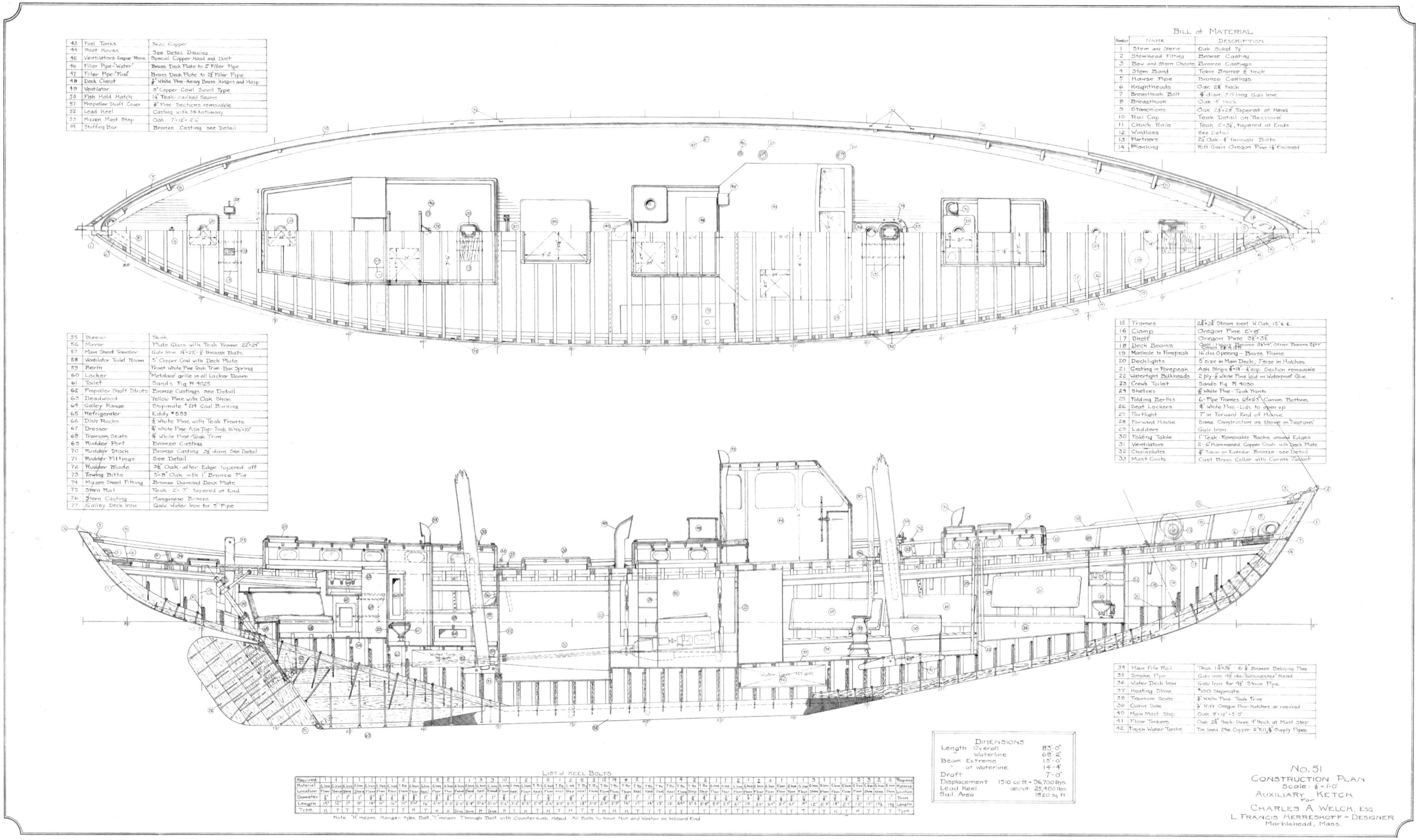

The construction drawing of the *Albatross.* As on some of his racing boats, Francis has eliminated a wooden keelson; the garboard planks were to be fastened directly to the lead outside ballast. She has six watertight bulkheads for compartmentation. The drawing has 77 numbered specifications to give the builder the needed details of materials, scantlings, and fittings. The table at the bottom gives specs for the vessel's more than 100 keel bolts, of 52 different sizes. None of this detail would be used, for the *Albatross* remained a dreamship. Sam Brown inked the drawings for the big auxiliary power cruiser between June 1931 and January 1932. (© Mystic Seaport, Daniel S. Gregory Ships Plans Library, SP38.144.3)

IN JANUARY 1929, Norman Skene left the office of L. Francis Herreshoff, Racing Yachts. He joined the firm of Howard and Munro in Boston. Francis would sometimes disparage Skene, because he didn't agree with Skene's mathematical approach to yacht design, but he must have missed Skene's fast drafting of finished drawings and his accurate calculations of the weights of all the parts of a yacht's construction. When Francis had to make such calculations, he complained about the inconvenience of having to change decimals of feet for the scantlings into feet and inches.[17]

By October 1929, Skene had joined Frank Paine, with whom he had worked alongside Francis at Burgess and Paine in Boston, and Frank's firm became Paine, Belknap, and Skene. Norman Skene had his name on the door and took an active role in creating yacht designs. Starling and Francis had done their own design work, so when Skene worked for them, he worked as a draftsman. Frank Paine came up with good general concepts for a design but usually left many of the details to others. So it was Norman Skene at Paine, Belknap, and Skene, who did much of the actual design work on, for example, the America's Cup contender *Yankee*, which came close to becoming the defender in 1930, and also on the great Gloucester racing fishing schooner, *Gertrude L. Thebaud*.[18]

As we have seen, Starling Burgess introduced Skene to kayaking at Provincetown in the early twenties. In 1923, Skene had designed an Eskimo kayak for *The Rudder*'s How-to-Build series, a boat he had built and paddled. Skene lived in Winchester, not far from Marblehead, and he liked to paddle a kayak around the islands outside Marblehead Harbor. One day in June 1932, he didn't come back. Searchers found his empty kayak a mile off the harbor entrance, in Cat Island Channel, between Cat and Eagle Islands. His body was not found.[19]

Starling had introduced Francis to kayaking also, and at the time when Skene was lost, Francis would often be out in his own kayak around the islands. His father worried about Francis's kayak paddling. He wrote to his son that Norman Skene's loss from his kayak "shows the folly of cruising in such craft." Francis replied: "The loss of Norman Skene is very sad, but several things indicate that it was a case of suicide, so this should not reflect too badly on all canoes." There is no way to know what were the "several things" that Francis referred to, or whether he was right or wrong about the nature of Skene's demise. Norman Skene was a far more accomplished yacht designer than Francis thought he was, but Francis had no reason to misrepresent his death. *The Rudder* stated simply that "America has lost one of its foremost yacht designers."[20]

TWO OF Francis's commissions to design racing boats for the 1929 season, a Q-boat and an M-boat, took him back to the Universal Rule. He had designed three R-boats and a Q-boat to the rule, as well as two M-boats that were not built, so at least these Universal-Rule boats had familiar parameters, compared to the 30-Square-Metres that he was called upon to design concurrently with them.

Before he started work on his 1929 racing boats, Francis had a good review of the Universal Rule. The Boston Class Q Association wanted to add some of its own restrictions to the rule and, in September 1928, appointed a technical committee of three yacht designers to formulate them. They were Frank C. Paine, John G. Alden, and L. Francis Herreshoff. Would that there were minutes of their meetings. The wealthy man of the world who liked to whip up designs for racing boats and then go race them in between his other sports; the outgoing enthusiast of the gaff-rigged schooner; and the proud, prickly, shy, artistic, competent son of the country's greatest designer of racing yachts, trying to build his own reputation in yacht design:

these three must have had some interesting discussions.

We can see Francis's hand in their decision to limit jib overlap to 2 feet, 6 inches. He believed that the entire area of the Genoa jib he claimed to have invented should be counted as measured sail area in the Universal Rule, but he couldn't sell that idea, so even better was simply to eliminate the big, overlapping jib. The group also decreed that a Q-boat's beam at the waterline must be at least 8 feet, and that the cockpit must be watertight. It was at this time when the construction of Universal Rule boats came under the inspection and approval of the American Bureau of Shipping. Francis would find their inspectors "much more agreeable, intelligent and helpful than [those of] Lloyds." As it turned out, each member of the technical committee would design

a Q-boat for the 1929 season: Frank Paine's *Cara Mia*, for Harold S. Wheelock; Alden's *Hope*, for his own use, but actually designed in his office by K. Aage Nielsen; and Francis's *Questa*, for the veteran Marblehead yachtsman and inveterate experimenter, Charles. H. W. Foster.[21]

FOSTER, for whom Francis had designed a schooner rig for his R-boat, was so interested in experimenting with rigs that he had a test tank with a fan set up in his basement for trying different rigs on models. "He and Mr. Herreshoff were always having heated arguments about sails," Foster's daughter remembered. Yet, other than her innovative main halyard arrangement, with sheaves built into the masthead and the sail's headboard, there was nothing experimental about the design of the *Questa*. *Yachting* reported, perhaps with a sense of relief, that "Unlike Mr. Herreshoff's recent boats, she has the customary transom [counter] stern, and the general design shows an extremely good-looking model of wholesome proportions."[22]

The *Questa* continued the trend in the Q Class toward bigger boats; she had the longest possible waterline allowed by the Universal Rule and had the most displacement of any of the Q-boats to date. Rather than designing her for Marblehead's light winds, Francis drew a Q-boat that would have as high a hull speed as possible when it blew hard. He wrote to Howard Chapelle that "the Q boat, *Questa*, was one of the best boats I have designed

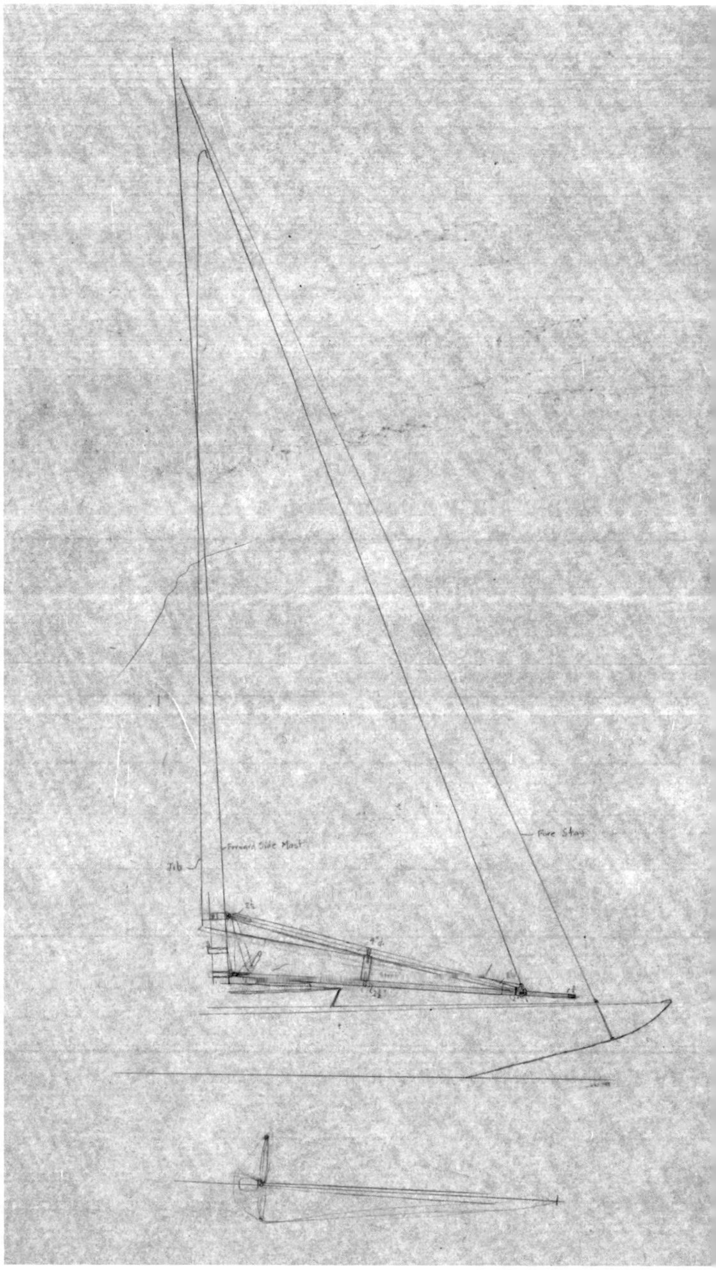

TOP LEFT: Charles H. W. Foster, for whom Francis designed the Q-boat *Questa*. (*Yachting* (June 1933): 67) BOTTOM LEFT and ABOVE: The outboard profile and sail plan of the *Questa*, Francis's design No. 33. Sail area is 895 square feet. The overlapping jibs of Francis's previous Q-boat, the *Nor'easter V*, are gone, since the Boston Q-Class Association had outlawed them. Francis made a pencil drawing showing the jib tacked down to a double pole that ran forward from the mast along and above the foredeck. This contraption could be swung outboard on either side to bring the jib's tack out to windward when reaching or running. The idea smacks of a Foster experiment, but it would have been outlawed for racing. (© Mystic Seaport, Daniel S. Gregory Ships Plans Library, SP38.59.4; pencil drawing, SP38.59.19.)

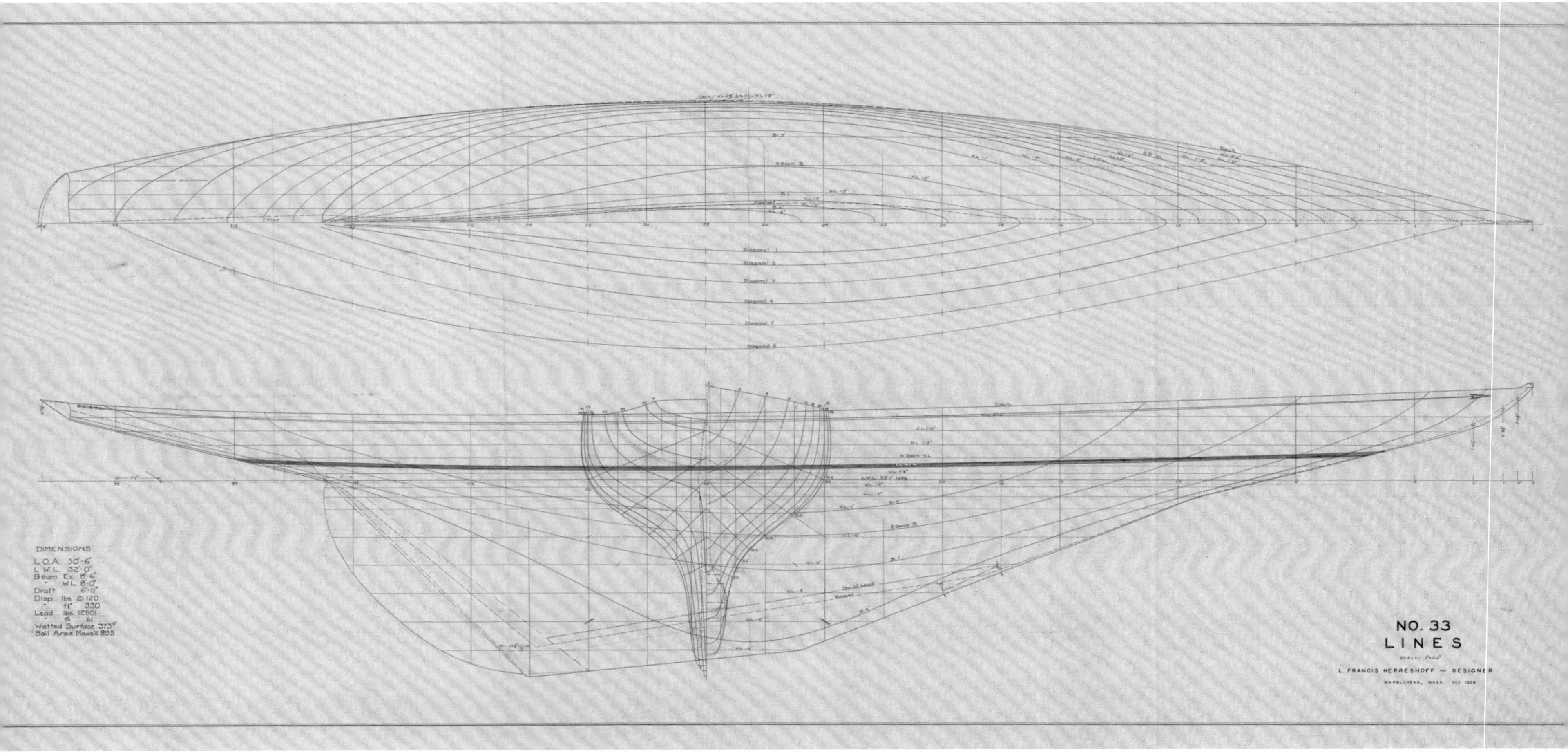
DIMENSIONS
L.O.A. 50'-6"
L.W.L. 32'-0"
Beam Ex. 8'-6"
" W.L. 8'-0"
Draft 6'-11"
Disp. lbs. 21120
" ft³ 330
Lead lbs. 12901
" % 61
Wetted Surface 373□'
Sail Area Meas'd 895
NO. 33
LINES
SCALE:
L. FRANCIS HERRESHOFF — DESIGNER
MARBLEHEAD, MASS. OCT. 1928

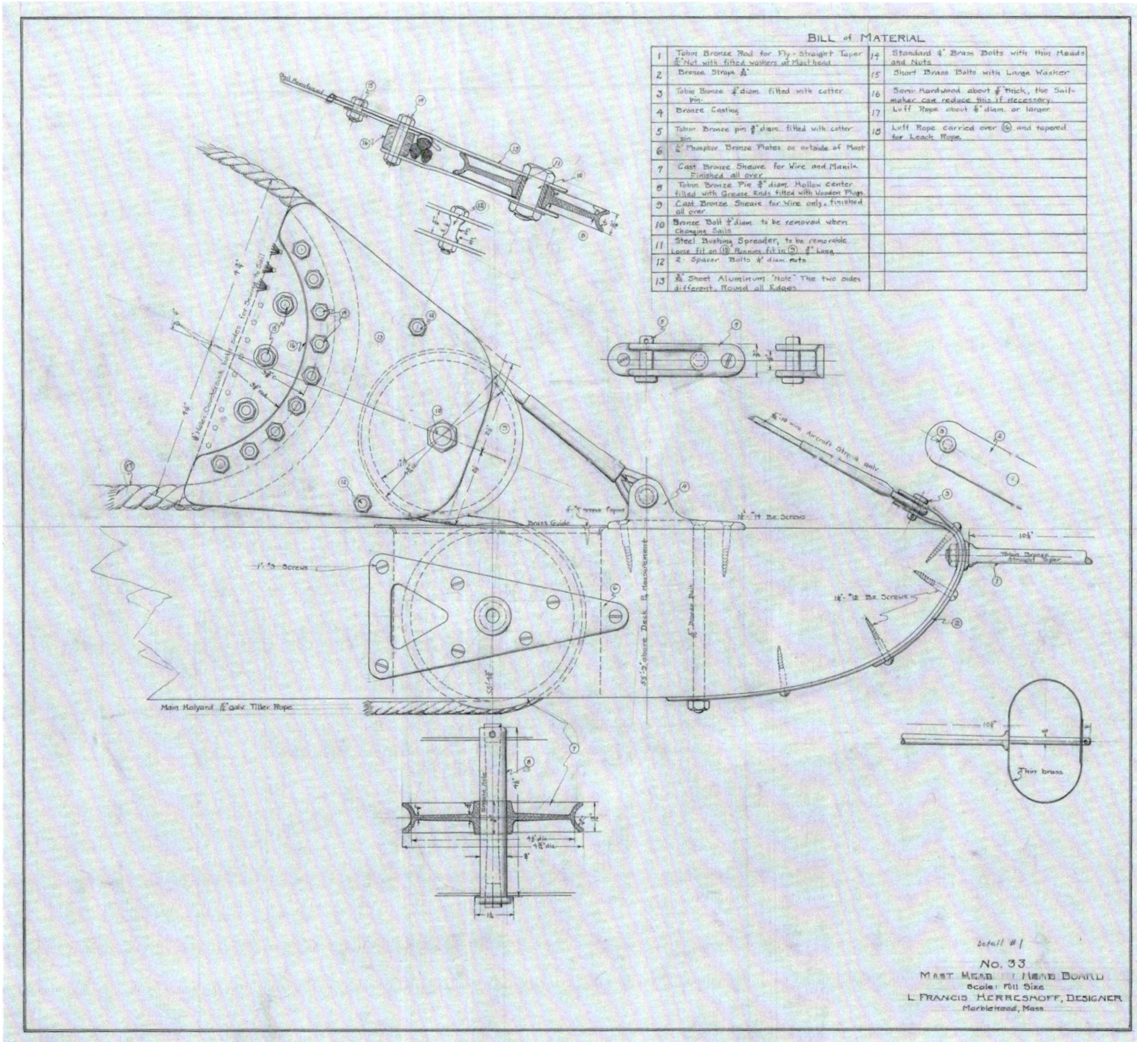

LEFT: The *Questa*'s lines. Even with her counter stern, she is the same length as the double-ended *Nor'easter V* on deck, at 50 feet, 6 inches, but she is 2 feet longer on the waterline, at 32 feet. Beam is 8 feet, 6 inches, and draft is 6 feet, 11 inches. Beam has been increased over that of the *Nor'easter V* by 9 inches to meet the Boston Association's minimum of 8 feet at the waterline. Displacement is 21,120 pounds, with 12,901 pounds of lead ballast, for a ballast-displacement ratio of 61 percent. The *Questa* displaced 2,400 pounds more than her predecessor and had a slightly lower ballast-displacement ratio. The biggest visual difference in the lines of the two boats, other than the different sterns, is in the sections. The increased beam of the *Questa* has forced Francis away from the rather straight, deep sections he had used on previous Universal Rule boats, to a more cutaway, wineglass shape. In the lines profile, the black boot top he shows, with its ends sheered up at the bow and stern, makes the boat's graceful ends look shorter. (© Mystic Seaport, Daniel S. Gregory Ships Plans Library, SP 38.59.1) ABOVE: Francis made a full-size drawing of the *Questa*'s masthead and special headboard for the mainsail. Instead of a pair of normal halyard blocks, he shows a sheave for the halyard built into the head of the sail, with another sheave built into the masthead. He has carefully worked out every detail of the design and construction of this streamlined, lightweight invention, with each part and fastening proportioned to be just strong enough. Francis described this aspect of his design work as "scientific." The headboard is an example of the artist's engineering ability. He made the device himself in the ground-floor shop at 20 Lee Street and sent it off to Ratsey's in Cowes, England, to be attached to the head of the sail. (© Mystic Seaport, Daniel S. Gregory Ships Plans Library, SP38.59.9)

under the Universal rule,“ and that “She could definitely beat all the other Qs in a strong breeze.”[23]

James E. “Al” Graves built the *Questa* at his yard at Little Harbor, the second of three coves on the northeast side of the Marblehead peninsula, just north of the entrance to the harbor. The Graves yard had been in business for about thirty years, expanding from dory-building to the construction of yachts, helped by commissions from the well-known Boston designer, Bowdoin B. Crowninshield, whose residence was on Peach Point, half a mile north of the yard. The Q-boat was far enough along by December 1928 that the inspectors from the American Bureau of Shipping could start making sure that she was being built according to the construction plan of the previous month that they had approved. The *Questa*'s building was the first time Francis had tried the Graves yard. He would write that she “was not particularly well built.” The *Questa* cost $14,000 to build, and her sails cost a further $1,100, so Francis would have earned total, ten percent commissions of $1,510 for his work and that of Sam Brown, who inked most of the eighteen sheets of the boat's plans.[24]

Although the *Questa* was undoubtedly fast when the wind blew hard, she was not a consistent winner. She did win the Eastern Yacht Club's series in her class of fourteen for Marblehead Race Week in 1929, but she never came close to a season championship. Francis wrote, “While it is true that *Questa* did not do well in racing this can be easily accounted for because she was very poorly sailed indeed and generally had poor sails.” Francis was frustrated, because Foster was a better experimenter than racing skipper.[25]

By 1935, the *Questa* was owned by Richard Harding, better known in Marblehead as a cruising sailor than as a racer. He opened up the forward cockpit and had an engine installed, but the whole arrangement, including off-center propeller and shaft, could be removed on the ways overnight to convert the boat from an auxiliary cruiser back to a racing boat that measured into the Q Class. Like others among Francis's racing boats, the *Questa* went to the Great Lakes, where she raced in a class of five Q-boats at least until 1961.[26]

In 1983, the *Questa* was owned in Milwaukee. Doug Averill, whom we have already met as the rescuer of Francis's Q-boat, the *Nor'easter V*, was accumulating flight hours for his pilot's license and landed in Milwaukee. He met a man who had a sailboat that he wanted to unload, and, after a few drinks, this man took it into his head that Doug's dude-ranch lodge at Flathead Lake in Montana would be the perfect resting place for his boat. He said he'd bring the boat to Big Fork and leave it there if Doug would take him deer hunting. Doug

RIGHT: The construction plan of the *Questa*. The hull structure is conventional, rather than longitudinal, probably to avoid problems with the American Bureau of Shipping inspectors. There is one web frame 12 feet back from the bow. She was double-planked, with 3/4-inch mahogany over 3/8-inch cedar. We see Francis's first use of diagonal bronze strapping to give the hull, deck, and cabin house extra strength against wringing. Hull and deck straps were 1/8-inch by 2-1/4-inches; those on the cabin house were 1/8-inch by 2 inches. There are no cavities in the lead keel for adjusting ballast. Note the hoisting eyes in the keel, with wire spans of specified length to balance the boat when lifted on a crane. The oval hatch in the forward end of the house is for the convenience of the spinnaker man. The separate watertight cockpits—a shallow one aft for the helmsman and a deep one forward for the crew working the main sheet and running backstays at its after end and the jib sheets forward—were Foster's idea. The scuppers in the forward end of the forward cockpit floor would have required plugs, for they are just below the waterline. A note on the plan says, “Jib sheet leads to be located by L.F.H.” The *Questa* was built right in Marblehead at the yard of James E. Graves. (© Mystic Seaport, Daniel S. Gregory Ships Plans Library, SP38.59.3)

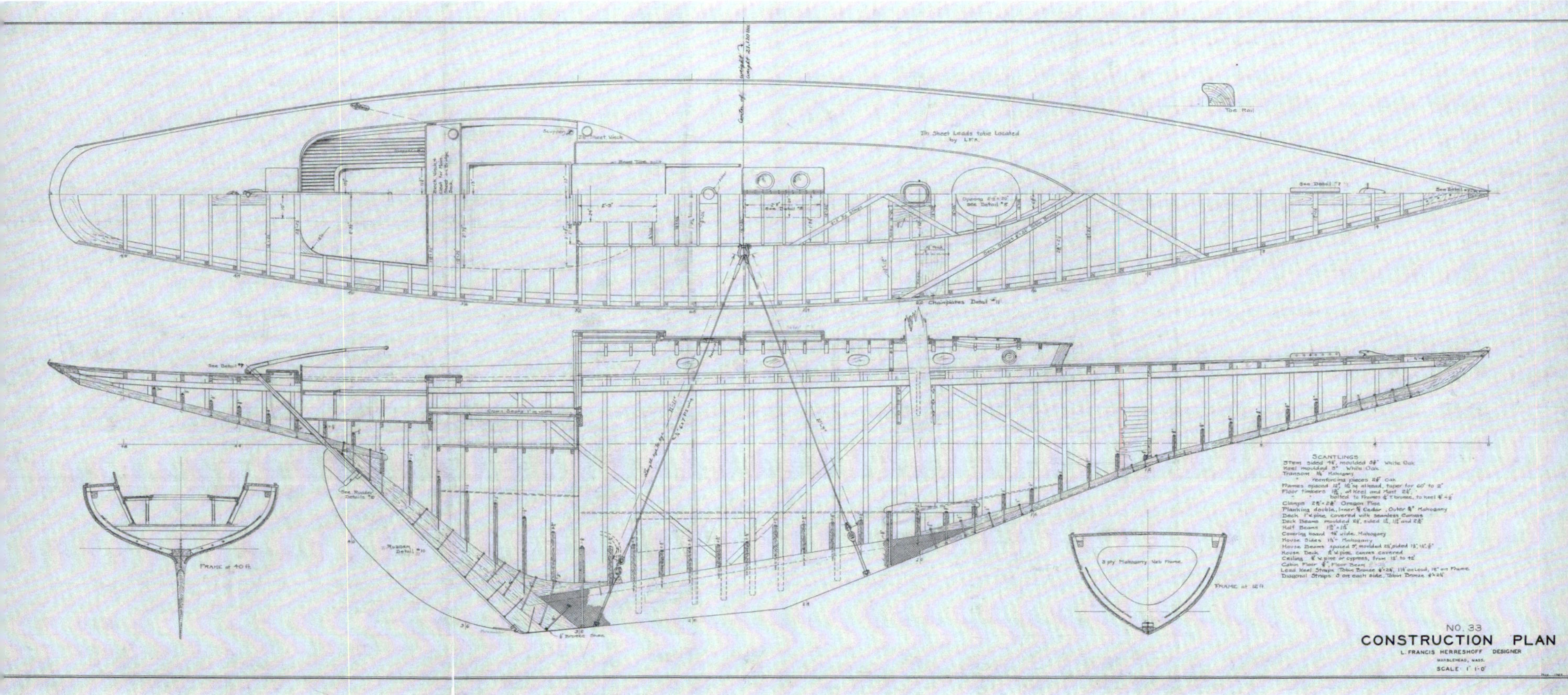
Toe Rail
SCANTLINGS
FRAME at 40 ft
FRAME at 12 ft
NO. 33
CONSTRUCTION PLAN
L. FRANCIS HERRESHOFF DESIGNER
MARBLEHEAD, MASS.
SCALE 1" 1-0"

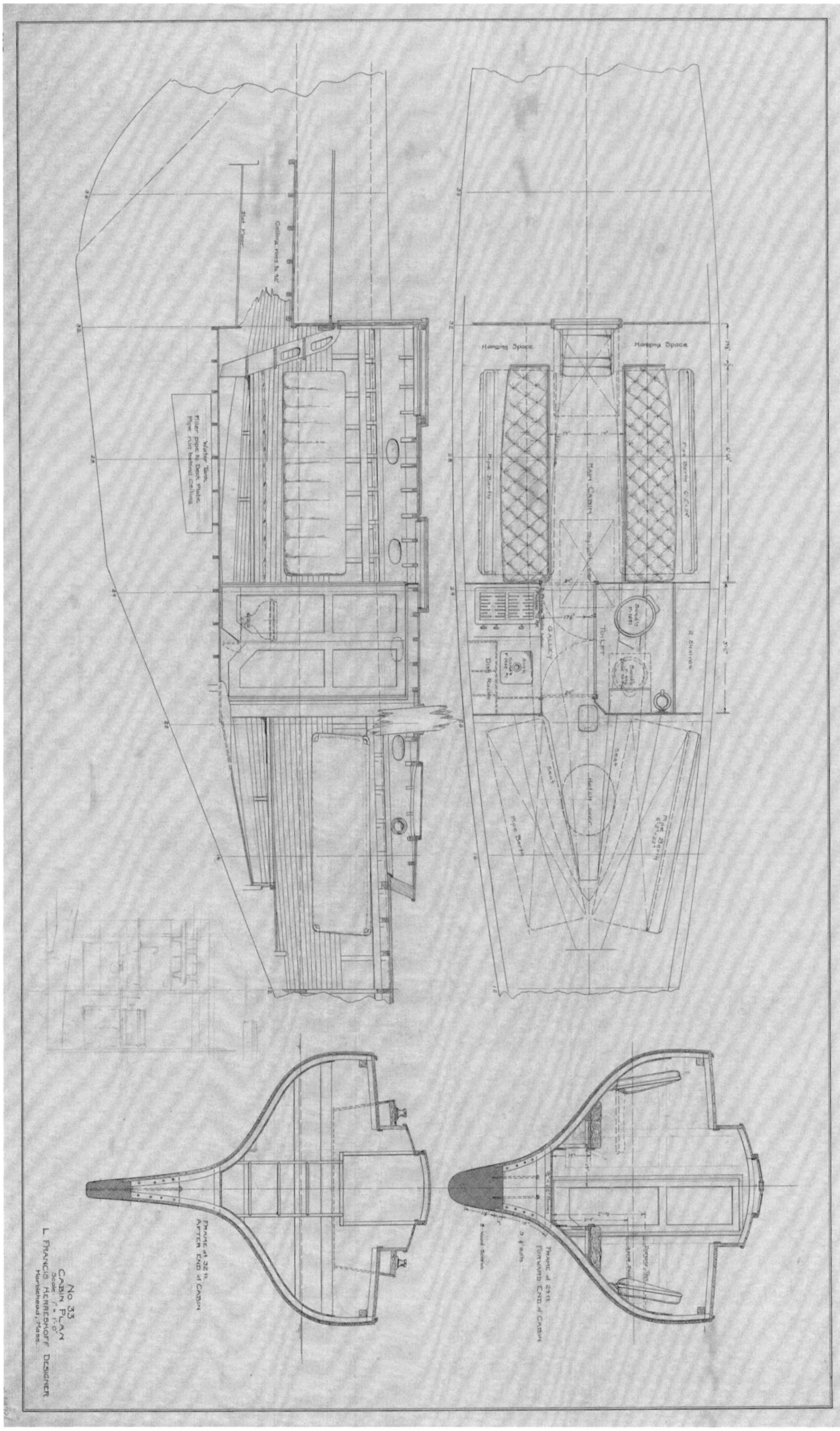
No 33
CABIN PLAN
L. FRANCIS HERRESHOFF DESIGNER
Frame at 32 ft.
After End of Cabin
Hanging Space
Hanging Space
Main Cabin
Galley
Toilet

went home and thought no more about it until, a few weeks later, the Milwaukeean pulled in at the lodge with his beautifully shaped, 50-foot classic racing boat in tow. There was a deer-hunt and then an exchange of $11,000. This was the *Questa*, and Doug Averill, the horseman, came to realize that he had a rare yacht indeed.

Averill learned that Herreshoff had designed another Q-boat, and the rumor was that she might still be sailing. He spread the word, particularly among his Lodge guests, to be on the lookout. And, as we have seen, the search succeeded in bringing the *Nor'easter V* to Flathead Lake.

In order to preserve the quiet beauty of sailing, both these boats now have electric motors for maneuvering in and out of the Lodge's tiny, land-locked harbor. Both are kept in outstanding condition by the Lodge's crew of carriage builders turned boatbuilders. Lucky is the person who can dismount a horse and step on board one Herreshoff Q-boat for a sail that includes watching the other Herreshoff Q-boat dancing alongside.[27]

THE BALTIC coast of Sweden, particularly in the region around Stockholm, is dotted with innumerable rocky islets, or skerries, providing a wonderful, protected, deep-water sailing area. By 1908, Swedish yachtsmen were developing a distinctive class of yacht for both racing and cruising to take full advantage of this natural treasure. The boats had to be seaworthy for sailing outside the skerries in the Baltic Sea, and they had to be nimble for sailing among them, in fluky winds and narrow channels. The rating of the boats for racing was based entirely on sail area, which encouraged a boat with a long, narrow, light hull and a deep keel to get the most speed from, and stability for, the restricted amount of sail. For cruising, the boats were required to have

LEFT: The *Questa*'s cabin plan. She has the required four bunks, all Francis's favorite tilting pipe berths, 6 feet, 2 inches long and a just-adequate 1 foot, 10 inches wide. The double doors to the toilet room open the cramped space to the galley, while closing it off from both the main cabin and forecastle. The racing boat's narrow cabin house allows plenty of deck space. (© Mystic Seaport, Daniel S. Gregory Ships Plans Library, SP38.59.5) ABOVE: The *Questa* heading home to Marblehead Harbor after a pleasant afternoon sail. She is running before a light southeast breeze with her jib tack wung out on its double pole, designed so it needs neither lift nor down-guy. This was not an idea that either Foster or Francis repeated. (Photo 4-92, Charles H. W. Foster Collection, Hart Nautical Collections, MIT Museum, Cambridge, Massachusetts)

a cabin house at least six feet long to provide sitting headroom over two bunks. There was a "suitcase rule"; the cabin had to be big enough so that a suitcase could be held crosswise in it. Not that a sailor would bring gear on board in such a contraption: there was plenty of storage space in the ends of the long hull. These Skargardskryssare, or Skerry Cruisers, as they were called in English, became popular not only in Sweden, but also in Denmark, Norway, and Germany. In the latter country, the name was Scharenkreuzer. By 1916, there were nine designated classes for racing, with measured sail areas of 15, 22, 30, 40, 55, 75, 95, 120, and 150 square metres. The most popular sizes were the 22- and 30-Square-Metre classes. Francis kept up on developments in European yacht design by reading the weekly German yachting magazine, *Die Yacht,* so he knew about the Scharenkreuzers and he liked the graceful, seaworthy, easily handled boats, fast for their sail area, that the Square-Metre Rule encouraged.[28]

In 1925, the Square-Metre Rule was changed and made far more complicated in order to place limits on the extreme hulls that were being tried. The new rule, written up by Swedish designer Karl Ljungberg, was adopted in 1928 by both the International Yacht Racing Union and the United States Yacht Racing Union. By then, there were over 100 "30-Squares" built under the new rule and racing in Europe, though none yet in the United States.[29]

Even with its new complexities, the Square-Metre Rule was appealing to Francis, because a yacht's rating was based solely on sail area, leaving designers free to experiment with different hull forms to try to make the fastest boat for a given amount of sail. Before the limitations of the 1925 rule, Swedish designers had tried 30-Squares more than 44 feet long with less than 6 feet beam. The new rule put twenty different limits on the hull of a 30-Square-Metre boat. Minimum displacement was 4,410 pounds. Maximum length at a point 7 inches above the waterline (approximating sailing waterline length in moderate conditions) was 29 feet, 10 inches, unless displacement, beam, freeboard, and keel length were increased according to proportions in the rule. The minimum beam measurement included the maximum beam at three different heights on the hull, fed into a formula with two constants. Draft was unlimited. Minimum freeboard was 1 foot, 6 inches. Minimum length of keel, measured at a point 1 foot, 10 inches below the measured-length line, was 7 feet, 6 inches. Cabin house and side deck dimensions had to meet minimums. Cockpit area could not exceed 23.68 square feet. There were extremely detailed minimum scantling rules. The measured sail area of 322.8 square feet included just 85 percent of the fore triangle, no matter how big a jib was set. Masthead height was limited to 36 feet, 5 inches. The clearest exposition of all this was in an article for the June 1929 issue of *Yachting,* in which Norman Skene presented the Square-Metre Rule in a diagram and tables for 22-, 30-, and 40-Square-Metre boats (as well as for one-sixth-size sailing models of these classes),

---

RIGHT: **Francis's design for a 20-Square-Metre boat, his No. 35. She is another of his lovely double-ended racing boats and as pretty as any of the far bigger ones. She is 30 feet long on deck, 18 feet on the waterline, with a beam of 5 feet, and a draft of 4 feet, 3 inches. Unlike most racing boats and daysailers of the time, she has a self-bailing cockpit, which, with her watertight bulkheads fore and aft, backs up Francis's claim in this drawing's label that she is nonsinkable. Her heavy, low ballast allows him to call her non-capsizable. These superlatives apply only to the conditions to which a day boat might reasonably be subjected. Note that the running backstays are set up by being hauled aft on a track, another of Francis's rigging innovations.** (© Mystic Seaport, Daniel S. Gregory Ships Plans Library, SP38.65.2)

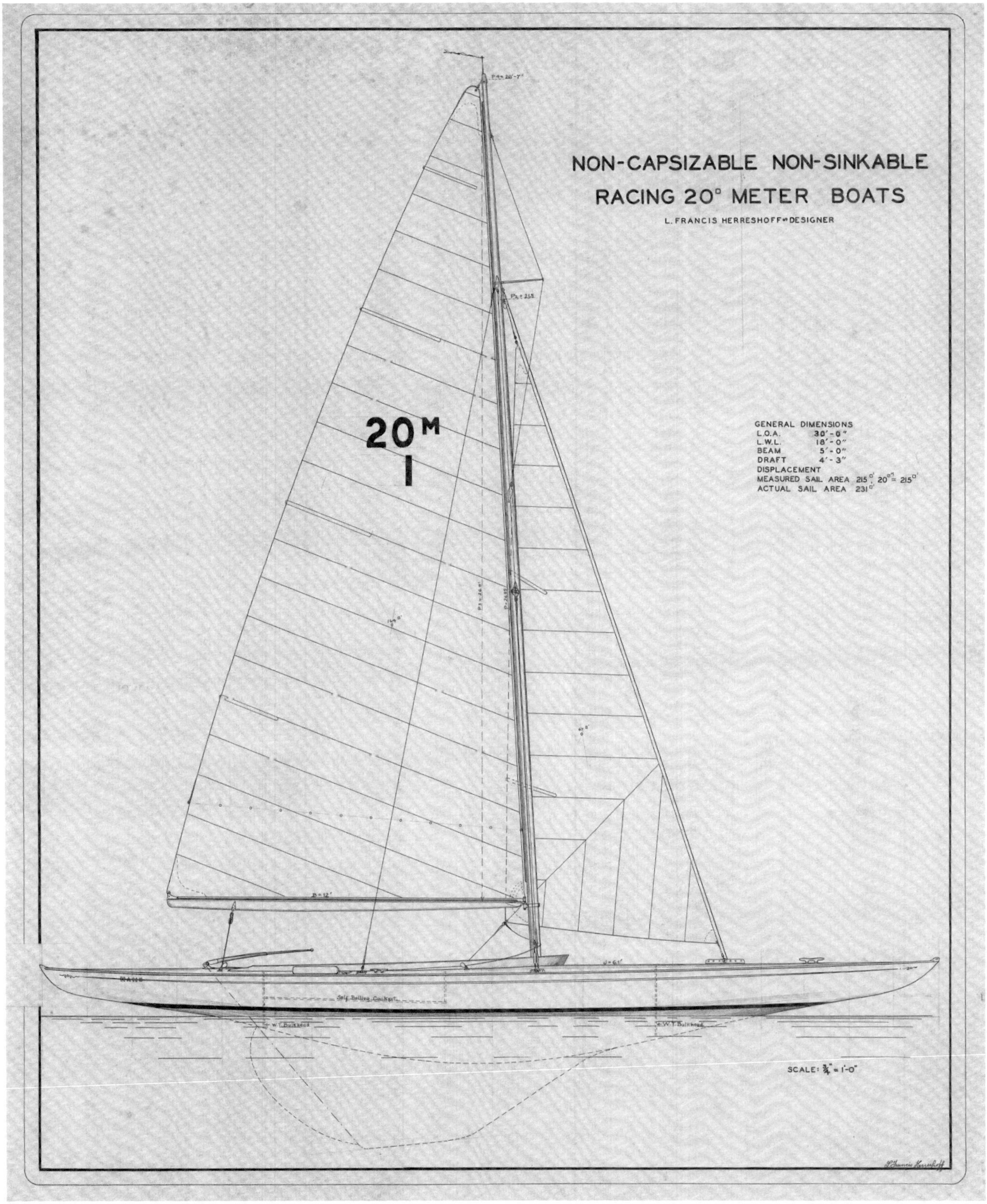
NON-CAPSIZABLE NON-SINKABLE
RACING 20□ METER BOATS
L. FRANCIS HERRESHOFF — DESIGNER
20M
1
GENERAL DIMENSIONS
L.O.A. 30′-0″
L.W.L. 18′-0″
BEAM 5′-0″
DRAFT 4′-3″
DISPLACEMENT
MEASURED SAIL AREA 215□′, 20□M = 215□′
ACTUAL SAIL AREA 231□′
Self Bailing Cockpit
W.T. Bulkhead
W.T. Bulkhead
SCALE: ¾″ = 1′-0″

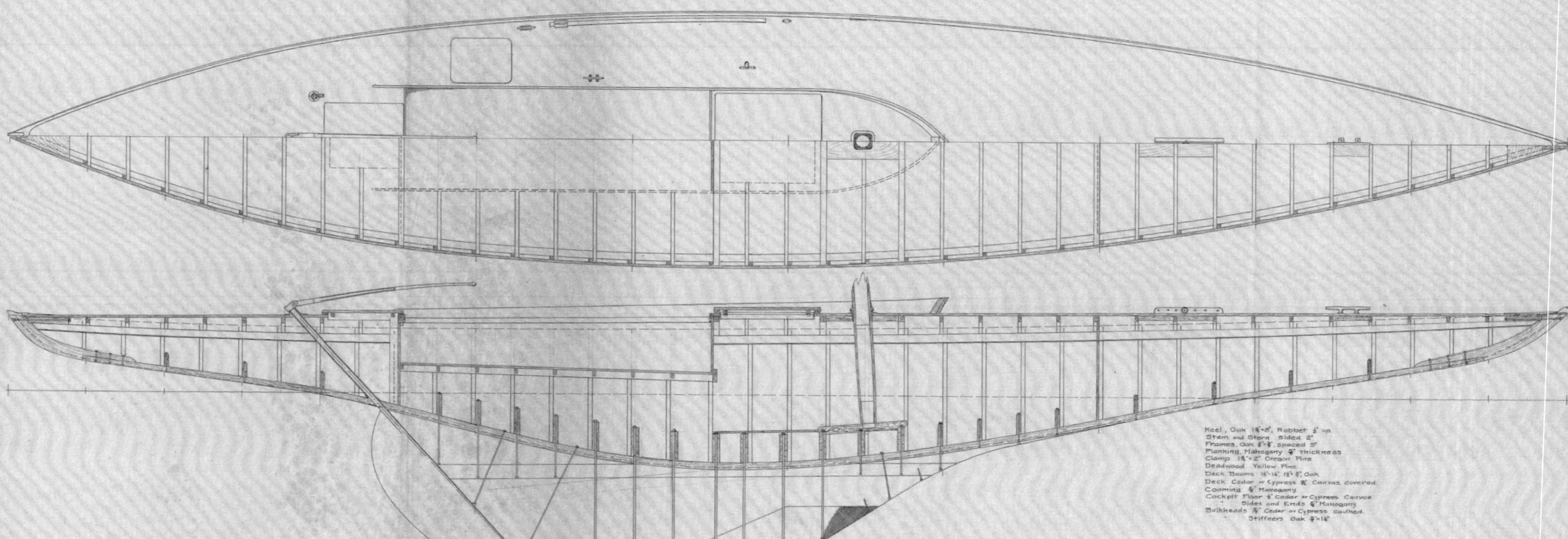

No. 35
CONSTRUCTION PLAN
Scale: 1½"=1'-0"
L. FRANCIS HERRESHOFF-DESIGNER
Marblehead, Mass

with his figures all converted to English measure for the convenience of American readers.[30]

Francis had been admiring plans and photographs of, in particular, the 40-Square-Metre boats of Germany and Sweden that were published in *Die Yacht,* and had extolled their virtues to his father: "They appear to me to be the prettiest boats I have ever seen. I imagine they are delightfully easy in a sea and extremely dry." In the summer of 1928, Francis made a design for a 20-Square-Metre, his design No. 35. This was his attempt to start a square-metre sail-area racing class in the United States, and, with the sail area fixed at 20 square metres, instead of the European 22 or 15 square metres, he was proposing a US class that would be different. He had in mind not a racer-cruiser, like the 30-Square, but a smaller, and thus cheaper, racer-daysailer, yet more of a boat than the 15-Square.[31]

The first 20-Square-Metre was to be built for Grafton Smith, but, evidently, he had enough on his hands racing the Q-boat *Nor'easter V*, and neither Smith nor anyone else ordered a boat to be built from Francis's design. The only publicity the 20 Square got was publication of the design in Billy Atkin's August 1928 issue of *Fore an' Aft*, not a publication of wide circulation. Francis must have been disappointed that the world of racing sailors didn't beat a path to his door to have "Non-Capsizable, Non-Sinkable Racing 20 Square Metre Boats" built. He noted on his plans list that the drawings for No. 35 were destroyed, but fortunately at least the sail and construction plans escaped the flames. It was a great design.

IN SEPTEMBER, at the end of the racing season of 1928, Hanns Stinnes, a German industrialist and yachtsman of the Kaiserlicher Yacht Club in Kiel, brought his 30-Square-Metre boat, the *Gluckauf IV*, to Marblehead to demonstrate her and try to foster interest in the class for future international racing. The *Gluckauf* was the first 30-Square-Metre boat seen in the United States. She had been designed by Henry Rasmussen and built in his yard in Lemwerder, Germany. Rasmussen and Francis were friendly correspondents; since the mid-twenties, Rasmussen had presented Francis with annual bound volumes of *Die Yacht*.[32]

Francis gave Herr Stinnes a warm welcome, and the two soon found that they shared many of the same views on yacht design and construction. They formed a friendship that, though interrupted by World War II, lasted all their lives. And Francis was smitten with the *Gluckauf.* Although William U. Swan reported to readers of *The Rudder* that in demonstration races the German 30-Square was beaten by R-boats both on and off the wind, and was "slightly bettered by Alden Triangles and a Herreshoff S-boat to windward, but outran and outreached her rivals with started sheets," Francis wrote to Nathanael that only the R-boats beat her to windward, and that she "beat S-boats easily in all conditions." We don't know who was the more accurate reporter of these informal races, but we can notice a put-down by Francis of his father's S-boats.[33]

Stinnes planned to leave the *Gluckauf*

LEFT: The 20-Square-Metre's conventional construction plan. The forward watertight bulkhead is not shown in this drawing. Note the wide side decks; she would have to be heeled way over before water came into her watertight cockpit. The cockpit floor, like the deck, was to be canvas-covered. The helmsman has a seat on either side, so he can sit out on deck on a level with the top of the low coaming. Sam Brown inked this plan. (© Mystic Seaport, Daniel S. Gregory Ships Plans Library, SP38.65.1)

Francis sailing his 30-Square-Metre boat, the *Visitor*, designed and built in Germany by Henry Rasmussen. German yachtsman Hanns Stinnes brought her over to Marblehead late in the 1928 season to demonstrate how a racing boat designed to a measurement rule based on sail area alone would fare against yachts built to the Universal and International Rules. At the end of the season, Francis bought the *Gluckauf* and changed her name. She is long (37 feet, 10 inches on deck), narrow, and of relatively light displacement. The sail area, of course, is 30-Square-Metres (324 square feet). The mast is curved, the mainsail has roller reefing by rotating the boom, and the jib is small. The Corinthian Yacht Club's race committee called the 30-Square-Metres the "X" Class, evidently thinking that a boat with a hull that was much longer than her sail plan was merely an experiment. In this light breeze, Francis has chosen to sit to leeward, hold the tiller over his shoulder, and study the luff of the jib to know whether to head up a mite or off a mite, as he works his boat to windward. This type of yacht had become popular in Scandinavia and was very different from an R-boat or a 6-Metre; the *Visitor* provided a new sailing experience for Francis, one in which he delighted. (Photo 19-31, Charles H. W. Foster Collection, Hart Nautical Collections, MIT Museum, Cambridge, Massachusetts)

in Marblehead over the winter, hoping that Americans would build a few 30-Squares for him and other German yachtsmen to race against the next season. Francis arranged to buy the boat. The name *Gluckauf* had significance for Stinnes, who was in the coal business; it was a salutation for miners going down, meaning "good luck" coming back up. Marblehead wits couldn't resist calling her the "Glue Cough." Francis changed her name to the *Visitor*.[34]

However the Rasmussen 30-Square-Metre boat fared against Marblehead racers in other classes, Francis was impressed by her performance. He bought her so that he could try her out thoroughly. For the next two seasons, he sailed the boat as often as he could, keeping her in commission from early May until well into October. He raced and cruised in his boat, often taking for crew his draftsman, Sam Brown, or Oisten Lie-Nielsen, a nineteen-year-old Norwegian sailor who had arrived in Marblehead in the spring of 1927.[35]

Lie-Nielsen had accompanied his father's 8-Metre, the *Sans Ca Tout*, stowed on the foredeck of the passenger steamer *Christiania Fjord*, from Norway to Halifax and had then sailed the boat to Marblehead single-handed. The idea was to sell the boat at a profit in the United States, bringing her in through Canada to save on the import duty. Francis, spotting a new, interesting boat in the harbor, kayaked out to inspect her. He and Lie got acquainted, and Lie decided to stay in Marblehead to see what he could do around boats. He taught sailing at the Eastern Yacht Club, took out parties in the 8-Metre, and got to know and crew for Charlie Welch. O. Lie Nielsen's arrival in Marblehead marked the start of another lifelong friendship for Francis, although Lie would recall later that Francis, eighteen years his senior, was not an easy man to get to know; Lie described him as "a very serious man."[36]

And the young Katherine Jones would sometimes go for an afternoon sail with Francis in the *Visitor*, as she had in his Development boat, the *Dragon Fly*. With Katherine, Francis was not an autocratic skipper. As she would recall many years later, he would let her sail the boat and would not correct her unless he saw that she was about to do something crazy. To her surprise, he would even let her shoot the mooring in the *Visitor*. "He said, `Now Katherine, you've never sailed a boat this big—you take her up to the mooring.' So I did. No other person with a brand new boat would have said to a twelve-year-old, `You take her up to the mooring.' He'd challenge you to do something, and he'd help you if you got stuck."[37]

While Francis preferred Universal Rule boats to those designed to the International Rule, he came to like the Square-Metre boats best. He wrote of his 30-Square:

> *She is extremely easy to handle and very much livelier and more fun to sail than the R or 6-Meter boats, as the displacement for the length is about half as much as in these other two classes. [She] is very dry, and an extremely good sea boat. On Columbus Day we were caught off Marblehead in a very strong, northerly squall of wind, about force 8 [34-40 knots]. We took in the jib and with the roller reef, rolled down about one-half the area of the mainsail; we then tacked home dead to windward in very difficult going. The way the little ship went to windward and tacked was a revelation to me compared with what a heavy R or Six-Meter would do under the same conditions.*[38]

In a race in a forty-knot sou'wester on Buzzards Bay, 30-Square-Metres did in fact beat 6-Metres.[39]

Apparently, the *Visitor* figured in an incident that led to one of Francis's flights from conflict. He had joined the Corinthian Yacht Club, where his friend Charlie Welch was now vice commodore, in order to be able to race his 30-Square, and perhaps in a half-hearted attempt to make contacts for his business. The *Visitor*'s mooring was off the club. One late afternoon, Francis needed to go out to the boat to secure the cockpit cover. The club's launch-driver wouldn't take him for some reason. Rather than press the issue, Francis resigned from the club. It is not known what Charlie Welch thought of either Francis's or the launch-driver's behavior.[40]

The 30-Square-Metre *Visitor* was the only sailing yacht that Francis would own. He could afford to buy her because he was busy with design work in 1928. He sold the boat in the spring of 1931 to Ernest B. Dane Jr. for what he paid for her. Dane would become an important client for Francis three years later.[41]

FRANCIS CLAIMED credit for starting the square-metre sail-area classes in the United States by his purchase of the first 30-Square to arrive in the country. He also designed the first two boats in the class, for the 1929 racing season. The Corinthian's new vice commodore, George E. McQuesten, ordered the design of a 30-Square from Francis, as did Alfred E. Chase, another Marblehead yachtsman. Francis could have shared credit for starting the class with Hanns Stinnes, to be sure, as well as with the other Marblehead yachtsmen who ordered 30-Square-Metres for the 1929 season.[42]

Charlie Welch, promoted to commodore at the Corinthian, wanted one, but instead of starting Francis on the design, he went to Professor George Owen of MIT, an accomplished designer of racing yachts. Francis would not have argued with Charlie's choice. He would write: "Professor Owen is unique among yacht designers inasmuch as he has never designed a freak or an undesirable yacht," and that he designed several yachts "which could even be said to be beautiful, and this adjective can only be truthfully applied to few things in this world." Charlie was always looking for a different boat, and perhaps he felt that Francis was busy enough at his drawing board not to need another order from him. Owen drew a long, pointed stern on this 30-Square for this regular client of L. Francis Herreshoff. Charlie used the name *Yankee* again for his Owen 30-Square. There were no hard feelings: Francis and Charlie sailed together in the new *Yankee*. And E. Arthur Shuman, a member of the Corinthian Yacht Club, ordered a 30-Square, to be named the *Tippler III*, from the Boston designer, Gordon Munro.[43]

SHORTLY AFTER the racing season of 1929, Francis received a letter from Henry Rasmussen calling attention to his recent design of a 75-Square-Metre boat and suggesting that Francis promote the idea of a class of 75-Squares in the United States. Rasmussen allowed as how he'd be glad to build the boats in his yard in Germany. Promotion was not Francis's forte. He replied promptly to Rasmussen: "I have been quite busy lately and have not done much about getting an order for the 75 Square Meter boat. I will see what I can do, though."[44]

Francis liked the idea enough to draw a preliminary plan of a 75-Square-Metre. He superimposed on his drawing a profile of the Q-boat he had recently designed and made up a table comparing specifications, including cost, of the 75-Square-Metre, the Q-boat, and a typical 8-Metre. He was hoping to demonstrate some advantages of the Square-Metre Rule over the Universal and International Rules. With her greater length and lighter displacement, the 75-Square would be faster than the other boats, even though she had less sail area. The 75-Square had the most cabin space. And she would cost, Francis estimated, 15 percent less than the Q-boat and 8 percent less than the 8-Metre. It is not known that Francis's comparative drawing and table got any publicity. If any yachtsman saw it,

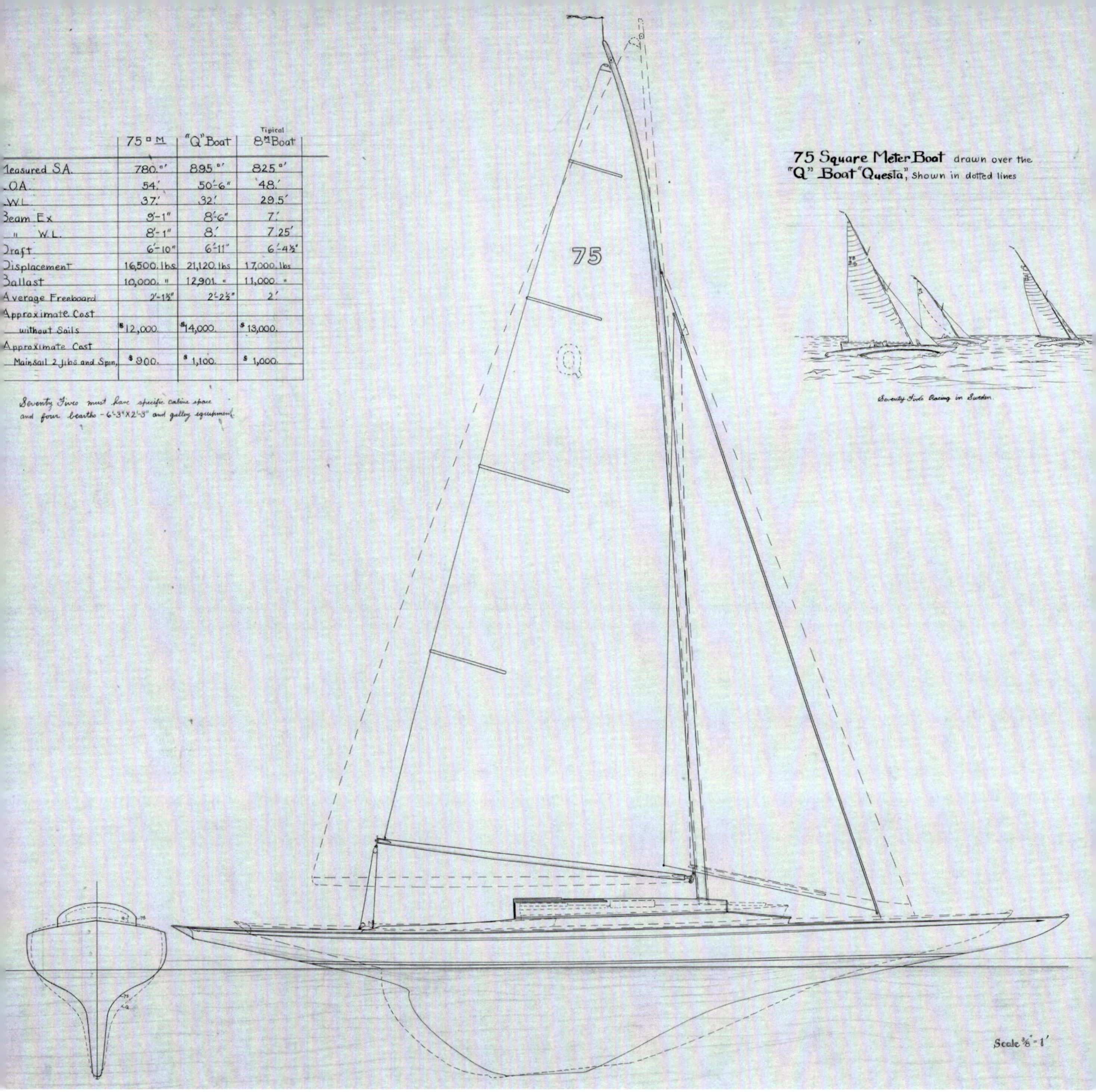

The outboard profile and sail plan of Francis's proposed 75-Square-Metre boat. Length on deck was 54 feet; length on the waterline, 37 feet; beam, 9 feet, 1 inch; and draft 6 feet, 10 inches. Displacement was 16,500 pounds, with 10,000 pounds of ballast, for a ballast-displacement ratio of 60 percent. The sail area was 780 square feet. The boat Francis has drawn for comparison in dotted lines is the Q-boat *Questa* that he had designed for the 1929 season. His sketch in the upper right corner shows three 75-Squares on a tight windward leg, racing in enough breeze so that two of them have rolled in reefs, shallow on the left-hand boat, and deeper on the leader. (© Mystic Seaport, Daniel S. Gregory Ships Plans Library, SP 38.40.1)

he didn't bite. The design for the 75-Square-Metre went no further, and Henry Rasmussen got no orders for American 75-Squares.[45]

THE DISAPPOINTMENT of the abortive 20-Square-Metre design in 1928 and of the 75-Square the next year was counterbalanced: four racing sailors did beat a path to Francis's door. For the 1929 season, Francis was designing not only two 30-Square-Metre boats, but also the Q-boat, *Questa,* and a big M-boat, one that would be built this time. Francis didn't replace Norman Skene, so he and his draftsman, Sam Brown, had all they could handle. Francis, himself, was not a fast worker. He was methodical, painstaking, and not overly concerned with the passage of time. He would write: "It takes me a month to make a construction plan for a yacht 40 feet on the waterline," and that "A construction plan is harder for me than all the rest of the design put together." His construction plans were detailed and intricate, more so than those of most designers. Never in a hurry, he accomplished much.[46]

Francis was well acquainted with George McQuesten, who ordered the first US 30-Square-Metre boat. McQuesten was a bachelor who lived on Marblehead Neck, the peninsula that protected the harbor from ocean swells. Francis first encountered him when the two would chance to meet at F. N. Osborne & Company, grocers, at the corner of School and Pleasant Streets. Francis shopped at Norris Osborne's emporium daily, buying his half-pound of ground beef, his corn flakes, his quart of milk, his melon, and, occasionally, his bottle of S. S. Pierce New England rum. McQuesten was there to show off one of his automobiles, maybe a grand Rolls Royce one day, and his specially designed Cadillac sedan the next. Francis, with orders in hand for racing boats, was thinking of buying a Packard, so he and McQuesten would stand in Osborne's parking lot, talking cars. McQuesten also liked to talk boats, for he was a yachtsman who was interested in the science of yacht design. Francis didn't like talking about his favorite subject with McQuesten, however, because he said he never could follow McQuesten's theorizing. When the two talked boats, there seemed to be no connection between their remarks. They did connect, however, on the appeal of the 30-Square-Metre Class.[47]

Like Grafton Smith with his Q-boat, McQuesten wanted his 30-Square to be short on the waterline to reduce hull resistance for Marblehead's typically light, summer winds. Francis complied, though he knew that a short waterline would mean reduced speed in more than light winds. The *Oriole,* as McQuesten named his new racer, had a waterline length of 22 feet, over a foot shorter than the average in the class at the time. Francis gave her a long overhang in the bow and the long, pointed stern that was becoming his trademark on racing boats. As with all these double-enders, the diagonals, the lines that show the hull shape on which the boat sails when heeled, have gentle and very fair curves. Other than ensuring that these basic factors were incorporated into the design as well as possible, there was little Francis could do to produce a fast boat. He wrote to Nathanael: "I think this [30-Square-Metre] rule is very interesting and do not know how to beat it." The *Oriole* was built at the George Lawley yard at Neponset. She was planked with mahogany, and Francis thought the builders made a nice job of it.[48]

Francis's second 30-Square-Metre boat for the 1929 season, for Alfred Chase, was named the *Rima*. She had a hull shape identical to that of the *Oriole*, including the short waterline, except that she had a small counter at the stern instead of being a double-ender, and the bottom of her keel was flat instead of curved. The rigs of the two boats were identical, as were their construction and interior arrangements. The *Rima* was built by Henry Vincent at Warren, Rhode Island.[49]

Shortly after working out the designs for the

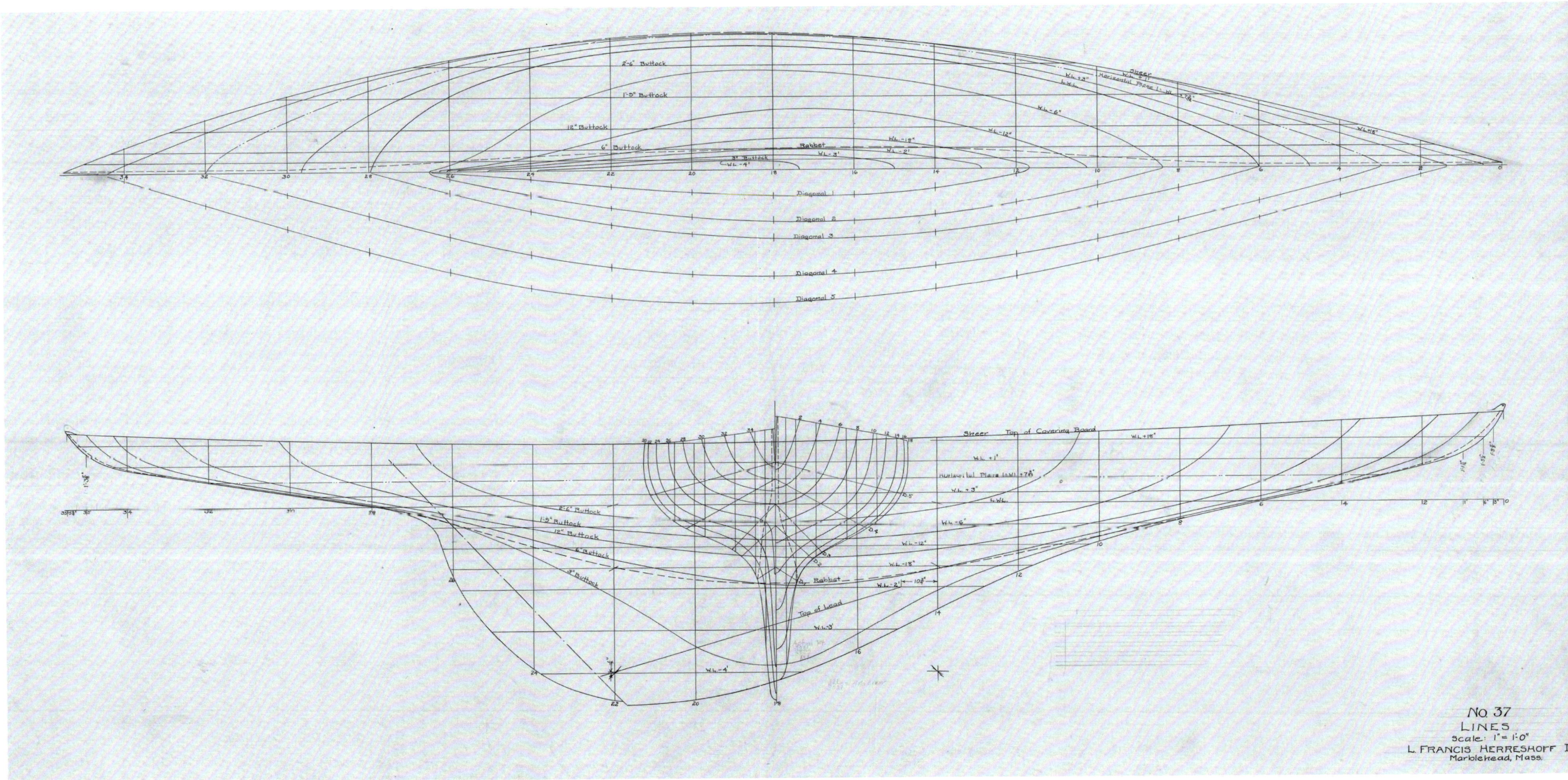

The *Oriole*'s lines. It is interesting to compare this 30-Square-Metre boat with a 6-Metre. With the exception of displacement and sail area, her dimensions are not that different from those of Francis's 6-Metre *Wasp*. Her midsection is far more cutaway than that of the *Wasp*, and she has 2,800 pounds less ballast, and 100 square feet less sail than the *Wasp*, but her length on deck, length on the waterline, beam, and draft are close to those of the 6-Metre. In light and moderate weather, the two would be on equal terms for speed, but in a hard breeze, the 30-Square could be driven faster than the 6-Metre. The *Oriole* is 35 feet, 6 inches long on deck; 22 feet on the waterline; with a beam of 6 feet, 6 inches; and a draft of 4 feet, 9 inches. Displacement is 5,470 pounds, with 3,021 pounds of ballast, for a ballast-displacement ratio of 55 percent. Sam Brown inked the lines and dated them November 24, 1928. (© Mystic Seaport, Daniel S. Gregory Ships Plans Library, SP38.62.1)

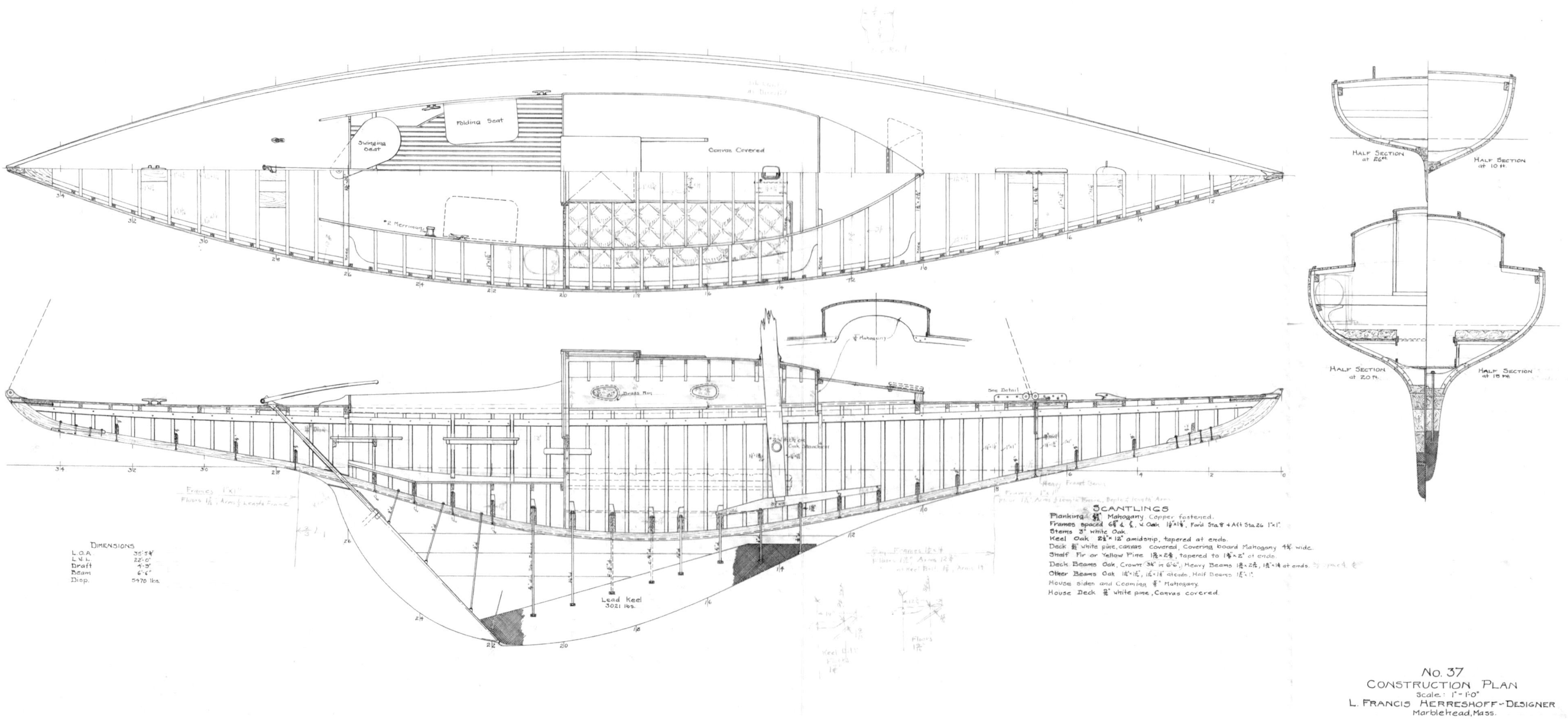

The *Oriole*'s construction plan. The dimensions of the parts of the boat's conventional construction were dictated by the scantling rules of the Square-Metre Rule. Unlike Francis's 20-Square-Metre, her cockpit is open to the bilge. Note the swinging seat aft, so that the person steering can sit on either side of the tiller. The crew has folding seats. The high-crowned cabin house allows for the required sitting headroom on the two bunks. This is another tracing by Sam Brown. (© Mystic Seaport, Daniel S. Gregory Ships Plans Library, SP38.62.3)

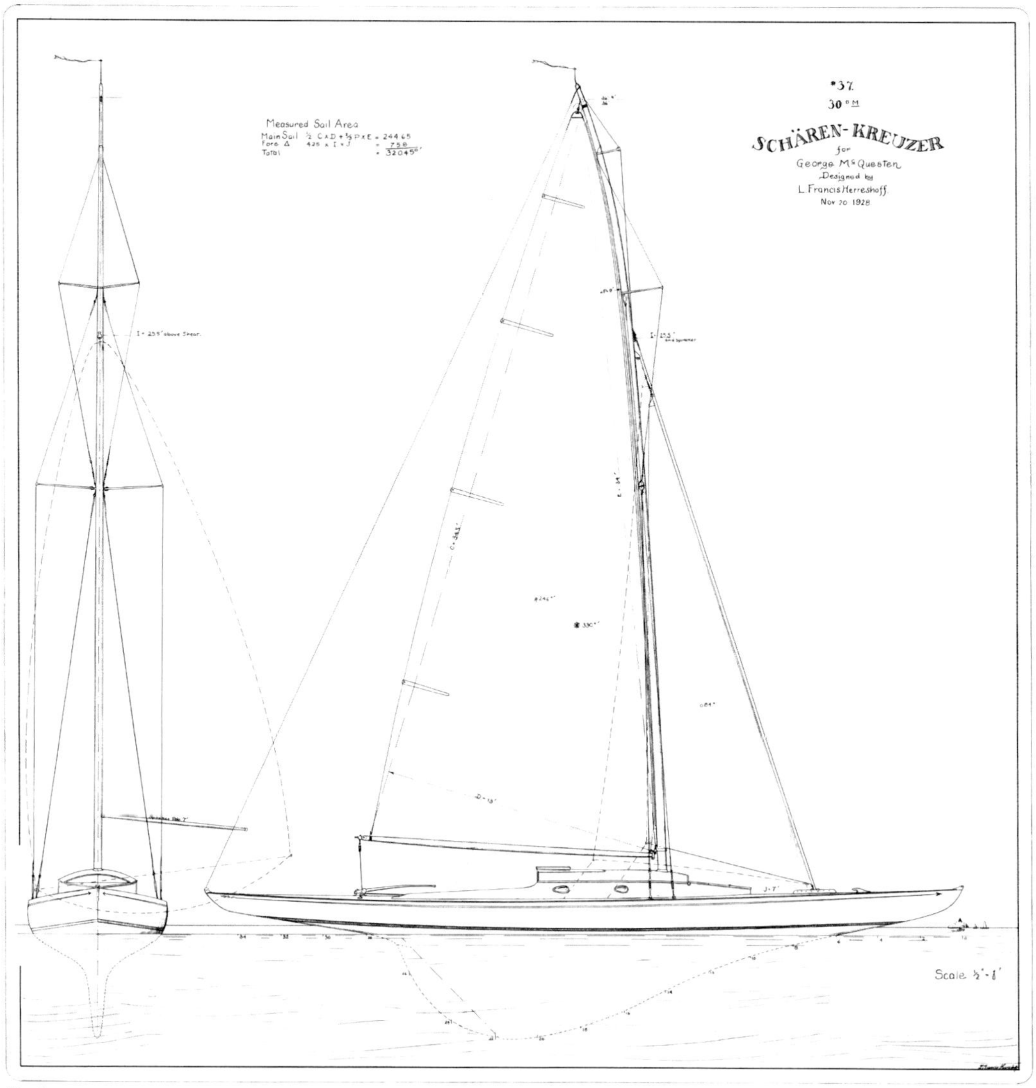

38.62.4

The outboard profile and sail plan of the first US 30-Square-Metre, the *Oriole*, Francis's design No. 37 for George E. McQuesten. Francis has given her the curved mast that became popular in the class. The spar is hollow and rectangular in section. A 30-Square, with a curved mast and a permanent backstay led to the long stern, had no need of running backstays. Francis designed roller-reefing gear for the mainsail, and, taking no chances, made the patterns for its fittings and finished the castings himself. The measured sail area is 320.45 square feet. With the working jib shown in the plan, the actual sail area was 330 square feet. The single-luff spinnaker shown in dotted lines at the left is all the rules would allow. The sheet (to the lower, left-hand corner of the sail) had to be led inside the forestay, and the length of pole was limited to the length of the base of the fore triangle. Francis has dated his drawing November 20, 1928. (© Mystic Seaport, Daniel S. Gregory Ships Plans Library, SP38.62.4)

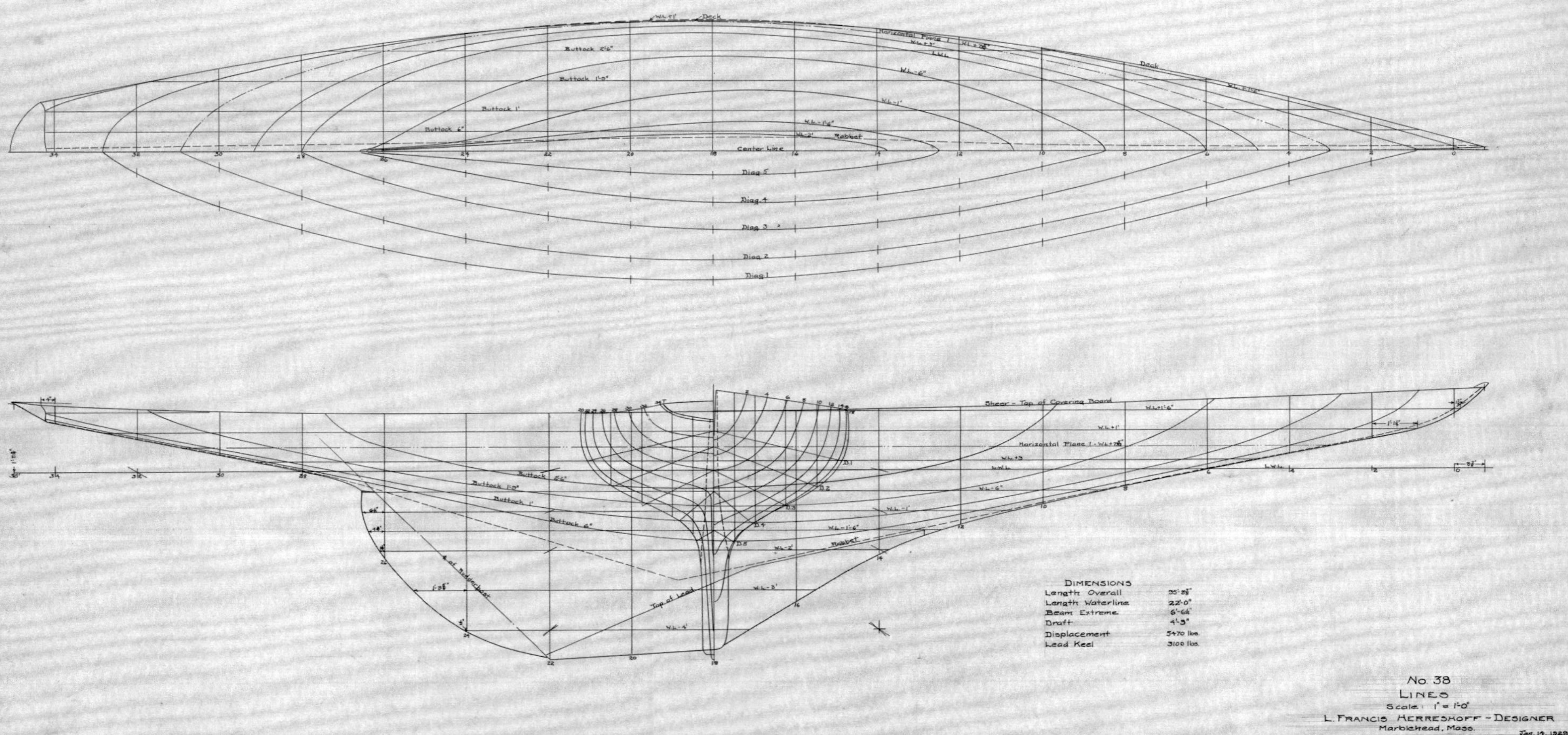
Dock
Horizontal Plane 1
Buttock 2'-6"
Buttock 1'-6"
Buttock 1'
Buttock 6"
Center Line
Rabbet
Diag 5
Diag 4
Diag 3
Diag 2
Diag 1
Sheer - Top of Covering Board
Horizontal Plane 1
Top of Lead
DIMENSIONS
Length Overall 35'-8⅝"
Length Waterline 22'-0"
Beam Extreme 6'-6¼"
Draft 4'-3"
Displacement 5470 lbs.
Lead Keel 3100 lbs.
No. 38
LINES
Scale: 1" = 1'-0"
L. FRANCIS HERRESHOFF - DESIGNER
Marblehead, Mass.
Jan 14 1929

Oriole and *Rima*, Francis wrote briefly about them to Nathanael and said that he would probably be designing more 30-Squares and would be glad to have his father's suggestions for improving hull form. No such suggestions were forthcoming, however, for Nathanael, at age eighty, wasn't interested in immersing himself in a new and very different rating rule for racing yachts.[50]

Hanns Stinnes's demonstration of his fourth *Gluckauf* in Marblehead had the desired effect. In the summer of 1929, he brought a new 30-Square, the *Gluckauf V*, to Marblehead, accompanied by two other German 30-Squares, Leo Ross's *Kickerle* and Johannes Theede's *Hathi*, and a Swedish 30-Square, Eric Lundberg's *Bacchant*, and found a team of three American 30-Squares ready to race them. While the European 30-Squares had been selected from sizable racing fleets, the three American boats were chosen from among a mere four boats. The *Rima* was eliminated, leaving the *Oriole, Yankee, and Tippler III.* George McQuesten had been persuaded to charter the *Oriole* to Chandler Hovey for the international series. She was sailed by his daughter, Elizabeth "Sis" Hovey, who, still in her teens, was the first woman to skipper a racing yacht in an international series. Francis, who preferred crewing to skippering when it came to competitive racing, did not campaign his *Visitor* for the international team-racing series, but he did enter her in the final free-for-all race, coming in last. The tactics of racing did not interest him, but he was glad to be in a position to observe the performance of the yachts, both of his own design and of his competitors. That said, he did win the 30-Square-Metre Class regular season racing of the Eastern Yacht Club for 1929 in the *Visitor*.[51]

Francis apparently intended to crew in the *Oriole* in July during the international series elimination races, when she earned a place on the American team, and again in August during the series itself against Germany. He mentioned his plans to race in letters to his father, but it is unlikely that he was in the *Oriole*'s crew, for though he was sometimes invited to lunch at the Hovey house, he didn't know the Hoveys as well as he knew McQuesten. Besides, Sis Hovey already had an expert advisor and main-sheet-trimmer in the boat, Frank Paine.[52]

The racing must have been disappointing to Francis, the observer, for Marblehead produced nothing but light airs, so that it was the drifting-match skills of skippers and crews that were tested, more than the designs of the boats. The *Oriole* was the second highest point scorer in the team racing, thanks to brilliant, sacrificial tactics by Shuman in the *Tippler III,* but the German boats won the cup sponsored by President Herbert Hoover for the event by a score of 57 to 48. The Swedish *Bacchant* was barred from the team racing but won everything else. She had an exceptionally tall mast, allowing the mainsail to be raised a good four feet higher than those of her competitors and had a bigger spinnaker than the other boats had, both of which differences helped her in the light going. Charlie Welch bought the *Bacchant* as soon as the races were over, but when he lowered her rig four feet to comply with the rule, he found her to be just ordinarily competitive. The *Oriole* raced until World War II; in 1937, as the *Pintail*, she became the first of a class of 30-Squares on Narragansett Bay.[53]

LEFT: **The lines of the 30-Square-Metre *Rima*, Francis's design No. 38. Her hull has the same dimensions as those of the *Oriole*, except that because she has a counter stern, her on-deck length is 2 inches less. Her lead ballast keel has a straight-edged profile rather than the more expensive curved shape of the *Oriole*'s keel. The *Rima*'s flat keel would make her easier to haul out and would not harm her sailing qualities.** (© Mystic Seaport, Daniel S. Gregory Ships Plans Library, SP38.60.1)

US
X
I

FRANCIS HAD been instrumental in starting the 30-Square-Metre Class in the United States. Hanns Stinnes and Charlie Welch deserve more credit than Francis for stimulating the American acceptance of the European concept of rating racing boats by sail area alone, but L. Francis Herreshoff's enthusiasm for the square-metre boats, his owning and sailing the first imported 30-Square, and his designing of the first two boats in the American class gave him some right to the founding-father role that he claimed. And the enthusiastic founding father

LEFT: During the 1931 Marblehead Race Week, *Pintail* ex-*Oriole* sails with the working jib set, close-hauled and footing fast in a gentle breeze. Her sail number indicates that she is qualified to represent the United States in the 30-Square-Metre Class (called the "X," or Experimental Class, in Marblehead), and is the first boat in the class. (© Mystic Seaport, Rosenfeld Collection, 1984.187.47839F) ABOVE: The *Rima*'s sail number shows that she was the second boat in Marblehead's Experimental Class of 30-Square-Metres. Her owner, Alfred E. Chase, has her going nicely on the wind in a gentle breeze. She has conventional reefing for the mainsail, rather than the *Oriole*'s roller reefing. (Willard B. Jackson photo, 19-21, Charles H. W. Foster Collection, Hart Nautical Collections, MIT Museum, Cambridge, Massachusetts)

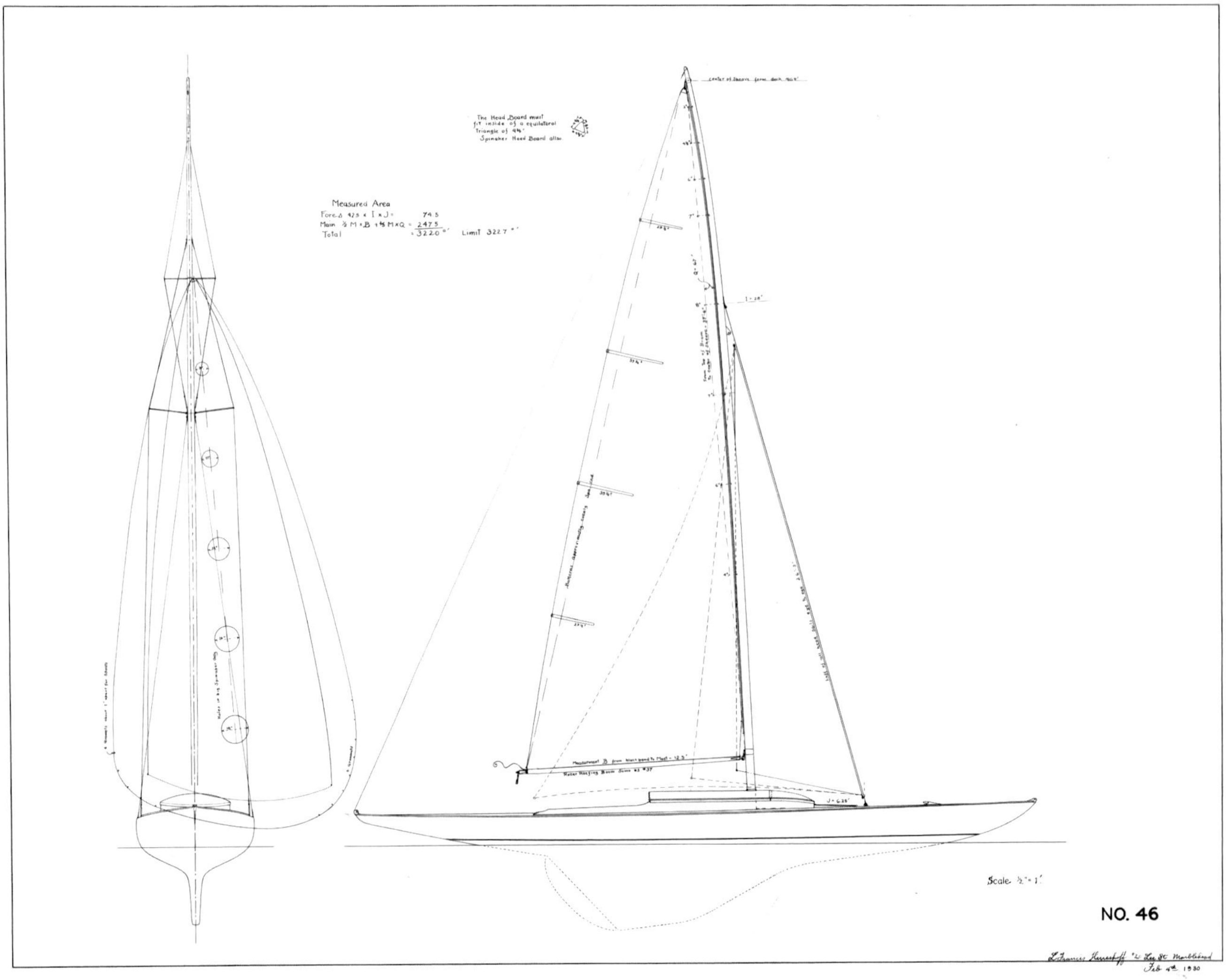

ABOVE: The sail plan of the *Oriole II.* Francis's original pencil drawing of this plan (SP38.63.8 in the Daniel S. Gregory Ships Plans Library at Mystic Seaport) is a good example of his preliminary plans from which his draftsmen produced finished tracings in ink. With Norman Skene gone and Sam Brown busy on other designs, Francis traced this drawing himself. We see the normal curved mast of the 30-Square; it has internal halyards running below to winches in the cabin. The backstay is shown running through a sheave; Francis later changed the sheave to a fitting that slid on a track. The mainsail runs in slots on mast and boom and is fitted with roller-reefing gear. He has drawn a huge Genoa jib with a concave leech, the clew coming back close to that of the mainsail. He shows two spinnakers, a standard-sized one, as big as it could be using the short pole prescribed by the rule, and a bigger sail to be set flying, because the rule didn't say you had to use a pole. To help the big spinnaker set better without the benefit of a pole, Francis tried a vertical row of ventilation holes, a scheme that was a short-lived experiment by several designers at the time. Measured sail area is the maximum allowed by the rule at 322 square feet. (© Mystic Seaport, Daniel S. Gregory Ships Plans Library, SP38.63.4) RIGHT: The lines of the *Oriole II.* Her underbody is more cut away than that of the first *Oriole*, and she has sharper sections at the bow. She does not have quite the beauty of her predecessor, whose long, knuckled bow profile has been replaced by a shorter, less interesting curve, and whose elegant sheerline has been replaced by one that is very nearly flat from amidships to the stern. The *Oriole II* is 39 feet long on deck; 28 feet, 9 inches on the waterline; with a beam of 6 feet, 10 inches; and a draft of 4 feet, 10 inches. (© Mystic Seaport, Daniel S. Gregory Ships Plans Library, SP38.63.1)

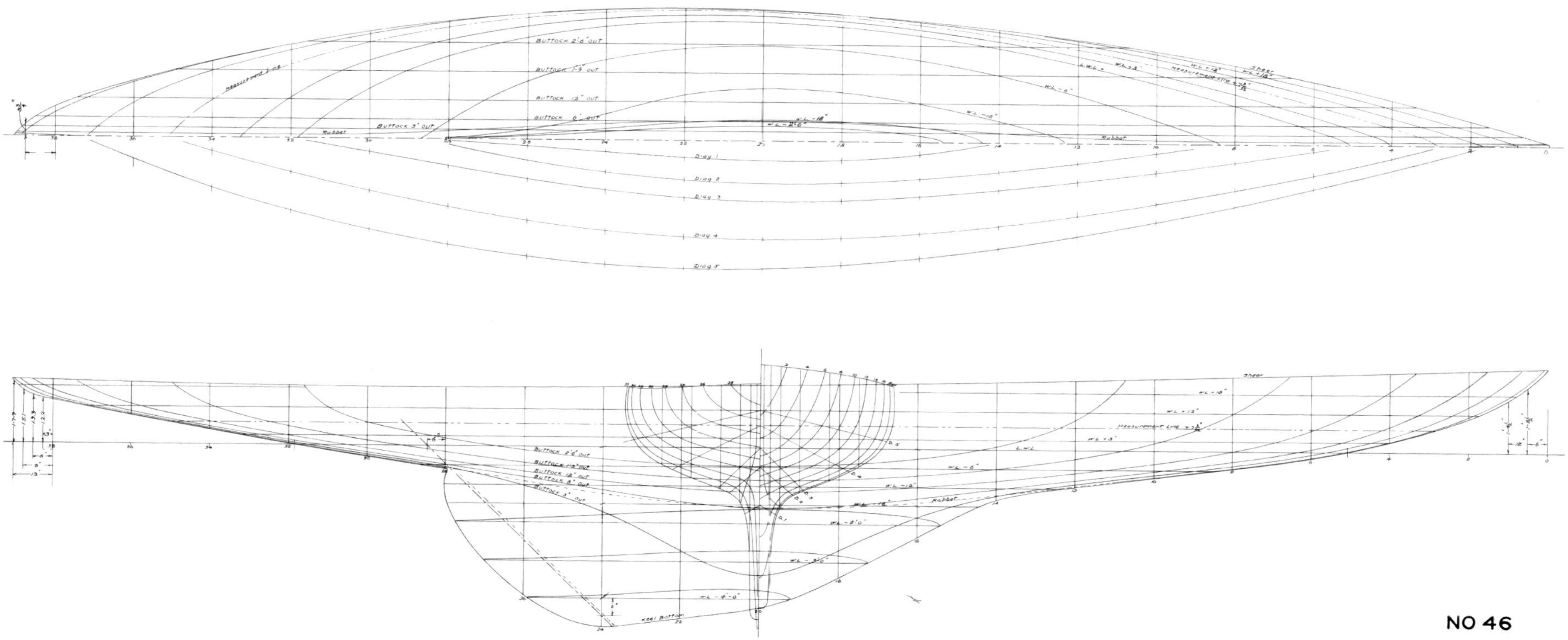

NO 46
LINES

L. FRANCIS HERRESHOFF. DESIGNER.
MARBLEHEAD. MASS.

SCALE. 1 INCH = 1 FOOT. FEB. 20'30.

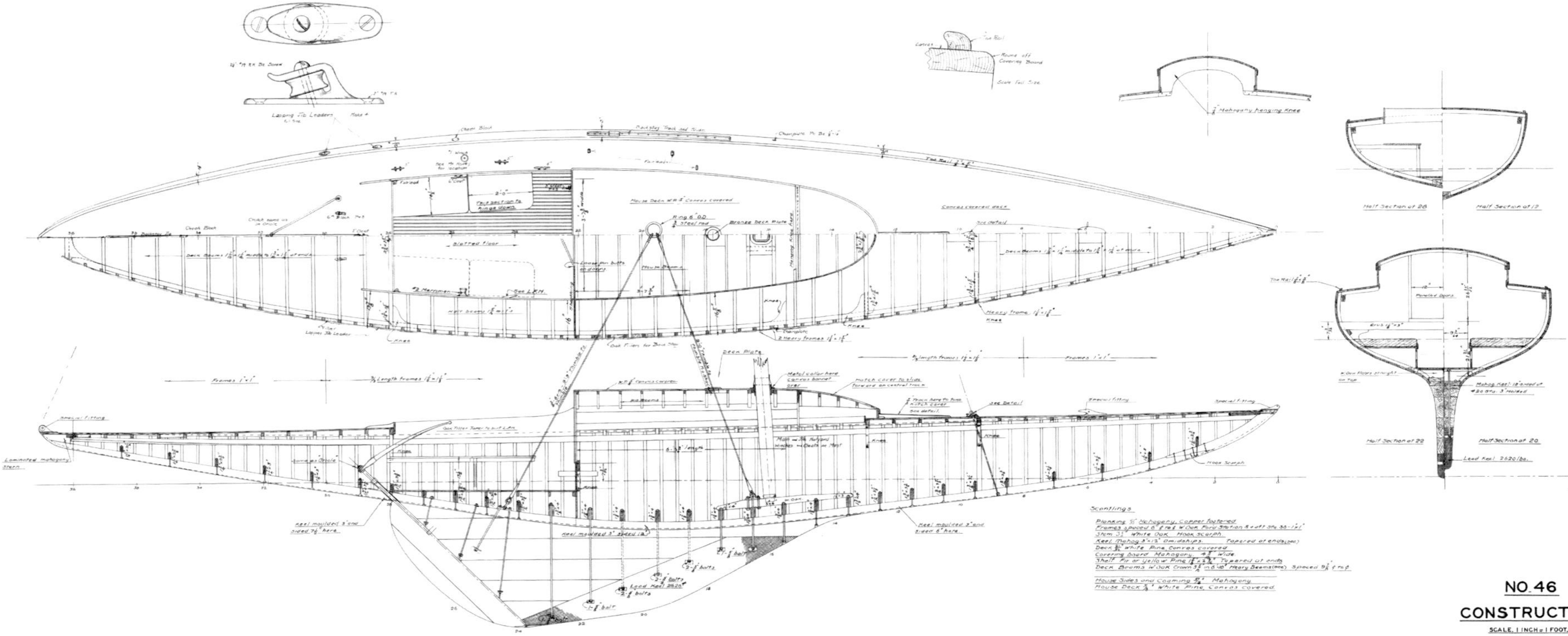

NO. 46
CONSTRUCTION

SCALE. 1 INCH = 1 FOOT.

L. FRANCIS HERRESHOFF, DESIGNER.

MARBLEHEAD, MASS.

would continue designing for the class: one of the two boats he designed for the 1930 racing season would be another 30-Square, a second *Oriole,* for Chandler Hovey, and, two years after that, he would draw the plans for a one-design class of 30-Square-Metre boats.

As the design for the *Oriole II* took shape, Francis sent his drawings to Nathanael and got a reaction: "The b.p. [blueprint] for a 30 sq. m. for Miss Hovey to take abroad is very interesting indeed! But what extraordinary narrow sails you are giving her. Can you keep them set? And can you make them at all efficient with sheets lifted in strong breezes? I see there are holes in the spinnaker. What for? Do they help as much as the Chinaman's eyes painted on the bows?" Francis explained to his astonished and amused father the theory that air passing through the spinnaker's holes was supposed to create a partial vacuum on the lee side of the sail and thus help keep the big, full sail from collapsing in a light breeze. The designers of spinnakers soon accomplished this by careful sail shape, and the idea of the ventilated spinnaker didn't last long. Francis left his father's questions about high-aspect-ratio sails unanswered. Nathanael G. Herreshoff, who had made so many innovations in yacht design, was, at last, being overtaken by events.[54]

In the summer of 1930, at Kiel, Germany, with Sis Hovey at the tiller in strong winds, the *Oriole II* did well enough to win one race. At Sandhamn, Sweden, in light weather, her big spinnaker scared the race committee into setting up triangular courses instead of windward-leeward races. The problem was that on the runs, the *Oriole II* could "fly the sail like a kite," in Sis's words, and ran away from everybody. Sis Hovey loved that spinnaker. She also liked the boat's "biggest, biggest" jib, as she called the one that overlapped so much. She went so far as to believe that in 1930 the sail was the first of its kind and became responsible for the name Genoa jib. She had help in this misunderstanding from L. Francis Herreshoff. We have seen how he claimed that he was the inventor of the sail, and he told the Hoveys "that it should have been called the 'Hovey' jib." In any event, as we have seen, Genoa jibs had been in use since 1927.[55]

Back in Marblehead, Sis Hovey raced the *Oriole II* successfully for a few more seasons. The 30-Square-Metre was her favorite boat to sail. Sixty years later, she proved that she hadn't lost her touch at the tiller. The *Oriole II* survived, and, in 1991, under the sponsorship of the Museum of Yachting at Newport, with help from Sis, she underwent a 90 percent restoration by Frank McCaffrey's Narragansett Shipwrights. In a series of match races against another 30-Square, the *Cythera*, designed in 1937 by Knud Reimers of Sweden, Sis Hovey, at age seventy-nine, won two out of three with her old boat.[56]

IN THE SPRING of 1931, Francis started a design of a 30-Square-Metre for the 1932 season for Charlie Welch, to replace his Owen-designed *Yankee*. She was to have a long waterline for the class of 28 feet and a shorter-than-normal base to the fore triangle. But Charlie changed his mind, and the design was another abortive one for

LEFT: The construction plan of the *Oriole II*. Francis shows a hoisting rig, for the boat was to be shipped to race in Germany. The streamlined forward end of the cabin house is a hatch that can slide forward on a track on deck, giving the spinnaker handler a good place to work. Planking is 23/32-inch mahogany; the deck is 21/32-inch white pine covered with canvas. The tiller was of oak with "taper to suit LFH." The boat was built at the Lawley yard. (© Mystic Seaport, Daniel S. Gregory Ships Plans Library, SP38.63.3)

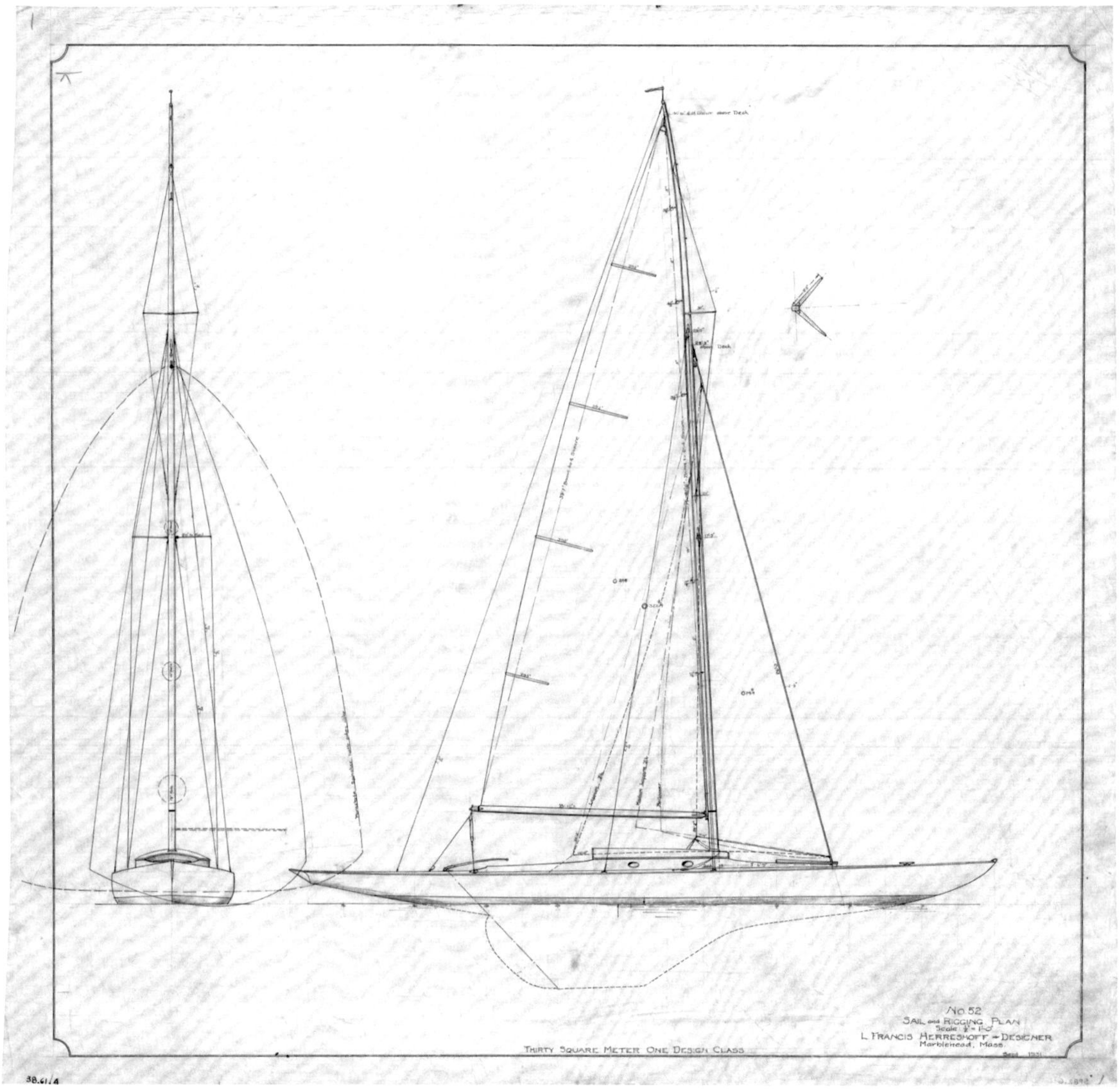

The sail plan for the 30-Square-Metre one-design class that Francis designed for the Beverly Yacht Club at Marion, Massachusetts, on Buzzards Bay, his design No. 52. The rig is standard for a 30-Square, tall and narrow, with 322 square feet of area, with just the fore triangle measured. Francis has drawn a huge, symmetrical, parachute spinnaker, with ventilation holes. The Square-Metre Rule put no limit on the area of light sails, but the big spinnaker would have to be set with the short pole shown, and the sheet would have to stay inside the forestay. Besides the working jib, Francis shows three overlapping jibs, the smallest of which is cut full for reaching in a strong breeze. He has omitted a sail with the huge overlap of the *Oriole II*'s "biggest, biggest" jib, as Sis Hovey called it. The jib-sheet lead blocks are adjustable fore and aft on tracks on the rails. The main sheet is rigged with the middle block fixed on a bridle, instead of sliding on a traveler. Each leg of the bridle runs through a lead block at the rail and then forward to a jig tackle. Thus, when close-hauled, the boom can be positioned on the centerline or to windward of it, as well as to leeward. Francis wrote, "results have undoubtedly shown that when the boom is held close to the centre line and to windward in moderate weather the boats are faster." The shrouds are set inboard 8¼ inches with turnbuckles below deck. The forestay and backstay run over sheaves in the deck to jig tackles below, for adjustment. The running backstays slide on tracks. The upper end of the permanent backstay and those of the jumper stays are spliced around the mast, instead of being secured to tangs; evidently, Francis wanted a little give at the masthead. (© Mystic Seaport, Daniel S. Gregory Ships Plans Library, SP38.61.4)

Francis. Instead, he went to work on a design for a one-design class of 30-Squares for the Beverly Yacht Club at Marion, on Buzzards Bay. The agreement stipulated that Francis had to complete the plans by October 15, 1931, and that the boats had to be built by April 1, 1932, at a cost of no more than $3,000 each. The intent was to build ten boats, but, in those depression days, only four yachtsmen came forward with orders: Paul Dudley Dean named his 30-Square the *Fleetwing*, William Bross Lloyd had the *Ngauruhoe* ; S. Wiley Wakerman, the *Monsoon II*; and H. Nelson Emmons, the *Gem*. The builder was the George Lawley Company. Lawley's had the exclusive right to build to Francis's design No. 52 and had to pay Francis a commission of 2 ½ percent of the cost on each boat, or $75 per boat. So Francis, who had hoped to make extra money for a design that might become popular, got $300 in commissions for the four boats, merely the equal of his normal 10 percent commission on a single boat costing $3,000.[57]

Perhaps because the design was for multiple boats, Francis did take the first one completed out for a test sail from the Lawley yard. On the way back, the southwest wind breezed up hard. Francis had to beat up a narrow channel to the dock and was glad that 30-Square-Metres had roller-reefing gear.[58]

The four Beverly Yacht Club 30-Squares raced from Marion for seven seasons, though they were soon joined by other 30-Squares, including, by 1936, the *Oriole,* then owned by Richard Dane, and, by 1939, two Swedish 30-Squares, so the one-design racing was short-lived. It lasted long enough, however, for one disgruntled owner, whose boat was losing, to write Francis "some pretty disagreeable letters." "He seems to be under the impression," Francis wrote to Nathanael, "that I have made his boat different from the others." The Beverly Yacht Club 30-Squares also raced against 30-Squares from other Clubs, for, by 1937, there were classes not only in Marblehead and Marion, but also in Northeast Harbor, Maine; Edgartown, on Martha's Vineyard; Nantucket; and Narragansett Bay.[59]

The *Monsoon II*, despite her short waterline, was second of ten boats in the race for the President's Cup, put up by Franklin Delano Roosevelt, sailed in Buzzards Bay late in August 1934. The *Ngauruhoe* won the Beverly Yacht Club's class of six boats in 1935.

Waldo Brown, with and for whom Francis had designed the schooner, *Joann*, bought the *Gem* from Nelson Emmons. For one series of races in Buzzards Bay, four 30-Squares, including the *Gem,* were towed down from Marblehead through the Cape Cod Canal. The towboat was Charlie Welch's *Walrus*, and Francis was running her. At the west end of the canal, he found high, steep waves, caused by a fast current coming out of the canal into a strong southwest wind. Back on the towline, the 30-Squares were taking a beating, pounding into it. But they were fine heavy-weather boats, so they all made sail, let go the towline, and beat to Marion, a lot more comfortable under sail than they had been under tow.[60]

Waldo and his children used to take short cruises in the *Gem*. Once, they set off from Provincetown in a strong northeaster to go through the canal to Marion. Running before it with just the full mainsail, the boat was under good control, surfing down the big waves. When they got to the canal entrance, the authorities came out in their picket boat to do the usual formalities. One of the blanks Waldo had to fill in was for the type of power in the transiting vessel, for you weren't supposed to sail through the canal. Waldo had no dinghy with him, but he did have the dinghy's outboard motor, so "Evinrude, 1 h.p." was dutifully recorded. Then the little eggbeater, not running, was lashed to the *Gem*'s side, and she sailed on through.[61]

And there is the story of how once, when Francis was sailing in the *Gem* on Buzzards Bay with Waldo, they got into a heated argument about exactly how the jib should be trimmed. At the end of the day, when they were going ashore to

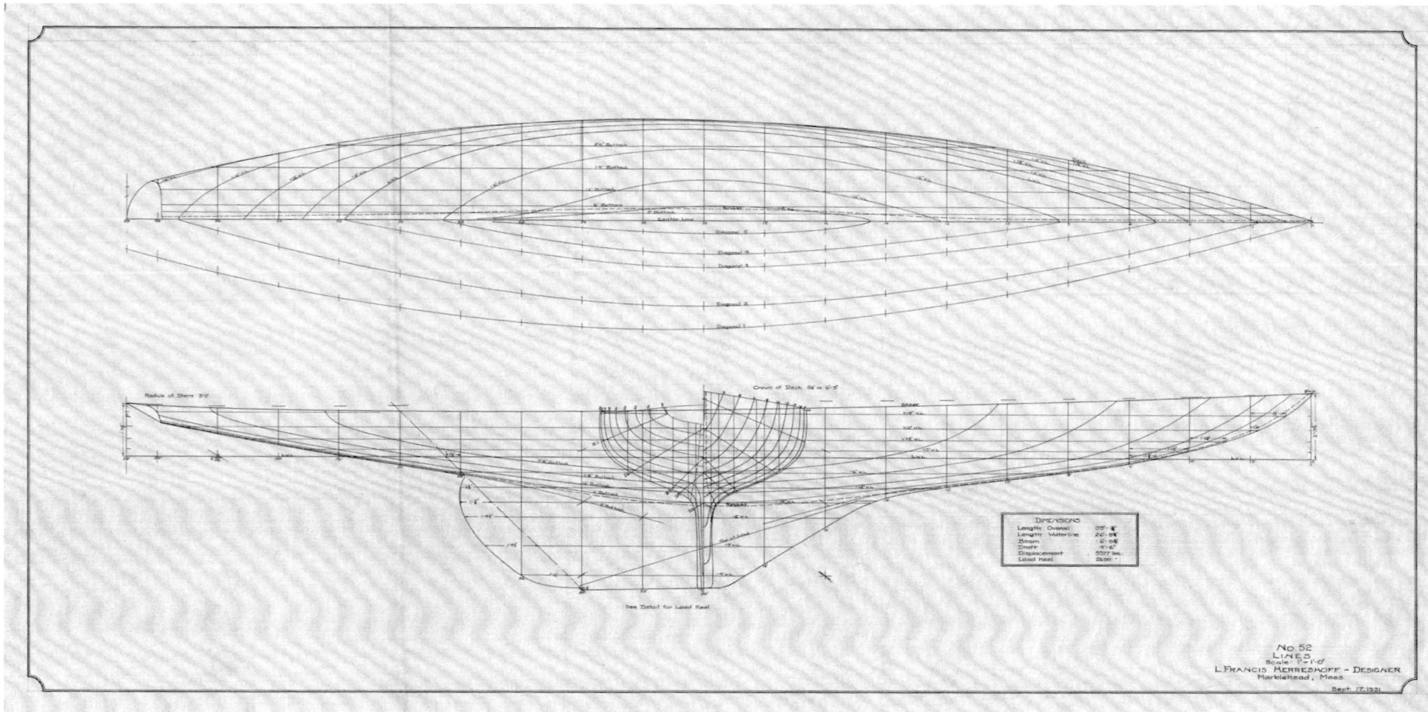

The lines of the 30-Square-Metre one-design. The hull is shaped much the same as that of the *Oriole II*, but her waterline is two feet shorter. This would be a disadvantage if the boats were raced against longer 30-Squares, but, of course, would make no difference in the one-design class. Other changes from the *Oriole II* are that the bottom of the keel is flat instead of curved, and she has a counter stern instead of being a double-ender. Francis hoped that many boats would be built from this design, and he probably feared that a pointed stern might put people off. The one-design is 39 feet, 3/4 inch long on deck; 26 feet, 8-3/4 inches on the waterline; with a beam of 6 feet, 9-3/4 inches; and a draft of 4 feet, 6 inches. Displacement is 5,577 pounds, with 2,690 pounds of lead, outside ballast, for a ballast-to-displacement ratio of 48 percent. The drawing is dated September 17, 1931. (© Mystic Seaport, Daniel S. Gregory Ships Plans Library, SP38.61.1)

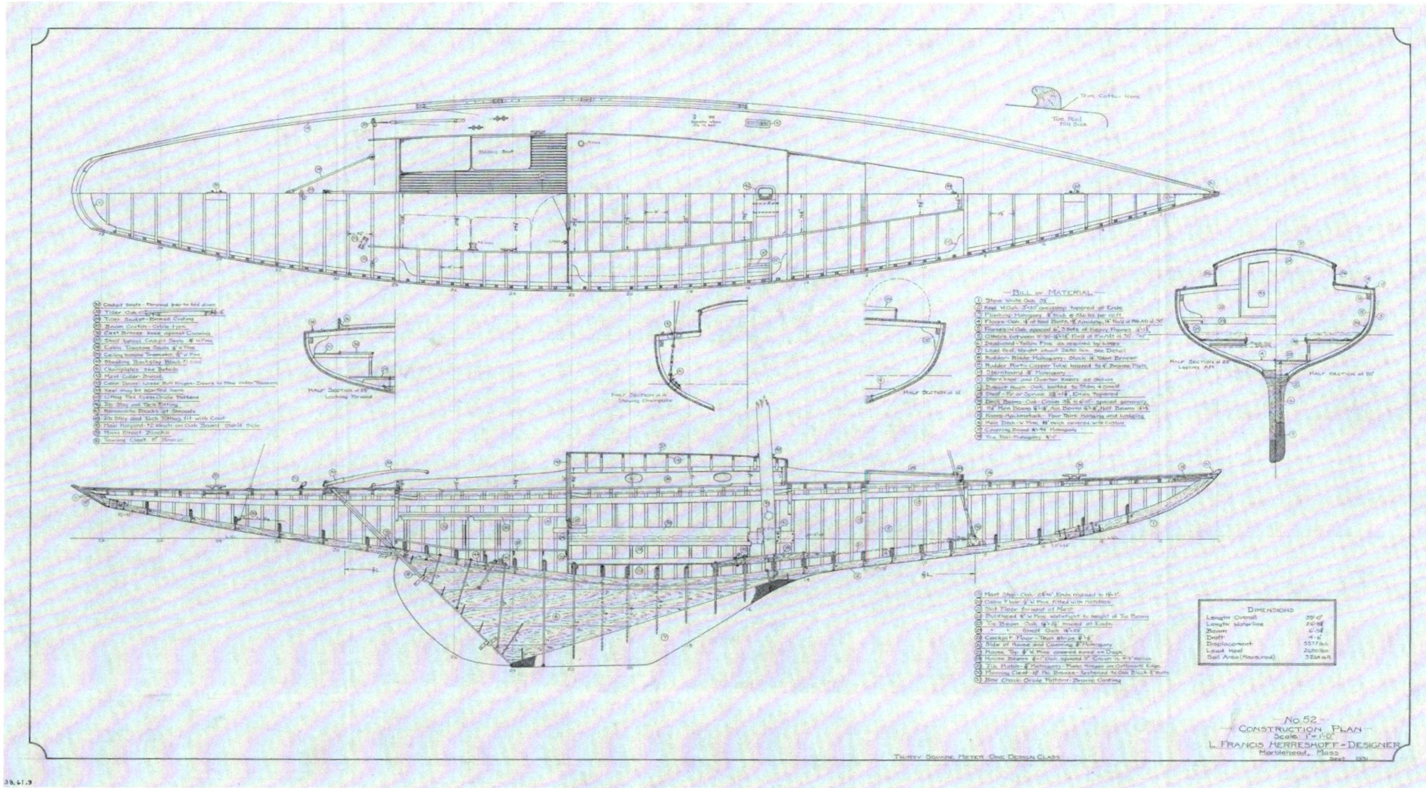

The 30-Square-Metre one-design's construction plan. Francis has used his system of numbering the parts and including corresponding descriptions, with dimensions and materials, on the drawing. Builders—in this case the men at Lawley's—appreciated this clarity. The two halves of the long, trapezoidal forward hatch open athwartships on piano hinges. The low coamings between this hatch and the forward end of the cabin house would be helpful to the foredeck man. Planking is 3/4-inch mahogany; the big deadwood is yellow pine; the deck is 23/32-inch white pine covered with canvas. There are padeyes to take a lifting span, in case the boat might be shipped to race abroad. This plan and the sail plan were published in the July 1932 issue of *Yachting*. (© Mystic Seaport, Daniel S. Gregory Ships Plans Library, SP38.61.3)

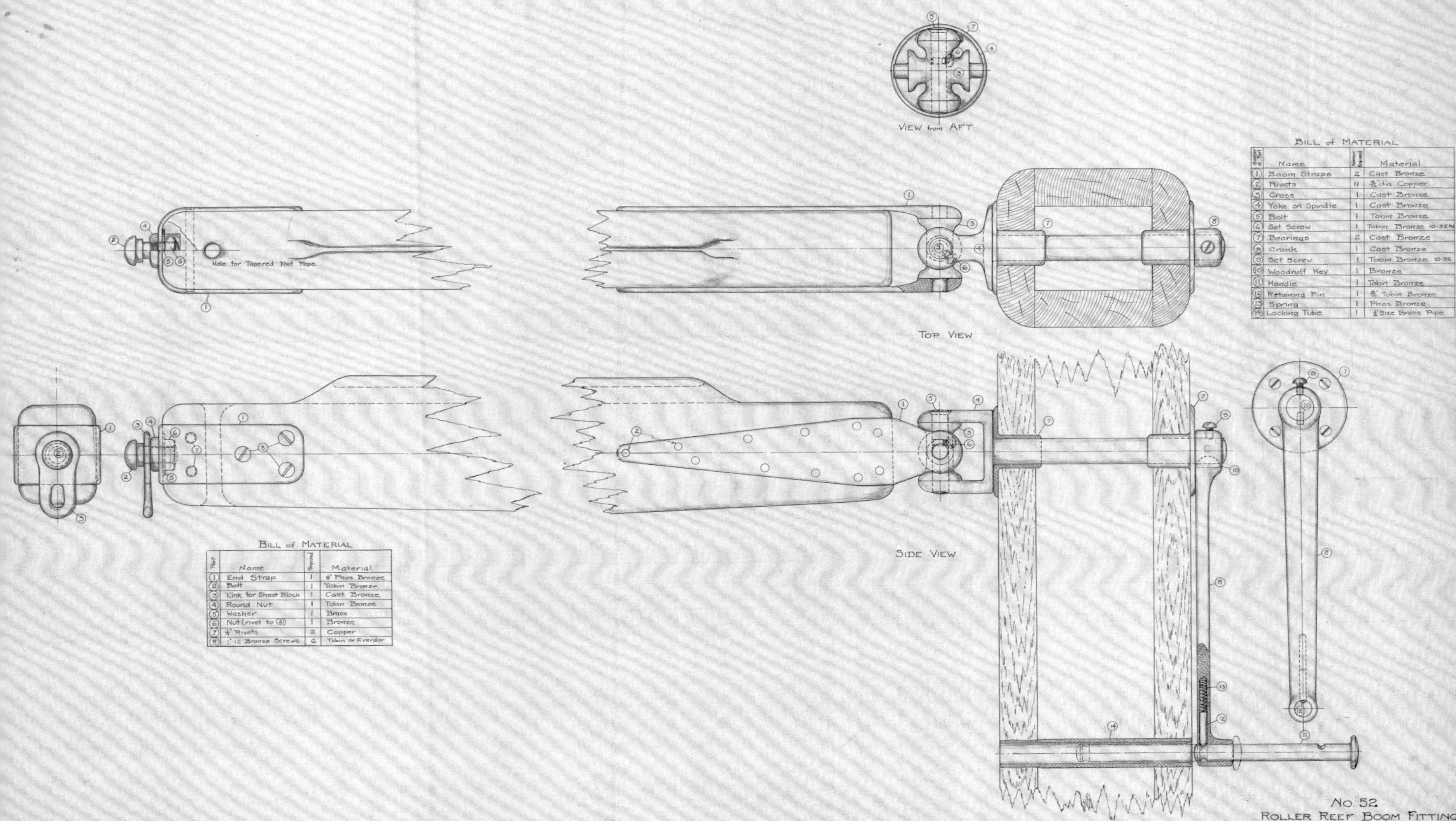

BILL of MATERIAL

Part	Name	Required	Material
1	End Strap	1	¼" Phos. Bronze
2	Bolt	1	Tobin Bronze
3	Link for Sheet Block	1	Cast Bronze
4	Round Nut	1	Tobin Bronze
5	Washer	1	Brass
6	Nut (rivet to ②)	1	Bronze
7	¼" Rivets	2	Copper
8	1"-12 Bronze Screws	6	Tobin or Everdur

BILL of MATERIAL

Number of Part	Name	Number Required	Material
1	Boom Straps	2	Cast Bronze
2	Rivets	11	$\frac{3}{16}$" dia Copper
3	Cross	1	Cast Bronze
4	Yoke on Spindle	1	Cast Bronze
5	Bolt	1	Tobin Bronze
6	Set Screw	1	Tobin Bronze 10-32N
7	Bearings	2	Cast Bronze
8	Crank	1	Cast Bronze
9	Set Screw	1	Tobin Bronze 10-32
10	Woodruff Key	1	Bronze
11	Handle	1	Tobin Bronze
12	Retaining Pin	1	$\frac{3}{16}$" Tobin Bronze
13	Spring	1	Phos Bronze
14	Locking Tube	1	¼" Size Brass Pipe

No. 52
ROLLER REEF BOOM FITTINGS
Scale: Full Size
L. FRANCIS HERRESHOFF – DESIGNER
Marblehead, Mass.
Oct. 1931

LEFT: The roller-reefing gear that Francis designed for the 30-Square-Metre one-design. With the crank on the forward side of the mast, the gooseneck can be small, so that the luff of the mainsail comes nearly straight down onto the boom as it rolled. The boom was shaped straight on top, but with a slight convex curve on the bottom; by rolling the sail down to one side of the boom or the other, you could adjust the draft of the sail. Sam Brown traced all the drawings for the 30-Square-Metre one-design. (© Mystic Seaport, Daniel S. Gregory Ships Plans Library, SP38.61.5) ABOVE: Waldo Brown's 30-Square-Metre one-design *Gem,* running in a light breeze with her ventilated parachute spinnaker drawing nicely. (Willard B. Jackson photo, Mystic Seaport, 1974.577.32)

the Beverly Yacht Club in Charlie Welch's launch *Gadget*, Francis, perhaps still seething, stalled the engine in the middle of an uncharacteristic, high-speed landing. He got no reverse, the *Gadget* crashed into a granite wall, and she sank. Luckily, only feelings were hurt, and the launch lived on. Despite such shenanigans, Waldo said that of all his boats, he got the most pleasure from the 30-Square-Metre *Gem*.[62]

DESIGNING and sailing 30-Square-Metre boats had given Francis pleasure, also. They had opened his eyes to what a fine boat could be designed on the principle of combining a long, narrow hull of light displacement with a small sail plan. The result would be a relatively inexpensive boat that would sail well enough in light and moderate weather and that would have the great advantage of coming into her own when it blew hard, being easily handled and able to be driven at high speed, if her skipper so chose.

Francis's involvement with the 30-Square-Metre Class ended, however, on a sour note. This is how he told the story:

Some of these oversize Swedish boats were imported to this country and one of their owners, realizing that it would be expensive to have her cut down to the rules which we had for the class, got up at a meeting of the 30 square meter association and proposed that measurement be done away with, and this suggestion was accepted so that each year after that the imported Swedish boats came bigger and bigger. Under this childish condition the class was bound to become a failure. Of course the American boats, which had to be built to the only rules we had and were measured to these rules, were easily beaten.

The late Swedish freaks in this class were a most miserable type of boat only good for exhibitionism. With a supposed measured sail area of some 320 square feet, they often sailed with 450 square feet of sail area and required a crew of from four to six to handle their freak sails. On the whole they were the most miserable and most uncomfortable boats imaginable, so that the class, which I had started in this country, turned out one of the greatest disappointments of my life.[63]

CHAPTER 10

MEASURED SAIL AREA
Area Fore △ = .425×28×77 = 916□'
" Mainsail = .5 × 92×42 = 1932
2848
Detail #3
Detail #4
Detail #5
Detail #6
Detail #7
Detail #11
Detail #12
Detail #13
Detail #2
2080□' actual area including roach
Total 3205□'
Try Sail Reef
Mainsail Reef
Spinaker Head Board not More Than 3"
Spinaker Pole 28' to ℄ of Mast
B=42'
J=28'
Scale ¼"=1'
Nº 34
SAIL PLAN - CLASS M YACHT
L. FRANCIS HERRESHOFF, Designer
Marblehead, Mass.
Sept 25 1928

THE ISTALENA

Istalena was…capable of slightly faster average speed than the other yachts of her class.

—L. FRANCIS HERRESHOFF, 1944

George Mallory Pynchon, head of a prominent New York brokerage house, had been a yachtsman for many of his sixty-six years. He lived on Long Island Sound in Greenwich, Connecticut, was a member of the New York Yacht Club, and had been a faithful customer of Nathanael G. Herreshoff and the Herreshoff Manufacturing Company. Each time the Wizard of Bristol came out with a new one-design racer for the Club, Pynchon had to have one. He raced in the 30-, 40-, and 50-foot classes (waterline lengths). His *Istalena* was one of the three Herreshoff 65-footers that had come out in 1907, and with her he had won the King's Cup in 1909 and the Astor Cup in 1912. He had last raced, in his New York 50, another *Istalena*, in 1922. Now, in 1928, he wanted a big boat to race for the 1929 season in the Universal Rule's Class M, in which there was growing interest on the Sound.[1]

Nathanael was, for the most part, retired, but the Herreshoff Manufacturing Company had been brought back to life by Rudolph Haffenreffer and his sons Carl and Rudolph III, so Pynchon naturally wanted his new boat built at Bristol. He hoped he could persuade Nathanael at least to cast his experienced eye on the project. For a designer, he turned to Nathanael's son, Francis; after all, Francis had designed three R-boats, including the champion racer *Yankee,* to the Universal Rule. Evidently, the *Live Yankee*'s unconventional design didn't bother Pynchon. He may or may not have been aware of Francis's two previous abortive designs for M-boats or of his designs for two Q-boats. Francis credited the *Yankee*'s success with bringing him the commission to design an M-boat for George Pynchon.[2]

The M Class in 1929 would consist of seven yachts. Starling Burgess was the designer of four of them. Two, like Pynchon's boat, would be launched for the new season. The other two Burgess boats were already racing, one of them being Harold Vanderbilt's *Prestige*, the boat to beat in the class. Then there was a Herreshoff New York 50 with a Marconi rig, rated at 46 feet under the Universal Rule. And Charles D. Mower was designing an M-boat for 1929 for Junius Morgan, the yachtsman who had been "scared off" by Francis's innovative M-boat design, his No. 31.[3]

For his M-boat, Pynchon again used the name *Istalena*, a North American Indian word for the water lily. To Francis, it was one of those tiresome names that needed always to be explained. As he set to work on the design in August 1928, he heard from Nathanael that Pynchon was "very enthusiastic" about the new boat. It must have been heartening for Francis to be designing a large racing yacht that would actually be built and tested on the racecourse. It was also doubtless encouraging to him to be working toward a substantial commission. He would earn $5,000 for designing the *Istalena*, a considerable sum in the late twenties.[4]

As we have seen, Francis had already drawn the lines of two M-boats that weren't built, his No. 22 in the spring of 1927, and No. 31 in the spring of 1928. Both had been double-enders, and Francis again chose the pointed stern that he liked so much for the *Istalena*. He wrote, "Some of the advantages of a double-ender are that the construction at the stern is as easy as it is at the bow, and it stays in shape, does not leak or rot; it is cheaper and lighter

ABOVE: George Mallory Pynchon, who commissioned Francis to design a new Class-M racer for the 1929 season. Pynchon and Company was a Wall Street stock and bond brokerage firm. Pynchon had owned and raced three large one-design racing boats designed and built by Francis's father, so, with Nathanael Herreshoff retired, Pynchon turned to a Herreshoff son for his next boat. The new *Istalena* would be raced by an experienced skipper. (© Mystic Seaport, Rosenfeld Collection, 1984.187.35522F)

and double-enders are good sea boats as a narrow stern lets the bow raise to meet a sea." He might have added that the narrow stern depresses the bow less in a following sea. He did add that "she does very well in a seaway as her bow is just flat enough to prevent her from pitching deeply." The *Istalena*'s flattish bow, encouraged by the Universal Rule, was an enlarged version of the bow of the *Yankee*. Francis drew the *Istalena*'s sections with the wineglass shape of No. 31, not the elongated triangle of No. 22. George Pynchon would get essentially the M-boat that Junius Morgan would have raced had he decided to build to Francis's design No. 31.[5]

Nathanael involved himself with Francis and Pynchon carefully and tactfully. In mid-August 1928, he offered to make a half model of the *Istalena* from Francis's lines, a model that Pynchon wanted for the New York Yacht Club's display room. Francis accepted the offer, writing, "It may, however, be one or two weeks before I get the lines out as I have here some other work in hand now." The other work in hand, as we have seen, was on Charlie Welch's *Walrus*, the Development Class, a new rig for the big schooner *Speejacks*, and, particularly, work on the Q-boat *Questa*. Three weeks went by, and Nathanael, growing impatient, wrote to Francis urging him to get on with it. But his letter crossed one from Francis announcing that the *Istalena*'s lines were all worked out and being traced. A week later, Pynchon had seen the blueprint and proposed to Nathanael that they meet with Francis at the Herreshoff yard office in Bristol to go over the yacht's lines. Francis must have bristled at this, but he was probably also glad to have his father involved. The last thing he wanted at this point was another owner getting cold feet.[6]

The meeting took place on October 3, 1928. Would that we had a record of it. We know that changes were made, because a new lines drawing was completed on October 11. We can assume that the changes were minor; the lines are obviously Francis's work, but it would be fascinating to know what Pynchon may have proposed and what role Nathanael may have played as instigator or mediator. In any event, the meeting seems to have gone well from Francis's point of view: he wrote to his father: "I enjoyed very much the few hours I spent with you." Nathanael had already made the half model from Francis's original lines, having it all shellacked four and a half days after receiving the blueprint, but, inadvertently, he had made it for the port side, whereas the New York Yacht Club wanted it starboard-side to be consistent in its collection. Now Nathanael made a starboard-side model to reflect the changes. An indication that the modifications agreed to on October 3 were minor is that Pynchon kept the port-side model to hang on his own wall.[7]

And Nathanael had an afterthought: he suggested extending the flat keel forward a bit to make the boat easier to haul out, "losing nothing in performance." Francis liked the idea, and the change was made on the lofting floor and on both of Nathanael's models. Nathanael wrote to Francis: "I want to congratulate you on the sweetness of the present form. I believe it is a model that will be hard to beat." L. Francis Herreshoff was now, indeed, his father's chosen son.[8]

Under the Herreshoff Manufacturing Company's contract No. 1131, the yard was to deliver the *Istalena*, ready to sail, by April 15, 1929, for $50,000. The document added: "Upon completion of this yacht a trial under sail will be made to demonstrate that spars and rigging are complete and in proper working order." Nathanael warned Francis that he would have to hustle to produce drawings without delay after the contract was signed so the shops could meet the deadline.[9]

As work on the yacht started in Bristol, Nathanael wrote to Francis: "as I have just written to Mr. Pynchon, I will be glad to act as your and his agent to repeat your instructions or report progress, but I will not direct without your advice and word. The design must be entirely yours. Of

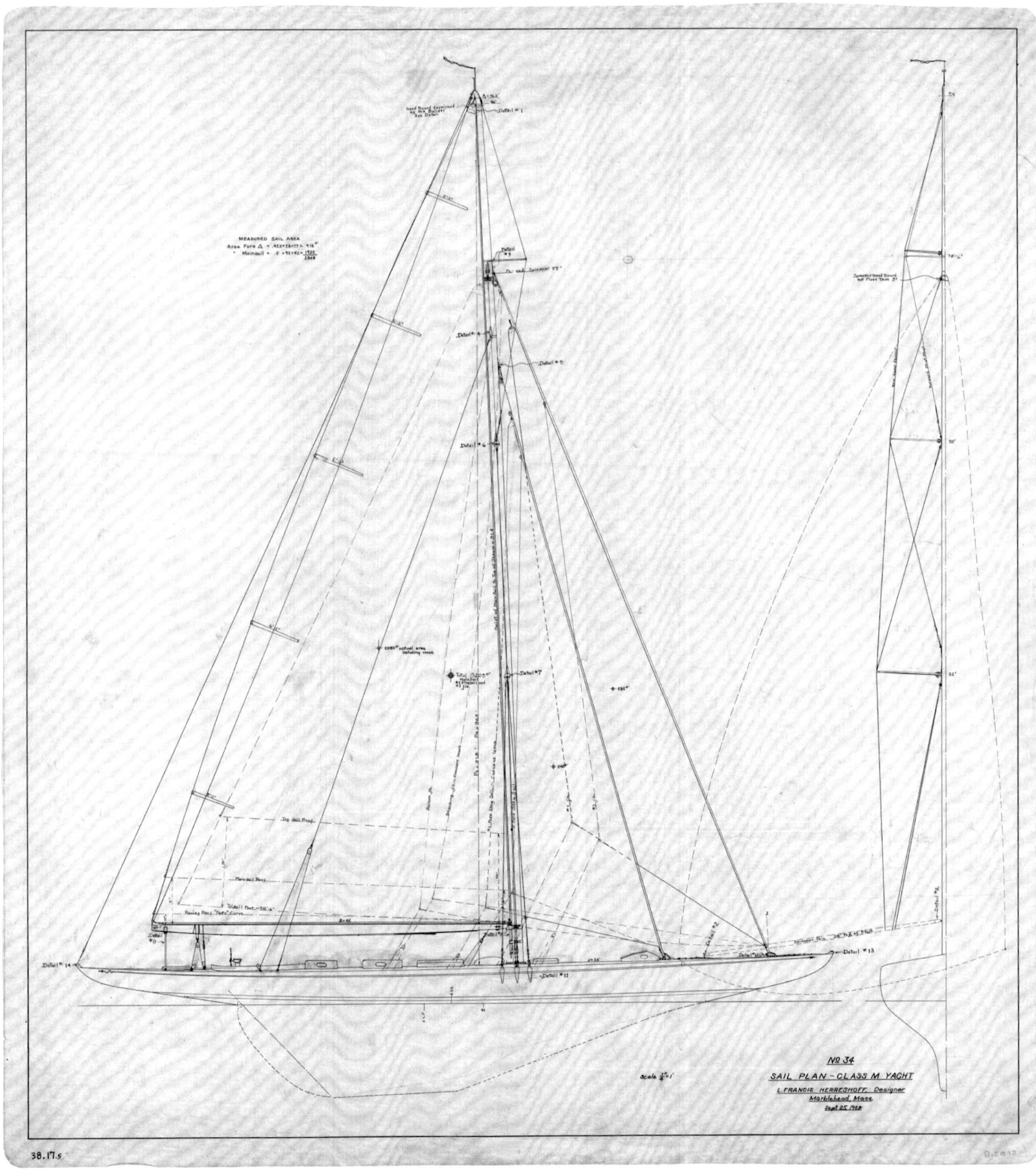
No 34
SAIL PLAN - CLASS M YACHT
L. FRANCIS HERRESHOFF, Designer
Marblehead, Mass.
Scale 1/4" = 1'
MEASURED SAIL AREA

course I will be glad to advise when asked to." As Francis worked out the details of the *Istalena*'s design, he did ask for his father's advice. He sent many of the drawings to Nathanael for comment and got back suggestions, some of which he accepted and some of which he rejected, tactfully, explaining his reasons.[10]

Along with Nathanael's clear statement of his role in the project, he made his first report: "They are laying down the lines of the M and they come very nice indeed and fair-up almost exactly to the figures given in table of offsets." In addition to his father's reports, Francis had another advantage: he knew many of the men who were building the *Istalena*. Peter Gasper, a man whom Francis liked and respected, lofted her lines. But Francis thought that Construction Superintendent Charles Nystrom, an experienced hand at the Herreshoff yard, was overstepping his authority. On his own inspection trip to Bristol on November 22, Francis discovered that Nystrom was making changes to construction details, some at the suggestion of Lloyd's Inspector Bennett and others on his own.[11]

IN JANUARY 1928, the New York Yacht Club had adopted new scantling rules for the construction of racing yachts. The American Bureau of Shipping (ABS), expert at supervising the construction of large, steel merchant vessels, had written the rules at the request of the Club and of the North American Yacht Racing Union. Francis had seen the new scantling rules before they went into force, and he wrote, "in general they describe how a yacht was built thirty or forty years ago." The *Istalena* was one of the first boats built to the new rules. Certification that she adhered to them would have to be obtained from the inspectors of both Lloyd's, the huge British marine insurance firm, and the ABS. As George Pynchon's yacht began to go together at the Herreshoff yard, the Lloyd's

LEFT: The *Istalena*'s sail plan. Francis claimed that the *Istalena* was the first racing yacht with the double-head rig and nearly parallel headstays, but, in fact, that distinction belonged to the *Prestige*, the M-boat of 1927 designed by Starling Burgess. It is true that at about the time Starling was designing the *Prestige*, Francis was drawing his proposed, modernistic M-boat, his design No. 22, with not only a double-head rig, but also a forestaysail set on a luff spar and a quadrilateral jib, but that design was not built. The *Istalena*'s mainsail has an area of 2,080 square feet. The total sail area, with the full-sized working jib and forestaysail, is 3,205 square feet. Measured sail area under the Universal Rule is 2,848 square feet. Note the curved "racing reef" in the mainsail, from nothing at the tack to 12 inches at the clew, more to flatten the sail in a breeze than to reduce it; and see the hatch just forward of the mast, for hoisting the spinnaker from below. Because the *Istalena* was to be built in Bristol at the Herreshoff Manufacturing Company, Francis felt he could be less painstaking than usual with her specifications. For standing rigging to support her hollow, wooden, 106-foot mast, he gave a choice of either Extra-Galvanized Plough Steel wire or 1x19 Airplane Wire Rope. Of her fittings, 152—including her steering gear, anchors, and some of her winches—were made from standard Herreshoff Manufacturing Company patterns, the sizes to be selected by his brother Sidney, as Francis didn't know the yard's pattern numbers. But Francis did design many special fittings for the *Istalena*. She has his folding metal boom crutch, "always ready for immediate use and can never get adrift," for which he provided a separate detailed drawing. She had a new type of turnbuckle that Francis designed, with a single fine-threaded adjustment bar in the center instead of the usual barrel, these to be made, not of bronze, as were the Herreshoff Company's turnbuckles, but of galvanized nickel steel, for extra strength. She had specially designed fittings on the foredeck for adjusting the stays and tacks of both jib and staysail, and a threaded tightener for the permanent backstay. Francis drew a beautifully curved bow chock for the anchor chain or towline. The men who built the *Istalena* in Bristol had fifty-eight of his drawings to work from. (© Mystic Seaport, Daniel S. Gregory Ships Plans Library, SP38.17.5)

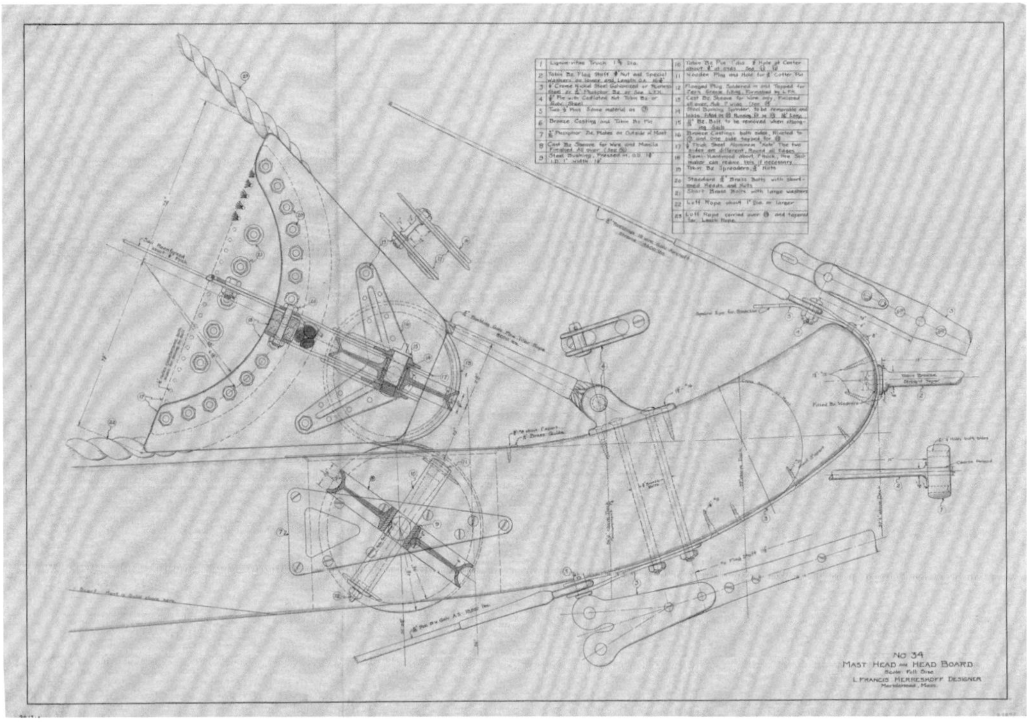

ABOVE: **This drawing shows details of the *Istalena*'s masthead and mainsail headboard. He used a similar arrangement on the Q-boat *Questa*, but with a straight masthead. The wire main halyard dead-ends on the curved masthead, runs through the single sheave in the headboard, up over the single sheave in the mast, and down outside the forward side of the mast to Francis's winch, which hoisted the big sail with the two-part halyard. The halyard was to be of 7/8-inch galvanized plow-steel, tiller rope, made by Roebling (he of the Brooklyn Bridge), with a breaking strain of 8,200 pounds. Crowning this elegant masthead, Francis placed a carefully designed, 16-3/4-inch, tapered bronze flagstaff. When Nathanael saw this drawing, he wrote to Francis that with the *Istalena* sailing off the wind, his masthead design would put a "terrible twisting strain on the sailhead fitting." Francis calmly replied that it would be all right, and it was.** (© Mystic Seaport, Daniel S. Gregory Ships Plans Library, SP38.17.14) RIGHT: **The *Istalena*'s revised cabin plan. Francis's original drawing lacked a private double stateroom and a separate cabin for the yacht's captain, so, within three weeks, the owner intervened, with this result. Pynchon even got a "Wheeling combination bath" and two additional crew berths, and the crew now had a water closet. (The spinnaker would be set from the passage between the captain's room and the crew's head.) Many of Francis's cabin plans would have been improved by such editing. Nonetheless, Francis was given free rein with the yacht's interior decoration, and he had fun. "Below deck *Istalena* is nearly as novel as on deck," he wrote, "for most of her partitions and bulkheads are made of thin plain laminated wood panels [later called plywood] and covered with figured fabrics. This was done for lightness and to get away from that so fixed style which Queen Victoria invented and most all designers still copy. . . . in the main salon the motif is old Canton China with its ivory white background and its light and dark blue figures. In this room the partitions are covered with toile de Jouey with a blue Chinese nautical pattern which matches the china, which can be seen through the leaded glass of the buffets. The moldings and trim of the woodwork is Chinese in pattern and painted light blue, while the upholstery and carpet are dark blue, all giving a pleasing and nautical effect." Francis provided this description to English yacht designer Uffa Fox for his annual book of yacht designs in 1935, which was to include the *Istalena*. Fox used much of it verbatim without attribution.** (© Mystic Seaport, Daniel S. Gregory Ships Plans Library, SP38.17.7)

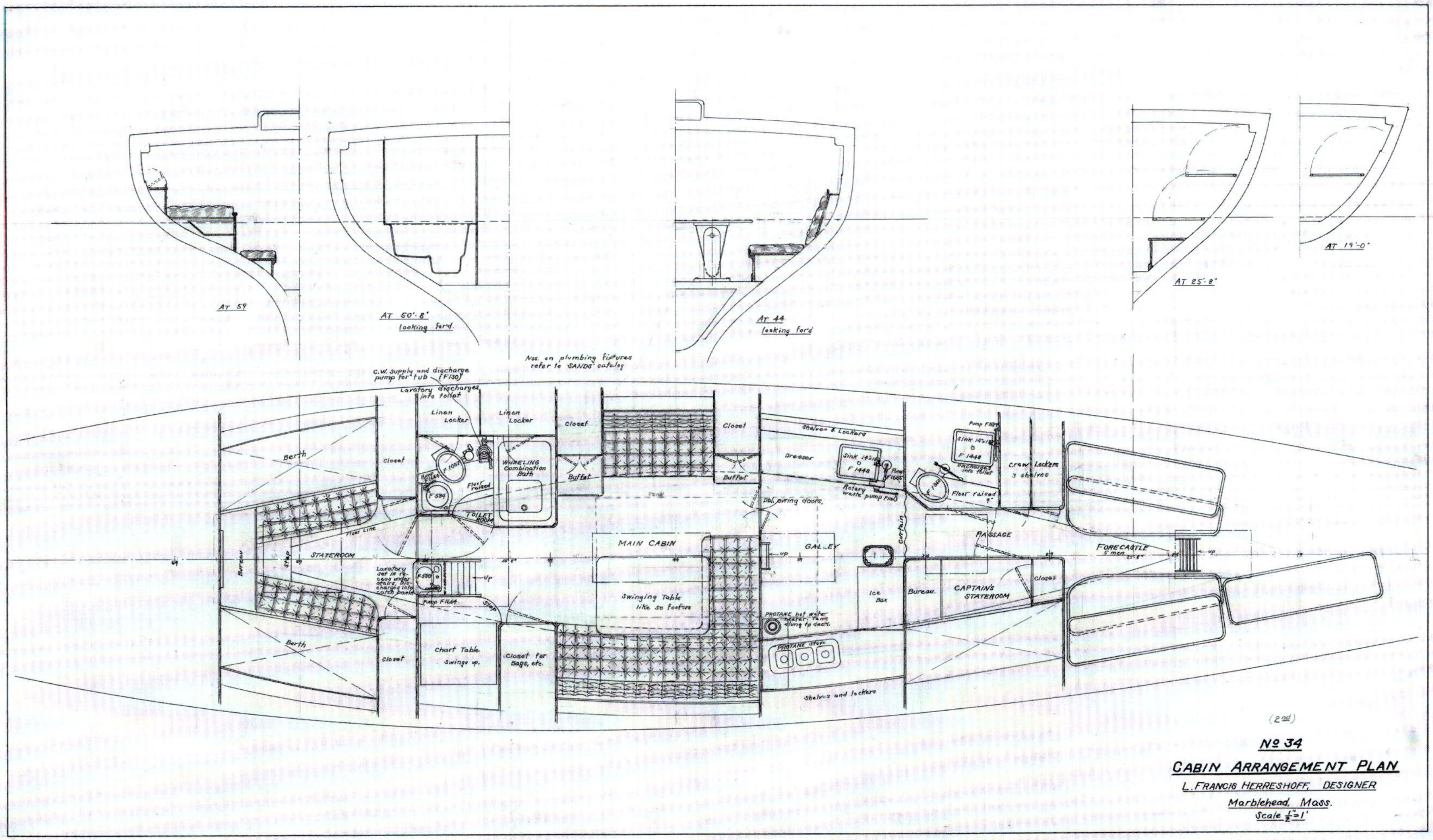
AT 59
AT 50' 8"
looking ford.
AT 44
looking ford
AT 25' 8"
AT 19'-0"
Nos. on plumbing fixtures refer to SANDS catalog
C.W. supply and discharge pump for tub (F130)
Lavatory discharges into toilet
Linen Locker
Linen Locker
Closet
WHEELING Combination Bath
Buffet
Closet
Buffet
Shelves & Lockers
Dresser
Berth
Closet
Floor raised
TOILET ROOM
Dbl. swing doors
STATEROOM
MAIN CABIN
GALLEY
Swinging Table like so fashion
Chart Table swings up.
Closet for Bags, etc.
Berth
Closet
Bureau
Ice Box
Bureau
CAPTAINS STATEROOM
PASSAGE
FORECASTLE
Crew Lockers 3 shelves
Floor raised
Rotary waste pump
curtain
Closet
PROPANE STOVE
Shelves and lockers
(2nd)
Nº 34
CABIN ARRANGEMENT PLAN
L. FRANCIS HERRESHOFF, DESIGNER
Marblehead, Mass.
Scale 1/2" = 1'

men were still studying the new rules and indicated that they could not yet approve or disapprove construction under them (though they could evidently suggest changes), and the ABS inspectors were, in Francis's opinion, totally ignorant of the construction of racing sailboats. Pynchon was in a hurry. Nathanael was sympathetic but was in no position of authority to break the log jam. Francis was in no way inclined to confront the situation by arguing with inspectors himself. In the end, it was Pynchon who forced the issue with Lloyd's. Dealing with the ABS would continue to be troublesome. Francis would later write: "scantling rules . . . are the *bete noir* of designing in the larger classes."[12]

In December, Nathanael wrote to Francis: "Have you figured out the easiest way to lighten the lead in case the boat goes too deep in the water? I am a little fearful of it." Francis wasn't fearful. He looked at the situation, thought it was all right, and replied to his father that if necessary, a slice could simply be cut off the keel. This was actually done after a few trial sails, for the owner thought that lightening the boat would make her faster, but at the end of her first season, the lead removed was replaced, at considerable expense, which Francis said "amused" him.[13]

At the same time, Nathanael sent to Francis his own scantling specifications for matching fastening sizes to various thicknesses of planking and explained his engineering reasons for them. Francis replied, "# 24 looks o.k. on the 'M' boat, but # 18 looks too large on the 'Q' boat." Here is the perfect example of Nathanael's engineering by formula set against Francis's engineering by eye.[14]

On December 18, Francis wrote to his father that he was having a hard time designing the connection of the rudder to the rudderpost. Four days later, Nathanael sent Francis a drawing of how to do it with the engineering explanation of why it would work. But by then Francis had devised his own solution, "not as good as the sketch you sent me," but all done and with the advantage that the rudder blade could be taken off without removing the rudderpost. Nathanael, by this time in Florida for the rest of the winter, examined Francis's rudder design and thought he could improve on the lower pintle that held the bottom of the rudder to the deadwood. Francis agreed with his father's suggestion, made a drawing of it, and sent it to Bristol with a note on the plan for the builders to get details checked by Sidney.[15]

In mid-January, Francis wrote to his father that he had been to Bristol to see how the *Istalena* was coming and reported that he was pleased with what he found. The yacht's frames were all set up and were fair without any planing and the hull was planked to six feet above the garboard. George "Sonny" Hodgdon, another builder whom Francis respected, was in charge of the planking. Hodgdon talked Francis into planking the M-boat single, instead of double, up to the waterline aft, because the bends were so sharp. A month later, Francis could report to his father: "She is all planked up and is a very nice job and looks extremely strong and fair. The scantlings are certainly sufficient to insure a boat that should hold her shape for some time." The ABS had beefed up some of Francis's just-strong-enough, intuitive engineering.[16]

For the *Istalena*'s tender, Francis chose the pram type. He had rowed one in rough water in the Solent in 1921 when racing in England and had been most impressed with her seaworthiness. He wrote in 1957 that this boat "was the one that started the rage in this country for pram dinghies." At any rate, sailors caught on that a short pram could carry safely the same load as a longer dinghy of the day. This one is 8 feet, 3-1/2- inches long, with a beam of 3 feet, 10-1/2-inches. She could carry 720 pounds with 6 inches of freeboard. For perfect stowage, upside down, the top edges of both transoms had concave curves to fit the crown of the *Istalena*'s deck. (© Mystic Seaport, Daniel S. Gregory Ships Plans Library, SP38.17.A.1)

OFFSET TABLE

Sta.	Heights from L.W.L. Rail	12" But.	6" But.	Rabbet	Half Breadths Rail	9" W.L.	6" W.L.	3" W.L.	L.W.L.	Rabbet
Bow	1.2.0	0.9.6+	0.7.1	0.6.6	1.2.0	0.11.0				0.0.7
1	1.1.2	0.4.1	0.2.6+	0.2.4	1.6.1+	1.5.0+	1.3.0	0.7.3		0.0.7
2	1.0.2	0.0.6	0.1.4	0.1.5+	1.9.7	1.9.4+	1.8.7+	1.7.1+	1.2.6	0.0.7
3	0.11.5+	0.1.7	0.2.3	0.2.5	1.11.0	1.11.0	1.10.5+	1.9.4	1.6.6	0.0.7
4	0.11.3	0.1.3+	0.2.0	0.2.3	1.10.3+	1.10.3+	1.10.1	1.9.4	1.6.0	0.0.7
5	0.11.4	0.0.1+	0.0.4	0.0.7+	1.8.3	1.8.2	1.7.6	1.5.7+	0.10.4+	0.0.7
Stern	1.0.1	0.3.4+	0.1.6	0.0.6	1.5.3	1.4.7+	1.3.4	0.10.5		0.0.7

Note: The Bow and Stern's upper edges are concaved to fit the crown of th deck

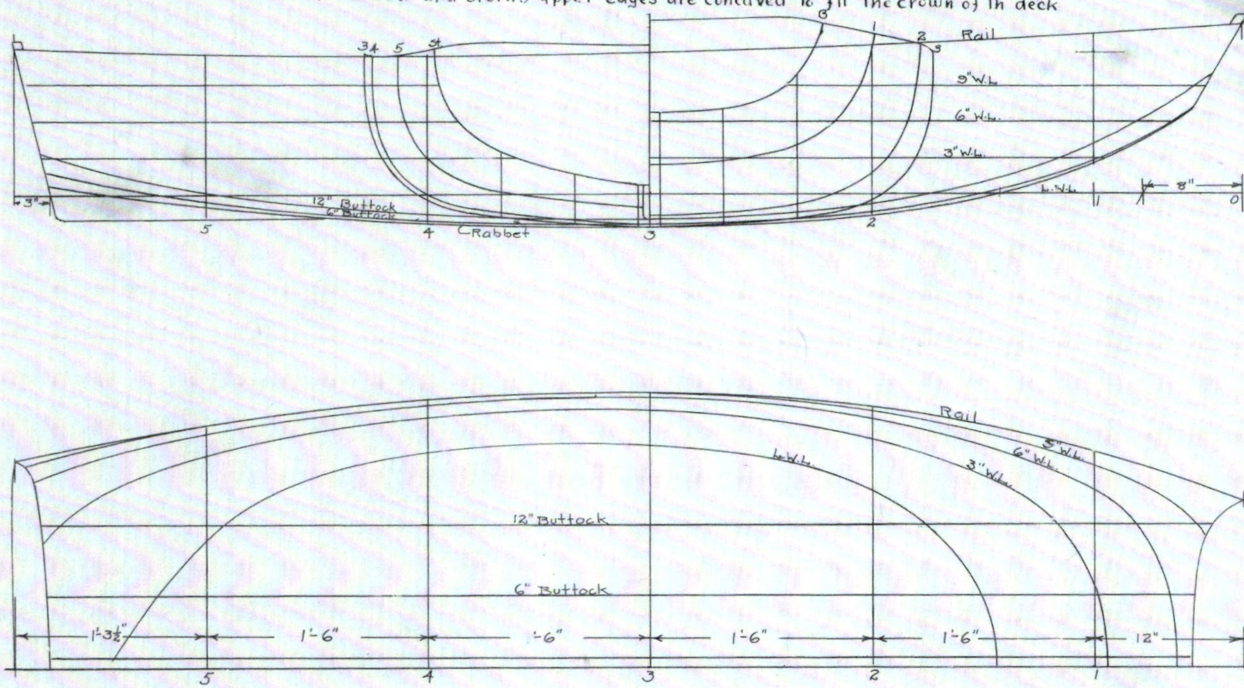

LOA 8'

No. 34
ROWBOAT
Scale: 1½" = 1'-0"
L. FRANCIS HERRESHOFF DESIGNER
Marblehead, Mass.

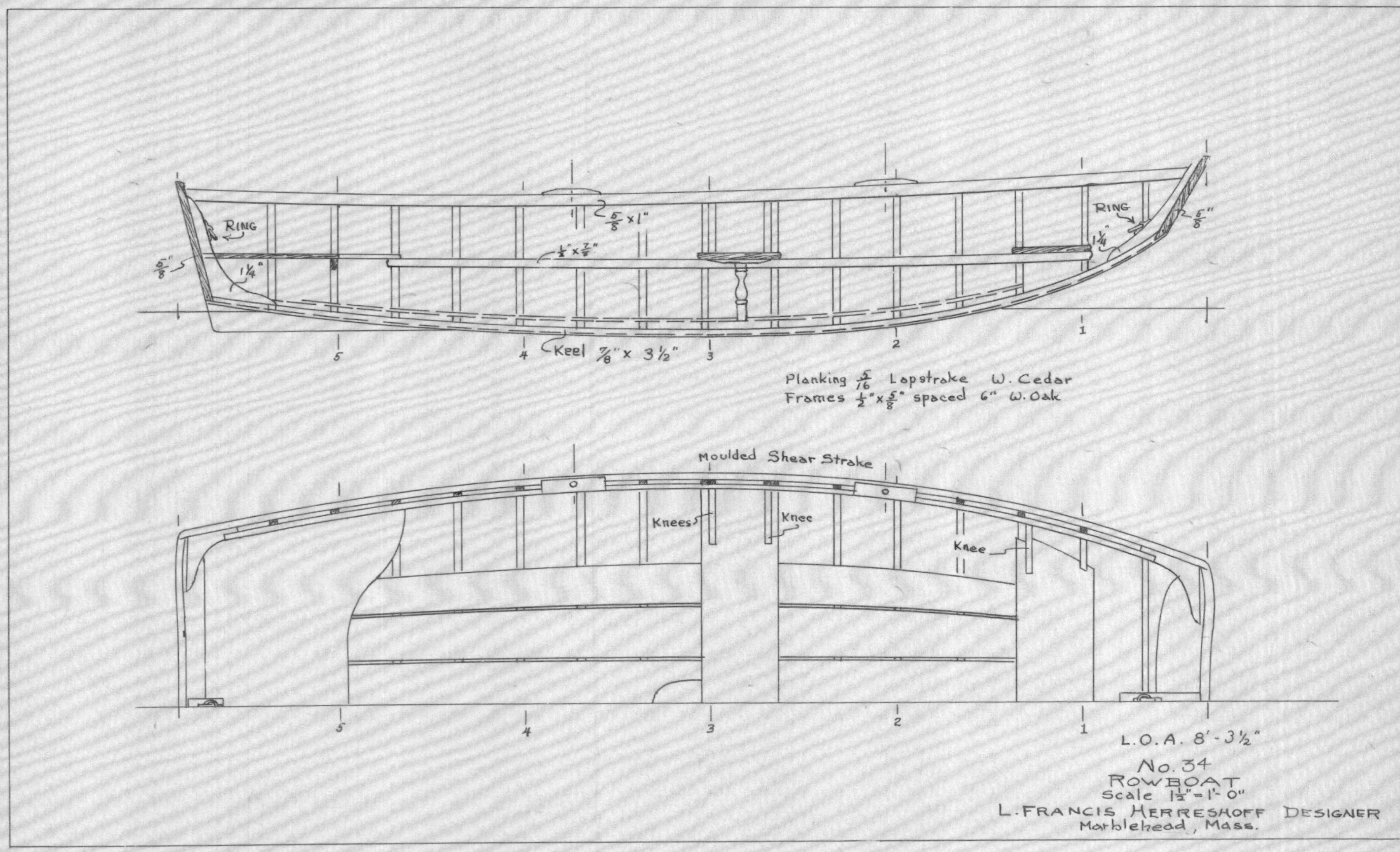
Ring
Ring
5/8 x 1"
1/2" x 7/8"
1 1/4"
1 1/4"
5/8"
5/8"
Keel 7/8" x 3 1/2"
5
4
3
2
1
Planking 5/16 Lapstrake W. Cedar
Frames 1/2" x 5/8" spaced 6" W. Oak
Moulded Shear Strake
Knees
Knee
Knee
L.O.A. 8'-3 1/2"
No. 34
ROWBOAT
Scale 1 1/2" = 1'-0"
L. FRANCIS HERRESHOFF DESIGNER
Marblehead, Mass.

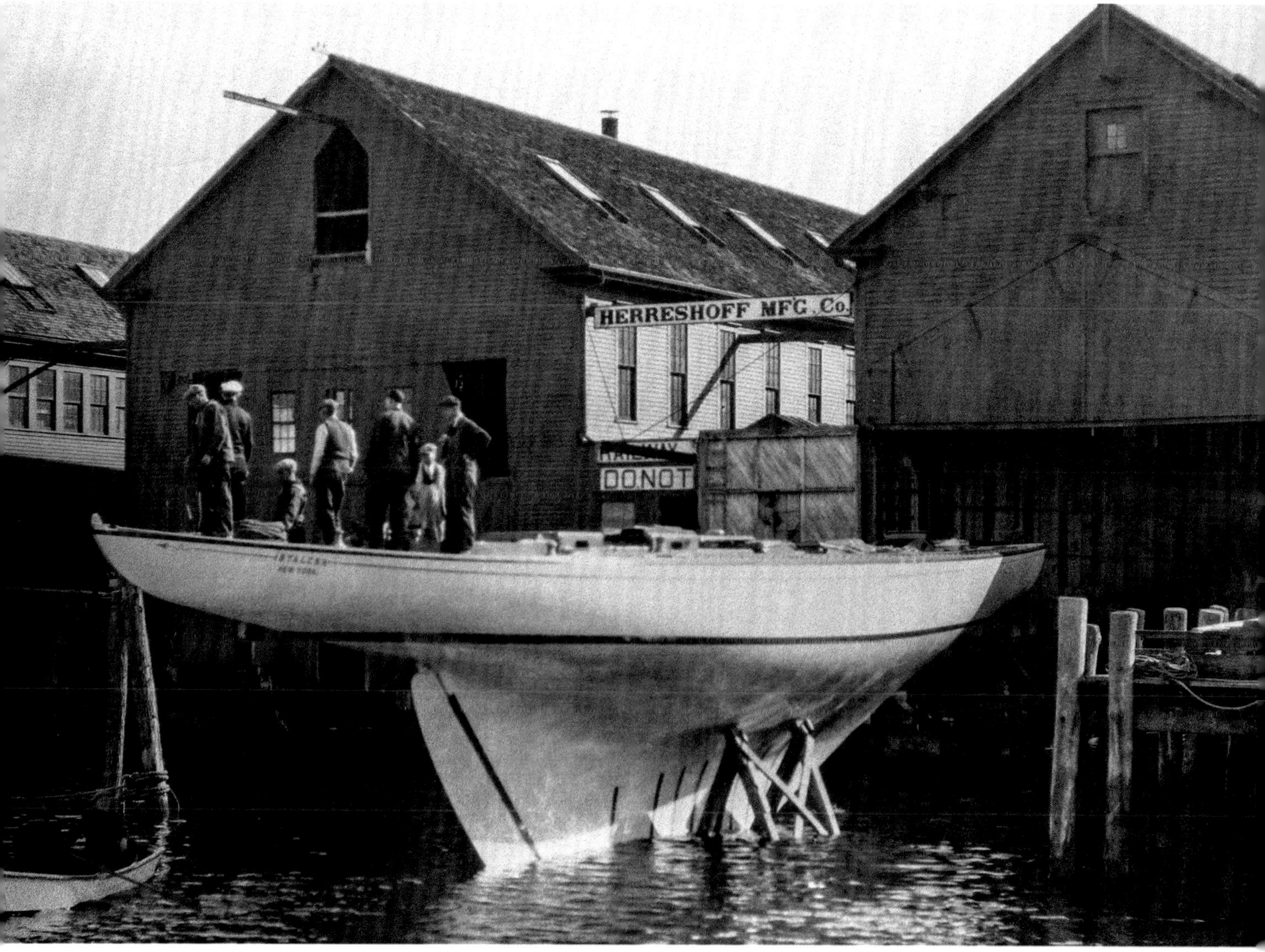

LEFT: The construction plan of the *Istalena*'s tender. She was planked lapstrake with 5/16-inch white cedar. Frames were 1/2-inch-by-5/8-inch white oak, spaced on 6-inch centers. She weighed 100 pounds. This was Francis's favorite tender design, the one he would have chosen for his own use. Fine little rowing craft are still being built to the design by discerning amateurs. This was Francis's first drawing on Mylar. Most of his finished drawings were on either the Eugene Dietegen Company's "Fulton" heavy, smooth, yellowish drawing paper from New York, or on extremely durable linen. (© Mystic Seaport, Daniel S. Gregory Ships Plans Library, SP38.17A.2) ABOVE: The *Istalena* being launched from the south construction shop at the Herreshoff Manufacturing Company in mid-May 1929. The scene looks somber for what should be a day of celebration and hope. Two weeks later, during her first race in Long Island Sound, off Rye, the big new racing yacht would be dismasted. (Probably Thomas P. Brightman photo, Herreshoff Marine Museum, Bristol, Rhode Island)

Unofficial inspection and testing was also carried out on the *Istalena*. Francis had made a design for a new type of turnbuckle for the yacht, and his brother wondered how strong they were. "Mr. Sidney" as Francis referred to him when he thought his brother was being too persnickety, "tested one of the turnbuckles spliced into the ½ [inch] 19-strand wire for the lower shrouds." And Francis went on to report to their father that the wire had failed at 28,000 pounds and the turnbuckle at 33,000. Francis wrote later, "the turnbuckles . . . are probably the strongest in the world for their weight." Philip C. Bolger, a boat designer who was a great admirer of L. Francis Herreshoff, told of testing to destruction one of these turnbuckles made in later years to Francis's design and specifications. The turnbuckle broke in the necks of the threads where the machine shop hadn't been able to cut as fine a thread as Francis had specified. Every other component of the turnbuckle showed some form of distortion. Bolger believed that if the turnbuckle could have been made exactly as designed, it would have, in his words, "vanished in a fine molecular mist like the proverbial one-hoss shay."[17]

Francis would later write to a builder of one of his designs: "As for the turnbuckles, be sure to have the diameter of the threaded part at least as big at the base of the threads as the diameter of the wire. In other words, if coarse threads are used quite a large diameter will be necessary to make the turnbuckle as strong as the wire. By the way, the turnbuckle does not have to be as strong as wire because the splice weakens the wire about 85%, and wire also depreciates and looses strength where the turnbuckles do not." The "fine molecular mist" would not have been an accident.[18]

The *Istalena*'s professional skipper, Captain Howell, insisted that the yacht's main boom be rigged with old-fashioned quarter lifts to support the boom when the sail was down. Nathanael, unaware that the quarter lifts were Howell's idea, advised Francis to change them for a single topping lift. Francis was quick to agree, and wrote to his father that he would tell Captain Howell that N. G. Herreshoff thought the boom should be supported with a single lift and "everything will be all right."[19]

The contract completion date of April 15 came and went with the *Istalena* sitting in the south construction shed of the Herreshoff yard, with considerable fitting-out work still to be done. Things were not moving so efficiently at the Herreshoff Manufacturing Company as they had when John and Nathanael were running the yard. And the sails didn't arrive from the Ratsey loft in England until the end of the month. Francis had them shipped to Marblehead, put them through customs in Boston, and drove them to Bristol. The *Istalena* was launched three weeks late.

GEORGE PYNCHON'S first day of racing in the M Class was May 31,1929. It was not a happy day on board the *Istalena*. In Long Island Sound off Rye, a strong northwester was gusting to more than strong. As the big yacht heeled to an exceptionally heavy blast, a mahogany spreader broke and a hundred feet of mast crashed overboard. There were no injuries, but doubtless plenty of disappointment and frustration. *The Rudder*'s reporter, "Davy Jones," wrote: "If her luck holds, she'll get the name of a hoodoo ship for fair."[20]

The Henry B. Nevins yard at City Island went right to work on a new mast. The spar was built to the same specifications as the original, except that the spreaders were made of Oregon pine instead of mahogany. Francis made two inspection trips to City Island and reported to Nathanael that the workmanship on the new mast was "very much better" than on the one built by the Herreshoff Manufacturing Company.[21]

Despite this setback, Pynchon was pleased with his new racing yacht. He gave Francis credit for creating a great design. The praise didn't come

The *Istalena* was always photogenic. There is no better shot of her long ends doing their work as she knifes to windward under a big jib. If the stern wave rose one foot, she would gain seven feet of speed-giving waterline length, which seems to be about what is happening here. Yet Francis wrote that when he looked at photographs of the *Istalena* sailing, he was disappointed that she didn't seem to gain as much waterline length from her overhangs as he expected she would. (Edwin Levick photo 107330, The Mariners' Museum, Newport News, Virginia; Mystic Seaport, 1949.1758)

directly to Francis, however: Francis heard of his customer's satisfaction through his father. Mentally, George Pynchon was still dealing entirely with the Herreshoff Manufacturing Company.[22]

By the time the *Istalena* got going again, she had missed the Eastern Yacht Club's cruise. And when she did meet the other M-boats on the racecourse, she was beaten by most of them. One reason was that Pynchon hadn't steered a racing boat in seven years. Moreover, the *Istalena* was his first boat with the Marconi rig. Pynchon had to adjust his thinking and reactions when beating to windward, for the new *Istalena* could point up closer to the wind than could his previous gaff-riggers. But just how much closer? Pynchon had to experiment, but Harold S. Vanderbilt, for one, already had experience with sailing a Marconi-rigged M-boat.

As he learned to sail the *Istalena*, Pynchon got no help from her designer. Unless a client of Francis's was also a good friend, like Charlie Welch or Waldo Brown, Francis was not inclined to go sailing with him. He knew that there would be differences of opinion about just how to sail the boat, and he had no taste for conflict with the owner. Nor did he need wonder about the perfor-

The *Istalena* on the wind, sometime during the 1929 racing season. Her owner, George Pynchon, has ensured that her headsails are trimmed just perfectly. (© Mystic Seaport, Rosenfeld Collection, 1984.187.34702F)

mance of one of his designs. He knew instinctively how a boat he had created should sail. By the time he finished a design, he would have traveled many miles in the boat in his imagination, and he would have stored up a bank of perceptions on her performance in many different conditions of wind and sea. Once Francis had completed the design of the *Istalena*, none of this unusual ability of his helped George Pynchon.

Nathanael chided Francis for not sailing in the *Istalena*. And he relayed to Francis that "Pynchon has great faith in you as a designer and inventor and only regrets that you didn't spend more time sailing in *Istalena* [he didn't spend any] when she first came out." As we have seen, N. G. Herreshoff had made a habit of trying out his new boats himself and often raced in them to ensure that they did their best. But Francis did not have his father's reputation. He doubted that, if he went on board the *Istalena*, he would be put in charge.[23]

Nonetheless, Pynchon began doing better. On the New York Yacht Club cruise in August, the *Istalena* came alive. The run on August 9 was thirty-four miles from New Haven, Connecticut, to Greenport, on the North Fork of Long Island, in a light southwester, which gave the racers a long reach, followed by a beat. "To the surprise of everyone," *The Rudder* reported, "*Istalena,* which has done very little in the way of winning races, ran through the entire fleet almost at once, and at the finish the only yacht ahead of her was [the much bigger] *Vanitie*." A 10-Metre won out over the *Istalena* on corrected time, but she beat all the M-boats. Pynchon then proceeded to rack up four more victories in a row over the other M-boats: on the run from Newport to Mattapoisett, in Buzzards Bay; on the return run to Newport; and in both the Astor and King's Cup races off Newport. In the next three-race series just for the M Class, however, Vanderbilt's *Prestige* scored the most points.[24]

One reason why the *Istalena* began to sail faster was that Pynchon had adopted the single-big-jib arrangement that two of the other M-boats were using successfully. So much for the double-head rig that Francis liked. Pynchon even wanted to remove the *Istalena*'s forestay, so that it would be easier to tack with a big headsail. Francis learned of this proposal from his father. By then, he had returned to his "other work." Francis put a great deal of thought into a design, and when he finished it, he considered his work on it to be complete, the best he could do. He had no interest in returning to a design to try to improve it. Francis told Nathanael to go ahead and change the *Istalena*'s rig if he wanted to, reminding him that if the forestay were removed, the support it gave the mast would have to be replaced somehow. The forestay remained, but Nathanael drew a plan for a new jib with a foot 30 feet, 6 inches long.[25]

Pynchon now decided that he wanted a new mast for the *Istalena*. He may have been worried about another dismasting, or he may have wanted a stronger mast so that the forestay could be released when racing with a single big jib. Francis did return to the project to design the new mast. Perhaps he felt guilty about the loss of the original spar. All he did, though, was add half an inch to the fore-and-aft section of the mast he had designed in the first place. Neither mast number two nor this new mast number three gave trouble.[26]

The *Istalena* continued to do well in the 1930 season. Pynchon won the Long Island Sound Championship and Larchmont Race Week in the M Class. When Clinton Crane wrote about his experience of racing a boat of his own design in Class M, he concluded: "The *Istalena* proved, when finally tuned up, the outstanding boat in the M class."[27]

After the 1930 season, with Nathanael in Florida for the winter, Pynchon's comments on the *Istalena* finally came directly to Francis. Nonetheless, son and father continued their consulting on the boat. Francis wrote to Nathanael: "Mr. Pynchon reports she steers so hard in strong breezes going to windward that he thought this was one of the causes of her not doing so well

Here she is on a close reach in a fine breeze and smooth water during the 1930 Block Island Race, with a big ballooner pulling her along at or near hull speed. But shouldn't her main sheet be eased a mite? (© Mystic Seaport, Rosenfeld Collection, 1984.187.40929F)

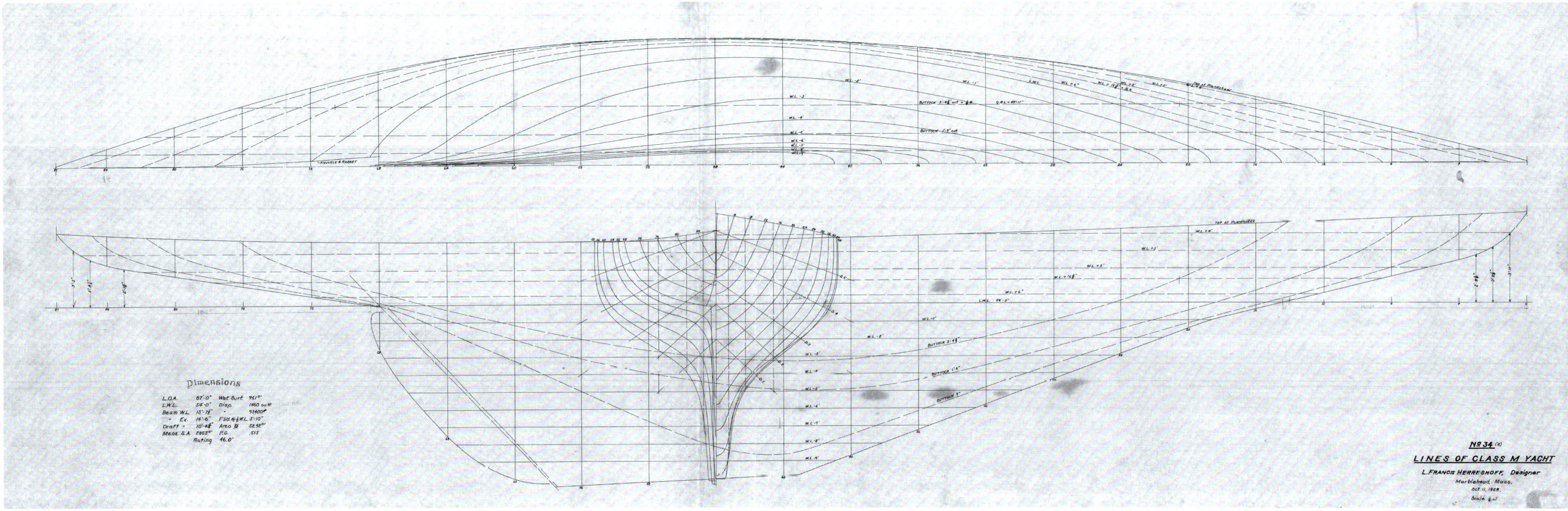

The *Istalena*'s final lines, which are much like those of his design No. 31, the M-boat that Junius Morgan shied away from. Francis believed that Pynchon trusted him to design a big, new racer not so much because he was a Herreshoff as because of the success of the R-boat *Yankee*. The *Istalena*'s lines are similar to those of the Yankee, except for the M-boat's pointed stern. We see the same wineglass midsection and the same long, knuckle bow with its snubbed-in waterlines and sections, to save waterline length. But, instead of the *Yankee*'s sweeping profile curve from the bow down to the forward end of the keel, the *Istalena* has a straight line more than 20 feet long. She is 87 feet long on deck; with a waterline length of 54 feet; a beam of 14 feet, 6 inches; and a draft of 10 feet, 5 inches. Displacement is 93,400 pounds with outside lead ballast of 50,500 pounds, for a ballast-displacement ratio of 54 percent. Because of the shape of her above-water profile, the *Istalena* earned the nickname, "The Cleat," presumably a jam cleat, not a Herreshoff cleat. Norman Skene traced Francis's lines drawing in ink in six hours on October 11, 1928. (© Mystic Seaport, Daniel S. Gregory Ships Plans Library, SP38.17.1)

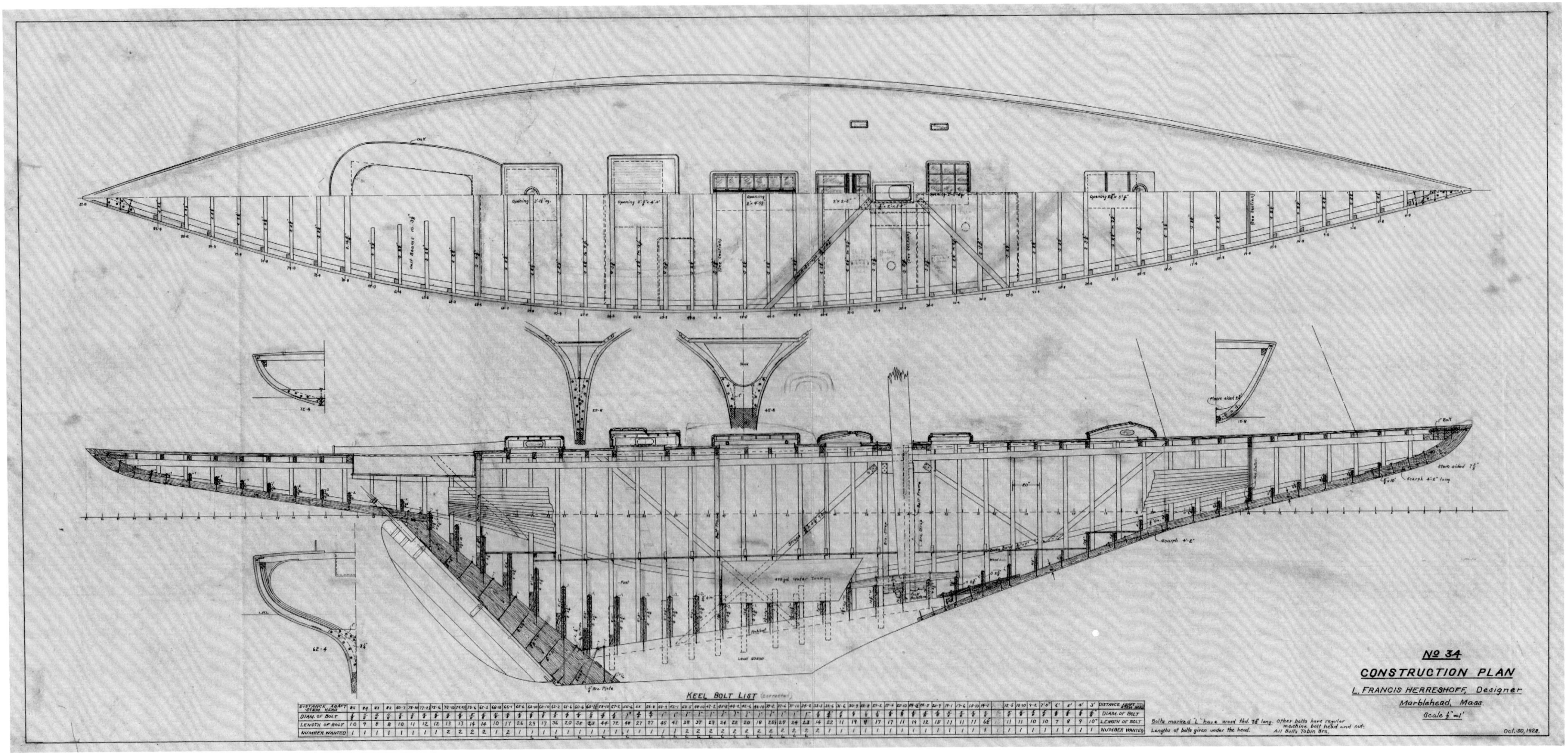

The *Istalena*'s construction plan. On a separate construction section drawing, Francis wrote, "Notice. These plans must be approved by N. G. Herreshoff and the inspector of Lloyd's or the American Bureau of shipping and signed on the blue print before used for construction. L. Francis Herreshoff." Pynchon naturally returned to the Herreshoff Manufacturing Company to have his new yacht built, and both he and Francis wanted the stamp of approval of the great N. G. Herreshoff himself before proceeding. The *Istalena* was double-planked, with California sugar pine inside and Honduras mahogany outside to a total thickness of 1-29/32 inches. The garboard planks were fastened directly to the lead keel (hardened with antimony), the method Francis had found to be successful on smaller racers. The deck was also double-planked, both layers of white pine, glued together and covered with canvas. The streamlined deck structures were of butternut or mahogany, the hatches themselves being of airplane-window celluloid. She had three extra-heavy belt frames each side, whose molded dimension was doubled by three-ply lamination and which were further strengthened by bronze straps fastened into the keel, these special frames being in way of the mast, amidships, and in way of the rudder. There was also a web frame in the bow, just forward of the waterline. Francis made much use of bronze strapping to strengthen the *Istalena*'s hull: besides the six straps use to strengthen the key frames, she had five diagonal straps on each side, let into the planking, with the two longest ones, amidships, also fastened into the keel; and two straps on each side in the deck, in way of the mast. This plan is dated October 30, 1928. (© Mystic Seaport, Daniel S. Gregory Ships Plans Library, SP38.17.3)

under these conditions." It may have been fortunate that the *Istalena* was the only M-boat that was steered with a wheel instead of a tiller.[28] Francis took this criticism so seriously that he considered a bizarre solution: two daggerboards, one on each side of the boat, toed in at a slight angle from the yacht's centerline. Only the board on the leeward side would be used. The idea of this novel arrangement was that the lee daggerboard would be like an additional rudder, set permanently to head the boat off the wind. Placed far enough aft, it would give the stern lift, so that less weather helm would be needed. Francis tried his notion on his father, adding that the daggerboard would also provide additional lateral plane to reduce leeway. Nathanael didn't think much of the scheme. He advised his son that the daggerboards would merely increase hull resistance and that the only way to reduce leeway was to deepen the keel.[29]

Pynchon was worried, because he had heard that changes were being made to the *Prestige* and to the *Valiant,* Winthrop Aldrich's Burgess-designed M-boat, at the Herreshoff Manufacturing Company. Francis went to Bristol to see what was up. Starling was deepening the keel of each of his M-boats, in effect, by adding a centerboard. And he was trying experiments with a boom as an endplate, beyond the T-section that Francis had developed, in order to capture downdraft off the mainsail. Francis was not impressed. He wrote to his father that he was trying to persuade Pynchon not to change the *Istalena.* "I am still confident that if she is maneuvered properly she will beat the other two boats. However, if Mr. Vanderbilt outmaneuvers her why she will be beaten." He doubted that the *Prestige* and *Valiant* would be faster as modified. He predicted that if their speed did improve, it would be because their owners sailed them better, but that the credit would go to the modifications.[30]

George Pynchon was not to have the pleasure of racing the *Istalena* against the modified Burgess boats. As the Great Depression worsened, his business failed in April 1931. He chartered the *Istalena* to Chandler Hovey of Boston for the 1931 season for $8,000, with an option to buy for $38,000, the charter money to apply to the purchase price. The agreement gave Hovey the right to make "minor changes and adjustments in the deck leads and rigging which the Architect and Owner also believe will increase the speed of the boat." And with Pynchon and Francis's approval, he could convert the port transom in the saloon into a double berth. We are reminded of the times by paragraph eight of the agreement: "The Charterer agrees to protect and indemnify the Owner for any loss from any consequences of the violation of the Eighteenth Amendment [Prohibition] by the Charterer or his party." Francis's reaction, when he read all this in his copy of the agreement, is unrecorded. At least, he must have been glad to know that the *Istalena* would be well sailed, for the Hovey family, for whom he had designed the 30-Square-Metre *Oriole II*, were good sailors. The young Sis Hovey, who had had the pleasure of racing two exquisite double-ended 30-Squares designed by L. Francis Herreshoff, must have been thrilled by the prospect of steering his magnificent, 87-foot double-ender.[31]

With Sis at the wheel, the *Istalena* cleaned up in 1931. The Hoveys arranged for a race for Class M at Marblehead in July. Nathanael had sent Francis a good pair of binoculars, and Francis wrote to thank him: "From the upper window of my place [20 Lee Street] I can see a great many yachts, including *Istalena*, and to have some powerful glasses to look things over is very useful." Francis would have taken his new binoculars and gone out to see how the *Istalena* did in the race, particularly against the modified *Prestige* and *Valiant.* He could report to Nathanael that the changes didn't seem to help them. The *Istalena* won.[32]

She also won the William H. Vanderbilt Cup for Class M in a Narragansett Bay regatta. And off Newport, she won both the King's Cup and the Astor Cup. In the latter race, Sis Hovey

Elizabeth "Sis" Hovey steering the *Istalena* to windward. Her father, Chandler Hovey of Boston, chartered the yacht for the 1931 season and turned the wheel over to his teenaged daughter, already a seasoned racing skipper in smaller boats. When Nathanael wrote his congratulations to Francis on the *Istalena*'s success that summer, he also congratulated Miss Hovey, and commented, "I always thought I did my best handling of sailing yachts when in my teens." (© Mystic Seaport, Rosenfeld Collection, 1984.187.48069F)

sailed the graceful double-ender to victory around the thirty-eight-and-a-half-mile triangle in a moderate breeze to beat thirteen of the best racing sloops in the country. The *Istalena* saved her time on Nathanael's America's Cup defender *Resolute* and on the great *Vanitie*, designed by William Gardner and sailed by Secretary of the Navy Charles Francis Adams, the dean of New England racing skippers. Sis Hovey made *Time* magazine. And Francis won indirect affection from his father. Nathanael wrote to him, "I have been very much pleased at *Istalena's* success."[33]

Pynchon was unable to sell the *Istalena* until 1934, when William J. Strawbridge, of the Philadelphia department store, bought her. Strawbridge raced her successfully on Long Island Sound that summer, out of Greenwich, Connecticut. Nathanael, noting her success under a new owner, wrote to Francis: "It has been gratifying to me that *Istalena* is doing so well and it shows the ability of the boat." But what was more important than Strawbridge's winning races was that sailing the *Istalena* made him a devotee of L. Francis Herreshoff. He would become an important customer to Francis, as well as a good friend.[34]

The next year, Strawbridge sold the yacht to Reginald B. Lanier, and her hailing port became Newport. By 1941, the Sparkman and Stephens yacht brokerage had sold *Istalena* to an owner on the Great Lakes. From their quarters near the New York Yacht Club, Sparkman and Stephens combined a thriving yacht brokerage under Drake Sparkman with a top yacht design office under Olin J. Stephens. Nineteen years younger than Francis, Olin Stephens became a yachting celebrity at twenty-two when his seventh design, the yawl *Dorade*, won the 1931 Transatlantic and Fastnet Races. While Francis dreamed up innovative boats in Marblehead, it was Olin Stephens and his brother Rod who got a ticker-tape parade on Broadway when their *Dorade* did so well in 1931. It was Olin Stephens who helped Starling Burgess design the J-Class America's Cup defender *Ranger* in 1937. Francis received no such honors for his exquisite, artistic work. The contrast made him paranoid about Stephens and the New York yachting scene. He later wrote: "Then to remove her [the *Istalena*] from the Atlantic seaboard, the Sparkman and Stevens Company sold her to the Great Lakes, and designed a poor sail plan for her, apparently to hamstring her permanently."[35]

The *Istalena* was one of only two big-class racing yachts that L. Francis Herreshoff designed. As we shall soon see, she was the only successful one. As such, she may be considered one of the pinnacles of his career. His own words are her best epitaph: "*Istalena* was a fine, quiet and dry sea boat when jogging under a trysail in a lop of a sea, and still capable of slightly faster average speed than the other yachts in her class."[36]

THE BUILDING of the *Istalena* at the Herreshoff Manufacturing Company in Bristol in 1929 brought Francis into more than the usual contact with his father and also with his brother Sidney. Francis made at least seven trips to Bristol in connection with Pynchon's yacht. He wrote to Nathanael in Florida: "Mr. Sidney was feeling quite cheerful yesterday and showed Mr. Welch and myself a new electrically driven lathe he has purchased for himself." And Francis expressed concern about his brother's eyesight: "Some one [not I] should see that he has his eyes examined soon." He even went on to suggest to his father that Sidney's "sluggish elimination" might cause him rheumatism. During this time Sidney made a rare visit to Francis in Marblehead. Such personal concerns would not have been raised between the shy brothers. They might have spoken about the *Istalena,* or about a power craft being designed by Sidney, or about one of the few sailing yachts that their father was still designing in retirement. They would certainly not have mentioned Sidney's relationship with Rebecca Chase, whom he would marry the next year.[37]

"For something to do," Nathanael made up a baker's dozen of small T-squares that he thought would be useful for sketching out ideas for boats on pads. He kept a pair for himself, gave a pair to his friend Ralph Munroe, and sent a pair to each of his four sons. Francis and Sidney could certainly use them, and they might also be helpful to Griswold and Clarence.[38]

In the spring of 1927, Griswold had left his engineering job in New Jersey to go to work for the Chrysler Corporation in Detroit. He lived on the water in nearby Grosse Point. In September 1929, Nathanael told Francis of Griswold's promotion to "Director of all Truck and Buss Construction in the Chrysler Works, which is very nice indeed." Clarence, who had started his drafting career at the Herreshoff Manufacturing Company working on plans for yachts, had changed over to big-ship work. He left his job at the Fall River Shipyard in 1929 to work in the Hull Department of the Marine Engineering Corporation in Philadelphia. Clarence, like Francis, enjoyed kayaking. He had built himself a small kayak that he had used on Narragansett Bay. In Philadelphia, he had a folding kayak from Germany that he would take to paddling sites by train on weekends. Nathanael used Francis's and Clarence's mutual interest in kayaking to try to bring them together, at least by mail. And he succeeded, somewhat, for Francis did send Clarence photographs of his own kayaks.[39]

Clarence soon moved on to a brief stint with the Newport News Shipbuilding and Drydock Company in Virginia. In 1930, he was laid off as work dried up due to the Great Depression. He returned to Love Rocks in Bristol and, after the long separation from his mentally unbalanced wife, he divorced her in 1931. Now in his mid-thirties, Clarence experienced three years of unemployment, for even at the Herreshoff yard there was no work for him.[40]

Francis and his father were now in continual contact about both professional and personal matters. Francis had a "standing order" from Robert Myer, the son of a Herreshoff Manufacturing Company customer, to design him a catamaran. Expecting to draw the boat in the summer of 1929, Francis asked Nathanael for ideas, but nothing came of the project. Nathanael's wife, Ann, sent Francis papaya candy from Florida, and Francis, sensitive to his independence, dispatched $2.00 in return. Nathanael replied: "Just let us know when you want more, don't bother about sending any money." The candy kept coming with no further payment. Francis reported that he liked its boxes: "very nice to keep small tools in."[41]

As he approached forty, Francis was beginning to wear glasses. There was no question of the blindness that had affected the previous generation of Herreshoffs, although the fear that the cause might be hereditary must have crossed his mind. He wrote to his father, "I use glasses on all work close to, and although I could see all right it takes some strain off of my nerves." He wore glasses for reading as well as for working at his drafting board. Despite his dyslexia, Francis was a great reader. He read slowly, with great concentration, in part a pace forced upon him by the dyslexia. His bachelorhood provided him with the undisturbed time that he valued for examining a book. The extensive library that he was acquiring was well thumbed and included many of the classics of literature, along with a large collection on maritime technology, history, and art. And along with vision, there was always the business of digestion to be discussed in those days. "I have found a rest before eating has helped me more than anything," Francis reported to Nathanael, "but one must take his mind off his work to get complete rest or change.

CHAPTER 11

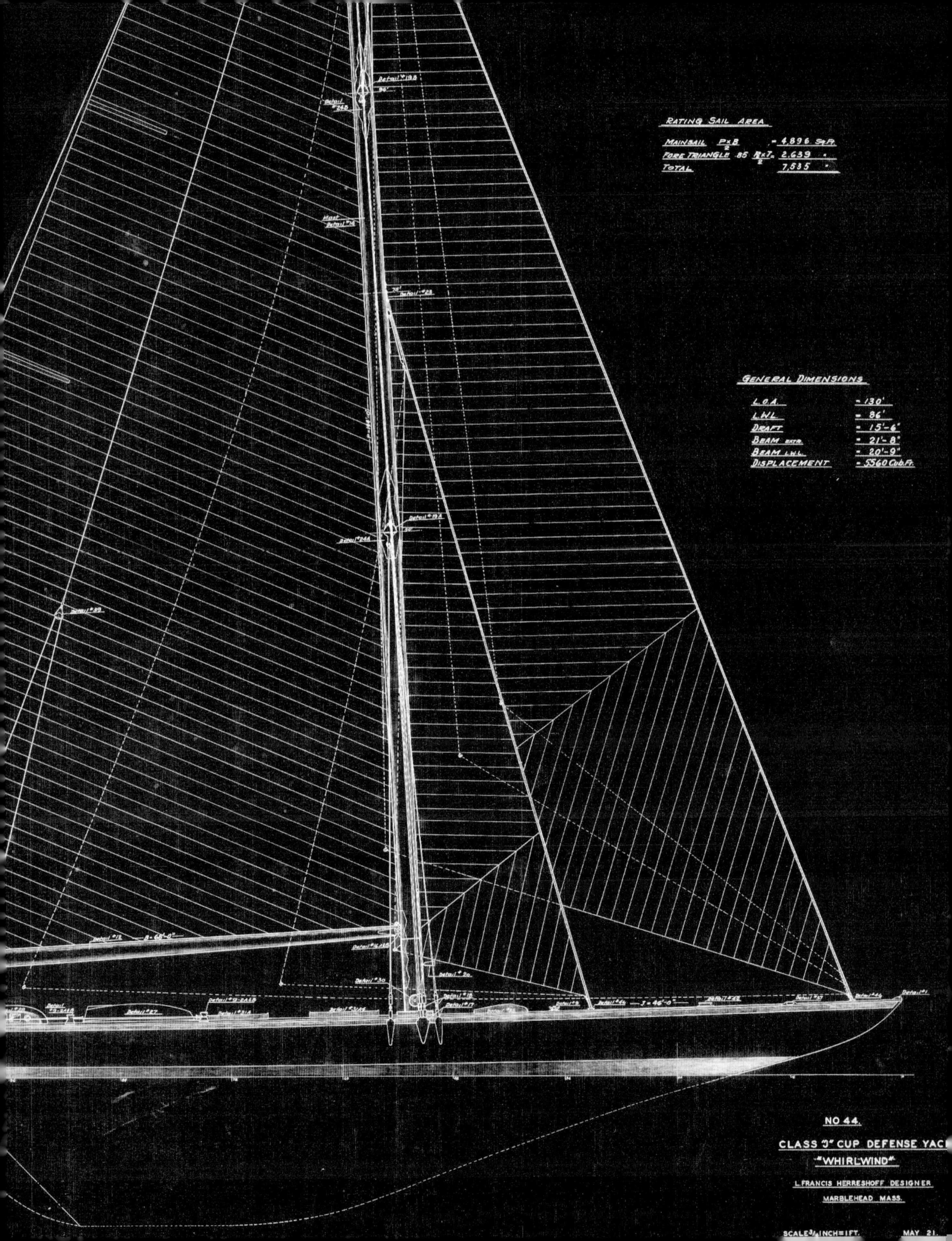
RATING SAIL AREA
MAINSAIL P×B/2 = 4,896 Sq.Ft.
FORE TRIANGLE .85 P×T/2 = 2,639 "
TOTAL 7,535 "
GENERAL DIMENSIONS
L.O.A. = 130'
L.W.L. = 86'
DRAFT = 15'-6"
BEAM EXTR. = 21'-8"
BEAM L.W.L. = 20'-9"
DISPLACEMENT = 5560 Cub.Ft.
NO 44.
CLASS "J" CUP DEFENSE YACH
"WHIRLWIND"
L. FRANCIS HERRESHOFF DESIGNER
MARBLEHEAD MASS.
SCALE 3/16 INCH = 1 FT.
MAY 21.

THE WHIRLWIND

"We will never know whether she was fast or slow.

—L. FRANCIS HERRESHOFF, 1935

A British maritime tradition that has proved valuable to the advancement of naval architecture was the practice of taking off and preserving the lines of superlative vessels as the opportunity arose. One such opportunity was the arrival in England in 1851 of the 102-foot schooner yacht *America*. George Steers, the thirty-one-year-old modeler of fast pilot schooners in New York, had designed her for a five-member syndicate headed by John C. Stevens, commodore of the recently formed New York Yacht Club. Steers designed magnificent vessels. If he had not been killed in a carriage accident five years after designing the *America*, he, in Francis Herreshoff's opinion, "might have become the greatest yacht designer of all time and eclipsed George L.Watson and N. G. Herreshoff, for there is no doubt he was a great artist." The *America* was so-named, because the purpose of her crossing the Atlantic was to be exhibited as a product of her country in London at the world's first World's Fair. While in Cowes, the *America* joined, on August 22, 1851, a fleet of seventeen yachts of the Royal Yacht Squadron for a fifty-three-mile race around the Isle of Wight, the prize being a silver cup valued at 100 guineas. The *America* won the cup. The syndicate brought it home and decided, in 1857, upon Stevens's death, to deed it to the New York Yacht Club as a challenge cup for other countries. The America's Cup has been, and perhaps still is, the world's premier yacht-racing trophy, although in the modern era it has sometimes been won by lawyers rather than by designers, builders, and sailors.[1]

The lines of the *America* stayed behind in England. Sailmaker Thomas Ratsey had a copy, learned of Francis Herreshoff's interest in the great Steers schooner when they met at Cowes in connection with the 6-Metre racing in 1921, and sent him a set. Francis admired the shape of the *America*'s hull more than that of any other vessel. George Steers's design was an inspiration to him.

Up through 1920, the America's Cup was contested thirteen times; twice by Canada, seven times by England, and four times by Ireland. No challenge was successful. The Cup was defended six times by designs from Francis's father and three times by designs from Starling Burgess's father; Frank Paine's father had been principal owner of the Burgess boats. The fourteenth challenge, in 1930, came again from Ireland, for Sir Thomas J. Lipton, the tea magnate, despite having lost four challenges with four *Shamrocks,* was coming back with the *Shamrock V.* Edward Burgess and General Paine were long gone, and Nathanael Herreshoff was eighty-two. The fourteenth defense of the America's Cup would be up to the next generation.

In the summer and early fall of 1929, with the fun and games of the twenties still roaring, public interest in the new challenge from "the gallant Tommy Lipton," as the press liked to call him, was high. There hadn't been a Cup race for ten years. Since 1899, the Wizard of Bristol, with his *Columbia, Reliance,* and *Resolute,* had turned back four *Shamrocks*—two designed by William Fife Jr., the others by George L. Watson and Charles E. Nicholson. In the last Cup race, delayed from 1914 to 1920 by World War I, the latter's *Shamrock IV,* had won the first two races in a best-of-five series. And Nicholson was the designer of the *Shamrock V.* Everyone wondered who would be able to take the place of Captain Nat Herreshoff.

The 1930 America's Cup races were to be contested by yachts designed to the Universal Rule rating of 76 feet, Class J. This would be the first America's Cup contest with no time allowance, for both yachts would necessarily have the same rating. They were the first of the 125-foot, 150-ton J-boats with their 170-foot masts. Four of them were built by American syndicates of owners and launched in the spring; they would race against each other during the summer, and in August the New York Yacht Club's Selection Committee would choose the defender for the September Cup races.

The J-boat with the racing number "1" was the *Weetamoe.* Clinton Crane took time off from running the St. Joseph Lead Company to design her for a New York Yacht Club syndicate headed by J. P. Morgan, and including Junius S. Morgan Jr. and Cornelius Vanderbilt. George Nichols, a former commodore of the New York Yacht Club, was the managing owner and skipper. Crane was in her afterguard, as were Junius Morgan, John Parkinson, Robert N. Bavier, and Augustus H. Eustis. Their J-boat would be built with a bronze-plated hull by the Herreshoff Manufacturing Company.

No "2" was the Boston boat, the *Yankee,* the other three being funded by New York syndicates. Frank Paine designed her, with plenty of help from Norman Skene, for partners John S. Lawrence and Chandler Hovey. The partners served in her afterguard, along with helmsman and secretary of the navy Charles Francis Adams, Paine, who also had money in the boat, and the young sailor and future yacht designer C. Raymond Hunt. Adams, a descendant of two US presidents, was

LEFT: **Clinton H. Crane, designer of the *Weetamoe.*** (*The Match for the America's Cup,* supplement to *The Sportsman* 7, no. 5 (1930): 27) MIDDLE: **Frank C. Paine, designer of the *Yankee.*** (*The Match for the America's Cup,* supplement to *The Sportsman* 7, no. 5 (1930): 27) RIGHT: **L. Francis Herreshoff, designer of the *Whirlwind.*** (*The Match for the America's Cup,* supplement to *The Sportsman* 7, no. 5 (1930): 27)

an outstanding helmsman and tactician who was good at calling wind shifts. He claimed that his main asset in yacht racing was preparedness. The George Lawley Company would build the *Yankee*, also of bronze.

George M. Pynchon, who had headed an unsuccessful syndicate for the 1914 Cup defense, formed a syndicate with Paul L. Hammond. Francis was well acquainted with both. He knew Pynchon through the *Istalena*. He first met Hammond when the latter returned from naval service in England at the end of World War I and would have seen him again in 1920, when he took delivery of Herreshoff S-boat No. 1 to start the fleet at the Seawanhaka Corinthian Yacht Club at Oyster Bay, for Francis had conducted the trials of the new boat in Bristol Harbor. The two would have become better acquainted the following summer on the United States team during the 6-Metre racing in Cowes, England, where Hammond raced his Burgess-designed, Herreshoff-built *Sheila*, and Francis crewed for Frank Paine in the *Jeanie*. Soon after, Hammond went into big-boat racing: he sailed two successive New York Yacht Club Fifties, and, in the second one, the *Iroquois II*, he won the King's Cup in 1924. And in 1928, he had sailed the 59-foot staysail schooner *Niña*, designed by Starling Burgess, to victory in the small class to win the Queen's Cup in the Transatlantic Race to Spain.[2]

The Pynchon-Hammond syndicate also included Alfred L. Loomis, a New York banker and inventor, who had his own private laboratory in Tuxedo Park, New York; lawyer Elihu Root Jr., son of Theodore Roosevelt's secretary of war and Nobel Prize recipient; and the extremely wealthy investment banker, *Chicago Sun* publisher, Thoroughbred horse breeder, and department-store heir, Marshall Field III. Based on the success of the *Istalena*, Pynchon and Hammond chose L. Francis Herreshoff to design the syndicate's J-boat No. "3."

The stock market crashed on October 24, 1929, and by the following spring, Pynchon's brokerage business was in trouble. He was forced to sell most of his interest in the syndicate, and he never got to sail the new J-boat, though, as we have seen, he was able to hang onto the *Istalena* and race her in the 1930 season. Loomis brought his brother-in-law and business partner, Landon K. Thorne, into the syndicate. These two investors had realized that the stock market was unstable and had sold out before the crash. Thorne, whose membership in the New York Yacht Club dated from two months after the crash, became the principal owner of the J-boat and placed himself at her helm, though he agreed to share it with Paul Hammond in the tight spots. Up to this time, Thorne had raced only in the 23-foot Star Class boats, and apparently not as owner or skipper. He got to choose the J-boat's name, selecting that of an ancestor's extreme clipper ship that had made several fast passages from New York to Melbourne, Australia, in the 1850s, the *Whirlwind*.[3]

J-boat number "4" was the *Enterprise*, designed by W. Starling Burgess for a New York Yacht Club syndicate headed by Harold S. "Mike" Vanderbilt, with Winthrop W. Aldrich, Vincent Astor, George W. Baker Jr., and George Whitney. Vanderbilt, the experienced M-boat racer, would be helmsman and skipper. His afterguard would consist of Burgess, along with naval architect and veteran yachtsman C. Sherman Hoyt, banker Winthrop Aldrich, and Charles S. Havemeyer. An important asset to the *Enterprise* was the yacht's professional skipper, George H. Monsell, a longtime employee of Vanderbilt's and a good sailor, who trained a crew of twenty-six Scandinavians and North Fork (of Long Island) Yankees. The Herreshoff Manufacturing Company would build her of bronze.[4]

One of these four would have to beat Lipton's *Shamrock V.* Her designer, Charles E. Nicholson, was head of the major yacht-building yard, Camper and Nicholsons, Limited, at Gosport, England, and so enjoyed the same advantage that N. G. Herreshoff had held for so many years: being

able to superintend the construction of the yachts he designed at his own yard. None of the American J-boat designers had this opportunity. Set against this advantage of Nicholson's was his inexperience in designing to the Universal Rule, in which the American designers, except for Crane, were well versed. Like the *Whirlwind,* the *Shamrock V* would be of composite construction. The challenger's team was really just Lipton and Nicholson. The businessman, yachtsman, and philanthropist left everything but money matters to his designer-and-builder. He even put Nicholson in charge of the yacht after she was launched.

IN JUNE of 1929, when it became public knowledge that Lipton had again challenged the New York Yacht Club for the America's Cup through the Royal Ulster Yacht Club in Belfast, Ireland, Nathanael wrote to his chosen son, Francis, advising him to "make a study" for a Cup defender. But by the end of August, perhaps fearing that Francis was not suited to dealing with rich yachtsmen under intense pressure, he backed off and wrote that he doubted that it would be wise for Francis to get involved. But Francis was already involved. By September 10, he was able to take blueprints of the basic plans of the J-boat he was designing for Pynchon's syndicate, his design No. 44, to Bristol to show to his father. With Francis committed, Nathanael tried to help him all he could.[5]

Francis gave his J-boat an ultra-modern rig. While the three other defense contenders and the challenger all had the traditional three-headsail rig, Francis did away with the jibstay entirely and all but eliminated the forestay as well, shortening it drastically and moving it well aft. He relied entirely on the long headstay, from the bow almost to the masthead, to carry the boat's racing jibs. Francis was far ahead of his competitors with this essentially single-headsail rig, but some of the credit belongs to George Pynchon, for Francis must have been aware of Pynchon's success in racing the *Istalena* with a single, large jib, drawn for him by N. G. Herreshoff.[6]

As to the hull, Francis's experience with designing to the Universal Rule had shown him that bigger was better. In juggling the elements of hull design according to the rule, he judged that it was worth choosing the longest possible waterline and suffering the drawbacks of more displacement and slightly less sail area, while enjoying more draft to fight leeway. Because of her long waterline, the biggest boat that could be built to the rule ought to be the fastest, even with a little less power from her sails, provided she had a fine-lined, well-balanced hull. Francis gave his J-boat a waterline length of 86 feet, within a foot of the maximum allowed by the Universal Rule. Nathanael didn't agree. After seeing Francis's plans and making a half-hull model from the lines, he thought Francis's hull was too big for her sail area. He continued to argue for a smaller hull, but Francis replied, "In regard to the size of the boat, I still think it is all right." Nathanael didn't give up: he pointed out that while his *Reliance* had had a sail-area-to-wetted-surface ratio of 5.5, that of Francis's J-boat was only 3.15. Francis would not be moved. He believed in his work and hated to change a design. The other J-boats were all smaller, and Francis's mentor, Starling Burgess, had designed the smallest. Compared to Francis's design, the *Enterprise* was 6 feet shorter on the waterline, had 30 tons less displacement (a difference of almost 20 percent), and set a little (33 square feet) more sail.[7]

OPPOSITE PAGE: **Landon K. Thorne (left) and Paul Hammond (right), who headed the syndicate and formed the afterguard of the *Whirlwind* after George Pynchon had to bow out. Hammond was an experienced racing skipper, but Thorne had never raced anything bigger than a 23-foot Star boat. Yet, except for starts and close maneuvers, he would be at the J-boat's wheel. Between the two yachtsmen is the *Whirlwind*'s captain, John Muir, a sound professional new to the Marconi rig.** (© Mystic Seaport, Rosenfeld Collection, 1984.187.39121F) RIGHT: **W. Starling Burgess, designer of the *Enterprise*.** (*The Match for the America's Cup*, supplement to *The Sportsman* 7, no. 5 (1930): 27) FAR RIGHT: **Charles E. Nicholson, designer of the *Shamrock V*.** (*The Match for the America's Cup*, supplement to *The Sportsman* 7, no. 5 (1930): 27)

Francis had made a careful study of the hull form of racing boats, not by tank tests, which some designers were starting to use, but by observation of the boats themselves. From a motorboat, he had watched R-boats and Q-boats sailing hard and had noted that they were well balanced fore and aft, neither down by the head nor stern. He thought it might be advantageous to give a racing boat more reserve buoyancy aft than forward, by means of a "raking mid-section," so that when she heeled the stern might be raised slightly so the boat would ride down her quarter wave. A raking mid-section was achieved by giving a hull its section of greatest area aft of her mid-section. Pynchon and Hammond also wanted a raking mid-section on their J-boat based on their experience with New York Yacht Club 50-footers, which had plenty of buoyancy aft, but also plenty of weather helm. During visits from Hammond in January and February, Francis allowed himself to be persuaded further in this direction and drew in full waterlines and wide sections leading back to a pointed stern. Much later, he wrote: "While this wide after body is all wrong to go with a sharp stern, I thought I could get away with it." But Francis had clearly been toying with the idea of a raking midship section for the *Whirlwind* on his own.[8]

The design of the J-boat was a huge project for Francis. It took fifty-six complex drawings to put her hull, rig, interior, construction details, and all her special fittings on large sheets of linen for the builders. Francis and Sam Brown were busy. They must have missed Norman Skene, but he was helping Frank Paine with the particulars of the *Yankee*. Francis wrote to his father: "I have not made any calculations on stability and I am still very short handed and haven't time to bother with that sort of calculations." But Francis's design for the J-boat was a prodigious piece of engineering that impressed his father. Nathanael wrote to Francis: "I have looked over #44 blueprints you have sent. They show a remarkable amount of study and ingenuity in working up the details and you must have put in long hours on them." Francis had come a long way from The Farm in the eyes of his father, but Nathanael was still praising effort and aptitude, not accomplishment.[9]

PYNCHON, Hammond, and Francis would all have preferred to see Francis's No. 44 built at the Herreshoff Manufacturing Company, but Harold Vanderbilt and George Nichols had beaten them to it. The *Enterprise* and *Weetamoe* would be built at Bristol, while the *Yankee* and No. 44 would take shape at the Lawley yard at Neponset. Not that Lawley's was lacking; 700

RIGHT: The sail plan of the *Whirlwind*, the J-class racer that Francis designed to contend for the defense of the America's Cup in 1930. He has leaped far ahead of his time in giving her essentially a single-headsail rig. The huge sails that could be set on her headstay in moderate weather could be easily brought round the inboard forestay when tacking. That stay is just to support the mast; setting a small sail on it is like an afterthought, for it has no opposing backstay. Her hollow, wooden mast stands 154 feet, 1 inch above the deck. The boom is 67 feet, 6-7/8 inches long. She carries a 46-foot spinnaker pole. Rated sail area is 7,535 square feet, of which 4,896 square feet are in the mainsail. Francis put his sense of proportion to the ultimate test with the *Whirlwind*: the stresses on the rig would be far outside his experience, as would be the stakes. He drew three-ply chainplates, specifying 3/16-inch nickel steel, galvanized, with a tensile strength of 120,000 pounds. Each would be fastened with a single 3/4-inch bolt and 35-5/8-inch bolts. Each lower shroud tang was held to the mast by 222 screws. He enlarged the turnbuckles he had designed for the *Istalena* to a threaded-section diameter of 1-1/4 inches. The *Whirlwind*'s crew did experience one rigging failure during a race, but it was their own fault. (© Mystic Seaport, Daniel S. Gregory Ships Plans Library, SP.38.12.5)

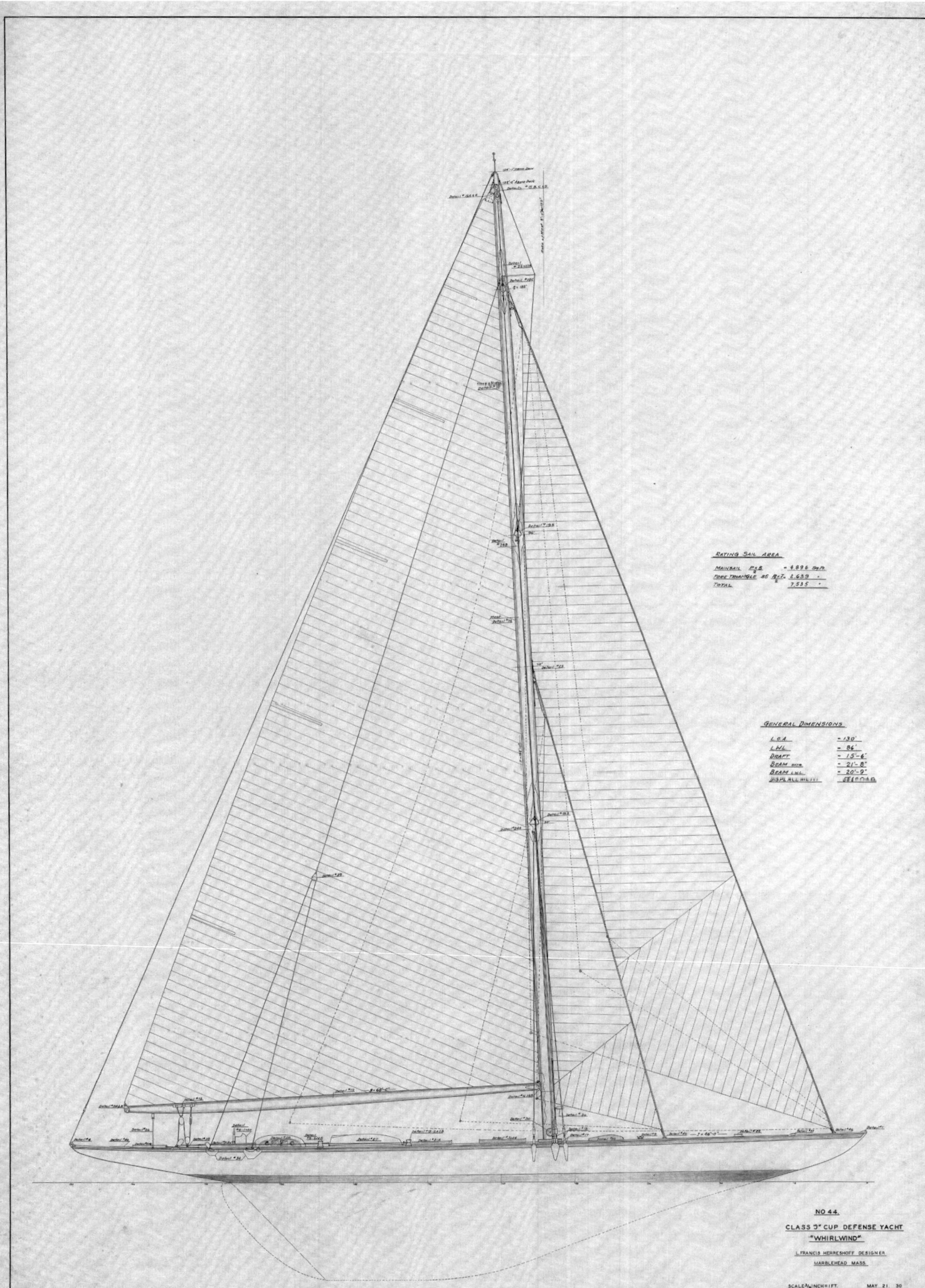
RATING SAIL AREA
MAINSAIL P×B/2 = 4,896 Sq.Ft.
FORE TRIANGLE .85 P×T/2 = 2,639 "
TOTAL 7,535 "
GENERAL DIMENSIONS
L.O.A. = 130'
L.W.L. = 86'
DRAFT = 15'-6"
BEAM = 21'-8"
BEAM L.W.L. = 20'-9"
NO 44.
CLASS "J" CUP DEFENSE YACHT
"WHIRLWIND"
L. FRANCIS HERRESHOFF DESIGNER
MARBLEHEAD MASS.
SCALE 3/16 INCH = 1 FT.
MAY 21 30

good men were on the payroll. And Bror Tamm, an outstanding Danish boatbuilder who had come over from Sweden and had become a regular at Francis's customhouse fireside in Marblehead, had the important job of supervising mast construction and rigging at the yard. Under his leadership, Lawley's would pioneer the construction and fitting out of the new, huge, Marconi rigs. In all other departments of yacht construction, Tamm regarded the Lawley yard as second best to the Herreshoff yard. "We copied all the Herreshoff stuff we could," he would remember many years later.[10]

By 1929, the George F. Lawley and Son yard had no more Lawleys superintending the work. The yard had been founded by George Lawley in 1866 at Scituate, Massachusetts. He had come to East Boston from England in 1851, perhaps crossing paths with the *America,* and had gone to work for Donald McKay, the builder of clipper ships. He moved his yacht yard to City Point in South Boston in 1874 and ran it until 1890, when his son, George Frederick Lawley Jr., took over. The third generation, Frederick D. Lawley, who learned yacht design at MIT, joined the firm in 1902. To gain space, the yard moved to Neponset in 1910. George Frederick Lawley II was the fourth generation of Lawleys to become involved. In 1926, these last three Lawleys sold out to Frank Paine and others and started a new yacht yard in Quincy, the F. D. Lawley Company. But the old George F. Lawley and Son yard at Neponset, now with Paine as investor and designer, would remain the premier yacht yard in the Boston area until World War II.

Bror Tamm, who built the huge wooden masts for the *Whirlwind* and the *Yankee* at the Lawley yard. (© Mystic Seaport, 2002.94.299)

The syndicate's contract with the George F. Lawley and Son company, dated September 26, 1929, provided that the vessel be built "to the classification of Lloyd's Rules for Composite and Metal Yachts and in accordance with requirements of inspectors designated by the New York Yacht Club." The fourteenth match for the America's Cup would be sailed under more equable conditions than had been the case in the previous contests. Not only would defender and challenger both be rated under the Universal Rule and race without time allowance, but also they would both be built to Lloyd's rules for construction. The challenger still had to sail from her home waters to the New York Yacht Club's racecourse, which for the *Shamrock V* meant crossing the Atlantic, just as the *America* had done. But, for the first time, the defender, although spared the ocean voyage, still had to be built just as strongly and heavily as the challenger. For all five J-boats built in 1930, Lloyd's surveyors and inspectors would be examining and testing all the materials that went into the yachts and making sure that it was all fastened strongly. They would not care what effect their findings had on the weight of the vessels they inspected, on their cost, or on the dates of their launchings.[11]

The *Whirlwind* syndicate was to pay Lawley's the cost of construction, plus 20 percent for overhead, plus another 10 percent of that total as profit, with a cap of $250,000. Francis's contract with the syndicate, dated October 7, 1929, provided him with a commission of $25,000 no matter what the cost of the J-boat, but this fee was to include, as usual, his expenses in connection with the work. If extra work was required after the completion of the boat, Francis was to get $25 per day, with $15 per day for "draftsmen," they being Sam Brown. Cost figures have survived for only three of the seven months it took to build the big yacht, but these indicate that she must have reached or come close to the $250,000 cap, so Francis's commission was about the normal 10 percent. This goodly sum must have been most welcome indeed to him at the start of the Great Depression.[12]

Francis claimed that when the Lawley yard shut down after World War II and the books were examined, it was discovered that the costs on his No. 44 had been padded by $20,000 and that Lawley's owners had to reimburse the syndicate that amount. "Some say," he wrote, "this overcharge was made because *Whirlwind*'s costs were running about this amount less than *Yankee*'s." In any event, in the month of February 1930 alone, Lawley's billed the syndicate for "Materials" that included $1,338.35 worth of tools, tools that would presumably stay on Lawley's shelves after the launching.[13]

The five-man syndicate that was to build Francis's design, with Landon Thorne taking over most of the financial burden from George Pynchon, would spend about $700,000 in total for its campaign with the *Whirlwind*. Francis, with his involvement in the defense of the America's Cup and with the biggest commission he would ever earn, was being carried on the crest of a huge wave at a time when the economy was ebbing fast. *The Rudder* estimated that with Lipton spending $500,000 to build and campaign the *Shamrock V*, and the New York Yacht Club shelling out $200,000 to put on the races, the total spent on the Cup in 1930 by the challenger, the four contenders for its defense, and the yacht club was $3,700,000. The America's Cup was that important, no matter what happened to the stock market. And it was becoming more expensive: just $6,500,000 had been spent on the previous thirteen matches combined.[14]

At Lawley's, in Neponset, construction was delayed on both the *Whirlwind* and the *Yankee*. The steel, bronze, and lumber that were delivered to the yard for the Cup boats sat outside the big building shed where the keels of the J-boats were to be laid, waiting for Edsel Ford's 132-foot power yacht *Sialia* to be finished and launched. For the *Whirlwind*, it was not an auspicious start for the construction of a big, complicated vessel whose builder's contract specified a launching date of May 1, only seven months away. But the most important word in her builder's contract was "Composite," because the other three syndicates had already contracted with Lawley's and the Herreshoff Manufacturing Company for "Metal"—namely bronze plating—and there were only so many skilled workers in metal available. The supposed advantage of metal construction was that it would be possible to achieve greater fairness and smoothness in such a hull, compared to wood planking. Francis later grumbled that he had been forced to specify wood planking for the hull of his J-boat rather than the exotic bronze that the other Js were using. But, as Lawley's men began following his drawings, he wrote to his father, Nathanael Greene Herreshoff, creator and superintendent of fine yacht construction at the Herreshoff Manufacturing Company for many years—including the first bronze-on-steel America's Cup defender, the *Vigilant* of 1893—construction that had been well observed by Francis: "The workmanship on everything so far is the best I have ever seen." And when his design was three-quarters planked, he reported to Nathanael that her wooden planking was fairer than the bronze plates on the *Yankee*, taking shape alongside her.[15]

Everyone had to work fast to meet the launching date. Francis and Sam Brown were certainly busy keeping ahead of the builders, Francis designing and drawing plans of all the construction details and innovations that he put into the J-boat, and Sam following Francis's penciled drawings to turn out inked, finished plans for the builders to follow. And the builders had to study and comprehend the plans; to cut and shape hundreds of pieces of steel, bronze, and wood; to fit them all together with precision; and to fasten them securely to each other, all on a tight schedule.

There was also work to do on two tenders for the *Whirlwind*. Paul Hammond admired Charlie Welch's *Walrus* and wanted a towboat like her. So Francis sketched a preliminary plan for a lengthened version of the *Walrus* with space for the sails that the crew would put on board the racer for daily use. Lawley's would build the *Twister*, as she was named, to the same shape as the *Walrus*, so all Francis needed to do was make a new construction plan for her; he didn't draw her lines until a year later. And to house the *Whirlwind*'s crew and store the rest of her sails, the syndicate purchased a 170-foot Nova Scotia tern schooner, the *Minas Princess*, and somebody had to work up her modifications for the purpose. This was left up to Lawley's.[16]

All materials for and workmanship on the *Whirlwind* had to be inspected and approved by Lloyd's. A further complication arose when the New York Yacht Club's America's Cup Committee decided that it would indeed designate inspectors to back up the Lloyd's men: inspectors from the American Bureau of Shipping, the experts on merchant ships. At times, Francis suspected the two organizations of vying with each other to see which could find a flaw that the other had missed.[17]

Nor was politics absent from the syndicates. Representatives of the *Enterprise* and *Yankee*, evidently believing that the ABS was letting the *Whirlwind* off lightly, put pressure on the Cup Committee to have Lloyd's increase their inspections of Francis's design. The *Whirlwind* syndicate fought back. Paul Hammond got Francis to enlist his father's help in persuading the Cup Committee that their boat's construction was sound, and Francis had the satisfaction of learning that George A. Cormack, a member of the Committee, did receive a wire to that effect, from the man who had done more than any other to keep the Cup safely in the New York Yacht Club's Manhattan headquarters.[18]

But Nathanael's intervention on Francis's behalf did no good. Between Lloyd's and the ABS, "a great many things on the boat are not made the way that I should have them but the way I am told they have to be," as Francis wrote to his father. The biggest difficulty was over the design

RIGHT: **The interior plan for the *Whirlwind*. Francis figured that if she was converted to a cruising yacht when her racing career was over, the midships cockpits, with their big portholes to let light below to where a racing crew would be turning winches, could be changed over to deck skylights to brighten a saloon and staterooms. Meanwhile, all she has for accommodations are one berth, a settee, a washroom, a chart table in the deckhouse, and four pipe berths and two crew's heads forward. The double-crank main halyard winch is just abaft the mast. On the after side of the mast is a worm and pinion gear to haul down the main boom gooseneck to tighten the luff of the mainsail. Forward is a winch and tackle for the forestaysail tack pendant, and further forward are two winches for the two jib tack pendants. Francis gave the five biggest winches—one forward to turn the anchor windlass, and four aft, two for the double-ended main sheet and two, further aft, for overlapping jib sheets or spinnaker lines—an unusual design. Each has a horizontal sheave 4 feet, 8 inches in diameter on a shaft that goes up to its corresponding winch on deck. Around the sheave is an endless line led through a block secured at the same height as the sheave to one of the vessel's structural stanchions. There is room for eight men to haul on this line if necessary. No need for gearing: Francis has taken advantage of the presence of a large crew, who can pull with just as much speed or power as the situation demands.** (© Mystic Seaport, Daniel S. Gregory Ships Plans Library, SP.38.12.7)

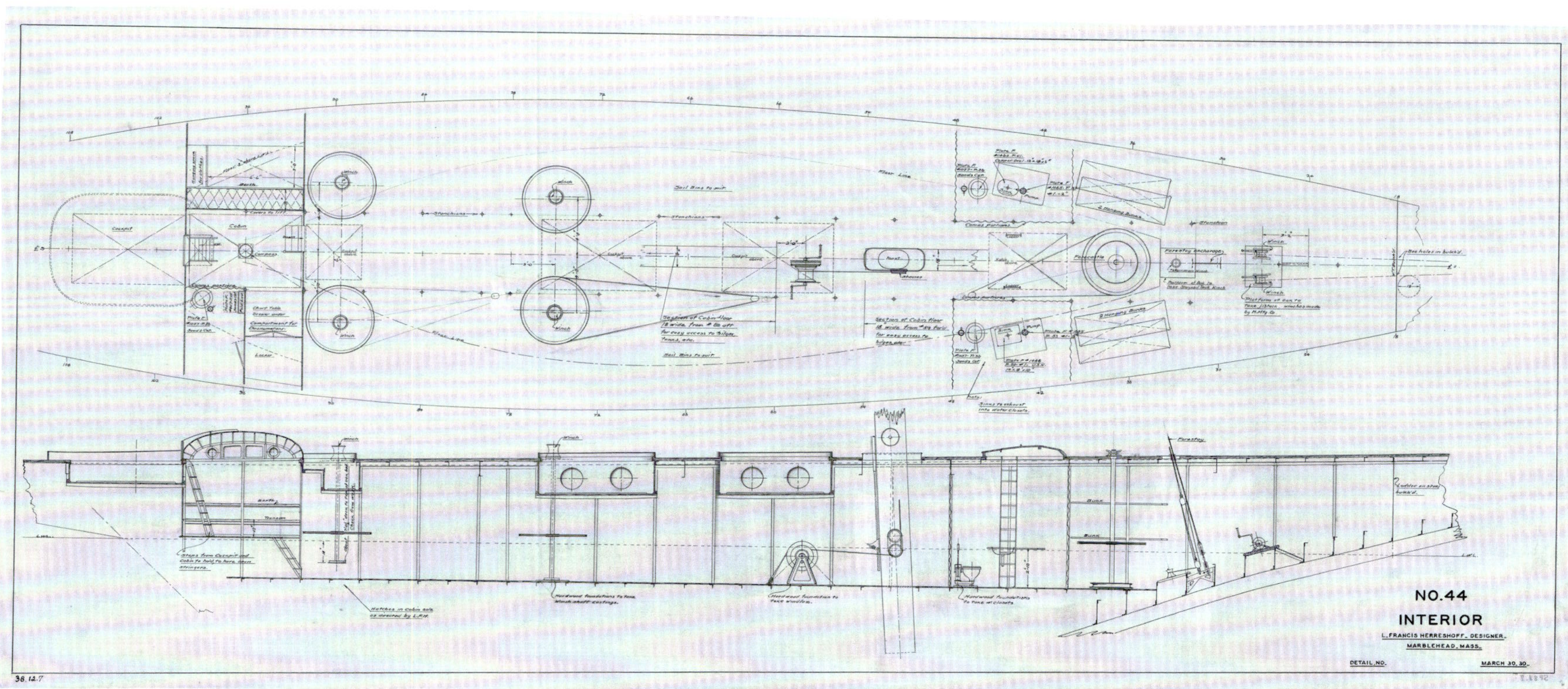
NO. 44
INTERIOR
L. FRANCIS HERRESHOFF, DESIGNER.
MARBLEHEAD, MASS.
DETAIL NO.
MARCH 30, 30.
38.12.7

and construction of the *Whirlwind*'s keelson. The Lloyd's rule, Francis wrote later, "called for a steel plate over a wood keel which in its turn makes bronze keel bolts wrong, and in many ways this combination is a perfect mess." So Francis substituted Everdur bronze for steel in his design for the keel plate and submitted his plan to both agencies of inspection. The ABS took two days to approve the design, provided that the thickness of the metal was increased from 1⅛ inches to 1¼ inches and that the weight of the structure per lineal foot be at least 166 pounds. Lloyd's took two months to issue its approval, with the proviso that the metal be tested to withstand a pressure of 55,000 pounds per square inch. The Everdur proved not to be that strong, so the first keel plates that were cast had to be scrapped. It was mid-January by the time Francis had the Bethlehem Shipbuilding Corporation, in nearby Quincy, cast keel plates of manganese bronze that tested to over 80,000 pounds per square inch. Francis wrote later: "These were quite inferior for this place, for manganese not only has ferrous metal in it but it generally is ductile and bends a long way without breaking, while stiffness in a keel plate is the quality desired."[19]

Looking back, thirty years after the event, Francis would write: "Thus it was quite plain that the [Lloyd's] inspector had been instructed to hamstring this yacht." At the time, though, after meeting with one of their surveyors, he had felt differently about the troubles with Lloyd's. Back then, he reported to his father: "I was much surprised, in talking with Mr. Bennett, to find out how little he knew about construction of any kind, and also how little he knew about Lloyd's rule. This, of course, accounts for most of the difficulty we have had with them; it is simply that they are so ignorant that they cannot understand the working of their own rule."[20]

Francis, in the cap, and Paul Hammond being ferried by Charlie Welch in the *Walrus* from Marblehead to the Lawley yard at Neponset, south of Boston, on April 5, 1930, to see how the *Whirlwind* is coming along. Hammond liked Charlie's motorsailer and wanted a tender like her for the *Whirlwind*. (© Mystic Seaport, #1973-3-393)

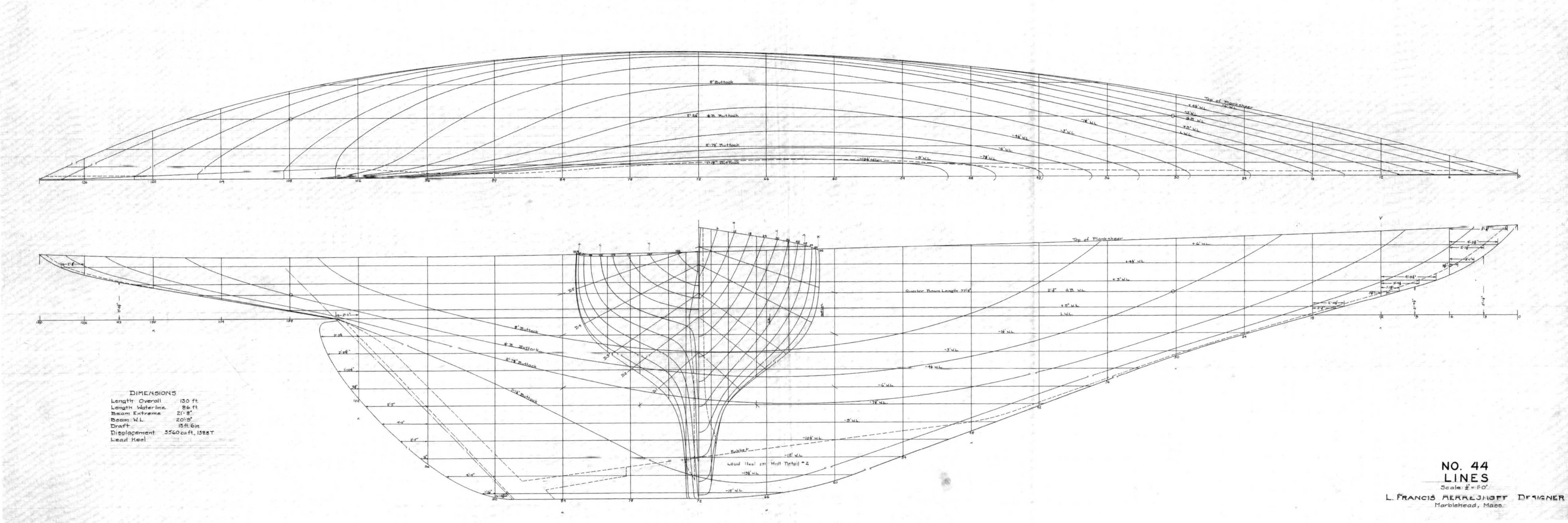

The lines of the *Whirlwind*. She is not just an enlarged *Istalena*, for she has wider, flatter sections in the stern than the M-boat had, giving her a raking mid-section, or more reserve buoyancy aft than forward. The *Whirlwind* also had slightly sharper sections in the bow compared to the *Istalena*, and Francis believed that the *Whirlwind* was built even sharper forward than he had designed her to be. Both these differences, particularly the raking mid-section, with the sections abaft the mid-section having slightly greater area than those forward of it, increased the J-boat's weather helm, but not to the point of being problematical. Most of that problem was caused by faulty sail trim. She is 130 feet long on deck; 86 feet on the waterline; with a beam of 21 feet, 8 inches; and a draft of 15 feet, 6 inches. Francis thought that she would increase her waterline by as much as 19 feet aft when sailing hard. Displacement was 158.8 tons. (© Mystic Seaport, Daniel S. Gregory Ships Plans Library, SP.38.12.1)

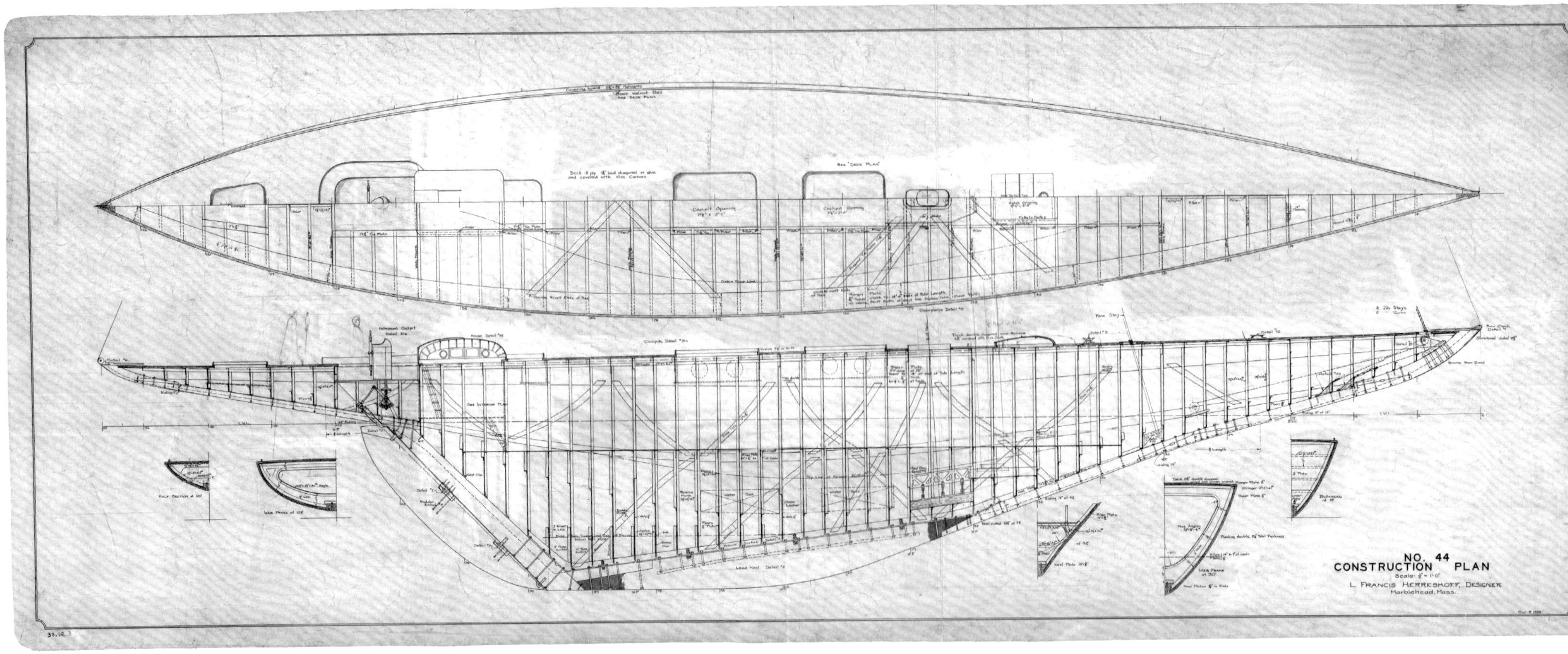
NO. 44
CONSTRUCTION PLAN
L. FRANCIS HERRESHOFF, DESIGNER
Marblehead, Mass.

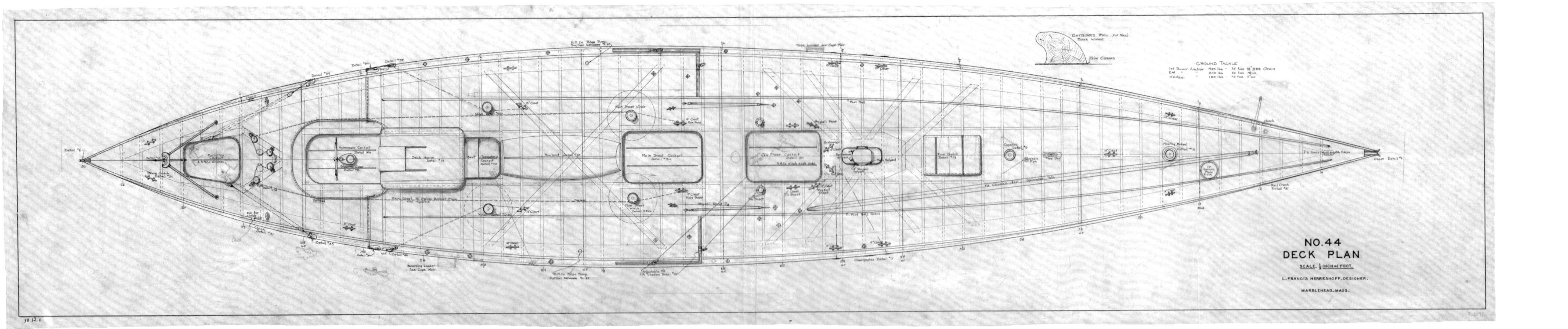
NO.44
DECK PLAN
L. FRANCIS HERRESHOFF, DESIGNER.
MARBLEHEAD, MASS.

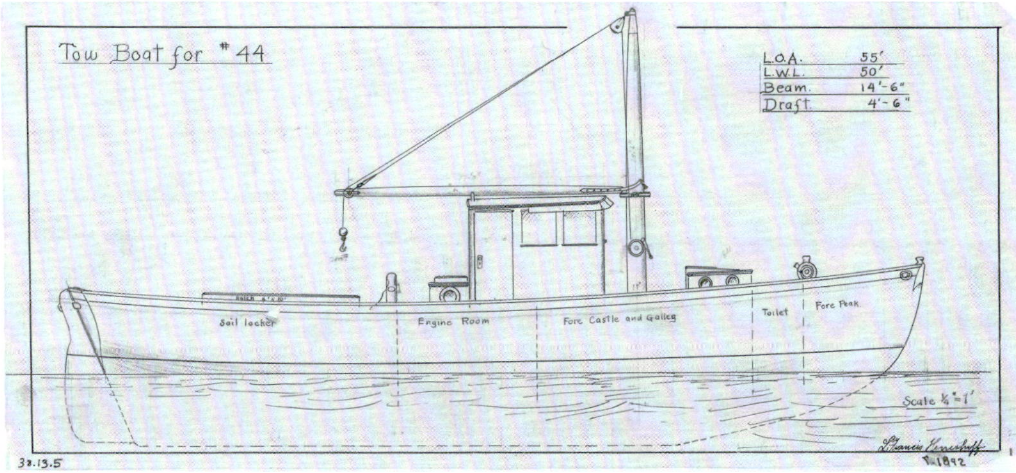

LEFT TOP: The *Whirlwind*'s construction plan. She was of composite build, with a bronze keel plate, floors, and diagonal strapping; steel frames, deck beams, interior columns, and struts forming trusses; steel longitudinal sheer, waterway, and bilge stringer plates; mahogany stem, sternpost, and double planking; and a double, plywood deck. There was a solid bulkhead in the bow at the waterline and three pairs of deep, web frames, in way of the mast, amidships, and aft, as well as one where the forestay was secured to the stem. Total planking thickness was 2-3/4 inches, fastened to the steel frames with bolts of the American Brass Company's new Everdur bronze alloy. The steel sheer plates, set on edge at the gunwale inside the topside planking and running from stem to stern, were 5/16-inch thick and tapered from 3 feet deep amidships to 18 inches at the ends. Along the top edge of this plate ran a 9-inch-wide sheer strake of black walnut that set off the yacht's subtle sheerline. The wooden mast was stepped in a steel casting that rested on a 1-foot-thick oak pad supported by a steel trough of 5/16-inch plate that spanned four frames, including two of the deep webs. The whole structure was backed up by three heavy turnbuckles on each side secured to further plates that also spanned the four frames. The gudgeon-and-pintle at the bottom of the rudder was suggested by Nathanael and agreed to by Francis, otherwise the bottom 7 feet of the rudder would have had no support. The water tanks in the bilge were shaped to the curvature of the hull to keep their weight as low in the boat as possible. Note, in the bow, the two jibstays and jib tack pendants leading below to winches and, at the stern, the adjustable, permanent backstay that leads through a sheave to a threaded rod turned by a lever in the aftermost cockpit. (© Mystic Seaport, Daniel S. Gregory Ships Plans Library, SP.38.12.3) LEFT BOTTOM: The deck plan of the *Whirlwind*. The toe-rails, to keep the crew from sliding to leeward when the yacht is well heeled over, are set far in from the gunwale, for safety and in deference to dry feet. The long spinnaker pole is a necessary tripping hazard when stowed on deck. She has five cockpits: one just abaft the mast for tending working-jib sheets; one amidships for tending the main sheet; one just forward of the deckhouse for the navigator; one at the wheel for the helmsman; and one at the stern for tending the running backstays. The pram dinghy stows between cockpits two and three. The double-ended mainsheet, of 3-1/2-inch (circumference) "Italian balloon rope," has a long lead forward to its winches on each side of cockpit number two and bears on the helmsman's cockpit coaming. The long lead allows putting twenty or so crewmen on the sheet to pull, if necessary, with far more power and speed than a winch could provide. The winches for overlapping jibs and for the spinnaker guy and sheet are abreast the navigator's cockpit, with plenty of deck space alongside the pram for a gang to tail on. Note the L-shaped tracks for the jib sheet lead blocks, giving a wide range of trimming positions. (© Mystic Seaport, Daniel S. Gregory Ships Plans Library, SP.38.12.6) ABOVE: The outboard profile of the *Twister*, the tender that Francis designed for the *Whirlwind*. She is a shoal-draft version of the *Walrus*, stretched out five feet. The Lawley builders used the *Walrus*'s molds, made more shoal, and lengthened the hull. She was fitted with a towing bitt amidships and had two 100-horsepower Type 150, "Mystic" Lathrops for pulling the big J-boat. (© Mystic Seaport, Daniel S. Gregory Ships Plans Library, SP.38.13.5)

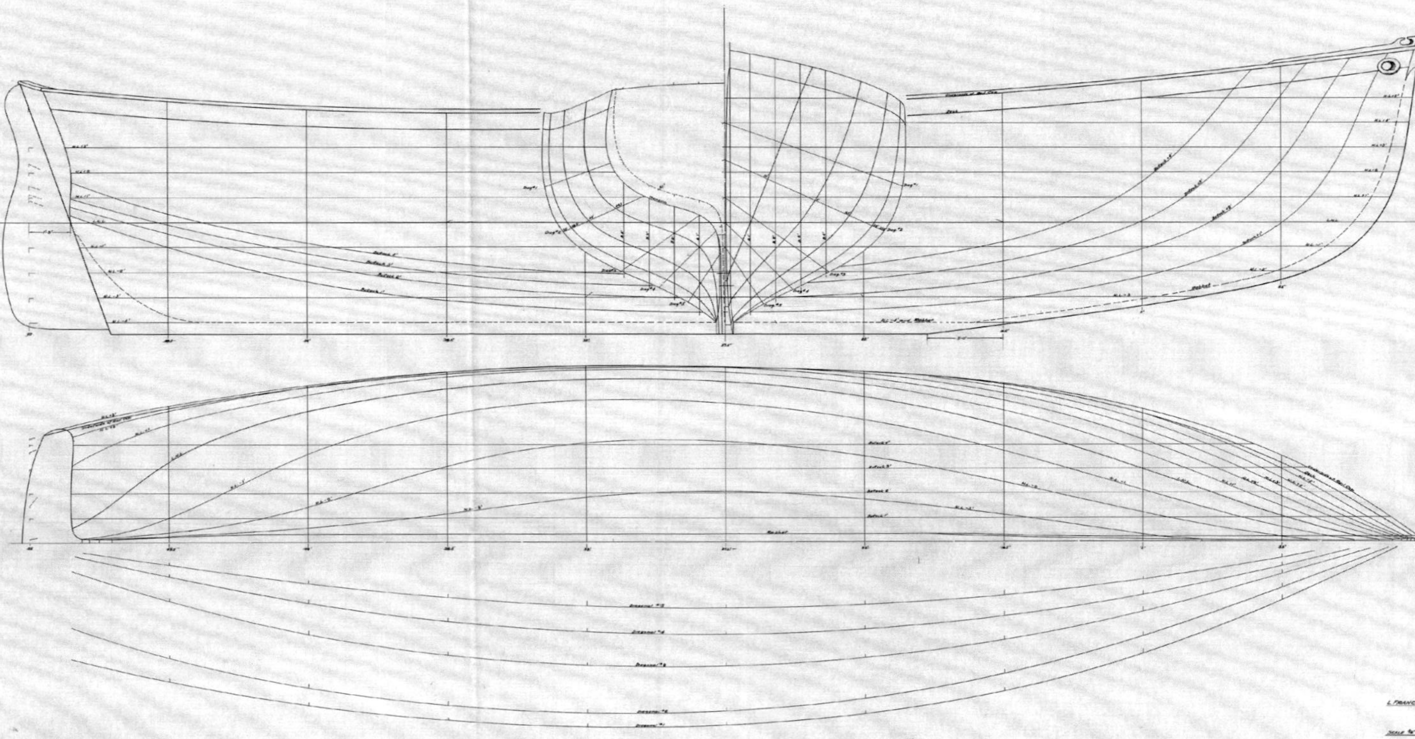

55 ft L.O.A. TOW BOAT

LINES

L. FRANCIS HERRESHOFF DESIGNER

MARBLEHEAD MASS.

SCALE 3/8" = 1'-0" DATE: FEB. 28. 1931

45A

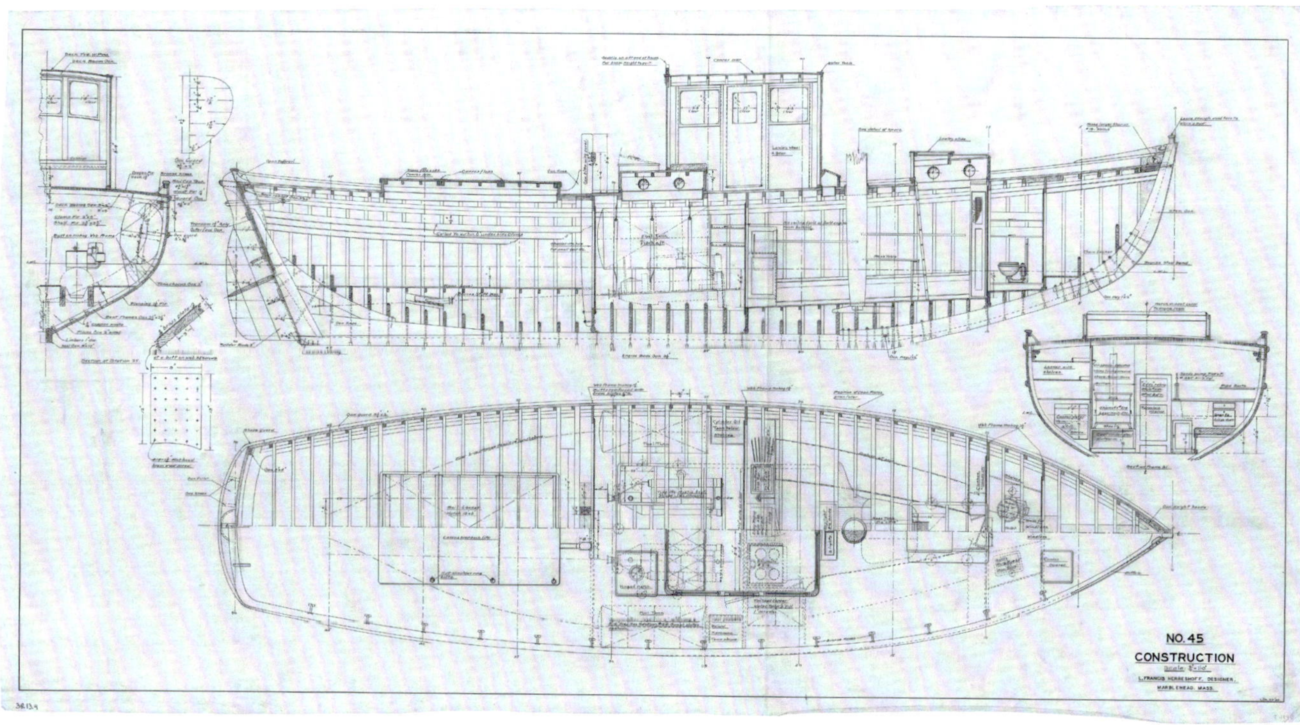

If Francis was unhappy with Lloyd's, he was at least more than satisfied with Lawley's. Working at top speed to Francis's detailed drawings, with two sets of inspectors under foot causing delays that played havoc with a production schedule, the men at the George Lawley Company built a yacht that in Francis's opinion was "a very good job . . . she should last forty or fifty years." And if Lloyd's had required that Lawley's build the *Whirlwind* more heavily than Francis designed her, presumably their inspectors were burdening the other J-boats with similar requirements.[21]

Another new element in the 1930 America's Cup races was the absence of the intense secrecy that had existed during many of the previous campaigns. Francis could report to his father that due to Lloyd's inspections Lawley's had to redesign most of the *Yankee*'s construction plan. As for the *Enterprise,* on January 13, Francis had the opportunity of inspecting her himself. He went to the Herreshoff Manufacturing Company to pick up backstay winches for his J-boat, and

LEFT: The lines of the *Twister*. Length on deck was 55 feet; with a waterline length of 50 feet; a beam of 14 feet, 6 inches; and a draft of 4 feet, 6 inches. (© Mystic Seaport, Daniel S. Gregory Ships Plans Library, SP.38.13.1) ABOVE: The *Twister's* construction plan. The whole stern of the boat was given over to a sail locker from which the crew could hoist sails up to the racing boat's deck through a 10-by-6-foot hatch with a three-piece cover. The engine room, with fuel tanks, was amidships, and forward was a galley and forecastle for eight men. Francis noted that the hawsepipes should be larger than those Lawley's installed on the *Walrus*. He gave the outboard rudder of this relatively plebian tender a nicely curved sectional shape and specified teak rail caps. (© Mystic Seaport, Daniel S. Gregory Ships Plans Library, SP.38.13.4)

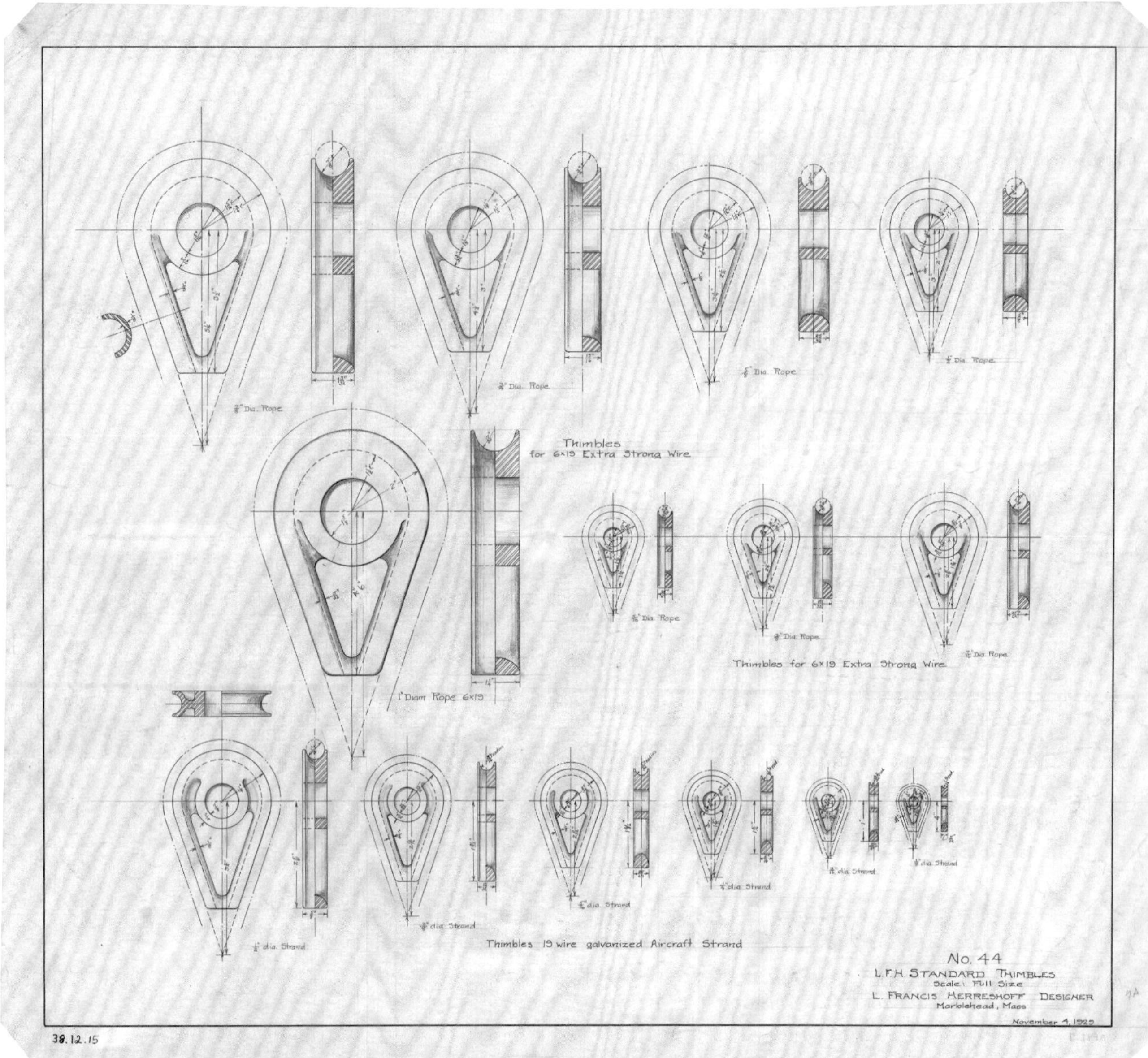

ABOVE: **For attaching the ends of the *Whirlwind*'s standing rigging, Francis designed a special thimble, with the strength of a solid casting, but with a triangular cutout to save weight. These he called "L. F. H. Standard Thimbles." For the *Whirlwind*, there were six sizes to take 19-wire galvanized aircraft strand, from 1/8-inch to 1/2-inch, and eight sizes for 6x19, extra-strong wire, from 5/16-inch to 1-inch. He proportioned each to be just as strong as necessary, compatible with its wire. This drawing is dated November 4, 1929.** (© Mystic Seaport, Daniel S. Gregory Ships Plans Library, SP.38.12.15)

RIGHT: **The plans of the *Whirlwind*'s pram dinghy. She is an enlarged version of the *Istalena*'s pram, stretched from a little over 8 feet out to 12 feet. As on the smaller boat, her bow and stern transoms have concave tops to fit the curvature of the *Whirlwind*'s deck, so she can keep a low profile when stowed upside down. Francis gave this boat a heavy, oak sheerstrake with the distinctive curved section that had graced so many of the small craft built by the Herreshoff Manufacturing Company.** (© Mystic Seaport, Daniel S. Gregory Ships Plans Library, SP.38.12A.1)

NO. 44

ROWBOAT

SCALE. $1\frac{1}{2}$" = 1 FOOT.

L. FRANCIS HERRESHOFF, DESIGNER.
MARBLEHEAD, MASS.

DRAWING NO. 27.

Row boat for "Whirlwind."

Jan. 27-'30.

Offset Table

	Height from L.W.L.				Half Breadths					
Sta.	Rail	14" But	7" But	Rabbet	Rail	$10\frac{1}{2}$" W.L.	7" W.L.	$3\frac{1}{2}$" W.L.	L.W.L.	Rabbet
Bow	1.5.5	1.0.0	0.6.0	0.7.5	1.3.6	1.0.4				
1	1.4.4	0.5.2	0.5.4	0.3.0+	1.8.4+	1.6.7+	1.4.4+	0.7.0		
2	1.3.1	0.1.0	0.2.0	0.2.1	2.0.5	2.0.1+	1.11.3+	1.9.3	1.4.6	
3	1.2.1+	0.2.5	0.3.2+	0.3.4	2.2.0	2.1.7	2.1.3+	2.0.4+	1.9.0	
4	1.1.6+	0.2.0+	0.2.6+	0.2.6+	2.1.4	2.1.4	2.1.0	1.11.6+	1.8.3	
5	1.2.0	0.0.3	0.0.6	0.1.2	1.11.0	1.11.0	1.10.1	1.8.0+	1.0.0	
Stern	1.2.4	0.4.3	0.2.1	0.1.0	1.7.5	1.7.0	1.5.8	0.11.7		

Bill of Material.

Frames. White Oak. Spaced 5" – $\frac{7}{16}$" × $\frac{1}{2}$"
Keel. White Oak 4" × 1"
Bow Transom. Mahogany $\frac{3}{4}$"
Stern Transom. " $\frac{3}{4}$"
Floor Timbers. Oak. Over keel. 1" × $\frac{9}{16}$"
Planking. Cedar $\frac{5}{16}$" Lapped Strake.
Sheer Strake. White Oak 3" × $\frac{3}{4}$"
Gunwale. White Oak $\frac{7}{8}$" × $\frac{5}{8}$"
Seat Riser. White Oak $\frac{3}{4}$" × $\frac{3}{8}$"
Seats. Mahogany 8" × $\frac{5}{8}$"
Transom Knees. Hackmatack. $1\frac{1}{4}$"
Quarter Knees. " $\frac{3}{4}$"
Hanging Knees. Bent Oak $\frac{1}{2}$"
Footlings. Cedar $3\frac{1}{4}$" × $\frac{7}{16}$" Use screws. Oval head.
Foot Braces. Mahogany

Castings	No	Mat'l.
Rowlock Socket	4	Bronze
Rowlocks	4	"
Rings	2	"
Ring Socket	2	"
Screws.		"

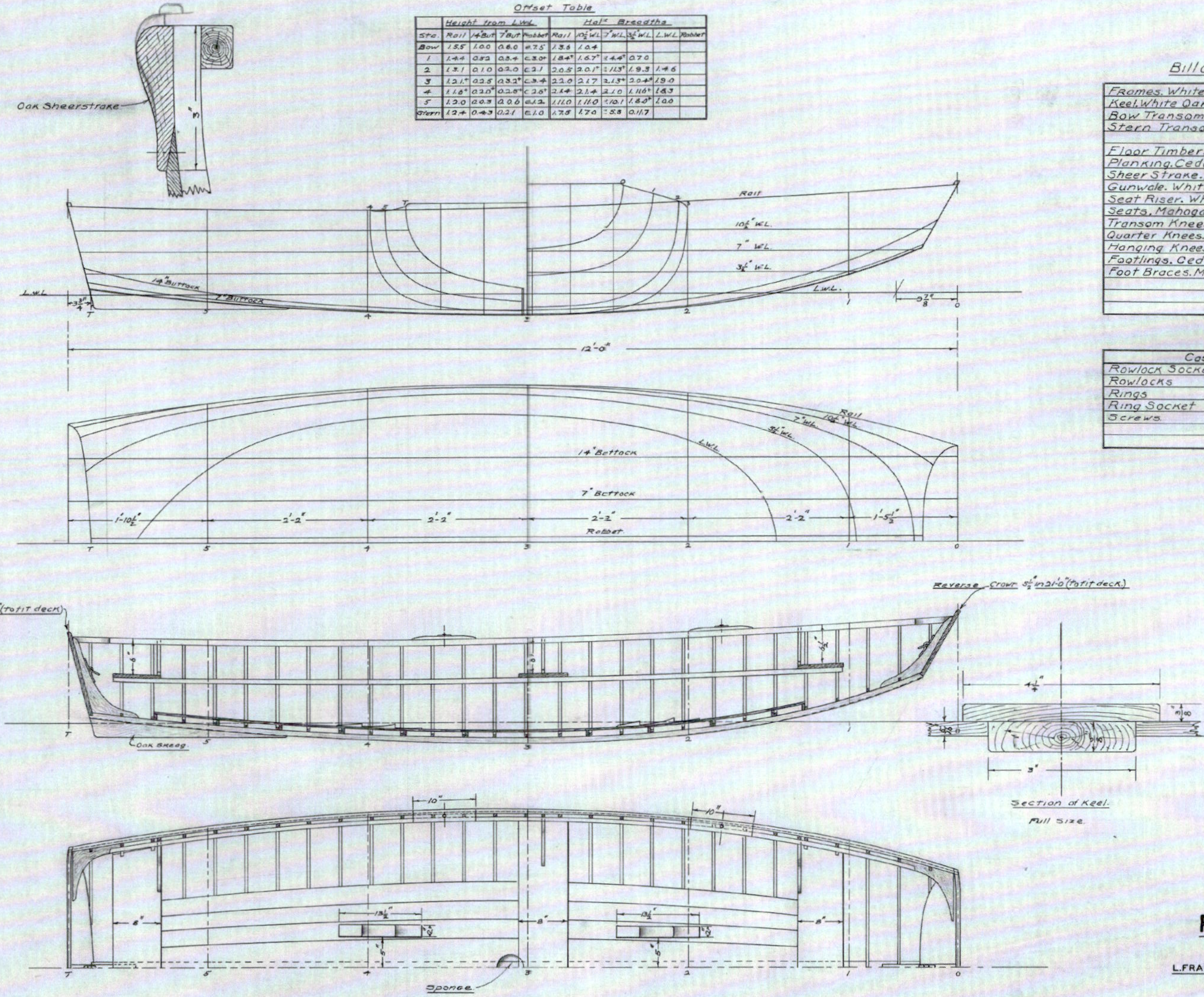

Sidney took him through Starling's design, set up in the South Construction Shop. Francis thought "she is none too strong," and wondered that the Lloyd's surveyors had passed her. But he wrote to Nathanael in Florida that "the Burgess boat is the prettiest model of all four."[22]

The masts of the Marconi-rigged J-boats, standing some 170 feet from keel to truck, would justify naming triangular-shaped sail plans after the inventor of radio, with its high antenna towers. Making the tallest single-section masts ever attempted for vessels would be a challenge. At Lawley's, it was up to Bror Tamm and his gang of sparmakers and riggers. Tamm had run the spar and rigging shops since 1920 and would soon become the yard's superintendent. Francis had met Tamm in 1923, when the Lawley yard built the *Stormy Petrel*. The same age, the two had different personalities, for "Tammy," as his friends called him, counterbalanced Francis's usual shy and gentle manner with great gusts of verbal energy. Yet they became fast friends, their divergent habits of conversation smoothed by strong, mutual respect. Each realized that it was worth listening to what the other had to say about boats. The difficult, urgent job of Tammy's building the *Whirlwind*'s mast to Francis's design would test their friendship.

Francis's design for the J-boat's hollow, wooden mast was basically a simple one: there were four sides held together and reinforced by eight corner pieces. But the spar had to be tapered precisely, and it had to be made up of many pieces of wood, glued together. Every one of hundreds of joints had to be perfect; for want of a perfectly fitted and glued joint, the Cup could be lost.

Bror Tamm thought Francis's mast design was too complicated. He described it many years later as "a darn good idea but difficult to do." When going over the project at 20 Lee Street with Francis and Paul Hammond, Tammy told Francis that he was not sure about his way of making the mast. Gluing the parts well would be troublesome, he thought, and the mast might not hold together. Francis flew into a rage, Tamm recalled, throwing his drawing on the floor, and saying, "If you're so smart, you go ahead and do it!" A week later, Tamm came back with a revised plan for the mast. Francis looked at it, appeared a little stunned, chuckled, and said, "Well, I doubt if it's any good, but if that's the way you want to do it, go ahead and do it your way." We don't have Francis's side of the story, and we don't know the nature of Bror Tamm's changes to Francis's mast design.[23]

As built, the *Whirlwind*'s mast weighed about 4,500 pounds and cost $11,000. It consisted of 1,100 separate pieces of spruce. Lengths of at least 20 feet were scarfed together to make the full 170 feet. Since the mast's wall thickness was only 2¼ inches, it took twenty men to move these 170-foot, spaghetti-like strips into place for gluing, without breaking them. When all the pieces were glued together, Tamm sent a small boy sliding inside the huge spar with a roller skate under his back and an electric torch in hand to see how the joints looked. The boy inspected 100 feet of the mast before its taper, or perhaps Tamm's nerve, stopped him. Francis was making frequent inspection trips to Lawley's at the time, so he may well have witnessed this re-enactment of his own much noisier, childhood journey inside the *Defender*'s mast.[24]

One complicating element of the *Whirlwind*'s mast design that Tamm couldn't change was the internal track for the mainsail luff slides that Hammond had to have. The track was made to Francis's design of extruded duralumin by the Baush Machine Tool Company in Springfield, Massachusetts. Duralumin was becoming popular for strong, light, metal structures, such as airship frames. The alloy had been invented in 1909 in Germany, where Alfred Wilm had discovered that adding 4 percent copper to aluminum made it resistant to ripping. Although he praised the track as "ingenious," Nathanael warned that it would be "elaborate and costly," and went on to write: "Think what would be the outcome if any untried details fail, and not give the craft the proper showing she should have and lose your reputation with your clients." Francis wasn't worried. He replied, "In regard to the untried gadgets on #44, I will try not to use any more if I can resist the temptation."[25]

Nathanael also disapproved of Francis's tangs on the *Whirlwind*'s mast. "Use eyes *around* the mast," he wrote. "Tangs may be ok in an R-boat, but not on such a big boat as a J." Again, Francis assured his father that he had worked out the details of his fittings so that they would be strong enough. And he wrote to the designer of the *Resolute* about her rigging eyes: "I might say that to me the mast and rigging on *Resolute* looked very clumsy and unscientific, and the rigging stretched a great deal in use." Nathanael gave up. "It appears as though I am too old fashioned and unscientific to give you any assistance about the rig and staying of spars on cup defenders," he wrote. "All I will say I hope all your inventions will be successful and that you will win out."[26]

The whole mast of the *Enterprise* was made of duralumin. It was 1,200 pounds lighter than the wooden masts of the other contenders, a huge advantage, especially for the smallest of the Js, because the lighter the mast, the more stability was reserved for the driving power of the sails. For the design of this mast, Starling turned to his brother, Charles P. Burgess, who had experience designing the metal structures for the navy's big airships. He applied "the elaborate mathematical theories" that he used in his aeronautical work to the metal structure of a 170-foot spar that would not buckle under the pressure of 7,500 square feet of sail in a 25-knot breeze. The Glenn L. Martin Company, of Baltimore, built the duralumin mast for $58,000.[27]

Francis wrote to Nathanael describing Paul Hammond's reaction, when he heard about the *Enterprise*'s duralumin mast: "So he got quite panicky. If he had heard that Burgess was making a mast of tight metal or celluloid, or anything else, he would have had to have had one right off." Francis must have realized that a lighter mast would be a significant advantage, but, despite the opportunity to compete for yachting's Holy Grail, he was not interested in trying to improve his design. He had applied his art to the utmost; what was done, was done. Nevertheless, Hammond pursued the idea. When Hammond received drawings of his proposed duralumin mast for the *Whirlwind* from a Dr. Arnstein—like Charles Burgess, an engineer working with lighter-than-air craft—he sent them to N. G. Herreshoff for comment, not to Francis. Nathanael pleaded ignorance of "this stuff," and was, wrongly, not impressed with saving 20 percent of the weight of the mast. Hammond dropped the idea for the time being.[28]

A key element for the successful racing of sailing yachts is to have well-shaped sails. For a yacht to do her best on the race course, particularly on the windward legs, where the skipper is engaged in the delicate balancing act of trying to sail fast while heading up as close to the wind as possible, the "cut of his jib" (and mainsail) is all-important. Too full—that is, too much curvature—and he couldn't point high and would have to sail extra distance to reach the weather mark. Too flat—that is, not enough curvature—and the boat would feel dead and slow. And the curvature had to be perfectly distributed, with most of the fullness forward, near the luff, gradually tapering off to almost nothing at the leach. There must be no hard spots or wrinkles.

The huge sails for all the contenders were cut and sewn by the only sailmaker capable of such work, the English firm of Ratsey and Lapthorn, and the work was done at their American loft at City Island at the head of Long Island Sound, established by George Ratsey, Sr. some five years earlier. The material for the sails of the *Whirlwind*'s three competitors was cotton duck shipped over from Ratsey's in Cowes, England; the *Whirlwind*'s sails were of Wamsutta duck made in New Bedford. In case a skipper might be dissatisfied with the shape a sail took in the wind, Ratsey and Lapthorn set up a re-cutting facility in Newport, for the New York

Yacht Club shifted the scene of the 1930 America's Cup races from the ocean course that had been used off Sandy Hook, outside New York Harbor, to an ocean course outside Narragansett Bay.

As the *Whirlwind* neared completion, so did her inventory of seventeen sails. Their importance may be inferred by the fact that they were stored in a vault. There were three mainsails and enough Wamsutta for a fourth; two forestaysails; seven jibs, three of them working jibs of progressive sizes, a small and a large Genoa jib, and a small and large balloon jib; and a large and small spinnaker. A small passage staysail and a storm trysail rounded out her wardrobe. The bill was about $80,000.[29]

THE *ENTERPRISE* got an important jump on her competitors when she was launched on April 14, nearly a month before the other J-boats. She was sailing five days later. The debacle with the *Whirlwind*'s keelson cost her a month, and since she was blocking the *Yankee* on the Lawley ways, it cost the Boston boat a month, too. But for the contretemps with the Lloyd's inspectors, the *Whirlwind* would have beaten the launch date of May 1 in her contract by three weeks. Instead, she was launched on May 7, still only a week late. The *Yankee* went down the ways three days afterward, on the same day when the *Weetamoe* took the water at Bristol. By then, the *Enterprise* had been tuning up under sail for three weeks and had been testing her speed against the Cup boats of 1920, the *Resolute* and *Vanitie*.[30]

At the launching of the *Whirlwind,* Francis was afraid that she would float lower than her designed waterline because of the added weight that Lloyds had required in her construction. After she "went down the ways very smoothly and steadily," however, he was "very much surprised to see that she floated about 10 inches high in the stern and 18 inches high in the bow." Her mast and rig would bring her down and level her, but Francis estimated that she could have the advantage of 10 tons of additional lead inside ballast without floating below her rated waterline. This would bring her ballast-to-displacement ratio up to about 63 percent. Francis wrote to Nathanael, "I think everything is working out very well on the *Whirlwind*." His father replied: "You are certainly to be congratulated in having *Whirlwind* float so high. It is a mighty good fault." Francis's sense of proportion had failed him this time, but, like his father, he seemed relieved rather than embarrassed by his design's unexpected buoyancy.[31]

But as the Cup boats began racing against each other off the New York Yacht Club's station at Glen Cove near the head of Long Island Sound, things did not work out well for the *Whirlwind*. The first meeting, on June 11, was between all the J-boats but the *Yankee,* and included the *Vanitie* and the *Resolute*. The *Whirlwind* carried the big jib and tiny forestaysail of Francis's advanced double-head rig. The afterguard and Captain John Muir quickly exhibited their strange notions of sail trim. When sailing close-hauled, they believed in trimming the mainsail in extremely flat and trimming the headsails with their sheets actually eased a little. This backwards combination prevented the sails from giving their maximum driving power and further slowed the boat by making her try to head up into the wind, so that extra rudder angle had to be used to keep her on course. At one point, that day, in an effort to trim the mainsail in more and more, the order was given to put twenty men on the mainsheet. They pulled so hard that the clew outhaul pendant ripped off the sail, releasing all tension on its foot, until a new outhaul could be jury-rigged. For much of the leeward leg, the crew failed to set a spinnaker. Even with these handicaps, the *Whirlwind* finished more than eight minutes ahead of the *Weetamoe*, but twelve minutes after the *Enterprise*. The misshandling of Francis's J-boat design did not augur well for the future.[32]

In an effort to correct the situation, the

Whirlwind's managers made a strange decision: they abandoned the double-head rig, and reverted to the traditional three-headsail rig that the other Js were using. Francis's reliance on a big jib had scared them from the beginning. Back in February, they had asked him to design an alternative sail plan with forestaysail, a normal-sized jib, and a small jib topsail. That drawing was now pulled out and followed to modify the *Whirlwind*'s rig. She would no longer have the pulling power of Francis's big jib as she tried to earn the right to defend the Cup.[33]

So, the *Whirlwind* evidently had too much weather helm. The cause was not Francis's hull design. He would have "gotten away with" the *Whirlwind's* raking mid-section had it not been for the actual cause: no one on board would trim the headsails in enough. It was perhaps not surprising that Landon Thorne didn't know better; the Star-boat sailor was out of his element in a J-boat. Nor is it surprising that Captain John Muir, the yacht's professional leader of the crew, chose to ease headsail sheets when beating to windward. He had no experience with trimming the flat-cut

ABOVE: **With her rudder well braced, the *Whirlwind* begins her ride down the Lawley ways into her element, May 7, 1930. The *Yankee* and *Weetamoe* will be launched three days later, but the *Enterprise* has been sailing since April 19. The four J-boats will start racing on June 11. This view shows off the *Whirlwind*'s underbody and her black walnut rail.** (© Mystic Seaport, Rosenfeld Collection, 1984.187.39125F)

ABOVE: The *Whirlwind* floated plenty high upon launching. Her rig will bring her down, but she will also need inside ballast. The high waterline shows that Francis was off on his estimate of where she would float, but the extra weight added to her stability. (© Mystic Seaport, Rosenfeld Collection, 1984.187.39131F) BELOW: The *Whirlwind* making her own breeze with a single headsail set. Edwin Levick's lens presents her stunning beauty reflected in a glassy Long Island Sound. (*Yachting* (July 1930): 48) OPPOSITE PAGE: Morris Rosenfeld's camera caught the *Whirlwind* on the wind, with the original, double-headsail rig. For once her sails are trimmed perfectly. (© Mystic Seaport, Rosenfeld Collection, 1984.187.39929F)

sails of a modern Marconi rig, designed to sail closer to the wind than any of the vessels he had commanded. What is mystifying is that Paul Hammond allowed Muir's penchant for not strapping in a jib to prevail. He certainly knew better, for example, from trimming the Burgess staysail schooner *Niña*'s array of headsails, sometimes four at a time, in her victory in the 1928 Transatlantic Race. But Muir was working for Thorne, and there may have been a fundamental clash between Thorne and Hammond; after all, Thorne was a Yale man whose World War I service had been in the army, while Hammond went to Harvard and was a naval officer.

And where was Francis? The designers of the other three J-boats were all in the afterguards of their creations, able to advise on sail trim or any other matter that might contribute to the speed of their yachts. Francis was ashore, except for one race. When the possibility of his son's designing a Cup defender had arisen, Nathanael, who had personally assured that his Cup boats were well managed, to the point of taking the helm himself on key occasions, wrote to Francis: "If you get involved with a Cup Defender, you should plan to spend a lot of time on board during her trials." And as the *Whirlwind* came closer to racing, Nathanael urged Francis to "keep aboard of her and sail in her all you can," and, "Do stick right to her and see that your designs have proper and successful treatment."[34]

Francis chose to ignore his father's advice. He allowed his reluctance to involve himself with owners who were not his good friends to get in his way. It is possible that if George Pynchon, whom he respected, had still been on board the *Whirlwind*, Francis would have spent more time on her himself, although he never sailed in Pynchon's *Istalena*. He had no respect for Thorne. Francis allowed the opportunity to help the *Whirlwind*

succeed pass him by. He did not have his father's force of personality or his reputation. He was not one to bend others to his will. Moreover, he was an artist who, once he had finished a work, did not want to revisit it, but preferred to shift his attention to the next design. Most yacht designers, including his father, sought perfection by attempting incremental improvements to successful boats; L. Francis Herreshoff sought perfection by leaps and bounds with new, different designs. Yet, no next design could possibly be as important to his career as the *Whirlwind.*

A greater problem than the *Whirlwind*'s weather helm was a byproduct of it, and it would

ABOVE: With the *Minas Princess* in the background, Francis (left) and Captain Muir discuss a detail with Lawley workers. If only Francis had been able to coach Muir on sail trim! (© Mystic Seaport, Rosenfeld Collection, 1984.187.39160F) RIGHT: The *Whirlwind*'s steering gear. This exquisite drawing shows Francis at his engineering best, for the gear performed exactly as he wanted it to, but it also shows Francis willing to risk too much innovation when the stakes were so high. He designed the Cup contender's unusual steering gear to be reversing, so that pressure on the rudder would turn the wheel, in order to give the helmsman a better "feel" for the balance of the boat. Her reversing steering gear made the big yacht hard to handle, until it was corrected after the initial observation races. (© Mystic Seaport, Daniel S. Gregory Ships Plans Library, SP.38.12.17)

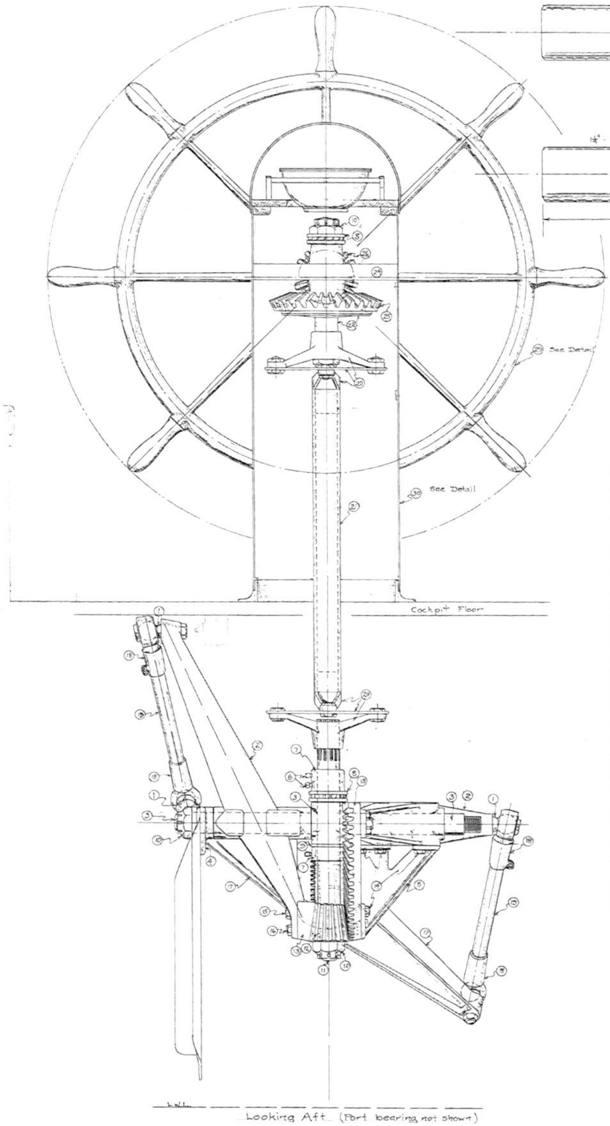

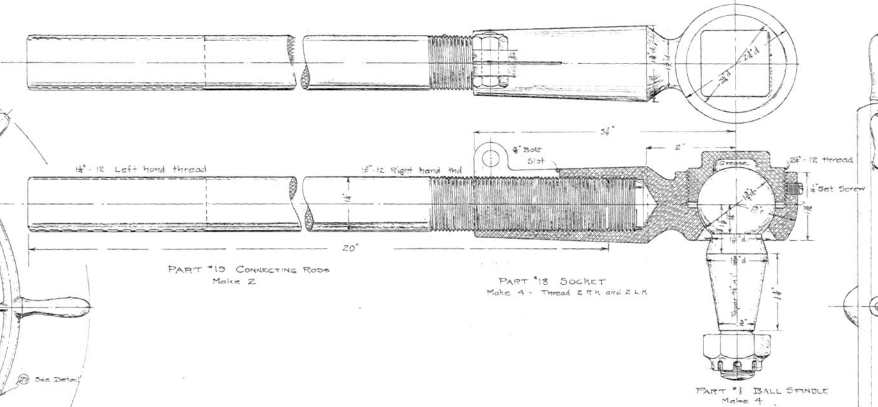

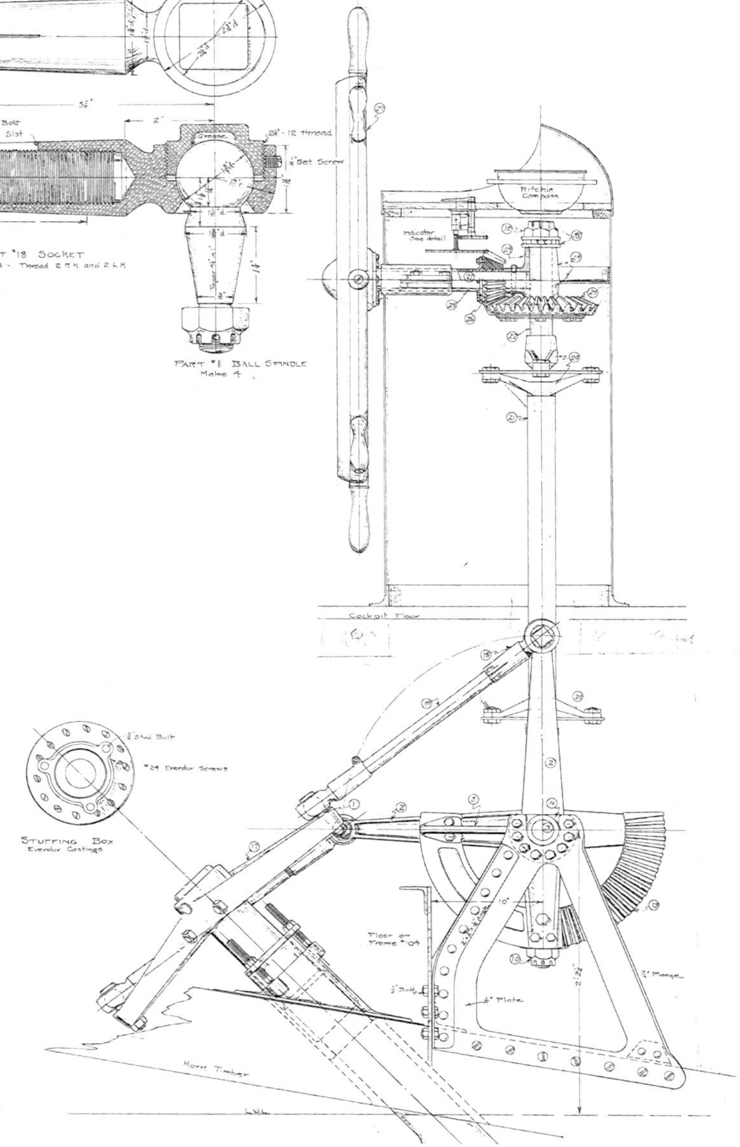

Part Number	Number Required	Name	Material	Remarks
BILL of MATERIAL				
1	4	Ball Spindle	Nitralloy Steel	
2	2	Steering Levers	Everdur	Machine for Starboard and Port
3	1	Counter Shaft	Steel	
4	2	Bearings	Everdur	Fastened with 8 - ½" Bolts
5	2	Brackets	Everdur	
6	3	⅜" Set Screws	Steel	Spotted into Shaft #11
7	2	Thrust Collars		Upper one 2" with 2 set screws Lower " ⅝" " 1 " "
8	2	Ball Thrust Bearing		S.K.F. #311
9	1	Thrust Washer		¼" Thick
10	4	1½" Castellated Nuts	Steel	A.S.E. 12 thread
11	1	Vertical Shaft		Upper end Splined to Coupling Lower end Tapered fit to Gear #12
12	1	Bevel Pinion gear	Steel	
13	2	Toothed Sectors	Everdur	Machine for Starboard and Port
14	16	½" Tap Bolts	Steel	A.S.E. 20 thread
15	2	⅜" Tap Bolts	Steel	A.S.E. 18 thread
16	4	7/16" Tap Bolts	Steel	A.S.E. 20 thread
17	1	Yoke	Everdur	
18	4	Ball Sockets	Everdur	2 Threaded Right Hand 2 " Left Hand
19	2	Connecting Rods	Everdur	Right and left hand thread
20	2	Flexible Coupling	Steel and Bronze	
21	1	Tube - Hollow Shaft	Bronze	Brazed to Coupling
22	1	Flanged Shaft	Steel	Taper fit to Coupling
23	1	Thrust Bearing		S.K.F. #308 on #27
24	1	Diaphragm Bearing	Bronze	
25	1	Bevel Gear	Bronze	
26	1	" Pinion	Steel	
27	1	Stub Shaft	Bronze	
28	1	Hollow Shaft	Steel	
29	1	Hand Steering Wheel	Duralumin	
30	1	Column	Duralumin	

Note: Details are shown on separate Drawings

No. 44
DETAIL #8 STEERING GEAR
Scales: 3"=1'0" and Full Size
L. FRANCIS HERRESHOFF - DESIGNER
Marblehead, Mass
November 27, 1925

have existed even if her sails had been trimmed perfectly so that she had the normal amount of weather helm that every sailing yacht needs to do her best. The culprit was the steering gear itself. In an attempt to give the helmsman at the wheel the same feel for steering that a tiller gives, Francis designed the steering gear to be reversing, so that pressure on the rudder would turn the wheel. Steering gear is normally designed so that the helmsman can take his hands off the wheel and it will stay put, holding the rudder at the desired angle. That was certainly the case on the other J-boats, but on the *Whirlwind*, the helmsman had to hold the wheel constantly and maintain pressure on it against the weather helm being transmitted to the wheel from the rudder. Francis's innovation didn't work. The forces on a huge J-boat were too great. Steering the *Whirlwind* in a breeze was difficult. Paul Hammond later said, "She was a bitch to steer. I used to start her and then Landon Thorne took over and within half an hour he was worn out. Herreshoff made the fanciest [steering] gear you ever saw, it looked like a mass of gold all that wonderful brass gearing." Once, when she was hit by a squall, Hammond, trying to pull the wheel down on its lee side to keep her from broaching, was thrown up and over the binnacle as the wheel spun beyond his control. It may have seemed ironic to him, wrestling with the *Whirlwind*'s wheel, that the device itself was so gorgeous, while the gear it operated seemed wrong. The 50-inch-diameter wheel was made of cast duralumin, with black walnut trim to match the yacht's rail, and the walnut was inlaid with a pattern of white holly.[35]

And the problem of the reversing steering gear was intensified by the rudder itself. Francis admitted that he made a mistake by specifying that it be built of mahogany, with no ballast. When the boat heeled over and the weather helm naturally increased, the rudder tended to float, requiring more pressure from the wheel to hold it in place, thus adding to the feel of weather helm. This part of the problem could have been corrected by adding lead to the rudder, but it wasn't.[36]

The other J-boats each had a small centerboard that could be lowered out of the bottom of the keel to increase lateral resistance in order to prevent leeway when beating to windward. And the *Enterprise* and *Yankee* each had a second, even smaller centerboard that could be dropped from the after end of the keel. This second board would move the center of lateral resistance aft to decrease weather helm, if needed. Such a trimming centerboard to alter the boat's balance would have helped the *Whirlwind*, given her poor sail trim, but Francis eschewed the complication and expense of centerboards in her design, relying, instead, on the biggest keel area of any of the J-boats. The weather helm generated by erroneous sail trim on the *Whirlwind* might have been overcome by an aft, trimming centerboard, but the resulting impact on the boat's speed or ability to sail close to the wind with headsail sheets too slack and main sheet too tight would have been negligible.[37]

The *Whirlwind* quickly got a reputation for having too much weather helm, a reputation that persists to this day. She did have too much weather helm. It was caused by poor sail trim and was exacerbated by Francis's reversing steering gear and floating rudder. It was these factors, not faulty hull or rig design, that caused the problem.[38]

In the second meeting of the three J-boats and their two aging trial horses, off Glen Cove on the next day, June 12, the *Whirlwind* finished dead last. This time, the *Weetamoe* edged out the *Enterprise* for the win; the *Weetamoe* beat the *Whirlwind* by more than twenty minutes. Irony turned to action: Hammond called and asked Francis to design a proper steering gear that would hold the rudder in position without pressure on the wheel. On June 16 and 17, with the *Yankee* down from Boston for the latter race, the *Whirlwind* beat the *Vanitie* and *Resolute*, but she could not beat any of the other J-boats. These races were much closer, with the *Weetamoe* again winning both. The *Whirlwind* was only two minutes behind the

winner on the sixteenth and four minutes behind on the next day.[39]

At 8:20 a.m. on June 20, someone in the Gear Department of the Henry B. Nevins yard, at City Island, marked "Rec'd." on Francis's pencil drawing (there was no time for an ink tracing) for a modified steering gear for the *Whirlwind.* Presumably, by June 23, when the racing resumed off Newport, the *Whirlwind* had a non-reversing steering gear and was easier to handle. If so, it did her no good. On the twenty-third, she was last of the four J-boats, six minutes off the pace; the next day she was last again by the same margin; and on the twenty-fifth the *Vanitie* joined the other three Js in beating her, and this time she was more than ten minutes behind the winning *Enterprise.*[40]

The betting odds were now: *Enterprise,* 2-1; *Weetamoe,* 6-1; *Yankee,* 25-1; and *Whirlwind,* 60-1. It was a shame. In the opinion of *The Rudder*: "the *Whirlwind* must be regarded as the outstanding yacht of the season in expressing originality, ingenuity and skill in design and construction. No cup yacht or any other racing craft ever carried quite so many new-fangled ideas as L. Francis

Paul Hammond at the *Whirlwind*'s wheel in early June, before the steering gear was altered to the normal, non-reversing mode. This view shows the streamlined deckhouse. (© Mystic Seaport, Rosenfeld Collection, 1984.187.39630F)

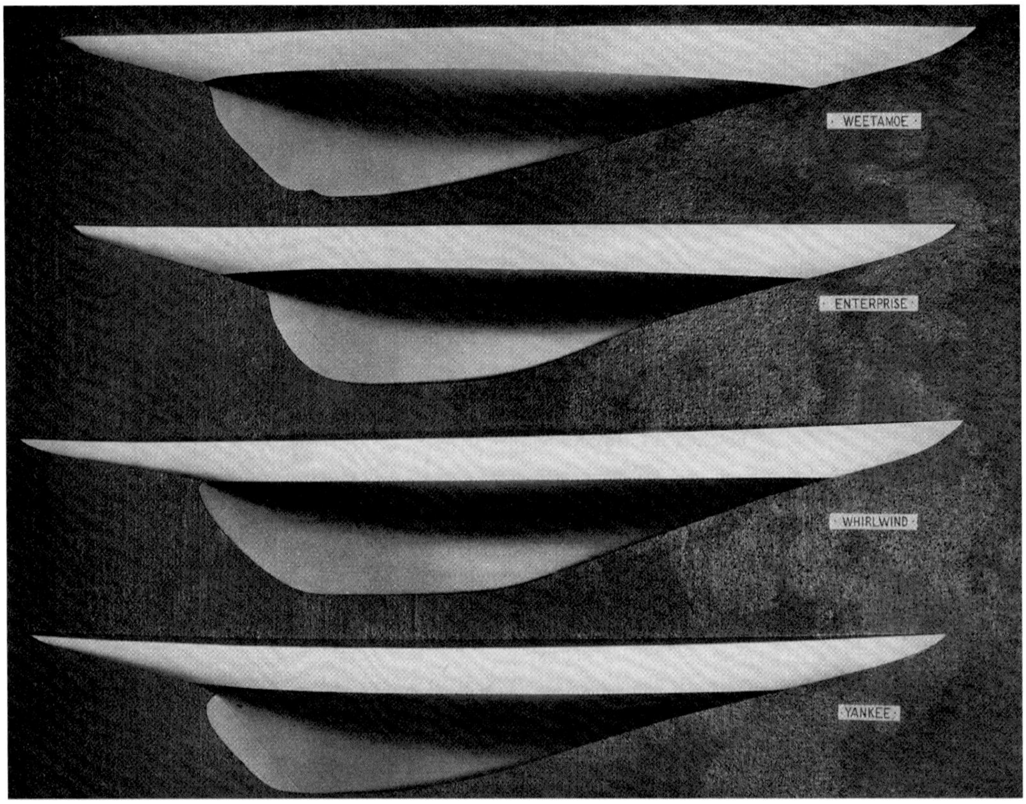

Herreshoff has installed on the Thorne-Hammond yacht." Unfortunately, Francis's originality, ingenuity, and skill were wasted on a syndicate that habitually trimmed the J-boat's sails to produce maximum weather helm and then wondered at what they had wrought. *Yachting*'s most experienced observer, W. P. Stephens, in correspondence with N. G. Herreshoff, wrote: "I would like to see her [the *Whirlwind*] win as the best boat in it [the J Class]. I am very sorry that she is not in abler hands as far as the development and actual sailing go."[41]

IN JULY, the New York Yacht Club staged a series of ten Observation races to begin the process of sorting out the four J-boats in preparation for selecting the Cup defender. In these match races in the ocean outside Narragansett Bay, where the Cup Races would be sailed, rotating pairs of contenders would be raced against each other, just two boats racing at a time, to duplicate the America's Cup format and see who could beat whom. Thorne and Hammond invited Francis to participate in the Observation series. He allowed himself to be "persuaded," the word he used in writing an account of the *Whirlwind* thirty years later, so he was on board her for the first Observation race on July 7 against the *Weetamoe*.[42]

Soon after the start, Francis was asked to steer, and he took the wheel. It was a windward leg in a ten-knot breeze. By both the feel of the boat and by watching the headsails, Francis realized that they needed to be trimmed in. He got permission from Paul Hammond to go forward to have the crew trim in the forestaysail, jib, and jib topsail to his liking. Hammond took the wheel, and Francis began directing the sheet trimmers. Here is the way he remembered what happened next: "While I was doing this the owner and captain [Thorne and Muir] came up to me and said in rather cross voices, 'You can't do that.' There was nothing for the designer of *Whirlwind* to do but go below which I did."[43]

Francis had come up against Thorne's and Muir's determination to sail his J-boat to windward without trimming the headsails in flat. We have only Francis's memory of what was said, but it is clear that he took the encounter as a rebuff. This was a very different situation for him than arguing with his friend Waldo Brown over trimming the jib of the *Gem*. Powerless to save the situation, he must have been angry, frustrated, and sad as he sulked, down in the *Whirlwind*'s cabin. By going below, he escaped a confrontation, but he couldn't escape the familiar pain of not being recognized for who he was and for what he knew. He was prone to avoiding confrontation; this was one of his more dramatic exits. And, as the race continued, Francis could add disappointment to his feelings: he must have realized that the *Whirlwind* would not be defending the America's Cup in September, for with her sail trim uncorrected, she had no chance. The *Weetamoe* won the match race by 3½ minutes. This incident ended Francis's participation in racing on the *Whirlwind*.[44]

July 7, 1930, was a disastrous day for L. Francis Herreshoff. The stakes were indeed high: Francis was striving to reach the America's Cup pinnacle that his father had long occupied. He needed to reach it in order to prove to himself, to his father and to the world, that L. Francis Herreshoff was as good a yacht designer as Nathanael G. Herreshoff. He had met his greatest challenge in his chosen profession of designing racing yachts with a superlative creation. The *Whirlwind*'s reversing steering gear had been corrected. Her floating rudder was a minor problem. But he had not developed a good working relationship with his clients. Ideally, he would have been able to present himself with the authority due the *Whirlwind*'s creator as the person best able to show the owners how to get the most speed out of the boat. He would have been able, long before July 7, to teach them, with tact, or cajolery, or threats of losing, how to trim the headsails. He would have been able to persuade them not to change his advanced headsail design. That he failed in these things meant that instead of having a chance to find success at the pinnacle of yacht racing, he found himself the creator of an also-ran. He knew that his design could be a winner, and so did W. P. Stephens and other experts. Nathanael G. Herreshoff wrote Stephens seven years after the debacle: "Francis sent me many of the blueprints to look over. I then decided, and still am of opinion she would have come out on top, had she been in good experienced hands." But none of this changed the fact that the *Whirlwind* was *not* a winner.[45]

At the end of the Observation Series, the point-score among the four J-boats was: *Weetamoe* 14, *Enterprise* 13, *Yankee 13, Whirlwind* 8. The latter's best performance was a decisive

LEFT: **The half-models of the four contenders to defend the America's Cup in 1930. The *Whirlwind* is the biggest of the four, with proportionally the most keel area. But the other three J-boats all had centerboards to increase lateral resistance when close-hauled, and the *Enterprise* and *Yankee* even had second centerboards, well aft, that could be lowered to reduce weather helm if necessary. When John G. Hanna, who wrote a monthly column for *The Rudder*, and who designed cruising boats so tubby that Francis called them "lightships," saw this photograph, he predicted that the *Whirlwind* would be the winner.** (*Yachting* (May 1930): 92)

7½-minute victory over the *Yankee* on July 8, the day after Francis's advice about headsail trim had been rejected. Is it possible that the *Whirlwind*'s brain trust had afterthoughts? No, the *Yankee* allowed them to split tacks and go inshore to find their own, private northwest breeze. On July 14, a 25-knot southeaster disabled both the *Whirlwind* and the *Enterprise*. The latter tore her sloppily reefed mainsail. On the *Whirlwind*, the mainsail headboard pulled out. It wasn't the elegant headboard that Francis had designed back in December with an internal double-sheave, but rather a simple attachment for an external double block that had been substituted in March.[46]

As soon as the Observation series had shown Thorne and Hammond that their boat needed marked improvement, they decided to take drastic action to decrease the *Whirlwind*'s weather helm. The tender, *Twister*, took the big J-boat in tow and proceeded up Long Island Sound to the Nevins yard at City Island for re-rigging. Far from taking Francis's advice to trim in the headsails, the *Whirlwind*'s managers had him make a new sail plan with the mast and headstay moved forward. And the mast was a new one, for Hammond had pressed for a lightweight, duralumin spar. Dr. Arnstein's design was built by the Goodyear-Zeppelin Corporation in Akron, Ohio. When the racing among the four J-boats resumed in August, the *Whirlwind* was ready with a new rig. Francis believed that it would make no difference to the yacht's performance. He was right.[47]

On the New York Yacht Club cruise during the first week in August, the J-boats raced as a class on the port-to-port runs between New London, Connecticut, and Martha's Vineyard, with one race over a triangular course in Buzzards Bay. The *Enterprise* won three of the five races. The *Whirlwind* technically beat the *Yankee* in one race and the *Weetamoe* in another, when both were disqualified, and she beat the *Weetamoe* in a further race, when the Crane boat had to maneuver to pick up a man overboard. Otherwise, the *Whirlwind* was always last. And when the Club's Selection Committee ran off a second series of match races

The *Yankee* crosses ahead of the *Whirlwind* in an Observation Series race on July 11, 1930. The latter's headsails are not trimmed in enough, a crippling error that was repeated many times during her racing season. Yet the *Yankee* beat her that day by only a minute and a half. (Photo by Edwin Levick. *Yachting* (August 1930): 57)

off Newport starting on August 20, the members needed only two victories of the *Yankee* over the *Whirlwind* to warrant their coming on board the latter after the race of August 21 to inform Landon Thorne that his yacht's presence at the trials would no longer be required. The *Whirlwind*'s racing career of two months and ten days was over. Her mainsail would never be hoisted again. On August 29, Francis wrote to Nathanael, "I am greatly relieved that the strain of being with the *Whirlwind* is over." By then, the Committee had chosen the *Enterprise* to defend the America's Cup against the *Shamrock V*.[48]

FRANCIS DID blame others for the *Whirlwind's* lack of success, with justification, but his sulking of July 7 did not continue. When it was all over, he wrote to Nathanael: "You would be quite surprised if you knew the foolish things I have had to persuade the afterguard of the *Whirlwind* not to do, but I will tell you about some of this when I see you." Francis stayed involved, but we don't know what "the foolish things" that he prevented were, only that they were not sufficiently important to make a difference.[49]

Francis even got some social pleasure out of his involvement. He wrote to his father: "I think everybody but the *Yankee* crew are well satisfied with the choice of *Enterprise*, and the crew of the *Weetamoe* were very nice about it. I was calling on Mr. Burgess on board the *Vara* [the Vanderbilt power yacht] when the *Weetamoe* crew came over to congratulate Mr. Vanderbilt." And he went on, "We had a very pleasant supper party on board the *Minas Princess* the other night and Mr. Nicholson and Mr. Burgess were there and both showed the lines of their 'J' boat." Francis also had a tour of the *Shamrock V* with Charles Nicholson, another "very pleasant time."[50]

After losing four straight races to the *Enterprise*, Tommy Lipton had his last *Shamrock* brought alongside the victor so that he and his crew could give the winners three cheers, cheers that were handsomely returned. The great Cup was saved again.

When the next challenge came, in 1934, from T. O. M. Sopwith, the English manufacturer of aircraft, with the *Endeavour*, the *Whirlwind* had been laid up for four years. There she stayed, while Burgess and Vanderbilt won the Cup again, with the *Rainbow*. Nathanael wrote to Francis, "I wish *Whirlwind* could have been in good hands and properly fitted for the Trial races." Doubtless Francis did too. He was proud of his creation and put up on the wall of his drafting room at 20 Lee Street a large, framed photograph of the *Whirlwind*. When the J-boats came to Marblehead after the 1934 Cup races, Francis paddled out in his kayak to look them over. Harold Vanderbilt spotted him from his big tender-yacht, the *Vara*, and called out, "Francis! Francis!" The *Whirlwind's* designer wouldn't look up. Carrying a cargo of hurtfulness, he just kept paddling away.[51]

At this time, English yachtsman Thomas B. F. Davis, who owned the big Herreshoff racing schooner *Westward*, asked Nathanael to design him a J-boat with which to continue his rivalry with King George V's *Britannia*. At age eighty-six, Nathanael declined and asked Francis if he would like to be recommended for the job. Francis replied: "I really do not feel able to undertake so much responsibility, and do not think it would be good policy for me under any varying conditions. If I just did the lines and sail plan, leaving construction to others, the design would probably be a failure. If I should make a very detailed design I am sure the difficulty of having it built abroad, so that it functioned properly, would be too much for me." Nathanael suggested to Davis that he buy the *Whirlwind*, but Davis was set on a new J-boat. He never did get one, for King George's death in 1936 ended the friendly competition, and Davis lost interest in racing.[52]

In 1935, Thorne, Loomis, and Hammond

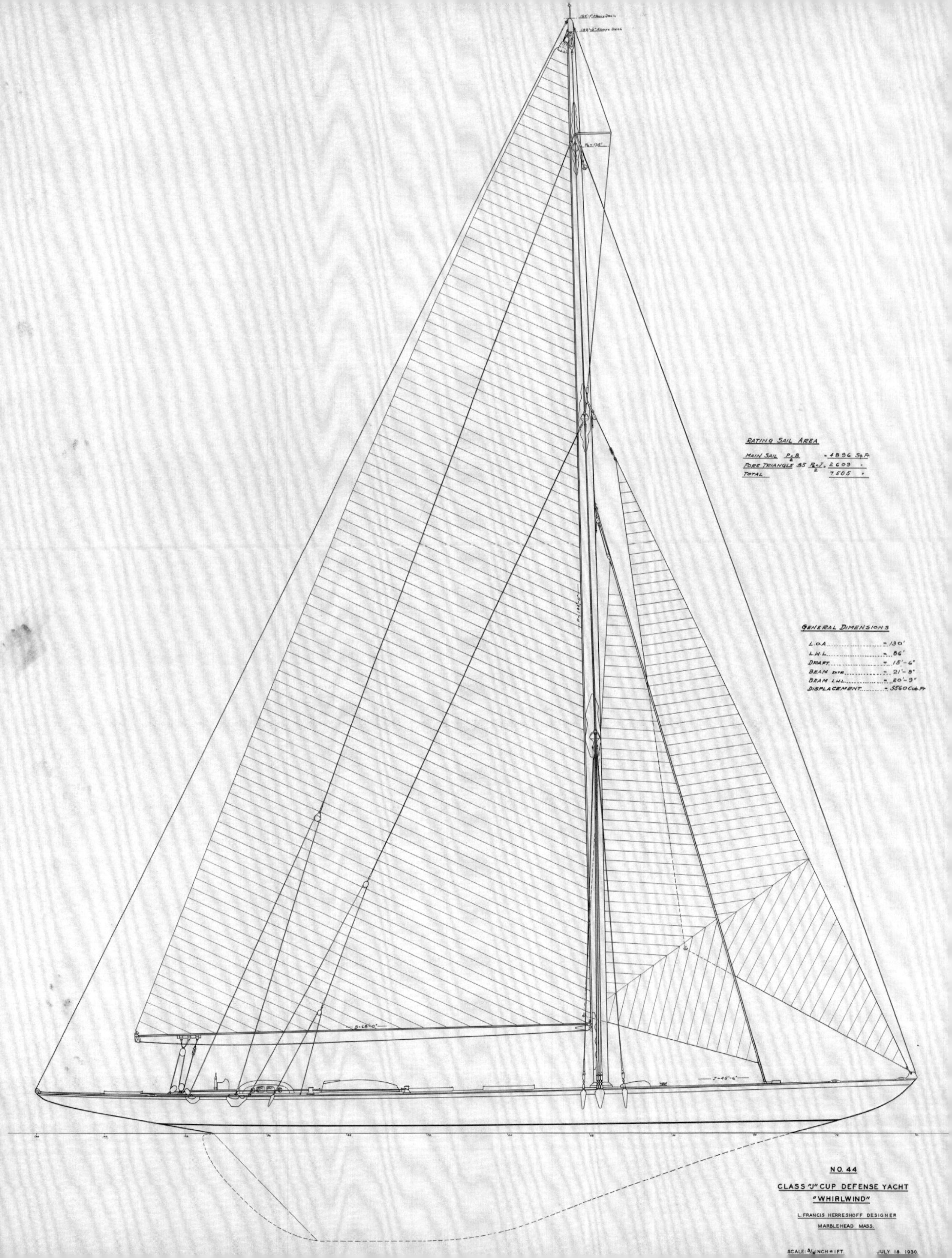

RATING SAIL AREA
MAIN SAIL P×B/2 = 4896 Sq.Ft.
FORE TRIANGLE .85 P×J/2 = 2609 "
TOTAL 7505 "
GENERAL DIMENSIONS
L.O.A. = 130'
L.W.L. = 86'
DRAFT = 15'-6"
BEAM EXTR = 21'-8"
BEAM L.W.L. = 20'-9"
DISPLACEMENT = 5560 Cub.Ft.
NO. 44
CLASS "J" CUP DEFENSE YACHT
"WHIRLWIND"
L. FRANCIS HERRESHOFF DESIGNER
MARBLEHEAD MASS.
SCALE: 3/16 INCH = 1 FT.
JULY 18 1930.

sold the *Whirlwind* for scrap for $9,000. She was purchased by an employee of the Jacobson yard at City Island, where she had been laid up, on condition that she not be sailed and that she be broken up. W. P. Stephens, on top of the situation as usual, wrote to Nathanael, "I understand that in selling her to be broken up the idea was to remove as quickly as possible all evidences of the crime [the mismanagement of the boat in 1930] without attracting attention." And he went on to refer to "the wanton destruction of *Whirlwind* without a thorough trial." The *Whirlwind* syndicate succeeded in making it impossible for anyone to show them up. Francis wrote, "*Whirlwind* has been broken up and we will never know whether she was fast or slow."[53]

Sopwith challenged for the America's Cup again in 1937 with a new *Endeavour*. Harold Vanderbilt and Starling Burgess teamed up once more, this time with help on the design from Olin J. Stephens, to win the Cup with the *Ranger*. The dimensions of the big *Ranger*, which earned the reputation as the best of all the J-boats, were close to those of the *Whirlwind*. It was not a case of Starling copying Francis. Seven years later, Starling simply arrived at design conclusions similar to those of Francis by mathematics and tank-testing, instead of by intuition. By then, changes in the J-Class measurement rule had increased the advantage of a larger boat. But the *Ranger*'s outstanding performance emphasized the possibility of what the *Whirlwind* might have been.

Francis blamed the afterguard of the *Whirlwind* for her failure. He may well have singled out Paul Hammond as the chief culprit, for he knew that Hammond should have been capable of sailing the boat at her best. And Hammond, himself, may have felt some chagrin at his own performance, although chagrin was hardly his habit. At any rate, he did not hold Francis responsible for the J-boat's poor showing. If he had, he would not have come back to L. Francis Herreshoff the very next year for the design of his dreamboat, the 71-foot ketch *Landfall*.

Landon Thorne perhaps got more pleasure at the wheel of the *Twister* than he did at the *Whirlwind*'s helm. In 1932, he had a bowsprit with pulpit added to the tender, lookout stations installed aloft on a schooner rig with steadying sails, and a new steering wheel mounted atop her pilothouse. He and Loomis went swordfishing.

Francis got no pleasure from the *Whirlwind*. He had put all his knowledge and his artistic and scientific skill into her design, and he knew what a wonderful racing yacht he had created. Her failure was a huge disappointment to him. It was some consolation that his father shared that disappointment. Yet, next to having been sent to The Farm by that father, the poor performance of the *Whirlwind* was the most crushing instance of Francis's not being recognized for who he was. The what-ifs are almost inevitable: what if the stock market hadn't crashed and the skilled big-boat sailor Pynchon had continued as managing owner of the *Whirlwind*? What if someone on board—anyone—had trimmed the J-boat's headsails

---

LEFT: The *Whirlwind*'s modified sail plan of July 18, 1930. The change included a new, lighter duralumin mast and was effected between the observation series and the trials for selection. Thorne and Hammond thought the boat had too much weather helm, so the mast was moved forward 7 feet, 2 inches, and the headstay was moved forward to the stemhead. The mainsail was not changed, just moved forward. She lost 30 square feet of sail area in the fore triangle. By this time, Francis knew why the *Whirlwind* usually carried too much weather helm, but it was the crew's sail-trim problem, not a design problem, and, though he tried, he could not fix it. The new rig did not improve the *Whirlwind*'s performance. (© Mystic Seaport, Daniel S. Gregory Ships Plans Library, SP.38.12.102)

properly? But also, what if Francis had been able to make himself part of the *Whirlwind*'s afterguard and see to it that the yacht was raced competently? But a complete change of Francis's personality was no more likely than the stock market continuing to rise forever.

Francis thought it strange to name a vessel for a wind she would hope never to meet, but *Whirlwind* was an accurate name for his greatest creation: she blew into and out of his life with a great rush, and he would never be quite the same yacht designer again. Had the *Whirlwind* been able to compete on an equal footing with the *Enterprise, Yankee,* and *Weetamoe,* even if she hadn't been selected as the defender, Francis would have been recognized as one of the top designers of racing yachts, along with Starling Burgess, Frank Paine, and Clinton Crane. The design of the *Whirlwind* should have been the pinnacle of his career, but, instead, it was the nadir. After the debacle of 1930, L. Francis Herreshoff turned almost exclusively away from the design of racing yachts and toward the design of cruising yachts. That course change would guide him to a very different pinnacle, one that perhaps was less exciting than racing for the America's Cup, but one that was more in keeping with the quiet, sensitive artist that he was.

The *Twister* on her mooring. Langdon Thorne would have more fun with her than he did with the J-boat she tended.
(© Mystic Seaport, Rosenfeld Collection, 1984.187.41078F)

Chronology
Endnotes, Bibliography
Index

AN L. FRANCIS HERRESHOFF CHRONOLOGY, 1890–1930

1890

November 11: Lewis Francis Herreshoff is born to Nathanael Greene and Clara A. DeWolf Herreshoff at Bristol, Rhode Island. He has four siblings: Agnes, six; Sidney, four; Nathanael, two; and Griswold, one.

November: *The Rudder* magazine publishes its sixth monthly issue.

November: Herreshoff Manufacturing Company contracts to build the *Vamoose*, William Randolph Hearst's 27-knot (!) steamer.

1891

February 27: Herreshoff Manufacturing Company contracts to build the *Gloriana* and the *Dilemma*, the first fin-keeler.

July 12: Edward Burgess dies.

1893

February 9: Herreshoff Manufacturing Company contracts to build the *Alerion*, Nathanael Herreshoff's 32-foot sloop.

September 3: Francis is baptized at St. Michael's Episcopal Church, Bristol.

October 7-13: The *Vigilant*, Nathanael's first America's Cup boat, defeats the *Valkyrie II* off Sandy Hook.

1894

June 17: Herreshoff Manufacturing Company contracts to build the *Alerion II*, Nathanael's 28-foot sloop.

1895

February 22: Francis' brother, Clarence Herreshoff, is born.

Spring: If his later memory is correct, four-year-old Francis works inside the *Defender*'s mast as it is riveted together.

September 7-12: The *Defender* defeats the *Valkyrie III* to win the America's Cup.

September: Herreshoff Manufacturing Company contracts to build the *Kildee*, Nathanael's 18-foot sloop.

October: Herreshoff Manufacturing Company contracts to build the *Porter* and the *Du Pont*, torpedo boats for the US Navy.

November 15: Herreshoff Manufacturing Company contracts to build the first of the Newport 30s.

ca. 1895: Starling Burgess, at about age seventeen, makes the first of his visits to the Herreshoff family to pay homage to and seek advice from Nathanael; he bounces the child Francis on his knee. (Francis will go on to work for Starling, his true mentor, from 1920 to 1926. They will remain friends until Starling's death in 1947.)

1895: Andrew Patterson becomes managing editor of *The Rudder*, a position he holds until 1950.

1896

Summer: Nathanael starts Francis working in the Row Boat Shop at the Herreshoff Manufacturing Company.

October 27: Francis enters 1st grade.

1897

August: Francis cruises with his family in the *Neckan*, a Herreshoff steam yacht chartered from her owner.

September: Francis must repeat 1st grade.

1898

February 20: Francis sends a drawing of the USS *Boston* to his maternal grandmother, Clara DeWolf.

June 27: The *Spray* enters Newport after Joshua Slocum's single-handed circumnavigation.

September: Francis enters 2nd grade.

1899

September: Francis enters 3rd grade.

October 11: Herreshoff Manufacturing Company contracts for the first of the New York Yacht Club 70-footers.

October 16–20: The *Columbia* defeats the *Shamrock* in America's Cup racing.

1899: Herreshoff Manufacturing Company contracts for the first of the Buzzards Bay 15-footers, the E Class.

1900

September: Francis enters 4th grade.

ca. 1900: Nathanael buys Francis tools, using some of his savings from working in the Row Boat Shop.

ca. 1900: Francis and Nick Potter become boyhood friends. (Later, they will work together briefly at Burgess, Swasey, & Paine and will maintain contact throughout Francis's life.)

1901

September: Francis must repeat 4th grade.

September: Herreshoff Manufacturing Company contracts for the *Roamer*, Nathanael's 94-foot steam yacht.

September 28–October 4: The *Columbia* defeats the *Shamrock II* to keep the America's Cup.

1902

Summer: Francis cruises with his family in the *Roamer.*

September 8: Francis enters 5th grade.

October 3: Herreshoff Manufacturing Company contracts for the Bar Harbor 31.

Winter: Francis witnesses a major fire at "The Mount," Bristol.

1903

Summer: Francis cruises with his family in the *Roamer.*

August 22-September 3: The *Reliance* defeats the *Shamrock III* in defense of the America's Cup

September 14: Francis enters 6th grade.

1904

April: Francis joins the Rhode Island Audubon Society.

Summer: Francis cruises with his family in the *Roamer.*

September 12: Francis enters 7th grade.

November 15: Herreshoff Manufacturing Company contracts for the New York Yacht Club 30-foot class.

1905

May: The three-masted schooner yacht *Atlantic* (designed by William Gardner) sets a record in the transatlantic race.

Summer: Francis cruises with his family in the *Roamer.*

Summer: Francis crews in race on a New York Yacht Club 30.

September: Francis enters 8th grade.

November 28: Francis's mother, Clara DeWolf Herreshoff, dies.

ca. 1905: Francis is "laying in bed the best part of the days," according to Nathanael.

1906

Summer: Francis cruises with his family in the *Roamer.*

September 10: Francis enters 9th grade.

1907

June: Francis carves a half model of a long, slim, lovely racer.

September: Francis enters high school (10th grade).

1908

June: Francis graduates from high school (11 grades).

September: Francis enters the College of Agriculture and Mechanic Arts (now the University of Rhode Island) at Kingston, Rhode Island.

1909

October 1: Herreshoff Manufacturing Company contracts to build the schooner *Westward.*

1910

February: Francis carves a model of a Sonder boat (Herreshoff Manufacturing Company Hull No. 695).

April: Francis sails on trial trip of the schooner *Westward.*

May: Francis finishes the two-year course at the College of Agriculture and Mechanic Arts.

Fall: Francis starts running The Farm, which he will do until 1917.

1911

January: Francis carves a model of the *Pollywog*, Buzzard's Bay 21 (Herreshoff Manufacturing Company Hull No. 707).

1912

January 20: Francis takes Christine Howe out for a ride on his iceboat and has a crack-up. She is badly injured.

March: Herreshoff Manufacturing Company contracts to build *Helianthus*, Nathanael's 64-foot power cruiser.

September 13: Herreshoff Manufacturing Company contracts to build the New York Yacht Club 50s, including the *Pleione.*

October 19: Herreshoff Manufacturing Company contracts to build the *Alerion III*, Nathanael's 22-foot sloop.

1913

Winter: Francis accompanies Nathanael to Bermuda to help his father rig the *Alerion III.*

1914

March 28: Herreshoff Manufacturing Company contracts to build the Buzzards Bay 25s.

November 14: Herreshoff Manufacturing Company contracts to build the first of the 12 ½-footers.

1915

June 25: Francis watches the Harvard-Yale Race in the Thames River on board the *Helianthus.*

July 20: Francis's uncle, John Brown Herreshoff, dies.

August 5: Francis watches the Astor Cup Race off Newport on board the *Helianthus.*

October 7: Nathanael marries Ann Roebuck.

October 14: Herreshoff Manufacturing Company contracts to build the New York Yacht Club 40-foot class.

1916

June 23: Francis is on board the *Helianthus* for the Harvard-Yale Race. The cruise continues, calling at Newport, and watching races off New London and Block Island.

ca. 1916: Francis owns a Baby Blitzen Benz racing car.

1916: Marconi rig comes to America.

1917

April 6: The United States declares war on Germany.

May 28: Francis enters the US Naval Reserve Force as an ensign. Assigned to the Equipment Office, he supervises alterations to yachts turned over to the navy for patrol work.

June 25: Francis becomes commanding officer of the Steam Patrol Boat No. 578, working near Block Island. He reports to Lt. (jg) Harold S. Vanderbilt.

November 1: Nathanael sails for Florida on board the *Helianthus II.*

December: Francis is put in command of Steam Patrol Boat No. 56, operating alternately with SP 578.

1917: Wealthy patrons buy John Brown Herreshoff's stock in the Herreshoff Manufacturing Company.

1918

March 11: Francis is ordered to the Inspection Station, Second Naval District, where he inspects naval vessels.

July 13: Francis is ordered to the Experimental Station, New London, where he develops underwater shapes for naval devices.

1919

Winter: Francis is assigned to a board to determine peacetime uses for recent naval inventions.

March 14: Francis is released from active duty in the US Navy.

Fall: Francis designs a 14-foot sailing skiff for the Bristol Yacht Club.

December 28: Herreshoff Manufacturing Company contracts to build the first S-boat, the first Herreshoff Manufacturing Company boat with a Marconi rig.

1920

Winter: Francis designs a 20-foot keel day sailer for Narragansett Bay—with Marconi rig (not built until 1985).

March: Francis delivers Nathanael's *Alerion III* from New York to Bristol.

July 15-27: The *Resolute* defeats the *Shamrock IV* in defense of the America's Cup.

November 20: Francis designs a modernistic catamaran.

ca. 1920: Francis makes the preliminary design for a 45-foot deep-sea cruiser (double-ended ketch), his design No. F-5 (not completed).

December: Francis goes to work for Starling Burgess in Provincetown.

1921

January: Frank Paine joins Burgess. Francis becomes good friends with Paine. (There's a twenty-year hiatus in their friendship after Burgess, Swasey, & Paine closes down in 1926. They will reconnect in 1946, and their friendship will continue until Paine's death in 1952.)

March 1: Francis gets a bonus of $100 from the state of Rhode Island for his service in World War I.

May: Trials of the Burgess-designed 6-Metre, *Sheila,* take place at the Herreshoff Manufacturing Company.

July: Francis at Cowes, England, where he crews for Frank Paine in the 6-Metre *Jeanie.*

October: Frank Paine joins Burgess as a partner to form Burgess and Paine.

1922

ca. January 1: Francis makes a freehand drawing of the racing fishing schooner *Puritan* (B & P design No. 227).

February 5: Francis designs an 85-foot auxiliary fishing ketch (not completed).

April 19: Francis designs a 101-foot three-masted schooner (No. F-16, not completed).

May 17: Francis designs a 61-foot centerboard ketch at Burgess & Paine (not completed).

June 9: Francis makes a preliminary design for a 62-foot shoal-draft Marconi-rigged schooner (including foresail) for Paul Hammond at Burgess and Paine.

Summer: Francis works on plans for the *Undertaker*, a 6-Metre for Charles A. Welch (Burgess & Paine No. 229). He begins what will grow into a close friendship with Charlie Welch, for whom he will design sixteen boats into the mid-1930s. Their friendship will continue until Welch's death in 1945.

August 31: Francis designs a 49-foot schooner (Burgess & Paine, not completed).

1923

Francis makes a study of a 130-foot steel steam yacht.

January 1: Francis designs the pond model *Dilemma*, 500 square inches.

Early 1923: A. Loring Swasey joins Burgess and Paine to form Burgess, Swasey, & Paine.

March 15: Francis designs the rig, with the first tangs, for the R-boat *Gypsy* (Burgess, Swasey, & Paine No. 237).

1923: Francis invents the rectangular, hollow spar.

April 22: Francis designs the *Stormy Petrel* for Charles A. Welch (Design No. 18).

Spring: Francis meets Bror Tamm, rigger at Lawley's. They will establish a friendship that continues until Francis's death.

November: Burgess, Swasey, & Paine's offices move from Provincetown to 585 Boylston Street, Boston.

December: Francis designs noiseless winch at Burgess, Swasey, & Paine.

December 1923-July 1924: Francis, with Waldo Brown, designs the *Joann* (Burgess, Swasey, & Paine No. 257) for Brown. This is a landmark design, precursor of the *Tioga*s. Francis begins friendship with Waldo Brown, for whom he will design the *Tioga* in 1930 and who will involve him in the *Yankee* One Design project in 1937. Their friendship will last until Brown's death in 1939.

1924

January 2: Francis designs a 33-foot ketch (forerunner to the *Santee* and the H-28) at Burgess, Swasey, & Paine (not built).

January 6–March 4: Francis designs the *Manana*, a 61-foot centerboard schooner (Burgess, Swasey, & Paine No. 262).

April 8: Francis designs the *Santee*, a 33-foot sloop (Burgess, Swasey, & Paine No. 269).

August 21, 22: Herreshoff Manufacturing Company is bought at auction by Rudolph F. Haffenreffer.

October 8: Herreshoff Manufacturing Company contracts for the *Pleasure*, Nathanael's 30-foot sloop.

October 22-April 12, 1925: Francis designs the R-boat *Yankee* for Charles A. Welch (Burgess, Swasey, & Paine No. 272), representing the first use of wooden longitudinal construction.

1924: Francis makes a preliminary design for a 104-foot brigantine.

1924: Francis makes a preliminary design for a fast seagoing cruiser at Burgess, Swasey, & Paine.

Winter 1924-25: Francis lives aboard the *Joann* on the Charles River.

Winter 1924-25: Nathanael and Ann Roebuck spend their first winter in Commodore Ralph Middleton Munroe's cottage at Coconut Grove, Florida.

1925

January: Francis designs the iceboat *Slipper* for Charles A. Welch (Burgess, Swasey, & Paine No. 285).

February 2: Francis designs a 44-foot lifeboat ketch for Charles A. Welch (Burgess, Swasey, & Paine No. 288, not built).

March 19: Nathanael writes to Francis from Florida, their first contact since Francis went off to work for Starling Burgess at Provincetown in 1920.

April: Francis acquires a Hjorth lathe.

Summer: Francis races sailing canoes on the Charles River.

August 4: Francis makes preliminary design for 40-foot fishing launch at Burgess, Swasey, & Paine.

September: Francis makes preliminary design for the 50-foot motorsailer *Walrus*, proposed winter cruiser and summer tender for the *Yankee*, for Charles A. Welch (Design No. 19). Design not finished until late 1929 (Welch put her on hold, and the *Dispatch* becomes the summer tender).

November 11: On his thirty-fifth birthday, Francis designs R-boat with patent streamlined rig, forerunner of the *Live Yankee* (Burgess, Swasey, & Paine 303, not built).

December 6: Francis's brother Clarence (age thirty) has been left by his wife. He lives in East Braintree, Massachusetts.

1925-26: Francis lives with Frank and Virginia Paine at 11 Beacon Street.

1926

January 11: Francis designs new rig for the *Hayseed VIII*, a Q-boat, at Burgess, Swasey, & Paine.

February 20: Francis designs schooner rig for the *Pleione*.

April: Francis's brother Nathanael dies of pneumonia at age thirty-eight.

April: Francis thinks he has "a leaky heart."

April 13-September: Frank Paine, Francis's "most intimate friend in Boston," is away for five months in Africa.

April 19: Nathanael writes Francis of his disappointment that none of his sons finished MIT and none qualified to take over the Herreshoff Manufacturing Company.

April 19: Nathanael writes Francis a pep talk: look ahead; assume direction; cater to the needs of the public, etc., etc.

April: Francis loves working on the lathe.

April 29: Francis designs 40-foot motor launch for George Upton (Burgess, Swasey, & Paine, not built).

Summer: Francis goes out in a powerboat to watch R- and Q-boats sail, watching behavior in generated waves.

Summer: Francis races in the R-boat *Yankee* off Newport.

July 9-October 8: Francis designs the *Dispatch* (Burgess, Swasey, & Paine No. 314, then Francis's Design No. 20), tender to the *Live Yankee* for Charles A. Welch.

Fall: Starling Burgess closes down Burgess, Swasey, & Paine and starts what will be Burgess, Rigg, & Morgan in New York. Francis establishes his own design business. He moves from Boston to 20 Lee Street, Marblehead, the brick, attached building down on the water side of 20 Lee Street proper.

October: Francis employs Norman Skene as draftsman. The author of *The Elements of Yacht Design*, Skene had been draftsman at Burgess, Swasey, & Paine.

October: Francis employs Helen Bolster as secretary. Previously employed as office manager at the Burgess aircraft plant in Marblehead, she will work for Francis until retiring in March 1968.

October: Francis designs new sail plan for the R-boat *Scapa II*, designed by Johan Anker.

1927

January: *Yachting* publishes short article by Nathanael on the Universal Rule.

January: Francis designs new sail plan for the *Hawk* (Burgess, Swasey, & Paine No. 280), a Q-boat that had been designed by Norman Skene.

January 11-April 22: Francis designs the *Live Yankee*, an R-boat for Charles A. Welch (Design No. 21). Her streamlined rig with rotating mast and jib luff spar are patented on January 11.

January 14: Francis is on good terms with yachting reporter William U. Swan.

January: Francis attends the New York Motorboat Show and a dinner at the New York Yacht Club to discuss R-boat racing.

January: Francis designs a new sail plan for the *Leonore*, a Q-boat designed by Johan Anker.

January 29: Francis asks Nathanael to write some history of American measurement rules (which he does).

February 1: Francis designs new mast and boom for the *Hayseed VIII* (Burgess, Swasey, & Paine No. 294), a Q-boat (also used on the *Dawn*, Burgess, Swasey, & Paine No. 299).

February 1: Francis designs an M-boat for Clinton Crane, as subcontractor (Design No. 22, not built). Design is a modernistic knock-out. Francis sends blueprints to Nathanael, who refuses to be impressed, at least in his response to Francis. He decorates plans of No. 22 with seahorses, dolphins, and scallop shells for the first time.

February: Francis designs new rig for the *Nor'easter IV*, a Q-boat designed by Alden in 1926 (the first of six new rigs he would design for her). This one has a jib luff spar.

February 16: Francis designs new rig for the *Mary*, (Burgess, Swasey, & Paine No. 281), an R-boat owned by C. H. W. Foster. Jib and mainsail both set on one boom pivoting around the mast.

February 18: Francis writes scathingly to Nathanael about the cruising boats of the day as "lightships."

February 18: Francis is doing a small, local brokerage business. He agrees to try to sell the *Pleasure* for Nathanael.

1927: Francis designs lapping jib for the *Gypsy*, Frank Paine's R-boat. In letter to Nathanael of August 14, 1933, he claims this was the first Genoa jib.

March: Francis attends dinner at New York Yacht Club to discuss R-boat racing.

March 22: Francis makes preliminary design for 35-foot launch for J. V. Santry (not built).

March 26: Francis is reading foreign yachting magazines (German, Swedish, Norwegian, and French—also English). He refers (in letter to Nathanael) to rapid progress Europeans are making in racing boats, particularly with experiments in sail plans derived from aeronautical knowledge.

Spring: Francis's brother Griswold leaves the Rushmore Company in Plainfield, New Jersey, to go to work for the Chrysler Corporation in Detroit.

Spring: O. Lie-Nielsen, a young Norwegian, sails into Marblehead in an 8-Metre, makes the acquaintance of Francis. (He will take room and board with Francis in 1931-33, working as his general assistant, not in design work. The friendship will continue to Francis's death.)

May 6: Francis designs 36-foot launch for J. V. Santry (Design No. 23, not built).

July-October: Francis designs *Siva*, a 91-foot power yacht (Design No. 25).

August: Francis hires designer Samuel H. Brown as draftsman because of the workload imposed by the *Siva*.

October 2: Francis designs new rig for the *Mary*, an R-boat owned by C. H. W. Foster, including a modest lapping jib.

October: Francis designs the *Nor'easter V*, a Q-boat, for Grafton Smith (Design No. 26).

November: Francis designs two new rigs for the *Mistral*, a Lawley schooner. One is for a staysail schooner with gaff mainsail.

November: Francis designs the *Wasp*, a 6-Metre, for W. A. W. Stewart (Design No. 27).

1928

Winter: Francis makes two pond models.

January: Francis designs rig changes for the *Pleione.*

January: Francis draws lines for the *Bonnie Lassie*, an R-boat for Dr. Prince (Design No. 28).

February: Francis designs the *Retriever*, a launch for Charles A. Welch (Design No. 30).

March: Preliminary plan for the *Walrus* published in *Yachting*. Welch has decided to have Francis finish the design.

March: Francis takes out a full-page ad in *Yachting* to sell the *Dispatch.*

March 12: Francis designs an M-boat for Junius Morgan (Design No. 31, not built).

April: *Yachting*'s "Directory of Naval Architects" lists L. Francis Herreshoff, Racing Yachts, 20 Lee St., Marblehead.

April: Francis designs fast motor launch for the Dyer Motorcraft Corporation of Providence, (Design No. 29). An advertisement in *Yachting* for Dyer lists "L. Francis Herreshoff, Designing Engineer."

April 11: Francis files for patent for longitudinal construction, prompted by the use of the method for the Dyer motor launch (first used in the *Yankee*, 1925, and in eight subsequent designs).

Summer: Francis meets Katherine Jones, a twelve-year-old Marblehead girl who keeps her sailing dinghy at Charlie Welch's float.

June: Dyer motor launch, Francis's Design No. 29, published in *Yachting.*

July 4: A gale at Marblehead blows 70 knots from the west. Nine boats capsize while sailing outside the harbor.

July: Francis designs Development Class boat (Design No. 32).

August: Francis visits Nathanael, who is 80, at Bristol. Plans to pick up books and "the small steam engine that is over at the farm" (the Simpson Strickland).

August: Francis designs new sail plan for the 127-foot Hand schooner *Speejacks.*

August: Design for the *Walrus* is proceeding. Sam Brown is doing the finished drawings. This is the first design for which Norman Skene makes the calculations.

September: Francis, Frank Paine, and John Alden are on a technical committee for Q-boat rules.

September: Francis designs a 20-Square-Metre boat (Design No. 35, not built).

September: Francis designs a 25-foot, centerboard, gunter-rigged sloop (not built).

September 5: Hans Stinnes, a German, has the 30-Square-Metre boat *Gluckauf* at the Corinthian Yacht Club, Marblehead. He demonstrates her abilities. Francis meets Stinnes, is most interested in this sail-area measurement rule. (This begins a friendship that will continue to Stinnes's death, ca. 1970, interrupted only by World War II.)

Fall: Francis designs the *Istalena*, an M-boat for George M. Pynchon (Design No. 34).

Fall: Francis buys the 30-Square-Metre *Gluckauf* from Hans Stinnes. He changes her name to the *Visitor.*

September 29: Races at Marblehead between Marblehead and Huntington Development Class boats. Marblehead sweeps the series. Order of finish: 1. Francis; 2. Charlie Welch; 3. Lawrence A. Percival.

October: Francis designs the *Questa*, a Q-boat for C. H. W. Foster (Design No. 33).

October: Samuel H. Brown Jr., working for Francis, designs the *Albacore* for G. N. Gregory.

October 9: Francis asks Nathanael and Ann Roebuck Herreshoff to please find his copy of W. P. Stephens's canoe and boatbuilding book. Ann finds it, but, as usual, it's missing the folding plans from the back pocket.

November: Francis designs the *Oriole*, a 30-Square-Metre boat for George E. McQuesten, (Design No. 37). Francis begins acquaintanceship with McQuesten. They meet and talk cars.

December: The American Bureau of Shipping is inspecting the construction of the *Questa* at Graves boatyard, Marblehead.

December: Herbert L. Stone, editor of *Yachting*, asks Francis to write an article about the Development Class (which he does, published in February 1929 issue).

December: Francis designs 16-foot, 6-inch punt for Charles A. Welch.

December 14: Francis asks Nathanael for ideas for hull shapes for the Development Class.

December 16: Sidney visits Francis in Marblehead.

Christmas: Francis gets candy from Ann Herreshoff, the first candy he's eaten in six months.

Christmas: Francis sends money to his Aunt Grace to help repair damage to her house in Puerto Rico from the 1928 hurricane.

1929

January 8: Francis receives patent for the longitudinal construction he used on the Dyer motorboat.

January: Francis designs the *Rima*, a 30-Square-Metre boat (Design No. 38).

January: Norman Skene leaves Francis's office and goes to the office of Howard and Munro in Boston.

January 22: Francis is working on the following designs: *Questa*; *Istalena*; *Oriole*; *Rima*; and a 55-foot ketch (Design No. 42, not built).

Winter: Francis makes preliminary design for a 75-Square-Metre boat.

February 10: Francis designs 17-foot knockabout, similar to the Development Class (Design No. 39).

February 27: Francis designs *Manatee*, a 28-foot launch (Design No. 40).

February: Francis is studying the 30-Square-Metre rule.

Spring: Francis has five boats being built to his designs: *Questa*, *Istalena*, *Albacore*, *Oriole*, and *Rima*.

April: Francis designs second new rig for the *Taygeta* (ex-*Nor'easter IV*).

April 24: Francis goes sailing with Charlie Welch in his 30-square-Metre boat, the *Yankee*, designed by George Owen.

April 25: Francis goes to the Herreshoff Manufacturing Company to inspect the *Istalena*, accompanied by Charlie Welch.

April 26: Francis writes Nathanael that his design work is slacking up a little, so he can machine parts for the roller reefing gear he designed for the 30-Square-Metre boat *Oriole*.

Late April: The *Istalena* is launched, three weeks late.

April 30: Francis receives small T-squares for use on pads, made for him by Nathanael.

May 1: The *Istalena* breaks her mast.

Early May: Francis puts the *Visitor* in commission.

May 8: Francis designs a fitting to tighten permanent backstays, threaded for adjustment, with a handle to produce tension.

May 14: Francis makes his first drawing on mylar (instead of paper or linen).

May 18: Francis first uses glasses "on all work close to." He can see all right; the glasses are to take the strain off his nerves. He is concerned about Sidney's eyesight.

Week of July 15: Francis takes off from work to race the *Visitor*.

August: Francis races in the 30-Square-Metre boat *Oriole*.

August 19: Nathanael designs jib for *Istalena*'s single-head rig.

August 23: Francis has been resting before eating.

August 27: Francis designs 48-foot ketch for E. Parsons (Design No. 42, not built).

August 28: Francis designs the *Carpenter* for Charles A. Welch (Design No. 41).

August 30: Francis makes third mast design for the *Istalena*, "New Big Mast."

September 1-November 4: Francis designs the J-boat *Whirlwind* (Design No. 44).

Early September: Francis visits Nathanael in Bristol.

September: Griswold promoted to Director of Truck and Bus Construction at Chrysler; Nathanael is pleased.

October 14: Francis buys a Packard.

October 22: Francis visits Nathanael in Bristol.

October 24: The Stock Market crashes.

November 25: Nathanael brings Francis and Clarence into contact over canoes.

December 7: Francis designs rig changes for the *Pleione*.

December 8: Clarence is working at the Marine Engineering Corporation in Philadelphia as a draftsman in the Hull Department.

December 17: Francis designs modifications for the 170-foot *Minas Princess* to convert her into a tender to the *Whirlwind* with accommodations for the racing crew.

1930

January: Ad for "L. Francis Herreshoff, Yacht Designer and Broker, 20 Lee St., Marblehead, Mass" published in *Yachting*.

February: Francis designs the *Oriole II,* a 30-Square-Metre boat for Charles Hovey to race in Germany (Design No. 46).

February 22-23: Francis goes for a cruise in the *Walrus*.

March: Brother Sidney and Rebecca Chase decide (finally) to marry.

April 5: Francis and Paul Hammond travel to Lawley's in the *Walrus* to inspect the *Whirlwind.*

April 23: Francis is making a pond model.

May 7: The *Whirlwind* is launched.

June: Francis designs new, simplified steering gear for the *Whirlwind.*

June 14: Francis designs Development Class boats *Butterfly* and *Flutterby*, the first for himself and the other for Charles A. Welch (Design No. 48).

July 7: Francis sails on the *Whirlwind* during the first Observation race, confirming his belief that the owners do not know how to trim her sails.

August 21: The *Whirlwind* is eliminated from America's Cup competition for the defense (she will be scrapped in 1935).

ENDNOTES

Abbreviations

Throughout the notes, L. Francis Herreshoff will be abbreviated as LFH, and his father Nathanael Greene Herreshoff will be abbreviated as NGH. LFH published "The Common Sense of Yacht Design" as a continuing series in *The Rudder* and as stand-alone volumes. Citations in the notes normally list the *Rudder* issue, with the corresponding volume listing in parentheses.

The Daniel S. Gregory Ships Plans Library at Mystic Seaport is abbreviated as DSGSPL.

The G. W. Blunt White Library at Mystic Seaport is abbreviated as GWBWL.

Citations to box and folder locations in the L. Francis Herreshoff Collection, Collection 138 at the G. W. Blunt White Library at Mystic Seaport, are abbreviated as 138:box number/folder number.

The Herreshoff Marine Museum in Bristol, RI, is abbreviated as HMM.

Prologue

1. Train and trolley details, Christopher Parker, Cape Cod Central Railroad, e-mail to author, January 16, 2001; Frederic Tudor, interview by Maynard Bray, November, December, 1971, transcript, GWBWL.
2. Stewart Benedict, ed., *The Literary Guide to the United States* (New York: Facts on File, 1981), 21-23, 81; Frederic Tudor, interview by Maynard Bray, November, December, 1971, transcript, GWBWL.

Chapter 1

1. L. Francis Herreshoff, *Capt. Nat Herreshoff, The Wizard of Bristol: The life and achievements of Nathanael Greene Herreshoff, together with an account of some of the yachts he designed* (New York: Sheridan House, 1953), 30; Samuel Carter III, *The Boatbuilders of Bristol: The Story of the Amazing Herreshoff Family of Rhode Island: Inventors, Individualists, Yacht Designers, and America's Cup Defenders* (New York: Doubleday and Company, 1970), 6; see also Charles Rappeleye, *Sons of Providence: the Brown Brothers, the Slave Trade, and the American Revolution* (New York: Simon

and Schuster, 2006); Frances Fitzgerald, "Peculiar Institutions: Brown University Looks at the Slave Traders in its Past," *The New Yorker*, September 12, 2005, 72.

2. LFH, *Capt. Nat Herreshoff*, 34-35; it was renamed Brown University in 1804, in honor of John's nephew Nicholas Brown Jr.; Carter, *Boatbuilders of Bristol*, 7.
3. LFH, *Capt. Nat Herreshoff*, 35.
4. Nathanael Greene Herreshoff III, "The Real Reason Why the Charles Frederick Herreshoff Family Left Point Pleasant Farm in 1856," *Herreshoff Marine Museum Newsletter*, January 2014, date corrected from the usually stated 1763 (the reason involved a quarrel between Charles and his older brother, John); NGH III, interview with author, March 15, 1996 (the descendants were Norman Herreshoff and John Nicholas Brown); see also Westcote Herreshoff Chesebrough, *Random Recollections* (privately printed, 1976), 10; LFH never claimed Frederick the Great as an ancestor; William Richard Cutter, comp., *New England Families: Genealogy and Memorial* (New York: Lewis Historical Publishing Company, 1915), 2176; see also Alfred Lee Donaldson, *A History of the Adirondacks,* 2 vols. (New York: Century Company, 1921), in which the author credits Francis's uncle, Lewis Herreshoff, for his story of Charles Frederick Herreshoff; LFH, *Capt. Nat Herreshoff*, 27, 28; see also Carter, *Boatbuilders of Bristol,* 3-6, 9-11; I have followed a middle course between these two accounts, steering clear of LFH's sometimes sanitized statements and Carter's sometimes sensationalized ones. Neither book gives sources for facts. LFH detested Carter's book, in which he made twenty-one scathing marginal notes (none of which apply to the facts cited above).
5. LFH, *Capt. Nat Herreshoff*, 28; Carter, *Boatbuilders of Bristol*, 10.
6. LFH, *Capt. Nat*, 29; see also Chesebrough, *Random Recollections*, 10.
7. Chesebrough, *Random Recollections,* 12; LFH, *Capt. Nat Herreshoff*, 28, 29; Carter, *Boatbuilders of Bristol*, 15-21; LFH never wrote of his great-grandfather's suicide, but he didn't dispute it in the margin of Carter's hated book; see also Donaldson, *A History of the Adirondacks.*
8. LFH, *Capt. Nat Herreshoff*, 36.
9. LFH, *Capt. Nat Herreshoff*, 36.
10. LFH, *Capt. Nat Herreshoff*, 60; *New York Herald*, October 9, 1898; Carter, *Boatbuilders of Bristol*, 63.
11. LFH believed the cause was glaucoma, but that is far from certain; see LFH, *Capt. Nat Herreshoff*, 43; others in the family have speculated on a virus; NGH III, interview with author; LFH, *Capt. Nat Herreshoff*, 36; Carter, *Boatbuilders of Bristol,* 36; Chesebrough, *Random Recollections,* 8; *New York Herald*, October 9, 1898.
12. NGH, Discussion of W. P. Stephens, "Yacht Measurement: Origins and Development," Society of Naval Architects and Marine Engineers, *Transactions* 43 (1935): 35.
13. LFH, *Capt. Nat Herreshoff*, 38, 39, 41; for a description of how the ballast car was handled when tacking, see LFH, "The Common Sense of Yacht Design," *The Rudder* (July 1947): 35 (vol. 2: 119).
14. NGH to LFH, October 29, 1935, 138:17/11, GWBWL; see also Maynard Bray and Jim Giblin, "The Herreshoff Anchor," *WoodenBoat* 231 (March/April 2013): 44.
15. Carlton J. Pinheiro, ed., NGH, *Recollections and Other Writings* (Bristol, RI: Herreshoff Marine Museum, 1998); to place James's very early and important innovation with the V-bottomed boat in context, it is useful to review Howard I. Chapelle's summary in *American Small Sailing Craft,* (New York: W. W. Norton, 1951), 338: "The appearance of the V-bottom in the Revolution and in some Canadian lumber bateaux, in the modified sharpie style of hull, suggests that the V-bottom was produced step by step from the colonial type. Yet this attractive and orderly development cannot be supported by available evidence and it seems very certain that the development of the V-bottom in American workboats did not take place in a single area or section of the coast alone and that there was much local evolution that did not occur through copying of a 'master invention'"; LFH, *Capt. Nat*

Herreshoff, 47–51, 49, 74; Maynard Bray and Carlton Pinheiro, *Herreshoff of Bristol: A Photographic History of America's Greatest Yacht and Boat Builders* (Brooklin, ME: WoodenBoat 1989), 14.

16. NGH, Biographical notes and reminiscences, etc. (ca. 1926), 138:16/13, GWBWL; NGH III, interview with author; Carlton Pinheiro, interview with author, 12 February 12, 1996; see also Pinheiro, *Recollections,* 5, 38; LFH, *Capt. Nat Herreshoff*, 43; [Clara DeWolf Herreshoff?], "[Glim]pses from The Life of Nathanael Greene Herreshoff," 4, Collection 138, Box 16, Folder 12, GWBWL; Pinheiro, *Recollections,* 38; see also LFH, *Capt. Nat Herreshoff*, 43, 52, 63; see also NGH to Stephens, August 31, 1935, in John W. Streeter, *Their Last Letters 1930-1938: Nathanael G. Herreshoff and William P. Stephens* (Bristol, RI: Herreshoff Marine Museum, 2001), 71, 72.
17. LFH, *Capt. Nat Herreshoff*, 63; NGH to Stephens, in Streeter, *Their Last Letters*, 71, 72.
18. LFH, *Capt. Nat Herreshoff*, 38; see also Herreshoff, "[Glim]pses from the Life," 3; Carlton Pinheiro interview with author; LFH *Capt. Nat Herreshoff*, 43, 44, 52; see also Pinheiro, *Recollections*, 8.
19. LFH, *Capt. Nat Herreshoff*, 44, 57; see also Herreshoff, "[Glim]pses from a Life," 5; see also Pinheiro, *Recollections*, 13, 14; NGH to Charles H. W. Foster, March 6, 1932, 138:16/25, GWBWL. The *Sprite* is on display at the HMM.
20. LFH, *Capt. Nat Herreshoff*, 63; see also NGH, Biographical notes, Collection 138, GWBWL; Arthur Brendze, interviews with author, May 26, 27, 2007, May 11, 2008, Sausalito, California. Brendze was a close friend to LFH in the last four years of his life. He later became a boatbuilder and is now an experienced psychotherapist. More than anyone else, Brendze was able to break through LFH's reserve and reticence and get him to talk about himself and his father.
21. LFH, *Capt. Nat Herreshoff*, 63, 80, 81; see also Herreshoff, "[Glim]pses from a Life," 10.
22. LFH, *Capt. Nat Herreshoff*, 64.
23. LFH, *Capt. Nat Herreshoff*, 65, 66; NGH to J. Vechten Waring, July 27, 1934, 138:16/25, GWBWL.
24. LFH, *Capt. Nat Herreshoff*, 66; see also Herreshoff, "[Glim]pses from a Life," 22; NGH to Stephens, August 31, 1935, in Streeter, *Their Last Letters*, 74; a similar Corliss engine is on display at the Owl's Head Transportation Museum, Owl's Head, ME; George H. Kellner and J. Stanley Lemons, *Rhode Island: The Independent State*, (Woodland Hills, CA: Windsor Publications, 1982).
25. NGH to Foster, March 6, 1932, 138:6/25, GWBWL; see also Herreshoff, "[Glim]pses from the Life," 19; LFH, *The Common Sense of Yacht Design*, vol. 2 (New York: Rudder Publishing, 1946), 40.
26. LFH, *Capt. Nat Herreshoff*, 77, 78; see also LFH, *Common Sense of Yacht Design*, vol. 2: 122-27; "A New Era in Yachting: The Patent Catamaran or Double Hulled Boat," May 1, 1877, 138:16/30, GWBWL.
27. LFH, *Capt. Nat Herreshoff*, 74-77.
28. LFH, *Capt. Nat Herreshoff*, 52.
29. LFH, *Capt. Nat Herreshoff*, 53, 94, 95; Streeter, *Their Last Letters*, 75.

Chapter 2

1. NGH, Diary, November 11, 1890, copy at GWBWL; Clara Herreshoff, Notebook, HMM.
2. Anne Lawrence Bondy, interview with author, June 26, 1998; Katherine Jones Vosburgh, interview with author, Newburyport, MA, March 4, 1995; NGH III, interview with author.
3. Bray and Pinheiro, *Herreshoff of Bristol*, 14; LFH, *Capt. Nat Herreshoff*, 114.
4. NGH III, interview with author; Agnes was named for her great-great-grandmother, and the spelling of her middle name varies from Mueller (the most commonly accepted) to Clara's Muhler to LFH's Muller, to the Müller that Agnes herself used in the albums of her photographs; LFH, "The Common Sense of Yacht Design," *The Rudder* (November 1944): 36; John Gardner, interview with author, January 23, 1995; Arthur Brendze, interview with author, July 1, 1999, Bucks Harbor, ME; see also reference to "a single child who had never been

exposed to ridicule," probably an envious comment by LFH in his "The Compleat Cruiser," *The Rudder* (January 1953): 61; Tom Davin, "He Carries On The Great Herreshoff Tradition," *Boats* (September 1956): 19; Arthur Brendze, interview with author.

5. NGH to LFH, April 19, 1926, 138:17/2, GWBWL.
6. Herreshoff, "[Glim]pses From the Life," 28; NGH, Diary, previously cited; *Boston Globe*, June 11, 1967; LFH, *Capt. Nat Herreshoff*, 125; C. Seaver Robinson, interview with author, Port Clyde, ME, May 27, 1999.
7. LFH to unidentified correspondent, undated, 138:6/7, GWBWL; Carlton Pinheiro, interview with author; Proposed Division of "the Farm," 138:16/11, GWBWL; NGH, *Recollections*, 16, 17.
8. Arthur Brendze, interview with author.
9. Arthur Brendze, interview with author.
10. Arthur Brendze, interview with author.
11. Davin, "He Carries On," *Boats*, 19.
12. LFH to Malcolm MacNaught, March 7, 1947, March 26, 1951, December 23, 1958, 138:3/1, 4/2, 4/9, GWBWL; see also LFH to Jim Tiffany, February 16, 1969, 138:6/4, GWBWL; Boris Lauer-Leonardi to LFH, August 23, 1946, 138:2/10, LFH to Malcolm MacNaught, October 12, 1953, 138:4/4, GWBWL.
13. John Gardner, interview with author; LFH to NGH, June 14, 1934, 138:1/4, GWBWL; Davin, "He Carries On," *Boats*, 19.
14. LFH to NGH, June 14, 1934; Bray and Pinheiro, *Herreshoff of Bristol*, 35; Paul Glynn, interview with author, Georgetown, MA, June 6, 1999.
15. Bray and Pinheiro, *Herreshoff of Bristol*, 32, 36; LFH, *Capt. Nat Herreshoff*, 148.
16. LFH, *Capt. Nat Herreshoff*, 138; see also *Herreshoff Marine Museum Chronicle*, Fall 1999; LFH, "The Common Sense of Yacht Design," *The Rudder* (November 1944): 36; LFH, *Capt. Nat Herreshoff*, 129-33.
17. LFH, *Capt. Nat Herreshoff*, 205, 210.
18. Davin, "He Carries On," *Boats*, 19.
19. LFH, "Yachting in the 1900s," *The Rudder* (July 1948), reprinted in *An L. Francis Herreshoff Reader* (Camden ME: International Marine Publishing, 1978), 21. The island was Walker's Island, just off the eastern shore of Bristol Harbor.
20. LFH to Sidney Phillips, July 14, 1965, 138:5/7, GWBWL.
21. LFH, *Capt. Nat Herreshoff*, 116, 117; see also NGH, *Recollections*, 55, 95, 96; Bray and Pinheiro, *Herreshoff of Bristol*, 50, 146; the *Coquina* remained in the Herreshoff family until September 21, 1938, when she was destroyed in a hurricane. Her replica is on display at the HMM; NGH Diary, copy at GWBWL; LFH, *Nathanael Greene Herreshoff 1848-1938: A life and appreciation of his work by his son, L. Francis Herreshoff* (Hartford: Wadsworth Athenaeum Marine Room, Publication 2), 2 (published in concert with the exhibit, "The Art and Genius of Nathanael Greene Herreshoff" in the Tapestry Hall of the Morgan Memorial).
22. LFH, *Sensible Cruising Designs* (Camden, ME: International Marine Publishing, 1973), 50; NGH, Diary, July 5, 1892, copy at GWBWL; Clara DeWolf Herreshoff, Diary, August 1897, HMM; LFH, *Capt. Nat Herreshoff*, 119; see also Herreshoff, "[Glim]pses From the Life," 45; LFH, "Yachting in the 1900s," *An L. Francis Herreshoff Reader*, 18, 19.
23. LFH, *Capt. Nat Herreshoff*, 119; see also Herreshoff, "[Glim]pses From the Life," 45; Bray and Pinheiro, *Herreshoff of Bristol*, 125; Agnes M. Herreshoff, Photo Album, 1902-1904, HMM; LFH, "Yachting in the 1900s," *An L. Francis Herreshoff Reader*, 20.
24. LFH, *Capt. Nat Herreshoff*, 71; Herreshoff, "[Glim]pses from the Life," 21; like the *Coquina*, the *Riviera* was destroyed in the Love Rocks boathouse in the hurricane of 1938.
25. Arthur Brendze, interview with author.
26. LFH, "Yachting in the 1900s," *An L. Francis Herreshoff Reader*, 21; NGH, *Recollections*, 67, 68; Bray and Pinheiro, *Herreshoff of Bristol*, 58; see also LFH to NGH, September 22, 1933, 138:17/9, LFH to Boris Lauer-Leonardi, February 7, 1944, 138:2/5, GWBWL; LFH, "The Common Sense of Yacht Design," *The Rudder* (July 1944): 37; Davin, "He Carries On," *Boats*, 19; LFH, "The Common Sense of Yacht Design," *The Rudder* (November 1945): 41.
27. LFH to John B. McCurdy, August 23, 1970,

138:6/5, GWBWL. All lengths given of Herreshoff Manufacturing Company boats follow the company's practice of using waterline lengths as the basic measure of size, rather than the later practice of using on-deck lengths. For non-Herreshoff Manufacturing Company boats, on-deck lengths are used, unless otherwise specified (on-deck length is often called length overall, but, to add to the confusion, the term "length overall" has also come to mean, in some quarters, the length of a boat including any overhanging spars, a usage avoided herein.); LFH to C. Lowndes Johnson, April 19, 1948, 138:3/4, GWBWL; see also LFH, "The Common Sense of Yacht Design," *The Rudder* (September 1946): 44; LFH, "The Common Sense of Yacht Design," *The Rudder* (November 1944): 36.

28. Davin, "He Carries On," *Boats*, 19.
29. Transcript of LFH's Bristol Public Schools Record, Bristol Warren Regional School District; Carlton Pinheiro, interview with author; "H-28—Or the Building of the Snarke," *The Rudder* (April 1943), reprinted in *The Writings of L. Francis Herreshoff* (New York: Rudder Publishing, 1946), and in *An L. Francis Herreshoff Reader* (Camden, ME: International Marine Publishing, 1978), 165; LFH to Malcolm MacNaught, December 13, 1951, 138:4/2, GWBWL.
30. Anne Lawrence Bondy, interview with author, April 25, 1995; Adrienne Franklin, interview with author, June 24, 1997; Mark Selikowitz, *Dyslexic and Other Learning Difficulties* (New York: Oxford University Press, 1993), 46-61. In quoting LFH's unpublished writings, I have not corrected his misspellings. He had to cope with dyslexia all his life; NGH III and Carlton Pinheiro, interviews with author.
31. Arthur Brendze, interviews with author.
32. LFH, *Capt. Nat Herreshoff*, 262, 263; Bray and Pinheiro, *Herreshoff of Bristol*, 101; *Bristol Phoenix*, November 28, 1905; quote from "The Perfect Wife," Proverbs, 31:31.
33. Anne Lawrence Bondy and Katharine Jones Vosburgh, interviews with author; LFH, *Capt. Nat Herreshoff*, 263; Natalie Herreshoff and Carlton Pinheiro, interviews with author; the former had the story from her mother, Helen Warren, Nathanael, Jr.'s wife; the latter, from Francis's brother, Clarence; LFH, "The Heights," 10.
34. Arthur Brendze, interview with author.
35. See LFH, *The Compleat Cruiser: The Art, Practice, and Enjoyment of Boating* (New York: Sheridan House, 1956), 127; LFH, "The Common Sense of Yacht Design," *The Rudder* (November 1944): 33; Davin, "He Carries On," *Boats*, 19; this model is in the collection of the HMM; Arthur Brendze, interview with author; see Sylvia Nasar, *A Beautiful Mind* (New York: Simon and Schuster, 1998), 69.
36. Model 90.253, HMM. Nathanael was a far better speller than Francis, but he may have had a trace of dyslexia himself; Arthur Brendze, interview with author.

Chapter 3

1. Cutter, *New England Families*, 2179; Carle M. Bigelow to LFH, September 18, 1953, Collection 138:4/4, GWBWL; Carlton Pinheiro, interview with author; there seemed to be a certain Spanish influence in the Herreshoff family, NGH naming his own favorite boat the *Coquina*, for example. The first big contract secured by the Herreshoff Manufacturing Company in 1878 had been to build a gunboat for the Spanish government to use against insurgents in Cuba; LFH, *Capt. Nat Herreshoff*, 95.
2. NGH III, interview with author.
3. *Boston Globe*, June 11, 1967; Dale Calloway, interview with author, February 8, 1995; Arthur Brendze, interview with author.
4. Katherine Vosburgh and Arthur Brendze, interviews with author.
5. *Bulletin of Rhode Island State College* (Kingston, RI, 1910), 27, 29, 88; LFH, "The Common Sense of Yacht Design," *The Rudder* (February 1945): 33.
6. FH, "The Common Sense of Yacht Design," *The Rudder* (April 1944): 24.

7. LFH, "Captain Charley Barr," *The Rudder* (May, June 1948), reprinted in *An L. Francis Herreshoff Reader,* 94, 95.
8. Anne Bondy, interview with author.
9. The model is at the HMM; see also LFH to Marguerite S. Britter, September 19, 1960, note at bottom, October 4, 1960, 138:5/1, GWBWL; *Forest and Stream,* September 24, 1910, 503; the other American representatives were the *Beaver*, a Burgess design, and the *Cima*, designed by Mower; Herreshoff Manufacturing Company Sonders seem to be design numbers 659, 660, 684, 695, 697, and 699; however, the dimensions given for the *Peg* (695) and *Toboggan* (697) differ from Sonder measurements.
10. LFH to J. F. Martin, July 13, 1970, 138:6/5, LFH, Memorandum to Commanding Officer, Naval Experimental Station, New London, CT, October 26, 1918, 138:16/8, GWBWL; LFH, "The Dry Breakers," *The Rudder* (April 1948); LFH to Roy C. Gumpel, January 13, 1970, 138:6/5, LFH to R. Thomas Paxton, December 6, 1965, 138:5/7, GWBWL.
11. NGH to LFH, December 8, 1929, LFH to NGH, December 13, 1929, 138:17/5, GWBWL.
12. Sidney Herreshoff to LFH, September 5, 1966, 138:5/8, NGH, "round robin" letter to Griswold Herreshoff, LFH, and Clarence Herreshoff, ca. October 1, 1930,138:1/9, GWBWL.
13. *Bristol Phoenix,* October 24, 1899.
14. Proposed Division of "the Farm," 138:16/11, GWBWL.
15. Membership card, April 1904, 90.164, HMM; LFH to John Ives Sewall, January 12, 1956, 138:4/7, GWBWL.
16. The model is at HMM.
17. *New York Times*, January 21, 1912.
18. NGH, *Recollections*; LFH, *Capt. Nat Herreshoff*, 122, 126; "Recollections of Nat Herreshoff," *Yachting* (February 1955): 46; the *Alerion III* is on display at Mystic Seaport; LFH to Richard Shew, September 10, 1969, 138:6/4, GWBWL.
19. Chesebrough, *Random Recollections,* 15; *New England Families*, 2179; NGH, *Recollections*, 32; Caroline Herreshoff Chesebrough to NGH, April 7, 1913, 138:16/25, GWBWL; see Streeter, *Their Last Letters*, 148; Noelle Duck, *Yachts Classiques* (Paris: Gallimard, 2004), 101.
20. *The Rudder* (September 1901): 363; plan in author's collection; Richard Henderson to author, March 11, 1996.
21. Caroline Herreshoff Chesebrough to NGH, March 3, 1914, 138:16/25, GWBWL.
22. NGH, *Recollections*, 73; LFH, *Capt. Nat Herreshoff,* 154, 155; *Providence Journal*, February 9, 1917, as quoted in Carter, *Boatbuilders of Bristol*, 166.
23. LFH, Life and Appreciation of NGH, 9; Bray and Pinheiro, *Herreshoff of Bristol*, 220; NGH III, undated typescript, "The Name Nathanael in the Herreshoff Family"; see also Halsey C. Herreshoff, commentary, *Providence Journal*, May 13, 1996, B5. I have used Nathanael's corrected spelling throughout, even for his son, Nat Jr.
24. NGH III, interview with author; Halsey C. Herreshoff, *Providence Journal.*
25. NGH III, Natalie Herreshoff, and Carlton Pinheiro, interviews with author; see also LFH, *Capt. Nat Herreshoff*, 292.
26. NGH III, interview with author; Bray and Pinheiro, *Herreshoff of Bristol*, xi; Cutter, *New England Families,* 2179.
27. LFH to Walter Hadley, May 10, 1965, 138:5/6, LFH to Percy Knauth, June 14, 1956, 138:4/7, GWBWL; Carlton Pinheiro, interview with author; Bray and Pinheiro, *Herreshoff of Bristol*, 144.
28. Paul Glynn, telephone conversation with author, June 14, 1999; Edmund Cutts, interview with author, Oxford, MD, April 19, 1996; C. Seaver Robinson, interview with author; LFH to George H. Waterman Jr., February 4, 1945, 138:2/7, GWBWL; Paul Glynn, interview with author, June 6, 1999.
29. NGH, *Recollections*, 118; see also LFH, *Capt. Nat Herreshoff*, 122; Bray and Pinheiro, *Herreshoff of Bristol*, 132.
30. LFH, Memorandum to Commanding Officer, 1, Commandant, Second Naval District, to LFH, May 28, 1917, 138:16/8, GWBWL.

31. LFH, Orders, June 23, 1917, LFH, Memorandum to Commanding Officer, 1, 138:16/8, LFH to Harold Sterling Vanderbilt, September 10, 1937, 138:1/7, GWBWL.
32. LFH to Albert C. Cleveland, January 11, 1945, 138:2/5 (should be 7), LFH to NGH, September 22, 1936, 138:17/12, LFH to David F. H. Watts, March 11, 1947, 138:3/1, GWBWL.
33. LFH, Memorandum to Commanding Officer, 2, 138:16/8, GWBWL; Paul Glynn, interview with author; see also LFH, "The Common Sense of Yacht Design," *The Rudder* (September 1944): 35; LFH, "The Common Sense of Yacht Design," *The Rudder* (February 1947): 41.
34. LFH, Orders, March 11, 1918, 138:16/8, LFH, Memorandum to Commanding Officer, 2, 138:16/8, LFH to F. Randolph Pearsall, February 4, 1947, 138:3/1, LFH to Percy Brewer, June 14, 1945, 138:2/7, GWBWL; Paul Glynn, interview with author.
35. LFH, Orders, July 13, 1918, author's collection; see also LFH, Memorandum to Commanding Officer; LFH to James P. O'Hare, July 26, 1960, 138:5/1, LFH to Mr. and Mrs. Walter Hadley, March 30, 1964, 138:5/5, GWBWL; LFH, "The Common Sense of Yacht Design," *The Rudder* (November 1944): 36 (vol. 1, 65); see also LFH to Mr. and Mrs. Walter Hadley, March 30, 1964, 138:5/5, GWBWL.
36. LFH to William Strawbridge, January 19, 1961, 138:5/2, GWBWL.
37. LFH, Orders, March 14, 1919, Collection 138:16/8, GWBWL; LFH, Orders, April 4, 1919, author's collection.
38. *Acts and Resolves of Rhode Island*, 357.
39. Llewellyn Howland III, "Herreshoff Manufacturing Company: The Irresolute Years: 1915-1925," unpublished MS, 15, 16, 18; see also LFH, *Capt. Nat Herreshoff*, 155.
40. LFH, *Capt. Nat Herreshoff*, 147, 148.
41. Thomas G. Skahill, "Nick Potter," *WoodenBoat* 83 (July/August 1988): 38.
42. LFH, "A Sail in the *Alerion*," *The Rudder* (September 1943).
43. LFH, *Capt. Nat Herreshoff*, 306; LFH to John E. Fitzwell, April 22, 1965, 138:5/6, GWBWL; when LFH's nephew Halsey's S-boat *Coquina* went on the rocks at Marblehead in a gale in 1960, Francis consoled him with the remark: "Don't worry, she's only an S-boat, not one of your grandfather's better designs."
44. In 1985, David Broadhead, in British Columbia, built the *Nadia* to Francis's plans. This boat—as of 1995 kept at Victoria and renamed *J. Marie* by her owner, Tony de Goutiere—has a cuddy cabin and straight mast, but otherwise follows the design. Tony de Goutiere reports his boat to be seaworthy and fast, Tony de Goutiere to author, January 18, 1995.
45. SP38.235.1, DSGSPL not reproducible; Carlton Pinheiro, interview with author.
46. SP38. 147.1, DSGSPL
47. NGH, Discussion of W. P. Stevens, "Yacht Measurement: Origins and Development," *Transactions of the Society of Naval Architects and Marine Engineers* 43, 36; see also NGH to C. H. W. Foster, March 6, 1932, 138:17/8, GWBWL; Herreshoff, "[Glim]pses from the Life," 19; Howland, "The Burgess Legacy, Part I," *WoodenBoat* 71 (July/August 1986): 59; Howard I. Chapelle, *The History of American Sailing Ships* (New York: Putnam, 1936), 341.
48. Howland, "The Burgess Legacy, Part II," *WoodenBoat* 72 (September/October 1986): 45; Ann Burgess Hopps, interview with author, October 29, 1998; Marjorie Young Wolff, interview with author, February 15, 1999.
49. Howland, "The Burgess Legacy, Part IV," *WoodenBoat* 74 (January/February 1987): 45.
50. LFH, "A Sail in the *Alerion*," *The Rudder* (September 1943); *Boston Globe*, August 31, 1924.
51. SP38.299.1, DSGSPL; see LFH, "The Common Sense of Yacht Design," *The Rudder* (August 1947): 38 (vol. 2, 125, 126); Francis would later draw a proposal for another catamaran with a rig for each hull, but the rigs were vertical, rather than tipped inboard, and they were simple Marconi sloops, LFH, *The Common Sense of Yacht Design*, vol. 2, fig. 343; a somewhat similar catamaran was developed in the

1980s for fishermen of Sri Lanka by Edwin Gifford, Southampton, England, Nigel Calder, *The English Channel* (New York: Penguin Books, 1986), 272.

52. LFH, Memorandum to Commanding Officer, 138:16/8, LFH to James E. Craig, February 19, 1948, 138:3/4, GWBWL; LFH, "The Common Sense of Yacht Design," *The Rudder* (November 1944): 36; LFH to David J. Reiber, April 30, 1969, 138:6/4, GWBWL; LFH, "The Common Sense of Yacht Design," *The Rudder* (October 1945): 40.
53. Anne Bondy, interview with author.
54. NGH to LFH, August 24, 1929, MSM, 138:17/5, GWBWL; Natalie Herreshoff, interview with author.

Chapter 4

1. Ann Burgess Hopps, interview with author, October 29, 1998; Frederic Tudor, interview by Maynard Bray, November, December, 1971, transcript, GWBWL.
2. Llewellyn Howland III, "The Burgess Legacy, Part II," *WoodenBoat* 72 (September/October 1986): 45; H. K. Rigg, "Profiles: Man of Ideas," *The New Yorker,* May 31, 1947, 20-22; Howland, "The Burgess Legacy, Part IV," *WoodenBoat* 74 (January/February 1987): 42, 44; William H. Taylor, "W. Starling Burgess," *Yachting* (May 1947): 80; see also John Lenger, "Conquest of the Air," *Harvard Magazine* (May-June 2003): 33, 34.
3. Howland, "The Burgess Legacy, Part II," *WoodenBoat* 72 (September/October 1986): 49; see also Charles P. Burgess to LFH, October 16, 1950, LFH to Charles P. Burgess, October 23, 1950, 138:4/1, GWBWL.
4. LFH, "A Sail in the *Alerion*," *The Rudder* (September 1943).
5. Howland, "The Burgess Legacy, Part IV," *WoodenBoat* 74 (JanuaryFebruary): 44, 45; Llewellyn Howland III, telephone interview with author, January 24, 2002; Ann Burgess Hopps, telephone interview with author, March 2, 2002.
6. See LFH, "The Compleat Cruiser," unabridged typescript, 138:12, GWBWL; Arthur Brendze, interview with author.
7. Carlton Pinheiro, interview with author; LFH, *The Compleat Cruiser: the Art, Practice and Enjoyment of Boating* (New York: Sheridan House, 1956), 155.
8. LFH to Walter Hadley, October 31, 1966, 138:5/8, GWBWL; Davin, "He Carries On," *Boats*, 52; biographical sketch in description of the Paine Collection, Hart Nautical Collections, MIT Museum, Cambridge, MA; LFH to Georgina Paine Fisher Howland, ca. January 1, 1956, 138:6/7, GWBWL; Georgina Paine Fisher Howland, *Afterthoughts* (New Bedford, MA: privately printed, 1955), 236; Llewellyn Howland III, interview with author, March 21, 1999.
9. Howland, *Afterthoughts*, 244, 245; see also Howland, "The Burgess Legacy, Part IV," *WoodenBoat* 74 (January/February 1987): 40; Llewellyn Howland III, *No Ordinary Being: W. Starling Burgess (1878-1947), a Biography* (Boston: David R. Godine, 2014), Chapter 12, p. 196.
10. LFH, *NGH: A Life,* 21.
11. Frederic Tudor, interview by Maynard Bray, November, December, 1971, transcript, 28, GWBWL.
12. Robert J. Walsh to Norman L. Skene, July 12, 1921, 138:16/9, GWBWL; *The Rudder* (September 1932): 51, (January 1918): 28.
13. Howland, "The Burgess Legacy, Part III," *WoodenBoat* 73 (November/December 1986): 38.
14. LFH to H. F. Newman, October 24, 1955, 138:4/6, GWBWL; Howland, "The Burgess Legacy, Part IV," *WoodenBoat* 74 (January/February 1987): 45.
15. Alan Viner, *A History of Rating Rules for Yachts: 1854-1931* (Greenwich, England: National Maritime Museum, 1979), 14-17; see also, LFH, *The Common Sense of Yacht Design*, vol. 2, 33-35; Bray and Pinheiro, *Herreshoff of Bristol,* 159; LFH to Charles Nicholson, August 4, 1950, 138:4/1, GWBWL; LFH, *The Common Sense of Yacht Design*, vol. 2, 52.
16. Howland, "The Burgess Legacy, Part IV," *WoodenBoat* 74 (January/February 1987): 45.
17. Charles Nicholson to LFH, July 17, 1950, LFH to Charles Nicholson, August 4, 1950, 138:8/5, GWBWL; see also LFH passport visa, HMM; see also LFH to Walter Hadley, January 30, 1957, 138:4/8, GWBWL; Howland, "The Burgess Legacy, Part IV," *WoodenBoat* 74 (January/February 1987): 45; LFH to Robert D. Schultz, August 14, 1961, 138:5/2,

LFH to Charles E. Nicholson, July 5, 1950, 138:4/1, GWBWL; LFH, "The Common Sense of Yacht Design," *The Rudder* (July 1946): 43.

18. LFH, "The Common Sense of Yacht Design," *The Rudder* (July 1946): 43; *The Rudder* (November 1921): 56.
19. LFH to NGH, May 8, 1936, 138:17/12, GWBWL.
20. LFH, "The Design of Fishing Vessels," *Maine Coast Fisherman* (January 1951); "Cutters, Laying To, Etc.," *The Rudder* (November 1943): 12; the *Mayflower* was Burgess's design No. 218 and the *Puritan* was No. 227; this drawing so impressed English yacht designer Uffa Fox that he used it on the cover of his *Uffa Fox's Second Book* (1935).
21. LFH, "A Few Comparisons of *Puritan* and *Mayflower*," and "To the Knockers of the Schooner *Mayflower*," *An L. Francis Herreshoff Reader* (Camden, ME: International Marine Publishing, 1978), 259-65; Keith McLaren, *A Race for Real Sailors* (Boston: David R. Godine, 2006), 93, 94, 120, 164, 216; LFH, *An L. Francis Herreshoff Reader,* 131.
22. LFH, "The Design of Fishing Vessels," *An L. Francis Herreshoff Reader,*" 268; SP38.212.1, DSGSPL; see William M. P. Dunne, *Thomas F. McManus and the American Fishing Schooners* (Mystic: Mystic Seaport, 1994).
23. SP38.151.1, DSGSPL; Bray and Pinheiro, *Herreshoff of Bristol*, 160.
24. SP38.161.1, DSGSPL; LFH, "Preliminary Description of 40' LWL Schooner—#F-13," 138:16/19, GWBWL.
25. David Slater, e-mail to author, October 1, 2011; Llewellyn Howland, III, unpublished MS on LFH, 6; Hope Welch Slater and Edith Welch Potter, interview with author; Welch family photograph albums; Anne Lawrence Bondy, interview with author; *Boston Globe,* January 2, 1927.
26. *Yachting* (January 1923): 29; original plan at the Hart Nautical Collections, MIT Museum, Cambridge, MA.
27. Robert W. Carrick and Richard Henderson, *John G. Alden and his Yacht Designs* (Camden, ME: International Marine Publishing, 1983), 363.
28. Arthur Brendze, interviews with author. This is an opinion with which the author agrees. Applying the same standards that judged 55 of LFH's 125 designs to approach perfection (in the Introduction) produces 35 designs in that category of the Alden company's 900 designs; LFH to Allan Vaitses, February 6, 1956, 138:4/7, GWBWL.
29. Construction Record for LFH Designs, 138:15a/14, GWBWL.
30. SP138.118.2, DSGSPL; LFH, *The Common Sense of Yacht Design*, vol. 1, 129; see also Llewellyn Howland III, unpublished MS on LFH, 20; LFH, "Shroud Attachments," unpublished typescript, April 20, 1935, 138:16/17, GWBWL.
31. LFH to H. G. McKinney Jr., March 25, 1946, 138:2/9, GWBWL.
32. James S. Rockefeller Jr., e-mail to author, February 18, 2005.
33. LFH to NGH April 16, 1929, NGH to LFH, April 21, 1929, 138:17/5, GWBWL.
34. LFH, "The Common Sense of Yacht Design," *The Rudder* (October 1945): 40 (vol. 1, 113, 114.); LFH to NGH, January 4, 1928, 138:17/4, GWBWL.
35. LFH to NGH, January 4, 1928, 138:17/4, GWBWL; see also LFH, "Box Section Spars," unpublished typescript, ca. April 1935, 138:16/27, GWBWL.
36. William U. Swan, "The Marblehead Season," *The Rudder* (November 1923): 21, 22.
37. Howland, "The Burgess Legacy, Part IV," *WoodenBoat* 74 (January/February 1987): 45; Bray and Pinheiro, *Herreshoff of Bristol*, 151; Llewellyn Howland III, interview with author.
38. Skahill, "Nick Potter," *WoodenBoat* 83 (July/August 1988): 40.
39. SP38.288.1, DSGSPL; LFH, *The Common Sense of Yacht Design*, vol. 2, 79; LFH, "The Common Sense of Yacht Design," *The Rudder* (January 1948): 45; 138:15/34, GWBWL; SP38.288.3, DSGSPL.
40. One could assume that LFH must have previously designed F-1 through F-17, but if so, only F-5 and F-16—both of which we shall meet in a later chapter—have survived. When he designed his next boat on his own, she was No. 19, without the F, the simple numbering system that he would continue; SP38.45.2, DSGSPL.

41. SP38.45.1, SP38.45.4, SP38.45, DSGSPL
42. LFH to Boyd Donaldson, May 21, 1945, 138:2/7, GWBWL; see also LFH, "The Common Sense of Yacht Design," *The Rudder* (April 1946): 44.
43. *Yachting* (February 1925): 46; LFH, *The Common Sense of Yacht Design*, vol. 1, 25.
44. LFH to NGH, June 3, 1933, 138:17/9, GWBWL; LFH, "Cutters, Laying-to, etc.," *The Rudder* (November 1943), reprinted in *An L. Francis Herreshoff Reader*, 133, 134; see also LFH, *The Compleat Cruiser*, 74.
45. LFH to NGH, June 9, 1933, 138:17/9, GWBWL; Edith Welch Potter, interview with author; Arthur Brendze, interview with author; see LFH, *The Common Sense of Yacht Design*, vol. 1, fig. 61.
46. *The Rudder* (March 1925): 80, (April 1926): 91. The *Stormy Petrel* was listed in *Lloyd's Register of Yachts* until 1972.
47. William U. Swan, "Joshua Brown: 1828-1901," unpublished typescript, 1937, commissioned by Waldo H. Brown
48. Waldo Hayward Brown, Memorandum to Bureau of Navigation, "Application for appointment as Lieutenant, Sr. Grade Aviation Volunteer Special, USNR," June 7, 1927, 2, 3, courtesy Paul Gray Brown, Duxbury, MA; Paul Gray Brown, interview with author, Duxbury, MA.
49. John N. Brown, interview with author, North Chatham, MA; Paul Brown, interview with author; Ora James Mulford, Obituary, *The Rudder* (September 1943): 75.
50. Waldo Brown, Memorandum to Bureau of Navigation.
51. *Lloyd's Register of American Yachts*, 1923, 64; LFH to John Hertz, April 5, 1951, 138:4/2, GWBWL; "The Other Man's Boat, *Circe*," *Yachting* (October 1967): 53.
52. Waldo Brown, Memorandum to Bureau of Navigation.
53. The plans of the *Joann* are SP38.145, DSGSPL; Waldo Brown, Memorandum to Bureau of Navigation.
54. SP38.145.22, SP38.145.1, DSGSPL.
55. John N. Brown, Paul G. Brown, interviews with author.
56. LFH to Ralph Reed, February 24, 1968, 138:6/2, LFH to Peter M. Harris, June 20, 1967, 138:6/1, LFH to Ralph Reed, March 2, 1970, 138:6/5, GWBWL; Len Hornick built a fine schooner, the *Mary Harrigan*, to the design of the *Joann*, and he added a centerboard. This writer can attest, after some memorable cruising in the *Mary Harrigan*, that, with the centerboard, she sails to windward like any other Herreshoff boat: exceedingly well.
57. SP38.145.26, DSGSPL; see previous note on the *Mary Harrigan*.
58. This may have been so the *Joann* could squeeze under the fixed bridge at Warren Avenue, Boston, in case Waldo wanted to put her in the Charles River Basin for the winter; yet a photograph of the schooner so ensconced shows her with masts removed; SP38.145.5, DSGSPL; *The Rudder* (June 1928): 83.
59. SP38.145.8, DSGSPL.
60. SP38.145.2, DSGSPL.
61. Paul G. Brown, photocopy, Mystic Seaport, 1996.10.4; SP38.145.7, DSGSPL.
62. Check stub, Ralph Reed and Sons, November 11, 1958, 138:8/9, GWBWL.
63. *Lynn Item*, June 21, 1906; Andrew W. Britt, "Britt Brothers: The Pinnacle of Boatbuilding as Art," *WoodenBoat* 167 (July/August 2002): 59; Andrew B. Britt, "Britt Brothers: Boatbuilders, 1904-1941," unpublished notes.
64. LFH, "The Common Sense of Yacht Design," *The Rudder* (July 1944): 35; LFH, *An L. Francis Herreshoff Reader*, 253; LFH to NGH, April 13, 1926, 138:17/2, GWBWL.
65. Arthur Brendze, interview with author; see also Thomas G. Skahill Jr., "Ted Geary: More Than a Naval Architect," *WoodenBoat* 138 (September/October 1997): 44.
66. LFH to NGH, May 8, 1936, 138:17/12, GWBWL; *Boston Globe*, February 10, 1925; LFH, *The Common Sense of Yacht Design*, vol. 1, 38; his experience with the *Joann*'s stove, and others, enabled LFH to write "Small Coal-Burning Stoves Aboard Ship," a piece that finally saw publication in *An L. Francis*

Herreshoff Reader and that was summarized in his *The Compleat Cruiser*, 21.

67. Katherine Jones Vosburgh, interview with author, Newburyport, MA, May 2, 1999; Paul Glynn, interview with author, Georgetown, MA, June 6, 1999; LFH to Bror Tamm, December 1, 1960, 138:5/1, GWBWL.
68. *Boston Globe*, February 10, 1925. The photos also appeared in the *Providence Sunday Journal* on February 22.
69. NGH to LFH, March 19, 1925, 138:17/1, GWBWL.

Chapter 5

1. LFH, *Capt. Nat Herreshoff*, 156, 157, 308.
2. NGH to LFH, March 19, 1925,138:17/1, GWBWL.
3. SP38.187.1, DSGSPL.
4. SP38. 287.1, DSGSPL; LFH, "The Common Sense of Yacht Design," *The Rudder* (February 1947): 41 (vol. 2, 80).
5. SP38.286.2, DSGSPL; LFH, "Discourse on Displacement, Etc.," *An L. Francis Herreshoff Reader*, 244; SP38.285.1, 2, DSGSPL.
6. *The Rudder* (October 1927): 11.
7. SP38.79.1, DSGSPL.
8. LFH, *Capt. Nat Herreshoff.* 129; LFH to Allan Vaitses, September 10, 1957, 138:4/8, GWBWL; O. Lie Nielsen, interview with author, August 31, 1998; John N. Brown, interview with author; LFH, *Capt. Nat Herreshoff*, 128; LFH, "The Common Sense of Yacht Design," *The Rudder* (February 1946): 37.
9. Dale Calloway, interview with author, East Lyme, CT, February 8, 1995.
10. Llewellyn Howland III, interview with author; Frederic Tudor, interview by Maynard Bray, transcript, 35, GWBWL; Arthur Brendze, interview with author.
11. LFH, "The Common Sense of Yacht Design, *The Rudder* (September 1946): 42, 43 (vol. 2, 46); Stephens, "Yacht Measurement," 28.
12. Stephens, "Yacht Measurement," 27, 28; W. P. Stephens, *The Match for the America's Cup: 1930*, Supplement to *The Sportsman* 3, no. 5 (1930); Streeter, *Their Last Letters*, 36, 108; see Jonathan Rice, "The Q Class," *WoodenBoat* 207 (March/April 2009): 58, 59.
13. LFH to NGH, August 4, 1933, 138:17/9, GWBWL; SP38.67.1, DSGSPL.
14. SP38.67.4, DSGSPL.
15. Two years later, C. Sherman Hoyt would take the enlargement of the fore triangle to what was then considered a ridiculous extreme, with his rig for the 6-Metre *Atrocia*, whose mast was so far aft that her club-footed, masthead jib was bigger than her mainsail. The *Atrocia* raced poorly. It was several decades before "the most peculiar rig ever seen on Long Island Sound," as it was called in *The Rudder* (August 1927): 42, 43, unfortunately became commonplace.
16. *Yachting* (June 1933): 67; Stan Grayson, "A Vanished Era—Catboat Sailing in the Late 19th Century: Photographs from the C. H. W. Foster Collection Hart Nautical/MIT Museum," in *Catboats*, 2nd ed. (Marblehead, MA: Devereux Books, 1996), 107; Matthew P. Murphy, *Glass Plates and Wooden Boats: The Yachting Photography of Willard B. Jackson at Marblehead, 1898-1937* (Beverly, MA: Commonwealth Editions, 2006), 46, 47.
17. LFH, *The Common Sense of Yacht Design*, vol. 1, 127; see also LFH to Evers Burtner, November 30, 1961, 138:5/2, LFH, unpublished statement on measurement rules, 138:14/21, GWBWL; LFH, "The Common Sense of Yacht Design," *The Rudder* (October 1945): 38, (vol. 1, 127).
18. LFH, "The Common Sense of Yacht Design," *The Rudder* (October 1945): 21.
19. LFH, "The Common Sense of Yacht Design," *The Rudder* (August 1945): 27, 28, (vol. 1, 118, 119); see also LFH to NGH, August 4, 1933, 138:17/9, GWBWL; LFH, "The Common Sense of Yacht Design," *The Rudder* (May 1947): 40 (vol. 2, 96, 97).
20. SP38.67.3, DSGSPL; LFH, "The Common Sense of Yacht Design," *The Rudder* (May 1944): 39.
21. LFH, "The Common Sense of Yacht Design," *The Rudder* (December 1945): 29, 30; LFH to Arthur Fiveland, April 3, 1967, 138:6/1, GWBWL.

22. LFH, "The Common Sense of Yacht Design," *The Rudder* (November 1944): 35; SP38.67.14, Ships Plans worksheet 38.67, DSGSPL; LFH, Notebook, 138:15a/14, GWBWL; see also LFH, "The Common Sense of Yacht Design," *The Rudder* (November 1944): 34, 35; *Yachting* (March 1926): 45; a disadvantage that did not concern LFH was the necessity of curling up around a web frame in the *Yankee*'s bunks, described to the author by a member of her racing crew years later on Lake Michigan; *Yachting* (May 1925), (June 1925).
23. NGH to LFH, October 29, 1935, 138:17/11, GWBWL; NGH, *Recollections*, 65.
24. LFH to NGH, April 12, 1927, 138:17/3, LFH to David Pierce-Jones, June 25, 1969, 138:6/4, LFH to NGH, December 27, 1929, 138:17/5, GWBWL; LFH, "The Common Sense of Yacht Design," *The Rudder* (December 1944): 42, 43; Bray and Pinheiro, *Herreshoff of Bristol*, 162.
25. LFH, *Capt. Nat Herreshoff*, 143.
26. Construction Record for LFH Designs, 138:15a/14, GWBWL.
27. LFH to NGH, May 6, 1925, NGH to LFH, 138:17/1, GWBWL.
28. LFH, *Capt. Nat Herreshoff*, 309; see also Bray and Pinheiro, *Herreshoff of Bristol*, 163; NGH to LFH, November 3, 1925, 138:17/1, GWBWL.
29. *New York Times*, August 6, 1925; Z. W. Hauk, *Schenley Yachting and Trophy Championship Book* (New York: Schenley Products, 1935), 55, 60, 61; see also LFH to NGH, August 4, 1933, 138:17/9, GWBWL.
30. William U. Swan, *Boston Transcript*, October 2, 1925.
31. NGH to LFH, November 3, 1925, 138:17/1, GWBWL; SP38. 67.13, DSGSPL; NGH to LFH, April 10, 1926, 138:17/2, GWBWL; LFH, *Capt. Nat Herreshoff*, 309.
32. Carrick and Henderson, *John G. Alden*, 353, 423.
33. LFH to NGH, April 13, 1926, 138:17/2, GWBWL.
34. LFH to NGH, April 13, 1926, 138:17/2, GWBWL.
35. SP38.67.5; patent drawing, 138:16/3, GWBWL; see also LFH, "The Common Sense of Yacht Design," *The Rudder* (May 1944): 39, 40.
36. NGH to LFH, April 10, 1926, LFH to NGH, April 13, 1926, 138:17/2, GWBWL.
37. *Boston Transcript*, June 28, 1926; Leonard M. Fowle, *Boston Globe*, August 29, 1926.
38. Unidentified newspaper clipping (probably from *Boston Transcript*) August 15, 1926, from a Welch family scrapbook; Allen D. Slater, interview with author; see also LFH to NGH, October 29, 1935, 138:17/11, GWBWL; Edith Welch Potter, interview with author; Arthur Brendze, interview with author.
39. *New York Times*, September 14, 1926; *Yachting* (October 1926): 24.
40. NGH to LFH, September 17, 1926, 138:17/2, GWBWL.
41. LFH to NGH, March 26, 1927, 138:17/3, GWBWL.
42. Larry Bates, telephone interview with author, Huntington, New York, January 13, 1995; Edward W. Schnobel to LFH, January 8, 1937, 138:1/7, Muriel Vaughn to David Pierce Jones, March 2, 1969, 138:6/4, GWBWL.

Chapter 6

1. SP38.125.1-9, DSGSPL.
2. Nat Wilson, interview with author, January 22, 2000.
3. LFH to NGH, February 18, 1927, 138:17/3, LFH to J. Thurston Eaton, April 7, 1947, 138:3/1, GWBWL.
4. Nat Wilson, interview with author; *Windcheck* (February 2012): 12.
5. W. H. Bunting, "Project *Slipper*," *WoodenBoat* 182 (January/February 2005): 56-59.
6. SP38.78.1, SP38.78.3, DSGSPL; LFH to Siegfried Hannah, February 20, 1947, 138:3/1, GWBWL; drawings in author's collection; LFH to Walker A. Settle Jr., July 10, 1968, 138:6/3, GWBWL.
7. LFH, *The Common Sense of Yacht Design, The Rudder* (December 1947): 27 (vol. 2, 147); see also Edwin J. Schoettle, *Sailing Craft* (New York: Macmillan, 1942), 118, 119; LFH to NGH, January 29, 1929, 138:17/5, GWBWL.
8. LFH, *The Common Sense of Yacht Design,* vol. 2, 144, 145.
9. LFH, "The Common Sense of Yacht Design," *The*

Rudder (July 1947): 32.

10. Plan at Hart Nautical Collections, MIT Museum, Cambridge, MA.
11. Plan at Hart Nautical Collections, MIT Museum, Cambridge, MA.
12. LFH to Georgina Paine Fisher Howland, ca. January 1, 1956, 138:6/7, GWBWL; see also Howland, *Afterthoughts*, 47.
13. LFH to NGH, April 13, 1926, 138:17/2, GWBWL.
14. LFH, "The Common Sense of Yacht Design," *The Rudder* (February 1947): 41 (vol. 2, 80).
15. SP38.213.1, DSGSPL.
16. SP38.244.1, SP38.245.1, DSGSPL
17. Carlton Pinheiro, interview with author; Bray and Pinheiro, *Herreshoff of Bristol*, xi.
18. NGH to LFH, April 10, 1926, 138:17/2, GWBWL.
19. Bray and Pinheiro, *Herreshoff of Bristol*, 139; NGH to LFH, November 3, 1925, 138:17/1, GWBWL.
20. NGH III and Carlton Pinheiro, interviews with author; NGH to LFH, December 6, 1925, 138:17/1, GWBWL.
21. LFH to NGH, April 13, 1926, 138:17/2, GWBWL.
22. Sidney had gone further "thru the course" than had his brothers, but he had not graduated; NGH to LFH, April 19, 1926, 138:17/2, GWBWL.
23. NGH to LFH, April 19, 1926, 138:17/2, GWBWL.
24. LFH to NGH, April 27, 1926, 138:17/2, GWBWL.
25. NGH to LFH, May 2, 1926, 138:17/2, GWBWL.
26. *The Rudder* (September 1926): 15; see also *Yachting* (April 1961): 91; LFH to NGH, April 13, 1926, NGH to LFH, May 2, 1926, 138:17/2, GWBWL.
27. After ten years on display at Mystic Seaport, the *Pleione* was scuttled in deep water outside Fishers Island, New York, in 1967 in accordance with the terms of J. V. Santry's will.
28. LFH to NGH, April 13, 1926, 138:17/2, GWBWL; Llewellyn Howland III, interview with author; Marjorie Young Wolff, interview with author, Middletown, Rhode Island, February 15, 1999; Rigg, "Profiles," *New Yorker*, 25.
29. *Yachting* (November 1926); Rigg, "Profiles," *New Yorker*, 24; see also LFH to Jacob D. Cox Jr., June 25, 1935, 138:1/5, GWBWL.
30. Llewellyn Howland III, interview with author, Jamaica Plain, MA, June 12, 2003.
31. When LFH gave Bror Tamm at the George Lawley Company a copy of Kunhardt's *Small Yachts*, he inscribed it "A gift of Francis L. [sic] Herreshoff of Bristol, R. I., 1925."

Chapter 7

1. Priscilla Sawyer Lord and Virginia Clegg Gamage, *Marblehead: The Spirit of '76 Lives Here* (Philadelphia: Chilton, 1972), 223.
2. See William U. Swan in Schoettle, *Sailing Craft*, 701-03.
3. A. L. Widger, *Historic Marblehead* (Wellesley, MA: Thurlow S. Widger, 1957), 17, 18.
4. Stan Grayson, e-mail to author, February 2, 2005; see also Llewellyn Howland III, "Is Yacht Designing an Art or a Science?" unpublished MS, 8; the building became the clubhouse of the Boston Yacht Club in 1956; LFH to NGH, March 14, 1933, 138:17/9, LFH to Boris Lauer-Leonardi, March 5, 1943, 138:2/4, GWBWL.
5. Arthur Brendze, interview with author; O. Lie-Nielsen to parents, June 16, 1931, courtesy of O. Lie-Nielsen, Rockland, ME.
6. LFH to NGH, May 6, 1925, 138:17/1, LFH to NGH, May 15, 1936, 138:17/12, GWBWL; O. Lie-Nielsen to parents, June 16, 1931; Peter Coe, interview with author, January 22, 2000.
7. Dale Calloway, Arthur Brendze, and Peter Coe, interviews with author.
8. Katherine Vosburgh, interview with author, Newburyport, MA, May 2, 1999.
9. NGH to LFH, September 3, 1926, 138:17/2, GWBWL.
10. LFH to Walter Hadley, June 11, 1965, 138:5/6, GWBWL; Anne Bondy, Katherine Vosburgh, interviews with author; LFH to Georgina Paine Fisher Howland, ca. January 1, 1956, 138:6/7, LFH to Virginia Paine, November 13, 1951, 138:4/2, Agreement with George Lawley and Son [for construction of the *Albacore*], 138:15/6, GWBWL; Anne Bondy, interview with author.

11. Francis remembered their time together at Burgess, Swasey, and Paine inaccurately as "about four years," LFH, "The Common Sense of Yacht Design," *The Rudder* (July 1944): 36 (vol. 1, 37).
12. LFH, "The Common Sense of Yacht Design," *The Rudder* (March 1944): 60 (vol. 1, 6); LFH, "The Common Sense of Yacht Design," *The Rudder* (July 1945): 25 (vol. 1, 114); LFH to Harry G. Blake, November 19, 1943, 138:2/4, GWBWL; LFH, "The Common Sense of Yacht Design," *The Rudder* (September 1946): 45 (vol. 2, 49); LFH to Edgar P. Bainbridge, March 29, 1945, 138:2/7, Miscellaneous and Unidentified Calculations, Scantlings, etc., 138:16/9, GWBWL.
13. Hope Welch Slater, interview with author.
14. Advertisement for the *Dispatch*, *Yachting* (March 1928): 17.
15. Advertisement for the *Dispatch*, *Yachting* (March 1928): 17; LFH, *The Common Sense of Yacht Design*, vol. 2, 76.
16. LFH, *The Common Sense of Yacht Design*, vol. 1, 102, vol. 2, 76.
17. Van Wyck Brooks, *The Flowering of New England: 1815-1865* (New York: E. P. Dutton, 1936), 415.
18. Murphy, *Glass Plates and Wooden Boats*, 70; see Herbert L. Stone, "Editorial," *Yachting* (December 1927): 66.
19. LFH to NGH, March 26, 1927, 138:17/3, GWBWL; SP38.6.30, DSGSPL; LFH to Walter Hadley, February 8, 1965, 138:5/6, GWBWL.
20. *The Rudder* (June 1928): 24; "Heard Through the Porthole," *Yachting* (August 1927): 67.
21. LFH, "The Common Sense of Yacht Design," *The Rudder* (May 1946): 43.
22. SP38.6.1, DSGSPL; see also LFH to H. G. McKinney Jr., March 11, 1946, 138:2/9, GWBWL; LFH, "The Common Sense of Yacht Design," *The Rudder* (May 1946): 43; the cube root of the displacement, in cubic feet, could not exceed 20 percent of the waterline length, plus 0.5 feet; for the *Live Yankee,* both figures came out at 5.8 feet; see also Carrick and Henderson, *John G. Alden*, 271.
23. "Miscellaneous Calculations," 138:16/9, GWBWL; SP38.6.1, DSGSPL.
24. SP38.6.1, DSGSPL; *Yachting* (August 1927): 57.
25. Thomas G. Skahill Jr., "Ted Geary: More Than a Naval Architect," *WoodenBoat* 138 (September/October 1997): 53; LFH to NGH, April 12, 1927, 138:17/3, LFH to H. G. McKinney Jr., 138:2/9, GWBWL.
26. NGH to LFH, February 10, 1927, March 21, 1927, LFH to NGH, April 12, 1927, 138:17/3, GWBWL.
27. LFH to NGH, January 29, 1927, January 14, 1927, March 26, 1927, 138:17/3, GWBWL
28. LFH, *The Common Sense of Yacht Design*, vol. 1, 21; LFH, "The Common Sense of Yacht Design," *The Rudder* (May 1944): 39 (vol. 1, 112); Edith Welch Potter, interview with author, Martha's Vineyard, MA; LFH to H. G. McKinney Jr., March 4, 1946, 138:2/9, GWBWL.
29. Arthur Brendze, interview with author, June 20, 2014, Sausalito, CA.
30. LFH, "The Common Sense of Yacht Design," *The Rudder* (May 1944): 39 (vol. 1, 112); LFH to L. W. G. Wertheim-Symes, February 16, 1969, 138:6/4, GWBWL.
31. *Yachting* (August 1927): 57; as Philip C. Bolger has pointed out ("L. Francis Herreshoff," *Nautical Quarterly* 9 (Winter 1980): 75) Francis's work was akin to that of the builder of Oliver Wendell Holmes's wonderful one-hoss shay in "The Deacon's Masterpiece or, the Wonderful 'One-Hoss Shay': A Logical Story," Oliver Wendell Holmes, *The Autocrat of the Breakfast-Table* (Boston; Phillps, Sampson, 1858) every single part of which turned to dust on its hundredth birthday; Francis was in the *Stranger*; LFH to NGH, July 14, 1927, 138:17/3, GWBWL.
32. *Yachting* (August 1927): 57; John Graham Jr. to LFH, August 8, 1944, LFH to John Graham Jr., August 11, 1944, 138:2/6, GWBWL.
33. "Construction Record for LFH Designs," 138:15/40, GWBWL; the provision of the Rule was: "The cube root of the total displacement [in cubic feet] below the sheerline must be more than 60 percent of the square root of the sail area plus three"; LFH, "The Common Sense of Yacht Design," *The Rudder* (April

1945): 26; LFH to H. G. McKinney Jr., 138:2/??, GWBWL.

34. "Heard Through the Porthole," *Yachting* (August 1927): 67.
35. LFH to Walter Hadley, February 8, 1965, 138:5/6, GWBWL.
36. LFH to NGH, July 14, 1927, 138:17/3, GWBWL; Howard I. Chapelle, *History of American Sailing Ships* (New York: W. W. Norton, 1935), 354; Bruce King, interview with author, Damariscotta, ME, March 13, 1996.
37. LFH to T. R. Mason, August 24, 1945, 138:2/8, GWBWL.
38. *Yachting* (October 1927): 45.
39. *Boston Globe*, January 30, 1928.
40. *Boston Herald*, January 28, 1928; *Boston Globe*, January 30, 1928; J. Scott Rohrer, "The Pacific Northwest Yachting Photography of Asahel Curtis," *WoodenBoat* 204 (September/October 2008): 48; *Yachting* (June 1928): 85.
41. LFH to NGH, May 1, 1928, 138:17/4, GWBWL; *Yachting* (October 1927): 45.
42. NGH to LFH, May 7, 1928, 138:17/4, GWBWL.
43. *Yachting* (October 1928): 87; David Slater, e-mail to author, October 1, 2011.
44. *Yachting*, December 1930, 106; Hauk, *Schenley Yachting and Trophy Championship Book*, 55, 59, 60, 61, 63, 64, 71; Skahill, "Ted Geary," *WoodenBoat* 138 (September/October 1997): 53; John Graham, Jr. to LFH, August 8, 1944, 138:2/6, Arthur J. Atkinson to LFH, September 10, 1948, 138:7/1, GWBWL.
45. H. Y. McKinney Jr. to LFH, March 20, 1946, 138:8/4, GWBWL.
46. SP38.119, DSGSPL; NGH to LFH, April 7, 1928, 138:17/4, GWBWL.
47. SP38.39.1, SP38.35.1, SP38.37.2, SP38.176.1, 2, 3, 14, 15, and 4, DSGSPL.
48. Ben Martin, interview with author, St. Michael's, MD, June 25, 1999; Johan Selmer-Larsen to author, August 21, 1995.
49. Martin Black, *G. L. Watson: The Art and Science of Yacht Design* (Limerick, Ireland: Peggy Bawn Press, 2011).
50. LFH to Charles Francis Adams, October 25, 1932, 138:1/2, GWBWL.
51. LFH to NGH, August 14, 1933, 138:17/9, LFH, notes for a meeting, August 1964, on "A Rule for Measuring and Rating Racing Sail Boats," 138:14/21, LFH to "Dear Sir," November 25, 1968, 138:6/3, LFH to Gordon Thomson, January 8, 1969, 138:6/4, GWBWL; Robert J. Shekter, "L. Francis Herreshoff," *Popular Boating* (September 1957): 71.
52. SP38.6.5, DSGSPL.
53. SP38.69.5, SP38.69.2, DSGSPL.
54. Olin J. Stephens II, *All This and Sailing Too: An Autobiography* (Mystic: Mystic Seaport, 1999), 23; May Fife McCallum, *"Fast and Bonnie": A History of William Fife and Son Yachtbuilders* (Edinburgh: John Donald, 1998), 117; see also Herbert L. Stone, "Editorial," *Yachting* (November 1927): 66.
55. Manfred Curry, *Yacht Racing: The Aerodynamics of Sails and Racing Tactics*, 5th ed., (New York: C. Scribner's Sons, 1948), 64; LFH to NGH, March 26, 1927, 138:17/3, GWBWL; *Yachting* (July 1927): 59, 60.
56. LFH, "The Common Sense of Yacht Design," *The Rudder* (May 1947): 36; *Yachting* (February 1930): 80; Philip C. Bolger, interview with author.
57. LFH, *The Common Sense of Yacht Design*, vol. 2, 126, 127.
58. Curry, *Yacht Racing*, 64.
59. LFH, "The Common Sense of Yacht Design," *The Rudder* (May 1944): 37, 38 (vol. 1, 17-19).
60. LFH, "The Common Sense of Yacht Design," *The Rudder* (May 1944): 37, 38 (vol. 1, 17-19); see also Philip J. Roosevelt to LFH, December 16, 1935, LFH to Philip J Roosevelt, December 20, 1935, 138:1/5, LFH to Boris Lauer-Leonardi, May 7, 1959, 138:4/10, GWBWL.
61. LFH to Boris Lauer-Leonardi, May 7, 1959, 138:4/10, GWBWL; LFH, "The Common Sense of Yacht Design," *The Rudder* (October 1945): 39.
62. For the counterargument see M. Heckstall-Smith's report on the International Yachting Conference of 1928, at which the unmeasured area of the Genoa jib was retained, *Yachting* (December 1928): 34; Charles

Francis Adams to LFH, November 10, 1932, 138:7/1, GWBWL.

63. Robert M. Steward, Jacksonville, FL, to author, October 14, 1982.
64. *Yachting* (October 1928): 87; LFH to NGH, February 18, 1927, 138:17/3, GWBWL; *Yachting* (November 1927): 9; the *Pleasure* still sails out of Bristol, now owned by the HMM.
65. Stan Grayson, "A Vanished Era—Catboat Sailing in the Late 19th Century," typescript, 1; SP38.69.1, DSGSPL.
66. LFH to NGH, February 21, 1933, 138:17/9, GWBWL; SP38.69.5, DSGSPL.
67. "Dr. Curry's Latest Experiment," *Yachting* (March 1928): 85; Roger Stollery, "Swing Rig," *Yachting World* (November 1984): 84-87.

Chapter 8

1. Stephens, *All This and Sailing Too*, 17, 65.
2. Boats designed to a Universal Rule class naturally had similar dimensions. Vanderbilt's *Prestige* did have "exactly the dimensions" of No. 22 as to waterline length and beam and drew only one inch less. But the *Prestige* had a conventional counter stern instead of the long, pointed stern of No. 22, so she was 5 feet, 6 inches shorter on deck; LFH to NGH, February 18, 1927, 138:17/3, GWBWL; LFH, "The Common Sense of Yacht Design," *The Rudder* (July 1947): 32.
3. LFH to NGH, March 26, 1927, NGH to LFH, April 3, 1927, 138:17/3, GWBWL.
4. LFH, "The Common Sense of Yacht Design," *The Rudder* (April 1946): 44.
5. I have retained Nathanael's spelling.
6. Howland and Company, Jamaica Plain, MA, *Catalogue 56*, November 1996, 29, Item 301; LFH, "The Common Sense of Yacht Design," *The Rudder* (June 1944): 28, fig. 40.
7. LFH to NGH, May 10, 1927, 138:17/3, GWBWL.
8. SP38.215.1, SP38.41.1, DSGSPL.
9. SP38.76.47, DSGSPL.
10. Katherine Jones Vosburgh, interview with author, Newburyport, MA, May 2, 1999; O. Lie-Nielsen, interview with author, Rockland, ME, August 31, 1998; see, for example, *The Rudder* (July 1920): 24, (December 1923): 24, (April 1927): 54, (December 1927): 57; see *The Rudder* (January 1925): 37; *Yachting* (April 1927): 75
11. NGH to LFH, December 12, 1928, LFH to NGH, December 18, 1928, 138:17/4, GWBWL.
12. Construction Record for LFH Designs, 138:15/5, GWBWL.
13. *Yachting* (December 1931): 80-82; see also LFH, *Sensible Cruising Designs*, 240; *The Rudder* (April 1931): 58; *Yachting* (December 1933): 58, 59; *The Rudder* (March 1935): 56, (February 1945): 75.
14. SP38.76.3, DSGSPL; LFH, "The Common Sense of Yacht Design," *The Rudder* (January 1947): 38.
15. Katherine Vosburgh, interview with author.
16. *Winton News*, April 1929, Ships Plans Folder 38.76, DSGSPL.
17. *The Rudder* (June 1928): 80; SP38.76, DSGSPL; LFH, "The Common Sense of Yacht Design," *The Rudder* (April 1945): 24; Andrew W. Britt to author, January 19, 2001.
18. *MoToR Boating* (April 1929): 112.
19. LFH to B. W. Lamson, February 17, 1937, 138:1/7, GWBWL; Davin, "He Carries On," *Boats*, 52.
20. LFH to NGH, January 14, 1927, 138:17/3, GWBWL.
21. *Yachting* (December 1927): 51, (April 1928): 88, (March 1928): 89.
22. LFH to Howard I. Chapelle, January 5, 1937, 138:1/7, LFH to William F. Schanen, May 6, 1948, 138:3/4, GWBWL.
23. LFH to A. M. Herrmann, October 13, 1936, 138:1/6, GWBWL.
24. SP38.16.24, DSGSPL.
25. *Yachting* (September 1928): 61, (December 1928): 42.
26. LFH to A. M. Herrmann, October 13, 1936, 138:1/6, GWBWL; NGH, *Recollection*, 56.
27. NGH, *Recollection*, 56.
28. SP38.16.7, DSGSPL; A. M. Herrmann to LFH, ca. October 1936, 138:7/8, GWBWL.
29. Deane Tank and Beverly Ford, ed., *Tales of the Chicago Mackinac Race: 1898-1998* (Chicago: Island

Goats Sailing Society, 1998), 128, 172, 173; Bruce Grant, "Forty-Third Annual Mackinac Race," *The Rudder* (September 1950): 11.

30. Ships Plans Folder 38.16, DSGSPL; Johan Roe, "Q Boats in the Rockies," *Sailing* (April 2002): 81.
31. Doug Averill, interview with author, Big Fork, MT, October 11, 2013; Jon Derry to author, no date, received January 17, 1995; see also, Dan Spurr, "Ladies of the Lake," *WoodenBoat* 170 (January/ February 2003): 58.
32. Clinton H. Crane, *Clinton Crane's Yachting Memories* (New York: D. Van Nostrand, 1952), 193.
33. *Yachting* (March 1928): 128, (April 1928): 84.
34. *Yachting* (December 1928): 34, (March 1928): 128; Edwin J. Shoettle, *Sailing Craft* (New York: Macmillan, 1942), 322, 323.
35. *Yachting* (December 1927): 60.
36. LFH to NGH, January 14, 1927, 138:17/3, GWBWL; *The Sportsman* (April 1927).
37. NGH to LFH, January 23, 1927, 138:17/2, GWBWL; LFH, *Nathanael Greene Herreshoff*, 23; LFH to NGH, 138:17/2, GWBWL.
38. LFH to H. F. Newman, October 24, 1955, 138:4/6, GWBWL; LFH, "The Common Sense of Yacht Design," *The Rudder* (September 1946): 45, (January 1948): 46.
39. Miscellaneous and Unidentified Calculations, Scantlings, etc., 138:16/9; LFH to NGH, May 1, 1928, 138:17/4, GWBWL.
40. LFH to NGH, April 20, 1928, 138:17/4, GWBWL.
41. LFH, "A Rule for Measuring and Rating Sailboats," 138:14/21, GWBWL.
42. LFH to NGH, May 1, 1928, 138:17/4, GWBWL.
43. LFH, "The Scharenkreuzers," *Yachting* (December 1928): 67.
44. LFH to NGH, May 1, 1928, 138:17/4, GWBWL; by the time of this letter, LFH could have added two motor launches to the *Yankee, Dispatch, Live Yankee, Siva, Siva*'s launch, *Nor'easter V,* and *Bonnie Lassie.*
45. *The Rudder* (November 1928): 29, (December 1928): 43; LFH, "The Common Sense of Yacht Design," *The Rudder* (September 1946): 76.
46. Howard I. Chapelle, *The American Fishing Schooners, 1825-1935* (New York: W. W. Norton, 1973, 1995), 235, 236.
47. NGH to LFH, April 21, 1928, 138:17/4, GWBWL.
48. Edmund Cutts, interview with author.
49. Patent No. 1,698,304, January 8, 1929 to Lewis Francis Herreshoff of Marblehead, MA, Assignor to Dyer Motorcraft Corporation of Providence, RI.
50. *The Rudder* (January 1929): 146.
51. Contract, December 23, 1927, 138:15/3, GWBWL; *The Rudder* (March 1928): 148; one of these boats was offered for sale in 2012 for $45,000; *Yachting* (April 1929): 96; one of these boats, the *Quickstep*, is on display at the Museum of Yachting in Newport, RI; *The Rudder* (October 1930): 86.
52. LFH to Boris Lauer-Leonardi, October 20, 1944, 138:2/6, GWBWL.
53. William Atkin, "The Suicide Fleet Looks in at Marblehead," *Fore an' Aft* (November 1928): 6, 8.
54. LFH, "An Interesting Experiment in Rigs," *Yachting* (February 1929): 74; this article also appeared in the German magazine *Die Yacht*, March 2, 1929.
55. LFH, *The Common Sense of Yacht Design*, vol. 2, 65
56. Atkin, "The Suicide Fleet," *Fore an' Aft* (November 1928): 8; LFH to George P. Publow, December 6, 1945, 138:2/8, LFH to Boris Lauer-Leonardi, February 26, 1948, 138:3/4, GWBWL.
57. LFH, "An Interesting Experiment," *Yachting* (February 1929): 73.
58. *The Rudder* (August 1928): 88; Katherine Vosburgh, interview with author, Newburyport, MA, May 2, 1999; LFH, *The Common Sense of Yacht Design*, vol. 2, 65.
59. LFH, *The Common Sense of Yacht Design*, vol. 1, 22; LFH, "An Interesting Experiment," *Yachting* (February 1929): 138.
60. LFH, "An Interesting Experiment," *Yachting* (February 1929): 73, 74; Atkin, "The Suicide Fleet," *Fore an' Aft* (November 1928): 9, 12.
61. NGH to LFH, April 7, 1928, LFH to NGH, December 14, 1928, 138:17/4, NGH to LFH, January 19, 1929, LFH to NGH, February 11, 1929, NGH to LFH, February 15, 1929, LFH to NGH, February 26, 1929, 138:17/5, GWBWL.

62. John Brown, interview with author, Chatham, MA, March 20, 1996; William Cannell built a boat to design No. 39 in his boatshop in Camden, ME.
63. *Yachting* (January 1931): 96; Hanns Stinnes to LFH, October 3, 1949, LFH to Hanns Stinnes, October 31, 1949, 138:3/6, GWBWL.
64. LFH to NGH, August 29, 1930, 138:17/6, LFH to G. H. Green, September 8, 1947, 138:3/3, GWBWL.
65. LFH to NGH, June 24, 1932, May 5, 1933, July 28, 1933, 138:17/8, 9, Woodbury E. Burd to LFH, October 16, 1946, 138:2/10, LFH to G. H. Green, September 3, 1947, 138:3/3, GWBWL.
66. Wirth M. Munroe, "The Wishbone Rig in the Development Class," *The Rudder* (July 1935): 50; *The Rudder* (September 1933): 37, (April 1934): 40.
67. LFH to Uffa Fox, December 23, 1934, 138:1/4, LFH to Boris Lauer-Leonardi, August 28, 1944, 138:2/6, LFH to Thomas M. Buerrmann, June 19, 1944, 138:2/5, GWBWL.
68. SP38.171.10, SP38.171.9, DSGSPL; William Strawbridge III, interview with author, Easton, MD, April 19, 1996.
69. The Mystic Seaport collection includes another Development Class dinghy that Strawbridge designed on his own in 1933. The *Butterfly*'s accession number is 1988.78; that of the Strawbridge boat of 1933 is 1980.14.

Chapter 9

1. Katherine Vosburgh, interview with author, Newburyport, MA, May 2, 1999; LFH to John W. Nicholson, February 12, 1951, 138:4/2, GWBWL.
2. Katherine Vosburgh, interview with author; Suzy Fernberger, interview with author, Marblehead, MA, September 25, 1999; Arthur Brendze, interview with author.
3. LFH to NGH, August 3, 1928, 138:17/4, GWBWL.
4. NGH to LFH, April 21, 1928, LFH to NGH, May 1, 1928, 138:17/4, GWBWL.
5. LFH to NGH, August 14, 1928, September 18, 1928, October 9, 1928, 138:17/4, GWBWL.
6. Grace Herreshoff to LFH, December 26, 1928, 138:17/4, GWBWL.
7. SP38.52, SP38.200, DSGSPL.
8. LFH to NGH, March 28, 1930, 138:17/6, LFH to William Strawbridge, October 26, 1954, 138:4/5, GWBWL.
9. LFH to NGH, April 7, 1930, NGH to LFH, April 15, 1930, LFH to NGH, April 10, 1931, 138:17/7, LFH to Lathrop Engine Company, August 13, 1935, 138:1/5, GWBWL.
10. *The Rudder* (May 1930): 188; LFH to NGH, December 31, 1930, 138:17/6, GWBWL.
11. Francis C. Welch (Charles Welch's nephew) to author, February 15, 1980.
12. LFH to NGH, February 25, 1930, 138:17/6, LFH to NGH, March 16, 1931, 138:17/7, GWBWL.
13. Edo Potter, *The Last Farm on Chappaquiddick* (Edgartown, MA: Vineyard Stories, 2010), 36; *The Rudder* (May 1931): 136; Edith Welch Potter and Hope Welch Slater, interview with author.
14. LFH to NGH, April 10, 1931, 138:17/7, GWBWL.
15. Letters from LFH to NGH of April 10, 1931 and April 24, 1931, MSM, 138:17/7, GWBWL.
16. *Yachting* (April 1937): 27; Latham to LFH, August 24, 1944, 138:2/6, GWBWL; Ships Plans worksheet 38.81, DSGSPL: *Yachting* (January 1955): 69.
17. *The Rudder* (March 1929): 138; LFH to NGH, June 6, 1936, 138:17/12, GWBWL.
18. *The Rudder* (October 1929): 88, 90, (September 1932): 51.
19. *The Rudder* (June 1923): 20; Anne Bondy, interview with author.
20. NGH to LFH, June 19, 1932, LFH to NGH, June 24, 1932, 138:17/8, GWBWL; *The Rudder* (September 1932): 51.
21 LFH to NGH, December 29, 1928, 138:17/4, GWBWL; Jonathan Rice, "The Q Class," *WoodenBoat* 207 (March/April 2009): 62.
22. Lloyd Bergeson, telephone conversation with author, March 29, 2000; Edith Foster Farwell, quoted in Joe Garland, *The Eastern Yacht Club: A History from 1870 to 1985* (Marblehead, MA: Eastern Yacht Club, 1989), 179; "The 'Q' Class at Marblehead," *Yachting*

(March 1929): 85.

23. LFH to Robert C. Strassman, July 6, 1949, 138:3/6, LFH to Howard I. Chapelle, September 24, 1935, 138:1/5, GWBWL.
24. Murphy, *Glass Plates and Wooden Boats*, 60; LFH to Howard I. Chapelle, September 24, 1935, 138:1/5, GWBWL.
25. *Yachting* (October 1929): 69; Leonard M. Fowle Jr., "The Racing Season at Marblehead, *Yachting* (December 1930): 69; LFH to Howard I. Chapelle, September 24, 1935, 138:1/5, GWBWL.
26. Ed Earle, "Massachusetts Bay Flashes," *Yachting* (May 1935): 112.
27. Doug Averill, interview with author, Big Fork, MT, October 11, 2013; see also Johan Roe, "Q Boats in the Rockies," *Sailing* (April 2002): 80-82; Dan Spurr, "Ladies of the Lake," *WoodenBoat* 170 (January/February 2003): 58-64.
28. LFH, "The Scharenkreuzers," *Yachting* (December 1928): 67.
29. LFH, "The Scharenkreuzers," *Yachting* (December 1928): 67; see also "An Outline of the Square Meter Rule," www.sskf.se/regein/online.htm.
30. Norman L. Skene, "The Scharenkreuzers," *Yachting* (June 1929): 63; see also "An Outline of the Square Meter Rule"; Knud H. Reimers, "Thirty Square Meters," *The Rudder* (May 1931): 141.
31. LFH to NGH, March 26, 1927, 138:17/3, GWBWL.
32. Dieter Empacher, interview with author, Marblehead, MA.
33. William U. Swan, "International Racing," *The Rudder* (December 1928): 90; LFH to NGH, January 29, 1929, 138:17/5, GWBWL.
34. Margrete L. Stinnes, interview with author, Rockland, ME; Arthur Brendze, e-mail to author, March 5, 2010.
35. LFH to NGH, April 26, 1929, 138:17/5, GWBWL.
36. O. Lie-Nielsen, interview with author, Rockland, ME, August 31, 1998.
37. Katherine Vosburgh, interview with author, Newburyport, MA, May 2, 1999.
38. See Schoettle, *Sailing Craft*, 578; LFH, "The Scharenkreuzers," *Yachting* (December 1928): 67.
39. LFH to NGH, February 6, 1931, 138:17/7, GWBWL.
40. Jay Greer, interview with author, Port Townsend, WA, September 13, 1999. Greer had the story from Muriel Vaughn.
41. LFH to NGH, April 10, 1931, 138:17/7, LFH to George Fisher, November 2, 1966, 138:5/8, GWBWL.
42. LFH, "The Common Sense of Yacht Design," *The Rudder* (November 1946): 42; LFH to George Fisher, November 2, 1966, 138:5/8, GWBWL; *Yachting* (February 1929): 78.
43. LFH, "The Common Sense of Yacht Design," *The Rudder* (September 1946): 43.
44. Henry Rasmussen to LFH, September 25, 1929, LFH to Henry Rasmussen, October 1, 1929, 138:1/1, GWBWL.
45. SP38.40.1, DSGSPL.
46. LFH, "The Common Sense of Yacht Design," *The Rudder* (November 1944): 50; LFH to Boris Lauer-Leonardi, January 7, 1942, 138:2/3, GWBWL; John Gardner, interview with author.
47. Bobby Russell, interview with author, Marblehead, MA.
48. LFH to NGH, February 26, 1929, 138:17/5, LFH to Walter Hadley, June 10, 1970, 138:6/5, GWBWL.
49. *Yachting* (April 1929): 97.
50. LFH to NGH, January 29, 1929, 138:17/5, GWBWL.
51. *Yachting* (October 1929): 52, 71.
52. LFH to NGH, July 17, 1929, 138:17/5, GWBWL; see also, *The Rudder* (May 1929): 112; LFH to NGH, August 6, 1929, 138:17/5, GWBWL; see also *The Rudder* (June 1929): 126, (October 1929): 98.
53. *The Rudder* (October 1929): 52, 98, 100; *Yachting* (September 1935): 89; *The Rudder* (December 1936): 54.
54. NGH to LFH, April 2, 1930, LFH to NGH, April 7, 1930, 138:17/6, GWBWL.
55. Elizabeth Hovey-Morss, interview with Joseph E. Garland, quoted in his *History of the Eastern Yacht Club*, 187, 188; see also Virginia Macomber, "30 Squares: The Greyhounds of Yacht Racing," *Spinnaker* (Summer 1996): 8, 9.
56. Elizabeth Hovey-Morss, interview with Dave Philips, *Providence Journal*, February 12, 1991; Macomber,

"30 Squares," *Spinnaker,* 9.

57. LFH to NGH, March 5, 1931, 138:17/7, Construction Record for LFH Designs, 138:15/9, GWBWL.
58. LFH to NGH, May 6, 1932, 138:17/8, GWBWL.
59. Ships Plans File 38.61, DSGSPL; LFH to NGH, August 1, 1932, 138:17/8, GWBWL; *Yachting* (May 1935): 116.
60. John Brown, interview with author.
61. John Brown, interview with author.
62. John Brown, interview with author.
63. LFH, "The Common Sense of Yacht Design," *The Rudder* (November 1946): 42 (vol. 2, 55).

Chapter 10

1. *Yachting* (October 1929): 83.
2. LFH to Walter Hadley, October 31, 1966, 138:5/8, GWBWL.
3. *Yachting* (June 1929): 84.
4. *An L. Francis Herreshoff Reader,* 181; NGH to LFH, August 19, 1928, 138:17/4, GWBWL.
5. LFH to Uffa Fox, January 14, 1935, 138:1/5, GWBWL.
6. LFH to NGH, August 14, 1928, NGH to LFH of September 7, 1928, LFH to NGH, September 8, 1928, NGH to LFH, September 14, 1928, 138:17/4, GWBWL.
7. LFH to NGH, October 23, 1928, NGH to LFH, September 19, 1928, 138:17/4, GWBWL.
8. NGH to LFH, October 23, 1928, 138:17/4, GWBWL.
9. Design No. 62 [and No. 34], 138:15/11, NGH to LFH, October 9, 1928, 138:17/4, GWBWL.
10. NGH to LFH, October 9, 1928, 138:17/4, GWBWL.
11. NGH to LFH, October 23, 1928, 138:17/4, LFH to Malcolm MacNaught, December 17, 1956, 138:4/7, LFH to NGH, November 23, 1928, 138:17/4, GWBWL.
12. LFH to NGH, March 26, 1927, 138:17/3, GWBWL; LFH, "The Common Sense of Yacht Design," *The Rudder* (January 1945): 70.
13. NGH to LFH, December 22, 1928, 138:17/4, LFH to NGH, October 14, 1929, 138:17/5, GWBWL.
14. NGH to LFH, December 22, 1928, LFH to NGH, December 29, 1928, 138:17/4, GWBWL.
15. LFH to NGH, December 18, 1928, NGH to LFH, December 22, 1928, 138:17/4, NGH to LFH, February 7, 1929, LFH to NGH, February 11, 1929, 138:17/5, GWBWL.
16. LFH to NGH, January 18, February 26, 1929, 138:17/5, GWBWL.
17. LFH to NGH, April 2, 1929, 138:17/5, LFH to Uffa Fox, January 14, 1935, 138:1/5, GWBWL; Philip C. Bolger, "L. Francis Herreshoff," *Nautical Quarterly* 9 (Winter 1980): 74, 75; see also Oliver Wendell Holmes, "The Deacon's Masterpiece or, The Wonderful 'One-Hoss Shay': A Logical Story," *Autocrat of the Breakfast-Table.*
18. LFH to William A. Heine Jr., March 30, 1948, 138:3/4, GWBWL.
19. LFH to NGH, April 6, 1929, 138:17/5, GWBWL.
20. *The Rudder*, July 1929, 106.
21. LFH to NGH, June 14, 1929, 138:17/5, GWBWL.
22. NGH to LFH, June 19, 1929, 138:17/5, GWBWL.
23. NGH to LFH, August 24, 30, 1929, 138:17/5, GWBWL.
24. *The Rudder* (October 1929): 17, 20, 21.
25. *Yachting* (October 1929): 40; SP38.17.36, DSGSPL.
26. SP38.17.15, DSGSPL.
27. *Clinton Crane's Yachting Memories*, 167, 168.
28. LFH to NGH, November 20, 1930, 138:17/6, GWBWL.
29. LFH to NGH, November 13, 1930, NGH to LFH, November 17, 1930, 138:17/6, GWBWL.
30. LFH to NGH, January 22, March 30, 1931, 138:17/7, GWBWL.
31. Design No. 62 [and No. 34], 138:15/11, LFH to Charles H. Truscott, September 26, 1967, Collection 138, Box 6, Folder 1, GWBWL. Humbled but resolute, Pynchon (1862-1940) sold his boats and his country house, moved into a small Park Avenue apartment, and went to work as a low-level employee in another brokerage firm, according to news reports of the day.
32. LFH to NGH, June 26, July 20, 1931, 138:17/7, GWBWL; *Yachting* (November 1931): 34.
33. *Yachting* (October 1931): 102; LFH, "The Common Sense of Yacht Design," *The Rudder* (September

1946): 76; *Time*, August 31, 1931; NGH to LFH, July 24, 1931, 138:17/7, GWBWL.

34. NGH to LFH, June 21, 1934, 138:17/10, GWBWL.
35. *The Rudder* (June 1941): 46; LFH to Charles H. Truscott, September 26, 1967, 138:6/1, GWBWL. Under the name *Sabre*, Francis's Design No. 34 had a long and successful racing career in her new, fresh-water environment. In 1984, she was being restored at Dearborn, MI. There were rumors of another more recent restoration, but the *Istalena* seems to have disappeared.
36. LFH, "The Common Sense of Yacht Design," *The Rudder* (April 1944): 24.
37. LFH to NGH, April 26, May 18, August 23, 1929, 138:17/5, LFH to NGH, December 18, 1928, 138:17/4, GWBWL.
38. NGH to LFH, April 21, May 7, 1929, LFH to NGH, April 30, 1929, 138:17/5, GWBWL.
39. NGH to LFH, September 30, 1929, 138:17/5, GWBWL; NGH III and Carleton Pinheiro, interviews with author; NGH to LFH, December 8, 1929, 138:17/5, GWBWL; Streeter, *Their Last Letters,* 146, 147; NGH to LFH, November 19, 1929, LFH to NGH, November 25, 1929, 138:17/5, GWBWL.
40. NGH III, interview with author.
41. LFH to NGH, May 2, 1929, NGH to LFH, January 25, 1929, LFH to NGH, April 30, 1929, 138:17/5, GWBWL.
42. LFH to NGH, May 18, August 23, 1929, 138:17/5, GWBWL.

Chapter 11

1. LFH, *An L. Francis Herreshoff Reader*, 3; W. P. Stephens, *The Match for the America's Cup,* Supplement to *The Sportsman* 7, no. 5 (1930): 7, 8.
2. LFH to Paul Hammond, December 4, 1958, 138:4/9, GWBWL. Paul Lyman Hammond (1883-1976) was born in Scituate, MA, and graduated from Harvard in 1906. Moving to New York, he entered real estate, finance, and business, and became a member of the Seawanhaka Corinthian Yacht Club. During World War I he was an ensign in the US Naval Reserve, and through the 1920s he was a supporter of sea scouting. A longtime bachelor, he married Susan Sedgwick in 1929; *Yachting* (August 1929): 75.
3. *The Rudder* (April 1930): 114. Alfred Lee Loomis (1887-1975), the son of a New York City physician, graduated from Yale in 1909 and from Harvard Law School, then practiced corporate law in New York until his service in the US Army during World War I. He developed improvements in artillery. After the war, he and his brother-in-law, Landon Thorne, became partners in the investment firm Bonbright & Company. Loomis also built a laboratory at his Tuxedo Park home, where his experiments in physics included an early concept for what would become LORAN, Luis W. Alvarez, *Alfred Lee Loomis, 1887-1975: A Biographical Memoir* (Washington, DC: National Academy of Sciences, 1980). Landon K. Thorne (1888-1964), son of New York industrialist Edwin Thorne, graduated from Yale in 1910 and was a partner with Alfred L. Loomis in Bonbright & Company. He was also on the board of directors of Bankers Trust. Loomis and Thorne owned Hilton Head Island, SC, which they used as a private hunting preserve. Built at Medford, MA, in 1852, the very sharp, round-stern clipper *Whirlwind* made two fast passages from New York to Melbourne, Australia, of 80 and 72 days in 1857 and 1858, Octavius T. Howe and Frederick C. Matthews, *American Clipper Ships, 1833-1858*, vol. 2 (Salem, MA: Marine Research Society, 1927), 690-91.
4. Display at the East End Seaport Museum and Marine Foundation, Greenport, NY, July 1997; Monsell (1882-1951), son of a Southold, Long Island, coasting schooner captain, learned to sail in his father's vessel. He began working for Vanderbilt in the early 1920s. His motto, displayed on the later J-boat *Ranger*, was "try to find in your mate that which you hope he may find in you," Obituary, *Newport Daily News*, April 13, 1951.
5. NGH to LFH, June 19, 1929, August 30, 1929, 138:17/5, GWBWL.
6. It is puzzling that although Francis clearly believed in the efficacy of the single-head rig for a large

racing boat in 1930, on February 11, 1937, he would write to Clinton Crane with regard to the L Class (between, in size, a J-boat and an M-boat): "I believe there should be a rule requiring the foretriangle to be divided up, as I am afraid only one head sail will be used and 'L' boats are too big for this when close hauled in a breeze."

7. NGH to LFH, September 22 and 30, October 16 and 20, 1929, LFH to NGH, October 17, 1929, 138:17/5, GWBWL; Stephens, *Match for the America's Cup*, 26.
8. LFH to NGH, January 29, 1927, 138:17/3, LFH to NGH, January 28, 1930, 138:17//6, LFH, "Whirlwind," unpublished typescript, August, 1961, 138:15/7, GWBWL.
9. LFH to NGH, October 17, 1929, 138:17/5, NGH to LFH, April 2, 1930, 138:17/6, GWBWL.
10. Llewellyn Howland, III, "A Farewell to Bror Tamm," *WoodenBoat* 46 (May/June 1982): 33.
11. Design No. 44, 138:15/7, GWBWL.
12. Design No. 44, 138:15/7, GWBWL.
13. LFH, "Whirlwind," 3, 138:15/7, 138:15/6, GWBWL.
14. *The Rudder* (June 1930): 147.
15. *The Rudder* (December 1929): 116; the *Sialia* was launched in mid-November, *Benton Harbor News Palladium*, November 20, 1929; LFH, "Whirlwind," 1, 138:15/7, LFH to NGH November 25, 1929, 138:17/5, see also LFH to NGH, February 8, 1930, LFH to NGH, March 21, 1930, 138:17/6, GWBWL.
16. SP38.13.6, DSGSPL.
17. LFH to NGH, December 27, 1929, 138:17/5, GWBWL.
18. LFH to NGH, December 9, 1929, 138:17/5, GWBWL.
19. LFH to NGH, October 17, 1929, 138:17/5, GWBWL; LFH, "Whirlwind," 2, 138:15/7, Design No. 44, 138:15/7, LFH to NGH, January 14, 1930, 138:17/6, see also LFH to NGH, January 2, 1930, 138:17/6, GWBWL.
20. LFH to NGH, January 2, 1930, 138:17/6, LFH to NGH, January 28, 1930, 138:17/6, GWBWL.
21. LFH to Uffa Fox, March 5, 1935, 138:1/5, GWBWL.
22. LFH to NGH, January 2 and 14, 1930, 138:17/6, GWBWL.
23. Charles Mason, "It Was All New Ground," *SAIL* (August 1974): 79.
24. Mason, "All New Ground," *SAIL* (August 1974): 80, 81.
25. NGH to LFH, January 3, 1930, LFH to NGH, January 6, 1930, 138:17/6, GWBWL.
26. NGH to LFH, January 11, 1930, LFH to NGH, January 14, 1930, 138:17/6, GWBWL; NGH to LFH, January 21, 1930, 138:17 (misdated as 1929 and thus filed in Folder 5), GWBWL.
27. Charles P. Burgess, "The Mast of 'Enterprise,'" *Yachting* (December 1930): 84; Mason, "All New Ground," *SAIL* (August 1974): 81.
28. LFH to NGH, ca. mid-March 1930, NGH to LFH, March 23, 1930, 138:17/6, GWBWL.
29. 138:15/40, GWBWL.
30. *Yachting* (May 1930): 51, (June 1930): 48; *The Rudder* (June 1930): 147.
31. LFH to NGH, May 8, 1930, NGH to LFH, May 14, 1930, 138:17/6, GWBWL.
32. Streeter, *Their Last Letters*, 174; Harold S. Vanderbilt, *Enterprise: The Story of the Defense of the America's Cup in 1930* (New York: Scribner's, 1931), 90; see also Herbert L. Stone, "America's Cup Aspirants Do Battle," *Yachting* (July 1930): 45, 46.
33. LFH, "Whirlwind," 5, 138:15/7; SP38.12.92, DSGSPL; see also *Clinton Crane's Yachting Memories,* 183; *Uffa Fox's Second Book*, 13.
34. NGH to LFH, August 30, 1929, 138:17/5, NGH to LFH, May 14, June 1, 1930, 138:17/6, GWBWL.
35. LFH, "Whirlwind," 6, 138:15/7, GWBWL; as it happens, the author has had the experience of steering a sizable sailing vessel with reversing steering gear, albeit of very different type than a J-boat. She is the *Lois McClure*, a replica of a Lake Champlain canal schooner, with a simple, tiller-rope-to-wheel arrangement that is reversing. She is hard to steer in a breeze; quoted in Ian Dear, *Enterprise to Endeavour: The J-Class Yachts* (New York: Sheridan House, 1999), 56; Bolger, "L. Francis Herreshoff," *Nautical Quarterly* 9 (Winter 1980): 74.
36. LFH, "Whirlwind," 6, 138:15/7, GWBWL.
37. Stephens, *The Match for the America's Cup, 1930,* 28.

38. Streeter, *Their Last Letters,* 95, 180.
39. Vanderbilt, *Enterprise,* 92, 95, 97.
40. Vanderbilt, *Enterprise,* 104, 106, 107.
41. Streeter, *Their Last Letters*, 29.
42. LFH, "Whirlwind," 7, 138:15/7, GWBWL.
43. LFH, "Whirlwind," 7, 138:15/7, GWBWL.
44. Vanderbilt, *Enterprise*, 116.
45. Streeter, *Their Last Letters,* 180.
46. Streeter, *Their Last Letters*, 119, 135.
47. SP38.12.48, DSGSPL.
48. Vanderbilt, *Enterprise,* 142, 145, 147, 148, 151, 172, 181; LFH to NGH, August 29, 1930, 138:17/6, GWBWL.
49. LFH to NGH, August 29, 1930, 138:17/6, GWBWL.
50. LFH to NGH, August 29, 1930, LFH to NGH, August 29, 1930, 138:17/6, GWBWL.
51. NGH to LFH, August 30, 1934, 138:17/10, GWBWL; Anne Bondy, interview with author.
52. NGH to LFH, September 24, 1934, LFH to NGH, September 26, 1934, 138:17/10, GWBWL.
53. Streeter, *Their Last Letters,* 43, 93-95, 200; LFH to Uffa Fox, October 22, 1935, 138:1/5, GWBWL.

BIBLIOGRAPHY

PRIMARY SOURCES

The *raison d'etre* of this book is the L. Francis Herreshoff Collection at the Mystic Seaport Museum. The heart of the book is Francis's design drawings from the Ships Plans Collection, Collection 38, Daniel S. Gregory Ships Plans Library. Its soul is Francis's letters, contained in 90 folders, in Collection 138, G. W. Blunt White Library. Most of them are copies, with the incoming letter to which he was replying on their versos, a researcher's dream come true. I made so much use of Francis's plans and letters that the Fellows of the G. W. Blunt White Library gave me a prize. Collection 138 also has 137 folders of Francis's writings, some unpublished, and of his descriptions and specifications of his designs.

Although it is not usual to list published books as primary sources, Francis's own books seem to me to qualify. In the absence of a diary, we cannot get closer to his thoughts and ways of being than in his writings. His books, particularly *The Common Sense of Yacht Design*, are a window into his mind.

Herreshoff, L. Francis. *Capt. Nat Herreshoff, The Wizard of Bristol: The life and achievements of Nathanael Greene Herreshoff, together with an account of some of the Yachts he designed.* New York: Sheridan House, 1953.

———. *The Common Sense of Yacht Design*. New York: The Rudder Publishing Company, 1947.

———. *The Compleat Cruiser: The Art, Practice, and Enjoyment of Boating*. New York: Sheridan House, 1956. Also, unabridged MS. at G. W. Blunt White Library.

———. *An L. Francis Herreshoff Reader*. Camden, ME, International Marine Publishing. 1978.

———. *Nathanael Greene Herreshoff 1848-1938: A life and appreciation of his work by his son L. Francis Herreshoff.* Hartford, CT: Wadsworth Athenaeum, no date.

———. *Sensible Cruising Designs*. Camden, ME: International Marine Publishing, 1973.

———. *The Writings of L. Francis Herreshoff*. New York: The Rudder Publishing Company, 1946.

ADDITIONAL UNPUBLISHED SOURCES

Bray, Maynard. Transcript of interview with Frederic Tudor. G. W. Blunt White Library.

Bristol Public Schools Record. Transcript on L. Francis Herreshoff.

Britt, Andrew W. "Britt Brothers: Boatuilders, 1904-1941." Unpublished notes.

Burgess, Swasey, and Paine. Plans, Hart Nautical Collections, MIT Museum.

Grayson, Stan. "A Vanished Era: Catboat Sailing in the Late 19th Century." Unpublished MS.

Herreshoff, Clara DeWolf. Diary. Herreshoff Marine Museum.

——— (probable author). "[Glim]pses from the Life of Nathanael Greene Herreshoff." Unpublished MS, Herreshoff Marine Museum.

———. Notebook. Herreshoff Marine Museum.

Herreshoff, L. Francis. "The Heights." Unpublished autobiographical poem, Herreshoff Marine Museum.

———. "Whirlwind." Unpublished MS, G. W. Blunt White Library.

Herreshoff, Nathanael Greene. "Biographical Notes and Reminiscences, etc." Unpublished MS, Herreshoff Marine Museum.

——— "Diary." Herreshoff Marine Museum.

Herreshoff, Nathanael Greene, III. "The Name Nathanael in the Herreshoff Family." Unpublished MS.

Howland, Llewellyn, III. "Herreshoff Manufacturing Co.: The Irresolute Years: 1915-1925." Unpublished MS.

———."Is Yacht Designing an Art or a Science?" Unpublished MS.

Paine Collection. Biographical sketch of Frank C. Paine. Unpublished MS, Hart Nautical Collection, MIT Museum.

Swan, William U. "Joshua Brown: 1828-1901." Unpublished MS.

SECONDARY SOURCES

Books

Black, Martin. *G. L. Watson: The Art and Science of Yacht Design*. Limerick, Ireland, Peggy Brown Press, 2011.

Bray, Maynard, and Carleton Pinheiro. *Herreshoff of Bristol: A Photographic History of America's Greatest Yacht and Boat Builder*. Brooklin, ME, WoodenBoat Publications, 1989.

Brooks, Van Wyck. *The Flowering of New England: 1815*-1865. New York: E. P. Dutton, 1936.

Calder, Nigel. *The English Channel.* New York: Penguin Books, 1986.

Carter, Samuel III. *The Boatbuilders of Bristol: The Story of the Amazing Herreshoff Family of Rhode Island: Inventors, Individualists, Yacht Designers, and America's Cup Defenders.* New York: Doubleday and Company, 1970.

Chapelle, Howard I. *The American Fishing Schooners*. New York: W. W. Norton, 1973, 1995.

———. *American Small Sailing Craft*. New York: W. W. Norton, 1951.

———. *History of American Sailing Ships*. New York: W. W. Norton, 1935.

Chesebrough, Westcote Herreshoff. *Random Recollections*. Privately printed, 1976.

Crane, Clinton H. *Clinton Crane's Yachting Memories*. New York: D. Van Nostrand, 1952.

Curry, Manfred. *Yacht Racing: The Aerodynamics of Sails and Racing Tactics,* 5th ed. New York: C. Scribner's Sons, 1948.

Cutter, William Richard, comp. *New England Families: Genealogy and Memorial.* New York: Lewis Historical Publishing, 1915.

Dear, Ian. *Enterprise to Endeavour: the J-Class Yachts.* New York: Sheridan House, 1999.

Donaldson, Alfred Lee. *A History of the Adirondacks.* New York: Century Company, 1921.

Duck, Noelle. *Yachts Classiques.* Paris: Gallimard, 2004.

Dunne, William M. P. *Thomas F. McManus and the American Fishing Schooners.* Mystic: Mystic Seaport, 1994.

Fox, Uffa. *Uffa Fox's Second Book.* New York: Scribners, 1935.

Garland, Joseph E. *The Eastern Yacht Club: A History from 1870 to 1985.* Marblehead, MA: Eastern Yacht Club, 1989.

Hauk, Z. W. *Schenley Yachting and Trophy Championship Book.* New York: Schenley Products Corporation, 1935.

Henderson, Richard, and Robert Carrick. *John G. Alden and his Yacht Designs.* Camden, ME: International Marine Publishing, 1983.

Herreshoff, Nathanael Greene. *A New Era in Yachting: The Patent Catamaran or Double Hulled Boat.* Bristol, RI: author, 1877.

Howland, Georgina Paine Fisher. *Afterthoughts.* New Bedford, MA: privately printed, 1955.

Howland, Llewellyn, III. *No Ordinary Being: W. Starling Burgess, Inventor, Naval Architect, Poet, Aviation Pioneer.* Boston: David R. Godine, 2014.

Kellner, George H., and J. Stanley Lemans. *Rhode Island: The Independent State.* Woodland Hills, CA: Windsor Publications, 1982.

Lord, Priscilla Sawyer, and Virginia Clegg Gamage, *Marblehead: The Spirit of '76 Lives Here.* Philadelphia: Chilton, 1972.

McCallum, Mary Fife. *Fast and Bonnie: History of William Fife and Son Yachtbuilders.* Edinburgh: John Donald, 1998.

McLaren, Keith. *A Race for Real Sailors.* Boston: David, R. Godine, 2006.

Murphy, Matthew P. *Glass Plates and Wooden Boats: The Yachting Photography of Willard B. Jackson at Marblehead, 1898-1937.* Beverly, MA: Commonwealth Editions, 2006.

Pinheiro, Carlton, ed. *Recollections and Other Writings by Nathanael G. Herreshoff.* Bristol, RI: Herreshoff Marine Museum, 1998.

Potter, Edith Welch. *The Last Farm on Chappaquiddick.* Edgartown, MA: Vineyard Stories, 2010.

Rappeleye, Charles. *Sons of Providence: the Brown Brothers, the Slave Trade, and the American Revolution.* New York: Simon and Schuster, 2006.

Schoettle, Edwin J. *Sailing Craft.* New York: Macmillan, 1942.

Selikowitz, Mark. *Dyslexia and Other Learning Difficulties.* New York: Oxford University Press, 1993.

Stephens, Olin J. *All This and Sailing Too: An Autobiography.* Mystic: Mystic Seaport, 1999.

Streeter, John W. *Their Last Letters 1930-1938: Nathanael G. Herreshoff and William P. Stephens.* Bristol, RI: Herreshoff Marine Museum, 2001.

Tank, Deane, and Beverly Ford, ed. *Tales of the Chicago Mackinac Race: 1898-1998.* Chicago: Island Goats Sailing Society, 1998.

Vanderbilt, Harold S. *Enterprise: The Story of the Defense of the America's Cup in 1930.* New York: Scribner's, 1931.

Viner, Alan. *A History of Rating Rules for Yachts 1854-1931.* Greenwich, England: National Maritime Museum, 1979.

Widger, A. L. *Historic Marblehead.* Wellesley, MA: Thurlow S. Widger, 1957.

Periodicals

The Rudder and *Yachting* have been valuable for accounts of races, developments in rating rules, descriptions of particular yachts, and movements of yacht designers among the various firms. *Lloyd's Register of American Yachts* traced boat ownership.

Articles:

Atkin, William. "The Suicide Fleet Looks in at Marblehead." *Fore an' Aft,* November 1928.

Bolger, Philip C. "L. Francis Herreshoff." *Nautical Quarterly,* Winter 1980.

Bray, Maynard, and Jim Giblin. "The Herreshoff Anchor." *WoodenBoat* 231, March/April 2013.

Britt, Andrew W. "Britt Brothers: The Pinnacle of Boatbuilding as an Art." *WoodenBoat* 167, July/August 2002.

Bunting, W. H. "Project *Slipper*," *WoodenBoat* 182, January/February 2005.

Burgess, Charles P. "The Mast of Enterprise." *Yachting,* December 1930.

Davin, Tom. "He Carries On the Great Herreshoff Tradition." *Boats,* September 1956.

Fitzgerald, Frances. "Peculiar Institutions: Brown University Looks at the Slave Trade and the American Revolution." *The New Yorker*, September 12, 2005.

Grant, Bruce. "Forty-third Annual Mackinac Race." *The Rudder,* September 1950.

Herreshoff, L. Francis. "An Interesting Experiment in Rigs." *Yachting*, February 1929.

———. "Cutters, Laying To, Etc.," *The Rudder*, November 1943.

———. "The Design of Fishing Vessels," *Maine Coast Fisherman*, January 1951.

———. "The Scharenkreuzers." *Yachting,* December 1928.

Herreshoff, Nathanael G. Discussion of "Yacht Measurement: Origins and Development," by W. P. Stephens. The Society of Naval Architects and Marine Engineers. *Transactions,* Volume 43, 1935.

Howland, Llewellyn III. "The Burgess Legacy." *WoodenBoat* 71, July/August 1986; 72, September/October 1986; 73, November/December 1986; 74, January/February 1987.

———. "A Farewell to Bror Tamm." *WoodenBoat* 46, May/June 1982.

Lenger, John. "Conquest of the Air." *Harvard Magazine,* May-June 2003.

Macomber, Virginia. "30 Squares: the Greyhounds of Yacht Racing." *Spinnaker*, Summer 1996.

Mason, Charles. "It Was All New Ground." *SAIL,* August 1974.

Munroe, Wirth M. "The Wishbone Rig in the Development Class." *The Rudder*, July 1935.

Reimers, Knud H. "Thirty Square Meters." *The Rudder*, May 1931.

Rice, Jonathan. "The Q Class." *WoodenBoat* 207, March/April 2009.

Rigg, H. K. "Profiles: Man of Ideas." *The New Yorker,* May 31, 1947.

Roe, Johan. "Q Boats in the Rockies." *Sailing*, April 2002.

Rohrer, J. Scott. "The Pacific Northwest Yachting Photographs of Asahel Curtis." *WoodenBoat* 204, September/October 2008.

Shakter, Robert J. "L. Francis Herreshoff." *Popular Boating,* September 1957.

Skahill, Thomas G. "Nick Potter." *WoodenBoat* 83, July/August 1988.

———. "Ted Geary: More Than a Naval Architect." *WoodenBoat* 138, September/October 1997.

Skene, Norman L. "The Scharenkreuzers." *Yachting*, June 1929.

Spurr, Dan. "Ladies of the Lake." *WoodenBoat* 170, January/February 2003.

Stephens, William P. "The Match for the America's Cup. 1930." Supplement to *The Sportsman* 3, no. 5, 1930.

Stone, Herbert L. "America's Cup Aspirants Do Battle." *Yachting*, July 1930.

Swan, William U. "International Racing." *The Rudder*, December 1928.

Taylor, William H. "W. Starling Burgess." *Yachting,* May 1947.

INDEX

Italic numerals indicate illustrations

A

Adams, Charles Francis, III, 133, 141, 208, 241, 357, 362
Advance (staysail schooner), 162
Akaba (6-Metre), 258
Albacore (ketch, design 36), *222, 223, 224, 225-26, 228,* 230
Albatross (double-ended power cruiser, design 51), 294, 295, *opposite 296, 297, 298*
Alden, John G., 81, 135, 202, 209, 242, 250, 285, 299
Aldrich, Winthrop, 355, 363
Alerion III, 50, 60
Alert (steam yacht), 58, 87
Alexander, C. D., 205
Amaryllis (catamaran), 21, 65
America (schooner), 27, 361
American Bureau of Shipping (ABS), 300, 304, 341, 344, 370, 372
America's Cup, 64, 74, 361, 362, 393, 395; cost of 1930 competition, 369
Amory, Robert, 202
Angelita (8-Metre), 244
Anker, Johan, 201, 202
Arnstein, Dr., 381, 392
Atkin, William J., 230, 266, 270, 276, 311
Atkinson, Arthur J., 201
Audubon Society of Rhode Island, 47
Avenger (cutter), 45-46
Averill, Doug, 251, 304, 307

B

Bacchant (30-Square-Metre), 321
Barker, B. Devereux, 241
Barr, Charley, 34, 45-46
Bay Bird (sloop), 277
Bernoulli effect, 207
Beverly Yacht Club, 277
Beverly Yacht Club 30-Square-Metre (design 52), *328,* 329, *330, 331, 332, 333*
Bibelot (Sonder), 46
Blue Bill (Development Class), *269*
Bluenose (schooner), 75
Bolger, Philip C., 348
Bolster, Helen, *177*
Bonnie Lassie (R-boat, design 28), 259, *260, 261, 262*
Boom, T-section, 129, 206, 259
Brigantine (104-foot), *117,* 119
Britt Brothers, 109, 110, 133, *185,* 193, 233, 234, 244
Brown, James, 13
Brown, John, 9, 10
Brown, John, 277
Brown, Joshua, 99
Brown, Moses, 9, 10
Brown, Samuel H., Jr., 227, 229, 230, 231, 244, 277, 304, 316, 369, 370
Brown, Waldo Hayward, *98,* 99-100, 103, 106, *109,* 169, 277, 329
Brown, William H., 264
Brown Trust, 10, 11
Brown University, 9
Burgess, Charles, 381
Burgess, Edward, 64
Burgess, Edward II, 70, 71
Burgess, Rosamund, 70
Burgess, W. Starling, 64, 65, *72,* 83, *88,* 100, 155, 162, 166, 206, 209, 215, 251, 277, 337, 355 357, 363, *365,* 393, 395, 396; as mentor to LFH, 69, 70, 71, 121, 129, 178, 181

Burgess, Rigg, and Morgan, 162, 209
Burgess and Paine, 74, 76, 77, 81
Burgess Model A aircraft, 69
Burgess, Swasey, and Paine, 87, *88*, 89, 99, 100, 107, *111*, 117, 119, 125, 132, 135, 145, 151, 155, 157, 162, 166, 202, 203
Butterfly (Development Class, design 48) *275*, 277, *278*, *279*, 280
Buzzards Bay 15 (sloop), 48
Buzzards Bay 21 (sloop), 48
Buzzards Bay 25 (sloop), 52

C

Canoeing, 71-73
Cara Mia (Q-boat), 301
Carpenter (tender, design 41), *291*, *292*, 294
Cassandra (steam yacht), *51*
Catamaran, 21, 65, *66*
Centerboard schooner (62-foot), 77, *80*
Chapelle, Howard I., 197, 263, 301
Chase, Alfred E., 314, 316
Chase, Rebecca, 358
Chesebrough, Albert Stanton, 50-51, 89
Clarence Barclay (schooner), *98*, 99, 102
Columbia (schooner), 75, 76
Columbia (sloop), 32
"Common Sense of Yacht Design, The," 89, 117
Constitution (sloop), 131
Coquina (cat yawl), 33
Corinthian Yacht Club (Marblehead), 71, *171*, *172*, 313-14
Corliss Steam Engine Company, 18, 19
Cormack, George A., 370
Crane, Clinton H., 213, 215, 251, 258, 351, *362*, 396
Crowninshield, Bowdoin B., 304
Cruising ketch (46-foot, design F-5), 60
Cruising ketch (61-foot), 77, *78*
Cruising ketch (45-foot), *96*
Cruising ketch (50-foot), *97*
Cruising launch (ketch rig, 40-foot), *157*
Cruising launch (sloop rig, 40-foot), 157, *158*
Cruising R-boat (design 24), 227
Cruising schooner (49-foot), *81*
Cunningham, John H., 200
Curry, Manfred, 129, *206*, 207, 208, 209
Curtis, Harry M., 241, 251, 253, *258*
Curtiss, Glenn L., 69
Curved headboard, *260*, 261
Customhouse (Marblehead home of LFH), 171, 172, *173-76*
Cyrus P. Brown (iceboat), 45, 48-49
Cythera (30-Square-Metre), 327

D

Daiquiri (Development Class), 276
Dandelion (R-boat), 133
Dane, Richard, 329
Davis, Thomas B. F., 393
Day launch (design 23), *220*, *221*, 227
Dean, Paul Dudley, 329
Deck-stepped mast, 196
Defender (sloop), 28, 30, 380
Derry, Jon, 251
Development Class (design 32), 266, *268*, 269, 270, 276, 277, 280
DeWolf, Algernon Sidney, 47
DeWolf, Clara Dimon, 38, 47
DeWolf Farm (The Farm), 25, 28, 47, *48*, 284
Dispatch (launch, design 20), *179*, *180*, 181, *182-86*, 207, 209
Displacement, calculations for, 191-93, 258, 287
Don Lee Cup (R-Class trophy), 200, 201
Dorade (yawl), 357
Dragon Fly (Development Class, design 32), *269*, *270*, 277
Double-ended hull, benefit of, 231, 244, 316
Duralumin, 380, 381
Dyer, William J. H., 264
Dyer launch (21-foot), *263*, 264, *265*, *266*
Dyer Motorcraft Corporation, 265

E

Elements of Yacht Design, 71, 177, 178
Ellis, Ralph, 251
Emmons, H. Nelson, 277, 329
Emmons, Robert W., 45, 52
Enaj III (SP-578), *55*, *56*
Endeavour (J-boat), 393
Endeavour II (J-boat), 395
Enterprise (J-boat), 363, 366, 381, 382, 388, 389, *390*, 391, 392, 393
Eschoff, Corporal, 10

F

F. N. Osborne & Company, 316
Field, Marshall, III, 363
Fife, William, Jr., 362
Fishing ketch (85-foot), 76, *77*
Fishing schooner (100-foot, design 33), 85
Flathead Lake, MT, 251, 307
Fleetwing (30-Square-Metre, design 52), 329
Flutterby (Development Class, design 48) *275*, 277, *278*, *279*, 280
Fore an' Aft, 230, 276, 311
40-Square-Metre boats, 311
Foster, Charles Henry Wheelwright, 126, 171-72, 205, 209, 230, *300*, 301
450 Class model yacht, 202, *203*
Fowle, Leonard M., 112, 199, 200, 241, 249
Francis, John, 10

Frederick II, King of Prussia, 10
Fredonia (fishing schooner), 64, 74

G

Gadget (launch), 334
Game Cock (R-boat), 133, 142
Gardner, William, 71, 357
Gasper, Peter, 341
Geary, L. E. "Ted," 200, 201
Gem (30-Square-Metre, design 52), 329, *333*
Genoa jib, 205-08, 327
George F. Lawley and Sons Company, 91, 244, 287, 316, 329, 363, 366, 368, 369, 377, *383*
Gertrude L. Thebaud (fishing schooner), 299
Gillespie, Schuyler W., 201
Gloriant, ex-*Nor'easter V* (Q-boat), 250
Gluckauf IV (30-Square-Metre), 311, 313
Gluckauf V (30-Square-Metre), 321
Goodwin, Dexter, 203
Gossoon (R-boat), 141
Graham, John, Jr., 201
Graves, James E. "Al," 304
Gray, Frances M., 99, 102
Gray, John Simpson, 99
Gray, Paul, 99
Gray Gull (iceboat), *44*, 45
Gray Marine Motor Company, 99
Gray Motor Company, 99
Grayling (sloop), 132
Grayling (R-boat), 135, 142
Gregory, George N., 229, 230
Gruber, Henry, 119
Gypsy (sloop), 71,
Gypsy (R-boat), *82*, 87, 126, 133
Gypsy (II, R-boat), 201
Gypsy (III, R-boat), 261

H

Haffenreffer, Rudolph F., 115, 159, 337
Hammond, Paul L., 73, 78-79, 363, *364*, 366, 370, *372*, 380, 381, 385, 388, *389*, 390, 393, 395
Hand, William H., 186, 285
Har (sloop), 230
Harding, Richard, 304
Hathi (30-Square-Metre), 321
Havemeyer, Charles S., 363
Hawk (Q-boat), 202
Hayseed VIII (Q-boat), 202
Helianthus (motor yacht), 54
Hell No! (Development Class), 276
Henry B. Nevins yard, 348, 388, 392
Herreshoff, pronunciation of, 53
Herreshoff, Agnes Muller, 26, *27*, *30*, 43
Herreshoff, Alexander Griswold (Griswold), 26, *27*, *29*, *30*, *35*, 37, 43, 53, 112, 159, 358
Herreshoff, Algernon Sidney DeWolf (Sidney), 26, *27*, *30*, *35*, 43, 51-52, 53, 159-60, 357, 358
Herreshoff, Ann Roebuck, 53
Herreshoff, Caroline, *12*, *22*
Herreshoff, Charles Frederick (II), 51, 53
Herreshoff, Charles Frederick (III), *12*, 14, 21, *22*
Herreshoff, Charles Frederick (Herreschoff, Karl Friederich), 10, *11*
Herreshoff, Charles Frederick Jr., *12*, 13, 14, 16, *22*
Herreshoff, Clara Ann DeWolf, *22*, 25, *26*, *38*, 47, 53
Herreshoff, Clarence, *27*, *29*, *35*, 37, 43, 53, *54*, 159, 358
Herreshoff, Grace, 285
Herreshoff, Halsey C., 54
Herreshoff, Helen Warren, 158
Herreshoff, James, *12*, 14, 21, *22*
Herreshoff, John B., *12*, 13, 14, *16*, 21, 22, 52, 160
Herreshoff, John Brown Francis, *12*, 13, *22*
Herreshoff, Julia Ann Lewis, 11, *12*, 13, *22*
Herreshoff, Julian Lewis, *12*, 13, *22*
Herreshoff, Lewis, *12*, 13, 47
Herreshoff, Lewis Francis, birth of, 25; childhood of, 25, *26*, *27*, 28, *29*, *30*, *38*, *39*; rivets *Defender*'s mast, 28, 30, 380; work at Herreshoff Manufacturing Company, 28, 30-32, 39, 46, 58, 65; boating activities of, 33, *34*, *35*, 36, *54*, 276, 280, 283, 290-91, 299, *312*, 313, 314; schooling of, 36, 37; dyslexia of, 36-37, 39; personality of, 66, 238, 251, *258*; difficulties with father, 26, 38-39, 40, 49, 66; vessel modeling of, 39, *40*, 46, 48, 60, 119-21; college career of, 43, 44-45, 47; farming activities of, 47, 52, *59*; iceboating activities of, *44*, 45, 48-49; travels to Bermuda with father, 50; learns from Albert Chesebrough, 51; and automobiles, 53; in US Navy, 54, *55*, *56*, 57, *58*; early designs, 60; meets Starling Burgess, 64; works for Starling Burgess, 65, 75, *88*, *111*; races 6-Metres in England, 73-*74*; observations on fishing schooners, 76; designs fishing vessels, 76, *77*, *85-86*; opinion on John G. Alden, 81; designs first mast tangs, 83, *84*, 87; comments on *Stormy Petrel*, 95; comments on *Joann*, 103, 110-12; reconciles with father, 112, 115, 133, 135, 142, 159-62; "scientific" approach to design, 123; introduces longitudinal construction, 131; develops streamlined rig, 135, *136*, *139*, *140*, 141; opinion on female sailors, 141-42; and sailing canoes, 151-52; lives with Paines, 155; opinion on powerboats, 155; distant relations with brothers, 159, 161, 215, 217, 357; correspondence with father, 87, 115, 133, 159-61, 162, 176-77, 193, 200-01, 209, 215, 217, 220, 253-54, 259, 261, 264, 277, 280, 284, 291, 316, 327, 339, 341, 351, 357, 364, 369, 380-81, 382, 393; moves to Marblehead, 169, 171; appearance, 176; invents deck-stepped mast, *188*, 189, 191,

196; opinion on boat colors, 191; opinion on *Live Yankee*, 197; patents awarded, 141, 191, 264, *265*; designs 450 Class model yacht, 202, *203*; claims to design first overlapping jib, 203, 205-08; behavior toward Manfred Curry, 206, 207; as yacht broker, 209; designs M-boats, 213-17, 338-39; adornment on plans of, 215; compensation for designs, 227, 230, 234, 304, 329, 338, 368-69; opinion on *Albacore*, 230; opinion on *Siva*, 238; advertising and self-promotion, 241, 285; and double-ended hulls, 244, 338-39; opinion on *Nor'easter V*, 244, 250; opinion on International Rule, 253, 256; "Suggested Rule" on scantlings, 258-59; works as designing engineer for Dyer, 264; and Development Class, 266-80; opinion on children, 283-84; and telephone, 284; reunion with father, 284-85; comments on *Walrus*, 291; comments on *Carpenter*, 294; serves on Boston Class Q technical committee, 299-300; comments on *Questa*, 301, 304; comments on Square-Metre boats, 311, 313; comments on construction plans, 316; as a racer, 321; comments on 30-Square-Metres, 334; assisted by father on *Istalena* construction, 339, 341, 344, 351; comments on turnbuckles, 348; rarely sails with clients, 350-51, 385-86; considers daggerboards for *Istalena*, 355; comments on *Istalena*, 357; wears glasses, 358; enjoys reading, 358; opinion on George Steers, 361; decisions on *Whirlwind* design, *362*, 365-66, 369, 370, *372*, 380-81, *386*, 388; comments on other J-boats, 377, 380; comments on *Whirlwind* mast, 380; sails on *Whirlwind*, 390-91; comments on America's Cup trials, 393; declines Davis's J-boat project, 393; reaction to *Whirlwind*'s failure, 395-96

Herreshoff, Nanthanael Greene, *12*, 16, *17*, *18*, 19, 21, *22*, 25, *26*, 32, 33-34, 50, 51-53, 60, 64, 65, 66, 71, 115, 120, 125, 131, 132, 133, 153, 337, 338-39, 341, 351, 358, 362, 365, 369, 370, 382, 385, 391, 393, 395; half models of, 120, *122*, 339; disappointment with sons, 160-61; compliments LFH, 339, 366

Herreshoff, Nathanael (Jr.), 26, *27*, *30*, *35*, 43, 53, 158

Herreshoff, Sally, *12*, 13, *22*

Herreshoff, Sarah Brown, 9, 10, *11*

Herreshoff Anchor, *14*

Herreshoff Manufacturing Company, 16, 21, 30, *31*, 32, 36, *44*, 46, 52, 64, 65, 73, 89, 115, 159, 337, 339, 341, *347*, 348, 355, 362, 366,

Herrmann, A. M., 250

Hildegarde (schooner), 51

Hill, Cora, 36

Hodgdon, George "Sonny," 344

Hope (Q-boat), 250, 301

Hovey, Chandler, 321, 327, 355, 362

Hovey, Elizabeth "Sis," 321, 327, 355, *356*, 357

Howe, Christine, 48-49

Howell, Captain, 348

Hoyt, C. Sherman, 363

Hunt, C. Raymond, 362

I

Iceboat, *44*, 45, 145-49

International Fishermen's Races, 75

International Measurement Rule, 73, 251, 252, 255, 256

Invader (schooner), 51

Iroquois II (NY 50), 363

Istalena (NY 50), 337

Istalena (M-boat, design 31), 338-39, *340*, 341, *342*, *343*, 344, *347*, 348, *349*, *350*, 351, *352*, *opposite 352*, *353-54*, 355, *356*, 357; tender of, *345*, *346*

J

J Class, 362

Jeanie (6-Metre sloop), 73, 363

Jenks, Richard P., 201, 227

Jib-luff spar, 196, 205

Joann (schooner), 100, *101-110*

Jones, Katherine, 283, 313

Julia (catboat), 13, *14*, *15*

Julia II, 13

Jumper stay, 126

K

Katoura (schooner), 52

Kayaking, 299, 358

Keelson, elimination of, 132

Kickerle (30-Square-Metre), 321

Kildee (sloop), 36,

L

Lanier, Reginald B., 357

Lathrop Engine Company, 287

Lawley yard, see George F. Lawley and Sons Company

Lawrence, John S., 162, 362

Leilana, ex-*Walrus* (motor sailer, design 19), 294

Lenore (Q-boat), 202

Lewis, Joseph Warren, 11

Lie-Nielsen, Oisten, *199*, 313

Lifeboat-cruiser (44-foot), 149, *150*, *151*

Lifeboat-cruiser (33-foot), 151

Lillian Woodruff (schooner), 126

Lipton, Thomas J., 362, 364

Live Yankee (R-boat, design 21), 186, *187-88*, *opposite 188*, *189-90*, 191, *192*, 193, *194-95*, 196, *197-200*, 201, *204*, 205, 206, 209, 217, 220, 253, 263

Ljungberg, Karl, 308

Lloyd, William Bross, 329

Lloyd's Bureau of Shipping, 254, 258, 341, 344, 368, 370, 372, 377, 382

Longitudinal construction, 131, *132*, *137-38*, 233, 261, *262*

Loomis, Alfred L., 363, 393

Love Rocks, 25, 26, 27, *33*, 159
Lundberg, Eric, 321

M

Manatee (runabout, design 40), *268*
M-boat (design 22), 213, *214*, 215, *216*, 217, *opposite 224*
M-boat (design 31), 217, *218, 219*
M Class, 213
MacGregor, Charles G., 83
MacNaught, Mac, 31
Mañana (schooner), *118, 119, 120, 121*
Marblehead, MA, 169, *170, 171*, 244
Marblehead T Class, 152, *153, 154*, 155, 203
Marconi rig, 74, 79, 126, 206, 350, 380
Mary (R-boat), 126, *128*, 205, 209, *210*
Mason, Mark, 148
Massachusetts Institute of Technology (MIT), 18, 43
Mast, curving top, 129
Maxwell, Henry L., 135
Maybe (6-Metre), 205
Mayflower (schooner), 75, 76
McCaffrey, Frank, 327
McManus, Thomas F., 76
McQuesten, George E., 314, 316, 321
Meteor (sloop), 14
Minas Princess (schooner), 370, *386*, 393
Mistral (schooner), 285
Monsell, George H., 363
Monsoon II (30-Square-Metre, design 52), 329
Morgan, Junius, 217, 337, 362
Morton, Jessie P., 201
MoToR Boating, 236, 238
Mower, Charles D., 133, 217, 266, 276, 337
Muir, John, *364*, 382, 383, 385, *386*, 391
Muller, Agnes, 10
Munro, Gordon, 314
Munroe, Ralph Middleton, 115, 358
Myer, Robert, 358

N

Narragansett Bay daysailer (sloop), 60, *62-63*
Neckan (steam yacht), 34
Nevada (cutter), 51
New York Yacht Club, 125, 142, 193, 337, 339, 341, 351, 361, 362, 370
Ngauruhoe (30-Square-Metre, design 52), 329
Nichols, George, 362, 366
Nicholson, Charles E., 73, 74, 362, 363, *365*, 364, 393
Nielsen, K. Aage, 81, 83, 301
Niña (schooner), 83, 363, 385
Nor'easter IV (Q-boat), 202, 241
Nor'easter V (Q-boat, design 26), *239, 240, 242, 243*, 244, *248, 249*, 250, 251, 259; tender of, *247*
North American Yacht Racing Union (NAYRU), 251, 253
Nye, Harry G., Jr., 251
Nystrom, Charles, 341

O

Oriole (30-Square-Metre, design 37), 316, *opposite 316, 317-18, 319*, 321, 329
Oriole II (30-Square-Metre, design 46), *324, 325, 326*, 327
Outlaw (Beachcomber dory), 229
Outlook, 69, 125
Overlapping jib, *154*, 155, 202-03, *204*, 205, 206
Owen, George, 314
Owl (sloop), 71

P

Paine, Charles Jackson, 70, 71, 362
Paine, Frank Cabot, 70-71, 73, 74, 83, 87, *88*, 117, 133, 155, 162, 166, 186, 201, 261, 299, 321, *362*, 368, 396
Paine, Belknap, and Skene, 299
Peg (Sonder), 46
Percival, Lawrence F., Jr., 269, 276
Peterson, Murray, 81
Pintail, ex-*Oriole* (30-Square-Metre), 321, *322*
Pleasure (yawl), 209
Pleione, schooner rig (New York 50), 162, *163, 164, 165*, 208
Point Pleasant Farm, 10, 16, 21
Post, Ernest F., 294
Potter, Nicholas S., 60, 87, 155, 166, 244
Power cruiser (57-foot, design 76), *296*
Prestige (M-boat), 215, 337, 351, 355
Prince, Morton, 241, 259
Priscilla (6-Metre), 251, 258
Provincetown, MA, 70
Puritan (schooner), *75*, 76
Puritan (sloop), 64
Pynchon, George Mallory, 337, *338*, 339, 344, 348, 350, 351, 355, 357, 363, 365, 385

Q

Q-boat, 201, 202, 244, 314, *315*
Questa, (Q-boat, design 33), 251, *300, 301, 302, 303*, 304, *305, 306, 307*
Quiver (R-boat), 135

R

R-boat, double-ended, streamline rig, 135, *136, opposite 136*
R-boat, schooner rig, *128*
R Class, 87, 123, 133
Rainbow (J-boat), 393
Raking mid-section, 366
Ranger (J-boat), 357, 395
Rasmussen, Henry, 311, 314
Ratsey, Thomas, 74

Ratsey and Lapthorn, 131, 205, 208, 348, 381-82
Redd's Pond, Marblehead, 202, *203*
Reimers, Knud, 327
Reliance (sloop), 34-35,
Resolute (sloop), 52, 64, 71, 357, 388
Retriever (28-foot launch, design 30), 266, *267*
Rhode Island State College (University of Rhode Island), 43, 47
Rigg, J. Linton, 162, 209, 294
Rima (30-Square-Metre, design 38), 316, *320*, 321, *323*
Riviera (sloop), 35,
Roamer (steam yacht), *33*, 34,
Roamer, ex-*Siva* (motor yacht), 238
Rockwell, Carl B., 38
Roller reefing, 329, 332
Root, Elihu, Jr., 363
Ross, Leo, 321
Roue, William J., 75
Rudder, The, 107, 241, 251, 164, 290, 299, 311, 348, 351, 389

S
Sailing canoe, 151-52
Salen, Sven, 205
Sans Ca Tout (8-Metre), 313
Santee (sloop), 117
Santry, Joseph V., 162, 202, 208, 220
S-boat, 60, *61*, 311
Scapa II (R-boat), 201
Scharenkreuzers, 308
Seagoing cruiser, (power, 135-foot), *116*, 117
Seawanhaka Rule, 125
75-Square-Metre boat, 314, *315*, 316
Shamrock V (J-boat), 362, 363, 364, 368, 393
Shadow (sloop), *19*, *20*, 64
Sheila (6-Metre sloop), 64, *72*, 73, 363
Shuman, E. Arthur, 314, 321
Sialia (power yacht), 369
Sir Tom (R-boat), 200, 201
Siva (motor yacht, design 25), *229*, 230, *231*, *232*, *233*, *234*, *235*, *236*, 238, *opposite 244*, *245-46;* tender of, *237*
6-Metre sloops, 73, 251, 258
Skene, Norman L., 71, 125, 131, 155, 177, *178*, 191, 192, 193, 202, 203, 220, 231, 244, 256, 258, 277, 287, 290, 299, 316
Skerry Cruisers (Skargardskryssare), 307-08, 311
Skipper, effects of skill, 263
Slipper (iceboat), 145, *146*, *147*, *148*, 149
Slocum, Joshua, 45
Smith, Grafton, 202, 241, 244, 249, 250, 311
Sonder boat, 46
Sopwith, T. O. M., 393, 395
SP-56 (patrol boat), 57
Sparkman & Stephens, 357
Spars, hollow, 87, 129, 141, 189, 380
Speejacks (schooner), 285
Spindle, ex-*Nor'easter V* (Q-boat), 250, 251
Spook (Development Class), 276
Spray (yawl), 45
Sprite (sloop), 16,
Square-Metre Rule, 308
Staysail schooner, 162, *164*, *165*
Steam yacht (138-foot), *opposite 84*, 88-89
Steers, George, 361
Stephens, Olin J., 357, 395
Stephens, W. P., 390, 391, 395
Stevens, John C., 361
Stewart, W. A. W., 241, 251, 253, 256, *258*
Stimson, Cully, 201
Stinnes, Hanns, 311, 313, 321, 323
Stone, Dexter S., 21
Stormy Petrel (ketch, design F-18), 89, *90*, *91-95*, 99, 135
Strawbridge, William J., 280, 357
Streamlined rig, 135, *136*, *139*, *140*, 141, 145
Suicide (junior racer, design 39), *272*, *273*, *274*, 277
Suicide Class, see Development Class
Swan, James, 52
Swan, William U., 87, 142, 241, 311
Swasey, A. Loring, 52, 58, 64, 87, *88*, 166
Swing rig, 209, *210*
Swordfisherman, 40-foot, 155, *156*

T
Tadpole, 14
Tamm, Bror, 176, 244, *368*, 380
Tangs, 83, *84*, 87, 129
Taygeta, ex-*Nor'easter IV* (Q-boat), 202
Taylor, Edward Thompson, 186
Taylor, William H., 253
Theede, Johannes, 321
30-Square-Metre Rule, 259, 323
Thomas, Vitas S., 250
Thorne, Landon K., 363, *364*, 369, 383, 385, 388, 391, 392, 393
Tippler III (30-Square-Metre), 314, 321
Tranquilo (steam yacht), 34
Tripp, Donald F., 227, 238
20-Square-Metre boat (design 35), *309*, *310*, 311
25-foot sailboat for William Taggart, *271*
Twister (*Whirlwind* tender), 370, *375*, *376*, *377*, 392, 395, *396*

U
Undertaker (6-Metre sloop), 81
Universal Rule, 123, 125, 189, 192, 193, 197, 203, 299, 300, 301, 364
Upton, George, 119, 157, 158, 169

V

Valiant (M-boat), 355
Vanderbilt, Harold S., 55, 213, 215, 337337, 338, 350, 351, 363, 366, 393, 395
Vanitie (sloop), 64, 71, 351, 357, 388
Vara (power yacht), 393
Vega (sloop), 51
Ventura (sloop), 77, *79*
Vigilant (sloop), 369
Vincent, Henry, 316
Violet (sloop), 18
Visitor, ex-*Gluckauf IV* (30-Square-Metre), *312*, 321

W

W. Starling Burgess Company, 69
Waimarie (Development Class), *269*, *270*, 277
Wakerman, S. Wiley, 329
Walrus (motor sailer, design 19), 151, 285, *286*, 287, *288*, *289*, *290*, 293, 294, 329, 370, *372*
Wasp (sailing canoe), 152
Wasp (6-Metre, design 27), 251, *252*, *254*, 256, *257*, *258*
Watson, George L., 74, 88, 361, 362
Weetamoe (J-boat), 362, 366, 382, 388, 389, *390*, 391, 392, 393
Welch, Charles A., II, 79, 81, 89, 91, *95*, 98, 123, 133, 135, 141, 142, 145, *148*, *149*, 151, 169, 176, *178*, 181, 189, 196, 197, *199*, 200, 201, 205, 220, 241, 263, 264, 266, 269, *270*, 276, 283, 285, 287, 290, 293, 294, 313-14, 321, 323, 327, 329
Welch, Josh, 148
Welch, Ruth, 141, 148, *149*, *199*, 200, 201
Westward (schooner), 46-47, 393
Wheelock, Harold S., 301
Whirlwind (clipper ship), 363
Whirlwind (J-boat, design 44), 363, 365, 366, *367*, 368, 369, 370, *371*, 372, *opposite 372*, *373-74*, 376, 377, *378*, 381, 382, *383*, *384*, *385*, *386*, *387*, 388, *389*, *390*, 391, *392*, 393, *394*, 395, 396; mast of, 380-81, 392; pram dinghy of, *379;* steering gear of, *387*, 388, *389*
Williams, Fenwick, 81, 176
Wilm, Alfred, 380
Wilson, Nat, 148
Windward (M-boat), 217
Wychmere Harbor, Harwich Port, MA, 102-03

Y

Yacht, Die, 191, 202, 206, 308, 311,
Yacht Racing: The Aerodynamics of Sails, 206
Yachting, 81, 91, 135, 206, 241, 253, 259, 264, 269, 285, 294, 301
Yankee (R-boat), *124*, 125, 126, *127*, 129, *130*, 131, *132*, 133, *134*, 135, *137-38*, *140*, 141-42, *198*, 259
Yankee (J-boat), 299, 362, 363, 366, 382, 388, 389, *390*, 391, *392*, 393
Yankee (30-Square-Metre), 314, 321
Young, Charles, 276

CHRONOLOGICAL INDEX

of L. Francis Herreshoff Designs

Half model, 40
Peg (Sonder), 46
Buzzards Bay 21 (sloop), 48
Narragansett Bay daysailer (sloop), 60, *62-63*
Cruising ketch (46-foot, design F-5), 60
Catamaran, 65, *66*
Fishing ketch (85-foot), 76, *77*
Cruising ketch (61-foot), 77, *78*
Centerboard schooner (62-foot), 77, *80*
Cruising schooner (49-foot), *81*
Mary, mast tangs (R-boat), 83, *84*
Steam yacht (138-foot), *opposite 84*, 88-89
Stormy Petrel (ketch, design F-18), 89, *90*. *91-95*, 99, 135
Joann (schooner, design BSP 257), 100, *101-110*
Mañana (schooner, design BSP 262), *118*, *119*, *120*, *121*
Seagoing cruiser, (power, 135-foot), *116*, 117
Brigantine (104-foot), *117*, 119
Yankee (R-boat, design BSP 272), *124*, 125, 126, *127*, 129, *130*, 131, *132*, 133, *134*, 135, *137-38*, *140*, 141-42, *198*, 259
R-boat, schooner rig, *128*
Slipper (iceboat, design BSP 285), 145, *146*, *147*, *148*, 149
Lifeboat-cruiser (44-foot, design BSP 288), 149, *150*, *151*
Lifeboat-cruiser (33-foot, design BSP 293), 151
Marblehead T Class (sloop, design BSP 295), 152, *153*, *154*, 155, 203
R-boat, double-ended, streamline rig, (design BSP 303), 135, *136*, *opposite 136*
Cruising ketch (45-foot, design BSP 310), *96*
Swordfisherman (40-foot), 155, *156*
Cruising launch (ketch rig, 40-foot), *157*
Cruising launch (sloop rig, 40-foot), 157, *158*
Pleione, schooner rigs (New York 50), 162, *163*, *164*, *165*, 208
Dispatch (launch, design BSP 314, LFH 20), *179*, *180*, 181, *182-86*, 207, 209
Walrus (motor sailer, design 19), 151, 285, *286*, 287, *288*, *289*, *290*, 293, 294, 329, 370, *372*
Live Yankee (R-boat, design 21), 186, *187-88*, *opposite 188*, *189-90*, 191, *192*, 193, *194-95*, 196, *197-200*, 201, *204*, 205, 206, 209, 217, 220, 253, 263
Scapa II, sail plan (R-boat), 201
Hawk, sail plan (Q-boat), 202
Hayseed VIII, sail plan (Q-boat), 202
Lenore, sail plan (Q-boat), 202
Nor'easter IV, sail plan (Q-boat), 202, 241
450 Class model yacht, 202, *203*
Mary, swing rig (R-boat), 209, *210*
M-boat (design 22), 213, *214*, 215, *216*, 217, *opposite 224*
Day launch (design 23), *220*, *221*, 227
Cruising R-boat (design 24), 227
Siva (motor yacht, design 25), *229*, 230, *231*, *232*, *233*, *234*, *235*, *236*, 238, *opposite 244*, *245-46*; tender of, *237*
Nor'easter V (Q-boat, design 26), *239*, *240*, *242*, *243*, 244, *248*, *249*, 250, 251, 259; tender of, *247*
Wasp (6-Metre, design 27), 251, *252*, *254*, 256, *257*, *258*
Bonnie Lassie (R-boat, design 28), 259, *260*, *261*, *262*
Dyer launch (21-foot), *263*, 264, *265*, *266*
Retriever (28-foot launch, design 30), 266, *267*
M-boat (design 31), 217, *218*, *219*
Istalena (M-boat, design 31), 338-39, *340*, 341, *342*, *343*, 344, *347*, 348, *349*, *350*, 351, *352*, *opposite 352*, *353-54*, 355, *356*, 357; tender of, *345*, *346*
Development Class (design 32), 266, *268*, 269, 270, 276, 277, 280
Dragon Fly (Development Class, design 32), *269*, *270*, 277
25-foot sailboat for William Taggart, *271*
Fishing schooner (100-foot, design 33), 85

Questa, (Q-boat, design 33), 251, *300, 301, 302, 303*, 304, *305, 306, 307*
20-Square-Metre boat (design 35), *309, 310*, 311
Albacore (ketch, design 36), *222, 223, 224, 225-26, 228*, 230
75-Square-Metre boat, 314, *315*, 316
Oriole (30-Square-Metre, design 37), 316, *opposite 316, 317-18, 319*, 321, 329
Rima (30-Square-Metre, design 38), 316, *320*, 321, *323*
Manatee (runabout, design 40), *268*
Suicide (junior racer, design 39), *272, 273, 274*, 277
Carpenter (tender, design 41), *291, 292*, 294
Whirlwind (J-boat, design 44), 363, 365, 366, *367*, 368, 369, 370, *371*, 372, *opposite 372, 373-74*, 376, 377, *378*, 381, 382, *383, 384, 385, 386, 387*, 388, *389, 390*, 391, *392*, 393, *394*, 395, 396; mast of, 380-81, 392; pram dinghy of, *379;* steering gear of, *387*, 388, *389*
Twister (*Whirlwind* tender), 370, *375, 376, 377*, 392, 395, *396*
Oriole II (30-Square-Metre, design 46), *324, 325, 326*, 327
Butterfly (Development Class, design 48) *275*, 277, *278, 279*, 280
Flutterby (Development Class, design 48) *275*, 277, *278, 279*, 280
Albatross (double-ended power cruiser, design 51), 294, 295, *opposite 296, 297, 298*
Gem (30-Square-Metre, design 52), 329, *333*
Ngauruhoe (30-Square-Metre, design 52), 329
Monsoon II (30-Square-Metre, design 52), 329
Fleetwing (30-Square-Metre, design 52), 329
Beverly Yacht Club 30-Square-Metre (design 52), *328*, 329, *330, 331, 332, 333*
Taygeta, ex-*Nor'easter I*, sail plans (Q-boat), 202
Power cruiser (57-foot, design 76), *296*
Cruising ketch (50-foot), *97*

ROGER C. TAYLOR met L. Francis Herreshoff while a student at Milton Academy. He went on to study maritime history at Harvard, then served in the United States Navy as a deck officer in a destroyer and a diesel submarine. He was a leader at the U. S. Naval Institute in the 1960s and founder and leader of International Marine Publishing Company in the 1970s and '80s, where his publishing list included two books by Herreshoff. In "retirement," he has lived mostly afloat with his wife, Kathleen Carney, and he has worked his captain's license, adding to his life list of a couple of hundred boats sailed, including fourteen designed by L. Francis Herreshoff.

OTHER BOOKS BY ROGER C. TAYLOR

Good Boats (1977)

More Good Boats (1979)

Still More Good Boats (1981)

The Elements of Seamanship (1982)

The Fourth Book of Boats (1984)

Thirty Classic Boat Designs: The Best of the Good Boats (1992)

Knowing the Ropes (1993)

The author checking notes for his book in the wheelhouse of the Dutch canal cruiser *Water Lily* somewhere in France. (Kathleen Carney photo)